Critical Praise for *When Pride Still Mattered*

"A masterful, soulful biography, one that traces how a flawed and driven man was also able to construct football's most storied dynasty.... Maraniss has crafted a superlative work."—David Davis, *San Francisco Chronicle*

"Unexpectedly rich and provocative.... [Maraniss] sheds remarkable light not only on what Lombardi meant to the NFL but to the entire country in the nasty days of the '60s.... It all comes to life in this voluminous, artful retelling: the games and the glory, the protests and the bluster.... Nobody who lived through the era can read [Lombardi's] story and not hear the awful echoes."—Bill Brashler, *Chicago Sun-Times*

"A thoughtful, engaging and well-written biography of a complex, contradictory man.... Maraniss does a great job re-creating Lombardi's life and times, rescuing the man from the myth."—Bob Minzesheimer, *USA Today*

"Maraniss painstakingly reveals the underpinnings of the coach's philosophy.... [He] has a superb eye for detail.... *When Pride Still Mattered* stands in stark contrast to most other books by and about coaches. Maraniss shows ... that winning isn't everything, it's not even what it's cracked up to be."—Allen St. John, *The New York Times Book Review*

"Maraniss went after this project as Lombardi himself would, with a religious passion for methodology and an insatiable curiosity for detail.... There is a great humanity to Maraniss' book.... [A] masterful character study. Great sports books are virtually an oxymoron in this culture, but *When Pride Still Mattered* deserves a place ... on the top shelf of the genre."—Gene Collier, *Pittsburgh Post-Gazette*

"[T]he book soars like a game-winning field goal."—Daniel Okrent, *Time*

"Maraniss' sympathetic yet unsparing portrayal of a sports legend and his family ... transcends the narrow world of yard markers and end zones. In Maraniss' deft hands, it is an American tragedy."—Michael Skube, *The Atlanta Journal-Constitution*

"A sharply focused rearview mirror on the life of a complex and even paradoxical man, *When Pride Still Mattered* is more than a sports book on a nostalgic errand—it's an unflinching look at a man and the myth surrounding him.... A fluid narrative about a fascinating individual."—Tom Perry, *Green Bay Press-Gazette*

"Remarkably insightful.... The football follower finds old myths punctured, fundamental truths revealed."—Earl Gustkey, *Los Angeles Times*

"We get all we could ever hope for on this topic.... Maraniss chronicles the making of the myth as well as the man."—Tim Long, *The Miami Herald*

"Maraniss offers the sort of full-scale biography routinely written about great thinkers and statesmen but rarely about a sports figure.... *When Pride Still Mattered* gives us not just the man on the sidelines ... but a full-scale account of the forces that shaped Lombardi's life and ideas.... [A] fine biography."—Michael Oriard, *The Philadelphia Inquirer*

"Crammed with anecdotes and surprising observations ... Maraniss' book reads like a novel. But it's not just a football story. It's about an American icon, the John Wayne of the gridiron, successful on the football field, flawed off it."—Scott Anderson, *Seattle Post-Intelligencer*

"Ambitious and definitive.... Maraniss' research is daunting.... He gets his man down fully and finally."—John Powers, *The San Diego Union-Tribune*

"[Maraniss] gets behind the legend and reduces Lombardi to flesh and blood, strengths and flaws. [He] gives us the humanity, not just the legend."—Bill Reynolds, *Houston Chronicle*

"In his remarkable biography ... Maraniss captures this man of prayer and paradox. ... [A] wonderful work that will force people who read books to take another look at football and force football fans to take another look at the idea of reading a book." —Lester Munson, *Chicago Tribune*

"[This] remarkably researched biography strips an icon down to his all-too-human parts.... Sharply written and rich in imagery.... A gritty portrait of a paradoxical figure, a father for his boys in the locker room who was rarely around for his own kids.... Maraniss plays it all beautifully against the backdrop of the 1960s."—Bill Briggs, *The Denver Post*

"Because of Maraniss' descriptive prowess, the Lombardi saga more closely resembles a carefully stitched together, gripping novel instead of a meticulous work of scholarship.... Maraniss rekindles the passion and the pride that this remarkable man brought to football and to life and recalls the glorious days when football was still a game, and not yet so blatantly a business."—William K. Marimow, *The Sun* (Baltimore)

"[Maraniss'] narrative is rich in scenes and personalities and seamlessly catches the sound and feeling of the United States during Lombardi's life.... It reads like an epic novel. The result is a triumph, a classic American biography."—Robert W. Creamer, *The Washington Post Book World*

"Maraniss' work might be the best sports biography ever written."—Les Carpenter, *The Seattle Times*

"Stunning, brilliant, well-written. . . . Maraniss holds nothing back. . . . For anyone who remembers Lombardi, this book will bring the memories rushing back."—Richard C. Crepeau, *The Orlando Sentinel*

"Absorbing . . . wonderful . . . like a lengthy, fascinating fireside chat."—Donn Esmonde, *The Buffalo News*

"A brilliant biography."—Charlie Patton, *The Florida Times-Union* (Jacksonville)

"Maraniss . . . employs meticulous research and a sweeping narrative style that shatters some of the myths surrounding Lombardi. . . . [He] does a splendid job of separating Lombardi the coach from Lombardi the man."—Everett J. Merrill, *The Star-Ledger* (Newark)

"That Old Man—who coached the Green Bay Packers to five championships in nine years—is a compelling subject, and Maraniss an equally compelling analyst. . . . A daunting task, and Maraniss is more than equal to it. . . . A classic."—Steve Dunn, *The Oregonian* (Portland)

"In David Maraniss' exhaustively researched, thoroughly absorbing biography, a very fallible, almost fragile man emerges from behind the larger-than-life legend."—Michael Sauter, *Biography* magazine

"*When Pride Still Mattered* reads like a historical biography worthy of Robert Caro or Stephen Ambrose. . . . Maraniss does a great job of explaining the reasons for Lombardi's success, while clearly highlighting his failures. . . . Maraniss' excellent analysis of Lombardi points out that victory in football is not the same as victory in life."—Steve Galpern, *The Daily Camera* (Boulder)

"A thorough look at Lombardi in all his complexity. . . . An insider's view of classic moments in NFL history."—Sam Hieb, *Greensboro News & Record*

"A great biography, fascinating even for readers who don't care about football." —Susan Larson, *The Times-Picayune* (New Orleans)

ALSO BY DAVID MARANISS

They Marched Into Sunlight
The Prince of Tennessee (with Ellen Nakashima)
The Clinton Enigma
"Tell Newt to Shut Up!" (with Michael Weisskopf)
First in His Class: A Biography of Bill Clinton

DAVID
MARANISS

Simon & Schuster Paperbacks
New York   London   Toronto   Sydney

WHEN

PRIDE

A Life

of

Vince Lombardi STILL

MATTERED

SIMON & SCHUSTER PAPERBACKS
Rockefeller Center
1230 Avenue of the Americas
New York, NY 10020

SIMON & SCHUSTER PAPERBACKS *and colophon are*
registered trademarks of Simon & Schuster, Inc.

For information about special discounts for bulk purchases,
please contact Simon & Schuster Special Sales:
1-800-456-6798 or business@simonandschuster.com.

Designed by Edith Fowler
Manufactured in the United States of America

30 29 28 27 26 25 24 23 22

The Library of Congress has cataloged the
hardcover edition as follows:

Maraniss, David.
  When pride still mattered: a life of Vince
Lombardi / David Maraniss.
    p.   cm.
  Includes bibliographical references and
index.
  1. Lombardi, Vince.   2. Football coaches
—United States Biography.   3. Green Bay
Packers (Football team)—History.   I. Title.
II. Title: Life of Vince Lombardi.
GV939.L6M37   1999
796.332'092—dc21
[B]   *99-37859*
                                                    CIP

ISBN-13: 978-0-684-84418-3
ISBN-10:   0-684-84418-4
ISBN-13: 978-0-684-87018-2 (Pbk)
ISBN-10:   0-684-87018-5 (Pbk)

To Wendy
My sister forever

Contents

Preface

THE TITLE of this book was taken from a scene in Richard Ford's novel *Independence Day* in which his main character, a former sportswriter named Frank Bascombe, makes a pit stop at the Vince Lombardi Service Area at exit 16W on the New Jersey Turnpike. The "Vince," as Ford called it, then had a collection of Lombardi memorabilia from days when pride still mattered. Ford put the phrase inside parentheses, and I thought when I first read the passage that he intended it with a certain irony, a suspicion that he later confirmed when I asked him. That is the spirit in which I use it as well.

Lombardi was a great and fearsome presence of my youth, always there above me up in Green Bay, true north, standing firm on the frozen earth of Lambeau Field as I skittered free and feckless down below in the Madison of the sixties. America was at war during much of that decade; we all were in various ways, and though our wars were vastly different I always counted myself on Lombardi's side. The Packers were his first platoon, yet his troops numbered greater among the masses, including students like myself who were rebelling against authority, discipline, the establishment—most of what the coach was supposed to represent.

Part of the bond could be explained by cultural geography. It seemed so unlikely and glorious that he was winning in Wisconsin. If life is comprised of a million small battles waged endlessly in our imaginations, in mine, every Sunday that Lombardi won, he won for me, defeating not just the Giants and Colts and Rams, but deeper foes, the forbidding East, class expectations, fate and also L.A., and everything else that seemed transient or unsettling compared to our place in Middle America. I realize now that I also thought he was winning for my father. They both had big, open faces and chain-smoked cigarettes and paced the winter in trench coats and talked tough. My dad was a newspaperman, a city editor, who came from Brooklyn and got his best chance late in life, and in Wisconsin, as did Lombardi.

Nearly three decades have passed since Lombardi's death. Other great coaches, George Halas, Bear Bryant and Woody Hayes, have receded with their passing, confined to the narrow world of football, but Lombardi alone seems to live on, larger than his sport. His bronze bust at the Pro Football Hall of Fame in Canton, Ohio, has the shiniest nose, touched more than any other by the faithful, the sporting world equivalent of rubbing St. Peter's foot in Rome. Walk into the office of an insurance salesman in Des Moines, or a college financial officer in Richmond, or a hockey-team president in New Jersey, and there is the Lombardi credo, framed and hanging on the wall. Turn on ESPN and there is John Facenda, the voice of God, declaring, "Lombardi, a certain magic still lingers in the very name. It speaks of duels in the snow and the cold November mud." Green Bay's run to the championship in 1996 brought more attention to Lombardi, but he is always there anyway, lurking in the national psyche at a deeper level.

Many yearn for Lombardi out of a sense of longing for something they fear has been irretrievably lost. Every time a sporting act seems graceless and excessive, every time a player dances and points at himself after making a routine tackle, or a mediocre athlete and his agent hold out for millions, whenever it seems that individual ego has overtaken the concept of team, the question can be asked: What would Lombardi do about this? Why isn't there anyone like the Old Man out there anymore? Others think Lombardi represents something less romantic, a symbol of the American obsession with winning, a philosophy that if misapplied can have unfortunate consequences in sports, business and all of life. From this perspective come other questions: Did Lombardi really believe that winning isn't everything, it's the only thing? What does his life say about the modern ethos of competition and success? The questions from both sides are valid, and the stereotypes from which they arise are equally misleading. Lombardi was more complex and interesting than the myths that surround him. It is that contradiction, the ambiguity of his meaning in American culture, that drove me as I researched this biography.

WASHINGTON, D.C.
MAY 1999

1

Tattoos

EVERYTHING BEGINS with the body of the father. At the turn of the century, when Harry Lombardi was a rowdy boy roaming the streets of lower Manhattan, his chums called him Moon. He had a face that reminded one of a full moon, a round ball that surely would bounce on the sidewalk if it could be yanked off his shoulders. His thin lips, slatted eyes and disjointed nose seemed painted on, or imagined—as if they had been made by looking up at the moon and creating facial features from shadows of gray on a white-lit orb. His spherical face rested atop a frame that grew boxier year by year, evoking a second nickname given to him in adulthood: Old Five by Five. This was said mostly behind his back by members of his own family, including his children. To be precise, he stood several notches above the five-foot mark, the top edge of his brush cut reaching five five, and though his stomach protruded generously, his body seemed more square than fat. The little strongman was so powerful that he once loaded two kids on a coal shovel and lifted it up with one hand.

The ornamentation of his flesh is what truly announced Harry's presence. He was covered with tattoos. They rose up from his forearms, a swirling blue and red mural of devotion to family and country, each splotch symbolizing another of his simple beliefs. He even had messages tattooed onto his hands, one letter per finger in a row above the knuckles. The letters appeared upside down and backward from his perspective, looking down, but in legible order to someone reading them from the front. On the index finger of the left hand was a W, followed by an O on the middle finger, R on the ring finger and K on the pinky. His right hand lettering began with P on the pinky, then L and A, ending with Y on the index finger. WORK and PLAY, competing for attention on the beefy digits of an immigrant meatcutter in New York. There could be no more fitting passwords at the creation of an American myth.

What Harry thought of his ink-stained body, which he acquired during his early teenage years, has been a matter of dispute within the family. It is known that his widowed mother, Michelina, was horrified by the tattoos, ordered him to wash them off (even the MOTHER on his bicep) and prohibited him from paying further visits to a tattoo parlor near their tenement house on Mott Street. Harry apparently scrubbed and scraped to little avail. The lasting image of maternal concern was a vestigial American bald eagle on his chest, only half complete. Some relatives insisted that he was embarrassed by the tattoos later in life, while others remembered that he displayed them with pride, wearing short-sleeved shirts when he might have concealed the artwork on his arms. In either case, the patriotic tattoos expressed his loyalties. He was born in 1890 with a foreign-sounding name in another country, Enrico Lombardi of Italy, but he arrived in New York at age two and from then on considered himself every ounce an American. He was Harry on city records, Harry to federal census takers, Harry to customers at his meat market. He said little about his Neapolitan ancestry and rarely spoke Italian, attaining fluency instead in a peculiar New York dialect in which these was *dese*, those was *dose*, them was *dem* and things were *tings*.

By his thirtieth birthday in 1920, Harry Lombardi seemed to be living the modern American life. He and his brother ran their own business, selling wholesale meat from a shop on the Hudson River waterfront. He was married and the head of a household of four: wife, Matilda; son, Vincent, seven, and daughter, Madeline, three. Three more children were to come. The Lombardis lived behind a white picket fence in a gray two-story wood-frame house at 2542 East Fourteenth Street in Sheepshead Bay, a pocket of southeast Brooklyn nestled between Flatbush to the north, Manhattan Beach to the south, Gravesend to the west and Marine Park to the east. Shops and fruit markets throbbed along Sheepshead Bay Road. An array of restaurants lined bayside Emmons Avenue, including Lundy's, a fish palace that occupied an entire block and attracted the diversity of Brooklyn to its tables: families, priests, businessmen, movie stars, boxers, Dodgers, gangsters. Across the street were rows of fishing shanties leading down to the docks where charter boats went out for snapper and flounder. Breezed by the sweet salt air of the nearby Atlantic, Sheepshead Bay had once served as a resort for New York's gilded class, but now it was playing a more egalitarian role: a decompression chamber between old world and new for first-generation immigrant families who seemed as eager as Harry Lombardi to fit in.

Next door to the Lombardis lived old John Murphy, who had escaped the poverty of Ireland as a boy. Two houses down was the family of Frank

Rich, who emigrated from Austria. On the other side lived Ben Brandt, whose parents left Germany, and Thomas Wright, one generation removed from Scotland. While there were notable concentrations of Italians and Irish in that part of Brooklyn, the diversity of blocks like the Lombardis' on Fourteenth Street seemed to hasten the Americanization of the people who lived there, and perhaps drew them to Sheepshead Bay in the first place, away from the ethnic density of Little Italy and Hell's Kitchen. They were entering the middle class, turning away from some parts of their pasts. All the women stayed home except a young telephone operator, boarding with her parents. One man sold cars, two others brokered real estate, another clerked for Kings County. Most were craftsmen with skilled hands: barber, telegraph operator, bricklayer, stonemason, butcher.

Matilda Lombardi, Harry's wife, was a member of what many regarded as a first family of Sheepshead Bay, not in wealth, but in size and fraternity. She was born an Izzo in a brood of thirteen children—four sisters: Delia, Betty, Nicolina and Amelia; and eight brothers: Frank, Joseph, Richard, Louie, Jimmy, Pete, Anthony and Mikey. Their parents, Antonio Izzo and Laura Cavolo Izzo, were immigrants who had arrived at Ellis Island as teenagers from Vietri di Potenza, a tiny mountain village nestled in a brilliant green gorge of olive and oak trees below Mount La Serrapula, sixty-five miles east of Salerno in southern Italy. Many Izzos and Cavolos, who had been farmers, millers and carpenters, fled the impoverished and earthquake-ravaged village in an early wave of Italian immigration in the late 1870s and early 1880s. They were lured to New York by advertisements seeking laborers for the construction of the Brooklyn Bridge, which was celebrated as the longest suspension span ever conceived, an eighth wonder of the world.

The union of Antonio and Laura Izzo eventually created a new world wonder of its own. As the thirteen Izzo siblings reached adulthood and accumulated spouses and children, they all settled within a mile radius of their parents' house on East Sixteenth Street in Sheepshead Bay, a homestead that throbbed with the daily rituals of a prodigious Italian Catholic family: engagements, weddings, birthday parties, picnics, feast days, Sunday dinners, comings, goings, births. That is where Vincent Thomas Lombardi was born, the eldest son of Matilda and Harry, named for his paternal grandfather in the Italian custom. He was delivered into the world in a second-floor bedroom on the night of June 11, 1913, and the Izzo homestead served thereafter as the womb of his childhood. Like his sister Madeline and the three other Lombardi children when they came along, brothers Harold and Joe and sister Claire, Vinnie grew up in the protective and unavoidable embrace of his mother's extended family.

There was unceasing commotion at the Izzo homestead on weekends as the thirteen siblings came in and out with their families. Grandma Izzo was a big-busted woman who wore thick black shoes and tied her deep black hair in a bun. She greeted her grandchildren by grabbing hold of their cheeks and squeezing tight while shouting "Bella! Bella!" Matty, as people called Matilda, and her sisters Nicky and Millie played the piano. Nicky loved ragtime; Matty improvised popular songs and sang in a sharp soprano voice. One of the Cavolo cousins plucked his banjo. Harry Lombardi joined the Izzo brothers down in the basement, where they shot billiards and late at night rolled dice on the green felt of the pool table. Grandma Izzo was a formidable card shark, fond of poker and tripoli, a form of rummy. She played for pennies against all takers, and month by month her glass penny jar shone with more copper coins, which she emptied at year's end to help pay the family taxes.

Vinnie and Madeline and their Izzo cousins, Richie, Dorothy, Wally, Freddy and Joseph, often made fun of the way their grandparents scolded them in broken English for playing rough inside the house. Sent out to play, they skipped down the front porch steps, darted through the fence gate past the cherry tree and out into the vast yard, where they hid and chased and tackled until they were called inside. Here before them was a childhood wonderland, a virtual farm-in-the-city, with shed and coop, side garden of tomatoes, eggplant, corn and string beans, a grape arbor overhanging the brick terrace in back, and a grassy field that extended down Sixteenth Street to the corner of Avenue Y. Grandpa Izzo kept chickens in a pen, and had taught Vinnie and his other grandsons how to prick holes in an eggshell and suck out the yolk. Also in the yard was a small barn for a black-and-white Shetland pony that belonged to Uncle Richard, who bought it from a bankrupt circus troupe. Young Vinnie delighted in the creature and treated it as his own. Once he slipped out the yard to a bridle path that followed Ocean Parkway up toward Prospect Park, a solo adventure that ended when he and the pony were clipped by a slow-moving truck. No injuries resulted, only embarrassment.

Sunday dinner was an endless feast consumed in shifts, with delegations of Izzos taking turns at the oblong mahogany table in the dining room, food and drink flowing for five or six hours. Matty and her four sisters did the cooking. The wine was homemade—Concord grapes picked from the back vineyard, featuring a strong and fruity bouquet that took some getting used to. After antipasto came homemade soup, usually minestrone, sometimes a tart dandelion, followed by spaghetti and meatballs with hot red peppers, or freshly made ravioli, then stuffed capons or braciola, and the Izzo specialty pies. Spinach Pie: Boil fresh spinach and dry. Place in piecrust with sautéed onions and olive oil, salt and pepper, add diced green onions and bake. Ricotta Pie: Mix ricotta with eggs and parsley, grated Parmesan cheese and Italian sausage. Array in piecrust and bake. There was no rush to leave the table.

Large Italian families were not uncommon then in Sheepshead Bay, but the Izzos stood out from the rest. The *Brooklyn Eagle* sent a reporter to a family gathering one Sunday in September 1924, and he came back with a story that ran on the front page with the understated headline: "IZZO FAMILY OF SHEEPSHEAD IS INTERESTING." The reporter found it especially interesting that for all of their Italian tradition, the thirteen siblings, who had been instructed by Antonio and Laura to speak only English at home, were now energetically merging with other ethnic groups in the community. "Father and mother Izzo are impartial to nationalities," the story noted. "One daughter married a son of Italy [Matty and Harry], another a son of Old Erin, another has married into an old Gravesend Yankee family; one of the boys married a Belgian miss," and yet another wed "a German butcher's daughter, pretty Molly Grenau; one of the younger sons expects to take unto himself a young girl from France." Still to come were spouses of Swedish, Polish and Scots heritage.

Grandpa Antonio Izzo was known by his identifying nickname: Tony the Barber. For more than three decades he had been the proprietor of Izzo's Barber Shop, a Sheepshead Bay landmark renowned for its close shaves and haircuts (one glowing account described Tony as a "tonsorial artist") and, even more irresistibly, as the place to go for inside information on the racing scene. During the Izzo Barber Shop's first twenty years of operation, from 1890 through 1910, Sheepshead Bay was a thoroughbred racing town, its mile and a furlong oval among the most popular on the East Coast. Jockeys, touts, trainers, owners, bookies—all found their way to the barbershop at the corner of East Sixteenth and Sheepshead Bay Road.

Inside Tony the Barber's, the saying went, "you not only got a shave, but you gave a tip and got a tip." If there was anything important to learn about an overnight starter, Tony's place got the dope and quietly passed it along to the right folks while lathering their chins. When the white-mustachioed Tony was preoccupied, you could deal with his able assistants along the seven-chair corridor of barbers, walking tip sheets all. Skeats the shoeshine man also had the news. Tony's clientele was a who's who of sporting figures: Snapper Garrison, Humming Bird Tyler, Cannonball Bald, Tom Sharkey, Philadelphia Jack O'Brien and Sunny Jim Fitzsimmons. Long after the Sheepshead Bay track closed, Tony maintained his line of steady customers and his sporting reputation, and passed the tradition along to another generation of Izzos: sons Frank, Louie and Pete all became barbers. It was not uncommon for customers to become family friends or even relatives. Frank Izzo, the oldest son, clipped Harry Lombardi's hair, introduced him to his sister Matty, served in their wedding party in September 1912 and settled down the block from them on East Fourteenth Street.

THE TRINITY of Vince Lombardi's early years was religion, family and sports. They seemed intertwined, as inseparable to him as Father, Son and

Holy Ghost. The church was not some distant institution to be visited once a week, but part of the rhythm of daily life. When his mother baked bread, it was one for the Lombardis, one for the priests, with Vince shuttling down the block between his house and the St. Mark's Rectory delivering food and tendering invitations. Father Daniel McCarthy took Vince and his best friend, Joe Goettisheim, to ball games in Flatbush and Coney Island. Harry Lombardi was not particularly devout then, but enjoyed swapping stories, eating and drinking with men of the cloth. Matty was a regular communicant. From an early age her son Vince revealed an equally strong affinity to Catholicism's routine. He accompanied his mother in prayers to St. Jude and St. Anthony, the family's patron saints, and toted his own prayer book to church for seven o'clock mass.

His mother's favorite picture of Vinnie as a child shows him standing in front of the house on confirmation day, resplendent in buffed black shoes, kneesocks, dark knickers, white shirt, striped tie and double-breasted suit coat, with a boutonniere pinned to his left lapel. The faint glimmer of a shy smile appears on his scrubbed face. His own clearest memory of his religious youth was the Easter Sunday when he and Joe Goettisheim, both twelve, served as altar boys. It was while standing there amid the color and pageantry, scarlet and white vestments, golden cross, scepters, the wafers and wine, body and blood, the obedient flock coming forward, that the inspiration came to him that he should become a priest. As an altar boy, he never wanted to be just another candle bearer, but up front in the procession, bearing the cross.

Vinnie was sponsored at church by Sunny Jim Fitzsimmons, a horse trainer and family friend who lived in the neighborhood and took a liking to Tony the Barber's grandson. Despite his nickname, Sunny Jim could appear stern, but to Vince it just seemed that he was taking his vocation seriously. The racing sheets were his catechism; he was a daily communicant at early morning workouts. Accessorized with hardboots, walking stick and stopwatch, he headed out to the training tracks on muddy spring mornings, often taking Vinnie along for the ride, godson and talisman. One August they went to Saratoga together for a spell of the upstate racing season. Horses had an esoteric appeal to Vince, but he was too heavy to be a jockey and never imagined amassing the wealth of an owner. He played basketball, but was too stiff to excel. In baseball, he was a rough-and-ready outfielder and catcher, but poor eyesight limited his skills with the bat. Football was his sport. He joined his first team when he was twelve, a sandlot outfit that represented Sheepshead Bay in a Brooklyn league. They wore helmets and shoulder pads and green and white uniforms, and though the games were organized, parents were blessedly absent; the SHB boys coached themselves. Vince played fullback and helped design the offensive plays.

"From the first contact on, football fascinated me," he said years later.

Contact, controlled violence, a game where the mission was to hit someone harder, punish him, knees up, elbows out, challenge your body, mind and spirit, exhaust yourself and seek redemption through fatigue, such were the rewards an altar boy found in his favorite game.

Contact and pain were not things from which the Lombardi family seemed to shy away. In later years Vince explained his own occasionally violent outbursts by portraying his father as a harsh disciplinarian who would "hit you as soon as talk to you." There was some truth to this if it described Harry's relationship with his eldest son, decidedly not with the younger Lombardi children. Harry showed a gruff exterior and talked tough about pain. "No one's ever hurt," he proclaimed when Vince came home from football practice with a bruised rib. "Hurt is in your mind!" When he had been drinking too much wine or his preferred scotch, Harry could alternate between verbal hectoring and didactic posturing: he sometimes lectured Vince and the others on his triangle of success—sense of duty, respect for authority and strong mental discipline. But behind his bluster and philosophical musings hid a soft touch who wanted to have a good time and knew that rules could be broken.

There was in Harry still a bit of the wiseacre Moon who marauded through the streets of lower Manhattan. One of his favorite stories was how he and his pals rumbled into restaurants in Chinatown and taunted chefs; one, he said, chased after them with a meat cleaver. And Harry was a prankster still. In Scrabble games with his wife, he invented words, many off-color. Nothing gave him more pleasure than his trick wine flask. After using it to fill his glass at Sunday dinner, he passed it around the table and laughed when it reached a first-time guest, who poured and poured with nothing coming out, unaware of a secret button that needed to be pushed. On Thursday nights, spaghetti night in the Lombardi house, Harry piled his plate high with noodles, smothered them with hot red peppers and dug in. A smile creased his moonface as he fanned himself, his mouth burning, and exclaimed in his throaty Brooklynese: "Hey, Matty! Matty! Whoa! Dis sure is good!"

Harry believed that his kids should not be deprived of the fun he was enjoying. Sometimes he came home late at night with Matty's brothers Mike and Pete, cooked a juicy steak and awakened the children to share in the midnight meal. *Tell us a story*, they implored him, and Harry invariably repeated the same one, about a man who got into a fight with an Indian and twisted the Indian's nose upside down and it rained and the Indian drowned. *No*, they would say, *not that one: Tell us another one!* Harry's effect on his first son was profound in many ways, but the image of him as a humorless autocrat pounding character into young Vince with his fists is mistaken, the first Lombardi myth, created later as part of a larger Lombardi mythology, which was steeped in patriarchy and needed a stern original father figure.

When a painful lesson was to be inflicted in the Lombardi house, more often it came from the back of the mother's hand. Matty was taller and more refined than her husband, with a taste for clothes and a manner that some relatives considered haughty, hence her nickname, the Duchess. She was nervous and domineering, barking out orders. Her family creed was that there was no time for lolling around. She assigned children the most menial tasks: one was responsible for polishing the base of her dining room table every day. Everything with her "had to be this way, the straight and narrow, all according to Hoyle; she had to make sure it was just right, even dessert, not a little whipped cream out of place," according to Joe, the youngest brother. Harold, the middle brother, was late arriving home once and got smacked before he could offer an excuse. "She would hit first and ask questions later," recalled Madeline, who was responsible for washing the dishes. Madeline remembered that her big brother Vince, as the oldest son, "which is a position next to God in an Italian family," had the fewest chores. But those he did have were strictly enforced. "If I didn't do them, I was rebuked," he said later of his mother's discipline. "And not orally, I might add."

By the time Vince became a teenager, his parents had transferred many disciplinary duties to him. He was foreman of the younger siblings. Madeline did the babysitting, but Vince was the enforcer, punishing them if they misbehaved when Mother was not around. Madeline's lingering memory of her brother during those years was that he was "mean." And though he was generally well behaved, his siblings knew that he was not the choirboy that he pretended to be. When he was fourteen, Madeline caught him sneaking a smoke behind the garage and informed her father. After being scolded by Harry, Vince set out to punish his little sister for snitching. "He chased me and caught me and let me have it but good," Madeline recalled. "I wasn't fast enough to get away from him." Meting out discipline was a role that he took to naturally and extended beyond the family, bossing around cousins and friends as well. Sometimes he could seem a bit much, more like an adult than one of them. But the older people loved him. Long before the outside world saw anything extraordinary in him, the family regarded Vinnie as the favorite son. He was the prized nephew of Izzo aunts and uncles; they saw in him Matty's intense perfectionism and the rustic physical features of Grandfather Tony: the distinct jawbone, dark and deep-set eyes, shining smile, piercing voice.

Harry and Matty worshiped their first son more year by year. He was given his own bedroom. His family stressed to him that being average was not enough, that he was better than the rest. They played to win, from Grandma Izzo at cards to Father Harry at Scrabble. You could see it in their eyes: beat Harry in Scrabble and his eyelids blinked violently, a trait passed on to Vince, whose buddies noticed it when they stuck him with the queen of spades in a game of hearts. He also had the churning stomach of his mother, which was one reason they both prayed to St. Anthony of Padua. Anthony was the patron saint of the poor, travelers and those who had lost property, but also, for the Izzos, the saint to turn to when overwrought with worries about the future. No one wanted Vince to spend his life cutting meat.

EVERY WEEKDAY MORNING at four-thirty, Harry Lombardi rose to make an hour-long commute through Brooklyn and across Manhattan to his place of business near the Hudson River waterfront at 23 Hewitt Avenue on the Lower West Side. There, down the block from the bustling Washington Market, he and his older brother Eddie ran Lombardi Bros. wholesalers, a variation of the classic immigrant success story. Family legend held that their father, Vincenzo Lombardi, had been a silk merchant in a village between Naples and Salerno and had come to the United States in pursuit of an associate who had stolen from him. The story was hazy and there were no records to substantiate it. The Lombardis, in any case, started over in America, in the commotion of a tenement house on Mott Street in Little Italy. Vincenzo hauled goods in a horse wagon before dying in early middle age, leaving his widow, Michelina, with four children. Eddie and Harry, the two oldest, had dropped out of elementary school and begun working in their early teens, holding jobs as haulers and delicatessen butchers before opening a market of their own.

Raw strength and street smarts were two qualities most useful in the wholesale meat business, both of which the Lombardi brothers had in abundance. Uncle Eddie was an intimidating hulk, well over 250 pounds, so massive, relatives said, that when he died they had to remove a door to get the casket out. He walked around with black olives in his pockets and dispensed them to customers and children as tokens of friendship. Whether Eddie was an entirely friendly sort is uncertain; family stories offer suspicions of connections to black marketeering. Harry was a miniature version of his brother, though his dealings seemed more benign. Eddie and Harry flexed their muscles all day, hoisting 225-pound half-steers from delivery trucks, placing the slabs on rail hooks outside the market, and taking them down again to be weighed and cut inside the refrigerator room, which was large and cold with sawdust on the floor. When Vince and his brothers and cousins were big enough, the heavy lifting was passed on to them. The two football-playing Lombardis, Vince and little brother Joe, could only laugh years later when asked if they had lifted weights. Never touched a barbell, they said. Only slabs of dead meat.

Bull meat was the Lombardi specialty, below top-grade fare that was sold to downscale chophouses and public institutions in the New York area for use as ground beef. Every Monday and Wednesday, Harry traveled to slaughterhouses in Secaucus, New Jersey, and Brooklyn, stamping LB into his selections with the company ring. The meat was soft and warm when it arrived at loading dock, and the trick was to get it inside, weighed, boned out and refrigerated quickly, so the blood would congeal. Lost blood diminished the weight, and the sale price. Although all the Lombardis knew their way around a side of beef, stories of accidents suffered by father and sons were part of the family lore. Working at the meat table one day, Harry cut his thigh when the knife slipped. Many years later the same misfortune befell Joe. Vince once got caught on one of the belt hooks and vowed never to work at the meathouse again.

The Lombardi boys were repelled and fascinated by their father's trade, as they were by the waterfront scene, a New York workingman's pasticcio of the ugly and the exotic: rats scampering behind crates in the wharf shadows, black-market jewelers hustling wares on the sidewalks, mob lieutenants stalking the corners, cops on the take, short-weighting con artists; and there, in the middle of Washington Market, anything one could imagine, a magnificent cornucopia of pheasants from New Jersey, colored birds from Manchuria, mallard ducks and Canadian geese, wild turkeys from Wisconsin, grouse direct from J. P. Morgan's private shooting preserve in Scotland, venison from Pennsylvania, reindeer meat from Alaska.

Harry, the grade school dropout, could read and write and showed sharp business sense. His transactions with wholesale customers were in pennies: half-cent, quarter-cent, seven and a half cents off here, a nickel there. He could check the scale and do the arithmetic in his head. No one tested his IQ, but anyone who encountered him knew he was no easy mark. He was financially conservative. His motto: If you can't pay for it, don't buy it. He instructed his family never to buy on credit, a directive that Matty followed, but not their daughter Madeline. As a teenager, Madeline enjoyed a few prodigious shopping sprees at Abraham and Straus department store, incurring debts that her doting father paid off for her. The imperatives of the industry required him to run the wholesale meat business on credit, but he hated to do so, especially after 1929, when many of the restaurants that bought from him collapsed in the Depression. He fumed when customers declared bankruptcy and reopened under different names. When President Franklin Roosevelt came along with programs to ease the way for debtors, Harry blamed the mess on him.

The tattooed butcher had created a comfortable life for himself and his family, and he had acquired the tastes of a middle-class self-made man. All through the Depression years he drove a black sedan. He registered as a Republican. After work he settled at the dining room table for a snack of sliced apples and toasted Italian bread, sipped a tumbler of scotch and read the *New York Evening Journal,* a step up from the sensationalist tabloids, chockablock with sports and columns. To ensure that his children would rise higher, he helped pay for almost everything they wanted, including private educations, and regaled them with aphorisms about freedom and responsibility.

• •

IN THE SUMMER of 1928, after Vince had finished eighth grade at P.S. 206 in Sheepshead Bay, he faced the first critical decision of his life. Where should he continue his education? The choice he made, Cathedral College of the Immaculate Conception, a diocesan preparatory seminary, reflected not only what he wanted to study but also whom he hoped to become. He thought he was on his way to being Father Lombardi. Pursuing the priest-hood was not an unusual calling for a studious Catholic boy then, not for an altar boy so earnest that he appeared at church an hour before mass, but it was out of the ordinary within his family. When Father McCarthy accompa-nied him to Cathedral's offices on Atlantic Avenue at St. James Place to reg-ister for the six-year high school and college program, Vinnie became the first among the Izzo and Lombardi clans to prepare for a religious life; not a priest or nun in the lot. There was one other curious aspect to the decision: the school had no football team.

Cathedral Prep was three stories of gray stone, long rows of ancient win-dows, topped by spires and gargoyles. Lombardi reached it by taking the Brighton Beach Line to Prospect Park, catching the Fulton Street Elevated to Atlantic and walking two blocks through a working-class neighborhood. A di-verse faculty of priests from the Brooklyn Diocese ran the school. Some of them were sarcastic, others gentle. The experience brought more discipline to Lombardi's days and instilled in him many rituals he continued into his adult life. He was required to wake before dawn to attend mass at St. Mark's, and his attendance was recorded with X's and O's in a book that the priests checked regularly. Daily mass became a lifelong practice, often cited as evidence of his extraordinary faith. True enough, but as Lombardi himself explained in later years, he was expected to worship every day when he was growing up, so it had become a habit; his religion was as much a matter of discipline and routine as devotion. The boys wore suit coats and ties, a formality that he maintained and expected of people around him in social situations thereafter. Along with academic subjects, he studied church doctrine, the Nicene Creed, martyrs in the church and articles of faith, and though the specifics of these lessons re-ceded with time, the essence of the dogma stuck with him. He was imbued with the notion that success came with faith and obedience to superiors.

He learned Latin from Father James Smith, nine parts taskmaster, one part humorist, whose teaching style, making the lessons clear to even the slowest pupil, was one that Vince would emulate. The coach in baseball and basketball, Jack "Jocko" Crane, was a levelheaded layman who treated the boys with respect, and drilled them in the importance of repetition and the necessity of mastering the fundamentals. The assistant coach, Father Mc-Goldrick, was Lombardi's sponsor and impressed him with an ability to make the boys believe in him without private doubt. That was not always an easy task; these would-be priests were full of vinegar. "We would try to get away with anything we could down there," said the Reverend Larry Ballweg, one of Lombardi's classmates. One teacher, a naive Irishman, tried to teach through dramatics, but "guys would run roughshod over the poor guy."

No student dared run roughshod over Spike Hyland, a priest with the disposition of a sweatshop foreman who was Cathedral's disciplinarian and oversaw "the Jug"—after-school detention. Hyland often kept an entire class after school and gave the boys tedious assignments as punishment: write out the principles of geometry but PRINT every third word. He was a skeptic who doubted that most of the boys wanted to be priests or had what it takes to be one. "None of you have the vocation," he would say dismissively to his charges. "You don't, your *mothers* do." There was a method to Hyland's madness. The Brooklyn diocese was then overflowing with aspiring priests, many of them, as Hyland pointed out, sent to seminary by Irish and Italian mothers who wanted one of their sons to wear the collar. Matty Lombardi was among them. "My son's going to be a priest," she boasted proudly to neighbors.

As a student and athlete at Cathedral, Lombardi was good but not outstanding, yet he stood apart from the boys anyway. He was scrappy and used his head. His grades were mostly B's. He stammered while reciting Latin and Greek, but plowed his way through both languages. He was surprisingly light of foot but rather uncoordinated in basketball, where he played center on a lackluster team. He could win the center jump by anticipating the referee's toss. His nickname was Two Points Lombardi. The derivation is unclear; more likely it meant that he might score two points a game than that he was a sure shot. As a utility outfielder and catcher, he barked out orders to his more talented teammates. He was also injury-prone. "Lombardi, by the way, has more injuries than Hoover has commissions," a student journal noted dryly. He was remembered at Cathedral for three characteristics: his smile, a sudden, wide flash of teeth that heated the room; occasional eruptions of anger; and his physical maturity. He had the body of an adult at age fifteen—his own adult body, in fact. He was the same height and almost the same weight as a freshman at Cathedral, five eight and 175 pounds, as he was in his senior year at college.

It was his intimidating physical presence, and his desire to lead, that helped Lombardi get elected president of his section of thirty-five classmates, known as Class B, four years in a row, unanimously every time. The student magazine proclaimed that he could have the job for as long as he wanted it. In his yearbook pictures—dark wavy hair, sharp suit and vest, arms folded in a menacing pose, always seated next to the priests in the front row—he appears several years older than his classmates. "He looked mature. He was a serious guy. He always had this smirk on his face," said classmate Joe Gartner. "When I saw him look at me, I would always wonder: Is that unveiled contempt or veiled admiration?" As class president, Lombardi's prime function was maintaining order, much as he did with his siblings and cousins in Sheepshead Bay. The boys stayed in one classroom throughout the day, with priests coming in to teach various subjects. Between periods they might be alone for five minutes, and Lombardi was determined to keep order. At the first rumbling: "All right, fellas, keep quiet." A minute later: "Come on, fellas, quiet." Then, if the hubbub persisted, he rose to his feet and let loose with a ferocious command: "SHUT UP!" Which everyone did, according to Larry Ballweg.

Vinnie's eruptions were often followed by "outbursts of laughter" that made him "a likable fellow," recalled another classmate, John B. Healey. In his third year annual he was described as "the guy who wise cracks his way through class." There was, along with his emotional manner, a bit of mystery to him during his Cathedral days. Few of the boys knew much about him outside the classroom. They called him Tony, a nickname that he used nowhere else. They knew that he played football on a sandlot team on Sunday afternoons (the boys had Thursdays and Sundays off, but went to school on Saturdays). Every now and then he arrived at school with a black eye, which he earned boxing in a Golden Gloves program under a pseudonym. The Cathedral priests disapproved of violent sports; the only thing worse was going out with girls. Boys found to be dating faced suspension. This was an essential part of the culling process; only a third of the students survived the first four years of high school at the seminary. During a retreat at the end of their third year, a Franciscan priest led the boys in a vocational incantation: "I vant to be a priest!" he intoned in a thick German accent, directing the students to repeat the phrase with him. "I vant to be a priest! I vant to be a priest!"

In the end, Lombardi could not say the words with conviction. He left Cathedral in 1932 without completing the six-year program, overtaken by the realization, he said later, that he "was not intended to be a priest." As much as he had tried to direct his thoughts to the peaceful realm of God's salvation, he could not divert himself from earthly temptations. He loved physical contact more than spiritual contact, and could not shake his preference for the game of football. That sport was considered a virtual sin at Cathedral.

An essay on athletics in the 1931 *Cathedral Annual* explains the school's opposition to football, making a case that would echo through the decades:

> Many undesirable results and conditions, physical, moral and intellectual, are brought about by football. Athletes are very liable to physical injury and strain through overemphasis and overspecialization. Football tends to further the advancement of destructive and detrimental moral results. It indubitably leads to the adoption of questionable ethical practices and unsportsmanlike conduct. It sanctions the evasion of rules, trickery, undesirable recruiting practices bordering on professionalism, and a lack of courtesy. There is a regrettable psychological effect on the players. This effect is brought about by newspaper publicity, building

up individual prestige instead of praising the machinelike func-
tioning of a team. False attitudes are taken by the student body
which revels in its athletic accomplishments while neglecting the
real purpose of education.

None of this meant much to Lombardi. He simply loved football. At
the first opportunity, he persuaded friends to jump on the subway with him
and ride up to the Polo Grounds to watch the professional Giants and big-
time college matches between Fordham and Pitt. He followed football avidly
each fall in the sports pages. All through his Cathedral years, despite the dis-
couragement of the school's fathers, he kept playing sandlot football. As
some of his teammates turned eighteen, the good ones who played on major
high school teams told him stories about college recruiters dangling scholarships. Vinnie's resistance to the outside world was already weakened—by
uncertainty about a life of celibacy, by the demanding seminary curriculum
and by what he thought, somewhat ashamedly, was his unpriestlike temper—and finally it broke down. Football was out there, and he wanted in.

His timing could not have been better. The very summer that he went
looking for a place to play football and win a college scholarship, in essence
by repeating his senior year, St. Francis Prep was searching for boys like
him. He had heard of the little school, and had even visited its crumbling
yellow-brick building on Butler Street, because some of his Sheepshead Bay
friends already went there. St. Francis, the oldest Catholic school in
Brooklyn, was fighting to survive. At first it considered dropping football,
then set out on the opposite course, striving to make a name in football by
almost any means necessary, handing out scholarships to gridiron talent all
over the metropolitan area. Here could have been Exhibit A in the Cathedral essay about football's evils. Many of the athletes St. Francis recruited
did not meet its academic standards. With his good grades, Lombardi was an
honorable beneficiary of a dubiously conducted recruiting enterprise. He
was nineteen years old, with four full years of secondary school behind him.
The only reason he did not already have a high school degree was that
Cathedral was a six-year program. He was more mature than most of the
boys he would play against, a fact that would help him and his team. He took
a $150 scholarship to St. Francis for tuition and books and signed on to play
football.

The sporting world tends to cling to the nostalgic belief that everything
was simpler and cleaner in the old days. That is true in some ways, especially
in the realm of money, but not completely. It is the fallacy of the innocent
past. The sports of yesteryear might seem purer in retrospect because the
larger culture keeps changing: money increases, information comes faster,
and sources of temptation multiply. But human nature remains essentially
the same, no more or less pure from one generation to the next. Schools em-

ployed questionable methods to build winning football programs before Lombardi came along and after he left the game. Even as he followed a relatively straight and narrow path himself, the fallacy of the innocent past would be apparent throughout his career in football, starting at a desperate little Catholic school in Brooklyn.

THERE WAS NO practice field on Butler Street. The St. Francis boys trained for ten days in August at Camp Alverno in Centerport, New York, which felt like the Ritz compared with what they had to endure once school began. Back in Brooklyn, they put on their pads and cleats at school, then clambered into an old bus and jostled through the borough to what passed for a field on the edge of Todd's Shipyard along the East River waterfront. The skyscrapers of Manhattan soared in the middle distance. The field was actually a storage lot, a hazardous dirt yard littered with chunks of scrap iron that had to be cleared away. But if the conditions were difficult, the football was the real thing.

Harry Kane, the coach, ensured that much. He himself had been recruited to bring glory to St. Francis. He was an esteemed schoolboy tactician who had made his name coaching football and baseball at the High School of Commerce where, as he never stopped reminding later players, he had once instructed Lou Gehrig, the immortal Iron Horse of the New York Yankees. Kane was the prototypical football autocrat, a short bowling ball of a man with gray hair and a high-pitched voice who knew what he was doing and dismissed any alternative ways of proceeding. No patting on the head with Harry Kane. What he demanded of his players was undivided attention and commitment to winning. On the way back from the shipyard after a sloppy practice, furious at the way his boys were behaving, Kane shouted, "Stop the bus!" and ordered his players off, forcing them to walk the rest of the way back to Butler Street. It was a moment that Lombardi would recall with delight later, telling it to his own players when they complained that he was too unforgiving.

When the year started, Kane's top assistant, Tut Maggio, kept an eye on Lombardi, noticed the way he hit people and thought he should be moved to the line, which Maggio coached. Interior linemen who stood five eight and weighed 175 pounds were not undersized then. Vinnie wanted no part of the move. He survived the scare, playing in the backfield on offense as a spinning fullback, whose primary function in any case was to block, running only in short-yardage situations. There was another fullback on the team, a muscular, pug-nosed Irish kid with stunning speed, all light hair and laughter, who Lombardi realized had twice his own talent but none of his determination. Vinnie played. The gifted slacker mostly sat.

Though he was there for only one year, a ringer of sorts, Lombardi became a popular student at St. Francis. He was called the class Floyd Gibbons, thought of as a bold adventurer. His smile left the greatest impression. "Lombardi is famous throughout the school for his smile that only seems to become bigger under adverse circumstances," the *SanFran* yearbook said of him. "You must not think, however, that Lombardi's smile is like those ordinary ones that some people seem to wear eternally merely to appear pleasant, and with which they mask their true feelings. Lombardi can no more help smiling than the sun can help shining." The *SanFran* writer misunderstood young Lombardi, assuming that the smile reflected his "inner, happy nature." People in Vinnie's family knew that he was more complicated than that: the smile was also a product of the nervous energy and anxiety that drove him.

The St. Francis football team won five of six games that year on its way to the mythical Catholic school title, defeating both Brooklyn Prep and Brooklyn Tech, and Lombardi, on the field for almost every down, performed well enough to gain some all-city recognition. He had his own intense rooting section of Izzos and Lombardis at every game, led by the tattooed Harry, who lit up a Lucky Strike before the kickoff for good luck. But the most telling moment of the season for Vinnie came at the conclusion of an early game against powerful Erasmus Hall, a public high school then in the midst of a long winning streak. Led by the golden arm of its crackerjack quarterback, Sid Luckman, Erasmus shut out St. Francis, 13–0. Yet Lombardi, who smacked Luckman with a few good licks on defense, felt like anything but a loser when it was over. He experienced what he later described as a locker room epiphany. As he sat slumped on the bench in his grass-stained red and blue uniform, he was overcome by joy, a rare feeling for him. Nothing on the sandlots felt quite like this. He understood that he was not a great player, but he had fought hard, given his best and discovered that no one on the field intimidated him, no matter how big or fast. He was confident, convinced that he could compete, puzzled why other players did not put out as much as he had. He felt fatigue, soreness, competitive yearning, accomplishment—and all of this, he said later, left him surprisingly elated.

WORK and PLAY. It was an intoxicating sensation, one that he would want to experience again and again for the rest of his life.

2

Fordham Road

NEW YORK CITY once was the place to play college football. During the twenties and thirties, three schools there, Fordham, New York University and Columbia, all had major programs that attracted the best teams in the country to the Polo Grounds and Yankee Stadium. Their contests on autumn Saturdays were held in front of thunderous crowds and covered by the most influential sportswriters in America, who competed in prose and poetry to glorify the college game in more than a dozen metropolitan daily newspapers. When he accepted a scholarship to play at Fordham in the fall of 1933, choosing it over Columbia, Lombardi remained in New York, but he was a long way from home. The campus on Rose Hill was about as far from Sheepshead Bay as one could get within the city, forty-four miles from the bottom of Brooklyn to near the top of the Bronx. The trip by public transportation took an hour and a half of riding subways through three boroughs: aboveground on the BMT's Brighton Beach Line from Avenue U to Newkirk Avenue, down under Prospect Park to Myrtle Avenue, up in daylight again to rumble over the East River at Manhattan Bridge, and back in darkness as the Sixth Avenue Line rolled north under the West Side of Manhattan and the Bronx on the way up to the Grand Concourse. At the end of that trip came a half-mile walk down Fordham Road to the school's front gate.

Vinnie's cousin Richie Izzo, who had arrived at Fordham a year before him and had helped persuade him to enroll there, made that commute every day. Like most of the men of Fordham, Richie was a day hop, as commuter students were called. Many day hops traveled by train and subway from Brooklyn, Queens and outer Long Island. Another contingent hitchhiked or drove down in car pools from Westchester County; Ed Quinn, who inherited an old Ford from his aunt, took a group of four guys in from New Rochelle, often with just enough gas to reach the Bronx Zoo. In those days they could abandon the car in the middle of the street—"We wouldn't even push it to the curb," Quinn recalled—and hustle up the sidewalk to make their nine o'clock class, certain the car would still be there late in the afternoon when they returned with a canister of gas. Some day hops found their way across the Hudson River from New Jersey; Orville Leddy took the train down from Bergenfield to Weehauken, then rode across to Manhattan on a ferry, before shuttling north on the subway. And one of the 432 men in Lombardi's freshman class, Wellington Mara, whose father owned the New York Football Giants, was occasionally seen riding up from his family's luxurious residence at 975 Park Avenue in the back of a chauffeur-driven limousine.

Lombardi was among the lucky few spared the daily grind. There were no day hops on the football squad. Most of the players were recruited out of the factory towns of New England or Pennsylvania coal country, but even the few who came from the New York area were given room and board on campus. They were an elite within the school's boarding elite. Many of them, like Lombardi, had attended prep schools for a year or two after high school and were not only bigger but older than their classmates. They roomed on the same floors of Dealy or St. John's Halls (in alphabetical order: Lombardi's roommate was Jim Lawlor, a tackle from Astoria, Queens). They ate steaks and lamb chops together at the training table. They walked the campus in athletic brigades and played pool together in Dealy's smoke-filled recreation room. The first memory many teammates retained of Lombardi was of an incident at the pool table; he was leaning over to make a shot during their first week on campus, and someone goosed him. His pool cue flew across the table, and he turned around with a look that warned everyone that here was a serious fellow.

The Fordham campus and its surroundings seemed isolated from the grit of the metropolis. A calming preserve of natural beauty extended from the world-famous zoo to the New York Botanical Gardens and onto the school property itself, seventy acres of cobblestone paths, gray stone Gothic buildings and rolling greenswards shaded by graceful elms. The faculty of Jesuits, robed in full-length black cassocks, strolled the paths of the Quadrangle, carrying missals and saying their office. The athletic director, Jack Coffey, prided himself on memorizing the birthday of every student. "Hello, June 11," he chirped upon greeting young Lombardi. The campus was so evocative of academic serenity that it was a favorite choice for collegiate movie scenes. There was some clanging in the center of it all, where construction had begun on Keating Hall, but the noise was greeted as a sign of vitality, the majestic frontispiece of Keating rising skyward as a symbol that Fordham, founded in 1841 as the first Catholic institution of higher learning in the northeast United States, was flourishing even amid the economic hardship of the Depression years.

The Jesuits sought to impose strict discipline on the men who lived there, and Lombardi mostly accepted it. From his sparely furnished freshman room on the fifth floor of Dealy, high-ceilinged with a creaky wooden floor, he awoke each morning at six-thirty, dressed in coat and tie, put on his maroon-bowed miraculous medal depicting the Blessed Mother, and followed the path to chapel for daily mass before breakfast and class. He had few options in his coursework. Like many football players, he studied business administration, but only three courses separated that major from most others. All undergraduates essentially followed the same curriculum, the Jesuits' favored Ratio Studiorum, which emphasized the retention of knowledge in the first two years and an integration of that knowledge into a spiritual philosophy in the final two. Freshmen were loaded down with as many as eight courses per semester, while seniors had only four, with an increasing emphasis on philosophy, psychology, religion and ethics. All Fordham men were expected to have an acquaintance with classical languages, which Lombardi already had fulfilled by taking Latin and Greek at Cathedral and St. Francis. At Fordham he studied French.

There was no sleeping in or skipping class. Attendance was mandatory and tests came unceasingly. The Reverend Joseph Assmuth, S.J., biology professor for underclassmen, perhaps seemed inimitable, yet he was representative of the Jesuits who instructed Lombardi. Most of them had idiosyncratic touches; all were demanding. Assmuth was considered a world authority on termites. Students could not chew gum in his class. "Zat is for cows," he would proclaim in his German accent. "Ve don't chew!" He did not use textbooks, but scrawled everything on the blackboard for students to take down, essentially creating a textbook over the course of the year. And he kept everyone anxious. One never knew which day of the week he would stride in and bellow "Blitz!" as assistants passed out the dreaded surprise quiz.

After classwork and football practice Lombardi was expected back in his room no later than eight on weekdays, with lights out by ten-thirty. The Jesuits conducted room checks; to demonstrate their obedience, Lombardi and Lawlor stepped out into the hall, fell on their knees and uttered their nightly prayers. On weekends, the boarders could escape the campus, but had to return by eleven, midnight for upperclassmen, and report to the residence hall prefect or dean of discipline, Father John W. Tynan, S.J. (Black Jack, the students called him), on the way back to their rooms. John Barris, one of Lombardi's classmates, thought that it was "just like a monastery up there. They locked the gates. They wouldn't let you out. Everything was a sin. You had this stuff drilled into you." But football players often exhibit split personalities, willing to exist in an authoritarian environment, yet always looking for small ways to rebel. In their first weeks at Fordham, some freshman ballplayers learned how to sneak from room to room by climbing out the window and moving along the ledge while clinging to the mansard roof. Later many of them, including Lombardi, discovered they could fool the Jesuits, who checked their breath for alcohol at night, by chewing garlic cloves after drinking.

IT TOOK only one day of practice for the new head coach at Fordham to decide that his young recruit from Brooklyn was not going to become a backfield star. James H. Crowley watched Vinnie Lombardi play fullback that opening day, then motioned for freshman coach Ed Hunsinger to come over. Too slow, said Crowley, switch the kid to the front. The next day Lombardi was playing guard. He was frustrated by the move and had difficulty adjusting from the upright position of a fullback to the three-point stance of a lineman. His hip pads bothered him. Nearsighted and color-blind, he complained about what he saw up there on the line. The opponents looked too close to him, separated only by the width of the ball. But he became a guard.

That move of positions from fullback to guard in one sense marked the starting point of the mythology of Vince Lombardi. But the context of the Lombardi myth goes back another generation, to an earlier story involving his coach Jim Crowley. There is a remarkable circle of coincidence in Lombardi's life that began, long before he had ever heard of the place, in the small northeastern Wisconsin city of Green Bay. That is where Crowley launched his own football career. He was the backfield star of the 1920 Green Bay East High team that won the state championship when he threw four touchdown passes in the decisive game against Green Bay West, the precision of his spirals aided by a deformed pinky finger on his right hand, which he said helped him better steer the ball. His first high school coach was Earl "Curly" Lambeau, a local athlete who had dropped out of Notre Dame and was also starting up a new professional team back home called the Green Bay Packers.

At Lambeau's suggestion, Crowley left Green Bay to play for Knute Rockne at Notre Dame. There he became known as Sleepy Jim, a nickname that perfectly captured his appearance. His whole physical manner suggested relaxation: his ambling gait, his lazy hair parted down the middle, his tired, droopy eyes. It was Rockne who had coined the phrase by describing his recruit as "a sleepy-eyed lad who looked as though he were built to be a tester in an alarm clock factory." But Crowley's drowsy aspect disguised a quick wit. To the question of why he seemed so sleepy, he explained in deadpan: "I sleep all right at night and in the morning, but in the afternoon I toss and turn something awful." On the practice field at South Bend, Indiana, one day, Rockne, who was called The Swede by his players, lashed out at Crowley for missing a blocking assignment. "Is there anything dumber than a dumb Irishman?" asked the coach. From Sleepy Jim came the dry retort, "Yeah, Coach, a smart Swede."

Crowley was not just sleepy and funny, he was also a character in American mythology by the time he reached Fordham. He had been brought to fame in part by his own running skills, but more by the facile work of a publicist and the melodramatic prose of the greatest mythmaker in American sports, Grantland Rice, who over the course of a half-century wrote more than twenty-two thousand stories and seven thousand poems celebrating athletes and their games. Crowley played left halfback at Notre Dame in a backfield that included Don Miller, Harry Stuhldreher and Elmer Layden. The quartet, gritty and undersized, their average weight only 164 pounds, started twenty-two straight games from 1922 to 1924, losing only once. The fifteenth game in that streak came against a top-rated Army team at the Polo Grounds on October 18, 1924. Rice covered the contest amid the brotherhood of New York sportswriters in the press box, and in loose conspiracy with a sports information man for the Irish, he transformed Sleepy Jim and his backfield mates from mere mortals into football legends: the Four Horsemen of Notre Dame.

On the Wednesday before the game, back in South Bend, the Notre Dame players had traipsed over to the recreation center in Washington Hall for their ritual road trip eve movie. Playing on the screen that night was *The Four Horsemen of the Apocalypse,* a 1921 silent film starring Rudolph Valentino and based on the mystical book of the same title written by Vicente Blasco Ibáñez. It was a story of greed, hedonism, honor, love and war set in Argentina and France before and during World War I. In the movie's pivotal scene, the Valentino character encounters a Christlike prophet known as the Stranger who foresees "the beginning of the end," the coming of world conflagration, and evokes the Four Horsemen of the Apocalypse from Revelation. They appear as horrifying apparitions on horseback, the helmeted Conquest, the hideous War, then Pestilence, carrying the scales of famine, and finally the pale rider on the pale horse, Death.

George Strickler, the Notre Dame public relations man, said he "got goosebumps" watching the scene where the Four Horsemen, after appearing one by one, join together and thunder across the screen. The image stayed with him all the way to New York on the train. At halftime of the Army game, as he stood in the press box gossiping with a group of writers that included Grantland Rice and Damon Runyon, he mentioned that the Irish backs were running through the Army defense "just like the horsemen." The next morning, when he leafed through the Sunday edition of the *New York Tribune,* he realized that Rice had appropriated his idea for what would become the most famous football lead ever written:

POLO GROUNDS, New York, Oct. 18, 1924—Outlined against a blue-gray October sky, the Four Horsemen rode again. In dramatic lore they are known as Famine, Pestilence, Destruction and

Death. These are only aliases. Their real names are Stuhldreher, Miller, Crowley and Layden....

Strickler's work was not finished. After reading Rice's account he called his father in South Bend and arranged for him to rent four horses from a corral next to his saloon. At the first practice session after the team's return from New York, photographers were led onto the field to snap the picture of a publicist's dreams: Stuhldreher, Miller, Crowley and Layden on their mounts, wearing helmets and fearsomely stylish warmup coats. The shot was distributed nationally above the cutline: "The Four Horsemen of Notre Dame." That phrase and the symbolism of the photograph combined to denote something beyond the prowess of a talented college backfield. All the elements were there for a new myth, born from the old.

The leathery men on horseback not only summoned the allegorical riders of the Apocalypse from the Book of Revelations, they also connected football to something that had nothing to do with the movie but everything to do with the photographic image: the mythology of the American West. Swift justice and thrilling violence, the unambiguous world of black hats and white hats, valor and perseverance on the unspoiled plain—all that seemed endangered by the advent of the modern age. But here, within the hundred yards of a football field, was another way to play out America's enduring national myth, the freedom of the frontier. The Old West might be disappearing, but the Four Horsemen of Notre Dame rode on in the nation's romantic imagination, in league with the silent westerns then being filmed in Hollywood, yet with a more powerful combination of sport, legend and memory. High on horseback, invincible, Stuhldreher, Miller, Crowley and Layden became honorable warriors of a lineage that reached deep into the narrative archive, as eternal and illusory as knights of the Middle Ages. Their power in the sporting imagination, like that of medieval knights, arose from the contradiction of the heroic dream described by Dutch historian Johan Huizinga, whose seminal work on the legend of chivalric knights was published contemporaneously with Grantland Rice's rendering of the Four Horsemen. "Reality continuously denies the ideal," Huizinga noted, forcing culture to withdraw "further and further back into the sphere of festival and play."

Jim Crowley brought the mythology of the Horsemen with him to Fordham a decade after leaving Notre Dame. On the first day of practice, when he encountered Vince Lombardi and decided to move him to guard, he unwittingly provided the connection from past to future, from one myth to the next.

YOU DID NOT have to be a big lug to play guard. Crowley copied the system he had been taught at Notre Dame, preferring what were called "watch charm" guards, often four inches shorter and thirty pounds lighter than average linemen. The position demanded quickness and tenacity. Lombardi was squat and slow in sprints, with large feet that looked as though they belonged on somebody else's body, but he was quick in short bursts and indisputably tenacious, as was his fellow guard Nat Pierce. What was most unusual about Lombardi was that he was from New York. The other key recruits in Crowley's first class came out of New England factory towns: Pierce grew up in Biddeford, Maine, on a street whose name—Granite—would later define him; Leo Paquin, a rangy end, was from Brockton, Massachusetts; Joe Dulkie, a fullback, from Lowell; Andy "Handy Andy" Palau, a quarterback and kicker, and Albie Gurske, a halfback, both from Bristol, Connecticut; and Frank Mautte, another halfback, from New Haven. Among all the varsity and freshman players, only five were from New York, while eighteen were from Massachusetts alone.

During their freshman year, proscribed from varsity competition, Lombardi and his classmates spent most of their time on the practice field learning the Notre Dame box offense and mimicking the opposition in scrimmages against the varsity. The guards Lombardi and Pierce spent hour after hour practicing the crossover steps required of them when they pulled out to lead the blocking on sweeps. From his three-point stance at right guard, pulling right, Vinnie would drop his right foot back slightly at the snap, then cross over with his left foot and head out, swerving from the line enough so as not to interfere with other blockers, yet reaching the hole before the swiftest back would make his cut. Crowley's assistants, including line coaches Frank Leahy and Judge Carberry, who also came from Notre Dame, stressed that the key to good line play was the quick start, the sudden hit, taking the momentum away from the defender. One day in practice, Lombardi and Pierce learned just how quick they both were; mishearing the play, Vinnie pulled left while Natty pulled right. They met, full force, behind center, "like a head-on car collision," Lombardi later recalled. "We both went down. Our pride was hurt." His nearsightedness might have hindered him in that instance, but for the most part his coaches and teammates thought he was a superior blocker precisely because he could hardly see. He hit opposing linemen a split second before he realized he was upon them, which gave him a reckless abandon, never holding back to cushion the blow.

Butch was the nickname his teammates gave Lombardi. Appropriate, perhaps, for the grandson of Tony the Barber. And it reflected Vinnie's toughness. As rugged as he was, though, the history of his early career at Fordham is primarily a hospital report. He was held out of three freshman games with a broken ankle. During spring drills the next May, as Lombardi was preparing for his sophomore season, Crowley and the line coaches began mentioning him as a key backup, if not starter, and by fall preseason workouts his chances seemed bright. Upperclassmen on the line succumbed to injuries one after another: John Waldron dislocated his shoulder and was knocked out for the year, while Amerino Sarno, the roughneck tackle, fractured his ankle and was hobbling for several weeks. Butch Lombardi saw backup action at guard in the first varsity game of his college career, played at Yankee Stadium instead of the usual Polo Grounds, a 57 to 0 thrashing of tiny Westminster of Pennsylvania. Crowley used the mismatch to experiment, using a flexible shift formation in which the guards started in the backfield, aligned with the halfbacks, then jumped into gaps in the line before the snap. Neither the score nor Crowley's offensive creativity proved to be signs of things to come. For the rest of that year, Fordham would be a low-scoring outfit with a conservative offense that relied on a sturdy defense to win ball games.

The next weekend, on Columbus Day, Fordham made a rare road trip (every team wanted to play in New York, where the big crowds and sportswriters were), taking the train up to play at Boston College. Early in the game a starting tackle broke two bones in his hand, further depleting the crippled line corps, and was replaced by Lombardi, who performed admirably despite his lack of size for that position. In several stories the following Monday and Tuesday, as Fordham practiced for its annual visit from St. Mary's of California, Lombardi, projected to start at tackle, had suddenly ballooned into a bulky 200-pounder. Or so said the Fordham Rams publicity department and New York sportswriters. Butch actually still weighed about 183 pounds. The Lombardi buildup lasted one day.

In the day-to-day ritual of football practice, Wednesday was the most brutal day, the midweek session when the players went at it with game-situation ferocity. Crowley trained his men in secret, the workouts closed to students and the press. He was an adherent of long and physical practices, full of wind sprints and odd exercises like the one-legged bump, in which two players faced off against each other on one leg, holding the other behind them, and bumped shoulders until one hit the ground. Sleepy Jim thought it helped with balance. On Wednesday he kept the players on the field until they appeared as dim figures scrimmaging in the twilight, identified only by grunts. The final round was all hitting, with backs slamming into the line again and again, and blockers and tacklers, protected only by slender pads and leather helmets without face guards, pounding away in violent scrums at the line. The men often changed positions for the free-for-all; they were not rehearsing plays so much as toughening themselves for the bruises of Saturday and relieving the weekly boredom through unrestrained frenzy.

Lombardi loved Bloody Wednesday: out there on Fordham Field above the gymnasium on Rose Hill, trains from the New York Central rumbling along beyond the fence, Butch in the midst of his teammates, hours of work behind them, letting loose, darkness enveloping the Bronx, the smell of mud and grass and leaves and leather and sweat, thwack and thud, then a big heap on the ground, lying there, exhausted, and up for more.

But this time, on the Wednesday before the St. Mary's game, Lombardi did not get up. He had playfully switched to the backfield in the free-for-all and carried the ball. As players disentangled, Butch was on the bottom of the pile, motionless, groaning loudly, kicked in the gut so hard that he could not move. He had to be carried from the field. Enough, said Crowley, sending his men to the showers. That night Lombardi felt so queasy he could not eat. He returned the next day, determined not to lose a chance to start, but collapsed before drills began and was carried off again, semiconscious. At the infirmary, doctors determined that he was bleeding internally with an aneurism in his duodenum. If nothing else, a glowing article in Friday's *New York Post* must have cheered the young casualty, who had not started a game yet was portrayed as a most valuable player. "Fordham's dreams of football glory in tomorrow's intersectional gridiron classic with the highly-touted Galloping Gaels of St. Mary, which will pack the Polo Grounds to its historic rafters, were all but knocked galley west yesterday," the story began. "An injury to Vincent Lombardi, the powerful young Brooklyn sophomore whom Jim Crowley, the Ram coach, had nominated for a starting position at tackle, did it."

Lombardi was listed as a starting lineman in the game program, but in fact he was back in the campus infirmary when St. Mary's beat Fordham 14 to 9, consigned to a bedridden row of maimed football players that included three other linemen and the star halfback, Joe Maniaci. Lombardi was put on a diet of soft foods: ice cream, heavy cream, milk, bananas. The next week students in his public speaking and religion classes gathered below the window of his infirmary room and shouted up songs and get-well wishes. "Gave him the little rah, rah, rah," classmate Edward J. Schmidlein said. Inspired and still burning for his chance to play, Lombardi dragged himself out of the infirmary that Thursday and reported for practice, surprising Crowley and the Fordham beat writers, who hailed the return of "one of the cripples." But Lombardi was so weak that he could play little that week or the next. He was in and out of the lineup the rest of the year, which Fordham completed with a 5 and 3 record. The Rams lost to three intersectional foes, but won two important games near the end of the season, 13 to 12 over Major Bob Neyland's powerhouse Tennessee squad, and 39 to 13 against archrival NYU in the muck of Yankee Stadium on Thanksgiving Day. Most of the Fordham starting linemen graduated after that, opening the way for Lombardi and his cohorts to take over.

IT WAS NOT easy to meet women at Fordham, where even the cheerleaders were men. The Jesuits did not entirely discourage dating, but the only women on campus were a few elderly librarians and telephone operators. Joining an organization that traveled away from Rose Hill was the surest way to encounter women. The Fordham Glee Club was especially popular not just because of its musical tradition, but also its sex appeal. The male singers looked dashing in white ties and tails, and performed at the nearby women's schools, including Mount St. Vincent's and the College of New Rochelle. Most campus social clubs sponsored dances, none bigger than the spring formal held by the Brooklyn–Long Island Club. Four hundred Fordham men brought dates to the Hotel Pennsylvania's rooftop across Seventh Avenue from Penn Station, where couples danced in tuxedos and gowns to the big-band music of Woody Herman and Tommy Dorsey.

Lombardi's experience with women had been extremely limited. He played spin the bottle as an adolescent with his cousins over at Grandma Izzo's, but during his years at Cathedral Prep, as he trained for the priest-hood, even that innocent game would be considered sinful, material for his confessions. During his year at St. Francis Prep, he was allowed to date, but the girl he asked to the spring prom was his cousin Dorothy Izzo. Finally, at Fordham, largely because of the gregarious attitude of Jim Lawlor, his big, glad-handing roommate, Vinnie entered a new world of romance. Lawlor had a first cousin at Fordham named Arthur Planitz, whose two sisters, Marie and Marge, were then living with their mother in the Bronx in a first-floor apartment at 2564 Creston Avenue, a third of a mile up Fordham Road from campus. Marie had studied nursing at Roosevelt Hospital, but dropped out after getting sick. German Catholic on her father's side and Irish Catholic on her mother's (a Sheridan), she was tall, blonde and blue-eyed, with a figure, recalled several Fordham men, that elicited from them a famil-iar, ungrammatical locker room exclamation: "What a built!"

With the approval of Marie and Marge, Lawlor began bringing Vinnie and other football players to the apartment, sometimes on Saturday nights after the team's banquet of Italian food at the Riviera Restaurant on Kings-bridge Road, more often late on Sunday afternoons. Lawlor, Lombardi, Leo Paquin, Andy Palau and a half-dozen more pals sat around munching on pretzels, drinking beer and telling lies. Marie was quickly taken by Lom-bardi; overwhelmed, she said later, by his maturity, his dark curly hair and brilliant smile. She became his girlfriend, his first and only. Soon after Marie and Vin met, Lawlor accompanied them down to Fair Haven, the New Jer-sey shore town where the Planitz family came from and where they main-tained a residence.

As Marie told the story in later years, after a long day swimming and roaming the beach she said goodbye to Lombardi, walked into the house and announced to her father, "I'm going to marry that man."

"No you're not, Rep," she remembered her father answering sternly. "He's Italian."

"Rep" was Mortimer Planitz's pet name for his daughter, short for rep-tile. On the surface Mortimer Planitz appeared to be a reserved figure, conservative and status-conscious. He was a stockbroker who dressed in suit and bow tie every day, whether staying home to receive guests or heading to Wall Street to buy and sell on the New York Stock Exchange. He did not like the idea of his daughter dating the rough-looking son of an Italian butcher from Brooklyn. But Marie's father was in no position to dictate proper behavior to others. He had long been involved in an illicit intrafamily romance that haunted his wife, Mary, and Marie herself, for the rest of their lives. When Marie was entering high school at Red Bank (New Jersey) Catholic High near Fair Haven, her father became seriously ill with blood poisoning when his cut foot was infected from the dye in dark socks. He was cared for by Mary's sister, Cass, a nurse, at the family's apartment in the Bronx. During the recovery period he and Cass fell in love, and they stayed together from then on.

It was a debilitating family melodrama, played out in silence and shame. The Planitzes, Marie said later, did not yell and scream or even talk about what was going on. There was no divorce and remarriage, just an unofficial rearrangement. Marie blamed everything on her aunt Cass, not her father. Her mother, Mary, became a quiet alcoholic and eventually suffered a stroke. She stayed in Fair Haven until her children finished high school, then moved to the apartment in the Bronx, switching residences with Mortimer and Cass. Marie and Marge stayed with their mother while son Arthur attended school at nearby Fordham. Disaffected and confused by the family trauma, Marie tried to lose herself in fun: in search of the next dance, another party, a new young man to meet. Then she encountered Vin Lombardi, who seemed to offer everything that her life lacked: he was emotional, he had a huge family, he was full of life, a varsity athlete, religious and dependable, a relief.

Lombardi had been shy in his dealings with women, inarticulate about his deepest feelings, but Marie awakened his dormant romantic side. He showered her with gifts and pastel-colored greeting cards to "Rie Dear" from "Vin." She became, almost immediately, the first promoter of his career. During her high school years she had preferred to watch football games by standing on the sideline near the boys, and now she was figuratively standing next to her Vince. One day she was with him at an ice cream parlor near campus and saw big Ed Franco coming through the door. Franco, recruited to Fordham from Jersey City, New Jersey, a year after Vin, was also an interior lineman, with more raw talent, and loomed as a threat for playing time as Lombardi began his junior year. "So you're Ed Franco. You're the fellow trying to take away my boyfriend's job," Marie said to him. She bet Franco a box of candy that he would not be able to do it.

Vin brought Marie home several times in the summer after his sophomore year, when he worked as a lifeguard and special policeman at Brighton Beach, one beach down the shore from his family's summer locker at Manhattan Beach. The Lombardis by then had moved off Fourteenth Street to a new house at the corner of Avenue S and Twenty-ninth. Vin's brother Harold adored Marie, finding her more artistic than anyone in his own family. But the Lombardi women had trouble with her. Mother Matty seemed jealous of anyone who threatened to steal the love of her beloved son. "My mother was a very domineering woman and she would never relinquish Vin," said Harold. Sister Madeline befriended Marie and visited her at the Bronx apartment, occasionally sleeping over, but remained suspicious. If Marie had so much money, as she boasted, why did she keep borrowing clothes from Madeline? To her, Marie seemed a bit aloof. "I don't remember her ever showing emotion like I would," Madeline said later. "I thought she was pretty cold, but to an Italian if you weren't Italian I guess everybody seemed cold."

THE YEAR 1935 in the Bronx: Lombardi told the Fordham publicist that his favorite actors were Leslie Howard, Ann Harding and Helen Hayes. He claimed to be a "voracious" reader of the books of Richard Halliburton, the daring Hoosier who wrote adventure stories romanticizing his travels around the globe. Vinnie and his Fordham teammates paid a quarter to see motion pictures at the Paramount. Another quarter got them a sixteen-inch pie at the Italian pizzerias up on Arthur Avenue. They received free season passes to Giants games at the Polo Grounds (paying only the 20 cents federal tax). Old Golds, Luckies, cork-tipped Herbert Tareytons and menthol Spuds ("When Rah! Rah! Rah! makes your throat Raw! Raw! Raw! Light a Spud Cigarette") went for 15 cents a pack. A night out with Marie, dancing to Irving Conn and his Orchestra at Ben Riley's Arrowhead Inn on Riverdale Avenue, set Vin back a dollar per ticket. Subway fare: a nickel. The Bronx Buick Company on Jerome Avenue advertised a 1934 Pontiac Sports Coupe, eight cylinders and rumble seat, for $495. Tickets to Fordham football games at the Polo Grounds cost 50 cents for students; other fans paid $1.10 to sit in the bleachers, $2.75 for reserved seats and $3.30 for box seats. A pittance, in retrospect, but 50 cents was hard to get in the Depression; it was a half-day's work for Al Lucchi, one of Lombardi's classmates, who spent several hours before and after school as an elevator operator at the Barbizon Plaza in Manhattan.

The scale of life during Lombardi's college days now seems manageable and innocent, but that is looking through the distorted lens from present to past. Life did not appear entirely innocent then. In fact, as Lombardi began his junior year at Fordham, a dominant theme in American academic circles was the loss of innocence. Leading scholars feared that universities, reflecting changes evident in modern society, were deteriorating into incoherence, with an emphasis on the particular instead of the whole, on uninterpreted fact instead of fundamental principle, encouraging a hollow worship of fame and success. The inevitable results, they said, were confusion, greed and self-centeredness.

Robert Maynard Hutchins, president of the University of Chicago, delivered a paper asserting that bewilderment was becoming the characteristic feature of the modern world. If a university was to combat that, he said, it "must be intelligible as well as intelligent." But "if we look at the modern American university we have some difficulty seeing that it is uniformly either one. It sometimes seems to approximate kindergarten at one end and a clutter of specialists at the other." The fall from grace of American universities, declared Ralph C. Hutchinson, president of Washington and Jefferson College, was "evidenced by the shocking number of graduates who have been discovered in . . . corrupt professional practices, in the concealment of corporation assets or liabilities, in the watering of stock, the peddling of questionable securities, the evasion of income and other taxes, the distribution and acceptance of bribes, and the predatory exploitation of public resources."

The rise of major college football was part of the debate. After a brief slump at the beginning of the decade, the game had become increasingly popular and profitable again during Lombardi's college years: Attendance figures rose 10 percent every season from a Depression-era low in 1932, and bulging gate receipts loomed ever larger in the considerations of athletic directors and administrators. Notre Dame drew more than 53,000 spectators to every game. Navy led eastern schools with an attendance average of 44,000, with Fordham close behind. But along with enormous growth came complaints that the sport had compromised the integrity of the universities and made laughable the ideal of amateur competition. Even the Marx Brothers were laughing: their 1932 *Horse Feathers* was a send-up on the college recruitment of dumb football players.

The professionalization of college football dated back at least to 1891, when the University of Chicago hired the first coach at a professor's salary, Amos Alonzo Stagg. Now Chicago's president, Hutchins, was questioning the relevance of football to the educational mission. He had forced Stagg to leave in 1932 and was in the process of deemphasizing football; before the decade was out he would eliminate it at Chicago altogether. The college game was all but invented by Yale's Walter Camp, who conceived the modern scrimmage rules, attempted to deepen the significance of the game with his analogies to warfare and corporate management, and glorified the players with his annual All-American teams. But in 1931 the death of an Eli player had led some to conclude that the warfare analogy had gone too far, and now Yale's president, James Rowland Angell, stood out among the game's leading critics. During the 1935 season Angell lambasted the commercialization of collegiate athletics, saying that football had succumbed to a "hired man" policy. "College football has become in many instances big business," he said. "Today in college football it is the crowd, the winners, the receipts, that count above everything else in 70 percent of the institutions." Angell offered three alternatives: (1) seek endowments to make athletics independent of gate receipts; (2) allow athletics to carry on unaided by college; or (3) abandon college sports. His comments received major coverage. Most sports columnists ridiculed his preaching ("A careful perusal of the Constitution fails to reveal that the makers of that document were greatly concerned with the possible advantages which might accrue to a youth weighing more than 150 pounds and lucky enough to kick a football more than 40 yards," wrote Hugh Bradley).

Most editorial writers picked up the cause, however, as did other public officials. Governor Martin L. Davey of Ohio sarcastically called football "the supreme purpose of higher education" and complained that Ohio State players were stashed on the state payroll. To recruit top players, the university and its boosters found no-show or easy jobs for fourteen athletes in the state highway department, sales tax division and motor vehicle department, or at the capitol as legislative pages, elevator operators or clerks. The Reverend Patrick J. Mahan, S.J., of Creighton University said that big-time college football presented an inherent contradiction. "I am convinced, and reasonably so, that no regular player is on a big team without being paid. He does not, out of his own pocket, pay for his tuition, fees, board and lodging. Yet authorities of universities decry the subsidizing of athletics," said Mahan, concluding: "If you sit in at a crooked game you must be crooked if you expect to win."

During his first three years at Fordham, Jim Crowley heard no complaints from his Jesuit superiors about the dominance of big-time college football on campus. His problem with Father Aloysius J. Hogan, the school's president, was of an entirely different sort. Hogan had little use for academics who disliked football. Crowley's problem with his boss was that here was a Jesuit who thought he knew everything about sports. Every Monday during football season, shortly after lunch, Hogan would slip into Sleepy Jim's blue Packard parked outside the campus's Bathgate entrance, puff on his pipe and launch into a soliloquy on the tactics the coach might employ for the next game. Crowley ignored the advice but endured the lectures, which were a quiet source of amusement to others in the athletic department, though not to Jack Coffey, who faced the same situation with his baseball team. Once, after Coffey's ball club lost a game 18 to 2, Father Hogan was beside himself, saying there was no reason they should have lost by such a score. "I help out as much as I can," the father lamented. "But the exigencies of the job are endless, and I cannot be in two places at one time."

HIS JUNIOR YEAR was the most frustrating of Butch Lombardi's career. He began the season as the regular right guard, but injured his shoulder in a 13 to 7 victory over visiting Vanderbilt, and soon lost his job to Ed Franco. Whether this prompted Marie to pay off her bet and give Franco a box of candy is lost in history, but it did cause her boyfriend to sulk. Franco not only played, he became a star, part of a tough front line that shut out Pitt in a scoreless tie and stifled the offense of talented St. Mary's in a 7 to 7 tie. The front seven linemen performed so strongly that Fordham's publicist gave them a nickname, The Seven Samsons. Lombardi was relegated to a backup group of "shock troops" who spelled the regulars at the start of the game and again in the third quarter. Still, his injury jinx persisted, even with limited playing time. He twisted an ankle against Pitt and got elbowed in the mouth so hard in the St. Mary's game that his lower teeth were knocked loose. He wore a bridge for the rest of his life. He was the constant companion of trainer Jake Weber, the diminutive Dutchman known as Eighty Minute Jake, who could single-handedly tape the ankles of the entire forty-man squad, eighty ankles in eighty minutes. Harry Lombardi's old admonition to his son—"Hurt is all in your mind!"—was only partially true. Vinnie was hurting body and soul. One Saturday night, stuck alone in his room at St. John's with an injury, he spotted classmate James Ambury walking down the abandoned hallway and called him in for help. "Would you get me a priest?" Lombardi asked. "I need to go to confession but I can't move."

Sleepy Jim's entire team felt frustrated that year. The two ties and a 20 to 0 thumping by Purdue had dropped the Rams from the top national rankings. Thinking that Fordham had no chance against Jock Sutherland's Pitt team, New York's sportswriting fraternity had largely ignored what proved to be Fordham's finest defensive outing in years, choosing instead to take the overnight train to Columbus to cover the Notre Dame versus Ohio State matchup. But after stopping Pittsburgh, Fordham's players were convinced they were the best squad in the East going into the season finale against rival NYU, which, with an easier schedule, was unbeaten in seven games and anticipating a bowl berth. Before the game, the *New York Evening Journal*, Harry Lombardi's favorite paper, thought it had a scoop. Fordham's two senior stars, running back Joe Maniaci and tackle Amerino Sarno, reported that two "flashily dressed" gamblers driving an "expensive car" approached them outside the practice field at Fordham and offered them $1,000 each to throw the game.

As Maniaci told the story to the newspaper, "Sarno and I were on our way to the gym to change our clothes. Two fellows got out of their car. One guy asked, 'You guys need any money?' I said, 'Who doesn't?' The fellow asked me if I'd like to make a G for myself and made Sarno the same offer. We laughed. 'What do you want us to do?' The fellow said, 'We're a couple of bookies and we stand to make a lot of money on this game if we know which way it's going to go. All we want you guys to do is make it sure for us. You, Maniaci, you fumble that ball whenever you can and you, Sarno, make your tackles miss. In other words, dog it.'"

Hours before the game the next day, Maniaci and Sarno reported the bribe attempt to Sleepy Jim and their teammates. The story enraged the squad, pumping them up even more for the crucial contest, which was played on Thanksgiving Day before a boisterous sellout crowd of 75,000 at Yankee Stadium. Fordham dominated the Violets, winning 21 to 0, led by the offensive play of halfback Maniaci and quarterback Handy Andy Palau, who caught a touchdown pass, intercepted two passes, punted, returned punts and won the Madow Trophy as the game's most valuable player. Lombardi spent the first quarter on the sideline, but rushed the field with a band of teammates in the second quarter when Sarno got into a fistfight with NYU tackle Perry Gaffen. When the brawl ended, Sarno and Gaffen were tossed from the game, and the hole in the line gave Lombardi some unexpected playing time at guard. At midfield after the game, Crowley encountered NYU coach Mal Stevens, whose Rose Bowl hopes had just been crushed.

"I'm sorry, Mal," Crowley said.

"That's all right, Jim," said Stevens. "Maybe I can do as much for you someday."

Up in the press box, Damon Runyon, covering the game for the *New York American,* banged out his familiar telegram-style lead, addressing it to the Rose Bowl Committee:

> Dear Gents: Sorry will be unable to meet you in Rose Bowl stop We used everything possible against Fordham including our Dukes but were de-emphasized again stop They have tough chins stop Suggest worthy opponent for you would be Andrew Palau and any ten other fellows stop Love and kisses
> The Violets
> New York University

The next day Father Harold Mulqueen, the prefect at St. John's Hall where the football players lived, confronted Maniaci and Sarno after being told by police detectives that the bribe story appeared questionable. The seniors finally confessed to the priest. They had concocted it. Their only motive from the beginning, they said, was to inspire the team, which indeed they had, and the lopsided victory restored Fordham to national renown: the final polls ranked the Rams eleventh in the country.

There was one final bit of controversy for the Fordham football team that school year, and Lombardi was in the middle of it. It happened during spring practice, as the men were going through drills in preparation for the 1936 season, which would be Lombardi's last. He felt unsure of his standing on the team. Sleepy Jim had been picking on him, making him feel that he could do nothing right. Late one afternoon, after a discouraging session, Lombardi was taking a shower when he was approached by Richard Healy, another senior-to-be who was feeling equally frustrated after three years as a second-string end. Healy was known as a practical joker, and this time he went too far. He called Lombardi a wop and told another player to stand next to him to see who was darker. Lombardi was enraged. He tackled Healy to the hard shower floor and punched him several times before Leo Paquin and a few other teammates broke it up. Blood flowed into the shower drain as Healy and Lombardi were taken to the infirmary.

"I got an egg on my head and he got some stitches in his forehead," Lombardi later recalled. Healy said he "got the worst of it" in the exchange of blows, and carried the shame of what he had done for the rest of his life. "I agonized over it for years. It haunted me. It was another dumb trick. A dumb Irish trick. I regret that. It was a sad moment in my life." Fordham had a new president that spring, Father Robert I. Gannon, S.J., who did not think much of big-time college football. When he heard about the shower room fight, he considered it evidence that the violent game was making brutes of young men, turning them away from the responsible traditions of the Jesuits. He suspended both players from the team. Lombardi was stunned. "I thought," he said later, "that it was the end of my career."

3

We Do, or Die

TEN DAYS BEFORE the Fordham football squad opened its 1936 season, a young sportswriter for the Associated Press visited the practice field at Rose Hill to assess the team's prospects for the coming year. This cub reporter for the AP later gained journalistic renown as James B. Reston, Washington editor and columnist for the *New York Times,* but in his early days he covered sports under the informal byline Scotty Reston. Writing in the clipped and matter-of-fact style of the wire service, Reston centered his preseason account on a quote from the coach that was predictable both for its humor and pessimism. "I feel at home with this squad because they're big and I can't pronounce their names," said Sleepy Jim Crowley. "But we're playing so many tough teams that we can have a very good year and still lose almost every ball game." The eight-game schedule, Reston pointed out, featured first-rate teams from every corner of the nation: Southern Methodist from the Southwest, St. Mary's from California, Purdue from the Midwest and Georgia from the South, along with powerhouse Pittsburgh and NYU in the traditional finale. But Crowley had sixteen top lettermen returning, and not even his droll pessimism could diminish the great expectations for his team in his fourth year as coach.

Reston appraised this as Fordham's "biggest, fastest and most promising squad in years." His competitor at the *New York Sun,* Edwin B. Dooley, in a story headlined "Ram Team May Be Best in History of Institution," wrote his season-setter in more effusive prose: "Every one on the campus from the clerks in the office to the gardeners on the lawn was talking about it. All of them wanted to know if you had heard about the team Jim Crowley is going to have this year. If you hadn't it was a pity, for it was an absolute fact, you were informed, that the Maroon machine will be the best ever to set foot on Fordham's practice field." The stories noted that the strength of the team would be its seven-man line, led by a rugged junior who played center on offense and backer-up (what linebackers were called then) on defense. He was the player Reston identified as "the great unpronounceable": six-foot, 200-pound Alexander Franklin Wojciechowicz, who was being promoted for All-American honors as Wojy, his more pronounceable nickname. It was said that the sound of his blocks and tackles was so distinctive, a clean and sharp smack, that even a blind man could tell if Wojy had made the play. Starting up front with him would be ends Leo Paquin and Johnny "Tarzan" Druze, tackles Ed "Devil Doll" Franco and Al "Ali Baba" Babartsky, both of whom had been moved out from guard, leaving left guard for Natty Pierce and right guard for Vin Lombardi.

At last Lombardi was a fixture in the starting lineup, the beneficiary of the persuasive powers and football judgment of Crowley. First the coach intervened with Father Gannon to lift Lombardi's and Healy's suspensions. Then he and line coach Frank Leahy concluded that they could field the sturdiest forward wall by moving surplus guard talent to tackle, where two vacancies had been left by graduation. The new line Crowley built for the 1936 season from left to right: Paquin, Franco, Pierce, Wojy, Lombardi, Babartsky and Druze. Before the era of two-platoon football, these seven were almost sixty-minute men, playing both ways all season with occasional substitutions (the most frequent being Harry Jacunski at end for the oft-injured Paquin). On offense they responded fiercely to Crowley's familiar sideline refrain: "Blockers! More blockers!" he would shout. On defense they became known as the Seven Blocks of Granite, an evocative epithet that made the 1936 season memorable and blessed the Fordham linemen with a permanent place in football lore. For one among them, the scrappy right guard, already twenty-three years old, his uneven playing career nearing an early end, it served an even greater purpose: the figurative block of granite became a cornerstone in the construction of the mythology of Vince Lombardi.

On the eve of the season opener, Crowley paced the floor of his apartment on East Ninety-sixth Street in Manhattan. This late-night pacing had become a ritual for him, as he turned over in his mind every play that might go wrong the next day. Up at the Fordham campus, nine of his veteran players gathered in the St. John's Hall room of Dick Healy to tell stories and play craps for dimes on the bed. Butch Lombardi came, the bruises of his shower brawl with Healy forgotten. Paquin, considered the intellect of the group, was interviewing his teammates for a weekly column he wrote for the *Fordham Ram*. The players were in "fine physical and mental condition," Paquin determined, and were anxiously awaiting "the coach's signal to 'Go get 'em, boys.'" Wojy said he was eager for the St. Mary's Gaels "to blow into town." Frank Mautte, captain and halfback, was expecting trouble from Pittsburgh, which had already started its season and had rung up 53 points in the opener. Franco was nervous about his move to tackle and looking forward to playing the "Southern Methodist gang for thrills." Lombardi said he had "a score to settle with Purdue," which had dealt the Rams their only loss the previous season. Andy Palau, still frustrated by Sleepy Jim's cautious offense, said he expected to pass more this year. The answers were classic ballplayer clichés, none more so than the one Paquin elicited from Johnny Druze. "I'm not looking ahead to anyone but Franklin and Marshall," the opening day opponent, Druze said, noting that assistant coach Hugh Devore "saw them play last Saturday, and reports a great club."

Not so great, it turned out. The year before, Franklin and Marshall had surprised Fordham, losing only 14 to 7. This time Fordham ran up 66 points before the Diplomats from Pennsylvania finally scored in the closing seconds by falling on a blocked punt in the end zone. The Rams offense looked unstoppable, gaining 308 yards on the ground and another 98 through the air on six of seven passes. It was not entirely the wide-open attack Palau was hoping for, but impressive enough. But the offense created by Crowley, the old Horseman, turned from apocalyptic to meek after that first week. Southern Methodist came into New York next, and from the start all attention was on the visitors from Dallas, who arrived like a traveling circus, replete with mascot pony, marching jazz band and an official sweetheart named Mary Ann Collins. Riding east by train, the SMU pageant reached Grand Central Station at 10:45 Friday morning. While the players relaxed at the Hotel Croyden, the jazz band and its official sweetheart wowed New York, parading double time down Forty-second Street and performing at the Madison Square Garden rodeo.

At the Polo Grounds the next day, Southern Methodist revived the circus atmosphere by keeping the ball high. The Mustangs threw more passes than Fordham might attempt in a full season (forty-eight), and gained 213 yards passing, to zero for the Rams. But for all their showmanship, they could not score. Six times Fordham's defenders were pushed deep into their own territory; each time they stopped SMU from crossing the goal line. The visitors grew desperate as the afternoon darkened, until finally they threw one too many; Johnny Lock intercepted a long SMU pass and raced seventy-five yards for the game's only score. Fordham had been outplayed all day, but still won 7 to 0, maintaining its national standing. In the locker room afterwards, Sleepy Jim and his players acknowledged that they had been lucky. But Johnny Lock was a shaky hero, nauseous since reaching the end zone. In the excitement of the moment, dashing downfield on his run to glory, he had swallowed a wad of tobacco.

LOMBARDI WAS AN INVETERATE talker on the field. Always yapping. Aggressive. Barking. *Come on, let's go!* There were times when Andy Palau had to tell him to hold it down so he could call the play. No. 40 was the bossy older brother to his partners along the line, shoving them around even though they were all bigger, demanding more from them even though they were all better. "The better we became, the tougher and meaner Vinnie got all the time. He felt it was his obligation to instill religion in the younger players," said Tarzan Druze. The other members of the line were comparatively quiet. Wojy, a good-natured quipster out of uniform, turned mum in the locker room before a game and let his hitting speak for him until it was over. Natty Pierce, Druze and Devil Doll Franco occasionally threw wisecracks and taunts across the line to opposing players. But only Butch was incessantly talking to himself and his teammates. His eyelids blinked furiously. *Damn it, what's going on here!* When he missed a block or thought a play had been fouled up, he hustled back to the huddle seething "like a madman," in the words of his line coach, Frank Leahy, who worried that Lombardi was "always treading a thin line" between competitiveness and fanaticism. "There never was a more aggressive man who played for me than Vincent. There were times when I genuinely worried that he might be too aggressive." He impressed the more talented Wojy as a battler, a "fighting guard who never took any guff from anybody." But he rarely let his emotions interfere with his concentration for the next play.

As the quarterback in Crowley's Notre Dame box formation, Palau lined up a few yards behind center, then shifted to the left or right before the snap, often ending up behind the right guard. On many plays he and Lombardi had the same blocking assignment, pulling out to double-team an opposing tackle or guard, Vin hitting the defender from the inside, Handy Andy from the outside. They were not the most intimidating sight coming at you, Palau a bony 165 pounds, twenty less than Lombardi, and both were slow afoot, but they were persistent and smart. They developed their own internal blocking signals. If one thought he could handle the tackler alone, he would yell "Ice" and the other would turn upfield looking for a backer-up to block instead. "Vinnie was very smart that way," according to Palau. "Many times he called the play and got it right." His attributes of perfectionism and determination were more apparent to the team than to sportswriters in the press box, who dismissed Sleepy Jim's occasional comment that Vinnie was his most underrated player. Wojy and Devil Doll attracted most of their attention.

Lombardi's teammates could not see intimations of greatness in him, but they responded to his forceful character. He seemed mature beyond his years, carrying himself on campus like a young salesman moving briskly on his way to the next call. His shirts and suits were sharply pressed. He toted a snappy brown briefcase with neatly organized class notes and football diagrams. On game days he helped round up the team for mass, bringing along even Palau, a Lutheran. After the ritual ankle taping down in Jake Weber's barber's chair and a midmorning lunch of steaks and chops, peas, potatoes and milk, the Rams marched onto the bus for the ride up Fordham Road and down the Grand Concourse to the Polo Grounds. They sang most of the way, loud and joyous, starting with the playful ("She Told Me She Loved Me, but, Oh, How She Lied"), moving on to the sacred (the lilting Latin hymn, "Regina Coeli, Laetare") and ending with the school's emotional fight song. Lombardi would rise from his seat, flash his luminescent teeth and conduct the chorus of "The Fordham Ram."

> *Hail, men of Fordham, hail; on to the fray;*
> *Once more our foes assail in strong array,*
> *Once more the old Maroon, wave on high;*
> *We'll sing our battle song: WE DO, OR DIE!*

THE SOUTHERN METHODIST show was nothing compared with the coming of St. Mary's two weeks later. Led by its ebullient coach, Edward "Slip" Madigan, the team and an accompaniment of six reporters and 253 fans rode out of the Moraga valley in northern California on a fifteen-car special train, stopping to practice at Chicago's Soldier Field along the way. The eastbound party was preceded by Tom Foudy, an advance man born for the carnival circuit, who spread word that the Gaels had a new back, Jes Groux, who could throw the ball eighty yards "and when the wind is right he can make it one hundred," and pass with such accuracy that he knocked a nickel off a stake from fifty yards away. In this, their sixth trip east, Foudy noted, the Gaels would feature "the only Jew ever to play for St. Mary's," sophomore Harry Aronson, the son of a San Francisco tailor, and they would wear sensational new uniforms, solid silk in stockings, shirts and trousers, all of a shimmering emerald green with red, white and gold touches.

When the train reached Pennsylvania Station, Slip Madigan dashed over to the Waldorf to meet with his pals in the New York press corps. Stanley Woodward, the erudite sports editor of the *Herald Tribune* and president of the New York Football Writers' Association, was there, along with Allison Danzig of the *New York Times*, Bill Corum of the *Evening Journal*, Joe Williams of the *World-Telegram*, Frank Graham of the *Sun*, and Grantland Rice and Damon Runyon, among others. In one sentence, Runyon captured the philosophy of his brethren. "All of us dyed-in-the-wool New York sports writers from Pueblo, Colo., Memphis, Tenn., Waterbury, Conn., Chicago, Ill., Milwaukee, Wis., Boston, Mass., and way stations, are loyally pulling for the home team today, although it is pretty tough to pull against St. Mary's after you've met Slip Madigan," he wrote for his "Both BarrelS" column, published in the *New York American* the next morning. Wherever he went in the Waldorf, Runyon said, he was accosted by "inmates of California" wearing little red and blue caps, their "pockets stuffed full of pamphlets" about their home state. "As a matter of fact, we are commencing to suspect that St. Mary's annual pilgrimage to the big town on the excuse of a football game with Fordham is nothing more nor less than an insidious publicity campaign for California."

The Fordham men were thinking only football. The St. Mary's contest was the first of three games in the middle of the schedule that looked as though they would define this promising season: St. Mary's, then Pitt, followed by Purdue. After the first three games, the Rams had given up no touchdowns rushing and only two overall, both in the final minutes on fluke plays when the first string line was not in the game. But Crowley was still losing sleep over his offense and starting to take criticism for its lack of firepower. Dooley of the *Sun*, himself a former running back at Dartmouth, noted that Crowley "has never had an attack at Rose Hill which was even faintly reminiscent of the Four Horsemen." Slip was getting all the ink, but Sleepy Jim was certain he had the better story. He was searching, as he often did, for something to inspire his team.

Crowley was at heart a showman. Once he invited the heavyweight boxing champion Jack Dempsey to talk before a game. Whenever his friend and fellow Horseman Don Miller was in New York, Crowley ushered him onto the field for practice, but invariably dispelled the Horsemen myth with his instinctive sarcasm. "This is Don Miller, boys," he said once. "He used to play right halfback and block for me at Notre Dame. He is going to take the backs down to one end of the field and give them some tips. I want them to pay very strict attention—and when he has finished, forget everything he has said." Crowley even tried secret potions. Lombardi later told the story of how Crowley, before one game in 1935, claimed that he had been working with "a scientist from the Swiss Alps" and had invented "a pill that will impart superhuman strength." This was long before the era of uppers and greenies and steroids. It was a psychological con job; Crowley was using nothing more than sugar pills. The players came forward one by one, tongues out, to receive the wonder pill delivered on tweezers. Lombardi felt "HUGE," as though he could stomp anybody, when he took the field for warmups that day.

For the St. Mary's game, Crowley tried to inspire his men with stirring words. This was not his strong suit; he could never replicate the mystical oratorical powers of his old mentor Knute Rockne from the shadows of the Golden Dome. But in the locker room at the Polo Grounds on that October 24 Saturday, Crowley assembled his men and began a pregame speech that his players long remembered. There was a sellout crowd out there in the stands, he told them, and millions more would be listening to Ted Husing's radio broadcast. Out of the multitudes, he wanted them to think of one special fan, his elderly mother, "sitting in her rocking chair out there in Green

Bay, saying her beads" for her boy's good luck, waiting to hear whether Fordham could compete with the best. They must not let her down. Crowley paused, turned to the team manager and, in a low voice that rose to a crescendo, sent his players on a wild charge into the sunlight with the words, "Son, you better open the door and get out of the way fast. HERE COMES MY FORDHAM TEAM!"

Crowley also unveiled a new offensive plan, sending his backfield men in motion, which almost proved the team's undoing. Referee J. P. Egan determined that the Fordham backs were not coming to a complete stop after the shift, and he threw the flag on them seven times. Damon Runyon had his lead: "Penalty, penalty, who gets the penalty, seems to be the game the officials are playing this afternoon. . . ." St. Mary's took an early 6 to 0 lead, aided by the constant penalties and a powerful kicker, Lou Ferry, described by Runyon as "a human siege gun," who kicked field goals of eighteen and forty yards. But Ferry was "lugged off the field by six of his teammates" after being hurt in the second quarter. Handy Andy Palau brought Fordham back by throwing a touchdown pass and kicking the extra point, and the Rams held on to win 7 to 6. "The locker room afterwards was one mad scramble of backslapping, songs and shouts of 'What's hot tonight?—see you at the Commodore!' " Paquin, the end and newspaper chronicler, recalled. "Crowley in the meantime was congratulating each player and had the broadest grin of all."

The victory, Runyon noted in his game story, left "the team from Bronx county still undefeated and untied this season, with the old Rose Bowl dream flourishing up Fordham Road like a hot-house tomato." Also flourishing was the Fordham front line, which held St. Mary's to no touchdowns and only eight net yards for the afternoon. New York papers began running daily reports on Ram practices, focusing on the line. "Fordham Gets Blocking Drill in Scrimmage," read one headline. "The line may not be everything in football, but it is very important," wrote columnist Joe Williams. "It is practically impossible to score against the Fordham line." Willard Mullin, the sports cartoonist, drew a half-page cartoon that week with the caption, "Just a Line to Let You Know," over sketchings of Paquin, Franco, Pierce, Wojciechowicz, Lombardi, Babartsky and Druze. Below the players, Mullin sketched Sleepy Jim Crowley and a caption, "And So He Built a Line." James Cannon of the *New York American* paid a visit to Crowley and posed the pressing question.

How good is this team of yours?

The greatest defensive team I've ever seen, said Crowley.

Not the best Crowley had coached, Cannon reported. The best he had ever seen, with a line that was superior to the Seven Mules who played in front of the Four Horsemen.

Assistant coach Hugh Devore returned from Pittsburgh with a scouting report on the next opponent, a team that had already beaten Notre Dame and Ohio State. Pitt's program represented the best and most controversial aspects of college athletics in the 1930s. Under Jock Sutherland it played a precise, exciting style of football, but it was a de facto pro team. Pitt paid players so brazenly that Notre Dame complained and dropped the Panthers from its schedule after that season, while Sutherland soon decided to move on to the true professional ranks. The talent of that 1936 squad was made clear in Devore's scouting report. He analyzed each player in the starting lineup and posted the findings on a wall next to Jake Weber's barber chair in the basement of the Rose Hill gym, something for the Fordham players to study as they had their ankles taped. Jake added to the display, posting a picture of each Pitt player next to the report.

The prospects of a Rose Bowl, the emerging glory of a great line, the New York sports fraternity's hunger for a new local star—sometime that week Fordham's football team reached that ineffable moment when it was transformed into a phenomenon, the story people wanted to talk about, the team everyone wanted to see. Athletic director Jack Coffey noted a "salutary rush for tickets," with even the upper deck in the Polo Grounds selling out for Pitt. One night that week the players took in a double feature on the Grand Concourse, and between movies the lights went up, the manager pointed out the Fordham athletes, and the audience rose to cheer.

There was no surer sign of Fordham's new celebrity than the attention Damon Runyon paid the team. Now he was not only writing game stories, but also dipping into Fordham material for features and columns. Runyon's turn of phrase could make any story a corker, his humor evincing the universal in the particular. His story on Rameses VII, the team mascot, was a hilarious take on the use of animals on football field sidelines. "The Fordham boys up in the Bronx have a ram for a mascot, a ram being a gentleman sheep. This ram, whose name is always Rameses, is a sullen old bloke, who has to be dragged around by man-power whenever they want it to go anywhere, and it despises football. We believe Rameses would be much better off, and perhaps happier, as chops, or with curried rice."

By 1936 football was a sidelight for the prolific Runyon, who by one estimate wrote 73 million words in newspaper stories, columns, screenplays and works of fiction during his career. One problem with football was that it was played in daylight and outdoors. He preferred "jernts" like Lindy's restaurant to open air. He was on the town every night, usually stationed on a narrow stretch of midtown Broadway that he had adopted as his own since 1931, when he began writing short fiction about the "guys" and "dolls" who operated there. He could stay up all night, drinking forty cups of coffee, and look as fresh in the morning in his sharp clothes and glasses as his more subdued colleagues. From the hustlers and hacks he encountered at night came his characters, Harry the Horse, Sam the Gonoph, Bookie Bob. Runyon lived in the moment and wrote both his fiction and his Fordham game stories in the present tense.

But what can one write about a football game in which neither team scores and only once does either even threaten to cross the goal line? For the second straight year, Pitt and Fordham struggled to a scoreless tie. Runyon did his best: " 'Tis a great football pulling and hauling that Fordham and Pittsburgh put on in the Giants' yard this afternoon, with 57,000 customers teetering on the edge of their chairs throughout, but the upshot of it all is a dead heat, nothing to nothing. Ordinarily nothing from nothing leaves nothing, but in this case there remains to the observers the memory of one of the grandest gridiron shindigs in history—two teams battling each other to who-laid-the-chunk. You can't say at the finish that one is better than the other by as much as an eyelash." Runyon's prose was no more panegyrical than that of many of his press box colleagues. Stanley Woodward, writing in the *Herald Tribune,* said the game "came close to the claims of the press agents and it is doubtful if better or more savage football was played on any gridiron."

It was the front line, again, that stood out for Fordham: "transcendent," wrote Danzig of the *Times,* "against one of the hardest running attacks in football." The single scoring threat of the game came in the third quarter, when the spectacular Pitt running tandem of Marshall "Biggie" Goldberg and Bobby LaRue led the Panthers on a forty-six-yard drive, finally reaching the Fordham three-yard line. Fourth down, a yard and a half to go. Fordham had not given up a running touchdown all year. The front line was exhausted and wounded. Lombardi was playing hurt, a deep gash inside his mouth. He had been injured on offense earlier in the game, when Palau, to Vin's increasing dismay, kept calling the same play, the halfback inside tackle, in which the quarterback and right guard try to double-team Pitt's left tackle, an unmovable behemoth named Tony Matisi. One of Matisi's flying elbows had smacked Lombardi in the jaw, hashing the inside of his mouth into a fleshy mess that would require thirty stitches after the game. He had been on the bench, recovering, when Pitt began its charge, but Sleepy Jim called him back and now he was out there at his own goal line, swallowing blood. Next to him stood Babartsky, his wrenched right knee throbbing with pain. Behind them was Palau, woozy as well, having been kneed in the head earlier while making a crucial tackle on the high-stepping Goldberg. Here, for Lombardi, was the beautiful controlled violence of his game, holy war and bloody rite, refusing to yield, ignoring the body's fatigue. We do, or die.

On fourth down Pitt gave the ball to La Rue, running inside left tackle. Lombardi and Babartsky held firm. Wojy, the backer-up, came hurtling over, met La Rue with one of his blindman smacks and brought him to the ground two yards short of the goal. That was it for the game, no more scoring threats, and when it was over the Rams reacted as though they had won.

Their fans stormed the field as the marching band played late into the autumn afternoon. Andy Palau won a coin toss with Pitt's captain and brought the game ball back to Rose Hill on the bus.

As scores came in by Teletype from across the country that day, it became clear that Fordham stood as the finest unbeaten team in the East. This caught the attention of Henry Grantland "Granny" Rice, whose syndicated column, "The Sportlight," along with his magazine articles and monthly film shorts, made him the most influential chronicler of American sports. His cherubic face framed by the trademark Confederate gray fedora, his manner always gentlemanly, his wit soft and self-deprecating, Rice lived the playful sportswriter's life. He appeared at every major event, from boxing to horse racing to baseball to college football. He knew everyone, from presidents to jockeys; in any city he visited, his hotel room was the place to congregate after the games; and his prose and poetry were beloved by millions of readers. In the era before television, sportswriters served as the nation's tribe of storytellers, popular artists invested with enormous powers to reinforce cultural mores and shape the public imagination. Rice was the wise man of his tribe, "the bringer of good news about games," as he was later eulogized by William Randolph Hearst. It was Rice who had written the seminal bromide of good sportsmanship ("When the one great scorer comes/To mark against your name/He writes not that you won or lost/But how you played the game.") It was Rice who had watched the great Red Grange run and called him the Galloping Ghost. And it was Rice who had immortalized Sleepy Jim Crowley as one of the Four Horsemen of Notre Dame.

Rice translated into poetry what he saw on the playing fields not merely to elevate play to a more literate (if sappily romantic) realm; he saw a natural, ineluctable connection. "Verse and sport together make up the menu perfectly," he once explained. "Nothing else is needed where brain and brawn, heart and ligament are concerned. Rhythm, the main factor in both, is one of the main factors in life itself. For without rhythm, there is a sudden snarl and tangle." Now, after Fordham's front line had performed brilliantly for Jim Crowley, Rice looked down at a fresh piece of copy paper in his typewriter and found the rhythm for a new ode titled "Old Gibraltar." Not exactly the "Ozymandias" of one of his favorite poets, Percy Bysshe Shelley, but still moving to Fordham men everywhere.

> *Great, mighty Minnesota fell, upon a fateful day,*
> *Both Yale and Army felt the axe, and tossed their crowns away,*
> *Big Holy Cross, an early boss, hears no more winning hands,*
> *Yes, strange things happened everywhere, but the Fordham Wall*
> *   still stands.*
>
> *Once Carthage ruled an ancient coast, but where is Carthage*
> *   now?*

The Grecian Phalanx no more wears the winning olive bough,
And where are Persia's ruling hosts, that ruled all warring
*   lands?*
Their day is done, by sand and sun, but the Fordham wall still
*   stands.*

Who took the thrust of S.M.U. and rolled its chargers back?
Who stood the Gaels upon their heels and broke up each attack?
Who held young Goldberg at the line, with willing hearts and
*   hands?*
The answer rings from Coast to Coast: the Fordham wall still
*   stands.*

TIMOTHY SYLVESTER COHANE was already preoccupied with the Fordham wall and what he could do with it. Cohane, the school's fresh-faced publicist, had taken a job in the sports information department as a student a few years earlier after Jack Coffey cut him from the baseball team. He wrote witty articles in Fordham football programs during his school days, while also editing the sports section of the *Ram*. After graduating in 1935 he emerged as the favored press agent of New York sportswriters. More than anything, this lanky son of a New Haven dentist wanted to be part of the press box brotherhood, a keeper of the myth. He wore a fedora, drank scotch, smoked cigars and told stories with a deep voice, exhibiting great command of the language. His sensibilities were those of the tribe: respect for coaches, loyalty to the home team, glory to the game, but all with a leveling touch of sarcasm. He loved the pageantry of football. Every Saturday morning he arrived at the press box before anyone else and sat alone studying the teams and the numbers. He knew all the fight songs and tried to write some himself.

As an ace public relations man, Cohane understood that his mission was to make people remember his team and its players, and that the most effective way to accomplish this was through the imagery of metaphor and nickname, the semiotics of myth. The year before he had called Fordham's formidable front seven The Seven Samsons, but it failed to catch on, perhaps conjuring an image too archaic and hirsute. Cohane knew the myth of the Four Horsemen and Seven Mules, and he revered Granny Rice. The Seven Mules reminded him of something he had once seen in the *New Haven Journal Courier* back in 1930, when he was in high school. Fordham boasted of a powerful front line even then, under the coaching of Frank Cavanaugh, the Iron Major, whose teams went nearly two years without allowing a rushing touchdown. In the week between the Holy Cross and NYU games that 1930 season, an AP wirephoto ran in the New Haven paper under the cutline "The Seven Blocks of Granite." Cohane exhumed the phrase from the graveyard of sports metaphors and applied it to the 1936 Fordham line, first using it as a headline in the program for the Pitt game. Paquin, Franco,

Pierce, Wojciechowicz, Lombardi, Babartsky and Druze. The Seven Blocks of Granite.

Here, as with the Four Horsemen, phrase and image converged in the creation of a mythology that transcended its athletic reality. The number seven at once represented good luck and evoked an ancient and permanent lineage: seven seas, seven wonders of the world, seven blocks of granite. That the image was a wall of stone, an inanimate object, gave it a pureness beyond the human capacity, as philosopher Roland Barthes points out in his "Mythologies" essays: "We must not forget that an object is the best messenger of a world above that of nature: one can easily see in an object at once a perfection and an absence of origin, a closure and a brilliance, a transformation of life into matter (matter is much more magical than life)." There could be no better time for a perfect and permanent object than in 1936: dust storms rage in the American heartland, the Germans storm into the Rhineland, depression and totalitarianism threaten life all around, but the Fordham wall still stands.

Tim Cohane received notice for creating the Seven Blocks, but for the rest of his life he graciously refuted any claim to authorship, acknowledging that it was the work of a wire service cutline writer who never took credit for it himself. In all events, the phrase was transformed into myth. Sports sections competed for the fiercest-looking picture of the Seven Blocks of Granite: in three-point stance; charging downfield; standing tall and impenetrable. Other bards in the sportswriting tribe competed with Rice for memorable stanzas. Dan Parker, columnist for the *Mirror,* worked up a military analogy:

> *Hindy's well-known front wall*
> *Took a million troops to man it*
> *Whereas Fordham has but seven*
> *In its famous Wall of Granite.*

Linemen unaccustomed to the celebrity usually afforded gifted runners and passers were now treated as stars, worthy of feature stories in the press. Stanley Frank of the *New York Post* wrote a story on "the least conspicuous guard"—Vin Lombardi, whose Brooklyn boyhood provided a local angle.

"It is a pretty good stint for anybody to clinch immortality—for one season at least—as one of the Seven Blocks of Granite, particularly for a citizen whose speech is not distinguished by a broad 'a,' " Frank wrote. "The broad 'a' is almost standard equipment for a Fordham player since the majority of the squad and six regulars are pilgrims from New England. Lombardi comes from Brooklyn and can contribute only a broad beam to the panoramic picture." Butch was the least known of the Seven Blocks, Frank surmised, because "he doesn't wander at large in the manner of Wojy, the backer-upper; he hasn't Ed Franco's knack of getting into pictures, and he doesn't caddy fumbles as Nat Pierce does." He was just a "stout" fellow who kept plugging along without notice until "the epic battle in the Pitt game," when "opposition scouts went away speaking most kindly and at greatest length about Lombardi." At the start of the baseball season, Lombardi had correctly predicted that the Yankees and Giants would win the pennants, so Frank decided to ask him who would win the Rose Bowl: the champions of the Pacific or Fordham. "Lombardi maintained a complete and dignified silence. He probably knew the answer, but he is one of the gladiators who considers premature talk an ill omen."

Lombardi's reticence on the Rose Bowl issue seemed his alone. The motto at Fordham after the Pitt victory became "From Rose Hill to the Rose Bowl." Anticipating more of the national spotlight, the athletic department outfitted the Rams in brilliant new uniforms, with gilded helmets, bright yellow sateen pants, and maroon jerseys with gold numerals front and back. The expectations only increased that Saturday after Fordham gained revenge on Purdue, defeating the Boilermakers 15 to 0 in another impressive defensive performance that was keyed by Crowley's decision to shift his defense. He moved Lombardi out from his middle guard position to a post across from the strong-side end, where he could help thwart the sweeps of Purdue's star running back, Cecil Isbell. After the game, the Fordham band paraded out of the Polo Grounds blaring "California, Here I Come!" To the thousands of desperate families whose lives had been shattered by dust storms in Oklahoma and Texas that year, the popular tune was a bittersweet anthem of meager hope as they made their way west to California. To the football fans of Fordham, it was all rollicking fun as they marched behind the band. In their legion was Harry Lombardi, who had attended every game on a free ticket from his son (each player got two freebies; Harry sat next to Jim Lawlor's dad, while Marie Planitz was usually with Lawlor's girlfriend).

In the press box, looking down on the merriment below, Damon Runyon typed another of his telegram leads:

> POLO GROUNDS, New York, Nov. 7. Night letter to whom it may concern in Cal-i-for-ni-yay. Collect.
> If youse are looking for real football trouble in Rose Bowl New Year's day we got it for you. Stop. You spell it Fordham. Stop. Ask Purdue. Stop. Ask St. Mary's. Stop. Ask anybody. Stop. How are youse anyway? Stop. Love and Kisses. Stop.
> (Signed)
Little Old New York

All that remained after a week off were the last of the intersectional games, against Georgia, and the Thanksgiving Day grudge match with NYU.

Georgia had endured an uneven season. The Bulldogs had been drubbed twice early in the season, but were coalescing late in the year, defeating Florida and Tulane in the weeks before meeting Fordham. Grantland Rice and Damon Runyon suspected trouble. In his "Sportlight" column, Rice reported that Sleepy Jim "turned white and started to shudder" when someone told him the Georgia game would be easy. On the morning of the game, Runyon cautioned in his "Both BarrelS" column, "This one today may be the tough one for Fordham." His hunch was correct. Fifteen minutes before kickoff, the Fordham band strutted onto the field blasting out "California, Here I Come!" again. They played it while marching directly past the Georgia dressing room, firing up the visitors. After a scoreless first half, Georgia scored the first touchdown, on a pass against the Fordham second string, which Crowley had sent in because the first line seemed tired and uninspired.

Halfback Frank Mautte, the Fordham captain, sparked his team with a stirring catch and touchdown run to tie the score, and his superior play in the third quarter appeared to be making the difference. But it was a dirty game, and Georgia's roughneck tactics eventually got the better of Mautte. "I never lost my cool except in that game against Georgia," he said later. "We didn't wear masks in those days, and what Georgia was doing, three of them were on me at one time. One was scratching his nails in my face and smashing me while the other two were screening him from the ref. I complained to the ref. They stuck their fingers in my eye, really gouging me. But they weren't getting caught. I got a little excited and got in two good rights to the jaw. The ref gave me the thumb." Fordham's offense, not the most potent to begin with, sputtered without Mautte, and the game ended in a 7 to 7 tie. "Yes, suh, folks," Runyon opened his game story, "the perfume of the sweet magnolia blossoms wafting out of the dear old Southland today is too much for our stalwart boys, more accustomed to the fragrances of Bronx byways."

Lombardi had played vigorously, as usual, but was dismayed to see that some of his more illustrious linemates seemed lackadaisical or distracted. "Some of our better players . . . behaved as if we had already finished the season undefeated and had received and accepted the bid to the Rose Bowl we all wanted so badly," he lamented later. The Georgia tie hurt badly, but was not ruinous. A win against NYU could still send Fordham to Pasadena. But the Rams could not recover the spirit that had carried them through the difficult stretch from St. Mary's through Purdue. Instead, they performed even worse against their city rivals, when everything depended on the outcome. The Thanksgiving Day game, played in a quagmire of mud and sleet before 50,000 fans at Yankee Stadium, served as NYU's bowl, a means of redemption at the end of a disappointing 4–3–1 season and revenge for the 1935 loss that had ruined their perfect record and ended their own bowl run.

Fordham scored first, but missed the extra point because Palau, the regular kicker, had been knocked out with a lame ankle. NYU came back on a three-yard run by George Savarese, who thereby earned the nickname Stonecutter for being the first and only running back all year to rush for a touchdown through the Seven Blocks. Lombardi had hit Savarese at the one, but could not bring him down and rode on Stonecutter's back into the end zone. The extra point ended the scoring; Fordham spent the rest of the afternoon backed up near its goal line by the thunderous punts of NYU's Howard Dunney, who won the Madow Trophy as most valuable player. As the game ended with NYU winning 7 to 6, the Violets' raucous cheering section turned Fordham's chant around, shouting, "From Rose Hill to the Rose Bowl back to Rose Hill!"

To Lombardi and several other Rams, it appeared again that a few Fordham players had not put forth maximum effort. "Some of our better players were completely sour," Lombardi said. What happened? Was it overconfidence that did them in? No, there was more to it than that, a dirty little secret that would haunt the team for years. For several weeks that Depression-era season, some Fordham players had been sneaking off to New Jersey on Sundays to play for modest pay under fictitious names in a semipro league. Francis Caulkin, then the student manager for the football team, recalled that it was "common knowledge that some of those guys would scoot over someplace to play on Sunday." Dick Healy, an end on the team, remembered that "several of the guys were hurt in the semipro game the Sunday before the NYU game. Ed Franco was hurt in that game. But they covered it up." Handy Andy Palau grimaced in pain when asked about the incident more than six decades later.

"Sure, it's true," he said. "Ahhhhh, jeez! It's true. Three linemen and one back. Can't say who. Not Vinnie. That's probably why we lost it. Yeah. Ah, Jesus. Some of the players were banged up. And they were pooped and it's a shame. A shame! I was sure pissed off when I found out about it. A chance to go to the Rose Bowl and they screwed it up. Ahhhhh!"

FOR THE REST of his life, Lombardi was identified as one of the Seven Blocks of Granite. He was unarguably the least talented of the Seven Blocks in 1936. And that front wall, while outstanding, had the least impressive statistics of four exceptional Fordham lines that could make some claim to be known as the Seven Blocks. Tim Cohane, the Fordham publicist who went on to a long career in sports journalism, years later took out a pencil and sheet of paper and drew a grid of the four Fordham lines. The Iron Major's 1929 edition allowed no touchdowns on the ground while compiling a 7–0–2 record. In 1930 the line allowed one rushing touchdown late in the year while going 8–1. Sleepy Jim Crowley's 1936 line with Lombardi at right guard finished 5–1–2 with one rushing touchdown. And the 1937 team, which retained Wojy, Devil Doll, Ali Baba and Tarzan, but lost Lombardi,

Paquin and Pierce, was perhaps the best of all, with a 7–0–1 record and no touchdowns allowed.

The other three lines fell into obscurity, while the 1936 version entered the realm of football lore, a lasting symbol of fortitude and inviolability. Lombardi himself was partly responsible for this. He alone among the men of the four great Fordham front walls emerged as a large enough figure later in life to carry the legend. But this was also the work of the storytellers. Grantland Rice and Damon Runyon and their brethren glorified the 1936 line above all others, and their fraternal heir, Tim Cohane, continued the tradition. There is something to be said for the way they presented the world, looking for the romantic aspects of human nature through the playing of games, preferring it to what would come later, the cynicism of modern journalism and its life-deadening focus on money, controversy and man's inevitable fall from grace. The problem with the storytellers was not their exaltation of myth, but their pursuit of the ideal to the exclusion of reality, allowing for the perpetuation of the fallacy of the innocent past. Was the 1936 line inviolable? Not to hubris, not to heady distraction, not to temptation in the form of a few illicit dollars to be gained playing semipro ball across the river only days before the most important college game of one's career.

FROM HIS playing days at Fordham, Lombardi learned lessons that he carried with him into a life of football. His inner steel, he said later, was forged in those bloody college games, especially the scoreless ties with Pitt. "I can't put my finger on just what I learned playing . . . in those scoreless games, but it was something. A certain toughness." While he discarded the sarcasm of Sleepy Jim Crowley and the dourness of Frank Leahy, he came to understand from those coaches the importance of precision blocking, fierce tackling and the larger "truths of the game: conditioning, spartanism, defense and violence as distinct from brutality." He also discovered what he called football's fourth dimension. "The first three dimensions are material, coaching and schedule. The fourth is selfless teamwork and collective pride which accumulate until they have made positive thinking and victory habitual." But the importance of Fordham in Lombardi's life was far greater than learning what it took to play a game. From the Jesuits he acquired a larger perspective: duty, obedience, responsibility and the exercise of free will were the basis of a philosophy that shaped the way he looked at himself and his world.

That is not to say that he was in all respects obedient to the Jesuit way. He was a typical college student, and there was a hint of his freewheeling father in him, old Moon the marauder of lower Manhattan. Vinnie enjoyed the action, especially when he was around his roommate, Jim Lawlor. They had a regular craps game going in their dorm room, playing at night after the prayers and bed check, a game of which the Jesuit authorities were not entirely unaware. There would be monthly raids, seemingly without consequence other than the appropriation of the collection of dimes, which the rector declared would "go to missions." And the depth with which Lombardi absorbed Jesuit teachings was not obvious from his grades. His college transcript shows him to be at best a slightly above average student. In later years, friends, family members and publicists bragged that he excelled as a student; he was variously said to have been in the top 10 percent and to have earned Phi Beta Kappa or cum laude honors, none of which was true.

His highest grades came in his freshman year, when he received B's in seven subjects plus an A in French, making the dean's list for the only time, though he was shaken by a midterm D-minus in trigonometry. From then on most of his grades were C's, even in French. In his senior year he earned C's in both of his business classes, with low B's in psychology, religion and ethics. The highlight of his academic career was an A on the final exam in ethics, which was the school's most rigorous course, taught by Ignatius Wiley Cox, S.J., who had a reputation for never giving away an easy mark.

The values and ideas that became central to Lombardi's thinking all seem to have roots in the lectures and writings of Father Cox. He was not just another Jesuit professor, but the most renowned teacher at Fordham and an important figure in American Catholic thought. Cox had his own Sunday afternoon radio program in New York, wrote articles for *Liberty, America* and *Commonweal*, along with frequent letters to the editor at the *New York Times*. He had completed the seminal work of his career, a little red-covered ethics textbook entitled *Liberty: Its Use and Abuse*, in time for Lombardi and his classmates to study it in 1936. His course on ethics was mandatory and served as the pedagogical culmination of four years of Scholastic theology. He lectured the entire class of senior men for two hours every day inside the vast bowl-shaped auditorium at the newly opened Keating Hall. Standing up there on the podium, stern and imposing with black cassock, glasses, whitish-gray hair and a slightly reddish face, he appeared as the embodiment of rational Jesuitism, meticulously explaining every point and enunciating each word, occasionally pausing to formally inquire of a student, "Is that clear to you, Mr. Lombardi?" When Lombardi or a classmate nervously assented, Cox pressed again, "As clear as a mountain lake in springtime?"

Cox was often stereotyped as a staunch conservative, but that was not entirely true. He showed a strong distaste for his Catholic colleague Father Charles Coughlin, whose right-wing diatribes followed Cox's more thoughtful presentations on the radio. He expressed sympathies for the working man, arguing in favor of the right to strike, and supported Franklin Delano Roosevelt in his reelection campaign against Republican Alfred Landon. And he was an early outspoken critic of Germany's Adolf Hitler, not universally true among the Jesuit professors at Fordham, some of whom held anti-semitic views. But on many issues of the day that pitted modernism against Catholic tradition, especially questions of morality, birth control and abortion, Cox was a fierce defender of the old way, constantly warning that excessive freedom was not man's liberation but his ruination. He found himself in rhetorical battle with freethinking philosophers like Bertrand Russell and proponents of contraception like Margaret Sanger—even with the American Medical Association, which he said was providing "aid and comfort to the executioners of our American civilization" by condoning birth control. While a *Fortune* magazine poll indicated that two-thirds of all Americans favored birth control, Cox called contraception "sexual blasphemy" and argued that it went against God's order by "frustrating a faculty from obtaining its natural end."

His students, who called him Iggy, were in awe of Cox but not always receptive to everything he said, no more than many Catholics on the issue of birth control. They seemed most taken by his arguments on liberty and responsibility, which were at the heart of his lectures, and it was in that area that he had his most profound effect on Lombardi. Every day Lombardi heard Cox lecture on the meaning of character—"an integration of habits of conduct superimposed on temperament, the will exercised on disposition, thought, emotion and action." It was man's obligation, Cox said, to use his will "to elicit the right and good free actions and to refrain from wrong and evil actions." While man was blessed with intellect and free will, he was ennobled only when he sublimated individual desires "to join others in pursuit of common good." Cox lamented that the modern world was turning away from that notion, and "the vaunted liberty which was to make us free has eventuated in a more galling servitude to man's lower nature."

Cox's lectures were a distillation of four hundred years of Jesuit thought going back to Ignatius of Loyola, who founded the Society of Jesus in the sixteenth century after abandoning the unfulfilling life of a libertine Spanish army officer. When he formed his new order, Loyola transposed many of his military beliefs into his religious work, making the Jesuits the soldiers of Christ. There is a direct line in thinking from the Jesuits to football to what would become the philosophy of Vince Lombardi. The Jesuits rejected the notion of predestination, arguing that anyone could attain a state of perfection with enough zeal; perfection went to those who sought it most eagerly. They believed in man's liberty to choose between action and inaction, good and evil, but like the military and football coaches, they also maintained a hierarchical order in which the inferior submits willingly to the superior. This willingness to accept a rightful order required believing that the chief—God, the general, the coach—loved each member of the group with the same love. The seeming contradiction between free will and blind obedience was resolved by the Jesuits through the vision of a mystical goal: only those with free will could surrender it freely to achieve a higher ideal.

The line from Ignatius of Loyola to Vince Lombardi's life in football has two other threads. In his pursuit of perfection, Loyola paid strict attention to detail. It was said that he would rewrite letters twenty times. He concerned himself with the most trivial matters, such as engaging a cook, porter or nurse for his order. His most famous work, which came to be known as *The Spiritual Exercises of St. Ignatius of Loyola,* is predicated on spiritual discipline and precision. The exercises cover four weeks of meditations from sin and hell to divine love, perhaps the spiritual equivalent of a football training camp. Anyone attempting to follow the exercises, Loyola instructed, had to keep a daily chart of his sins and "the comparison between the rows of dots at the beginning of the exercise and the rows, shortened as much as possible at a later stage, shows the progress made in rooting out sinful habits and tendencies." Not unlike the grading system Lombardi later developed as a coach. Diego Laínez, Loyola's student and successor, stated that few great men had so few ideas as the founder of Jesuitism, but still fewer had been more thoroughly earnest in the realization of these ideas." That, too, had echoes of Vince Lombardi.

THE CLASS OF 1937 was graduated at Fordham at four on the afternoon of June 16, a gorgeous summery day, the outdoor ceremony on the green quadrangle framed by a soft blue sky above the towering frontispiece of Keating Hall. The ceremonies were presided over by the archbishop of New York, His Eminence Patrick Cardinal Hayes. Marie Planitz was there with her sister, Marge; Harry and Matty came with Madeline, Claire, Harold and little Joe. After arriving to the processional "La Reine de Saba," Vin received his bachelor of science degree. He was wearing his class ring, with garnet stone and Ram on the side, and had on a pair of bright white shoes, oblivious of how they glistened garishly in the sober congregation of black and maroon. After leaving the grounds to the recessional "Hail, America," he posed one last time with the graduating football lettermen, including Handy Andy Palau, Natty Pierce, Captain Frank Mautte, big Jim Lawlor and Leo Paquin, and once more he led them in song, "Once more the old Maroon, wave on high. We'll sing our battle song, We do, or die!"

4

Saints

THIS WAS ENGLEWOOD in the clean-slate sunshine of an autumn Saturday morning two years before the war. The town, nestled comfortably across the Hudson River in New Jersey four miles west of the George Washington Bridge and the cacophony of New York, still had a radiant sheen. Its unhurried avenues looped and dipped in the Seven Sisters hills, shimmering ridges with a red and yellow canopy of ancient elm, oak and hickory. Crisp piles of raked leaves smoke-simmered at the curb, sweetening the air with an intoxicating incense of order and yearning. The population of leaf rakers (including a superintendent of shade trees) was middle class in the most varied sense, balanced impartially between Manhattan commuters and well-settled families, Anglo-Saxon Protestants, second- and third-generation Irish, Italian and Polish Catholics, with a growing Jewish community and a small pocket of black citizens whose families had settled near downtown to work in the grand houses up on the Hill. That is where millionaire industrialists and Wall Street bankers had once lived, but they were mostly gone, retreated deeper into the sheltered countryside to ever more capacious homes. In the American suburban tradition, Englewood took much of its identity from its schools. The large public high school, Englewood Dwight Morrow, had a superior academic record and a campus so vast that it was often mistaken for a private college.

There was also St. Cecilia, a parochial school whose reputation far exceeded its size. Everyone in town, indeed in much of North Jersey, knew St. Cecilia as Saints, its nickname. Saints, which sat fortresslike on the slope of Demarest Avenue on the north edge of downtown, was constructed from blocks of granite, with a gray Gothic cast, its courtyard shadowed by the white marble Romanesque Revival clock tower of St. Cecilia Roman Catholic Church next door. The school was coeducational and had fewer than four hundred students, drawn from a wide swath of Bergen County. The girls wore uniforms of blue jumpers and white blouses; the boys dressed in coats and ties. The church and school were under the administration of fathers from the Carmelite order assisted by nuns from the Sisters of Charity, who lived in a nearby convent. The faculty included a few male teachers not in the priesthood. Two new lay teachers arrived at Saints in the fall of 1939, classmates from Fordham University named Andrew Palau and Vincent Lombardi.

Lombardi had been scuffling for two years before he found the little school in Englewood. We do, or die? Nothing had seemed so clear as his old fight song after graduation. At first he could not figure out what to do. Most of his classmates had assumed that he would make his way in the business world; he had dressed and acted like a corporate leader for years. But he had no interest in the one opportunity available to him, Harry's meat shop, and the only other job he could find was making collection calls on deadbeat borrowers, a task that was neither pleasant nor well paid. He was not talented enough to make a full-time living in pro football, but signed on to play in the second-rung American Professional Football Association for the Brooklyn Eagles, whose home games drew decent crowds at Ebbets Field and made him a minor Brooklyn celebrity. In a sense he was back home, bolstered by his father and the Izzos who appeared at every game. Vince even lived at home for a time, bulking up to 205 pounds on Matty's cooking, and occasionally, reluctantly, assisted his father on the waterfront.

This life inevitably began to feel suffocating, and he made one brief and futile effort to get away, venturing down to Delaware to play for the Wilmington Clippers, another semipro football team. He apparently worked temporarily in a research lab for Du Pont during his time in Wilmington, though the company has no personnel records establishing his employment there. In any case, he returned to New York before the fall of 1938 and enrolled at Fordham's law school, attending classes downtown on the twenty-eighth floor of the Woolworth Building. Another dead end. Vincent T. Lombardi, Esquire, might have been his old man's dream, but he had little desire to be a lawyer and less aptitude for the law. "He got tired of it fast. It wasn't his cup of tea," said Richard Izzo, his cousin, a third-year law student at Fordham when Lombardi began there. One semester and Lombardi was out, with poor grades that he tried to conceal ever after. Two lost years.

Andy Palau was also struggling by the summer of 1939. After graduation he had tried to make it to the big leagues as a catcher in the New York Yankees farm system, but fell short. Now he was shuttling between a semipro team in Vermont and his home in Connecticut, where he was pulling a shift in a Bristol factory. One night after work Palau received a call from Nat

Pierce, left guard of the Seven Blocks, who had been teaching and coaching football at a small Catholic high school in New Jersey, St. Cecilia. Sleepy Jim Crowley had just hired Pierce to return to Fordham as an assistant coach. Was Palau interested in taking over for him at St. Cecilia? So much so that the next day he rode the train down to Grand Central Station, caught a bus across the river to Englewood and presented himself to Father Basil Kahler in the St. Cecilia rectory. He was hired on the spot, then unhired, briefly, when a nun discovered that Palau was a Lutheran. It took a phone call from Fordham's Father Tynan to set matters straight with the mother superior.

One of Palau's first tasks was to hire an assistant coach. He tried several other Fordham classmates, with no luck, before placing a call of desperation to his old baseball coach, Jack Coffey. "Call Vinnie Lombardi," Coffey told him. "Vinnie's not doing anything. He's working for his father over on the waterfront and collecting money from poor people for some darn finance company." Lombardi? Palau had not thought of him. The last he had heard, Vin was considering the priesthood again. No, said Coffey, he was back in Brooklyn. Father Tynan had talked to Lombardi recently, Coffey said, and had the impression that he was searching for a new vocation. With nowhere else to turn, Palau made the call. Lombardi seized the offer. There was no master plan, just a call from Handy Andy, the Lutheran quarterback, looking for someone to help him out at a little Catholic school in New Jersey—that is how Vince Lombardi became a football coach.

Lombardi ended up staying at Saints for eight years. It was there, in the insular world of North Jersey schoolboy competition, that he developed many of the pedagogical skills that later allowed him to stand apart from the coaching multitudes. Year by year, as his reputation grew beyond Englewood, it became clearer to him that coaching was his life's calling. Football coach was not what Harry and Matty had expected of their son, nor what his old classmates had predicted. In some ways it was a job below his own self-image. All of which worked in his favor. During his years in Englewood, Lombardi was driven by a contradiction, consumed by a sport and somewhat embarrassed that it was considered merely a game. This had two consequences: it intensified his will to win, made it overpowering in him, while simultaneously pushing him to infuse football with something more serious, to find deeper meaning in the WORK and PLAY juxtaposition tattooed above his father's knuckles. In that mission he had much the same visionary motivation that philosopher Miguel de Unamuno, in a luminous phrase, ascribed to Ignatius Loyola, founder of the Jesuits, and other Catholic mystics—the perception of "an intolerable disparity between the hugeness of their desire and the smallness of reality."

WHEN HE TOOK THE JOB at Saints, Lombardi said later, his frame of mind was that he "wanted to be a teacher more than a coach," and he enrolled in courses at nearby Seton Hall to sharpen his classroom instruction. With a steady job in hand, he also felt secure enough to propose to Marie Planitz, and she accepted his engagement ring. His assignments at Saints left him with little free time and no spending money. He was Palau's top assistant, coaching the line, during football season, head coach of the varsity basketball team, and member of the faculty, teaching physics, chemistry and Latin. For all that, Saints started his pay at $1,700 a year. The salary was paltry, but not impossible to live on. On weekends there was always Matty's home cooking in Brooklyn or dinner with Marie. And housing in Englewood cost next to nothing. He and Palau started out sharing a boardinghouse room across the street from the church. The rent was a buck fifty each per week for the cramped quarters. "I hate to say this, but we slept in the same damn bed. Do that today, Holy Jesus!" Palau would say decades later. "A big king-size bed. We never had any trouble, really. We were so tired, slept right through."

The Saints lost the first two games of the 1939 football season, yet Palau and Lombardi emerged with positive reviews from the local press and intimations of better things to come based on the way their squad competed against heavily favored Ridgefield Park and St. Benedict's of Newark, who outweighed the Saints by fifteen pounds per man. The Lombardi-coached line impressed observers more than Palau's offense, which was based on the old Notre Dame box that he had learned from Sleepy Jim Crowley. The two Fordham teammates developed a rivalry even as they worked together compatibly and slept in the same boardinghouse bed. They competed intensely in chess matches before school in the morning and during class breaks, huddled in the corner of the locker room. At night, after dinner, they gathered empty beer cans until they had enough to field two teams, then arrayed the cans on the table, which served as a playing field, and tried to outsmart each other with new formations.

Before the third game against Tenafly, Palau asked Lombardi to give the team a pep talk, and when it was over realized that his assistant had a fire inside that he could not match. "I knew he was intense about the game and I knew he got excited," Palau said later. "But that pep talk was incredible. I had never seen anything like it before. I was shaking in my boots when it was over, and I know the team was, too." Eyes bulging, eyelids blinking, fists clenched, Lombardi finished his speech, approached the starters one by one, said that they had done nothing to impress him during practice that week and demanded more. "What are you going to do today?" he thundered. The Saints scored twice in the first period, then held firm the rest of the game for a 13 to 0 win. They did not lose again that season, which ended with the Saints establishing themselves as the new power in town with a 20 to 0 victory over crosstown rival Englewood Dwight Morrow on Thanksgiving Day.

What worried Lombardi most was the daunting task of coaching basketball. He was absorbed by football strategy and thought he understood it, but basketball was alien to him even though he had played on the Cathedral Prep team. Palau, a three-sport star who had captained the Fordham basketball squad, offered to help the first half of the season. He would teach Vince the zone defense, which was simple, he said. After football practice during the week, after games on weekends, they engaged in their basketball tutorials. Handy Andy could see that Vince had no feel for the game, but nonetheless was astute at picking up strategy and simplifying everything on court. After only five games he decided to leave Lombardi on his own. "I could see he was doing as good a job as I could have done. He had a brain."

In his first experience as head coach in any sport, Lombardi led the Saints to a winning season, though barely, at 10 wins and 9 losses. It took the players some time to adjust to him. Their previous coach had been "an easy rider," in the words of Mickey Corcoran, the team's star player, and when Lombardi came in as a strict disciplinarian "the change was a bit of a culture shock." His emotions were never far from the surface; his eruptions became legendary. Of all the stories about his temper, the one that Saints basketball players most enjoyed telling in later years concerned the time he leaped from the bench in a rage only to bang his head on a low-hanging steel girder in the Saints' cozy gym, a jolt that not only pained him but quieted him for the rest of the game. Red Garrity, the coach at rival Englewood Dwight Morrow, thought that it occurred in a game between the two schools when a referee made a crucial call against Saints. Corcoran had a different memory, believing that he inspired the head-banging when, as captain on the court, he chose to shoot foul shots instead of taking the ball out of bounds, defying Lombardi's instructions.

Corcoran, loose and cocky, with the natural basketball instincts his coach lacked, was Lombardi's pet, the first in a long line, and as such the most frequent witness to his mood swings. Before practice during the week, Lombardi enjoyed playing H-O-R-S-E with Corcoran, Fred Schoenfelder and Johnny Moon. *Match my shot! Make this one!* The outcome was usually the same, the boys outshot him, but Lombardi remembered the one trick shot he threw in, and boasted about it for days. After practice on Tuesdays he occasionally invited the boys over to his room to play hearts. If he stuck one with the queen of spades he "went hilarious," his big teeth flashing an irrepressible grin. On more than one Friday afternoon he found Corcoran after school and told him, "Call your mom, we're going out to Brooklyn for some home cooking." All the way out to the Lombardi house, they talked basketball: different defenses, college plays Vince had seen that week at Madison Square Garden.

Lombardi was warming to the role of coach. It was what he imagined being a priest might be like, he told friends. He could be a father figure and leader. And unlike the priesthood, the coaching profession did not force him to repress his emotions. If he wanted to blow off steam, he could bark at the kids and no one would be shocked. He made a point of challenging Corcoran the most, as a lesson to the others. After one loss, when Lombardi thought Corcoran had taken bad shots, he decided to punish him by making him take physical education for the rest of the semester, a course not required of varsity athletes. Two weeks later he realized that he had overreacted, apologized to Corcoran and released him from gym class. That was the method of Coach Lombardi. Corcoran learned it from his mentor and used it himself when he became a high school coach years later, then passed it along to his own disciple, a North Jersey boy named Bill Parcells, who also became a coach. "Rip your butt out, then pat you on the butt. Knock you down, then build you up," said Corcoran of Lombardi's style. "He understood human behavior better than any person I've ever met."

Late that first season Lombardi and his blue and gold Saints were involved in a game that secured a place in the annals of the world's strangest basketball contests. It happened on the Thursday night of February 29, 1940, when a powerful team from the North Jersey town of Bogota (pronounced Bu-GO-ta, not like the Colombian capital) visited St. Cecilia for a Leap Day game that meant very different things to the two teams. For the Saints, whose mediocre record precluded any chance of making the postseason tournament, a victory would enhance their late run to respectability. The mission for Bogota, at least as Coach Ev Hebel perceived it, was merely to survive the game without wasting energy, preserving his boys for a tournament game later that week. His Bucs had established themselves as the superior team, having trounced the Saints earlier in the year. What followed the opening tip was an extraordinary clash of wills between Lombardi and Hebel in an era before shot clocks or rules requiring a team to advance the ball upcourt.

Thirty seconds into the game Johnny Moon fired up a long set shot for the Saints. The ball bounced off the rim and the rebound was hauled in by Henry Baum of Bogota, who immediately revealed Hebel's strategy, which was for his boys to do absolutely nothing. One arm akimbo, the other cradling the ball, Baum stood in one spot, motionless, stone-faced. Lombardi ordered his defenders to back off and wait for Bogota to go into its offense. For seven and a half minutes Baum held the ball. Jeers and hisses hailed down from the stands. The second quarter was more of the same. The stall irritated Mickey Corcoran. He looked over at Lombardi and inched toward his man. Lombardi shook his head. "Stay back! Stay back!" He was furious at Hebel, but determined not to give in. The shorter the game, he figured, the better chance the outmanned Saints had for pulling an upset.

Saints won the tap to start the second half, and Corcoran, his fingers itchy from sixteen minutes without a shot, quickly pumped one from outside. No good. Baum of Bogota had the ball again, assuming his familiar frozen posture. Nineteen minutes without a point. The crowd grew rowdier.

Then Lombardi gave the signal, and the Saints moved up to press the ball. From then on, the game was normal basketball. The visitors had lost all energy to play even when they were instructed to do so. They took a total of seven shots and never scored a basket; a lone free throw prevented them from being shut out. The final score was 6 to 1. After the game an eerie quiet descended on the gym as Lombardi stalked across the court. He screamed at Hebel for his tactics, even though they had backfired. It was cowardly, he said, for the better team to hold the ball and make a mockery of the game. Hebel remained calm. He said he was merely saving his team for the tournament and making a point against zone defenses, which he detested. The two men had to be separated, but parted without blows. They did not acknowledge each other for several years.

AT NINE O'CLOCK one Sunday morning that spring, Palau was awakened by a pounding at the door. His roommate was not home. Just a minute, Palau said, and got up and opened the door. There stood Marie Planitz, dressed in Sunday clothes, tears streaming down her face. She and Vin had been fighting, she said, and the engagement was off. Where was he? She said that she was going across the street to attend mass at Saints. Would Palau please help them get back together? When Lombardi returned late that afternoon, Palau told him about Marie's visit. As his roommate later described the scene, Lombardi seemed distraught, complaining that everywhere he turned people were pressuring him to reconcile with Marie.

Even his mother, who had never expressed much appreciation for his girlfriend, now seemed to be urging him to make up. He was almost twenty-seven, she pointed out, he needed a wife, and Marie worshiped him. His younger brother Harold, studying fine arts at Fordham, had also been drawn to Marie's side. While Vince was working at Saints, Harold and Marie occasionally took outings in the city. Harold shared his brother's temper and perfectionism, but had a more artistic nature; he and Marie enjoyed sitting in the courtyard at the Plaza Hotel, sipping brandy Alexanders, talking about books and opera, American politics (they were Republicans; Vince supported Roosevelt) and the war in Europe (they thought America should keep out of it). To Harold, Marie was "the greatest woman ever," and he thought his brother would be lucky to have her.

Vince soon reconsidered. After another spat with Marie he wrote a note of reconciliation and left it at her apartment: "Darling Rie," it began. "I love you so much Rie. I'm sorry about last night. I'm with you 100 percent. . . . Have been here since 10:00 this morning. Alone since 11:30 A.M.—it is now about 1:00. Intend to leave soon. I even brought up some buns this A.M.—thought maybe you and I could have some coffee and—Sorry to have missed you, Honey. I love you with all my heart. I mean that. Sincerely, Vincent."

A date was soon set for the wedding. He and Marie were married on Saturday, August 31, 1940, at the Church of Our Lady of Refuge on East 196th Street in the Bronx. The nuptial mass was performed by the Reverend Jeremiah F. Nemecek, a Fordham football fan who idolized the Seven Blocks of Granite. Mary Planitz watched as her husband walked down the aisle with their daughter Marie and took a seat next to his lover, Mary's sister Cass. The other daughter, Marge Planitz, the maid of honor, was so upset with her father and Cass that she refused to acknowledge their presence. Most of the Izzo clan came up from Sheepshead Bay, filling the church with good will. But Matty Lombardi seemed less than overjoyed that day. After stepping in to restore the engagement, she could barely repress her earlier attitude that no one was good enough for her son. She and other family members privately worried that Vince was marrying Marie for the wrong reasons: she was blonde and buxom, a blue-eyed Irish-German, the daughter of a stockbroker, a step up the social ladder. None of that underlying tension was evident in the wedding pictures. Marie looks luxuriant in a white bridal gown with a seven-foot train that drapes the floor in a semicircle around the smiling Vince, in black tails and striped tie, proudly displaying his wedding ring, which had inscriptions of the Sacred Heart and Blessed Virgin inside the band.

The couple ventured to Maine for their honeymoon. Marie later confided that she was a virgin bride and that her first night in the conjugal bed was a difficult experience for her, as was the entire adjustment to life with her new husband. He seemed preoccupied with football even on their honeymoon, and cut it short to get back to Englewood before the first Saints practice. "I wasn't married to him one week," she related later, "when I said to myself, Marie Planitz, you've made the greatest mistake of your life." His temper, his obsession with sports, his compulsion to tell other people what to do, the tension between his dominant public persona and his innate shyness and private anxiety—all were apparent to her from the start. But she had married Vince because he seemed solid, religious and faithful, unlike her father. She believed, as he did, in the sacredness and lifelong commitment of marriage. She told herself that she would have to adjust.

Bored and stuck in a little second-floor apartment on Grand Avenue in Englewood, she scrambled for ways to fill the ocean of hours when Vince was working with his boys. She drank coffee and pink ladies, and played cards with the mothers of St. Cecilia players. She walked to Palisade Avenue with Palau's new wife, Margaret, a southern girl from North Carolina, who had just had a baby and lived in the same apartment building. On the way over, she taught Margaret how to talk northern (peh-nee, not pinny, for the coin. After they had shopped for both families at the market, Margaret carried the infant on the return trip while Marie pushed the baby carriage stocked with food. The hard part was lifting the loaded carriage up the four front steps. Once every few weeks Marie rode the bus back into New York to spend the day walking around Manhattan with Vince's brother Harold. She refined her artistic skills, crocheting and creating intricate Christmas ornaments. Late on weekend nights, when Vince was at last free from athletics, he took Marie out to his favorite haunts with the Palaus and other friends. They often drove up Route 9W to Englewood Cliffs for a late meal at Leo's and then some band music at the Rustic Cabin, where they fell into the habit of buying a beer and steak sandwich for a performer who came over to their table to chat after his closing set, a skinny young Italian crooner from Hoboken named Frank Sinatra.

In all of those ways, the evidence suggests that Marie adjusted admirably and tried to make the most of her marriage with Lombardi. She also learned quickly how to "give it back to him" and make him retreat after he had yelled at her. But on a deeper level she never adjusted. Haunted already by the trauma of her family history, by the unshakable reality that her father had run off with her aunt, she found only more heartache in her early efforts to create a family of her own. She became pregnant soon after her wedding, but at seven months the unborn infant died in her womb. With her doctor refusing to induce a birth, Marie carried the dead fetus inside her for several more weeks, a miserable period of prayer and mourning that she spent in bed at the Lombardi house in Brooklyn. In the aftermath of that tragedy, she began drinking heavily. Harold Lombardi, who tried to help, remembered that she was "in a perpetually troubled state of mind." She seemed distressed, her sister-in-law Madeline said later. "It had a terrible effect on her."

At times Vince was so preoccupied with teaching and coaching that he seemed unaware of his wife's troubles. He knew that she had a drinking problem, but considered it largely a matter of will and discipline. She was too weak, he told her. She either had to learn how to hold her liquor, as he did, or abstain from alcohol, an attitude that only led her to try to hide her drinking from him. Their relationship vacillated between hostility and adoration. They were a handsome and lively couple, their presence announced by their explosive laughter, but they snapped at each other over little things, unmindful that friends might hear them. They were chain-smokers, their ashtrays overflowing with butts, and incessantly blamed each other for burn marks on their Danish modern furniture. Vince attended mass at St. Cecilia's each morning and prayed for calm and control: of his temper, of her drinking. Once, in the car with his sister Madeline, a desk clerk at the Waldorf-Astoria, he cried in despair about his marriage.

When Marie became pregnant again, Vince's mother insisted that she return to the Lombardi house for bed rest a month before the due date. The pregnancy was difficult, but resulted in the successful birth of a son on the morning of April 27, 1942, at Prospect Heights Hospital. He was named Vincent Henry Lombardi. Vince and Marie had agreed on the first name, but she was surprised by Henry, a middle name that Vince had provided to the nurses without consulting her. Where did that come from? Vince explained that Henry (or Enrico) was his father's real name; it was traditional in Italian families for the first son to be named after the grandfather. Marie had wanted her son to be a junior: Vincent Thomas Lombardi Jr. In any case the arrival of the baby temporarily eased the tension in the marriage. The birth gifts included a carriage from Pop Lombardi, a crib from Gramps Planitz and a big leather football from the family doctor. Everyone said that Baby Vincent was going to grow up to be a football player. Marie had a family now—more than she expected. When she and Vince and the baby drove back to Englewood on May 7 in their old blue Buick, they were joined by Harry and Matty, who had moved out of Sheepshead Bay with little Joe and found a house on Knickerbocker Road not far from Saints and their oldest son, the football coach.

FOOTBALL AND RELIGION were conjoined at Saints in every manner possible. The team played on Sundays, the only time Saints could gain access to Winton J. White Stadium, since Englewood Dwight Morrow High laid claim to the municipal field on Saturdays. Before every game the preparation for battle resembled a holy rite. After the players put on their pads and uniforms, Coach Lombardi led them out from the dank basement locker room and directed them down the slope to church, their cleats clickity-clack-clicking on the sidewalk and up the marble steps as they entered the sanctuary to attend mass and receive communion. "The Few Minutes That Count Before a Game," noted the caption over a yearbook picture depicting the team on its knees, huddled in a semicircle of prayer near the front altar. At the end of pregame mass, a cluster of nuns greeted the squad out front on Demarest and distributed sacramentals, little bleeding hearts made of red felt. Some boys stuffed the hearts inside their pants or helmets; Lombardi tucked his under the sock of his left cleat. A man of superstition, he also was careful to wear the same coat and hat to every game.

The boys rode to the stadium standing in the open bed of an oil stock truck. On the way up Tenafly Road they sang, "On, Cecilia, on, Cecilia, Fight on for your fame!" to the tune of Wisconsin's familiar fight song. Before the opening kickoff, Lombardi gathered his charges at the sideline to recite the Lord's Prayer. The bleachers were aswarm with thousands of fans, in part because the Saints were a powerhouse team, but also because in that era, when television had not penetrated the American culture and professional football was considered a minor sport, the Saints were a main source of Sunday entertainment in North Jersey. Strangers traveled by bus from towns thirty miles away to watch them play. The grandstands nudged up to the team bench, and Harry Lombardi was always right there, lighting his good luck Luckies, sitting as close to his son as he could, along with his brood, which included Marie and Baby Vincent. In a tradition that defined his offbeat character, Old Five by Five climbed the cyclone fence and sneaked into games without paying. The ushers let it pass with a shake of the head: *There goes Lombardi's old man.*

On the ride home, the boys belted out the same raucous tune every week, "My Wild Irish Rose," and if they won, which was most of the time, the truck pulled into the half-circle driveway at the Sisters of Charity convent. As nuns streamed onto the broad front porch and peered out second-floor windows, the squad serenaded them with the school song.

> *Saint Suh-seeel-yuh!*
> *Saint Suh-seeel-yuh!*
> *We sing it in our way.*
> *We love our Alma Mater tried and true*
> *And all we are and all we have*
> *We give it all to you!*

The sisters had prayed for victory: how could Saints lose?

The 1942 season was Lombardi's first as head football coach. Palau had left that summer to return to Fordham to coach the Rams backfield. This was not the same program that Handy Andy and Butch had been part of back in the mid-1930s. Sleepy Jim Crowley had left for military service after Pearl Harbor, and many on his staff and squad had followed him. Within a year the Fordham program would close down for the remainder of the war, never to regain its previous stature. Still, Palau's leaving frustrated Lombardi even as it provided him with a new opportunity. He fretted that everyone was a rung ahead of him up the coaching ladder of success. First Nat Pierce, now Palau had made it back to the college ranks at Fordham; Johnny Druze was an assistant at Notre Dame. Leo Paquin was coaching at Xavier Prep in Manhattan. But the fact that Palau left ahead of Vince was no surprise. He had always been one of the Fordham administration's favorites, and his record at Saints did nothing to hurt his reputation. The team lost only one game in 1940 and went undefeated in 1941. It apparently did not occur to Fordham's new coach, Earl Walsh, that the brains behind the Saints operation was the old right guard, the forgotten Block.

Lombardi was bursting with ideas after Palau left, eager to assert himself as head man. He took his boys out to Hackettstown, New Jersey, for a two-week training camp and installed a new offense, merging the Notre Dame box with a variation of the T formation. He had learned the T himself the previous spring, after attending a coaching clinic and picking up a pamphlet co-written by Clark Shaughnessy and George Halas. First Shaughnessy at Stanford in 1940 and then Halas with the professional Chicago

Bears in 1941 had found great success with the T, which had been largely out of favor until they revised and restored it. In the T, the quarterback stands close behind the center to take the snap, with a fullback directly behind him and a halfback on either side of the fullback. The formation was as old as rugby, predating the American football game, but only with the innovations of Shaughnessy and Halas did it reveal its full offensive potential. There were two keys to their new T: putting a man in motion to distract the defense, and using the quarterback as a true field general who would handle the ball on every snap and control the field of play through sophisticated fakes, handoffs and passes. The T required precision and constant practice, but not great physical prowess, an offense that seemed made for Lombardi and his Saints, the first team in the area to use it.

Offensive football became Lombardi's mistress. Late at night, when Marie and Baby Vincent were asleep, he sat at his kitchen table, filling the ashtray with Chesterfield butts and studying plays. Sometimes he found a new variation that excited him so much that he could not even wait until practice the next afternoon to try it out; instead, he took a few boys out of class for a half hour in the morning and brought them down to the gym to run through the play. Repetition was at the core of his coaching philosophy. Doing the same thing over and over again, whether it was a play or a calisthenic, he believed, would make his boys fearless and instinctive. "He said, 'What I'm going to do, I'm going to drive you. I know the average level of conditioning at other schools. We're going to surpass that,' " Joe McPartland, a fullback on those Saints teams, remembered. "That was the genius of Lombardi that you could see right away. He pushed you and pushed you and made you strong."

The Saints campus did not have a practice field. When school ended at three o'clock, the boys dressed in the locker room and walked a half-mile to MacKay Park, a hike that took them through the heart of Englewood's downtown. Wearing pads and cleats and sometimes loaded down with equipment that did not fit into Lombardi's Buick, the Saints brigade made such a racket that homeowners and shopkeepers heard the squad approaching from blocks away; people came out to their porches or storefronts to trade quips with the boys and cheer them along. As they passed a downtown fruit stand, a few players inevitably swiped apples. Father Tim Moore, who served as Lombardi's assistant, knew what they were doing—he often took confession from them in the parking lot after practice—and pleaded with them to stop, saying that the poor fruit vendor was going broke. Once, when a ravenous lineman persisted in filching apples, the good Irish father calmly took off his collar, barked "Di'n't I tell ya!" and decked the wayward Saint with a hard right. Corporal punishment was not an everyday thing at the school, but neither was it forbidden.

Lombardi limited his hitting to the practice field. Nothing engaged him like the explosive moment of contact between blocker and tackler. He was his own blocking sled. One practice routine called for every boy to charge off the line and hit the head coach as hard as possible. "Hit me! Hit me!" he shouted, his voice echoing through MacKay Park, deep and intimidating. The boys felt conflicted by this demand. "When you would see him at practice you would say to yourself, Oh, my God, he's going to take me on today," recalled John "Gassy" DeGasperis, a Saints guard. "You had equal parts courage and fear. You wanted to go hard, but you could never hurt him. And if you did, he never let on to you." Al Quilici, a roughneck little Saints halfback, said that one of the lasting memories of his life was the day he cracked Lombardi in the jaw with a vicious elbow and the coach smiled and thundered, "That's the way to do it!" Football, Lombardi preached to his boys, was a lesson in life. They were going to get knocked down, but they had to drag themselves up and take another hit and do it right.

Rarely were there enough hours in the day for Lombardi and football. In the manner of Sleepy Jim, his old coach at Fordham, he kept his players on the field past sundown on autumn evenings, running plays over and over in the dusk. If it became too dark to see but he was still unsatisfied, he herded the team near the parking lot and illuminated the area with headlights from his Buick and the cars of townspeople who had come to watch practice. Soon enough he discovered the limits to how far he could drive young players. At one twilight practice, as he ran the same play over and over, shouting at a lineman who persisted in making the same mistake, the player suddenly burst into tears of frustration. Here was a youngster who tried hard but was less intelligent and athletic than many of the boys, and his response to criticism jolted Lombardi. He came to realize fully for the first time, he said later, that "there were limitations to the game due to mentality and physical ability and that the amount that can be consumed and executed is controlled by the weakest man on your team." There were ways to hide the physical liabilities of the weakest member of the team, Lombardi concluded, but every player "has to do his own thinking." From then on he tried to coach so that he was understandable to the slowest member of the squad.

The situation that Lombardi inherited from Palau was in some ways unenviable: a record that would be hard to match, including two state Catholic championships and a thirteen-game winning streak, and only three returning lettermen to lead the way. Furthermore, a fluke in scheduling found the Saints playing their fiercest opponent twice that season: they opened against rival Englewood Dwight Morrow and ended with them again on Thanksgiving Day. In his first game as a football head coach, Lombardi lost. Englewood beat his Saints 18 to 7, T formation and all, ending the winning streak and worrying the coach and the team's fans. "That night the St. Cecilia rooters were quiet," the school yearbook reported. "There was no blast of horns, or snake dance down Palisade Avenue, or bonfires. We could hardly believe that Englewood had won, but with determined minds we vowed that in the return game, the outcome would be reversed."

That completed the losing for the year. There were two ties, but no more defeats in a season marked by two notable triumphs: first, a 32 to 6 thumping of powerful West New York Memorial, during which Lombardi's T formation attack amassed 197 yards passing; and then a 7 to 0 shutout of Dwight Morrow, a season-ending victory that loosed the celebration that had been stifled by the earlier defeat. After serenading the nuns on Tenafly Road, hundreds of fans gathered at the school courtyard to cheer some more, then headed down the valley to Palisade Avenue, their "hearts full of joy" as they paraded along the downtown strip past Mac's Luncheonette and Pat's Toys, the Paramount Beauty Salon and Jabocus Shoes, the Young Colony Shop and Pearlman's Liquor, Charlie Wilson's bowling hall and Buckley's Drug Store, singing "On, Cecilia!" all the way. From there they worked their way up to the house Lombardi and his family had moved into that season. When the gleam-toothed visage of the new coach appeared at the door, "horns blew and the students yelled at the top of their lungs." Vince and Marie invited the students in for refreshments, and there was old Pop Lombardi, regaling the crowd. With their spirits still running high, the students drove back to the stadium and sprinted across the empty field, whooping it up. Later, the Englewood school board sent Saints its annual bill for alleged damages to the goalposts and scoreboard.

It was football glory for Lombardi and his Saints thereafter. The opening loss to Englewood turned out to be the last they would suffer in four seasons, until Seton Hall Prep beat them in the third game of 1945. It was a streak of thirty-two unbeaten games, including three ties, and inside that streak was another more spectacular one, twenty-five straight wins beginning with the rout of Memorial and ending with a scoreless tie in a bowl game against Union Hill at the end of 1944. The undefeated 1943 team, state parochial school champions and perhaps the best of the decade, surrendered only three touchdowns all year and outscored opponents by the overwhelming total of 267 points to 19 despite being outweighed in every matchup. With a new four-linebacker defense Lombardi had installed, they won eight games by shutouts, one of them a 6 to 0 win in the Legion Bowl against Jersey City Lincoln in front of 12,500 fans.

Little Saints challenged any school in the region during those years, the best of New York City and Hudson County, and beat them all, including a Brooklyn Prep team that featured a wily little back named Joe Paterno. Before the game against Prep, Lombardi gathered his squad in the locker room and read a series of nasty letters and telegrams that he said had been sent from Brooklyn. He did not tell his enraged players that he had concocted the defamatory material himself. That revelation came only years later in late night reminiscences with his friend and colleague Paterno, who had gone on to star at Brown University and begin a luminous coaching career at Penn State, reaching a status in the college ranks nearly equivalent to Lombardi's later in the pros.

Lombardi believed in fair play, he told his players, but not in the concept of good losing. He equated a loss with a sin. "I don't want any good losers around here," Joe McPartland remembered him telling the squad every year. "If you think it's good to be a loser, give the other guy the opportunity." Good losing, he said, was "just a way to live with yourself. It's a way to live with defeat." He was so intense that he would not even talk to the Englewood coach if he saw him in church. He was consumed with finding the edge that would assure victory. On Thursday nights he invited the quarterbacks and captains over to the house for a working dinner at which they studied plays for that Sunday's game. Between breaks in classes, he hauled a few more players into his office to talk football. When teams started to adjust to the T formation, he devised ways to switch it with the Notre Dame box at the last second so the defense would be off guard. When he entered the locker room with a smile on his face, the boys usually knew what was up. *Wait'll you hear this one.* He had stayed up all night diagramming a new play; sometimes he said plays came to him in his dreams.

In practice the first three days of the week before a big game against Xavier, he built up the opponents to make them seem like monsters. *They're gonna kill you. They're gonna wipe you guys up.* "It was like impending doom, disaster," said Iggy McPartland, one of his backs. "You didn't want to be disgraced in front of your family." But in the locker room before the game, after the referee stuck his head in to say it was time to take the field, Lombardi worked himself into a tear-inducing frenzy. Now his team could do no wrong. *You guys have worked so hard. They're a great team out there, but they'll never see the day they can touch you. You have more of what it takes than any ten teams I've seen.* His little Saints in blue and gold charged onto the field unbeatable.

While confident that he could take any group of boys and mold them into a football team, Lombardi was not naive about what made the difference. He was on an endless search for talent. Union City, Bergenfield, Cliffside Park, Clifton—he and Father Moore traveled the roads of North Jersey from one parish to another looking for players. John DeGasperis was in eighth grade in Cliffside Park when his teacher said there were two visitors who wanted to meet the class. "All of a sudden Father Tim and Coach Lombardi walk in. Father Tim talks first and says, 'I'd like you to meet the football coach.' When you saw Lombardi you were just awed by him. He had a smile, a voice, a big husky build. You said, 'Wow.' I had no intention of going to a Catholic school, but he had heard about me from another kid from my town who went there and at the end of the session he called me over and said, 'You're coming to Saints.' I told him my family had no money. He said, 'Don't worry. You're coming to Saints.'"

The local parish agreed to help pay DeGasperis's way. To save money, he hitchhiked to Englewood and back, often getting home after seven at night. But he became the best middle linebacker in North Jersey, proud to wear the Big Gold C. It was not just strapping specimens Lombardi sought, he also paid particular attention to scrappy youngsters from working-class families. He discovered Al Quilici from discussions with the local police, who told him about a kid who could outrun the law and was always fighting. Quilici had moved out to Englewood with his family from a cold-water flat in New York City. He helped bring in money for his parents, running up Englewood's hill at four in the morning to feed horses at stables owned by the town's equestrian elite. Lombardi promised him a scholarship and chance to wear the Saints uniform, and asked only that he confine his aggression to the football field. "You follow my way and I'll get you a scholarship to college," the coach told him. When Quilici arrived at Saints, Lombardi arranged for him to get into a typing class: it would help make his small hands more dexterous, the coach said, and also result in neater papers and better grades. It all proved true: Quilici starred at Saints, learned to type eighty-five words a minute on a manual typewriter and was recruited to play big-time college football at Arizona.

The truth about Lombardi was that his outward bluster barely concealed his soft spot for players, even in the classroom. When he encountered someone like Joe McPartland, a better student than athlete, he called on him daily in physics and pushed him to use his intelligence on the field. *Think, Joe! Use your head!* But when DeGasperis approached him after the first week of physics and confessed that he could not handle the material, Lombardi immediately transferred him to general science. "Otherwise he would have had to fail me," DeGasperis said later. "He turned out to be a friend." Iggy McPartland, Joe's less academic little brother, said Lombardi essentially gave him and many other football players a free pass in class during the season. "He did favor the football players. He didn't call on me until after Thanksgiving. He figured the football players were engaged in a sport that took a lot of time and that we were enhancing the image of the school, so he was considerate. The other students could be studying at home while we were still down at MacKay Park practicing under the headlights. After the season he'd look at me in class like he'd never seen me before and go, 'Hey you!' and I'd stand up and mumble something—I'd figure I was wrong, I didn't understand physics—and he'd say, 'Very good, sit down.' "

THE SISTERS OF CHARITY had such melodious names.

> Sister Symphrosa for history.
> Sister Theophane for mathematics.
> Sister Mary Aquinas for Spanish.

Sister Rose Magdalen for English.
Sister Anna Madeline for Latin.
Sister Louise Marie for French.

But the most memorable sister at Saints was known for more than her lyricism. She was Sister Louise Baptista, the principal. The students called her the Bap. A big-boned, intelligent woman with a sharp Boston accent, the Bap was fearless and fearsome, walking the halls of Saints in her black habit, her face framed in tight white cloth, a one-nun security patrol. Talk too much in class or act up in the hallway and the Bap would order you to kneel in humble contrition before she thwacked you with her punishment stick. Joe McPartland "got walloped a few times by the Bap. She had a good-sized arm," he said. There was no zone of privacy for students as far as the Bap was concerned. She inspected girls' pocketbooks looking for cigarettes, and if she suspected something awry in the boy's bathroom, she harrumphed, "Gentlemen, I'm coming in!" and barged through the swinging door.

The Bap understood her hormone-driven adolescent charges and seemed almost to mock them in her bluntness. "I found a pair of bloomers and they're not mine," she reported one day over the school loudspeaker. Then she paused ten seconds, anticipating the giggles her announcement would elicit, before scolding, "You filthy children!" The students at Saints made fun of her behind her back, imitating her tanklike build and unfamiliar accent, but what they never realized is that she was on to them as well. One of the favorite sisterly, if somewhat uncharitable, games at the convent was a variation of charades in which the Bap acted out the roles of students and others guessed who they were.

Not everyone subscribed to Sister Bap's authoritarian ways. Some officials in Englewood had begun to worry about the incipient problem of juvenile delinquency and expressed fears at public debates that "harshness and cruelly severe punishments for minor infractions" would only alienate the children further. What they shared with the nun and other disciplinarians was an inherent belief that it was the responsibility of teachers, parents and civic leaders to instill in the youth of Englewood a set value system through every means possible. The established code of ethics of the community, while often ignored in the private lives of town fathers, was articulated in a series of full-page advertisments printed in the *Englewood Press.* One Thanksgiving Day ad, under the blaring headline "SMALL SINS MAKE LIARS—LIARS MAKE CRIMINALS—FIRST OF ALL, TRUTH," sermonized that the compulsion to lie was at the root of most delinquency. "To tell the truth always is the principle that will take your son and daughter further than any other. In the school, on the playground, in the home—the boy or girl who abhors a lie is not likely to commit those sins which demand lying to avoid exposure."

At Saints, ethical values were largely passed on not by the priests and nuns but by Vince Lombardi, who found his pulpit everywhere, on the playing field, in the classroom and at schoolwide auditorium meetings. He was the one person to whom Sister Bap acceded. Dorothy Bachmann, salutatorian at Saints in 1944, thought "all the nuns loved him. They were not afraid of Vince, but they respected him for the way he presented his values to the students." Saints football, with its discipline, subservience and teamwork, was considered the ideal demonstration of proper teenage behavior, and Lombardi the purveyor nonpareil of the football philosophy. He was one of only four men on the Saints faculty of nineteen teachers. It was perhaps a typical ratio at a high school run by nuns, especially during the war years. That Lombardi was at Saints at all, rather than in the military, was unusual.

Though he was color-blind and nearsighted, other men with those liabilities were drafted into the service during World War II. Marie had expressed early reservations about the war and had attended an America First rally at Madison Square Garden in 1941, but Vince was adamant in his hatred of Hitler and in full support of the war effort. The Izzos were a patriotic lot; more than a dozen of his cousins and uncles had enlisted, including Tony Izzo, who was staying with Harry and Matty in Englewood while attending Fordham when he joined the Navy. Vince said that he tried to enlist but flunked a physical because of his poor eyes. That is possible. At least one of his friends, Francis Garrity, the basketball coach at Dwight Morrow, later said that he was with Lombardi when it happened. But there is no government record of any such event. Lombardi's Selective Service System records indicate that Bergen County Draft Board No. 7 gave him deferments throughout the war. The first deferment, in December 1941, was a II-A in the national interest for teaching. In 1943 he received a III-A deferment for dependency reasons. He was the sole provider then for Marie and Baby Vincent, but other young fathers were not deferred during the war. By April 1944, he had been reclassified IV-A, deferred by reason of age. He was then almost thirty-one years old.

The fact that he did not serve was not held against Lombardi in his community. The prevailing attitude was that the students at Saints were lucky to have a strong male figure available to mold them during those difficult years. Here was a paradox in Lombardi's character. He was never a soldier. He was never a priest. Yet he seemed the embodiment of the soldier priest, in the line of Ignatius of Loyola. The students at Saints regarded him with fear and respect. Their newspaper, the *Arcade*, applied popular song titles to personalities at Saints and matched "Mr. Lombardi" with "Mean to Me." He was known to throw an eraser at a daydreaming student, and his students came to learn the warning signs of a Lombardi eruption: "He would just stand there mute and his eyes would start blinking, harder and harder. That was the sign that an explosion was coming," recalled Don Crane, one of his students. "When his eyes started to blink, you stayed away." Only one student was truly in danger of suffering harm at Lombardi's hands: his youngest brother, Joe, who had enrolled at Saints as a freshman in 1943. Joe looked like his older brother and even played the same position in football, guard, but his disposition was the opposite: sweet and easy.

Being coached by his big brother was bad enough—"Lombardi! You're living on my name! You stink!" Vince screamed at him in practice—but it was in the classroom where Joe suffered most. In his sophomore year he coasted through school, thinking that as a football star he did not have to study. At an awards program at the end of the year, his brother disabused him of that notion. Vince was the master of ceremonies that day in the auditorium, calling students to the stage to receive scholastic honors and their report cards. As the program ended, Lombardi said that he had "one special mention" and brought up his brother. One by one, he read off Joe's poor grades. As Joe stood there sheepishly, Vince grew madder and redder, his eyes blinking violently, until finally he uncorked a wild swing at his little brother, who ducked and raced frantically for the exit, where one of his football teammates, Hooks Cerutti, had propitiously stationed himself, letting Joe through and then closing the door before Vince, huffing in pursuit, could catch him. The program ended right there in chaos with students scrambling out of the way of the raging bull, Mr. Lombardi.

Vince caught him later that night at home. The students were fearful about what would happen the following Monday, but Lombardi acted as though nothing had happened. For the most part, his intimidation was more a matter of demeanor than action. Dorothy Bachmann recalled that her lab partner in chemistry was so afraid of Lombardi that she never uttered a word all year. "She would never open her mouth and I had to do all the experiments because she was too scared." Lombardi tried to lighten things up with humor, but his jokes were always stale "groaners" that he laughed at harder than any of the kids. He was a believer in pop quizzes, and would stroll down the aisle singing "I'm Forever Blowing Bubbles," occasionally stopping to peruse someone's answer sheet. By all accounts, even though he scared some students, Lombardi was an effective teacher, able to explain physics and chemistry in comprehensible terms. He often spent a week repeating one concept until the slowest student in the class understood. "He made the subject clear and succeeded in communicating all the essentials so that all the students could get good grades," said Joe McPartland. "He had a great way of sensing whether you were getting it. He'd say, 'I don't think you really understood that,' and go over it again."

When not in the classroom, Lombardi spent most of the day in his office, which he shared with Father Tim Moore. Father Tim was a bright and lighthearted priest, more interested in forgiveness and redemption than the wrath of God. Although he did smack a football player for stealing one too many apples, his customary role as assistant football coach was to take players aside and reassure them after Lombardi had chewed them out. If he entered a classroom and noticed that a nun had marked down names for detention, he might back up to the blackboard and surreptitiously erase them. Since he heard confession at the church next door, he knew the secret lives of nearly everyone in the school, and handled their sins with equanimity. "He would open the sliding window and you would confess your sins to Father Tim without fear," recalled Don Crane, who played on the basketball team. "We used to steal our sweatpants and jackets and confess to him. He'd tell us to bring them back. We'd bring them back on Monday and steal them again on Friday."

For Lombardi, who attended mass daily and went to confession several times a week, Father Tim's proximity was particularly handy. "We'd be sitting there talking about something and all of a sudden Vinnie would say, 'Tim, I want to go to confession,' " the priest remembered later. "So I'd take his confession right there from my desk, and when he was done we'd start right back into the conversation we had going before." Father Tim used to say that when he was too busy to hear confession he just sent Lombardi over to church to substitute for him; people would laugh, but they were not sure that he was joking. Often it was hard to tell which of the two was the priest, especially during off-hours. Father Tim grew close to Lombardi's parents, and was a regular at their house on Knickerbocker Avenue. He stopped by on Saturday afternoons with a few of his brothers of the cloth, dressed in Hawaiian shirts. Vince often came over, too, much to Marie's dismay, but usually napped in a big chair as Pops and the priests entertained each other long into the evening, knocking down scotches, devouring an enormous pot of Matty's famous clam chowder and regaling one another with stories as they bickered over hands of gin rummy.

THE HEADLINE in the *Bergen Evening Record* ran across the top of the sports page on Tuesday, May 15, 1945: "LOMBARDI TO LEAD HACKENSACK GRIDMEN IN FALL." Underneath was a dour picture of the "New Comet Grid Tutor" and a story that began: "Vincent Thomas Lombardi is Hackensack High School's new football coach. The black-haired, bespectacled (but he hates wearing 'em and takes 'em off for pictures) 31-year-old coach comes to the County seat with a glittering record for his Englewood St. Cecilia–coached teams lost only one game in 3 years, tying three and winning 27 games." The move to the big public high school, the story went on, had been "kept under many Stetsons the last few days" as the Hackensack school board waited for Lombardi to get his release from St. Cecilia, where he still had two years to go on a four-year contract. Lombardi said he regretted leaving Saints, but felt compelled to make the move because Hackensack provided tenure and more earning potential. "I feel it's a move I must make when I consider my family," he told the *Record*.

The story was true in every respect—and ultimately wrong.

Hours after he had informed Hackensack officials, and the *Record* reporter, that he had been released by Saints, he changed his mind again, or had it changed for him. Father Tim refused to accept his decision. He said Vince was making a grievous mistake. By going to Hackensack he was resigning himself to a career in the high school ranks, the priest argued. "You have more ability than that." Marie also was opposed. The years at Saints had been traumatic enough for her. After the birth of Vincent she had endured another tragedy; her next pregnancy ended with the birth of a baby girl who died within two days of her birth. The fact that she saw this infant girl alive, and had to bury her, made it even more traumatic than the earlier stillbirth. An ill-informed doctor told her that she would never be able to have another successful birth, would never be able to have a baby girl. She had turned to alcohol again, and found that among the few things that made her happy were her husband's successes. The better his teams performed, the more recognition he gained, the better she felt about herself and her lot in life. One image stuck with her: sitting in the stands the day Vin's long winning streak ended, looking down at him on the sidelines where he stood in the middle of a puddle, looking smaller and smaller as the game wore on and the rain fell harder. Friends had suggested that she leave, but she insisted on staying: if he could take it, she could take it. There was some larger purpose. She worried that he might be satisfied as a high school football coach; furthermore, she was growing tired of sharing him with his family, especially Harry and Matty, who seemed more connected to the local high school culture than she was. Father Tim was right, she said: Hackensack is a dead end. Stay at Saints until something bigger than high school comes along.

That night little Joe and John DeGasperis and Al Quilici led a band of boys from the football team over to Vince's house on Mountain View Road and begged for Coach Lombardi to come out and talk with them. Gassy and Joe, known as the Gold Dust Twins, left guard and right guard, best friends and captains, had tears in their eyes when they asked Lombardi to stay with them through their senior year. He was brought to tears himself and relented, revealing a paradoxical pattern that persisted down through the years. Here was a man who seemed to the outside world to be in complete control, certain of what he was doing and where he was going. Internally it was never that way. Vince Lombardi was often conflicted, constantly changing his mind. Father Tim called Hackensack and said there had been a misunderstanding, Vince had not been let out of his contract at Saints. He would fulfill his obligation and stay two more years.

5

Lost in the Bronx

THE AMERICAN LIFE, abundant, was there for all to enjoy in the shade of the grape arbor behind the old Izzo homestead in Sheepshead Bay on the last Sunday of August 1947. Dozens of hot dogs and garlic-rubbed hamburgers from Lombardi Bros. sizzling on the grill, buns toasting, mounds of black olives, hot red peppers, sliced Bermuda onions and cold cuts heaped on picnic tables, barrels of draft beer flowing free and easy. All thirteen adult children of the late Antonio and Laura Izzo making the pilgrimage along with their spouses. J. C. Sapp, husband of Matty's little sister, Amelia, greeting everyone in barbecue apron and tall white chef's hat. Harry Lombardi, recovering rambunctiously from a heart attack he had suffered earlier in the year, arriving gaily in spatlike two-tone shoes with white laces and dress shirt rolled up to reveal his tattoos, a pack of smokes in his breast pocket. The swelling throng of thirty-three grandchildren (Vince and his cousins) and their families, including husbands, wives and twenty-one great-grandchildren. In all, the backyard on East Sixteenth Street pulsating with ninety-six Izzo relatives, six namesakes of the patriarch Tony the Barber among them, along with four Claras, four Richards, two Vincents and two Humberts. Not a long-lost stranger in the crowd; only two living beyond the boundaries of Brooklyn, one family out in Floral Park on the edge of Nassau County, and the Lombardis across the Hudson in Englewood.

Festively colored paper streamers were draped high from tree to tree. Dangling from the boughs were exotic Japanese lanterns brought home by some of the fifteen Izzo veterans who had been stationed in the Pacific during the war. As rumba tunes vibrated from the radio, young adults danced on a sheet of linoleum laid out on the grass and children competed nearby in potato sack and three-legged races. This was the first official gathering of the family in a dozen years, conceived for the Labor Day weekend as a way to honor the relevance of work in the Izzo family story: the older generation of barbers, beauticians, plumbers, tailors, carpenters, butchers, coal business operators, and the next generation's rising lawyers, teachers, coaches, insurance brokers, army intelligence officers. In the midst of their energetic consumption, three generations of Izzos also consecrated the memory of Laura and Antonio, the southern Italian immigrants from the mountain village of Vietri di Potenza, and toasted the family's continued good health, including the safe return of all its servicemen.

For Vince Lombardi at age thirty-four, the reunion was in line with an emerging theme of home and rebirth. He and Marie had two children of their own now, five-year-old Vincent and infant Susan, born the previous February 13 despite a doctor's ominous prediction that Marie would never bear a healthy baby. And while maintaining his home in Englewood, Vince had returned to work on familiar fields east of the Hudson. During his last year at Saints he had scoured the college ranks for an assistant coaching position, sending feelers as far away as St. Louis with no success. One rejection letter, from a former Fordham teammate coaching at a midwestern school, included a quote from their old coach, Sleepy Jim Crowley: "No future in coaching. Try something else." Among the jobs Lombardi sought was the head position at Fordham, which had resumed playing football in 1946 after dropping it for three years during the war. The school instead hired another football alumnus, Edward F. Danowski, who had been a senior during Lombardi's freshman year, then went on to quarterback the New York Football Giants from 1934 to 1941 before enlisting in the Navy.

Danowski had only one season of high school coaching experience and a modest interest in the profession. He began with a paltry $5,000 salary, a late start on recruiting and one assistant coach, and his first year at Fordham was a predictable disaster. After that season the football boosters raised money to fund thirty new scholarships and beefed up the coaching staff, bringing in Lombardi as one of several new assistants. The first day of fall practice was scheduled on Rose Hill for the Tuesday after the Izzo family picnic.

Lombardi's official responsibilities at Fordham were to teach physical education, coach the freshman squad and install the T formation offense, all for $3,500 a year. Behind the scenes came intimations from several influential alumni, as well as athletics director Jack Coffey, that Lombardi would be the head man himself soon enough, the one to lead a Rams football renaissance, returning the school to the pride of the days when Grantland Rice and Damon Runyon covered the Seven Blocks of Granite. This was the job Lombardi coveted. There was nowhere he would rather be, he told friends, than leading young men in maroon on the sidelines at the Polo Grounds on Saturday afternoons in late October, head coach of Fordham in games of national consequence against Tennessee or Syracuse or Army. Big-time football meant the same thing to Lombardi that it did to most sports fans in those early postwar days. It meant the college game.

Lombardi's dream in truth was more romantic than realistic. The fact that Fordham's Jesuit administrators had scrapped football for three years during the war was only one signal of their diminishing interest in the game, at least at the highest collegiate levels. The Reverend Robert Gannon, who had once suspended young Lombardi for fighting, was still Fordham's president, and his distaste for the professionalization of college football had only intensified in the decade since Vince's playing days. His philosophy corresponded with the latest concerns of the National Collegiate Athletic Association, which had recently adopted what was alternately called a Sanity Code or Purity Code calling for "strict amateurism" and limits on financial aid and recruiting. Scandals seemed to be erupting with regularity on campuses around the nation, some of them, too many for Gannon's taste, involving Catholic institutions. The coach of the University of San Francisco Dons was soon to resign with the announcement that twenty-two of his top players had been paid for their talents.

Gannon was so fearful of scandal that he hoped Fordham would never be good enough to get caught up in one. He had concluded, he acknowledged to one local alumni group, that football brought his school little benefit "financially, scholastically, socially or athletically." The more successful teams, he said, merely attracted gamblers and their corrupting milieu. With the intention of keeping Rams football "strictly collegiate," Gannon and his faculty adviser for athletics, the Reverend Kevin J. O'Brien, had developed a policy even stricter than the NCAA code. Along with a deemphasis on recruiting, the Fordham plan called for the construction of a small stadium on Rose Hill so that football would seem more connected to college life and less a separate business enterprise. Gannon was already withdrawing, rhetorically at least, from the addictive narcotic of sellout crowds at colossal city stadiums by calling the Mara family "extortionists" for the rents they were charging at the Polo Grounds.

The trend surely must have been apparent to Lombardi, but he plunged into his new job with only winning football on his mind. He had been separated from the college game for ten years, away from the tumultuous big-city crowds, the inflating Gotham press corps, the prospect of national recognition, and he told friends that he was determined to recover lost time. After accepting the Fordham position in late January 1947, he taught at Saints for the remainder of the second semester, but began commuting over to the Bronx in the afternoons to work out with the Rams and lead them through spring drills. On at least two occasions he brought along a carload of

Saints seniors and suited them up in Fordham uniforms to practice with the returning veterans, a surreptitious and perhaps illegal recruiting move that ran counter to Gannon's dictates. It was difficult to distinguish the college players from the Saints, Lombardi noted afterwards, boasting and complaining simultaneously, except that the Saints hit harder. One among them, his little brother, Joe, was eager to free himself at last after being physically and emotionally banged around by his big brother all his life, and escaped north to St. Bonaventure, but many of the Saints former backfield stars followed Lombardi to Rose Hill, in accompaniment with his T formation and his cause to rediscover lost Fordham glory.

FORDHAM HAD NEVER had a freshman class quite like the one that arrived in 1947. This was not just a collection of pink-faced teenage boys from Catholic prep schools. Here were many men in their twenties who had gone directly from high school graduation into the military during World War II and were now finally in college, as eager as their new freshman football coach to recoup lost time and move on quickly with their careers. Lombardi's squad of first-year players included three of his old backs from Saints, Dick Doheny, Billy White and Larry Higgins, all returned from the service, along with a twenty-three-year-old center named Herb Seidell, who had been in the Navy with Leo Paquin, left end in the Seven Blocks. Seidell certainly was not the poster boy for Father Gannon's restricted recruiting guidelines. He was a blatant ringer who had already played varsity football at Purdue before the war. In theory, he should have sat out a year before resuming his playing career, but in practice, as he later recalled, "all the rules were looser because of the war." Once again, the fallacy of the innocent past. Seidell not only played for Lombardi's freshmen, he was also elected their captain.

Again on Rose Hill with all the familiar sounds, sights and smells, dank gymnasium office, trainer Jake's old barber chair, the Keating Hall clock tower, Jesuits in cassocks clucking along, lunches of linguine and calamari on Arthur Avenue, leaves and mud on the practice field, thud and smack of leather upon leather as dusk enveloped the Bronx, maroon and gold, we do or die notes drifting over from band rehearsal—Lombardi was in his element, restored. Football as religion. The T a catechism from which he preached. And God was in the details.

In Lombardi's pedagogical style there was an exact method to hundreds of precise movements in the T. Some coaches concerned themselves with how laces were tied or shirts tucked or helmets held on the sidelines before a game. Lombardi concentrated on the minutiae of play itself. He had refined the T in the years since Doheny and White had played for him at Saints, and was refining it still. He was the patient scholar, devoting hours each day to breaking down and analyzing the elements again and again. The SNAP.

There had to be a quarter-turn rotation on the ball, no more or less. *Hold it right there! Let's see. Quarter-turn, Seidell. That's right! Now pop the ball against the fanny.* The CHEATER. The halfback three and a half steps back behind the quarterback. The fullback four. Now he got them to cheat up another half-foot to run them through the hole a split second quicker. Not a foot, that would throw off the timing completely; it had to be a half-foot.

The BALLET. Lombardi's favorite, he could work on it all day. He stood there with the center and his three quarterbacks and a posse of running backs and got out his stopwatch to time the play from snap to handoff. It was all in speed and dexterity, he said. The center had to anticipate the count to snap the ball in a split second. Then the quarterback had to jump-spin to the handoff position in time for the cheater running back. Faster. One fluid movement. The jump spin was ballet, he said. When Doheny did it right, beautiful ballet. And Doheny could do it right. He was unflappable, concise in everything he did. Not much of a runner, but Lombardi did not ask him to run. He had to hand off and pass. Not the greatest arm, but he knew when and where to throw it. His teammates called him "a cool cat." He was Lombardi on the field, the earliest coming of Bart Starr, the coach's star quarterback in Green Bay decades later.

There were blocking codes along the line, three or more options per position on a play, but also simple reads and reasons for every move. With repetition this seemed obvious, intuitive, and the young Rams learned their lessons well. They became so adept at the T that by October they were embarrassing the varsity in practice, galloping through the line at will during midweek scrimmages. They also appeared invincible in their two official games against other freshman teams, clobbering Rutgers and NYU in shutouts. The 12 to 0 defeat of Rutgers, during which the Fordham freshmen held the Scarlet Knights to negative yards on offense while compiling more than four hundred yards on the ground themselves and completing twelve of seventeen passes, prompted an article in the *New York Herald Tribune* boasting that "Coach Vinnie Lombardi . . . can feel justly proud for a job well done," that his "yearlings looked like a million dollars," and that they were certain to "lift the Rams to the prestige they knew on the gridiron before the war, come 1948." The NYU game, won by Fordham 33 to 0, excited the press boosters even more, especially in contrast with Danowski's uninspiring 1–6–1 record with the varsity that year.

At season's end Lombardi was rewarded with a new job, but not the one he expected. He was asked, belatedly, to step in and coach Fordham's freshman basketball team. The job had become vacant when Bob Mulvihill, who was slated to coach the freshmen, instead unexpectedly was declared eligible to play one final year with the varsity after returning from the Marine Corps as a twenty-five-year-old senior. Lombardi had been a successful high school basketball coach, leading one of his Saints teams to a regional championship during the war years, so he was considered the logical replacement. In fact, he had no interest in the job and knew less about the game than most of the Rams players. One of the freshman cagers that winter was Dick Tarrant, who later became a respected basketball coach at Richmond University. As Tarrant remembered that season, Lombardi was an odd mentor, largely preoccupied with football.

The players respected him and dared not challenge him. They learned that if practice was at three o'clock, they were wise to show up at two-thirty. He made them run laps ("which was absurd in basketball," Tarrant noted, since basketball scrimmages were nonstop running in any case), and set them up in a simple offense from which he would not stray. But for the most part he left the players alone, realizing that their skills surpassed his knowledge and interest in the sport. "He didn't know any of us and didn't really care to. He was babysitting us for that year," Tarrant said. Often, while the team was shooting baskets or running layup drills, Lombardi slipped off to a corner of the gym where a huddle of football players waited, and he went through the snap and ballet with his center and quarterbacks. The basketball team appeared bulky and overpopulated at times, as Lombardi brought linemen in to run laps with lanky forwards and guards. Sometimes at night, after studying football films for an hour, he walked across the campus hill against the howling winter wind and encountered a pack of athletes trudging back from dinner to their dorm in a former army barracks behind the gym. He would ignore the basketball players in the group and focus his attention on the shivering gridmen. *Did you work out today? Do your sit-ups?* The basketball players appreciated their anonymity; not only was Lombardi's energy elsewhere, but also his wrath.

Lombardi that winter was nonetheless, as usual, intense and nervous for better or worse. His will to compete was inevitably contagious, even in a sport that mattered less to him. During a meaningless freshman basketball game against Hofstra, Wagner or St. John's, played two hours before the varsity contest, with only a few girlfriends and student loiterers in the stands, a gym so empty that you could hear the vendor selling popcorn and Coke behind the stands on the other side of the court, Lombardi might launch into one of his eye-blinking spasms in response to a referee's ill-conceived foul call. There was one other characteristic that his basketball players never forgot about Lombardi the freshman basketball coach: he had a noticeably nervous digestive system. "Before every game he would be in the crapper. He would flush and we'd all giggle," Tarrant recalled. "And he spent most of halftime in the bathroom with the runs. I always wondered whether coaching placed an increasing strain on his colon. Lots of times, if you have colitis, the doctor will ask, 'Are you under stress?' "

POTATO ED, they called Ed Danowski, and that aptly described his coaching style. He had many attributes—athletic grace, handsome looks, sincere demeanor—but charisma was not one of them. No more sizzle than a half-baked spud. When Fordham's freshman class of 1947 moved up to the varsity the next season, so too did Lombardi, and though he was not promoted to head coach, he did most of the coaching, intellectual and spiritual, while Potato Ed, as one player described it, "stood in the corner and chewed tobacco." Fordham ran the T as Lombardi taught it, and entered the season with raised expectations, which were rudely dashed with an opening 53 to 14 loss to a middling Lafayette team. The situation deteriorated from there, with losses to Canisius, Georgetown, Boston University and Holy Cross. It was the first time in his career that Lombardi felt direct responsibility for losing, and with each loss he grew more intense and inventive, throwing as many trick plays as he could scheme up into his basic T. Fordham simply did not have the skill and depth yet to compete again at the big-time level. This mattered not at all to Father Gannon, who had already expressed his preference for safe losing and mediocrity, and it had no discernible effect on the disposition of Potato Ed, who shook it off with the sanest retort a losing football coach could summon, that it was only a game, not "life and death."

Alumni boosters and their cohorts in the press box were fed up, however, and began hectoring for change. There were suggestions of bringing back Hugh Devore, a former assistant to Sleepy Jim Crowley then coaching at St. Bonaventure, and even the fanciful notion that Frank Leahy, another former assistant, could be lured back from his prestigious post at Notre Dame. But most of the public speculation centered on Lombardi. "RUMOR MILL: DANOWSKI OUT?" queried a headline in the *New York Post* with two weeks to go in the season. The story said "Vin Lombardi, who gained fame as one of the Rams' renowned Seven Blocks of Granite, was said to be in line for Danowski's spot." The *New York Journal American's* Barney Kremenko followed up with the change as a *fait accompli,* saying Danowski's days were "numbered" and that "alumni had tabbed Lombardi as their man as far back as a year ago, when he coached the frosh to victories over NYU and Rutgers. But the fact that Danowski's contract had another year to run caused complications, and the embarrassing matter was dropped." In his "Sports Chatter" column, Harry Singer offered the opinion that Danowski's "lack of color and personality" were the main reasons he would be replaced by Lombardi, "who is rated just the opposite from the present Ram coach and who will make personal appearances and is a good mixer."

Lombardi neither pushed the speculation nor made an effort to quash it. Every morning during his commute from Englewood to the Bronx, he fretted aloud about the stressful situation he found himself in. He expected to be made head coach and wanted the job, but he did not want to be seen as Potato Ed's betrayer. He felt responsible for instructing the players, preparing them for each game, but it was still Danowski's team, and he was frustrated by not having true authority. As the controversy bubbled up around them, Danowski and Lombardi, barely on speaking terms, nonetheless devoted themselves to ending the season in respectable fashion. The Rams played spiritedly while losing to Rutgers in the penultimate game, after which a sympathy backlash for Potato Ed began to emerge. Leading sportswriters who had covered him during his days with the Giants began to comment on his good will and decency. President Gannon, working behind the scenes against the blatant move by some alumni to restore big-time football at Fordham, was only too willing to become a private source for pro-Danowski stories. Danowski was also aided by the neutrality of the most influential member of the alumni advisory board, Wellington Mara, owner of the New York Giants. Then and later, Mara's relationship with Lombardi was overstated by many: they had been classmates at Fordham, but were not pals. Mara felt just as close to Danowski, who had been one of his players with the Giants for eight seasons. "I don't know that I had any role," Mara said decades later of the dispute. "But I tried to stay away from that whole thing."

The players were torn. Some considered Potato Ed a dolt, a few thought Vince was a martinet, but most of them liked both men for decidedly different reasons: Danowski's ease, Lombardi's contagious will to win. On the weekend before the season finale against NYU, Herb Seidell, the team captain, was called home to Indiana to care for his father, who had fallen off a ladder. When he returned on the Friday after Thanksgiving, the day before the game, he could sense an "enormous amount of strain" in the locker room. Players were being called in one by one to talk to Father O'Brien about the coaching situation. O'Brien told Seidell that he was taking an informal poll and that the players seemed to be unanimous in their support of Danowski. Well, Seidell responded, all the players knew who was doing the coaching. It was Lombardi. He left the meeting convinced that "the cards were stacked against Vinnie" and that the administration was "trying to create the illusion of support" for Danowski. The next day Fordham played its finest game of the year, smothering NYU 26 to 0, and the salvation of Potato Ed was assured. "If Ed Danowski's job as head coach of Fordham wasn't saved by that endorsement his players gave him in chalking up the traditional game with the Violets for their beloved mentor," wrote Dan Parker in the *New York Mirror,* "then there's no balm in Gilead."

The balm arrived a week later, after a long Friday night meeting between Father O'Brien, acting on behalf of President Gannon, and Jack Coffey, the athletics director. It was arranged that Danowski would receive a new contract and a raise. He was to fire two of his assistants but keep Lombardi, even though Danowski had made it clear that he could not stand the sight of his threatening aide. If this was a compromise, it was "not a happy arrangement," noted Tim Cohane, who had been following the careers of Lombardi and other former Fordham athletes since his days as the school's publicist. Cohane had left Fordham in 1940 to enter the world of major sports journalism, his longtime ambition. He started at the *New York World-Telegram,* writing a column entitled "Frothy Facts" and covering college football and the Brooklyn Dodgers baseball team. Then in 1945 he moved on to *Look* magazine, where he served as sports editor. He was still plugged in at Fordham, and in fact had been lobbying for Lombardi's takeover of the football program. When that maneuver flopped, he received word that Vince and his dream of leading the Rams back to national glory were crushed.

Lombardi had not found his way home after all, but had merely drifted through two more lost years. He needed a way out again. The man who had created the mythology of the Seven Blocks of Granite soon had another plan for him. One school, one football program, stirred Cohane's soul as much as the old Maroon. On an afternoon in early December, he met his favorite coach, Colonel Earl H. "Red" Blaik of Army, at the Eastern College Athletic Association meetings at the Biltmore Hotel in New York. On the way to dinner Blaik casually mentioned that he was losing his offensive line coach and needed a replacement. Know anyone? Blaik asked. Yes, sir, Cohane said. He thought he knew just the right man for the job.

6

Fields of
Friendly Strife

LOMBARDI DROVE NORTH from Englewood up Route 9W high above
the Hudson River, the roadway along the Palisades framed by fresh snowbanks and slicked with sleet and ice. He was on his way to the United States
Military Academy at West Point on this December morning in 1948, a brave
new world for him, and the journey was not an easy one. When he reached
Thayer Gate at the south end of the academy, he declared that he had an appointment with the football coach, then negotiated his way up Mills Road
past Michie Stadium and Lusk Reservoir and down toward the gymnasium.
Even in the somber shroud of early winter, the panorama was at once majestic and intimidating: massive stone everywhere, barracks and cliff, Gothic
spire, long gray coats, vast snowy Plain, broad cold river. When Lombardi
reached the gym, he rode the elevator to the top floor and climbed another
flight of stairs to an office in the tower. There, in front of him at the secretary's desk talking to an aide, stood Colonel Red Blaik, the man Lombardi
had come to see. He was an imposing sight, six foot two, lean and immaculate at age fifty-one, with bronze hair and serious pale blue eyes.

"Sid, take a look at the hands on this man," Blaik said when Lombardi
extended his butcher-boy thick right hand in greeting. "Easy to see why he
was a block of granite." He was talking to Sid Gillman, his line assistant, who
was leaving to coach at the University of Cincinnati and whose position
Lombardi hoped to fill. Blaik's seeming familiarity with the Seven Blocks of
Granite was, in fact, rehearsed. He knew nothing of Lombardi before a recent briefing from Tim Cohane, who had brokered the interview, and he
harbored doubts that Lombardi's coaching background prepared him for this

job. The men retreated to the coach's inner sanctum: warm lighting, dark walnut paneling. On one wall, in bronze, hung a West Point coat of arms. Behind Blaik's mahogany desk, on which stacks of mail were neatly piled, was a large framed photograph of a saluting General Douglas MacArthur, commander of U.S. military forces in the Far East, who had been superintendent at West Point when Blaik played football there shortly after World War I. MacArthur was Blaik's hero, the No. 1 fan of Army football. Pleasantries quickly gave way to the substance of the job interview, a doctoral examination on football methodology.

What pulling technique do you teach your offensive guards? Blaik asked his prospective assistant.

The crossover step, Lombardi answered, rising from his chair to demonstrate the move he had learned under Sleepy Jim Crowley and Frank Leahy at Fordham, swinging his right arm back in a fluid motion to propel the quickest turn. The idea is to pull with speed and still be under control so you can assume a hitting position quickly, Lombardi explained.

Blaik pressed on: What technique do you teach guards for turning up into the hole?

Again, Lombardi returned to the fundamentals he had learned from Leahy, his former line coach, who was now gaining national renown as head coach at Notre Dame. Drop the outside shoulder, Vince said, and push off the outside foot.

On defense, Blaik asked next, do you favor the forearm shiver or the forearm left?

I think there's a place for both, Lombardi said, hedging slightly. But I personally favor striking the opponent under the shoulders with a forearm left.

Why? Blaik asked.

With the shiver, Lombardi answered, if you miss, they're into your belly right away. He tried to sound authoritative, but had no idea whether he was making points with the unrevealing colonel.

Blaik continued with the gridiron interrogation: What technique do you teach for downfield blocks?

The roll block. If you miss the target, Lombardi explained, he still backs away and it's enough to tie him up.

That's what we teach, Blaik said. The colonel was impressed. Lombardi seemed as taken with football nuance as he was.

The question-and-answer session persisted for nearly two hours until Blaik ended the interview and treated his guest to lunch at the officer's club. As Lombardi walked to his car for the drive back to Englewood, Blaik seemed noncommittal but encouraging. He said he would call.

That night Tim Cohane, curious about the results of his matchmaking, placed a call to Blaik to see how it went. As Cohane later remembered the conversation, Blaik said of Lombardi, "He's all right." Pressed further, Blaik added, "He's a rough soul." Cohane knew that Blaik was never impulsive in judgment, rarely effusive in praise, but was that a psychological assessment, a compliment, a criticism? Perhaps all three. The next day Blaik's office called Lombardi and asked him to return for another interview. This time Vince rode the train north through more icy weather and met with Blaik alone in the tower. Blaik discussed West Point, the history of the academy, the winning tradition of the football team since he arrived as head coach in 1941, and then went over Lombardi's background and salary at Fordham. He never asked how much Lombardi wanted, but stated that the job would pay $7,000, with free housing included. He also mentioned that there was a grade school on the post for young Vincent, who was six, and his little sister, one-year-old Susan, when she reached school age.

Blaik cautioned that he had to gain final approval from the athletic board, but Lombardi descended from the tower this time knowing that he had the nod. It was not the top job that he had yearned for, still just an assistant's position, but being hired by Blaik was nonetheless a significant achievement. Now he would be coaching in the big time and learning from the best. Blaik was the dominant college coach of the forties. He was an offensive wizard whose teams from 1944 through 1946, led by his famed tandem of backs, Glenn Davis and Doc Blanchard, Mr. Outside and Mr. Inside, had amassed prodigious point totals, a tie with Notre Dame the only blemish on their record. His sixth-ranked 1948 team had also finished unbeaten, though not perfect, having been tied by Navy in the season-ending rivalry. Blaik could hire virtually anyone he wanted, and he had selected an assistant less than two years removed from a small Catholic high school in North Jersey. Before leaving West Point this time, Lombardi was shown around the post by another assistant coach, Doug Kenna, who had played quarterback for Blaik during the war years. Kenna found Lombardi engaging, but nervous and uncertain that he could adjust to the military environment.

ON NEW YEAR'S DAY 1949, at eight in the morning, Lombardi attended his first meeting of the Army football staff. The holiday session was one of Blaik's annual traditions, reinforcing the idea that no team in the nation would get the jump on Army. That was the essence of Red Blaik, the most prepared man Lombardi had ever met. And there was much to get ready for this year. Blaik had two new coaches under him, Lombardi for offense and another young bull, Murray Warmath of Tennessee, for defense. Eighteen graduating lettermen had to be replaced, seven of them defensive starters, and the schedule was more difficult than usual, with early games against top-ranked Michigan and Penn State.

Lombardi and Warmath had met once before. Fifteen years earlier they had smacked each other around on a November afternoon in the Polo Grounds, Warmath lining up at left guard for Tennessee, Lombardi at right

guard for Fordham, which prevailed that day, 13 to 12. Now the two tenderfoot coaches shared a desk in a communal war room below Blaik's office, and
were brought together in a trying initial assignment: they were called up to
the blackboard several hours each day for the first week, diagramming plays
and formations, defending their ideas against Blaik's piercing questions. It
was a variation of Lombardi's first job interview, but this time for keeps. At
one point Lombardi found himself in a heated debate with Blaik and the
other assistants over the proper way to deliver the center's snap to the quarterback. Blaik had always taught the half-turn of the ball, presenting it to the
quarterback sideways. Lombardi preferred the quarter-turn, with the ball
reaching the quarterback at a slight angle. It was quicker, he said, and made
it easier for the quarterback to hand off or pass. Blaik disagreed, so they got
out a ball and practiced both methods there in the conference room outside
Blaik's office. The quarter-turn proved faster by a fraction of a second.

When spring practice opened on March 12, Lombardi began to appreciate the totality of Blaik's preparedness. The coaches reported at eight each
morning, spent the first hour on correspondence, then convened at 9:15 for a
staff meeting to establish the precise missions and chronology of that afternoon's practice, from the moment the players left the dressing room at 3:45
until they walked off the field at 5:15. The athletes had only a limited
amount of time for football in their regimented days, sandwiched between
final class and dinner formation at six o'clock, so nothing was left to chance.
A set amount of time was devoted to each drill. Fifteen minutes for line
blocks. Fifteen minutes for back blocks. Fifteen minutes for the blocking
sleds. Fifteen minutes at the end for all the units to come together and work
on new plays. Blaik discouraged assistant coaches from bringing papers with
them onto the field; they were expected to memorize the plays and blocking
assignments of every player. At first Lombardi had trouble keeping pace.
"Run No. 10!" Blaik commanded from the rear of the offensive unit, forcing
his assistant to confess that he had not yet found time to install play No. 10.
"Blaik just gave me his bland Scots stare," as Lombardi later described the
scene. " 'Run No. 11,' he'd order."

After practice the coaches broke for dinner and then often were expected to return to the gym, sometimes working until midnight. Photographs and motion pictures had been taken of that day's practice, and were
developed and waiting for the assistants to study in the evening, along with
films of future opponents. Blaik was a film fanatic, one of the first football
coaches to analyze the game play-by-play, position-by-position, methodically charting another team's tendencies on each down at various positions
on the field and tuning his offense and defense in response to what he had
seen. When studying films of their own team, Blaik and the assistants replayed the film to determine what every player did on each play, assigning
grades based on the degree of execution. Football was Blaik's life, his profes-

sion and only hobby. He largely disdained the social scene beyond West Point and his house on the hill, where he and his wife, Merle, hosted parties for out-of-town guests on football Saturdays and group suppers for cadets on Sunday afternoons. He seemed to think about football twenty-four hours a day.

Watching film was his idea of fun, WORK and PLAY. Once, after he and his staff had studied Michigan game footage for several hours in the projection room near his office, Blaik turned to Warmath and Lombardi and said, "You guys want to have some fun?" It was a hot afternoon and the assistants were restless. Warmath dreamed of a round of golf. "Heck," said the colonel to his projectionist, "open up the locker and get those Navy films out. Let's look at those for a while!" Even in the off-season the focus on football was relentless. Lombardi would be "halfway through dinner" when the phone might ring and it was Blaik saying, "I'll pick you up in fifteen minutes." They would drive to the gym and "discuss personnel or play ideas" late into the night. It was then Lombardi first realized that "football was a full-time twelve-month vocation."

In many ways the philosophy at West Point was similar to a way of life that Lombardi had learned earlier at Fordham from the Jesuits. There was a direct line from one to the next, from religion to the military to football, from the spiritual exercises of St. Ignatius to the football regimen of Colonel Blaik. Both emphasized discipline, order, organization, planning, attention to detail, repetition, the ability to adjust to different situations and remain flexible in pursuit of a goal while sustaining an obsession with one big idea. Lombardi was a daily communicant at both altars, absorbing what he learned from the Jesuits and Blaik to become the leading apostle of the mystical discipline of football. As integral as religion was to his sense of self, it was not until he reached West Point and combined his spiritual discipline with Blaik's military discipline that his coaching persona began to take its mature form. Everything he knew about organizing a team and preparing it to play its best, Lombardi said later, he learned at West Point. "It all came from Red Blaik."

Lombardi wanted nothing more than to please Blaik, a father figure who had the eminence and reserve that Harry Lombardi, Old Five by Five, lacked. Vince's bluster turned to obsequiousness when he was within range of the coach. At times he came across like a bootlicking corporal, snapping off refrains of "Yes, Colonel!" and "Yes, sir!" to Blaik's slightest requests. Yet it is hard to imagine two less similar personalities than Red Blaik, the Presbyterian Scotsman from the middle American town of Dayton, Ohio, and Vince Lombardi, the Italian Catholic from Sheepshead Bay.

Blaik was all understatement—reserved, aloof, stern, outwardly cool. He stood alone at practice, tall and straight in his Army baseball cap, sweatshirt, football trousers cut off below the knee and woolen socks, barking out crisp commands, rarely needing to modulate his tone of voice, just a nod and a look that said he could not be fooled. When he saw something that displeased him, he called the offender over and quietly explained what should have been done. He disciplined by way of teaching. His one curse word was "Jesus Katy!" More often "Jeebers Katy." And yet his "presence was overwhelming," said Doug Kenna. "He radiated authority. He was really in charge." Lombardi was overstated, emotional, enthusiastic, explosive, hungry for stories and action, quick to laugh and cry and yell, his deep, distinctive voice reverberating across the practice field. He thrived on resistance, another force pushing back at him, physically and mentally, and he confronted the players spontaneously, swearing and steaming, all hands-on demonstrations, just like with the high school boys at Saints, demanding that the linemen hit him, and he hit back.

The irony was that the cadets spent most of their hours at West Point with someone in their face, as they rehearsed drills on the Plain, and marched through archways to classes and meals, and made their beds and lined up for inspection, always with someone vociferously demanding more of them—and they looked forward to football practice as a respite from the daily grind. Lombardi threatened the equilibrium—he came in attacking—and there was some culture shock at first. The players were not accustomed to being confronted so vigorously; some hated him for it. This was part of the "rough soul" that Blaik saw in him and attempted to soften. "He toned down my temper, or tried to," Lombardi said of Blaik years later. "When I'd get too intense and explosive on the field, he'd call me into the office the next day and sit there and look at me and twirl his class ring—West Point 1920—and say, 'Vince, we just don't do it that way at West Point. You can't talk that way to cadets. You can't drive them that way because they're being driven all day.' "

There was one dominating characteristic that Blaik and Lombardi shared—an overwhelming will to win. "There was never any question that we were not allowed to lose," said Doug Kenna, who became one of Blaik's closest friends as player and assistant coach. "That was the general attitude. We did lose, but it was a bleak day at West Point when that happened." To the poetic sportsman's code of Grantland Rice, that wins and losses meant less than how you played the game, Blaik was once heard to reply with clean brevity: "Eyewash!" He was a miserable loser and proud of it. Blaik posted his Ten Football Axioms on the walls of the Army dressing room. Axiom No. 1 was about the distinction between losing and sportsmanship. "There never was a champion who, to himself, was a good loser. There is a vast difference between a good sport and a good loser." In Blaik's opinion the "purpose of the game is to win. To dilute the will to win is to destroy the purpose of the game." In this, as in most matters, he was influenced by General MacArthur. He never forgot MacArthur's words: "There is no substitute for victory."

MacArthur, or "Dauntless Doug," as he was known by fellow cadets at the turn of the century, had played baseball for three years at West Point, a right fielder with a weak bat who willed himself on base. During his senior year he managed the 1902 football team. By the time he returned to the Point two decades later to serve as superintendent from 1919 to 1922, he was a football man through and through, regarding it as another form of war-gaming. When Blaik and the other players of that era looked over at the side-lines during practice, invariably they caught sight of MacArthur pacing back and forth, riding crop in hand. Before he left that post for the Philippine Islands, his thoughts on the correlation between sport and war were carved in the stone portals of the gymnasium:

> UPON THE FIELDS OF FRIENDLY STRIFE
> ARE SOWN SEEDS THAT
> UPON OTHER FIELDS, ON OTHER DAYS
> WILL BEAR THE FRUITS OF VICTORY

He followed Army football religiously from then on, scouring press guides and magazines, watching highlight films whenever possible, memorizing the biography of every player, even third-stringers: height, weight, age, hometown. Even during the toughest days of World War II, according to his wife, he spent hours thinking about Army football, one of the few diversions that could relax his mind. After Army walloped Navy 23 to 7 in 1944 to finish undefeated, MacArthur sent Blaik a telegram saying that they had "stopped the war to celebrate" the "magnificent success" of "the greatest of all Army teams." He was fascinated by Blaik's coaching strategies and their parallels on the field of battle; when Blaik became an early proponent of two-platoon football, using specialists on offense and defense, MacArthur remarked that this "makes the game more and more in accord with the development of tactics of actual combat." Once, after Blaik informed him that he had lost both his line and backfield coaches, MacArthur lamented that "it could not have failed to be a great blow.... However, this again follows the technique of war, for you always lose your best men in the heat of battle."

Blaik and MacArthur were regular correspondents, their letters often touching on war, politics, friends, enemies, but always returning to their shared love of the minutiae of Army football. On July 30, 1949, as he made final preparations for the approaching season, Blaik sent a four-page single-spaced typed letter to MacArthur in Japan at General Headquarters of the Far East Command. He took note of the difficult schedule Army faced, the inexperience of his team, the arrival of two new assistants, Lombardi and Warmath, the weights of top performers along the defensive line, his preference for two-platoon football, and concerns that his defensive backs were too short and that his running backs were too "dainty." MacArthur wrote back on August 8, accurately reading between the lines of a coach's typical pessimism, saying that Blaik's report "fills me with hope that you will have a reasonably good season," an impression, MacArthur added, that was "fortified by the magnificent results you have always been able to produce in the past." In closing, he asked Blaik to "tell the Public Relations Officer to send me such literature as is put out about the team, and keep me in touch with the results of the games during the season. We are way out on the end of the line here, and little news of the Academy trickles through."

That exchange of letters came during the one brief period of the year when Blaik was on vacation of sorts, though he was not really away from football even then. During the final week of July and first week of August, he would retreat to Bull Pond, a fishing camp with two cabins on the West Point property about eight miles southwest of campus. This was by tradition a stag affair, just Blaik and his staff, a few Army Athletic Association officers and a handful of sportswriters. Lombardi was a first-time guest that year, and it was at Bull Pond that he developed friendships with two other West Point figures who later became significant influences on his life: Colonel Russell "Red" Reeder, a one-legged marvel, hero of D-Day, who taught history and psychology and was in charge of the athletic grounds, and Colonel Orrin C. "Ockie" Krueger, assistant graduate manager of athletics, who was Blaik's all-purpose aide-de-camp. From New York came Willard Mullin, the popular sports cartoonist for the *New York World-Telegram,* Stanley Woodward, sports editor of the *New York Herald Tribune,* and *Look* magazine's Tim Cohane.

Lombardi slept in Cabin No. 2, also known as the Mother Lodge, which was where most of the fun was. Bull Pond was the quintessential male-bonding experience of that time and culture. Every night the campers gathered on the screened-in front porch as an Army Signal Corps projectionist ran Army football highlights and Hollywood films. This was not a particularly artsy crowd; they preferred westerns and anything with Susan Hayward. Once when Blaik asked for a showing of *Julius Caesar,* most of the boys left to play cards and drink near the backroom bar, which was operated by the fun-loving Red Reeder and never closed. No one wanted to stay in Cabin No. 1 with Blaik, known to his cohorts as St. Blaik. He did not smoke or drink; furthermore, according to Ockie Krueger, "Blaik snored to beat hell." The group often took turns cooking. Lombardi and Mullin created a passable meal, by all accounts, but a gastronomic conspiracy of Blaik, Woodward and Cohane offered up a breakfast that "tasted as if it had been cooked in a drain pipe" and a lunch that elicited the immortal query from Murray Warmath: "Have I eaten this or am I supposed to?"

Along with the taciturn Blaik, Lombardi was the poorest storyteller in the gang, but he laughed the loudest at the jokes, including his own. He was the best audience possible for Cohane, the erudite, pipe-smoking scotch drinker who shared with his fellow Fordham grad a corny and romantic sense of humor. It was in the haze of a hangover one morning that summer that Cohane conceived the idea of a Bull Pond All-America team, the fictitious counterpart to the College All-Star teams he selected with Grantland Rice. The sensibility of the Bull Pond All-America team reflected Cohane's perspective on major college football, which was shared by the others: he revered it, despite its flaws, which he preferred to deal with through jokes rather than hand-wringing editorials and official investigations. On that 1949 Bull Pond team were players whose names made Lombardi laugh so hard that tears shot from his eyes. Excalibur Slime, the "maniacally aggressive" tackle from King Arthur's Knight School. Hairy Dog Staggerfoot, the "tipsy broken field artist" from Three A.M.&M. Percy Smog, the "X-ray-eyed quarterback" from UCLA. Increase Yardage, the "famed fullback and cum laude student in underwater fingerpainting" from Harvard. And the favorite of both Lombardi and Cohane, Chuckles Axemurder, the "murderous end" from Bedlam Hall.

NOT EVERYONE loved Red Blaik and his football program. His staff and players responded to him with reverence and undying loyalty ("You signed a lifetime contract with him," said Doug Kenna), but Blaik had adversaries scattered around the country, in the press box, in the academies and across the field, who considered him less than a saint. His critics complained that he was an egotist who would do anything to win and that the "brave old Army team" of the stirring fight song was not so brave after all; they played dirty, it was said, and bullied lesser teams on an easy schedule. Far from genuflecting to the patriots along the Hudson during the Blanchard-Davis era at the end of World War II, some people questioned publicly why Army had such brilliant athletes playing a game when they could have been saving the world overseas. Even Blaik's innovative two-platoon system was the object of scorn. The average football fan disapproved when Blaik implemented his system in 1948; while Army was destroying Stanford 43 to 0 at Yankee Stadium that year, thousands booed every time Army switched platoons from offense to defense.

Blaik's critics had reached full voice by 1949. Army began the season impressively, destroying Davidson and Penn State in its first two games. The T formation, tutored by Lombardi, looked impressive with Arnold Galiffa running the offense at quarterback. Galiffa was starting ahead of Blaik's son Bob, a talented sophomore who some alumni and sportswriters thought was a smarter signal-caller than Galiffa. But Blaik was disinclined to start his son over a veteran of Galiffa's talent, which he felt was considerable. In one of his letters to MacArthur, he had written, "In Galiffa, our quarterback and passer, we have a sharpshooter of unusual ability, who aside from a temperament which goes with the Italian youngsters, has all the qualities of an All American."

West Point then was dominated by the Anglo-Saxon culture of men like Blaik and MacArthur, and Italians were thought of in stereotypical fashion as fiery and emotional, which was more true of Lombardi than Galiffa. Early that season Lombardi had encountered the prevailing attitude when Blaik asked him to address the West Point Society of retired colonels and generals in Manhattan. It was his first appearance before the brass, and Lombardi was nervous on the drive down. After showing game films and appraising the team, he thought he had survived the ordeal, when an old warhorse rose from his chair and scolded him for starting Galiffa ahead of Bobby Blaik. "The only reason you're playing Galiffa is because he's Italian!" came the charge. Lombardi was so enraged by the accusation that he could "feel the hair standing up" on the back of his neck. He was never known for his quick wit, but this time he found an answer that calmed him down and made the others chuckle as well. "That's not the reason at all," Lombardi said. "I'm playing him because *I'm* Italian." In fact, Galiffa was starting because Red Blaik wanted him to start; Lombardi, like his grouchy old critic, privately preferred Bob Blaik at quarterback.

For the third game of the season in early October, the Army team rode the train out to Ann Arbor to face Michigan in the college game of the year. Michigan was top-ranked, unbeaten in more than two seasons, and Blaik had been preparing for this game for ten months, since that first staff meeting on New Year's morning. Every down and distance tendency that Michigan had revealed in previous games, what play they most likely would run on first and ten, third and long, third and short, what plays they preferred from left formation, what plays they relied on in their own territory, in their opponent's territory—all of that had been seen on film and plotted before the season by Lombardi, Warmath and the other assistants, Kenna, Paul Amen and Johnny Sauer (perhaps Blaik's finest staff ever; all but Kenna, who opted for the business world, became successful head coaches).

They also studied the Michigan offensive players individually, scrutinizing their movements for inadvertent tip-offs of what play was coming. The laborious process of looking at film with scientific precision was a revelation to Lombardi, who had done little of it at Fordham and none at Saints. "It's surprising how many players tipped by the position of their feet, the angle of their body. You could tell whether it was a wedge play, pass play, dive play, sweep," Lombardi said later. "You see whether a lineman can be had to the inside. You make notes on paper and put books together on the formations and the personnel." The key discovery from the Michigan game films was that their defensive linemen were inordinately tall, with high centers of gravity; Army's offensive line could handle them by blocking low, coming in under the forearm charge. In the week before the game Lombardi drilled the linemen relentlessly, taking the defensive position himself and having them charge at his shins and ankles. Such comprehensive analysis and adjustment would become routine among football coaches decades later, but it was rare then. It gave Blaik an advantage on the field not unlike a card-player who is expert at counting cards competing against opponents relying on the luck of the draw; the talent, or hand that is dealt, is of primary importance, but analysis can make a crucial difference between consistent winning and losing.

Blaik's signature talent was using all this data to create something clean and simple. He had what Lombardi called "the great knack" of knowing what offensive plan to use against what defense and then "discarding the immaterial and going with the strength." All the detailed preparations resulted not in a mass of confusing statistics and plans, but in the opposite, paring away the extraneous, reducing and refining until all that was left was what was needed for that game against that team. It was a lesson Lombardi never forgot, and the benefits of that system were apparent during the big game in Ann Arbor. Playing before a full house of 97,000 Michigan fans, Army defeated the seemingly invincible Wolverines 21 to 7. But the game did more than enhance Army's standing in the national polls. It also inflamed Blaik's reputation for dirty play. During a reverse play Michigan's passing right halfback, Chuck Ortmann, was knocked unconscious as he was trying to make a block. To Michigan fans, Ortmann's concussion became the symbol of West Point thuggery. After the game, the *Michigan Daily* printed an interview with W. H. Hobbs, an eminent professor of geology, who charged that Ortmann had been kicked between the eyes by Army's fullback Gil Stephenson. Hobbs wrote letters to colleagues around the country accusing Army of intentionally trying to cripple its opponents. He found an ally in a Harvard professor who watched Army defeat the Crimson 54 to 14 the following week and declared that in his twenty-two years working as an official, this Army team was the dirtiest he had seen.

"Army had more mud slung at it than a dredge could discover under the Mississippi," wrote Blaik's friendly scribe, Tim Cohane, in *Look*. Was it deserved? Army indisputably played a ferocious brand of football, its games marked by bruising tackles and bruised feelings. But Bennie Oosterbaan, Michigan's coach, disagreed with Professor Hobbs, saying that Blaik's team played hard but fairly. Game films later showed that Ortmann had been accidentally clonked on the head by the knee of one of his own blockers, and he could not have been kicked by Stephenson in any case, since he never got in the game and Karl Kuckhahn played the entire game at fullback.

Army's notoriety as a corps of bullies had been established nonetheless, and only spread further as the season progressed. A few more members of the New York press corps joined the anti-Blaik chorus after the Cadets overwhelmed Columbia 63 to 6; the next day's game stories sounded like reports from the front, elbows flying, Columbia players staggering from the field in a daze. This served as mere warmup for the commotion at Michie Stadium in early November when Army was host to Lombardi's old team, Fordham. The Rams came to West Point with much to prove. They had run through the season unbeaten to that point, surprising even themselves, and an upset of Army would bring national recognition for the first time since Sleepy Jim Crowley's final year at Fordham before World War II. Fordham's best players had played for Lombardi and wanted to show their old mentor that they could excel without him. This group included Joe Lombardi, who had transferred to Fordham only after his older brother's departure. Then there was the coach, Ed Danowski, to whom the game was a venue for revenge against the former aide who had tried to overthrow him. "We went up there with a chip on our shoulder," said Herb Seidell, Fordham's center.

In a sense Tim Cohane was responsible for it all. In his strategic position as Fordham alumnus and Blaik confidant, he had pressured both sides to schedule the game, thinking the prestigious opponent would help Fordham regain national stature. As was his custom, Cohane drove to West Point from his home in Scarsdale, New York, several hours before kickoff, singing college fight songs all the way up, and went directly to the press box to take in the thrill of a football Saturday. This was his notion of heaven on earth. No sight stirred him more than Michie Stadium and its environs along the Hudson. "They have likened its beauty to the Stade in ancient Athens," he once wrote in a letter to a friend. "The gridiron, running north and south, as well groomed as the front lawn of a palace. Along the west side, a tier of concrete stands roofless, slopes up to the wooded hills, and extends around to both end zones, forming a square cut letter C. Atop the steep wooded hill to the north sits old Fort Putnam, first built in 1798.... Michie was built less for size than for beauty. The spectator in the west stand repeatedly catches himself looking beyond to the breathtaking backdrop of the road, the reservoir, the knoll, the observatory, the colonial homes, and the Cadet chapel."

So much for the splendor of the setting. When the game started and Fordham and Army went at each other, there was nothing beautiful to be seen. Army eventually won 35 to 0, but the score was secondary; the fight was the game. Even Cohane had to confess that it was more brawl than football, as he wrote later in *Look:* "With a complete disregard for the sensibilities of the assemblage, including the Jesuits and the Army brass, the Cadets and the Rams went to work on each other with everything short of stilettos and strangling cords." Doug Kenna remembered the game as "probably the roughest I had ever experienced in college football. There were penalties all over and most of them for unnecessary roughness. I always sensed that part of it was because of Lombardi. Fordham wanted to show him." True enough, said Joe Lombardi. He felt that way about his big brother that day. "It was terrible and it was because of Vince's leaving and going to West Point. We wanted to show we could play them, but we just fought." We do or die, taken literally. Seidell, the Fordham captain who had been a strong Lombardi supporter during the power struggle with Danowski, said he "got the hell kicked out of" him by Army. "They called it the 'Donnybrook on the Hudson.' I was told that seventeen teeth came out of nine different mouths. I lost one. I got my whole face pranged when I was blindsided coming off the field after a punt. That was the kind of game it was."

One sportswriter acknowledged that he enjoyed the melee. "I hope there will be no hollering, bellowing nor deploring over the Army-Fordham game. After all, BOYS WILL BE BOYS," Frank Graham wrote in his game column for the *New York Sun*. But the brotherly feud was not dismissed so easily by the antagonists. Even Lombardi and Cohane found themselves in a shouting match afterwards over who started the mess. At a postgame dinner at Blaik's house, Cohane chided Lombardi and said Army precipitated the fighting; Lombardi said his alma mater was responsible. Blaik, as Cohane recalled it, "adopted the attitude of one who had been treated contemptuously by an old friend." But in the end, Lombardi took a lasting lesson from that game that had nothing to do with the fighting. For the rest of his career, he would remember how Fordham reacted late in the second quarter when it was trailing 7 to 0. "Fordham panicked," Lombardi said years later. Twice in a row the Rams tried to score quickly with passes and were intercepted both times, leading to quick Army scores. Instead of trailing by seven points at halftime, they faced an insurmountable three-touchdown disadvantage. "I never forgot this," Lombardi said. From then on, whenever a quarterback pleaded for a last-minute touchdown strike before the half, Lombardi said no, remembering Fordham's 1949 collapse at Michie Stadium.

The season ended perfectly for Army, with a 38 to 0 thrashing of Navy, and Blaik's maligned but victorious squad won the Lambert Trophy as the best team in the East. After two glum losing years on Rose Hill, Lombardi was feeling the thrill of WORK and PLAY again. At the postseason luncheon honoring the team, Red Blaik seemed untroubled by the controversy that had stalked him all year. He confessed that before the season began he had thought about retiring, but now he was glad he had stayed. "You have to pay the price," was his favorite motto, and he felt that he and his team had done so and were now reaping the reward. "Once in a while you are lucky enough to have the thrill and satisfaction of working with a group of men who are willing to make every sacrifice to achieve a goal, and then experience the achieving of it with them," Blaik said. "In this, believe me, there is a payment that cannot be matched in any other pursuit."

DUTY, HONOR, COUNTRY, FOOTBALL. What about family? The Lombardis were given a house at 1101 Bartlett Loop on the academy post, a cul-de-sac known informally as Coaches Loop. Most of the staff lived there, including the effervescent Red Reeder, who had a son about the same age as the Lombardi boy and three daughters with whom young Vincent was infatuated.

West Point was so different from Englewood, exotic and contradictory, rules about everything and yet wild and free, with a foreboding sense of danger and mortality. World War II was four years distant by the time the Lombardis arrived, but lingered in the culture. Most of the officers, like Red Reeder, had fought the Nazis in Europe. Their wives had been transformed by enduring four years on the post alone; they were accustomed to running the house without men. The kids tended to be independent, if not forgotten. "We probably fought a bit more than other kids," recalled Russell Reeder III, who was nine years old when young Vincent moved in down the street, and became his first West Point pal. "We probably had less support from our parents. It was an awkward place but a wonderful place at the same time."

Most wondrous was the sense of freedom. "Maybe it was the times, or maybe the community, but you could go anywhere and do anything," remembered Russell's sister Julia. Hide-and-seek up at Fort Put. Sardines in the Cadet Chapel. Swimming in the academy pool. Tennis courts. Young Vincent rode his bike everywhere, and always found something to watch. Cadets marching across the Plain, the football team practicing on the nearby field, a baseball game, Colonel Reeder, the assistant coach, hitting fungoes on a prosthetic leg, hurdlers scraping by at a track meet. Once young Vincent walked into the officer's club and ordered a hamburger and milk shake and put it on the Old Man's tab. This life, he thought, was "an ideal deal." Until his father examined the monthly bill, that is, and quickly put a stop to the freeloading. ("Geez," Vincent said decades later, remembering the scene, "he'd liked to have taken my head off.")

By the time young Vincent entered third grade, some of the roughness of the place had rubbed off on him. Wanting to be considered "one of the guys," he became a goof-off in school, and one day was ordered from his seat in the back of class to sit in confinement in the well under the teacher's desk. At recess, he made his escape and walked off the school property unnoticed. His teacher reported him missing when the class returned inside. School officials called Marie at home and Vince at the gymnasium. The post was mobilized to find Coach Lombardi's son. Had he been kidnapped? Students who could recognize him were taken out of class to help MPs comb the grounds. For hours, as the frantic search continued into surrounding woods, young Vincent sat hidden from view in the back of an abandoned building near their house on the loop, unaware of the commotion, taking in the sun, chewing on a stalk of grass. Near the end of the day, he got to his feet and walked over to his house and calmly said hello to his little sister and frantic mother. It was never easy being the namesake son of Vince Lombardi. That childhood moment of rebellion came to symbolize young Vincent's lifelong dilemma, trying to find his own quiet place in the sun.

To say that Lombardi was a strict father at West Point would be accurate and misleading. He had no qualms about hitting his son as punishment for apparent wrongdoing, the backhand thwacks of his mother, Matty, imprinted on his brain as an effective means of discipline. But mostly Lombardi was missing; he was largely an absentee father and husband, when not physically, then emotionally. At work from eight in the morning until late into the night. Away on road trips with the team, or recruiting prospective cadets in Pennsylvania, Ohio and Wisconsin (he found himself trapped in the snowdrifts of Green Bay on a recruiting mission with Doug Kenna and muttered, "Can you imagine living in this godforsaken place?"). When he did spend an evening at home, it often seemed to his family that he was not there, especially during spring drills, fall practice and the regular season—half of every year. The dining room was his extra office, strewn with papers, thick with smoke, two ashtrays crammed with cigarette butts before the night was out, three packs a day, four cartons a week, as he diagrammed plays and planned what he would tell his troops the next day.

Ten years into their marriage, even after all those years at Saints and Fordham, Marie was still uncertain about her place in Vince's football life. She desperately sought more of his time and attention, and alternately loved and hated the game that possessed him, now embracing it as the most effective means of reaching Vince, now rejecting it roundly as the temptress that lured her husband away from her. She often strolled down to the practice field to watch Vince lead the Cadets through drills. The practices were open to the public, and many wives and professors came out to see them. Blaik, by nature a secretive man, never liked the tradition and largely ignored the well-wishers. Lombardi was more gregarious, though not with Marie. Once she returned from a trip to Manhattan with Doug Kenna's wife wearing a tight new knit suit, and was delighted with her thin and striking appearance until Vin looked over at her and ruined her mood, shouting loud enough for heads to turn, "God, Marie, you look like a sausage!" If Marie was embarrassed, she did not take this abuse meekly. "She just leveled him, I mean totally leveled him" with words, said Doug Kenna, who had been standing next to Vince on the field.

Marie yearned for social standing. She wanted to be accepted by the elite and appreciated that West Point was a notch up the social ladder from Englewood. With other football wives, she made periodic trips to Manhattan, where they shopped on Fifth Avenue and dined at Leone's on West Forty-eighth Street, the boisterous Italian restaurant run by Gene Leone, who was Army Fan No. 2, if MacArthur was No. 1. Leone, whose son-in-law was a popular major at West Point, had been made an honorary member of the class of 1915, Eisenhower's class. He bought a nearby estate, catered at least one gourmet meal a year to the gang at Bull Pond, and made his restaurant the New York headquarters for all West Point officers and football coaches. Their wives were golden at Leone's: free parking in the lot, best tables and service. Marie enjoyed the special attention, but just as in Englewood, her Manhattan interludes could not fill the void. Nor could her children. She spent more time with young Vincent and Susan than Vince did, but she was not a doting mother. Rearing children was largely a distraction to her; she wanted to be with Vince and adults. It was the talk of the post once when little Susie wandered off unnoticed by her mother until a minister called and said he had found the toddler, stark naked and crying inside his church.

Marie's drinking worsened at West Point. She attended several Alcoholics Anonymous meetings and sought other counseling to help her deal with the frustrations of married life. "A lot of Army wives used to drink too much; they'd have these coffee klatsches or liquor klatsches in the early afternoons," said Vince's middle brother, Harold, who had long been Marie's confidant. "A lot of Marie's drinking came because she idolized Vin and he was off with his own little group." Marie spent many hours over at the Reeder house unloading her problems on Reeder's wife, Dort. Daughter Julia Reeder would eavesdrop. One day she heard Marie say, "Dort, I figured it out. He really *is* easy to live with—as long as he is not thinking about football." Which meant not often enough. When Vince was in a loving mood, sometimes his timing was off. Once at a tea for Army Athletic Association wives, Marie confessed that her husband was always in a rush. "Last week he came home from the football office at 11 a.m. when I was baking a cake. He wanted to make love to me and got flour all over the both of us."

For the most part, the outside world knew little of this. Vince and Marie were considered a fun-loving couple. In social settings, Lombardi was almost universally regarded as warm and jovial. Margaret Cohane, Tim's wife, considered him "very much a man's man" who paid little attention to the women in a room, but even she was taken by his enthusiasm, especially "that wonderful laugh that would start way down low and then expand." Vince was the godfather of the Cohanes' third child, Mary Therese. He seemed especially friendly with children other than his own. During the summer months families in the athletic department got together for ice cream socials, with five-cent movies and badminton tournaments, and Uncle Vince was always right there playing with the kids. Of course he could not just hit the shuttlecock back and forth. "If he was going to play, it had to be competition, a real game," said Russell Reeder, but his good-natured participation was appreciated nonetheless. When Doug Kenna's wife came to football practice with their six-month-old daughter, Vince "made a beeline to her and started dancing around the practice field singing 'Toot toot tootsie, goodbye, Toot toot tootsie, don't cry.'" The Kenna girl was known by her family as Tootsie for the rest of her life.

Lombardi certainly had strong feelings for family. Harry and Matty drove up from Englewood every few weeks, Old Five by Five hauling a few thick, delicious filets from the meat market, and various Izzo cousins were also frequent guests. Jim Lawlor, his roommate from Fordham, and several Englewood friends often dropped in. One of young Vincent's strongest memories of West Point was of his father and Tim Cohane sitting on the couch in the living room late at night, "talking and talking and talking. Tim did most of the talking. He was probably the forerunner of Howard Cosell— one of those guys who always had an opinion and it sounded better by virtue of the way he delivered it" with his deep, authoritative, melodious voice. Vincent and Susan were sometimes puzzled by how talkative their father could be with other people, how cuddly he was with other kids, in contrast to the way he acted at home. He was not the same person with them that he was with his players and friends. There were times when the wife and kids wondered whether they were at fault, somehow not living up to the concept of family that Vince carried with him from his childhood in Sheepshead Bay.

THE FIFTIES—nothing placid about the way the new decade began at West Point. By the end of June 1950, America was at war again, and many of the cadets who had played on the fields of friendly strife were now on muddy fields in Korea, led by General MacArthur, Supreme Commander Allied Powers, commander of United Nations military forces, fighting the North Koreans and Communist Chinese. At the academy, casualty lists were posted weekly, many of the names all too familiar to the cadets. As the football season opened in September, word arrived of the combat death of Tom Lombardo, captain of the 1944 national championship team. The players were distracted by events in Korea from then on. As part of his hazing duties as a plebe that year, Lowell Sisson, a tenderfoot end from Waterloo, Iowa, had to report to an upperclassman's room every day before meal formation, where he stood "in stiff brace" at the doorway and summarized all the dispatches from Korea in that morning's *New York Times.* "All the seniors knew they might be over there in a few months," Sisson recalled. "It was a very tense time for them."

Even in that anxious state of mind the football team began the season performing better than it had the year before. Lombardi, whom Blaik had entrusted with the Cadet offense, devoted himself to the development of the coach's son Bob Blaik, Galiffa's replacement at quarterback, and the effort paid off. Bob became the leader of a team that routed Michigan again and shut out five teams as it rolled through the first seven games undefeated. For the eighth game, Army took its first road trip by air out to California to play Stanford. It had rained unceasingly in northern California and the game was played in a blinding downpour, the field all mud and muck. Bob Blaik passed for the lone touchdown. That night, after the 7 to 0 Army victory, the old man and Lombardi and the rest of the staff partied in Blaik's suite at the St. Francis Hotel in San Francisco. Tim Cohane was there along with the aging Granny Rice and a coterie of eastern writers. They told stories and recited corny epic poems late into the night, Blaik and his men exhilarated by what was now a twenty-eight-game unbeaten streak.

The overconfident Cadets had two weeks to prepare for the game against Navy, the traditional season-ending rivalry. Scouting reports on the Midshipmen had been coming in all year, and they were invariably encouraging. Navy was becalmed, going nowhere in a miserable losing season. All prognostications were of an imminent rout. Blaik was nervous, as always, against Navy; the game could ruin an otherwise glorious season. "There was tension among the coaches," Lombardi said later, but "Blaik hid the tension from the players." He was nervous, fearing that his players were losing their "feel of the game" because heavy rains had forced them to practice indoors. Then, a few days before the game, during what was called Navy Week, when corps enthusiasm usually reached a feverish pitch, a report came in that Johnny Trent was dead, killed in action earlier that month in Korea. Trent had been the captain of the 1949 team, an ebullient end from Memphis who had begun the year as a graduate assistant working with the plebe squad before he and classmate Arnold Galiffa, the quarterback, were sent across the Pacific with the Eighth Army. The "ever increasing sad news from Korea, which has been brought closer to the cadets than to any group in the land," Blaik said, had "relegated thoughts of the Navy game to second place."

Perhaps they were excuses. The Navy team, which had received brilliant scouting reports on Army and played flawlessly, might have won anyway that day, and win they did, 14 to 2. There was a touch of poetic justice to the upset. Army was beaten at its own strong-arm game. "The Navy beat us and beat is the proper word, as our men took a physical beating which completely bewildered them," Blaik wrote later in a long letter to MacArthur. "[Gilbert] Reich, our only safety, went out the first five minutes of play and did not clear mentally until late Saturday night. Ordinarily we use three or four ammonia inhalers during a game, but against Navy our trainers used four dozen boxes. With Reich out, the only long pass for a score which had been made against the cadets in several years was completed. It was the play that gave Navy a surge which could not be denied."

It is doubtful that Blaik's lament moved MacArthur much in this instance, for at the same time that Army was losing to Navy, MacArthur's United Nations forces were at the Yalu River in Korea suffering a loss of incomparably greater dimensions. MacArthur, convinced that the Red Chinese would not enter the war, or if they did that it would be without much firepower, had pushed his troops to the Korea-China border. He ended up leading his men into a trap, and three thousand soldiers from the Second Infantry Division were killed or wounded as they retreated south through a gauntlet of Red Chinese guns firing down into a valley clogged with abandoned vehicles and the bloody detritus of war. Hardly in the same realm as Blaik's four dozen boxes of ammonia inhalers in the Navy game. If there was a comparison to be made, it was that both the coach and his favorite general were victims of their own success.

On the special academy train returning to West Point from the Army-Navy game in Philadelphia, Blaik entered a compartment shared by his assistants, Lombardi, Warmath and Kenna. He appeared utterly disconsolate. "I want to talk to you," he said in a deep, low voice. To Lombardi and Warmath's relief, he was looking at Kenna. Kenna knew that he was in trouble. He was in charge of the defensive backs, and they had been beaten on some key plays. "I thought he was going to chew me out, but he really didn't. He explained it was my fault, but that was that. He was in agony and wanted to talk to somebody. I sat and listened to him all the way back to West Point," Kenna said later. "I don't think Blaik ever lost a game that hurt that much." In his letter to MacArthur explaining the loss, Blaik acknowledged the depth of his despair. "There are many who had said that it is well that a friendly series such as ours should be more even, but I confess that there is no philosophy in me that accepts such a theory," he wrote. "We got the heck kicked out of us, and there is much to be done at West Point before we can get into the win column."

More, much more, than Blaik then realized.

7

Blaik's Boys

AN UNRAVELING had begun. The loss to Navy lingered at West Point for months, largely because of Blaik, who remained inconsolable. He could not forget what had happened that bleak afternoon in Philadelphia, nor would he allow himself to try. He might as well have installed a Navy blue neon sign on his furrowed forehead flashing night and day: 14 to 2! 14 to 2! He compulsively rehashed the loss and replayed the game films looking for explanations. He had "viewed the pictures and studied the individual performances of each man until the game is close to a nightmare," he confessed in a letter to General Dwight D. Eisenhower, the West Point alumnus who by then had become the president of Columbia University. Blaik's assistants had seen the game so many times that they had memorized the precise sequence from kickoff to final gun, every mistake, every moment when Blaik predictably stopped the film to draw an agonizing lesson one more time. It became ritualized, a morality play performed daily in the darkness of the projection room. The staff sat in the same seats and repeated yesterday's dialogue. Once Murray Warmath blurted something out of turn and was chided by Lombardi: "Hey, you stole my line!"

Navy was not supposed to win the game, they had not beaten Blaik's boys since 1943, but somehow every time the film ran to completion the final score came out the same. Anything was possible now. The Blaikian world of balance, order and certitude seemed shaken and vulnerable to collapse. In football, there is a natural tendency to develop an us-versus-them complex, but now "them" was not just Navy. Blaik believed there were forces inside West Point, especially officers in the tactical department, seeking to undermine his program and rid the academy of his best players. He noticed a warning sign before 1951 spring drills began in March when Warmath accompanied several players to Manhattan for dinner at Leone's. During the meal a West Point officer approached their table and berated the athletes, saying their social skills were embarrassingly deficient. As Warmath described the confrontation to Blaik, the coach mused aloud that the message was meant not for his free-spirited boys so much as for him.

He already seemed besieged when he received word the following month of a casualty on the political battleground. On April 11 his hero MacArthur was summarily fired from Supreme Command in the Far East by President Truman. The move was predictable, yet shocking to the general's acolytes; for months MacArthur had defiantly challenged military and foreign policy directives from the Pentagon and White House, pushing his troops beyond the defined limits in Korea and declaring that the United States had been too cautious in its dealings with China. Blaik was among his most ardent supporters. Hours after the dismissal, he cabled MacArthur at Tokyo headquarters: "AMERICAN PUBLIC IS STUNNED. TIME IS OF THE ESSENCE TO OFFSET ADMINISTRATION HATCHETMEN. MY AFFECTION AND DEVOTION TO YOU." In the weeks that followed, when he was not sitting in the darkness of the tower witnessing grainy footage of the Navy fiasco, Blaik busied himself with the task of ensuring that his favorite old soldier did not fade away. He believed that the best solution was for MacArthur to become the Republican candidate for president in 1952. Employing the metaphors of his sports universe, he wrote MacArthur that "the best hope for the future lies in fielding a new team in Washington." American military policy in Asia, he said, was "comparable to a football team with a strong ground game and air game always punting on first down and through fear presenting the initiative to the opponent."

Not long after MacArthur's forced return, Blaik visited him at his suite-in-exile atop the Waldorf-Astoria Towers in midtown Manhattan. At that meeting Blaik argued that the general, then seventy-one, was not too old to run for president ("The years have touched you so lightly," he wrote in a follow-up letter), and belittled the potential candidacy of MacArthur's longtime military competitor, General Eisenhower. As solicitous as the ever-political Blaik was in his separate running correspondence with Eisenhower, his private opinions of Ike were cutting. "I like Ike. We all like Ike—but not as president!" he wrote to one political associate that year. He called Eisenhower "the world's foremost compromiser," which in the political lexicon he had adopted from MacArthur was intended as a wounding insult. Lombardi watched Blaik's maneuvers with only moderate interest. He was intrigued by Blaik's readiness to transfer his philosophy to the political realm, awed by the strength of MacArthur's rhetoric, but less impressed with the specific politics. Since his days among the Jesuits on Rose Hill, Lombardi had been a

Democrat, and he shared with fellow Fordham grad Tim Cohane, also a Democrat, an ability to draw lifelong lessons from Blaik's philosophy and style without becoming submissive to his beliefs, to revere St. Blaik without following him blindly.

The spring of 1951 was a difficult time to follow him at all. Given Blaik's state of mind, agitated by the Navy loss and MacArthur's undoing, it was providential that Lombardi could escape West Point for a while. The opportunity came late in April, when he and five other members of the Army athletic staff were dispatched to the Orient to conduct football clinics. It began as a merry junket. The coaches lounged in luxury suites at the Mark Hopkins Hotel in San Francisco before boarding an old military transport plane that took them across the Pacific to Tokyo. The trip had been arranged before MacArthur's recall, during the days when he was trying to instill in the Japanese the traditions of American culture and democracy. The introduction of football, MacArthur thought, might ease the process. Lombardi and his colleagues were not burdened with the mission of selling democracy. Their goal was to teach football and enjoy the sights. Kenna, who had made several recruiting forays with Lombardi in the States, was not surprised to discover that Vince had connections in Tokyo. It seemed that wherever they traveled there was an old Fordham man—usually an FBI agent; Fordham was a dependable supplier of federal gumshoes—who knew the best places in town. Here it was even better: Vince found a Fordham man in charge of the officer's clubs in Tokyo. "Vin and I toured quite a few nightspots that the other guys didn't get to," Kenna said later. "We had a good time. This guy took us everywhere."

The football instruction was tedious. The Japanese had not played American football and were learning the game from scratch. They were earnest if bewildered and undersized students, and Lombardi, as ever, was an aggressive teacher. For the most part the instruction was mental rather than physical, which meant that he generally refrained from his hands-on methods of teaching blocking and tackling—and avoided injuring a student or himself. After three weeks in Tokyo, the Army coaches received a surprise telephone call from Arnold Galiffa, the quarterback for the undefeated 1949 team, now a decorated aide to General Matthew Ridgway, who had taken over the Supreme Command from MacArthur. Galiffa passed along word that "the Old Man"—in this case Ridgway; all brass in the military culture were the Old Man—wanted them to go to Korea and entertain the troops "like a USO tour."

Blaik would never allow it, Kenna responded. The colonel was uncomfortable having his assistants away this long. Certainly they had more Navy film to examine back at the gym. No problem, Galiffa said. It was already arranged. Ridgway sent a plane to retrieve them in Tokyo and take them to the war zone. Lombardi was dressed in military guise. Army fatigues, at least.

No stripes. Green cap askew, though not on backward the way the devilish Warmath wore it to irritate fussbudget lieutenants. Their first experience in Korea was unnerving; at the landing strip near Seoul, an American jet fighter-bomber came in right before them with its bombs jammed and about to explode.

At military posts in Korea they showed game films to the fighting men and told stories about the Army football team, the heroic backfield of Davis and Blanchard, how the Cadets seemed loaded again at the recently completed spring drills, oozing with so much talent, said Lombardi, that "no one in the country could touch us." From the troops they heard accounts of war and countless tales about MacArthur. They kept the negative comments to themselves and remembered the positive for retelling to Blaik back at West Point. Blaik treasured few things more than chances to praise and flatter his patron. (Indeed, in his first letter to MacArthur after debriefing his assistants, Blaik wrote: "This is the part that will interest you a great deal. They spoke with hundreds of soldiers, officers, as well as many civilians in Tokyo and Korea, and from all these sources without exception came words of respect and veneration for General MacArthur. Our coaches were amazed that it was so universal.")

What amazed them more was their nearness to real, rather than symbolic, warfare. One day the coaches were escorted by Army guides to advanced positions held by the First Marine Division under the command of Colonel Wilburt S. "Bigfoot" Brown. Here the distinction between football and war became patently obvious, and made any equating of the two seem preposterous. Colonel Blaik might draft battle plans in the secrecy of a tower, but he did not need the protective cover of sandbags piled ten feet thick like Colonel Brown's command bunker. Troops on the right and left had given way to enemy thrusts; Bigfoot (shoe size 14E) and his Marines were holding the precarious line when the coaches arrived. They were invited to his command bunker for lunch. With lanterns illuminating the scene, the guests sat on canvas cots as a captain prepared meals over a Coleman stove. Beans and franks. What the hell are we doing here? Warmath thought to himself. Just as the meal was to be served, an enemy bomb exploded nearby. Powerful concussion. Lanterns knocked out. Mess kits flying, food tossed. In the chaos of the moment, a shaken Lombardi reached up and felt "an awful mess" on his scalp. "God!" he shouted. "My brains are coming out!" He "really thought he had been hit," recalled Kenna, who had been standing a few feet away. Until, that is, he was informed that the hot mush simmering atop his head was not brain matter but an airborne serving of baked beans. Lombardi's military sojourn had its comic aspect, but it was also truly frightening; he was a civilian facing enemy fire, an experience thousands of servicemen never encountered.

After their Korean adventure the coaches split up for more football clinics. Lombardi was sent to the Philippines with Paul Amen. Kenna and Warmath went to Okinawa. It was July by then and they had been away two months. Bull Pond would be coming soon and then fall practice. By the time Lombardi reunited with the others in Tokyo, he seemed eager to return to West Point and begin work with his talented corps. Messages awaited in Tokyo; one from Colonel Blaik, urgent. Kenna called the Old Man, and when he hung up, he reported that Blaik was "absolutely sick" and wanted the staff to "get on back" as quickly as possible. Something about football players and violations of the academic honor code. Details would come soon enough, but one thing was obvious to the coaches as they scrambled back to West Point: this might be worse than any loss to Navy.

THIS WAS 1951, the beginning of what was later perceived through the lens of nostalgia as a decade of simplicity. This was West Point, garrison of traditional American values: duty, honor, country. And this was Coach Blaik, the Old Man, demanding and austere. It would be easy for someone nearly fifty years later, discouraged by the corrupted state of sports in America at the end of the twentieth century, and unmindful of the cycles of history, to take a fleeting look at that combination and make a backward leap of faith: now *there* was a time and place where sport was honest and clean, by the rules, when pride still mattered. But history has a way of mocking attempts to render it retroactively pure. That very trinity—1951, West Point, Red Blaik—could also be remembered for one troubling event: a massive academic honor code violation that resulted in, among other things, the devastation of Blaik's audacious football squad. Lombardi's role was peripheral. He was there and not there, he lived through the scandal, he survived it unscathed; his name does not appear in a single document related to it and he rarely spoke of it later in his career, as though he had repressed it. But the events of that episode are not immaterial to his larger story; they are central to understanding the mythology of Lombardi, the contradictory demands and expectations of football, and the fallacy of the innocent past.

THE TROUBLE for Blaik's boys began even before Lombardi and the other assistants left for the Far East, blissfully unaware. It was on the morning of April 2 that an honor representative for the first class, or seniors, visited the office of Colonel Paul D. Harkins and reported that some cadets had formed a ring to pass along unauthorized academic information—meaning questions and answers—for daily quizzes and midterm reviews. The cadet told Harkins that his knowledge of the scheme came originally from a third classman and member of the swim team whose own familiarity with the ring was more direct: he had been invited to join it. The swimmer believed the ring was operated by football players. After declining the offer to join the conspiracy, he became concerned about reporting fellow cadets, but also realized that failure to do so would be a violation of the honor code. *A cadet does not lie, cheat, or steal. A cadet who knows about someone who has lied, cheated, or stolen must report him for violating the code.* That was the honor code, as old as West Point and enforced by the cadets themselves. It was revered as the foundation of the academy's integrity, drilled into every plebe from the first week of orientation at Beast Barracks.

Colonel Harkins wrote a memorandum for the record detailing what he had been told about the ring and noting that he was "indeed shocked to hear of such a thing." As commandant of cadets and head of West Point's tactical department, Harkins was responsible for transforming college students into soldiers. His background for the job was unquestioned. He had been trained at the side of General George S. Patton, for whom he had served as deputy chief of staff with the Third Army during World War II, earning a nickname—the Ramrod—that reflected his determination to carry out Patton's wishes. In style and substance he was more Patton's opposite, unemotional and all by the book. What he excelled at was framing rules and following them. His feelings about Blaik and football were decidedly negative. It was Harkins who had confronted Warmath during dinner at Leone's, offended by the behavior of young officers-to-be. He considered the football department a discredit to the academy; it was favored with special privileges, flouted the rules of the corps, was stocked with athletes who belonged neither in college nor the Army, and was led by a coach whose power outstripped his position and whose rank exceeded his merit. Harkins was among the nonbelievers when it came to St. Blaik. The word among these heretics was that Blaik was at West Point when he could have been fighting in World War I, and became a colonel as a matter of show; after being recruited from Dartmouth to build the football program, he was recommissioned as an officer and during the war insisted on status equal to Navy's coach.

It was with that frame of reference that Harkins received the tip that Blaik's football squad might be involved in an academic scandal, and he responded with zeal. He quickly called a meeting of his immediate staff. "We had no tangible evidence and knew we would have to get some before we could prove anything," he wrote later in a confidential memorandum. "We discussed means and methods, we thought of everything from recording systems and hidden 'mikes' to having someone join the ring." They decided to "fight fire with fire" by asking the swimmer and two other trusted cadets to infiltrate the ring. The swimmer agonized about becoming a "stool pigeon." The request, he said later, seemed "unfair, unnecessary and undignified.... However, is the West Point Yearling privileged to doubt the judgment of the Commandant of Cadets?" He contacted an uncle, a corporate lawyer in New York, who drove to West Point that weekend to counsel him. They strolled up the path to Michie Stadium and stood by the low wall surrounding Lusk Reservoir as the cadet calmly outlined his dilemma. He said he felt trapped and wanted to quit West Point. His uncle urged him not to leave under fire since he had done nothing wrong: "Do as the colonel says." The tormented cadet agreed to go along with Harkins's plan.

By early May, the swim team cadet and other informants had gathered solid evidence on a handful of classmates and believed that as many as fifty to a hundred cadets were involved, most of them connected to the football team. Unauthorized information about tests, they told Harkins, was being "passed freely" at the football tables in the dining hall. They also said the ringleaders appeared to have rigged the system by strategically placing a few tainted cadets on the twenty-five-member committee that enforced the honor code. Professors of Spanish, math, mechanics and physics presented Harkins with evidence that test questions in their classes appeared to be known in advance. As the month wore on, rumors spread that a scandal was about to explode. Members of the ring became suspicious of the infiltrators and ostracized them. Harkins decided it was time to act: he went to Major General Frederick A. Irving, the academy's new superintendent, and received approval to launch an official investigation. Three officers were appointed to a board of inquiry, led by Harkins's ally in the tactical department, Lieutenant Colonel Arthur S. Collins Jr., who shared his distaste for Blaik and big-time Army football.

The board targeted fourteen cadets suspected of involvement in the ring and brought them in to testify under oath, one by one, starting at seven o'clock on the morning of May 29. The first witness was a third classman, who confessed immediately. "I first heard about this ring during Fourth Class [his freshman or plebe year, in 1949]," he began. He went on to say that the ring "was started by football players for football players," and that rings operated in both the First and Second Regiments. The way the process worked, he testified, was that ring members who took a writ (daily quiz) in an early period would pass along the questions to cadets who were to take the same writ later in the day. If there was time, the answers were then worked out by smarter members of the ring and slipped to cadets who were struggling academically. "Everyone has been scared to death, because they have had an idea it is going to break," the cadet said in concluding his testimony.

This first witness turned out to be the most forthcoming of the fourteen. The second said he knew nothing about a cribbing ring. The third said he would not say anything until he talked to Coach Blaik. "I'll tell you anything about myself but if it is football players you're asking about I won't squeal," he added. "There are people around here who don't like football players . . . my tactical officer is one of them." The remaining first-day witnesses insisted that they knew nothing of a ring.

The next afternoon, as Blaik strode across the Plain to attend a baseball game (his son Bob played second base), he encountered a football player who nonchalantly mentioned an honor code investigation. To Blaik it sounded minor, perhaps involving one cadet. He learned otherwise that night in an urgent phone call from another player saying that several sophomores needed to see him immediately. At 9:15 he was up in the projection room of the gymnasium tower, listening to twelve of his players tell him about the ring and their appearances before the board of inquiry. They said they were confused and would do whatever Blaik advised. By all accounts, he directed them to return to the board and tell the whole truth. "You know how we do business in the squad and at the military academy," he said. "Each one of you should state the facts to the board without equivocation." When the players left, Blaik remained in the film room, alone in the dark. Lombardi and his other assistants were on the other side of the world. His mentor MacArthur was off giving rousing political speeches. "No foreboding could have been greater than my own," Blaik later wrote of the dismay that overwhelmed him at that moment. "I had been in many a tough game, but this was not a game. It was a catastrophe."

When he left the gymnasium that night, Blaik walked next door to Superintendent Irving's house. All lights were out, but Blaik could not wait until morning; he flung pebbles at a darkened bedroom window, roused Irving from bed and sat in the "Supe's" living room recounting his meeting with the players. He pleaded with Irving to take the investigation away from the tactical department, arguing that the situation was "too important" for young officers to decide. Left unsaid was his concern that the board appointed by Harkins, an antagonist, was unlikely to give Blaik's boys a sympathetic hearing. He called Harkins a "black-and-white man with no shades of gray," and there was plenty of gray in this situation, Blaik maintained. He considered the honor system flawed because of its reliance on squealing, and he thought the academic system even worse, set up almost to ensure that the honor system would fail. Why give the exact same writs to different classes one day to the next?

Irving was consoling but noncommittal.

The next morning brought more bad news to the coach. Bob Blaik, his son and starting quarterback, confided that he was among those who had violated the honor code; he was a fine student who said he knew about the cribbing but did not report it. "My God!" said father to son. "How could you? How could you?" That same day the football players who had met with Blaik in the projection room notified Lieutenant Colonel Collins that they wished to reappear before his board of inquiry. This time they told the truth. They were followed by more cadets, football players and others, who also confessed. Suddenly the board had more information than it could process. The answers to Blaik's lament came gushing out. *How could they?* Their answers, as transcribed by a court stenographer and compiled in the confidential report of the board's proceedings, reveal the full range of human impulses, good and bad. They could violate the honor code out of fear, peer pressure, custom, laziness, academic inadequacy, loyalty, friendship, teamwork.

CADET 1: I did it to stay in the Academy; I could not have passed without it. . . . I knew this was a violation of the Honor System, but when I knew all these other people had done it and when I wanted to stay here so much it was either get help or go home.

CADET 2: At first I tried to be honest but after doing it a few times I just let things slide although I was aware of the Honor System and its requirements, my loyalty to my teammates seemed bigger. I was given the impression that the practice was passed on from upper classmen. . . . The football players tried to keep it among themselves. Someone said that there was one man on the Honor Committee who would warn us in time. Last night a number of us had a meeting with Coach Blaik. He was shocked. He told us to tell the truth and that is why I am back here.

CADET 3: I know it was wrong, but, after all, people cheat in civilian colleges so we thought it was okay to do it in West Point.

CADET 4: I became aware of it Plebe year during spring football. I noticed people talking about academic subjects at the table in the dining hall but I didn't know what to do about it. I knew it was against honor, but these men were my idols. When I arrived at West Point they told us to pick out a First Classman and be like him. I [picked one] and when I found out [he] was cheating it really shocked me; I had thought he stood for everything good.

CADET 5: I know everything; I saw everything. What I told you on the 29th was wrong. Coach Blaik told me to tell the truth and I will do whatever he tells me to. During the summer of 1949, soon after I entered West Point, I was approached by [a veteran football player] who told me how to do it: "You look like a dumb football player, kid—if you have any trouble in academics remember that the people in other regiments have instruction before you do. Get the poop. Then you'll get by." He was the greatest guy in the world to me. I would have done anything he told me to. . . . I know many cadets who couldn't do any problems. When they made good grades on writs I figured that the instructors knew about it and just let football players get away with it. . . . I couldn't turn all these people in. They were my best friends and when you play ball together you just get very close. Besides, when you see all those upperclassmen who you worship doing it you don't think it is so bad.

During the following week, the investigators expanded the probe, calling in cadets from all four classes. The seniors had just returned by train from a training mission at Aberdeen, Maryland, and were to graduate within a week. Although earlier witnesses had implicated members of this first class of 1951, to a man they denied knowledge of the ring. The investigative panel concluded that "a number of the members of this class are believed to have testified falsely but it cannot be established." They were all allowed to graduate June 5. The juniors from Bob Blaik's class of 1952 were not so lucky. The board called in dozens of members of that class, football players and others, and the portrait of a conspiracy grew wider and darker. Coach Blaik and his assistant coaches were never implicated directly, but witnesses spoke of players freely "passing the poop" in the projection room near Blaik's tower and in the locker room. The protective aura surrounding Blaik's program, some cadets said, made it easier for the scandal to develop.

> CADET A: "Passing the Poop" was a big thing. . . . Everyone in the Corps knows who Blaik's Boys are and anyone who tampers with them is in trouble. This is the impression one gets from the first day of Beast Barracks. You even hear remarks like that in the hotel before entrance. It is said that Colonel Blaik is so influential that no one had better cross him.

> CADET B: Any man on the football, basketball or baseball corps squad who tells you he didn't know unauthorized information was being passed is either lying or is too dumb to be in West Point. There were so many people in on it that it seemed almost to have official sanction. . . . I heard when I first got here that Blaik's Boys get by.

> CADET C: Colonel Blaik has always told the football team that they were the rock on which the Corps was built. This and other similar things had a tendency to set the football team apart from the Corps. . . . I believe the football team is the nucleus of this group.

THE THREE-OFFICER panel concluded its hearings the second week of June and filed a confidential report with Colonel Harkins just as the commandant of cadets was preparing to leave West Point for a new assignment at the Pentagon. The cheating conspiracy, according to the panel's findings, began as far back as 1947, was "centered in and perpetuated by members of the Football Corps Squad until the fall of 1950, at which time cheating began to spread," and eventually would have "destroyed the Honor System at West Point" had it continued. The findings listed ninety cadets who had been implicated in the ring for cheating, having knowledge of cheating or lying in sworn testimony, and suggested that they be "offered an opportunity to resign and be discharged"—immediately expelled, in other words. Among the ninety were all but two members of the varsity football squad.

Before sending the report to the superintendent and departing for Washington, Harkins added his own recommendations. "Separation from the academy," Harkins emphasized, was the "one and only" solution for the guilty cadets. He ended his comments with a final shot at Blaik and his boys. "I am sorry that the exposition of this group had to be my parting act as Commandant. However, having discovered it, proved it to be a fact, my duty to the honest cadets, to the Academy and to the country was to expose it, expel it and let the chips fall where they may. I think when the air clears, the whole thing will have a very salutary effect on West Point and the country. It will bring some of the athletic teams back closer to the Corps of Cadets. It will prove to all of us that, though we want to have winning teams and play to win, the teams must be made up of cadets who are members of the Corps and respect and live by the ideals and spirit of West Point. There can be no other way. In the final analysis, the honor system and the Academy will be the gainers and West Point will continue to live by high ideals and carry its banner with DUTY, HONOR, COUNTRY emblazoned on its crest at the head of the long gray line."

The confidential report moved up the military chain of command from Harkins to Superintendent Irving, who shared it with West Point's academic board and then sent it along to the Pentagon with his own conclusion on July 2 supporting the board's actions. The recommendation of expulsion would stick unless it was countermanded by higher-ups, and Blaik worked passionately to try to soften the penalties, urging what he called an "intramural" solution in which erring cadets would be disciplined privately within the academy. He tried to recruit MacArthur to help him in this effort, but the general was preoccupied with giving political speeches and unavailable to meet with him. Blaik was able to make several trips to Washington and meet informally with Army brass to repeat his case: He told his boys to tell the truth, which they had done, so why expel them when other cadets, who had blatantly lied, denying any knowledge of the academic cheating, were allowed to remain? The Army would have had difficulty getting enough evidence against most of these boys unless they had confessed. And the honor system was fatally flawed in any case, Blaik insisted, designed not to instill integrity, but to entice cadets to cheat and squeal.

During the third week of July, Lombardi, Warmath and Kenna returned from Japan. As Blaik began to outline the dimensions of the problem to them, he seemed beside himself, they said later, tormented in a way that they had never seen before. West Point was a starkly different place from when they had left. The granite fortress, symbol of right and might, now seemed cold and unforgiving, like the walls of a penitentiary. The incriminated cadets, many of whom had left for summer duties, were called back and confined to barracks, virtually under house arrest. Reporters had sniffed the faint scent of scandal and had begun visiting the academy looking for leaks. At the end of that week, Blaik appeared before what amounted to a final review board, a high-level panel consisting of two retired generals and

Learned Hand, the distinguished federal appeals court judge who had retired that May from regular bench duty in New York City. The Hand board stayed at West Point for two days, reviewed earlier findings, interviewed cadets and heard out Blaik. The coach left his session encouraged by a statement from one of the retired generals that his account was the first one to make sense. Finally, Blaik thought, his arguments hit home.

Some of them did, it seemed. In his report, Hand questioned the West Point custom of using the same written examinations in classes throughout one day and into the next, allowing cadets to pass along information. "This was the means by which all the cheating was done which has so far appeared. It offers a perpetual inducement, indeed a tempting bait, to those whose resistance is weak," Hand wrote. "And, although it is considered to be a part of the Honor System, it seems to us unnecessary and undesirable to so try the virtue of all, when that can ... be easily removed." The Hand report also sympathized with the inequity facing the cadets who happened to get caught. "Evidence indicates conclusively that nearly every cadet in this large group of honor violators fell into a practice already existing in violation of the code, were shocked and dismayed when they discovered it, and that in some instances through the usually commendable quality of loyalty to close friends, they did not have the courage to take action which they knew the code demanded. Evidence further shows without question that they were led into this situation by men in classes ahead of them, most of whom are now graduates and beyond anything but very complicated punitive action."

But Blaik's brief was seriously flawed. He had been making his pleadings based on his belief in his players and what they had told him, without access to confidential documents and interviews of the investigation. He believed, as his players insisted, that many of them only had knowledge of the wrongdoing but did not participate themselves, and that perhaps hundreds of cadets outside the athletic corps were also involved. He called it cribbing, not cheating, and sought to diminish the nature of the offense by saying that the cadets were merely passing along possible quiz subjects, not the answers. Blaik and his many supporters would make these arguments then and for decades to come, whenever the bitter subject of the 1951 scandal arose. The evidence that Hand and the others analyzed showed otherwise. Almost all of the implicated cadets, at least eighty-two of them, had confessed that they had succumbed to cheating themselves, rather than only having knowledge of the cheating ring, and in their testimony they established that the transgressions went far beyond merely passing along possible quiz questions. "Passing the poop" involved getting specific answers as well, in most instances. Similarly, the notion that academic cheating was an academy-wide problem proved to be an exaggeration spread by ringleaders in an effort to diminish their own responsibility.

Judge Hand and the retired generals understood the consequences of any decision they were to render. To dismiss the cadets, Hand wrote, "in effect wipes out the entire varsity football squad. With the great national prominence of West Point's football coach, the sports pages will comment and enlarge on the enormity of the disaster for a very long time to come. Moreover it will destroy West Point's football for at least 10 or 15 years." But any punishment short of dismissal, he concluded, would destroy West Point's honor code. Given a choice between honor and football, Hand's board chose honor and affirmed the superintendent's ruling. Blaik's boys had to go.

The coach received word of this decision as he was preparing for his annual vacation at Bull Pond; the news surprised him and left him deeply dispirited. Kenna had been staying at Blaik's house that week (his pregnant wife was back in Mississippi) and remembered that for three nights in a row, with Lombardi there for much of it, Blaik stayed up until dawn obsessed with his dilemma, looking for explanations, for a way out, burning at the notion that his enemies in the academy, the anti-football battalion, could get such ammunition. The colonel "never went to bed. He was under siege. He was miserable. Just absolutely emotionally wiped out." The discussions continued at Bull Pond, where the group was smaller than usual and the atmosphere less buoyant. No fictitious All-America squads. No guffaws for Chuckles Axemurder. The coaches played cards and commiserated, hiding from the world.

How did Lombardi behave during those bleak times? He and Murray Warmath, the two civilian coaches, seemed to be the last to hear about the emerging scandal—"Somewhere along the line, other coaches heard the scoop of things before Vince and I did," Warmath said later—and they had the most difficulty framing the issues. Particularly alien to them was the honor code mentality, which required classmates to squeal on one another. What Lombardi cherished about football was its fraternity, the sense of team and loyalty, one for all and all for one. He did not condone cheating, he told the others at Bull Pond, but from his understanding of the controversy (which was limited and one-sided; he had not read the investigative findings) it mostly involved helping athletes prepare for tests. This happened every day at other colleges. Why the fuss? What was new—or wrong—with that? Lombardi had become especially close to Bob Blaik, the quarterback, and the fact that such an able young man could be expelled for an honors violation bewildered him. During his college days at Fordham, he learned how taxing it was to study and play football; the demands at West Point seemed twice as difficult. He and Warmath had recruited several players involved in the scandal, talented athletes with modest academic training, many of them from Italian and Polish working-class backgrounds, the first in their families to go to college. It was easier for Lombardi to identify with them than with the aristocracy in the officer corps.

Lombardi was at Bull Pond with Blaik and the coaches at 12:50 on the afternoon of August 3 when Western Union transmitted a news release from West Point's public information office to all New York newspapers, the wire services, major radio networks and Dumont Television. After days of final deliberations in Washington, including notification of President Truman, the Army went public: "Breach of West Point Honor Code Announced," read the press release headline. Superintendent Irving was quoted as saying that approximately ninety cadets, among them many "who have been prominent in various activities including varsity football," had violated the honor code and would be discharged. It was a "stern and uncompromising" solution, Irving acknowledged, but officials saw no alternative. Within ten minutes the phones were ringing at the public information office. By three that afternoon members of the New York press corps had arrived "in considerable numbers" at Thayer Gate. The academy spokesmen said there was nothing to add to the earlier statement. Irving was not available for comment.

Out at Bull Pond, Lombardi was screening the calls. He took one from Tim Cohane, the sportswriting pal from *Look,* who had been vacationing with his family at Little Lake Sebago in Maine when the news broke. Lombardi gave Cohane the sorry picture: Blaik was convinced that he had to resign. They all might resign. They were suffering from shell shock. Warmath was grumbling and swearing, furious at the Army brass for being so cruel to the players. Vince was angry, too, but also depressed. Two and a half years after Cohane had helped him get hired at West Point, this might be the end. The assistants were supportive of Blaik, but they could not tell him what to do. Not even Cohane could. That level of influence belonged only to MacArthur.

Early the next morning, with his wife, Merle, accompanying him, Blaik set off to see the retired general in Manhattan. As he drove south on Route 9W and approached the George Washington Bridge, a tire on his car blew out. For Blaik, this was an uncharacteristic but fitting moment of disarray. He had always been a model of precision. He hated being late: Lombardi had watched in amazement once when Blaik drove away as a tardy assistant struggled to enter the car, one foot in, one foot dangling, the door flying wide open. But now Blaik's own wheels were coming off, literally and figuratively. Fearful of keeping the general waiting, he left his wife at the roadside to deal with the broken-down car and hitchhiked into the city, arriving at the Waldorf-Astoria Towers a half hour late. MacArthur greeted him with words of sympathy—"They have set the academy back twenty years," he proclaimed ("they" being Army officials, not the erring cadets)—then ushered the shaken coach into a vast living room adorned with the ornaments of his foreign campaigns. "Now," MacArthur said, settling into his favorite chair, "tell me the whole story." Blaik did, for two hours—at least his version. When he finished, the old soldier urged his disciple not to fade away. "Earl, you must stay on. Don't leave under fire."

Blaik returned to Bull Pond with the news. Four days later, on August 9, he agreed to meet the press for the first time since the scandal broke, not at an open press conference but at a private luncheon session with forty of his writing friends at his favorite Manhattan meeting place, Leone's. It was a main event in the city that day; newspaper photographers and newsreel cameramen jostled for position on the sidewalk outside on West Forty-eighth Street, and a lunchtime crowd stopped and gawked at the scene. "Jesus Katy!" Blaik muttered as he entered the restaurant flanked by Lombardi, Warmath and Kenna. Among the journalists inside was Walter Wellesley "Red" Smith, who was then beginning to replace the aging Grantland Rice as a leader of the New York sportswriting brotherhood. Smith was not a mythmaker in the same grand fashion as Rice and Runyon. His prose was less romantic, more literate and ironic, but the difference was of degree, not of kind. Smith came from Green Bay, the Wisconsin town that also produced Sleepy Jim Crowley, and had gone to college at the citadel of football glory, Notre Dame, as had Crowley. He sang from the same sports hymnal as his predecessors. Later he would solo in the sports chorus for Vince Lombardi. Now he sang sympathetically for Red Blaik, comparing the expulsion of Blaik's boys to "shooting a dog to rid him of fleas."

In his column describing the scene at Leone's for readers of the *New York Herald Tribune,* Smith depicted Blaik as "a shy man, inward turning, who never allows an outward sign of emotion," but whose face that day "bore the signs of strain." It was not until after lunch that Blaik addressed his handpicked audience, speaking with what Smith called "a grim eloquence" about his fallen players. He did not condone their actions; nor did he criticize the decision to separate them from West Point. But he wanted to ensure that they left with dignity. "I believe in the youngsters with whom I've been dealing," Blaik said. "I know their families. I know them, and I know they are men of character. . . . My entire endeavor from now on shall be to see that these boys leave West Point with the same reputations they had when they came in." Blaik then called on Doug Kenna to give the stellar histories of five athletes implicated in the scandal: their high school academic records and achievements, recommendations from their principals, teachers and coaches. Blaik said they were typical.

As the luncheon neared the end of its third hour, one reporter asked Blaik the single question that had drawn the crowd: What were his own plans? "Well, do you all want to leave now?" Blaik said, demonstrating a keen understanding of the press. He knew that his answer, one way or the other, would send them to the telephones. Then he responded in a deliberate voice: "I believe I can best make the public understand the boys, if necessary—and do the right thing—if I remain." Open cheering is customarily discouraged in the press boxes of American sport, but sportswriters cheered openly at Leone's that summer day in 1951 when Red Blaik said he would not resign.

There was no similar option for his varsity football players. All but two out of forty-five, including son Bob, were packed and gone by the end of the next week, among eighty-three cadets ultimately separated from West Point in the cheating scandal. Their discharges were by administrative order, neither honorable nor dishonorable. They left without courts-martial or due process hearings. They had no lawyers, agents, corporate sponsors or public relations firms to challenge the authorities or make their cases for them. There was no cable television with its sports channels or sports talk shows on radio to solicit public opinion on behalf of the players. They simply left, carrying conflicted sentiments of guilt, regret, bewilderment and rage at the system.

Blaik and his assistants tried in various ways to help them recover and get into other schools. Murray Warmath was busiest and boldest in that effort. He considered the expelled cadets "the finest group of young men" he ever knew and was outraged by the finality of their punishment. "I thought they were mistreated. I thought it was shoddy and still do," he said nearly fifty years later. Warmath left West Point himself later that year to coach at Mississippi State, then went on to receive national renown at Minnesota, but before he left he made scores of telephone calls to coaches around the country seeking programs that would accept Blaik's boys. "Kenna and Lombardi understood the system better than I did and knew when to keep their mouths shut. I said, 'Shit on this,' and started calling people. Blaik knew I was doing it and was happy about it. I had the football players going everywhere. I sent several players to Kansas State, another to Kansas. I hired two or three of them to work for me down at Mississippi State. Got them jobs." Warmath helped place nearly twenty of the players who were forced to leave.

Lombardi worked his strongest contacts with Fordham and the Catholic hierarchy in New York. Within days came a statement of sympathy from Francis Cardinal Spellman ("To err is human; to forgive divine," he said) and an offer to accept any of the cadets at Fordham, Manhattan or Iona. Kenna was on the phone several times with another Catholic benefactor who wanted to remain anonymous but said he would pay the way for discharged cadets to attend Notre Dame. This unnamed donor was Joseph P. Kennedy, patriarch of the political Kennedys. As Kenna remembered it, "Joe Kennedy thought it was terrible what happened to those kids. He had no connection to West Point. He was interested in Notre Dame, the Irish, a big fan. There was no small talk, he just wanted to help." The offer was made because it was "in the American tradition," Kennedy said, his quote attributed only to the anonymous donor. "A man who makes a mistake should have a reasonable chance to rehabilitate himself."

Several cadets responded to Kennedy's bequest and attended Notre Dame. Bob Blaik chose to go even farther away, enrolling at Colorado College. One night before leaving West Point, he asked his father, "Dad, do you now believe it would have been better to have lied?" It was an agonizing question for both Blaiks then; years later, after Bob had received his degree and become successful in the oil business, father and son would not have to swallow hard to answer "no." The shadow of scandal thinned over time and most of Blaik's boys eventually regained their footing, many of them in the same Army that had tossed them away. Because the cadets were separated by administrative order, not dishonorable discharge, they were not banned from further military service; some enlisted in ROTC programs at other colleges and returned to the officer corps, and one eventually reached the rank of general. Among those who returned to football in some fashion, backfield stars Al Pollard and Gene Filipski played briefly in the NFL and lineman Ray Malavasi rose to become head coach with the Los Angeles Rams.

Paul D. Harkins, the rigid colonel who launched the investigation and seemed determined to undo Blaik and the football program, wound up a dozen years later as the commanding general of American military forces in Vietnam, preceding the better known William Westmoreland. Life can turn around on people in unexpected ways. The officer who had disparaged some of Blaik's boys at Leone's that night in 1951, calling them a disgrace to the military, was derided himself in Vietnam. From his command post in Saigon, Harkins predicted easy victory and ignored any intelligence to the contrary. He constantly underestimated the troop strength and stamina of the Viet Cong and North Vietnamese, whom he dismissed as "those raggedy-assed little bastards." False bravado and inflexibility ultimately defined his conduct as an officer. After two years running the war, he lost the confidence of the White House and Pentagon, became an object of ridicule among American journalists in Vietnam and was quietly called home.

WITH EVERY national scandal come shock, surprise and lamentation on the fall of man. The event is seen by some as substantiation of decline, as though human imperfection were a modern-day phenomenon. Along with diatribes come complaints of public apathy; the righteous express bewilderment that no one seems to care. When the Army cheating scandal broke, one columnist attached it to a list of moral decline that he had been accumulating for decades. George E. Sokolsky, writing in the *Christian Science Monitor,* took what happened at West Point as proof that the world in 1951 was a wretched hell, nothing like the good old days. "When the morals of man are considered we are halted by the astonishing retreat of the 20th century with its excess of divorces, its broken homes, its emphasis on homosexuality, its acceptance of materialistic Marxism in wide areas that were so recently Christian, its avoidance of faith, honor, dignity, sacrifice. We need to know why our people are not outraged at the shameless corruption of our century. Something has gone terribly wrong with us and we need to know what it is and why it happened."

Colonel Blaik and General MacArthur, who shared some of that larger philosophy, might have taken exception to the manner in which Sokolsky linked the erring ways of Blaik's boys to all modern acts of perdition. On the other hand, nine Republican members of the House Armed Services Committee employed the red scare vocabulary of that era to blame the scandal on the Truman administration and Democrats soft on crime and communism. The cadets, the GOP legislators argued, "were scapegoats, while the real scoundrels—the appeasers, the fixers and the five percenters—not only have free rein in Washington but are defended and protected by the White House." Another debate focused on the narrower question: Did the troubles at West Point arise from an overemphasis on football? Senator J. William Fulbright, Democrat of Arkansas (and former placekicker for the University of Arkansas Razorbacks; whooh, pig, sooey!), was threatening to hold congressional hearings in Washington and called for the immediate suspension of the Army-Navy game. "It's a disgraceful situation," Fulbright said. "Intercollegiate athletics have become so perverted that it's a corrupting influence in the big universities."

In an effort to head off congressional action, West Point officials convened another board of officers, this one headed by a professor of electrical engineering, Colonel B. W. Bartlett, to probe the roots of the scandal and its relationship to big-time football. Blaik argued that his boys should receive sympathy because of the heavy load they carried in athletics and academics, but the Bartlett board found that the players were pampered from the time they entered West Point to the day they left. They were offered six-week cram courses (known as the "Monster Course") to help them pass the entrance examinations, provided with tutors throughout the year and exempted from dozens of minor rules that circumscribed the lives of other cadets. All of this special treatment, the board said, convinced the athletes that the success of the football team "was more important than anything else." The board was careful not to blame the football coaching staff for the cheating, but suggested that Blaik bore some responsibility for the academy's overemphasis on football because of the very characteristics that made him a successful coach—his "tremendous driving power, absolute singleness of purpose, and very strong personal convictions."

The summer of 1951 was a season of scandal in college athletics. Fourteen former basketball players at New York area colleges had pleaded guilty in July to conspiring with gamblers to fix games at Madison Square Garden. In August, while the Army scandal was breaking, a New York grand jury indicted eight more gamblers and three basketball players at Bradley University for fixing games. Those acts were criminal, infinitely more sinister than the academic misdeeds of Blaik's boys, yet they appeared less complicated, attributable to need and greed.

What happened at West Point, both what it signified and how it should have been resolved, raised complicated points of contention at the time that remain debatable even now. They raise larger questions that address the core mythology of football and of the man who went on to become its patron saint, Vince Lombardi. What is the value of competitive team sports? Where is the line drawn between a single-minded desire to excel and a debilitating obsession to win? Are football teams essential to the well-being of institutions and communities? Do athletes deserve special consideration because of this? In a realm where the ultimate measurement is wins versus losses, do ends justify means? The contradictory ideals of unity and independence, conformity and rebellion, run deep in the American psyche, and along that divide football is the sport most clearly aligned with unity and conformity, for better and worse. When asserting that football builds character, coaches invariably speak of teamwork, discipline, perseverance and loyalty. But even granting football those qualities, are they inherently positive? Or, as the Army honor code scandal suggests, can they also lead to group thinking, peer pressure, blind obedience and an emphasis on team solidarity over individual integrity? Those were the questions raised in 1951, and in one way or another they would follow Lombardi and define him for the rest of his life.

8

No Substitute
for Victory

NOTHING COULD HAVE seemed less relevant to Blaik and Lombardi on the afternoon of August 29 than a debate over whether West Point should put less emphasis on football. As the coaches looked out at the ragtag assemblage of athletic irregulars who reported on the first day of fall practice, it appeared that the question had been resolved. A team that would have been a contender, stocked with skilled players at every position, was prematurely gone. Here instead, as the raw material of the 1951 Army team, were the plebes of the year before, talented but untested, along with a few remaining fringe players promoted from the B squad and a legion of eager but overmatched cadet volunteers from the physical education intramural programs—"anyone who would agree to go out and get killed on Saturday afternoons," as one coach confessed. For seven seasons, from 1944 through 1950, Army had played the best football in the East, earning two national championships and five eastern titles while compiling a 57–3–4 record. Now mere survival was the first concern. As Blaik told the curious press corps on the practice field sidelines that first day, "We are only thinking of how we can field a team."

Blaik was so unfamiliar with his personnel that he was unable to present General MacArthur with his annual preseason analysis of the three-deep roster. "We have started our football," he wrote in a September 4 letter. "Soon I shall write you when I have better knowledge of the squad. At the moment the defense looks pitifully weak and our every effort will be to bring it along fast. Villanova is a burly outfit and our only chance to even contain them is with a good punter and a spirited defense." (Villanova was the first opponent on the schedule, and Blaik's bleak outlook went beyond his normal pessimism. During the glory years of the late forties, the schools had met five times and the cumulative score was Army 213, Villanova 0.) Blaik devoted the rest of the letter to reliving the scandal. He thanked MacArthur for persuading him not to resign after listening to his "sad story," denounced the "pious righteousness" of Pentagon officials, and urged the general and his wife to take in a few home games. "Any desire you may wish to eliminate official parties and crowd congestion is easily avoided by coming to our quarters which is adjacent to Lusk on a dead-end road about one block from the stadium," wrote the colonel. But there was no substitute for victory, and MacArthur stayed away.

For Lombardi, as he stood near Blaik during those first days of fall practice, all seemed uncertain and unexpected: the uncertain abilities of his charges and the unexpected fact that he and the colonel had returned to coach them. During the tense August days when the scandal was unfolding, Vince had prayed daily to St. Anthony and St. Jude to help the coaching staff find its way in what appeared to be a lost cause. He had told friends that he feared Blaik would resign. Imagining himself in the colonel's position, he wondered aloud whether he could have withstood that level of pressure as head coach. During his own unhappy spell at Fordham as top assistant to Ed Danowski, after all, he had bailed out after the first round of conflict. Decades later, looking back on his rise, Lombardi came to regard Blaik's decision to stay at West Point as a pivotal moment in his career. "If I ever needed a lesson, and I guess everybody does sooner or later, I got it with Colonel Blaik. Red showed me . . . what could be done by perseverance."

In truth the lessons flowed both ways, from Blaik to Lombardi and back again. In the profession of coaching, there are two essential challenges. One is to build a winning team from scratch, the other is to sustain excellence after a club has reached the top. They are distinct tasks, perhaps equally difficult, but usually requiring different intellectual and psychological skills. Even the best coaches are inherently more proficient at one than the other. Lombardi was by nature a builder and molder who during his first two seasons at West Point learned crucial lessons from the methodical Blaik on how to be a sustainer. In the aftermath of the honors scandal, the relationship changed, and Blaik became more reliant on his impassioned assistant to burn the white heat back into Army football.

The cadets on the roster of the 1951 squad found themselves in a more confusing situation than their coaches, torn as they were by contradictory pressures. Though not implicated in the academic scandal, they were the most visible reminders of it to the rest of the corps, and the players sensed a need to eradicate old stereotypes of Blaik's boys. This meant appearing unpretentious and self-effacing rather than apart and self-satisfied; not much of an act, given the dilution of the squad, but one that nonetheless had a psychological effect. Lowell Sisson, then a third classman, said later that the notion that football players were special "went straight down the tubes" that first autumn after the scandal. "We had to depress ourselves to a point where we began to get respected again. We had to keep bringing ourselves down until the corps decided that maybe these guys aren't so bad after all." Yet on the practice field, the coaches demanded more of them; especially Lombardi, who was relentless: yapping, roaring, laughing, encouraging, needling, teaching, pushing, in their face until the final drill before showers, the dreaded wind sprints: *Faster, give it your all, all the time, by God, don't let up now, faster, keep it up, be winners!*

Even with this makeshift crew, Lombardi established the goal of perfection. Always, every block: *Get your shoulder on* this *side and drive him* that *way.* He brought his backfield players into the projection room on Sundays and force-fed them hours of game film, showing not Blaik's depressing favorite, the ignominious 1950 loss to Navy, but rather the best and fleetest runners, his standards of the ideal, Doc Blanchard and Glenn Davis, Mr. Inside and Mr. Outside. Lombardi intended these films to work as positive reinforcement, but inevitably his narrations aroused stronger feelings in the Cadets. You can be as good as you want to be, better than you are, all you need is the desire and will to do it, he would say, while on-screen the incomparable Glenn Davis glided downfield against powerful Michigan. Watching Davis, listening to Lombardi, worrying about the distance between the coach's expectations and their own talents, many of the young Cadets felt intimidated; some thought of quitting, but, no, they couldn't quit, that would depress them even more; they became angry, determined to show that blankety-blank coach—and Lombardi had them right where he wanted them. As Blaik later said of the relationship between Vince and the players in 1951: "He was a driver. Not all the boys liked him, but he brought out the best in each of them."

Halfback Sisson broke his nose against Northwestern in the second game of the season and asked Lombardi at practice the next week whether he could wear a single bar across his helmet to protect himself. Lombardi took this request as a sign of meek surrender. Face guards were for sissies, he thundered. During his louder moments on the practice field, he could seem brutish, maniacal even, yet Lombardi usually knew where the line was that could not be crossed, where he would lose the respect of his players and of the even-tempered Blaik. His exhortations were counterbalanced by occasional hugs, unexpected pats on the back and shared laughter—and also by his brainpower, which by football coaching standards was superior. He could be screaming one minute and coolly dissecting an opposition defense the next, seeing things that no one else saw, quickly conceiving a counterattack that required complex thought and yet seemed so clear and obvious when he laid it out, the scholarly priest of the gridiron peering out at his students over his glasses, interpreting football's good book. He was "a very smart guy," said Gerald Lodge, then an offensive guard in his sophomore season. "He came across as an intellectual."

Working with a talent-drained corps, the coaches realized that their 1951 team had to rely heavily on intellect and ingenuity. From the Blanchard-Davis era through the seasons of Arnold Galiffa and Bob Blaik, Army tended to be quicker, deeper, faster and better organized than the opposition. The other team generally knew what was coming—three backs behind the quarterback in a tight T formation, straight ahead in the belly series or around the end—but could not stop it. Now Blaik and Lombardi improvised more, making use of the positive characteristics that all cadets possessed, even if they were comparatively slow, undersized and inexperienced, traits shaped by the repetitive physical and mental training of a military environment: first, they were all in top condition, fitter than the other team; and second, they were steeped in the tradition of receiving orders, memorizing them and carrying them out. As Gerry Lodge said: "Everybody was smart enough to remember his plays, so we could have relatively complex offensive schemes and change them weekly. That was one of their ploys that year—to have totally different plays every week and the element of surprise."

The technical aspects of the game had always intrigued Lombardi—his notion of a must read was a satchelful of offensive diagrams, all X's and O's and arrows—and he went out looking for new line splits, variations of the T formation, anything he could find in the vast uncatalogued library of technical football literature. To him this was both a vocational and an intellectual pursuit. Johnny "Tarzan" Druze, his old linemate on the Seven Blocks of Granite, was then an assistant at Notre Dame working under Frank Leahy, their former Fordham line coach who had risen to become an extremely successful head coach with the Irish. When Herb Seidell paid a visit to practice at South Bend, Druze quickly asked him, "What's with Lombardi?" Seidell drew a blank. What did Druze mean? "Well," said Druze, "there isn't a week that goes by that there isn't a pound of mail going from Vin to Leahy and back again." Lombardi and Leahy had been exchanging play diagrams, and Druze simply could not recognize that intense level of football curiosity—another manifestation of the drive that separated Lombardi from other assistant coaches.

There was still a limit to how far ingenuity and mental and physical conditioning could take the 1951 team. As Blaik had anticipated, Army lost the opener to "burly" Villanova by two touchdowns, beginning a four-game losing streak that included losses to Dartmouth and Harvard from the usually overmatched Ivy League. The winless slide stopped with a 14 to 9 victory over Columbia, prompting a congratulatory cable from MacArthur. "The team was thrilled over your telegram," Blaik quickly wrote in return. "Like all cadet football players of the past generation, they share my feeling that you are our number one rooter." But next came a trip down to Yankee Stadium to meet Southern Cal and its dashing star, Frank Gifford, who was posing for *Look* magazine as an All-America tailback. In his pregame missive to MacArthur, Blaik noted that he would employ an "unorthodox defense" to try to stop the Trojan attack, but added that "we are so completely out-classed physically there is reason to fear that we may not be able to with-stand the impact of such a fast and strong squad." Many in the press box observing that game thought Southern Cal could have scored 50 points, but stopped mercifully at 28. Looking back decades later on that trying season, assistant Doug Kenna spoke of "many long afternoons," but said it could have been worse: "The opposing coaches were good to us—they didn't run it up."

The Cadets were 2–6 by the time they boarded the train for Philadel-phia for the season finale against Navy. It was Blaik's worst record ever and more losses for Lombardi than he had suffered during any season in two decades, with the exception of his abortive attempt to resurrect Fordham under the somnolent Danowski. In the internecine world of service academy rivalry, this single contest was as meaningful as all other games on the sched-ule combined: a victory redeemed the most ghastly season, and an upset loss, like the one Blaik's boys had suffered the year before, ruined an otherwise exceptional year. To say that the outcome determined twelve months of bragging rights probably underestimated its significance: Army and Navy were in unending competition elsewhere—at the Pentagon, in the halls of Congress, in the realm of public opinion—fighting for prestige, new weapons, more money, recognition of singular prowess in battle, and all of those struggles were played out symbolically in the game of football. The only national setting where one branch could say indisputably that it was better than the other was on the playing field once each year in Philadelphia.

As the Army coaches, their families, the struggling team and the entire corps rode the train south to New York and down through New Jersey for the game, one uncomfortable thought prevailed. Could Army sink any lower? Still reeling from the academic scandal, too many of its recent gradu-ates slogging and fighting and dying in the confounding war in Korea, Blaik's adversaries around the country taking inordinate pleasure in his troubles—one game could ease some of the pain. If there was a shard of false hope, it was expressed by Lombardi's son, little Vincent, then nine, who, when the delegation reached Philadelphia, busily set about making a fleet of paper airplanes that he flew out the hotel window. BEAT NAVY was scrawled on the wings.

For the Navy game, as for all away games, Blaik followed his idiosyn-cratic practice of shepherding his team onto the field hours before kickoff and leading them on a leisurely stroll across the grass in their traveling clothes. He thought of this as a way to sharpen the focus, heighten the sense of anticipation, bring the boys together. Before they left the field for the locker room, Blaik gathered the team around him and gave them the first play to run during the game—something for the offensive players to think about as they put on their uniforms. But none of his psychology was of any use this time. Navy scored two touchdowns before Army could run an offensive series. In football, as in life, excessive fear and anxiety can dim the brightest mind. Army's young quarterback had been given the first play during the street clothes ritual, and Blaik and Lombardi went over it with him again before the first series. With a pat on the back, the signal-caller trotted boldly out to the huddle, then made a sudden U-turn and sprinted back to the sidelines, panting. "Coach," he said to the perplexed Blaik, "what did you tell me to do? I forgot." So much for the infallible memory of cadets. Yes, Army could fall lower. The final score was 42 to 7. There was only one blessing in the darkness of defeat: Lombardi and his colleagues were not forced to watch films of the game over and over for the next year. Not even Blaik could find a lesson in that loss.

THE NEXT JULY, one year after his return from Korea, Lombardi undertook a trip that he probably found even more daunting than the visit to Bigfoot Brown's war zone bunker. He took part in a father-son camping trip in the wilderness of Canada, driving in a three-car caravan up to La Vérendrye Provincial Park northwest of Montreal for a week of fishing, canoeing and sleeping outdoors. Lombardi had been a city creature for all of his thirty-nine years. The only camps he knew were football camps. He had never before spent a night without a roof over his head. Although he grew up near the fishing shanties of Sheepshead Bay, he had little interest in fishing. He had avoided the fishing hole at Bull Pond in previous summers, preferring to stay in the Mother Lodge where he would play gin with Tim Cohane and Stanley Woodward while Warmath and Blaik and Red Reeder sat out there in a rowboat for hours on end. Warmath could "fish you into the ground," as Reeder put it. "He didn't know when to quit. He could sit in that damn rowboat for eight or nine hours until you all got sick of it." Eight or nine minutes was all Lombardi could tolerate. Luckily for him, Warmath was not on this Canada trip; he had already left West Point to become head coach at Mississippi State. The July campers included the Lombardis, Reeder and his son Russ, Phil Draper (another Army colonel) and his son Stephen, and young Charles Summerall, Russ Reeder's cousin.

There was no question about who commanded this northern expedition: Red Reeder, still boyish and lean at age fifty, sandy red hair, jug ears, winning grin, sharp voice, clear blue eyes, natural-born wit and storyteller, prolific writer, lifelong Army brat "born at reveille," football dropkicker and baseball letterman in the West Point class of 1926. Red prepared the menus, fixing dry vegetables, beef jerky and other lightweight and durable food. He plotted the course, drove the front car, scheduled the wayside breaks, determined the overnight stops—all this with a prosthesis where his left leg used to be. Reeder was the real thing, an infantry colonel. Eight years earlier during the first week in June, he had readied his men of the Twelfth Infantry Regiment of the Fourth Division for their landing on Utah Beach in the Normandy invasion. What happened to him that fateful week was a story that Lombardi never tired of hearing, a romantic narrative of battle, football, pride and daring.

Before sailing from England for the landing in France, Reeder had gathered his regiment on a hillside on the edge of the coastal town of Plymouth and delivered what amounted to a pregame speech. First he addressed the sergeants, saying that noncommissioned officers had helped raise him since childhood and were the heart of the Army, the real leaders of fighting men. Then he described the landing at Utah Beach in football terminology: "The Eighth and Twenty-second regiments will land ahead of us and block to the left and right. The paratroopers are our downfield blockers. We will land and plunge through the hole and head for Cherbourg." His troops cheered, roaring even louder when Reeder declared that he would be at the front as they fought their way through France.

When their ship approached Normandy and the infantrymen assembled on deck near the landing crafts, Reeder took to the loudspeaker and read them a message from British Field Marshal Bernard Montgomery that ended with an old quatrain from the Earl of Montrose. War and sports—the words echoed the Fordham fight song, and the poetry easily could have been written by Grantland Rice up in the press box:

> *He either fears his fate too much,*
> *Or his deserts are small,*
> *Who dare not put it to the touch,*
> *To win or lose it all.*

Five days later, as Reeder led a patrol through the French countryside—"plunging through the hole"—he was hit by a German shell. He did not lose it all, just his left leg. For daring to put it to the touch, he won the Distinguished Service Cross, one of fourteen decorations he received during the war. Ten months later he was walking on an artificial leg. Within two years he was back at West Point, reorganizing the tactical department, teaching the psychology of leadership, hitting grounders to Army infielders as assistant baseball coach and writing a book with his sister Nardi Reeder Campion that would become the basis for John Ford's film classic *The Long Gray Line*. No small deserts for Red.

When Lombardi arrived at West Point, Reeder immediately befriended him. They lived near each other on the loop. Russ became pals with young

Vincent, Dort Reeder calmly kept the confidences of the troubled Marie, and Red watched after them all. Once the Lombardi basement flooded and Marie called in a panic—Vince was out of town (and was of little use around the house anyway)—and Red came over to fix the pipes and clean out the basement. He did not have Blaik's noble airs, but was more endearing and took on the role of Lombardi's playful mentor. For the rest of his life (he lived to age ninety-five) Reeder kept a picture of himself and Lombardi from the early 1950s, standing arm in arm at closing time at the Bear Mountain Inn, Lombardi in white suede shoes, ribbed socks, with his pant cuffs rolled way up past his shins, his right hand cradling both a cigarette and a Rheingold Extra Dry (the label upside down; long before the age of pull tops a can could be opened top or bottom), jaw agape in a teeth-flashing grin; Red impishly pulling the hat off Vince's head. When those two were on the premises, everyone at the Bear Mountain Inn knew it: Red would punctuate his stories with bursts of laughter, which caused Vince to guffaw so loudly that the table would reverberate, which made Red cackle even more, until it seemed that the entire drinking hall had caught the joyous contagion.

Anyone who spent time around Lombardi in those situations could only be puzzled by the prevailing image of him later in his career, when the human being could not be separated from a symbolic character created from his success. In the mythology of Coach Lombardi, the relentless winner, all gruff and bluff, there was little room for the mirthful and even giddy goofball that he sometimes surely was. Of course that aspect of his personality was seldom evident, usually seen only when he was in the company of close friends, in a bar, on a golf course, at a party. His own children rarely knew him that way. The camping trip to Canada was one of the few vacations Lombardi ever took with his son, and the memory stayed with young Vincent through the years as their relationship became more difficult.

There was nothing intimidating about Lombardi on that adventure. He was good-natured if inept, out of his element. After the campers had spent two days fishing along the river, eating their catch along with Reeder's wilderness food, Vince declared that he was "sick of this stuff," bolted for a shopping spree at a nearby general store and returned with a six-pack of beer, thick steaks and corn on the cob. The next day Reeder suggested that they break camp and canoe upriver to a lake. To minimize intrafamily bickering, he had separated fathers and sons, placing Lombardi in a canoe with young Draper. As Reeder later recalled the scene: "When we reached the lake we encountered a stiff wind and I looked back and there was Vince and his canoe was spinning around. Poor little Stephen Draper was up front, teeter-tottered up in the air, and couldn't get his paddle down in the water. Vince didn't know how to load a canoe. He had all the weight in the back and was just going around in circles, helpless." Reeder paddled back, steered the canoe to shore and helped Vince rearrange the load. That night they slept along the lakeshore and were serenaded by a loon. "Hear that?" Reeder said as the loon's lament echoed across the watery darkness. "That's the cry of a lost soul."

Lombardi felt more comfortable in landscapes tamed by man. There was a golf course on the academy reservation, an odd ten-hole layout cut into the woods that he played on Wednesday afternoons in the off-season with the other football assistants and occasionally Coach Blaik. Russ Reeder was the caddy, his profits based on a novel if somewhat coldly Darwinian system devised by Lombardi. He was paid a dollar a hole, which meant he could expect to make ten dollars a round—but only if no balls were lost. It was the youngster's primary responsibility to track down errant shots into the rough and woods; if he could not, the men would subtract the cost of the ball from his base salary. It seemed that Lombardi compulsively felt the need to give young people a test, an incentive. Golf became his favorite form of relaxation, stealing time that might have gone to his family, even seducing him away from the tower during slow summer days when Blaik was studying film and devising game plans.

With friends and assistants, as with players, Blaik seemed rigid but was in fact deceptively flexible, a trait that Lombardi slowly absorbed and used to his advantage later in his career. When subordinates thought they were fooling Blaik, more often than not he knew what was going on but let it pass, or delivered a subtle message to keep them from straying too far. One weekday summer morning Lombardi and Kenna slipped out to play golf at a country club near Tarrytown. "The old man will never find us here," Vince assured his nervous playing partner. As they finished the ninth hole and approached the clubhouse before making the turn, the club pro approached with a sly smile and said, "Colonel Blaik would like to buy you guys a beer." Kenna, horrified, thought they should quit and return quickly to West Point. Lombardi, after three seasons with Blaik, was less obeisant than he once was. We're here, he said, he knows we're here; might as well finish. But how did Blaik find out? "He knew anything that moved," was Kenna's explanation. That answer unavoidably provokes a harsher question. If Blaik was attuned to everything around him, how could he have been unaware that his players, including his own son, had been violating the honor code? One answer might lie in the simple fact that people develop an ability not to hear what they do not want to hear.

General Douglas MacArthur
Waldorf-Astoria Towers
New York, N.Y.

Dear General MacArthur:

They are mowing the stadium grass today and the air has that certain scent of autumn which reminds all football addicts that the

season is just around the bend. One of the penalties of city life is
the absence of nature's reminders, so this letter on the '52 season is
a less romantic way of your learning that soon another football
season will be with us. Politics and the state of the nation are out
as we discuss the football troops at West Point. The attached personnel charts will give you a team picture of our squad and these
additional random thoughts will supplement the charts.

So began a letter Blaik wrote to his general in the summer of 1952 as
Year 2 of the Army football recovery began. Although the coach now knew
enough about his personnel to offer a preseason guide, in contrast to the
previous year, it was still a characteristically bleak Blaik assessment: he informed MacArthur that there were only four talented players on offense,
one of whom was "the most immature youngster" he had ever coached, and
his defense was "far below par," with "only one man of the entire group who
normally would make a first West Point team." Defensive coach Murray
Warmath was gone. Potent Southern Cal was on the schedule again, along
with Georgia Tech. The opening day opponent, South Carolina, had "the
fastest backfield in the Southern conference." The Cadets would be "equal in
material" to only two opponents, Columbia and VMI. There was only one
way for Army to rise from its gridiron depression, Blaik asserted: by giving
the last full measure of devotion to winning.

"Unfortunately, too much experience in losing [gracefully] often low-
ers the resistance to defeat," he wrote. "Through the years I have found that
between equal teams the winning formula is a thin margin above which to
remain requires fidelity to fundamental principles and a team faith that abhors mediocrity and moral victories. I have often stated that there never was
a champion who to himself was a good loser; there is a vast difference between the good sport and the good loser, but today even at the Military
Academy we have a school of thought whose followers believe we should
place little emphasis on winning. They have never experienced the pride of
accomplishment which only comes from sacrifice and superior performance."

In other words, if you were against Blaik, you were a loser or wanted to
lose. There was an opposing faction at West Point, but while the academic
scandal had temporarily weakened the football team, it had not helped
Blaik's critics diminish his power. He signed a new contract in 1952 that gave
him even more control, as coach and athletic director, and his salary exceeded that of the dean of academics, a brigadier general. MacArthur con-
gratulated Blaik for his renewed contract and revised his earlier prediction
that it would take West Point ten or fifteen years to recover from the 1951
separation of Blaik's boys. By the end of another year, he now said, "the general athletic public will completely ignore the incidents" of the honors scan-

dal, and the football program will "come back into its own." The 1952 squad was in fact better than Blaik had predicted, though not all the way back. Army won and lost at an even rate and finished 4–4–1. After the Cadets upset Penn 14 to 13 in the penultimate game, MacArthur dispatched a congratulatory telegram to Blaik: "Your splendid team fills my old soldier's heart with pride. Remind them on November 29 there can be no substitute for victory." November 29 was the date of the Navy game, and though it was no substitute for victory, Army lost that day by only 7 to 0, a far less embarrassing score than the year before.

The Cadets were competitive in all but one contest, aided considerably by Lombardi's new positioning up in the press box during games, where he could analyze plays and send tips and recommendations down to the bench. Gerald Lodge, who played linebacker that year and called the defensive signals, said that Lombardi was as valuable on defense as offense because of his uncommon ability to notice several events simultaneously along the line of scrimmage as though they were happening in slow motion and in isolation. "I would come out after the first series of plays on defense and Lombardi would get me on the phone and tell me what to tell each of the players on the whole defense—what the opposing team was doing differently than we expected and how to adjust to it. The ends were too split; tighten up; the quarterback is tipping off his passing plays, subtle things like that. It is hard to watch more than one or two people at a time, but he could see everybody and just rattle it off."

Lombardi's ability to see everything on a football field served another purpose for him that year. After the games he often had the assignment of taking the film down to a studio on Long Island to be processed, and on the return trip, at Blaik's request, he stopped in midtown Manhattan for a special screening and play-by-play analysis in General MacArthur's commodious living room atop the Waldorf-Astoria. These were decidedly informal sessions (Doug Kenna, who performed the same errand at times, likened MacArthur to "a friendly old Dutch uncle"). There sat MacArthur, wearing his frayed gray flannel Army bathrobe with his varsity letter sewed onto it, at ease in his favorite chair, with Lombardi perched nervously nearby, and a military aide running the projector. The general was all questions: Why this play? What were you trying to do there? He had memorized the numbers of every Army player and knew more than Lombardi about their biographies. But it was not all football minutiae; MacArthur also talked about the difficulties West Point had endured and the value of competitive sports. Years later, when Lombardi was a national figure delivering speeches about the philosophical importance of football, he often reflected back on what MacArthur told him during those peculiar Waldorf screenings in the early fifties.

In one of those speeches, Lombardi said: "I can vividly remember him saying that 'competitive sports keeps alive in us a spirit and vitality. It teaches the strong to know when they are weak and the brave to face themselves when they are afraid. To be proud and unbowed in defeat and yet humble and gentle in victory. And to master ourselves before we attempt to master others. And to learn to laugh, yet never forget how to weep. And to give the predominance of courage over timidity.' I think they are great words from what I consider to be one of the great Americans." It is improbable that MacArthur, watching game films in his gray bathrobe, uttered precisely those words to Lombardi. This sounded more like the prose of one of MacArthur's carefully composed speeches. But the importance is one of lineage. In tracing the roots of Lombardi mythology, one significant branch leads back through Blaik to the melodramatic old soldier.

LOMBARDI WAS ANXIOUS and frustrated when the 1953 season arrived. This was his fifth year at West Point, and he had the quality of a postgraduate lingering on campus after his classmates had moved on. It was indisputable that he was Blaik's top aide and wielded more power than any previous second-in-command—the "prime minister to Blaik's king," as one player described the relationship—yet no matter how much influence he had, he was still an assistant coach. Three other former Blaik assistants had teams of their own by now. Why not him? Was it because he was Italian? Did they think he was too emotional? What did Murray Warmath have that he didn't have? These were among the questions he brooded over when Tim Cohane drove up to West Point to visit. The two Fordham Rams sat in Lombardi's living room late into the night and talked about life and football and the meaning of success. Their relationship "indulged strong differences of opinion" because they both believed in the benefits of discipline and hard work—and they both believed in Lombardi, Cohane said later. "I wanted badly for him to succeed. And he knew it." Cohane already had done more to promote Lombardi's career than anyone else. At Fordham, he had publicized Vinnie as one of the Seven Blocks of Granite. As sports editor at *Look* magazine, he had recommended him to Red Blaik. And he was still trying to help. When he noticed a coaching opening around the country, he called sportswriter pals and urged them to plug Lombardi, which they sometimes did, but to no avail.

In June, Lombardi had turned forty. He and Red Reeder had spent the summer working on a book about football. Red did most of the writing, but Vince provided the ideas. Reeder was impressed by the depth of Lombardi's knowledge of the game, the way he correlated tactics and strategy like a military general. But the New York publishers were not interested in a technical football book written by an assistant coach. Forty years old and still unrecognized. Few seemed to remember the glory of the Seven Blocks. Eight seasons at Saints. Two assisting back at Fordham. Four more in the shadows of the colonel. Lombardi was in danger of being permanently trapped in an image that he did not want, the football lifer, the valuable but anonymous man in the trenches. He burned for something more. He wanted to be Red Reeder leading his troops onto Utah Beach, to put it to the touch, to win or lose it all.

Not much was expected of Army's 1953 team. Six players, including the most talented back, Freddie Meyers, had been lost to academic failure. Would those setbacks have been avoided if the corps still passed the poop? Perhaps, perhaps not, but in a sense the team rendered that question irrelevant by playing above its abilities. Blaik sensed during fall practice that his players were jelling—"We are off to a good start in the face of some personnel problems," he wrote to MacArthur in his preseason letter—and the players, for their part, noticed that the coaches, especially Lombardi, had even more emotion than usual invested in the team's fortunes. Although Blaik was a proponent of two-platoon football, his squad clearly benefited from rules changes making substitutions more difficult in 1953, essentially going back to the days of sixty-minute men. This placed more emphasis on discipline and conditioning, the two areas where all Army teams were unmatched. The Cadets defeated Furman in the opener, 41 to 0, the most decisive win, and first shutout, since before the 1951 scandal. They were on their way to a win in the second game against Northwestern of the Big Ten, but were done in by two fumbles near the end zone and a dropped interception, which might have cost them three touchdowns and made the difference in a 33 to 20 loss. Lombardi took the loss especially hard, Blaik later recounted: "Vince was crying in the dressing room because individual mistakes had cost the game for a bunch of kids who had worked so hard to come out of nowhere."

Army rebounded in unexpected fashion, playing out the rest of the season unbeaten, with a lone scoreless tie against talented Tulane (whose star back was a future Green Bay Packer named Max McGee) and a stunning 20 to 7 victory over powerful Navy in the year-ending rivalry. It was the first Cadet win over the Midshipmen since 1949, and it brought with it a host of rewards: service academy bragging rights, a prized watch inscribed A 20 N 7 1953 that the players wore proudly for the rest of their lives, the Lambert Trophy as the best team in the East and some national coach-of-the-year honors for Red Blaik. But the upset over Navy was not the turning point. The emotional high in a passionate season had come earlier, in the heat of middle October, when Army played at the Polo Grounds against Duke, a national power, then ranked No. 7, with a brilliant backfield led by Red Smith and Worth (A Million) Lutz. On the eve of the season, Blaik had met privately with forty-five cadet captains and pleaded with them to help restore the academy to the days when the football team received unqualified support, a final reconciliation after years of estrangement. Team and corps needed to come together, Blaik told the captains, not just for competitive spirit, but for "a regaining of a soul for the academy."

The Duke game accomplished what words alone could not. The entire corps, 2,400 strong, rode down to New York for the game and stood as a thunderous wave of blue-gray, screaming from the moment the team set foot on the field until the final gun. The players gave them plenty to shout about: Tommy Bell plowing up the middle for the first score, quarterback Pete Vann ambidextrously switching the ball from right hand to left to make a crucial southpaw toss leading to a second score, Duke missing an extra point that would have tied the game at 14-all. It was a game worthy of golden era sportswriting, and Red Smith was there for the *New York Herald Tribune* to record the final act, which starred, felicitously, the Duke back of the same name. "The score held at 14 to 13 as the fourth quarter rolled out, and up in the press box historians burrowed in the records hunting another Army victory as unexpected as this. They couldn't find one. Then, suddenly, it appeared such comparisons would be vain, for here was Duke clamoring for another touchdown. There was a double reverse behind the line of scrimmage and Red Smith broke free, pursued only by Bob Mischak, a frustrated back who plays end and third base at West Point. Smith had a lead of at least eight yards when the pursuit began, but Smiths simply aren't fast. Seventy-three yards down the field, Mischak had him by the neck and dragged him to earth seven yards from the goal line."

In truth, sportswriter Smith underplayed Mischak's accomplishment at the expense of an irresistible joke about the running abilities of anyone named Smith. No one on the field or the sidelines expected Mischak to catch him. Gerry Lodge, pursuing from his linebacker spot, was ten yards behind Mischak as they ran after Smith and was shocked that his teammate made the tackle, one that he could remember vividly nearly a half-century later: "He grabbed Smith on top of the shoulder pads and pulled him straight down. The runner, and all of us, were so surprised." Duke had four downs to score from there, and bulled closer every time. On fourth down with two yards to go, Worth Lutz pounded forward on a quarterback sneak, and when the referee cleared the pile he had been stopped inches from the goal line. Blaik, fearful of a fumble, ordered a quick kick on first down and sent his defense out again for a final stand in its own territory. Forty seconds left. Cadets streamed down from the stands and gathered on the far sideline and behind the end line. Duke threw four straight passes, the last one broken up in the end zone. "Suddenly," wrote Red Smith, "the stained white jerseys of the West Point team disappeared, swamped under wave upon wave of blue-gray soldier suits. West Point cadets never break ranks. This time they practically broke their heroes to pieces."

When Bob Mischak made that unlikely play, what Blaik called "a marvelous display of heart and pursuit," Army's football team regained its soul.

Not just Lombardi, but all the coaches, even the stoic colonel, cried in the locker room after the game, and it was difficult at that moment to dispute that MacArthur was right: there was no substitute for victory. Not victory for its own sake; victories of this sort brought deeper feelings, for the game, for the school, for the team, for the human spirit. Tim Cohane was there with his young boys, who remembered the scene forever: Blaik smiling, a sight they had rarely seen before, and Lombardi roaring and shaking with laughter. For the athletes, this was the reason they played, this moment, sitting there exhausted in the dusty old dressing room above the south end of the field, lockers clanging, rounds of "On Brave Old Army Team" echoing in the din, T-shirts soaked with burning sweat sticking to their backs like extra layers of skin, and ... *here comes Vince,* beaming, holding scissors, shouting, "WE'RE GONNA CUT 'EM OFF, MEN!"—cut off the T-shirts. It was an honor, a symbolic gesture signifying that Blaik and Lombardi and their boys had everything to look forward to even though they had nothing left to give.

9

Cult of the New

Far off I hear the rolling, roaring cheers.
They come to me from many yesterdays,
From record deeds that cross the fading years,
And light the landscape with their brilliant plays,
Great stars that knew their days in fame's bright sun.
I hear them tramping to oblivion.

GRANTLAND RICE WROTE THOSE LINES as the closing stanza of a poem titled "The Long Road" that appeared on the last page of his final book, a memoir completed less than a month before his death. He died at 6:15 on the scorchingly hot evening of July 13, 1954, two hours after suffering a massive stroke while reading his mail at the "Sportlight" office on West Forty-eighth Street in midtown Manhattan. Rice was the romantic mythmaker of American sports, the creator of the Four Horsemen, but in the end he understood that everything he had glorified during his half-century in the press box would soon be tramping with him into oblivion, replaced by the new and the modern. "The best doesn't belong to the past," he wrote in the introduction to "The Long Road," though his tone seemed less expectant than resigned.

In the very month that Rice died at age seventy-three, wrecking balls were demolishing an archaic vestige of the newspaper culture he had entered at the dawn of the twentieth century, Joseph Pulitzer's New York World Building. It was the last original structure downtown along what had been known as Newspaper Row, former home not just to the defunct *World*, but also to the *Journal,* the *Evening Post,* the *American,* the *Tribune* and the *Sun.* Grantland Rice and the *World,* flesh and mortar of an obsolete era, gone at once. And here, suddenly, came the new age of television. By the summer of 1954 more than 350 broadcasting stations had started up in cities around the country, where three years earlier the national total was under fifty; in those same three years the ownership of TV sets in the average American home went from extraordinary to routine, from one in five families to nearly two of every three. Television profits rose by 25 percent that year, while radio and newspaper revenues declined. Perhaps Grantland Rice died at the appropriate time, just when the sportswriting style of his day was losing its dominant role to television as the teller of stories and shaper of myths.

Rarely did the old seem so old and the new seem so new as in 1954. The cult of the modern had been growing with the century, and now it was powerful and omnipresent, and television was just part of it. Corporations and their advertising agencies offered up the gods of science and progress to be worshiped in every aspect of American life.

"THE LIGHT OF A NEW AGE," blared a headline in *Newsweek* promoting the magazine above an eerie photograph "taken in the predawn dark, lit entirely by the flash of an A-bomb seven miles away." Another ad featured an alien hero of this new age, a scientific technician in protective plastic suit and mask, handling radioactive materials next to the promise: "As General Electric Sees It, the atom will produce power for homes in 5 to 10 years" and do so "without government subsidy." New chemicals, magic elixirs, were introduced to the public with religious reverence. Union Carbide sold its products with a mural depicting a huge hand reaching down from the clouds (man or God?) and pouring a chemical from a giant test tube onto a panorama of factories teeming with workers; the company boasted that its scientists were inventing a new chemical every month: "From the earth, air and water come new things for all of us—and new jobs." From Diamond Chemicals came an ad depicting a crowd gathered on the sidewalk of Main Street USA, peering into a dry-cleaning building, with someone shouting out the headline: "There's a revolution going on in the back room!" What revolution? A new dry-cleaning chemical named perchloroethylene. Environmental degradation was celebrated as progress. Southern Pacific Railroad developed an ad campaign based on the theme of man overpowering nature in "The Golden Empire" that stretched from Louisiana to California. "Eight years ago some rabbits called this Texas Gulf Coast plains 'home,' " proclaimed one ad showing the before-and-after effects of industrial expansion. "Now a multimillion-dollar chemical plant is located where the rabbits scampered only a few years ago . . . and right next door are other new plants, supplying the booming industries of the great Southwest."

New and modern everything: new vinyl handbags and pedigreed plastic furniture, new 1954 Mercury automobiles with "years-ahead styling" and "new ball-joint suspension" and "entirely new V-8 engines" and "new colors"—reds, yellows, blues and greens that seemed mixed into modern and sexy tints. New lightweight cans for soft drinks, new trailers for truck transports, new miracle-tip cigarette filters, new tubular all-steel folding chairs, new king-size baked-enamel tray tables, new water coolers with foot pedals, new central duct air-conditioning systems, new gear teeth for power transmissions, new aluminum pipes for farm irrigation, even a "new Chicago" undertaking a "great, new surge" with new expressways and skyscrapers.

IT WAS IN THE SPIRIT of the new that the New York Football Giants made a coaching change that year. Steve Owen had run the team for twenty-three seasons, since before Vince Lombardi entered Fordham. Once, long ago, the beefy Oklahoman with the gravel drawl and massive red face had seemed new and innovative himself, never more so than during the 1934 championship game played at the Polo Grounds against the Chicago Bears. Freezing rain and frigid temperatures that December day had turned the field into a skating rink. With his team trailing 10 to 3 in the first half, Owen, on the advice of the team physician, sent his equipment manager out to round up several dozen basketball shoes. The Giants wore them in the second half and gained tractional advantage over the slip-sliding Bears, coming back to win by the score of 30 to 13 in what became known as the Sneakers Game. But that story was a generation old. Owen was fifty-five now and had not won a championship since 1938. He was coming off his worst season, one in which his squad finished with 3 wins and 9 losses, and it seemed that the modern game had overtaken him. His varied offenses looked more desperate than imaginative. Even before the 1953 season was over, after a humiliating 62 to 14 loss to Cleveland, the Giants owners, father Tim and sons Jack and Wellington Mara, called Big Steve into the front office. "What's up?" he inquired, and they gave him the answer: his *time* was up. They were bringing in someone new.

In the *New York Daily News* the next morning, a two-column headline reported the firing along with a prediction: "GIANTS BOOT OWEN UPSTAIRS, LOMBARDI SEEN NEW COACH." The story began: "Steve Owen, long renowned as 'the coach without a contract,' yesterday was removed from the job as football boss of the Giants after one of the most disastrous campaigns in his 23 years at the helm. Steve comes off the field and into the front office following this Sunday's final game with the Detroit Lions in the Polo Grounds. It was learned by THE NEWS that president Jack Mara is seeking the services of Vincent Lombardi, backfield coach and highly regarded right-hand man to coach Earl (Red) Blaik at West Point. Mara already has contacted [Blaik] regarding the hiring of Lombardi, one of the famed Fordham Blocks of Granite who joined the Army coaching staff in 1949."

Lombardi, according to the story, "stacks up as just the injection of 'young blood' the Giants seem to need." By this account, he was born in Brooklyn, raised in Englewood and played as a starting guard for three seasons at Fordham. He was said to have graduated in 1937 "after making the Dean's list four straight years" and then gone on for "two years of postgraduate study" at Fordham law school. The article by sportswriter Gene Ward had every fact wrong except where Lombardi was born. It is unclear whether Lombardi himself fibbed about his academic record or merely never corrected the exaggerations and allowed them to become part of his résumé, but from then on, most articles describing his school years asserted that he was a cum laude graduate with two years of law school under his belt. Occasionally he was even said to have earned his law degree. But the most important fact that Ward had wrong—at least from Lombardi's perspective—was that he was being considered for the Giants' head coaching job.

He was not. The Maras hoped to hire Red Blaik, not Lombardi. Wellington Mara, who had been Vince's classmate at Fordham, said that Blaik turned them down and urged that they consider his top assistant—"Why don't you talk to my man Vince?" he said—but the Maras were hesitant to put Lombardi in the head job, worried that he was lacking in professional experience and unsure that he could be a disciplined leader. They were drawn instead to Jim Lee Howell, another of their former players, a lanky end from rural Lonoke, Arkansas, who was almost two years younger than Lombardi but had more of the aura of a pro. He was a former drill instructor in the Marine Corps who recently had been working two jobs: assistant with the Giants in the morning and head coach at Wagner College in the afternoon. "Now here is a guy who can come in and hammer things out," Well Mara said of Howell.

Contrary to later reports that they were close college chums, Wellington Mara had known Vince only casually during their Fordham years, when he spent most of his spare time scouting pro talent for his father's team. Vince and Well were in Ignatius Cox's ethics class together, but so were several hundred other students. In their senior year Mara was sports editor of the *Maroon* yearbook and wrote stories about the exploits of the Blocks of Granite, but considered Lombardi the least talented of the seven and never interviewed him. It was Steve Owen, in fact, who first alerted the Maras to Lombardi's coaching skills. Owen had been the guest speaker at a Saints football banquet one year in the mid-1940s. "You know that guy Lombardi who was in your class at school?" he told Well Mara after returning from Englewood. "They win the championship every year!" Mara became more familiar with Lombardi at West Point because of his relationship with Blaik. When Army played at the Polo Grounds, the Maras invited the coaching staff to stay overnight as guests of the Giants and watch the pro game the next afternoon. Blaik reciprocated by inviting the Maras to West Point.

Even if they did not want Lombardi for the top job, the Maras were interested in having him join their staff. Following Blaik's suggestion, Well Mara called Vince and set up an interview at the Bear Mountain Inn. Lombardi later remembered Mara saying to him during that phone call, "We've always wanted you on the Giants and we have an opening." According to Doug Kenna, Lombardi had told other members of the Army coaching staff that he wanted the head coaching job with the Giants "worse than anything in the world" and thought that was the opening Mara was talking about. It came as a "terrible disappointment" when Mara instead invited him to come to New York to run the Giants offense for Jim Lee Howell. It seemed that the football world was stocked with men who worked under Blaik and became head coaches: Murray Warmath at Mississippi State, Herman Hickman at Yale, Stu Holcomb at Purdue, Sid Gillman at Cincinnati, Andy Gustafson at Miami, Bob Woodruff at Florida, John Sauer at The Citadel. Why not Lombardi?

Mara's offer might have been flattering, but it was a disappointment. Lombardi told his former classmate that he needed to talk to Blaik before making a decision. Later that afternoon, in the gym tower office, he informed the colonel of his new job prospect, said that he preferred to stay at West Point and asked for a raise. It was only when Blaik rebuffed the raise request, saying that Vince already was paid the maximum for an assistant, that Lombardi decided to take the Giants job. "Another thousand dollars would have kept me at West Point," he said later. The story that he had joined the Giants broke in the newspapers on Christmas Day. In the *New York Herald Tribune* account, he was praised for his football intellect: "Lombardi now wears spectacles and gives the appearance of a studious professor. He is regarded as one of the smartest theorists in junior coaching." The *Daily News* said that he had "proven himself an outstanding handler and tutor of backs and was hired [to a two-year contract] for this particular talent," replacing Allie Sherman, the backfield coach under Steve Owen.

As it turned out, Jim Lee Howell would rather have retained Sherman. To ensure that the two men would get along, Mara sent Lombardi down to Arkansas to visit Howell during the week between Christmas and New Year's Eve. Lombardi felt out of place walking the winter pastures of Howell's large farm outside Lonoke, a town northeast of Little Rock, but the two men got along, especially after Howell said he would entrust the offense entirely to Lombardi. Howell also got to Lombardi through his stomach by feeding him an Arkansas version of an Izzo family meal, freshly shot wild duck and wild rice. Lombardi, as Howell later described it, "just couldn't believe it, and he kept saying over and over, 'You can't buy anything like this anywhere.' " On his return to the Giants offices at Columbus Circle, Lombardi let out "a huge guffaw" when he recounted his trip to "Lone Okie," as he called it, according to Well Mara. "I remember him laughing and laughing about all the cow shit in Lone Okie, Arkansas."

• •

THE NEW JOB brought the Lombardis back to New Jersey. They moved at the semester break, enrolling Vincent and Susan in a new school in Oradell, ten miles northwest of their former home in Englewood and an easy commute into Manhattan. It was a hurried move, and Marie was not delighted with the new town or her new house, a split-level brick rambler, less impressive than the stately colonial at the academy, but Vince was in no mood to look around. He was preoccupied with the transition to the new job. As confident as he was about coaching, he knew almost nothing about the pro game, and felt that he had much to learn in a short time. At West Point he had become proficient in studying film, and that is what he did now, following a more grueling schedule than ever. He brought home films of every Giants game of the past two years, set up a projector and screen in the den, sent the kids and even Marie down to the basement rec room if they appeared bothersome, lit up a cigarette and went to work, often not finishing until his eyes were sore and his ashtray was littered with packs of butts.

As Lombardi watched the grainy black-and-white film, he charted the movements of all twenty-two players on the field, using separate yellow notepads for each team's offense and defense, then indexing the notes so that he knew where to find a specific type of play. The notepads provided the original text of what later became known as Lombardi's bible, a tome written in the language of X's and O's, the chapters stored in a brown leather satchel that he kept from the winter of 1954 until the day he died. The Giants offense seemed anemic, but how could he revive it? He paid special attention to the games involving the Cleveland Browns, whose coach, Paul Brown, was considered the most thorough and innovative in the league. In Lombardi's bible, the chapters charting the Browns were the book of revelations.

From the films he had studied from January through June, Lombardi reached two conclusions about the offense he would try to develop for the Giants. The first involved the passing game. "The big point I realized was that whatever formation I used, I had to have a flanker back," he said. "You had to have the threat of a pass. Everyone in the league was using flankers." But it was the running game that needed the most work. "From pictures my sense was the passing game was great and the running game was only a half try. Everybody said, 'You can't run much in the pros.' Their defenses were too large and mobile to sustain a running game against them. I reasoned that the people we had on offense were every bit as big and every bit as mobile."

Lombardi took his first close look at the pro athletes that July at the Giants training camp at Willamette College in Salem, Oregon. It was also their first look at him, and it is fair to say that he was more impressed than they were. Here was a pro team that had won only three games the year before, yet Lombardi was awed by their athletic prowess. The gap in talent between

Army and the Giants was far wider than the one between Saints and Army; he had not seen anything like this in all his twenty years in football. At West Point, he and Blaik had operated on the theory that "the bigger the man, the less quickness." But watching pro linemen in drills he was "amazed by the speed, agility and quickness of the big men." The talents of backfield stars Frank Gifford, Kyle Rote and Charlie Conerly impressed him even more: "the fluid motion that Gifford had running. The great hands Rote exhibited ... catching the ball. The anticipation Charlie Conerly had in releasing the ball—anticipating where the defensive man would be." And beyond their athletic grace, Lombardi said later, he was "pleasantly surprised by the mentality of the pros."

The pros, for their part, were more surprised than pleased in their initial impressions of Lombardi. They considered him a college chump. For all his film study, he would not shed his Army playbook. He came in excited about delay plays in which the quarterback sprinted out and came to an abrupt stop, waiting patiently for his receivers to get clear downfield. Maybe that worked at West Point, but the Giants knew it was unsuited for the pros, where the quarterback would never get enough time. He installed another play from Army's split T formation designed to have Conerly, on thirty-three-year-old knees, fake a handoff and a pass and run around end. Conerly had no desire to run and changed the play whenever Lombardi sent it in. For offensive linemen, Lombardi taught rule blocking, another technique used at West Point. Instead of blocking a specific defensive player, each lineman blocked a zone, and if there was no one in that zone he fanned back to another area, following specific rules, hence the name. Army and other colleges were ahead of the pros in using rule blocking. It eventually became the norm in the National Football League, but the Giants had difficulty adjusting. "You had that first July that they didn't believe," Lombardi said later. "When I first explained it they looked at one another—'What's he doing?' "

The zealousness with which he sold his new schemes backfired at first. He appeared defensive about his credentials, and kept repeating that he had worked with the great Colonel Blaik at Army, as if that would impress the pros. Many of the players thought he was "loud and arrogant—a total pain in the ass," as Frank Gifford later described him. Behind his back, they mocked him, calling him the Little General and Little Mussolini. In the dorm rooms they enacted parodies of his coaching persona, his flashing teeth, his oversized feet and long arms, his barking commands, the way he lined up his blackboard chalk like a sixth-grade teacher (hiding his chalk became one of their favorite pranks). They were not afraid to tease him to his face, in milder fashion, dropping down to old-fashioned four-point stances and snarling their faces in pantomime of the old pictures of the Seven Blocks. The most memorable scene at the 1954 training camp came when veteran running back Eddie Price, fed up with the way Lombardi was trying to change his pass-blocking technique, muttered, "I'm getting the hell out of here," and ran off toward the locker room. Lombardi, angry but worried that he had gone too far, ran after him, shouting, "Eddie! Eddie! Come back, Eddie!" Offensive guard Bill Austin was stunned by the scene. "Lombardi chewing on Eddie like that, we just weren't used to that kind of discipline."

Young Vincent, a husky boy of twelve, accompanied his father to camp that year. He cleaned cleats, brought the balls out for practice, carried the water buckets and lived in a dorm room with a few other ball boys. He saw far more of the players than he did of his dad, which was fine with him, considering what it was like when they were around each other. "My father would chew me out in front of everybody. He'd scream that I didn't get the footballs, that I didn't do this or that," Vincent said later. This brought Vincent closer to the players, who empathized with what he was enduring. Although it embarrassed Vincent to see his dad screaming at his heroes, it was a revelation to him when he heard what they were saying about the Old Man. One day, standing on the sidelines next to two players, including one who had played at Army before being expelled in the cheating scandal, Vincent overheard an obscene rant against "that goddamned Lombardi." The second player gulped, realizing that the coach's son was next to them. Then, looking directly at Vincent, the first player said, "Well, the kid's gotta learn sometime that Lombardi's an SOB."

It was with Jim Lee Howell that young Vincent experienced his most anxious moment at training camp in Oregon. One morning he arrived at practice several minutes late, as did a few players. Howell knew that some players had lagged behind, but could not determine which ones, and insisted that Vincent tell him who they were. The team was gathered on the practice field, watching in amazement as Howell demanded that Lombardi's son squeal. Vincent refused, and Howell dismissed him, barking, "Don't come back until you're ready." Vincent left, proud that he did not give in, but fearful of his father's wrath. "I avoided my dad for as long as I could," he said later. His fear was groundless. Squealing had a deeper meaning to his father. It evoked the most unpleasant memory of his career, the West Point academic scandal, which centered on an honor code that required cadets to inform on cadets, a concept that offended Lombardi by running contrary to his sense of loyalty. When he finally caught up with young Vincent the next day, he surprised his son by saying that he was glad Vincent had refused to spill the names to Jim Lee Howell. Then he added, "If you had told, I'd have hit you." Even in praise there was a threat, but this time Vincent found it reassuring.

After his difficult early weeks at training camp, Lombardi began to earn the respect of the pros. He did it through persistence and adjustment. The will to succeed was his dominant characteristic, stronger in the end than his insistence on having things his way. If he had to adjust, he would find the means; it was a talent that he exhibited for the rest of his coaching career, though it often went unrecognized, overshadowed by his public image as the implacable leader who demanded that the world adapt to him. He began roaming the hall of the Willamette dorm at night, visiting with the offensive players. He acknowledged that he had much to learn and sought their advice, help and loyalty. He asked the veterans to work with him rather than second-guess him. "We would listen to him and he would listen to us," said Charlie Conerly. He tried to become one of the guys, not the authoritarian boss but the smarter older brother; they called him Vince or Vinnie, not Coach or Mr. Lombardi. He drank beers with them, laughed loudly at their jokes, told them how much he wanted them to succeed.

Frank Gifford was the key. Lombardi had seen him play in college when Southern Cal had defeated Army at the Polo Grounds in 1951. The field that day had been aswarm with photographers capturing every move of the graceful All-American from the West Coast. But when Gifford returned the next year to play for the Giants, he began two seasons of frustration. He never clicked with Steve Owen, and felt that he was being misused, shuffled from offense to defense. There were few rewards in pro football then. Gifford, one of the highest-paid players in the league, had just received a raise to $10,000 a year. He thought he could get more publicity and money in Hollywood, where he had been taking minor acting parts since his first year at USC. After the 1953 season he considered staying on the coast. He was "not unhappy" that Steve Owen was fired. "I might not have come back had there not been changes," he said later. But could Vince make him happy? From game films Lombardi had seen that Gifford was his ideal offensive threat, someone who could run, pass and catch. "You're my halfback" were the first words he ever said to Gifford after introducing himself. Still, the first weeks were tense. It meant little to Gifford to play halfback in a rinky-dink West Point offense.

Lombardi never lost his manic edge. Jim Lee Howell saw him pacing the dormitory roof before a preseason game, and from then on would shout, "Someone get a roof for Vinnie!" whenever his assistant seemed tense. But Lombardi did get the message the players were sending, and he adjusted and began building a pro-style game that let Conerly be Conerly and Gifford be Gifford, and from then on the players were on his side.

IF NOT THE DREGS of the athletic world, pro football began the 1950s closer to the bottom than the top. College football, major league baseball, horse racing and boxing all drew more ink, more attention on radio (and early television) and, with few exceptions, more fans in the stands. College football had been considered socially superior because of its attachment to academic institutions and its pretense of innocence. The pro gridder was thought to be a mercenary playing for meal money and free beer (Ballantine, sponsor of Giants games on WINS, provided the players with a case of beer every few weeks). It mattered not at all that many college stars were also mercenaries benefiting from lucrative, if illegal, financial arrangements. The amateur in American sports was protected by the prevailing myth that college boys played only for the love of the game and school spirit.

The lowly image of the workaday pro football bruiser had persisted for decades, since Jim Thorpe, the great Olympian and all-around athlete, and six owners gathered at Ralph Hay's Hupmobile auto agency in Canton, Ohio, on August 20, 1920, and conceived the beginnings of what would become the National Football League. But by 1954, as the spirit of the new came to dominate American culture, it seemed possible that pro football might be perceived in a brighter light. With the worship of the modern came a desire for the most technically proficient, the biggest, fastest and sleekest of everything—the professional. The amateur ideal seemed quaint, the concept of the exciting pro was taking hold. There were only a few signs of this transformation at first. One was in Cleveland, where Paul Brown had created the model of the new professional sports team: well organized and sharply outfitted, its players tested for intelligence as well as athleticism and treated more like corporate officers than factory tradesmen. The other was in Los Angeles, land of the new, where the Rams, led into the big time by a young publicist named Pete Rozelle, were the hottest game in town, luring massive crowds to the Coliseum. More than 93,000 fans saw the Rams play the San Francisco 49ers on the second Sunday of the 1954 season, an amazing figure; the other teams in the league that weekend drew between 17,000 and 27,000.

These were still only faint glimmers of what was to come. For the most part, the NFL remained endearingly unsophisticated. When Herb Rich joined the Giants roster during the second week of that 1954 season, after being acquired from the Rams, he was concerned that neither his new team nor his old one would pay him for the first game. So he called deBenneville "Bert" Bell, the NFL commissioner. Bell answered the phone, listened to Rich's concern and resolved it immediately, ordering the Rams to pay the salary. That is how simple life was in the league then—a defensive back picking up the phone and talking directly to the commissioner: no agents, lawyers, unions, league bureaucrats in the way. The NFL was not even based in New York, but housed in a small office in Philadelphia, because that was where Bell lived. He ran the league by letter and telegram, with a handful of aides helping him draft rules, keep track of the weekly transactions and negotiate the early television contracts. Every year Bell presented the same message to the NFL's rookies: Gentlemen, prepare yourselves for later life, because you aren't going to make a living playing football.

For the league to rise in the sports world, it needed not just Cleveland and Los Angeles in the vanguard, but also New York. The spirit of the new was created in the advertising offices of Madison Avenue and preached in national magazines and on television networks—all centered in Manhattan. Most of the admen and broadcast executives lived in the metropolitan area, and if they were to root for a pro team it most likely would be the New York Football Giants. The Maras understood this, and were striving to change the image of the team they had run since Tim Mara bought the club in 1925 with money he had earned as a legal bookie. In the first year of the new look, the results were modestly successful: Jim Lee Howell's inaugural team was superior to Steve Owen's last one, winning seven games and losing five. Attendance at home games at the Polo Grounds in 1954 was uneven but improving as well, twice exceeding 45,000. The most significant transformation was in the coaching staff, which was run on the corporate model. Howell was chairman of the board, but two chief operating officers ran the daily operations: Vince Lombardi the offense and Tom Landry the defense.

There were two schools of thought on Howell's leadership style. The harshest perspective was that he had little clue how to coach but was saved by the two finest assistants who ever worked on the same team at the same time. Howell readily acknowledged the talents of Lombardi and Landry, and joked self-deprecatingly that his main function was to make sure the footballs had air in them. The more complimentary view was that he was an expert at delegating authority. Most sportswriters subscribed to the second view, portraying Howell as a progressive thinker who had adapted to the spirit of the new, which in football terms meant the era of specialized platoons. "Mostly he is the administrator and coordinator, and that apparently is the way to do the job today," Red Smith wrote of Howell. Joe King, in the *New York World-Telegram,* noted, "If the question is offense, Howell says, 'Ask Lombardi about that.' Defense? Tom Landry is the man to see. U.S. Steel does fairly well on that plan, but it is unorthodox in football and therefore suspect by some." To King, Howell's platoon system of coaching was a "logical evolution—the pros have brought football to a peak of specialized skill. On the one squad the offense and defense platoons are considered separate items and play that way."

Lombardi and Landry running the same team—the Giants knew they had an extraordinary brain trust even then. Their coaching skills were undeniable; their personalities and styles as unalike as possible. Thomas Wade Landry was lean and spare, as dry as his mission homeland in the Rio Grande valley of Texas. He could be called a boy wonder of sorts—when the 1954 season began he was entering only his fifth season as a defensive back, and was not yet thirty years old—except that there was nothing boyish about him. From the moment he arrived in New York from the University of Texas, he struck his teammates as mature and rational, always thinking his way around the football field. He already had the respect of the other players when he was made a player-coach, and did not have to raise his voice to get it. Well Mara once said that "you could hear Vince laughing from five blocks away; you couldn't hear Landry from the next chair." But his mild appearance was deceiving. Landry was all science and innovation, daring to change. "He taught you not to be afraid to take chances," said Herb Rich, who played alongside him that first year in the defensive backfield. "The Rams [Rich's former team] loved to embarrass you if you took a chance. Tom would always say, 'Anticipate! Get there ahead of him. Go on the snap of the ball.' "

Landry insisted later that he and Lombardi had a good relationship, but many of the players felt a tension between them. Frank Gifford said there was "a lot of competition between Lombardi and Landry and I don't know if it ever turned into a friendship. That filtered through the team itself. There was tension. We didn't like them [the defense] very much, and they didn't like us much. And didn't really care. We were cliquey." Lombardi, always barking, could be heard at a tense point of a game shouting at the defense: "Get the goddamn ball back for us at least once!" Landry left the obscenity-laced slaps at the offense to his players. Howell felt the competition from both sides: "One day one of them would come in and tell me he hadn't been given enough time and the next day the other would.... They were fussing all the time." At various times during their coexistence, the defense was ahead of the offense, and when that was reported in the press, Lombardi fell into a deep funk. "It kind of dogged Vince that our offense wasn't thought of as good," Landry said decades later. "I remember a lot of times when we'd win ball games, if the offense didn't do well ... he wouldn't talk to Jim Lee Howell or me for two or three days." Landry came to think of Lombardi as a borderline manic-depressive. He gave him the nickname " 'Mr. High-Low'—because when his offense did well he was sky high; but, boy, when they didn't do well, you couldn't speak to him."

They were yin and yang in almost every respect. In film sessions during the week, Landry needed a fraction of the time Lombardi took to analyze the other team. Landry was quicker; Lombardi more thorough. It was Lombardi, borrowing on the tactics he learned from Colonel Blaik, who sold the Giants on the idea of taking pictures of enemy defenses during the game on a quick-developing camera and sending the shots down to the bench for instant analysis. (Wellington Mara, the handyman owner who loved being of use—he would shag punts if no one else was around to do it—often relayed the pictures himself, dropping them from the upper deck in an old sock attached to a string.) Lombardi showed the pictures to the quarterbacks, giving them "a different view and a good idea of how the defense is reacting. Visual education is much better than telling the quarterbacks the defenses." He was also more patient than Landry in the midweek skull sessions. He reverted back to the high school teacher pounding out the chemistry lesson at Saints until the slowest kid understood it. Landry was more the calculus professor addressing graduate students. "Vin was a great teacher," said Well Mara. "He could get on a blackboard and hammer it into the lower portion of the mentality. Landry would not do that. He knew there were only three or four people in the room who knew exactly what he was saying."

There was one essential characteristic that Lombardi and Landry shared: they were driven to win. Coaching together under Howell, they never had a losing season.

WE DO, OR DIE. The old college battle cry called out to Lombardi at the end of his first season with the Giants. On the first day of December 1954, Ed Danowski resigned as Fordham's head coach, closing a difficult nine-year reign with a hapless final season in which the Rams lost all but one game. Even more symptomatic of the school's football decline were the attendance figures. Fordham's four home games at the Polo Grounds were watched by an average of only 11,000 fans; more people attended a single Fordham game against Pitt or St. Mary's during the Seven Blocks of Granite era than the '54 club drew all season. The football program was dipped in red, losing more than $50,000 a year. With Danowski's departure came the brief shining idea of a return to the era when Fordham was a national power. New York newspapers the next day listed possible successors who could restore Fordham to glory, and most of the speculation involved former Blocks: Johnny Druze, end coach at Notre Dame; Leo Paquin, head coach at Xavier Prep in Manhattan; Harry Jacunski (Paquin's replacement on the line), end coach at Yale; and Vince Lombardi, offensive coach of the Giants.

Lombardi was at the top of the list and the candidate who most wanted the job. His last go-around at Fordham had ended inharmoniously, but he had been an assistant then, his ambition a threat to Danowski. Now he saw the opportunity to run his own program, and the prospect enthralled him. For all his gruffness, Lombardi was a football romantic. His athletic ideal was his senior year in college, and for nearly two decades he had been trying to re-create the intoxicating feelings that came over him that long ago autumn: up on the practice field, darkness enveloping Rose Hill, Butch and his mates banging and thudding and collapsing in the mud of a Bloody Wednesday; on the bus, a brilliant October Saturday, rolling down Fordham Road and the Grand Concourse toward the stadium, leading the Rams in joyous song; down on the playing field at the Polo Grounds, exhausted, hurting, Pitt driving toward the goal with the relentless thrusts of Goldberg and LaRue . . . but the Fordham wall still stands. To Lombardi, those sensations were the thrill of life, and even with all the power that Jim Lee Howell had ceded to him, he had not been able to replicate them to his satisfaction. He had not yet been fully indoctrinated in the cult of the modern; his vision was more nostalgic, linking the present with the past.

But the past was going, going, gone. Two weeks after Danowski's resignation, Lombardi negotiated a tentative salary agreement with Jack Coffey, the director of athletics. All that was needed to make his return official was a decision by the Jesuit administration on the larger question of whether Fordham would continue big-time college football. The answer came on December 15, in a letter from Fordham's president, the Reverend Laurence J. McGinley. "Fordham has enjoyed football" since 1883, McGinley wrote, but "the unfortunate fact remains that we have run out of money for football and must balance our books. And so, at long last, our head must rule our heart." Not even the prospect of Lombardi coaching the Rams could alter that harsh reality. Faced with competition from professional football and television and travel, college football programs were folding fast in the postwar era. Small private schools seemed especially vulnerable. The once-fierce Gaels of St. Mary's were no more. Extinct also were the programs at Duquesne, Georgetown, Santa Clara, St. Bonaventure, Niagara and New York University. Only Columbia remained among the teams that once made New York City a college football town. "From Rose Hill to Oblivion," read the headline of Arthur Daley's column in the *New York Times,* a phrase that mockingly evoked the old chant of optimism—"From Rose Hill to the Rose Bowl." Grantland Rice had vanished, and Fordham football, too, leaving behind only the lantern of mythology that forever lit the path back to Sleepy Jim Crowley, the Four Horsemen, Vince Lombardi and the Seven Blocks of Granite.

One person shared Lombardi's despair over the death of Fordham football. Tim Cohane had seen it as his life's mission to carry the torch for the college game, especially as it was played at his alma mater. He was also Lombardi's leading advocate, working furtively among influential alumni to strike the deal that would have had Vince succeed Danowski. Cohane was frustrated by the Jesuits and lamented that they seemed determined to transform Fordham into "a medieval study hall." But from his perch as sports editor at *Look* magazine, he saw a larger cultural trend that troubled him more. The cult of the modern was changing everything in his world, and he resented it. The money and power were shifting to television; the glamour of sportswriting was fading along with the clubby atmosphere that he cherished, the sense that they were all pals, the writers, the players, the coaches, all in it together and protecting one another. He knew which coaches were drunks and never wrote about their off-field antics, but that ancient unwritten code was being thrown aside by younger journalists. Not that he was utterly naive about the darker side of humanity—in the pages of *Look* he published stories about fixers and cheaters—but like his late idol Grantland Rice and his friend Vince Lombardi, he nonetheless clung to a romantic vision of the sporting ideal.

Lombardi and Cohane turned to each other for connections to that past. When they were together, they chatted in Latin, their shared language of Catholic school training, and belted out refrains of the Fordham Ram fight song. Although Lombardi could no longer attend Colonel Blaik's summer camp at Bull Pond, Cohane called him from the Mother Lodge to announce the latest selections for the Bull Pond All-American team, certain that the fictitious gridders would provoke "bellowing, infectious laughter" from Vince. He took to calling Vince "Conquering Longbeard," his stretched Latin translation of the words "Vincent Lombardi," and with Fordham no longer a possibility, he pushed Lombardi for head coaching jobs elsewhere. A few weeks after Fordham dropped football, Cohane was talking to the superintendent of the new Air Force Academy in Colorado Springs, who happened to be looking for a football coach. Cohane planted the seed of Lombardi, and it almost took root. The *Newark Star-Ledger,* whose sports editor then was Stanley Woodward, an old member of the tribe, ran a story saying that Lombardi would be the first head coach at Air Force. But at the last minute a veteran professional coach, Lawrence "Buck" Shaw, changed his mind and took the academy job.

It was with a growing sense of fatalism that Lombardi called Red Blaik a week later and inquired about the possibility of returning to West Point. If he could not reach his highest goals, he thought he might as well feel comfortable working at a lower level. Blaik greeted Lombardi's request with equal measures of surprise and delight. He had two openings—and one larger psychological hole—on his staff. He thought of Lombardi as his perfect alter ego, smart, committed, emotional, full of life, and he missed him. "Since you left we don't have any fun around here," the colonel confessed during a lunch at the officer's club. They shook hands on an informal agreement without discussing salary. Later that day Blaik called Wellington Mara to relate his discussion with Lombardi. Mara reacted with alarm. The Howell-Lombardi-Landry triumvirate seemed to be working perfectly. It was the new deal that would restore the Giants to the championship level. Over the weekend Well and his brother, Jack, talked with Lombardi three times, finally driving out to Oradell to make their case to Vince and Marie, saying that they intended for him to be head coach in New York someday. They had no intentions of dumping Howell that year, but they could reward Vince's patience with a significant raise.

Marie urged him to stay with the Giants. The raise boosted Vince's spirits, but he said he felt obliged to keep his agreement with the colonel. What was the right thing to do? That Monday he drove back to West Point to talk to Blaik again. The colonel realized from Lombardi's unanimated demeanor that something was wrong. "I have never gone back on my word in my life, and I don't intend to now," Lombardi began, fibbing in both respects. He had gone back on his word before and he hoped to now, though honorably, if Blaik would let him. After hearing the details of the offer from the Maras, and of Marie's excitement about it, Blaik quickly resolved the dilemma. Go back to the Giants, he said. Forget this ever happened.

One year later, at the end of the 1955 season, a season in which the Giants improved on the field but not in the standings, finishing 6–5–1, Lombardi was still looking around for a team of his own. Along with Fordham and Air Force, he had lost out at Penn and Washington, and his inability to land a head coaching job had thrown him into another depression. Mr. High-Low was down at the lowest of the low, moping around the Giants offices at 8 Columbus Circle in a self-absorbed funk. "I'll never get to be a head coach," he complained to Wellington Mara. "Here I am, an Italian, forty-two years old, and nobody wants me. Nobody will take me." Mara "didn't really buy" Vince's argument that prejudice against his Italian heritage was holding him back, but "didn't argue with him," he said later. During the Christmas break that year, he sent Lombardi to California to scout the Rose Bowl. Cohane was also in Pasadena, and after the game on January 1, 1956, the two old Rams went to dinner, driving out to the Tail of the Cock restaurant off Coldwater Canyon in the San Fernando Valley. Along the way, they reminisced back two decades to the season of 1936, remembering how Fordham almost made it to the Rose Bowl that year of the Seven Blocks. Eventually the conversation came around to Lombardi's coaching frustrations. "I'm wondering whether the right head-coaching job ever will open up for me," Lombardi said. "I know I can coach, but the right people never seem to know it."

"You'll get your chance," Cohane responded.

Lombardi hoped that Cohane was right, but he felt the faint chill of oblivion. "I'm not getting any younger," he said.

10

This Pride
of Giants

VINCE LOMBARDI, in the summer of 1956, was straddling the old and the new. He turned forty-three that June, no longer a young coach, but not wielding enough power for players to call him the Old Man. He had the same old job, but worked in a new place, not the ancient Polo Grounds, his traditional arena, where he had played and coached since his Fordham days, but a shinier venue that the Maras had found for their newly refurbished New York Football Giants across the Harlem River in the Bronx—Yankee Stadium, home of the pinstriped baseball Yankees of Casey Stengel, Mickey Mantle, Yogi Berra and Whitey Ford. No name in sports was as magical as the Yankees then. The Yankees worked and traveled first-class: they wore suits and ties, their dressing room was clean, modern and carpeted, they were not just jocks but celebrities, and they won and won and maddingly won. Lombardi had grown up a Brooklyn Dodgers fan. He hated the Yankees—and wanted nothing more than to be like them. He and his family also found a new home that summer, moving into a comfortable two-story white colonial on Lockwood Place in the borough of Fair Haven, nestled on the Navesink River between Red Bank and the Atlantic shore, forty miles south and around the bend from the suburban sprawl of North Jersey. It was a step up socially, the latest safe haven for commuters, and yet old and familiar to Marie. Fair Haven was her childhood home.

Marie had barely moved in when her husband drove away again, traveling north with young Vincent for preseason training camp, which began in mid-July at St. Michael's College in Winooski, Vermont, not far from Lake Champlain. Jim Lee Howell's corporate-style staff was entering its third season, and the players and coaches were exuding a newfound confidence. In the evolution of many great teams there comes a tipping point when success suddenly seems expected. The Giants had reached that point. Operating behind an experienced offensive line, the backfield was gifted and deep, with veteran Charlie Conerly and Don Heinrich at quarterback; Frank Gifford and the baby bulls, Alex Webster and Mel Triplett, at running back; and Kyle Rote shifted to end with Bob Schnelker and Ken MacAfee. Landry's defense was fortified with two promising rookies, Robert E. Lee "Sam" Huff from West Virginia and Jim Katcavage from Dayton, along with two veterans, Andy Robustelli from the Rams and tackle Dick "Little Mo" Modzelewski from the Steelers (writing in the *New York Times*, Gay Talese described the not-so-little Little Mo as "260 pounds of tough tenderloin with shoulders so broad that he often has to pass through doors sideways").

Huff, a two-way lineman who was the team's third-round draft choice, felt homesick in Vermont, was upset that Jim Lee Howell never seemed to stop picking on him, and felt undersized against behemoths like the Roosevelts of the line—offensive tackle Rosey Brown and defensive tackle Rosey Grier. He had a sore knee and missed the simpler life in rural West Virginia: the coal fields that his father once mined, the little grocery in Farmington where the checkout girl was Mary Fletcher Huff, his childhood sweetheart and bride since they were seventeen. One morning as Huff and another uneasy rookie, kicker Don Chandler, were resting on the beds in their dorm room listening to a country western station, Huff said that if a homesick song called "Detroit City" came on they should just pack up and leave training camp. "Damn if it didn't come on the radio right after I said it," Huff recalled. "And I said, 'Let's go.' Chandler was quiet and lonesome and ready to go with me."

The two rookies went downstairs to turn in their playbooks and found Lombardi taking a catnap in his first-floor room. "We walk in and say, 'Coach,' and he jumps out of bed and starts screaming, 'What the hell do you want!' " Huff said later. "Jesus. We held out our playbooks. We're quitting. He goes off on us. He says, 'We've got two weeks invested in you guys. You may not make this ball club, but you're sure as hell not quitting on me!' " While Lombardi was yelling at Huff, Chandler slipped out of the room and went back upstairs to pack. After listening to Lombardi and another assistant coach, Ed Kolman, Huff decided not to quit, but then Chandler changed his mind again and they made their escape in the borrowed station wagon of another rookie from Ohio. They were sitting in the airport lounge an hour later when Lombardi drove up like a truant officer, announced that he would not allow them to leave and escorted them back to training camp.

Huff and Chandler both eventually made the team and played in the NFL for more than a decade each. Huff was moved to middle linebacker, the key position in Tom Landry's mobile 4–3 defense, where he emerged as a star, the prototypical linebacker of his era, slashing violently from sideline to sideline. From then on, for the rest of his long career, even when he and

Lombardi were on opposing teams scrapping for championships, he considered himself a Lombardi man. So did Chandler, who ended up in Green Bay nearly a decade later, where his strong foot won one of the most important games of Lombardi's career.

For the most part it was the sophistication of his playbook, not the mental fragility of his players, that preoccupied Lombardi that summer. His satchel overflowed with new configurations of X's and O's, more plays to transpose from the page to the playing field, some exotic, others basic. There was the bedazzling belly 26 reverse pass that he had brought in for his triple-threat left halfback: the quarterback fakes a handoff to Triplett, the fullback, then to Webster, the right half, and finally gives the ball to Gifford, who at the snap moves left, then reverses field and glides right behind a pulling guard, looking to pass but with the option to run.

It was a play that could be used only a few times a year, but its success was dependent upon a simple concept that was now the foundation of Lombardi's offensive philosophy: freedom within structure. Get the running backs in positions where they could react to the defense with several options, run or pass, cut inside or outside. After watching Gifford dip to the outside and into the clear when a defensive end closed the off-tackle hole where one play was designed to go, Lombardi began to teach his running plays differently. "That was the first time that I realized that in the pro league it is to your advantage to run to daylight and not a specific hole," he explained later. "And that's the way I began coaching it."

Run to daylight—later the phrase would become the trademark of Lombardi's offense in Green Bay, but it was conceived in 1956 on the practice field in Vermont. And so was the seminal play of his pro offense, the power sweep. Before it became famous as the Packer sweep, it was the Giants sweep, and apparently before that it was the Rams sweep. Lombardi first saw the play while watching films of Los Angeles in 1955. He analyzed the movements of every offensive player, stuffed his research into his playbook satchel and showed it to the Giants that August. From the first time he taught it, Lombardi was in his element. This play defined him. It was at once old and new. It was seemingly simple and yet offered infinite complexity, demanding swift decisions by all eleven offensive players. It was not size that mattered— Bill Austin, the left guard, prayed for the sweep call because he weighed only 218 pounds and "wasn't big enough to go straight ahead" against the league's bigger tackles. Nor was it speed alone—if Gifford or Webster sprinted ahead of the blockers, the play was lost. The sweep required precision, teamwork and brains. Lombardi loved it. Once, at a football seminar, he talked about it nonstop for eight hours.

SPECIAL BULLETIN NO. 12A arrived at Giants camp that August from NFL headquarters at 1518 Walnut Street in Philadelphia. It was written by Bert

Bell, the league commissioner, and was intended for the Mara family and head coach Jim Lee Howell.

Wellington Mara had been sending notes to the commissioner every week. In his "Dear Bert" correspondence with Bell, a former colleague who had once owned the Philadelphia Eagles, Mara had passed along "constructive criticism for the good of our league" about bad officiating and cheap hits by opposing players. Bell usually took the notes in good humor, but this year he wanted to ensure that Mara's complaints stayed within the family. "You and I know that all the men connected with football are aggressive or they would not be in the game," Bell wrote. "And I can readily understand how, after losing a tough one, it is very easy for anyone to give off steam by criticizing the officials, the roughness of the other team, an individual player, the management, etc. . . . You will undoubtedly agree that this is not the way to build good public relations, as it certainly does not do anyone any good, and might do some person, a team, an official, a player, or the league itself, a great deal of harm." Bell went on to plead with the owner not to show game films to the press with the intention of pointing out mistakes by officials, and warned the coach that "abusive and/or foul language" on the field would result in penalties.

The bulletin had an unusual tone of urgency, and near the end Bell revealed why: "This year the Columbia Broadcasting System (CBS) and the local sponsors will present to the public all our games on television, giving us our greatest opportunity to sell the National Football League and professional football. Everyone must do all in his power to present to the public the greatest games in football combined with the finest sportsmanship." Bell anticipated that his league was on the cusp of something new, and he was nervous about the prospect.

It had been seventeen years since New York City's W2XBS, the NBC station, hauled two iconoscope cameras out to Randalls Island and undertook the first ever telecast of a football game. The event was mundane, though it had a synchronistic connection to Lombardi. It was a nonconference college match between Fordham, still coached by Jim Crowley and still a national power, and Waynesburg College of Pennsylvania, played in front of a small crowd at Triborough Stadium. The images from the two cameras, stationed on flatbed carts at the fifteen-yard lines, were sent by RCA, which owned NBC, to a nearby relay station and then by cable to a transmitter on the roof of the Empire State Building. There were perhaps a thousand television sets within broadcast range in metropolitan New York; TVs were rare and dearly expensive before the war (Piser's Furniture in the Bronx, in the vanguard of television retailers, offered a Clifton model for $600). It is doubtful that many viewers were tuned to the game anyway—the telecast was largely unwatchable because of regular patches of interference marring the already grainy black-and-white reception. One month later, at Ebbets

Field in Brooklyn, the first professional game was televised, another forgettable contest involving the mediocre Brooklyn Dodgers and the Philadelphia Eagles.

Another twelve years passed before the first national broadcast of an NFL game: the 1951 championship between Los Angeles and Cleveland, televised by the Dumont Television Network. Two years later, for the 1953 season, Dumont experimented with the first regular national broadcasts of NFL games, launching the *Saturday Night Game of the Week*. The broadcasts were sponsored by Westinghouse, which had tried the three other networks before settling on Dumont. CBS executives were approached first, but would not interfere with the Jackie Gleason show and instead offered to broadcast Monday night games if Westinghouse would move its *Studio One* live dramas to another night during the football season. No deal. NBC had a conflict with Sid Caesar's popular comedy show, and ABC was also unwilling to rearrange its programming. The play-by-play man for the 1953 Saturday night national games was Ray Scott, a former adman and pioneer local TV sportscaster from the Dumont-owned station in Pittsburgh. With his nasally resonant voice, Scott described a football game in spare but authoritative style, imbuing every run and pass completion with grave importance. He did this not by shouting or using dramatic voice modulation, but simply with earnest articulation. He loved the narrative of NFL football and was a believer in its future. By 1956, after Dumont folded, CBS and NBC negotiated deals with Bell to televise the regular season (CBS) and championship (NBC), bringing the sport into more living rooms than ever, and prompting the commissioner to send out his good-behavior bulletin. The nation's leading networks had their cameras in the stadium just in time for the rise of the New York Football Giants.

It was also in 1956 that *Sports Illustrated,* the national sports magazine, began publishing weekly reports on pro football written by Hamilton Prieleaux Bee Maule, whose byline was the more appropriate Tex Maule. As a former public relations man for the Rams and defunct Dallas Texans, Maule had had a career that paralleled pro football's rise, and he had become the game's resident expert. His column, "The Pros," reflected a transformation in sports journalism in the postwar era. Unlike the old scribes of the Grantland Rice mold, who offered impressionistic portraits of the rite of football, using romantic poetry as a favored device, writers at *Sports Illustrated* and other magazines were now taking readers deeper inside the game, describing the preparation and play in documentary style, placing less emphasis on outcome than on process. Among the masters of this new art was W. C. Heinz, a New York magazine writer who got his start when Damon Runyon, dying of throat cancer and unable to talk, was asked in 1946 by an editor for Hearst magazines to name the best young writer in the city, and scrawled "W. C. Heinz can write" on a cocktail napkin, underlining the name three times. Later, Heinz would write a memoir in the new style detailing a week in the workday life of Vince Lombardi. During 1956 he was writing a novel of natural realism about boxing entitled *The Professional*. What Heinz undertook in long form, Tex Maule, with help from his editors in New York, attempted in more modest fashion every week. His accounts were essentially positive, but in a modern way, glorifying the pros by documenting how mentally challenging the NFL had become.

As the Giants started winning in 1956, "The Pros" focused on the New York team. By the end of November the Giants were in first place with a 6–2–1 record, and *Sports Illustrated*, for its December 3 cover, ran a compelling photo of quarterback Chuck Conerly, chin strap tightened, a single face bar crossing his nose, his eyes intense and penetrating, reading a defense at the line of scrimmage. "Old Pros Don't Make Mistakes" declared the headline. At Yankee Stadium the previous Sunday, when the Giants had played the Chicago Bears, Maule had positioned himself on the bench near Conerly and watched the game unfold from there. "The noise of conflict could be heard clearly from where Conerly sat," he wrote. "This thunder in the line starts with the muffled slap of the football against the palm of the quarterback and, as much as anything, it is the difference between college and pro football. It comes from the solid thump of well-armored men in violent contact, and it is augmented by their grunts and groans and curses. It is one of the things a rookie back finds unsettling when he plays his first game of professional football."

Lombardi used his two quarterbacks as parts of the same machine that year. Heinrich, the second-stringer from the University of Washington, lean and sharp, started each game, probing the defense, testing out runs and passes, allowing Conerly to watch from the sideline until the situation required him. Heinrich was not overjoyed with his setup mission—"I'd pull him out and he'd be yelling 'You guinea sonofabitch,'" Lombardi later recalled—but he nonetheless performed his job well, giving Lombardi the information he could "spoonfeed to Charlie." Against the Bears, Maule wrote, "Conerly watched quietly" for three quarters, "hunched deep in the heavy sideline cape against the gray cold of the afternoon" as the Giants methodically rolled to a 17 to 3 lead. Lombardi inserted Conerly at the start of the fourth quarter, confident that he would not make crucial mistakes. "Be cautious out there," Lombardi said as Conerly trotted onto the field.

Old pros might not make mistakes, but relatively new pro coaches do. Conerly killed as much of the clock as possible in careful drives, but the Bears came back on two sensational touchdown catches by the winged Harlon Hill, and the game ended in a tie, 17 to 17. It was a lesson that Lombardi filed away for the rest of his career: Never try to sit on the ball for an entire quarter, needlessly stifling an offense. "From then on," Lombardi said later, "we played every game like the score was nothing to nothing."

The Giants offense scored 264 points in 1956, the most in the East, and Lombardi received more notice in the press. His image then was not of a ranting tyrant but a sporting intellectual, the bespectacled, chart-toting teacher of a thinking man's game. The *Daily News* ran a Sunday photo spread with a one-word headline—"THINK!" The top picture showed Lombardi from the back, gazing onto the field in trench coat and hat, his hands clasped behind him, clutching the plays "he'll call when opponents come up with anticipated defensive alignments." Next came a sideline shot of Lombardi huddling with Landry and Howell, the brain trust, who, it was said, looked "more like detectives than they do the traditional apoplectic, cigar-chewing coaches of old." Closer to home, the *Long Branch Daily Record* in New Jersey ran a feature describing Lombardi as "a genial, soft-spoken individual" who, as the headline said, "Cites Value of Brains for Pro Grid Success." The game had become so specialized, he told the reporter, that the pros needed to have brainpower to succeed and "the old type tobacco chewing burly ball players often referred to as tramp players are through."

This was indisputably true; the league was more specialized and the players more sophisticated. But Lombardi was not simply making a cultural observation, he was also filling a psychological need, still seeking absolution for his decision to dedicate his life to a game rather than to the priesthood, law or business. When he moved to the professional football ranks, it was more difficult for him to portray himself as a teacher who molded the values of young men, so he noted that he and the players were professionals in every respect: he and Frank Gifford worked in the insurance business during the off-season. Kyle Rote hosted a television show in New York and owned a kitchen cabinet franchise in Texas. Herb Rich was a lawyer with a degree from Vanderbilt. Landry and backs Jim Patton and Gene Filipski were engineers. Andy Robustelli owned a sporting goods store in Connecticut.

Lombardi did not have to wait long to seek redemption for the professional mistake he had made in the Chicago game. The Giants and Bears were to meet again at Yankee Stadium on December 30, this time playing for the 1956 NFL championship. When the Bears squad flew east on a chartered United DC-6 on the Friday before the game, they boasted the better record (9–2–1 to the Giants' 8–3–1), the best running attack in the league, led by the swift and powerful Rick Casares, and were established by oddsmakers as three-point favorites. But Lombardi was confident that the Giants would win. "I smell something," he said the week before the game. He sensed that his team had found what he was looking for, his holy grail—a perfect balance between new and old; the sophistication of a modern offense combined with old-fashioned team spirit and camaraderie.

The Giants not only played well together, they liked one another. Many of them lived in the Concourse Plaza apartment hotel near the stadium in the Bronx. Gifford, Conerly, Rote and Webster bonded even more with

Lombardi, driving south to Fair Haven frequently for a pasta dinner and a few hours of chalk talk and film study in the coach's den. Alex "Red" Webster, the six-foot-three, 225-pound bruiser from North Carolina State who had joined the team the year before after playing two seasons in Canada, had been a tough sell at first. A self-described "lazy" player, he initially bucked at Lombardi's insistent drilling, but eventually realized that it was making him a better running back. As the results of that forced labor became clear in 1956, his relationship with Lombardi improved. It was difficult for him to show affection for the coach, but he did it indirectly by playing harder and developing a special affinity for Lombardi's son. ("Alex Webster was my favorite," young Vincent said later. "He always had a kind word for me.") In any case, the closeness of the players had the effect Lombardi desired, what Webster called "a sensational feeling of unselfishness" on the field.

New York against Chicago usually offered something special. This was the fifth time they had played for the NFL title, going back to the inaugural championship match in 1933 involving teams from the Eastern and Western Conferences, a game the Bears won on what was called "the Stinky Special"—a fake line plunge and jump pass from the great Bronko Nagurski for the decisive score. They met again in 1934 in the renowned Sneakers Game in which the Giants outmaneuvered the slip-sliding Bears by donning basketball shoes. The Bears won the title games in 1941 and again in 1946, a postwar debacle in which New York gamblers attempted to fix the game by influencing the Giants fullback and quarterback. Now, ten years later, the two teams were competing for the title again. The Bears had practiced all through the Christmas holiday, while the Giants had taken five days off and seemed remarkably relaxed, an easygoing atmosphere encouraged by Jim Lee Howell, whose wife had given birth to a son two days before the game. Howell was passing out cigars in the locker room on the morning of the game, but he and Lombardi became concerned that perhaps there was "too much levity" among the troops. Rather than sitting alone at their lockers, silently steeling themselves for battle, the players were "laughing and joking" and "acting like a bunch of heroes already installed."

There was one hero among them already. Andy Robustelli, anchor of the defensive front four and part-time sporting goods man, had taken it upon himself to bring forty-eight pairs of basketball shoes down from Connecticut for the team to wear in case of icy conditions. The weather that Sunday was worse than predicted. It had sleeted all night, and the temperature plummeted to 13 degrees. The mimeograph machine in the press box froze. Fans warmed themselves by smuggling in pints of liquor; in the right-field stands they huddled around a raging trash fire. Red Smith set the wintry scene of 56,836 New Yorkers heading to their seats before kickoff. "They came trooping and whooping into Yankee Stadium in parkas and woolies and ski togs and furs with mufflers snugged about the ears, and everybody was ridiculing himself. 'Hi,' a guy would shout, meeting an acquaintance, 'how about this? Am I an idiot or what?' " There was "a light dusting of snow" on the sidelines, Smith reported, and the playing surface was "virtually clear but hard as a tackle's skull." He spotted Jim Lee Howell on the field ninety minutes before game time, testing the turf with two of his halfbacks, Ed Hughes in cleats and Gene Filipski in sneakers. "The cleats didn't hold," Smith noted, "so the Giants showed up for the kickoff shod like roundball players." The Bears came out in an assortment of cleats, none of which had the traction of Robustelli's footwear.

The one-sided nature of the game was established immediately by Filipski, the sneakers tester, a speedy back who had played for Lombardi at Army before being expelled in the 1951 cribbing scandal and finishing his college career at Villanova. Filipski took the opening kickoff and bolted between the skittering Bears on a fifty-three-yard return that set up the first touchdown two minutes later. Lombardi thought that single play by his fallen cadet proved that the Giants would win. "We were on our way," he said after the game. "That good criss-cross blocking for the runner, who went straight up the field, showed the team was out for a 33-man effort." Tex Maule described the rout that followed by drawing on his favorite theme of modern professionals at work. "For more than two hours of this gelid December afternoon the New York Giants played football with the savage precision of true professionals. Chuck Conerly, the old pro (*SI,* Dec. 3) who directs the Giants offense, loosed his aerial salvos with meticulous aim; the thunderous Giant runners moved with sure-footed power over this slippery field. The Giant lines—both offensive and defensive—administered a thorough cutting to the opposing Bear units, and the Giant secondary defense, which had given away two late and tying touchdowns in a regular season game between these two same teams, leaked not at all with the world championship in the balance. Against a team so well equipped and so well prepared, the Bears never really had a chance."

The final score was 47 to 7. Jim Lee Howell was the toast of the town after the game, but in large measure the championship win could be attributed to the coaching skills and persuasive powers of Vince Lombardi. The Giants offense was never better than on that ice-slicked afternoon. The quarterbacks Heinrich (who played the first quarter) and Conerly (on the field for the final three, wearing golf gloves at first) effectively changed plays automatically at the line of scrimmage, using Lombardi's system of reading and adjusting. Webster, with the new work ethic Lombardi instilled in him, banged in for two touchdowns. Gifford ran for daylight all afternoon and scored on a fourteen-yard pass from Conerly. Rote and Triplett also scored, demonstrating the balance of Lombardi's attack. And Sam Huff, the rookie middle linebacker whom Lombardi had refused to let quit back at training camp, "dogged Casares all afternoon," as Tex Maule reported, "keying on the Bear fullback with each play." Maule was right: these Giants were professionals.

The ascent of the modern—or what seemed modern in 1956—was evident in other ways that week. The *Chicago Tribune* sports section, unable to brag about the game itself, ran a front-page box detailing the speed with which it got action shots taken by veteran *Tribune* photographer Ray Gora into the paper overnight. "After shooting the game in Yankee Stadium, Gora took off from LaGuardia airport in New York at 5:25 p.m. (Chicago time) and arrived at Midway airport here at 8:35 p.m.," the *Tribune* reported. "A chartered helicopter, piloted by George Snyder, met Gora at Midway and took just five minutes to fly the films to Navy pier, from where they were rushed by car to the *Tribune* photo room." On the financial side, the game also set modern records, with numbers that appear exceptionally modest in retrospect but were substantial at the time. The total gate receipts were $517,385, with $205,000 of that coming from radio and television rights, and the Giant players took home unparalleled playoff shares of $3,779.19. A reporter suggested after the game that the Giants won because they were hungrier for that playoff money, but Jim Lee Howell disagreed. "It wasn't the money," he said. "It was their pride."

Money was just then emerging as a communal concern among the players. That very weekend player representatives from ten of the twelve NFL squads met with lawyer Creighton Miller in a suite at the Waldorf-Astoria and voted to form the National Football League Players Association. Kyle Rote represented New York, joined by Billy Howton of Green Bay, Norm Van Brocklin of Los Angeles, Y. A. Tittle of San Francisco, Adrian Burk of Philadelphia, Norb Hecker of Washington, Bill Pellington of Baltimore, Don Colo of Cleveland, Jack Jennings of the Chicago Cardinals and Joe Schmidt of Detroit. Miller, their counsel, a Notre Dame grad and former assistant coach in Cleveland, challenged the owners to accept the players organization as a logical step in the spirit of the professional. "The players obviously want a continuous improvement in their economic condition with some control over their own destiny," Miller said. "The football man, when dissatisfied, thinks not of revolt but of negotiation. It is hoped that the modern club executive, faced with player grievances, will think not of the divine right of management but of making feasible adjustments."

Van Brocklin, the veteran quarterback, took detailed notes during the Waldorf meetings and drafted a memo for his fellow Rams. The players, he reported, had agreed on three areas of primary concern: training camp expenses, a pension plan and compensation for injured players. It became apparent during the sessions that there were wide disparities in how players were treated from team to team. The Eagles were paid only five dollars a week during training camp. In Detroit, some players were paid for exhibition games, but not all of them were, which Schmidt said "causes dissension on the club." The Giants, according to Rote, received ten dollars a week in training camp, wanted severance pay for veterans cut during the final days of preseason and were "100 percent for the association." Redskins had laundry and cleaning paid during training camp, but those expenses were deducted from the salaries of players who made the club. Green Bay players had no complaints about preseason pay, but were pushing for a pension plan. The 49ers, according to Tittle, were nervous about asking the owners for more money, but felt strongly that they needed a clause assuring that injured players would be compensated. Colo said that Paul Brown in Cleveland was against the players association but felt that one was inevitable.

The prevailing attitude of the player representatives was one of mild consternation, as Van Brocklin's memo described it, not rebellion. They were not eager for Creighton Miller to turn them into a labor union. They were not seeking to negotiate with the owners as adversaries, but rather thought they "should get their confidence and friendship before taking further action." They were still open to the courtesies of Bert Bell, the commissioner, who told them that there was no need for an association, that he was for the players, and that his door was always open. If the meeting at the Waldorf forever rearranged the relationship between workers and owners in professional football, the ten men at that historic first meeting did not fully realize it, for as they were moving inevitably toward the new, their thinking was still shaped by the old.

ALL SMILES when the Lombardi family posed for the photographer from the *Long Branch Daily Record* that winter: Vince seated in his favorite Danish modern chair in the wall-to-wall carpeted living room, sharp in pressed gray slacks, blue sport coat and striped tie, wife Marie in sweater and skirt, perched on the chair's left arm, daughter Susan, nine years old, same pose on the right, son Vincent, fourteen, sentinel in back near the floor lamp, a strapping young man with the no-nonsense Lombardi jaw, and Wrinkles (known as little Ricky), the family dachshund, a brown sausage yapper at his master's feet. It seemed like the archetypal portrait of an American family circa 1956. Marie the housewife, driving her husband to the station in Red Bank every morning where he caught the 7:19 into the city, Vince playing gin in the club car on the ride north, reaching his office at ten minutes before nine, getting back to Fair Haven for supper Monday and Tuesday, but staying late at the office Wednesday through Friday as the workload piled up. Out of town all weekend half the time during the season. Selling insurance for the Equitable Insurance Company during the off-season; playing golf at Beacon Hill Country Club with his pals Johnny Ryan and Harold Kerr. The breadwinner doing what he thought he was meant to do, making a living, preoccupied with his job, the thoroughly professional man.

Marie had been married to Vince for sixteen years, and they had found an uneasy balance. They still argued frequently, most often when Vince put her down for something she said. "Shut up, Marie" and "That was a dumb thing to say, Marie" were common refrains. But she often stood up to him, giving as well as taking. She had long since accepted the fact that her husband was an obsessed football coach, and every year adapted herself more to his world. She tried never to miss a home game. Sometimes on the way up to New York she dropped Susan in Englewood at Matty and Harry's (Nanna and Poppop to the grandchildren), but more often she took her daughter with her to Yankee Stadium. This was not an occasion for mother-daughter bonding, however. As soon as she and Susan reached the stadium, she hired an attendant inside the ladies' room to babysit. Women entering the washroom would hand the attendant a tip and were given a towel; Susan sat on the counter and handed out the towels. For five years she went to Giants games and might never have seen a play, might never have known what action caused the roars she heard when the ladies' room door opened. She rarely left the washroom counter, not even for a hot dog and Coke—the attendant went out and bought it for her. She had little idea what her father did.

Susan said later that she enjoyed her Sunday afternoons inside the ladies' room at Yankee Stadium. It was in her nature to find entertainment in small things, which might have been a blessing considering her life situation. When her mother did show an interest in her, it was often to express concern about her appearance to the outside world: how she talked, how her hair looked, how much she weighed. For solace she carried around a security blanket, which she called her "ray-ray." She hated school from the start, struggled to learn to read and twice was held back in elementary school, repeating the first and fourth grades. At her first parochial school in Oradell, the nuns seated the smart students in front and the slow ones in back; Susan was pushed to the farthest row and largely ignored. At Fair Haven she took a battery of intelligence tests and was diagnosed with a learning disability.

In those few moments when Lombardi was there and not preoccupied with football films, he devoted himself to her. "Give Daddy a kiss," he would say, and make her rub her cheek against his beard to see if he needed a shave. He tried to find ways to teach Susan to read and count. "Being a schoolteacher himself, he tried to make me smarter," she later explained. "I'm not sure he didn't feel it was his fault sometimes that I was not that sharp. Maybe he felt he did something wrong, I don't know, but he was always trying to educate me." When they were riding in the car together, he pointed out road signs and asked her to read them along with him. He was always interested in making a competitive game out of life, and competed with her to find letters in billboards as a way to teach her the alphabet. At night he brushed her hair, counting aloud the strokes to one hundred and having her count along. He told her he loved her long hair. Marie was less fond of it, preferring Susan in short pigtails. Vin and Marie could argue about anything, and they bickered over Susan's hair; Marie cut it short once and when Vince came home and saw it "he hit the ceiling."

The tension in the family was felt most keenly by young Vincent, who had become accustomed to a house in which his father was rarely present. There are family pictures of Lombardi holding his toddler son proudly on his knee, handing him a football, but that image was not stored in Vincent's early memory bank. He went through childhood feeling distanced from his father. His dad had all the time in the world for players, but less for him— rarely read to him or played catch with him, never went through the daily rituals that other fathers performed with their sons. "We were not buddies," Vincent said decades later, his tone more matter-of-fact than resentful. Though more was expected of Vincent than of Susan, Lombardi expressed this mostly in a negative sense; Vincent did not feel pressure to excel, to "accomplish something that he didn't do," so much as pressure not to fail—not to misbehave in school, not to fumble on the football field, not to bring home a bad grade, all of which he did in the normal course of youth.

Vincent had conflicting feelings about his father's long work hours. His friends were envious of him for having a dad who worked for the Giants. Vincent would rather have had a father who was around every day. Yet he could not help feeling uncomfortable when his dad was home: "You knew he was in the house even before you saw him. You could feel it. He was there, you knew it, he changed everything, the air felt different. You were walking on eggshells most of the time. You never knew when he was going to be angry at you, or over what. You didn't know when he was going to overlook something or the next time when he wouldn't. It was how he would say it that would irritate you. He wouldn't say, 'It's raining out,' he'd shout, 'Put your boots on!' He would erupt over little things. A look. He'd take your head off for a look. He would swat you if you looked at him wrong." Like many fathers of that generation, Lombardi tried to discipline his son by hitting him. How often? "Quite often. It didn't hurt that bad, but it would hurt."

Once Vincent surprised himself by standing up to his old man. He was being ordered around and was tired of it, so he marched out of the house, slamming the door in defiance. Lombardi ran after him. Vincent could hear him coming, rage and righteousness churning down the sidewalk, and he sensed the pain that was about to be inflicted on him, and without considering the consequences, with the sort of move he might have made on the football field if he wasn't carrying the load of his father's judgment with him, natural and swift this one time, he boldly spun around with a hard right, punching his dad smack in the face. Lombardi was so stunned that he did not respond, returning silently to the house. Then he reconsidered, his face reddening, and went for Vincent again, but Marie stepped in and prevented another confrontation.

At Red Bank Catholic High, Vincent was an occasional underachiever (his dad grounded him for an entire marking period when he brought home poor grades). He did not get along with some of the nuns, and wanted no part of their plans for him to be a student leader. A leader is what his father was. Vincent did not much like the type; to him it meant constant tension, unrelenting pressure. He was tense enough already, but less directed and ambitious, more like his mother, and he believed that his dad thought less of him for that. "I think he thought I took after my mother in many respects. He thought she was weak. He thought I was weak." Once his father yelled at him in front of Frank Gifford; they were driving somewhere, Lombardi and Gifford in front, Vincent in back, and all of a sudden the Old Man laid into him for saying something wrong—one of the most embarrassing moments of his life.

It is not uncommon for fathers to misunderstand their sons, and for sons, their lives shaped by that difficult relationship, to wonder retrospectively whether they had misunderstood their fathers. That is how it went with Vincent Thomas Lombardi and Vincent Henry Lombardi. Looking back on his adolescence decades later from the perspective of his own adulthood, the son remembered not only the occasions when his father intimidated him, but also the time when the nuns sent him home from school for goofing off, and how fearful he was that his dad would hit him, and how instead the Old Man said something comforting and patted him on the back and let it go, and how that single pat on the back, an unexpected sign of love, meant the world to him.

There is no suggestion that Lombardi did not want to be a good father or that he had no interest in creating his own loving family. Few things in life meant more to him than family. He was born among the Izzos of Sheepshead Bay, when the whole world was family. But Marie, Vincent and Susan were victims of his obsessions and misdirected love. The football brotherhood could better satisfy his psychological needs: his longing for the adult equivalent of the embracing Izzo clan; his unslaked thirst to fight and prevail against the world. He tried to let his little brood into that more exciting world. He brought Vincent along to training camp and let him stand on the sidelines at every home game. He took Marie to dinner after the games, and brought players home sometimes rather than hanging out all the time at Toots Shor's or Mike Manuche's in midtown Manhattan. To his outside friends, who knew the social Lombardi, with his white-flash smile and contagious laugh, who heard him speak solemnly about the importance of family, he seemed to have a healthy balance in his life between God, family and profession. But like many people obsessed to achieve, his life listed heavily toward his profession. His little nuclear family saw him from the inside and found it hard to compete with the world: Susie struggling to read, Vincent stubbornly refusing to snap to, Marie, in the solitude of night, furtively tinkling two ice cubes into a tumbler and pouring her drink.

The frustration of good intentions often gone astray characterized the inner life of the Lombardis of Lockwood Place. In the comedy of grotesque, their saga might have been symbolized by the story of the duck. One Easter Sunday, Uncle Joe Lombardi gave young Vincent a duck as a present. All the duck did was sit at the bottom of the stairs and quack. While hurrying down the steps one morning, Vincent tripped over the duck and broke its leg. A quacking duck that couldn't walk. Marie took one look at it and told Vincent and Susan to leave the house while she resolved the crisis. She grabbed the duck and stuffed it into a paper bag, took it into the kitchen and opened the oven door. *What'd you do with the duck?* Vincent and Susan asked when they came back. The answer left them stunned, queasy. *You what? You gassed the duck?*

Lombardi's relationship to Harry and Matty seemed simpler. Old Five by Five swelled with pride over Vinnie's accomplishments. He became a vo-ciferous Giants fan and attended every game he could, still lighting his Lucky Strike before the opening kickoff, even though his doctor said he should stop smoking. He quit the meatcutting business, retired early, thought he had enough money, bought a sporting goods store in Englewood and turned it over to little Joe while he worked in his garden and watched Vince's games and enjoyed his grandchildren. Harry was surrounded by fam-ily. Madeline and her family lived upstairs, Claire and hers next door, and Harold, now teaching at Saints, occupied the basement rooms, filling the house with exultant arias from his collection of opera records. Little Joe lived nearby with his wife and kids, hating the sporting goods store and its obligations, but sticking it out, doing what his dad wanted. Joe was the duti-ful youngest son, always in his older brother's shadow, which was both op-pressive and beneficent. With Vince's connections, he sold equipment to Saints and Dwight Morrow and West Point, and served as a ticket outlet for the New York Football Giants, but when the store finally went up in smoke, no moans were heard from Joe; he went to mass at Saints and gave secret prayers of thanks and called the fire "a blessing in disguise."

Harry had been slowed by one heart attack and several occlusions dur-ing his years in New Jersey, but he was still a power-pack of energy. Chop-ping wood was his release. He would be outside on Saturday mornings, hacking away with his axe, then back and forth with the saw. His cardiolo-gists were "afraid to death" of him, according to Harold, and for good reason: one morning Doc Trainer came by the compound and saw Old Five by Five felling a tree. "You're not supposed to be doing that," said the doctor, to which Harry picked up his axe and made a feint toward the physician, bel-lowing, "Don't tell me what I'm supposed to do!" But Harry remained the lovable bully; his grandchildren teased Poppop, snatching tomatoes from his garden and pears from the fruit tree and giggling behind the house as he ran after them, his squat, short legs propelling him around the corner in comic search for the culprits.

• •

WAVES of talent washed into the National Football League during the second half of the fifties decade, but no pool of rookies did more to transform the pro game than the offensive stars who arrived in 1957. Jim Brown of Syracuse became the best and most feared runner of all time. Paul Hornung from Notre Dame, the triple-threat golden boy, established new standards for scoring and style. Ron Kramer from Michigan, hulking yet rangy, appeared as the new prototype for tight end. Quarterbacks Sonny Jurgensen from Duke, John Brodie from Stanford and Len Dawson from Purdue matured into All-Pro precision passers. Jon Arnett from Southern Cal was the less radiant version of Hornung, Tommy McDonald from Oklahoma showed there was still a place for agile little guys, and Jim Parker from Ohio State ushered in the era of huge and mobile pass protectors. This wave brought nothing for the Giants. They did not have a first-round pick and took little of value from the draft. Only one of their choices made the squad, but the Giants seemed unconcerned; they were stocked with skilled professionals and bound by uncommon togetherness which gave them a sixth-sense awareness of one another on the field. That was enough for most of the season, as they bolted out to a 7–2 start, but they tired near the end, losing their final three, with the Cleveland Browns overtaking them in a decisive year-ending game at Yankee Stadium, winning 34 to 28 behind the pounding rushes of Jim Brown, who was already, by the end of his rookie year, incomparable.

Lombardi's mind was quickly elsewhere, away from the playoffs once the Giants were eliminated. He had renewed his search for a head coaching position. The right college job still might have attracted him, but now he fully understood that there were fewer uncontrollable variables to coaching in the NFL. The players were bigger and smarter, yet he did not have to worry about losing them to honor codes, daily quizzes, midyear grades or graduation. An offer finally came that winter from Vince McNally, general manager at Philadelphia. Hugh Devore, one of Sleepy Jim Crowley's assistants at Fordham during the Seven Blocks era, had been dismissed by the Eagles after leading them through losing seasons in 1956 and 1957, and the owners were interested in either Lombardi or Buck Shaw, who a few years earlier had beaten him out for the Air Force Academy position, from which Shaw had now resigned. When Shaw delayed in his negotiations, seeking a clause allowing him to stay on the West Coast during the off-season, the Eagles turned to Lombardi.

At least some of them did. The management at Philadelphia was a mess, with a vast committee of partners elbowing for power. McNally was hamstrung in what he could offer Lombardi because of disputes within the ownership over salary and other terms. Even Bert Bell, the commissioner, who had once owned the Eagles and still kept a flame alive for the team, got involved in recruiting Lombardi, calling him on a Saturday morning while Vin was playing cribbage with Marie. Lombardi told Bell that he would take the job. Within minutes the Maras were on the line, pressing to keep him. Going to the Eagles was a mistake, Wellington Mara argued, because the ownership was rife with contentious politicians. "You'll never get along with them," Mara later remembered telling Lombardi. "They'll never let you run the team the way you want to do it. I don't think you ought to go there." No sooner had Mara hung up than the phone rang again and it was Mara's wife, Ann, urging Marie to persuade her husband not to leave the Giants. Vince began to reconsider. The phone kept ringing, with voices tugging and pulling at Lombardi to stay or go. Mara had promised him another raise, matching the $22,500 the Eagles were offering, and had jumped his life insurance policy to a cool $100,000. Finally, Marie told him to get out of the house and think about his future at St. James Roman Catholic Church in downtown Red Bank, where he attended morning mass. She said he should settle into a pew and just think for a while. "Don't pray," she said. "Think!"

Lombardi sat in the pew for several hours. Forty-four years old. Burning to lead. Impatient. Easily depressed when people could not see his greatness. Knew pro offenses cold. Thought he knew defense, too, always giving Landry an idea about that 4–3. Philadelphia had some talent, despite the losing record. The kids McDonald and Jurgensen and Clarence Peaks; the veterans Van Brocklin, who just came over from the Rams, and Chuck Bednarik, Tom Brookshier and Pete Retzlaff. Van Brocklin—what he could do with Van Brocklin! Chuck Conerly was an old pro, but the Dutchman was all-world. Overall, the Eagles were not as good as the still-loaded Giants. Gifford was the back you built an offense around. New York was Vin's town. He knew the restaurants, the sportswriters, the rhythms of the place. Philadelphia was East Coast, near enough, but not New York. The Maras were class owners, friends, like family. Who ran the Eagles? Jim Lee Howell was not going to stick around forever. Wellington Mara certainly implied that Vince might be next in line. Colonel Blaik was always talking about retiring and going into business. What a life that was at West Point! Maybe he could go back and run the show. The Giants paid him better than any assistant coach in the league. Something to be said for stability. Vincent and Susan had moved so often in their young lives. Marie was at home in Fair Haven. Hail Mary. Prayers to St. Anthony and to St. Jude. All the lost causes.

He left St. James and called Mara the next morning from Lockwood Place. The cautious choice, staying put again. "I think you're right," he said. "I won't take it."

THE START of the 1958 campaign seemed designed only to make Lombardi regret his decision. The Giants slogged through a miserable preseason, losing five warmup games. Vince sensed that the players were drained from expectations, banged up mentally and physically, too tight, and he arranged a beer-keg party for them at the Bear Mountain Inn up near West Point a few nights before the opener against the Chicago Cardinals in Buffalo. Red Reeder, the ebullient, one-legged colonel, was there, telling stories, and the evening worked just as Vince had hoped. It was the type of thing he would do if he were head coach, a perfectly timed surprise for the occasional release of tension, like the pat on the back for young Vincent, but it came easier for him with the players. The Giants, revived, walloped Pop Ivy's lowly Cards, 37 to 7, but then lost two early season games that they were supposed to win and dropped two games behind the Browns in the Eastern Conference standings. They saved themselves in late October and November, with consecutive close wins against the Browns in Cleveland and the Colts in New York, both games played in front of sellout crowds of more than 70,000 and watched by unprecedented millions on national television, then pulled out a last-minute win over the previous year's champions, the Detroit Lions, on a blocked field goal attempt. The eastern title depended on the outcome of the season finale against the Browns at Yankee Stadium. At first it looked like a repeat of last year's game, with Jim Brown performing another masterpiece—glide, weave, thrash, rumble, roar, score, chest out, No. 32 in brown and orange, sixty-five yards for the touchdown. But the Giants defense and a heavy snowstorm slowed the pace, and the game entered the final minutes tied 10 to 10.

Two minutes left and Lombardi's offense has the ball near midfield, though precisely where is uncertain; snow has whited out the sideline yard markers. A tie does the Giants no good; the Browns are one game ahead in the standings and can clinch the title. New York has to score. Conerly, the old pro, tries three straight pass plays, but all fall incomplete. Fourth and ten. What now? Howell and Lombardi huddle, disagree, and Jim Lee makes the call: Send in the field goal team. Lombardi stands back, shakes his head. No way, not even with Pat Summerall's powerful foot. A ten-yard pass is iffy, but a midfield field goal in a near blizzard with slippery footing seems impossible. Summerall is equally shocked by the call: On a bad field. So unrealistic. But what choice is there? Summerall is an Arkansas Razorback, same as Howell, who has confidence in him. Wellington Mara looks down on the desperate scene from the press box, bewildered. "He can't kick it that far. What are we doing?" the owner asks assistant coach Ken Kavanaugh, seated next to him. Summerall, with his straight-legged placekicking style, is now concentrating only on where he should hit the football with his right shoe. Not too low, or it will flutter high and short. Has to be addressed sharply in the middle, barely below center, but then sometimes it knuckles and wobbles from side to side.

He hits it dead center, and it starts flaring out, then knuckles back inside and pushes on and on, defying the resistance of the dank December air, floating over the crossbar. The stunned silence of disbelief, then a thunderous roar in the gray and white shroud of Yankee Stadium. As he walks off the field, his chest pounding with hero's blood, Summerall catches Lombardi's eye. Vince is smiling, and he says, "You know, don't you, that you can't kick it that far." Historians in the press box search for comparisons. Red Smith believes there is only one—the home run Bobby Thomson hit to beat the Dodgers in 1951 when the baseball Giants won the pennant. The New York Football Giants had to win, Smith writes. It was "do or die."

One week later the Browns were back, a coin toss determining Yankee Stadium as the home turf, same time, same place, do or die for both teams now in a tie-breaking Eastern Conference playoff. No snow, just a hard, frozen field. Huff and the defense were monsters again, stopping Jim Brown in his own backfield; only eight yards on seven carries all afternoon. Landry's boys threw a shutout and Lombardi's offense scored the ten points needed to win. Jim Lee Howell, handing out psychic rewards after the game, gave most kudos to the defense. He said he had never seen a game "where one defense overpowered the other team so completely." Vince could have fallen into a depression, even in victory, but he had just enough reason to strut. Gifford and Conerly and all his key players were banged up. Triplett had been thrown out in the second quarter, caught retaliating against two Browns who were kicking and yanking him. And the sportswriters all saw the Lombardi genius in the game's deciding play. The Giants were on the Browns' eighteen when Vince called a trick play he had devised just for this moment. Conerly took the ball and handed off to Webster, who handed it back to Gifford, who came around the end on a double reverse and soon lateraled to the trailing Conerly, who hobbled in untouched from the eight.

Vince was certain it would work; he had charted how the Browns tackles were pursuing blindly, leaving gaping holes. "We just put that play in to exploit the shift," he told the press after the game. But Conerly running the ball? Wasn't that the amateurish sort of play that Gifford and Conerly had ridiculed Lombardi about when he brought his naive college playbook to that first training camp in Salem in 1954? The old pro didn't complain this time; he crowed about how long it had been since "an old guy like me" had run it in. Gifford did not mind either. He was a blotchy mess when Red Smith spotted him in the dressing room afterwards, his legs and arms bruised and patched. What happened? "Ice. Tiny slivers of ice, like needles" made the field a frozen sheet of torture, Gifford said. "I'm cut up this way all over."

None of Red Smith's New York followers could read his column in the *Herald Tribune* the next day, nor follow any of the Giants' exploits in the New York newspapers. This was still a newspaper town, with nine dailies in the metropolitan area in 1958—four in the morning: the *New York Times,* the *Herald Tribune,* the *News* and the *Mirror;* and five in the afternoon: the *World-*

Telegram and Sun, the *Journal American,* the *Post,* the *Long Island Daily Press* and the *Long Island Star-Journal.* In normal times, 5.8 million local papers were sold each day, but none were to be found this Christmas season. The city had been without them since December 12, when a strike by delivery workers, which had begun four days earlier, forced the publishers to shut down. As far as the New York sportswriters were concerned, the Giants' two compelling struggles with the Browns had been oddly ephemeral, witnessed in the gloaming but not recorded and annotated for history. Only columnists with national syndication, Red Smith among them, were still writing for publication. Smith's work could be seen down the eastern seaboard in the *Philadelphia Inquirer*—the most popular newspaper in New York that month. To try to fill the vacuum, local television and radio stations pumped up their sports departments and doubled the time devoted to pro football on the nightly newscasts. Even more than in 1956, the rise of the Giants was watched and remembered as a television phenomenon.

Every aspect of life in the city was affected by the strike. Holiday sales were down along Fifth Avenue. Funeral service attendance dropped 20 percent without obituary notices. Travel agents reported business cut in half. Litter basket collections on the city streets, minus newsprint detritus, were 25 percent lighter. Ten thousand city newsstands were closed. Some sporting events in the area suffered dramatic attendance declines, as much as 25 to 50 percent according to a study by students at Columbia School of Journalism, but the Giants had no such troubles. Attendance throughout the NFL had risen another 5 percent in 1958, and the late rush by New York fueled the increase. Near the end of the third quarter of the playoff win over the Browns, with the Giants holding a 10 to 0 lead that appeared insurmountable, given the impenetrable nature of their defense, fans began leaving their seats to start the line for tickets to the NFL championship game against the Western Conference's Baltimore Colts, a game that would be held at Yankee Stadium the following Sunday, the third straight Sunday with a major game in the Bronx. The Giants sold 12,500 tickets late that afternoon and another 10,000 by ten Monday morning, when public ticket sales were halted.

Colts fans, in the grip of what Baltimore sportswriters called Coltaphrenia, bought another 15,000 tickets to follow their team to New York. Baltimore was seeking its first title in any major sport since before the turn of the century. The game had an obvious central theme, one that left Lombardi out. On one side was New York's swarming defense—the front four of Katcavage, Robustelli, Modzelewski and Grier, the linebackers Cliff Livingston, Harland Svare and Huff (known in the huddle as Sara, Wanda and Meg, respectively), the cornerbacks Lindon Crow and Carl Karilivacz, and the ballhawking safeties Jim Patton and Emlen Tunnell. On the other side was Baltimore's record-shattering offense, led by quarterback Johnny Unitas, end

Raymond Berry, tackle Jim Parker, and running backs Alan "The Horse" Ameche from the University of Wisconsin and Lenny Moore.

The weather on December 28 was chilly and windy, but there was no snow and a broad shaft of winter light lifted the Bronx morning—better conditions than for either of the Browns games. Old Five by Five stayed home in Englewood in any case, his heart doctors ordering him to keep as far away from the excitement as possible. And, they said, no Lucky Strikes! Since there was a television blackout within a seventy-five-mile radius of New York, Harry had to listen to the game on the radio. Commissioner Bell was adamant about the blackout rule; television might be the future, he said, but it was not everything. He felt an obligation to ticket holders at the stadium who had paid good money to see something that others should not see for free. Vince and Vincent, father and son, their discomfort soothed on Sundays by a shared passion for the Giants, headed out from Fair Haven early that morning in the family's big-fin '57 Chevy, two-toned in mauve and white (Vincent thought it looked almost pink), heading north in determined silence, from Route 35 to the turnpike and all the way north to the George Washington Bridge, then across the Cross Bronx and down to the stadium at 161st Street; walking through the players' gate, credentials out, into the dressing room, looking around at this pride of Giants: Frank, so cool, always, even now that he is hurting; and Alex, with the whisper of conspiratorial good will for Vincent; and Em and Rosey, friendliest of guys; and Little Mo and Kat, grinned killers; and Charlie Conerly, the old pro, taping up his Ole Miss bag of bones one more time.

New York was crazy for these Giants, and Baltimore for its Colts. Was this the old rah-rah of college or something more in the spirit of the new and professional? Looking down from the press box, Red Smith, among the few New York writers facing a deadline, tapped out his impressions of the pregame stadium fanfare: "From the start of the sunny afternoon, the playground had presented a spectacle rarely seen in this blasé town. Fog horns and sirens hooted and shrieked. Bands tootled and postured. Antlered ballet dancers in bright red union suits impersonated cottontail reindeer, a rare breed. Fillies of provocative design paraded wearing the letters COLTS across bosoms that pointedly contradicted that label." Vincent stood in his usual place, down the far end of the sideline, admiring those same fillies. His dad was up near Jim Lee, play chart coded and ready. Marie was in the stands with Johnny Ryan and his wife, family friends who had given her and Susan a ride to the game. Susan had finally graduated from washroom towel duty and was seated by her mother. The Giants scored first on a Summerall field goal, but then Gifford fumbled twice in the second quarter. Ameche rode in from the two and Unitas hit Berry at the end of another long drive, and the Colts held a 14 to 3 lead by the half.

Midway through the third quarter, the game looked nearly out of reach.

Unitas had moved the Colts downfield again, first and goal inside the five, but this time the defense held, and when Livingston tackled Ameche on fourth down several yards short of the goal, the Giants offense at last awakened. One long, loopy play brought them back: Rote went deep, caught Conerly's pass, raced toward the Colts goal, fumbled, and Webster, trailing amid a group of players, Colts and Giants alike, who seemed frozen for a second as they watched the ball bounce, finally picked up the loose ball and ran it all the way to the one—lucky improvisation, better than any trick play from Lombardi's bible. Triplett scored from there, and the Giants were back. From the press box, Tex Maule watched with satisfaction as Conerly, his favorite old pro, led New York downfield again early in the fourth quarter, hitting Schnelker on two long passes, then finding Gifford in the flat at the Colts five, where he outmuscled an arm tackler and glided in for the go-ahead touchdown. Red Smith, looking around, noted that "blizzards of paper whirled through the darkening canyon of Yankee Stadium."

The score was 17 to 14 now, Giants ahead, clock running, defense holding, Lombardi's offense fully engaged, getting the ball back, moving again. Two minutes, twenty-two seconds left. Third and a little more than three at the Giants forty-three. Sitting in his living room on Central Avenue, blood pressure rising, Harry's listening to the endgame on WINS. Vincent is on the far end of the Giants bench, gazing up at the sea of noise, shreds of paper falling from the upper deck, hot dog wrappers swirling onto the field, his mother and sister in the stands, his father checking the play chart again next to Jim Lee. Colts think pass, their linebackers drop back, Conerly goes with Lombardi's favorite, Gifford running for daylight, sweeping right, past the line of scrimmage and cutting upfield near the down marker. Gino Marchetti, the Colts' terrifying pass-rushing end, is off balance when Gifford cuts, but leans back awkwardly and makes the tackle. On the Giants side, they think Frank's got it, the first down that wins the game. But there is a distraction on the field. Big Daddy Lipscomb came to the play late and fell on his own man. Marchetti's hurt, writhing. His parents, watching pro football on television for the first time like millions of others, see it in their living room. They never wanted Gino to play football, and now his ankle's broken in the biggest game of his life and he's carried off the field on a stretcher and laid out in the dressing room where he cannot even follow the rest of the game on the radio. The ref spots the ball, and Gifford looks on in disbelief— the man's putting it back too far. *I made that first down,* Gifford would say, forever. *But the official ruled otherwise, so what can you do?* Inches short.

Howell and Lombardi decided to punt, figuring they had a great punter in Don Chandler and an even better defense. "Later, the wisdom of this decision would be debated," Red Smith wrote, "but it seemed wise then." The Colts took over at their own fourteen and Smith described the meaning of the drive: "Two years ago, Baltimore's Johnny Unitas was playing for six dollars a game on the Pittsburgh sandlots. Now he was throwing for the winners' share of $372,310. With a minute and a half left, he passed to Spats Moore for a first down. One minute, five seconds remained when the Colts reached midfield." The Giants front four knew Unitas was passing, but couldn't reach him; Robustelli spent all day trying to get around big Jim Parker, with minimal success. All Unitas needed was three seconds, and he got it almost every time. He kept working his passes to Raymond Berry, the skinny Colts receiver with "weak eyes, one leg shorter than the other and peculiar tastes like a preference for laundering his own football pants," as Smith described him. Borrowing a phrase that he had heard from another writer, his close friend W. C. Heinz, Smith called Berry an unprepossessing athlete who had but one incredible talent: he "catches passes ... the way most of us catch the common cold." Two Berry catches took the ball inside the twenty. The clock was down to seven seconds when big Steve Myhra lumbered out, head down, leg locked, and kicked a field goal.

Tied at 17 at the end of regulation. The first tie ever in an NFL championship, and it was in New York, on national television, with America caught up in the twilight drama, and there was more. This was the first year of use for Rule 14, Article 1: "Under this system, the team scoring first during overtime play ... shall be the winner of the game and the game is automatically ended upon any score. . . . When the regulation game ends in a tie, after a three-minute rest, a referee tosses a coin just as he does at the start of the game to determine which team is to receive. The visiting captain calls the toss."

Sudden death. Kyle Rote and Bill Svoboda met Unitas at midfield for the coin toss. Unitas, calling tails, lost the toss and the Giants received. Landry's boys were relieved; three minutes was not sufficient rest for them. Their fatigue was not merely physical. Unitas had worn them down. But the offense could not hold the ball, and on fourth and one Howell and Lombardi chose to punt again, and there came Johnny U, trotting onto the field one more time in his odd slump-shouldered lope, at his own twenty. "The tremendous tension held the crowd in massing excitement," wrote Maule. "But the Giants, the fine fervor of their rally gone, could not respond to this last challenge." Sam Huff felt the pressure of an entire season as he stared across the line into the Colts backfield. As the middle linebacker, he was responsible for Ameche's threat up the middle, wide slants by Moore or L. G. Dupre and short passes dumped into the center of the field. He did not know that Moore was being used only as a dangerous decoy now after suffering a brutal hit in the chest late in the first half. Huff found it almost impossible to outguess Unitas, and Ameche was such a running threat up the middle that he couldn't commit too soon on the pass.

Unitas sensed that he had the advantage, that the Giants were burdened with all the pressure. He made one calculated gamble after another, keeping

New York off balance, leading his offensive unit with what Maule called "the cool sang-froid of a card-sharp." On the key play of the drive, Little Mo charged through toward Unitas, finally eluding the pass-blocking wall that had stymied the front four so many times. But Unitas had suckered him in, deceived him, leaving a gaping hole on the left side, a free zone grown larger when Huff dropped off to cover Berry on what he expected to be a pass. And there was Ameche, galloping through the hole on the fullback trap. By the time Huff caught sight of him it was too late and The Horse had twenty-three yards. This happened on the far side of the field for young Vincent. All he saw was Ameche's back, more paper falling and swirling, the whole stadium thumping, sideline fillies leaping, his dad yelling, and Tom Landry, the handsome stoic, showing nothing.

When Ameche went down, finally, so did the broadcast. The exuberant crowd had knocked loose a power TV cable, and the sets went dark for the next two and a half minutes. During the blackout, the national television viewers in 10.8 million homes, the largest audience ever for an NFL game, missed a Unitas pass to Berry that took the ball down to the Giants eight, then a commercial, followed by a Dupre run stuffed for no gain. The sound and picture returned in time to catch Unitas arching the ball high over Livingston in the right flat, into the hands of tight end Jim Mutscheller, who was stopped at the one. No surprise what came next. "We all knew the next play was going to be a run, and that Ameche would be carrying, but it didn't do much good," Huff later recounted. Mutscheller blocked Livingston and Moore brushed Em Tunnell and no one even touched The Horse as he came through, and the Colts had won, 23 to 17. Thirteen plays of perfect offensive football, Lombardi watching helplessly from the sideline. Sudden death for his Giants. Gifford forlorn: two fumbles and the missed first down—he thought he had lost the game single-handedly, until Lombardi embraced him and said, "Frank, don't feel bad. We wouldn't have been here without you."

It was an uncommonly easy one-yard touchdown run, but one that immediately entered the realm of sports mythology. In that moment when Alan Ameche took the handoff from Unitas and churned across the goal line in the late December mist of Yankee Stadium, he ran pro football to a place in the American consciousness that it had never been before. The Colts' early lead, the Giants' comeback, Marchetti's broken ankle, Giff's bum-luck mark, the daring of Unitas, the hands of Berry, the speed and power of Lenny and The Horse, the cunning of Conerly and the grace of Gifford, the ferocity of Huff and Little Mo, the brilliance of Lombardi and Landry, the last-second field goal, the drive, the violence and sudden death, the rise of television, the cult of the professional—it all came together in what the headline over Tex Maule's story called the best football game ever played.

• •

THE NEWSPAPER STRIKE ended the next morning, and in the first days of the final year of the fifties more of the old gave way to the new. Colonel Blaik retired at West Point after a final unbeaten season. Tim Mara, the old man of the Giants, died. Toots Shor sold his old three-story sports saloon on Manhattan's West Side and began looking for a newer spot. And Vince Lombardi left the Giants, heading west to a place that he had once called god-forsaken, where at long last he could bust out of the category in which *Sports Illustrated* had placed him with its one-paragraph notice of his change of jobs. This might never have happened, a thousand flits of fate could have taken him somewhere else, yet his entire football life seemed to have readied him for this moment, when he could carry the mythology of the Four Horsemen and the Seven Blocks of Granite, the blood of the Izzos, the pragmatic discipline of the Jesuits, the faith of Saints, the order and clarity of Red Blaik, the no-substitute-for-victory philosophy of MacArthur, the professional cool of the Giants, the cult of the modern, with his leather satchel full of diagrams, his temper and fire and fearsome grin, his mauve and white Chevy and his struggling little family—take it all with him out to Green Bay, Wisconsin, where he had his one best chance to become more than just a face in the crowd.

11

The Foreigner

CHRISTMAS EVE 1958. Not yet half-past four in the afternoon, but already the drape of a long December night darkened the city: the old empty streets named for early American presidents, the widening yawn of the Fox River, the winter coal pile rising on the west bank, the northern firmament vaulted above the bay. Most of downtown had closed at noon, but lights flickered inside the two-story brick storefront office of the Green Bay Packers at the corner of Crooks and Washington. The staff was holding a party, a Yuletide football wake for the nicest guy who ever coached, Raymond "Scooter" McLean. Some of the men had ventured to a bar down the street and returned clinking bottles of gin and bourbon. One of the clerks brought in a phonograph and some big-band and polka records, and they cleared the furniture in the ticket office and had themselves a fine time dancing on the creaky soot-streaked floor. Verne Lewellen, the business manager, Tom Miller, the publicist, Art Daley, the *Press-Gazette* beat man, Ruth McKloskey and the other secretaries, all were there with Scooter and a few of his pals, brave and lonely souls in a town that had turned against them.

McLean had resigned under pressure one week earlier, following a season-ending loss on the coast to the Los Angeles Rams. In his only year coaching the Packers, he had established a new standard of ineptitude, compiling the worst record in team history, 1–10–1, a mark that New York sportswriter Red Smith, who had grown up in Green Bay, later immortalized with the phrase: "The Packers underwhelmed ten opponents, overwhelmed one, and whelmed one."

Now Scooter was fleeing to Detroit, where he could be an anonymous assistant again under his old Chicago Bears roommate, George Wilson. Packers coaches seemed to be packing up with depressing regularity; still vivid in McKloskey's memory was the sight one year earlier of her previous boss, the fired Lisle Blackbourn, trudging down the office stairs "with all his personal possessions, mumbling swear words all the way down." Blackbourn had lasted four losing years, and Gene Ronzani four losing years before that, and between those two and McLean the Packers had lost seventy-two games during the 1950s while winning less than half that many. The team had become pro football's provincial joke. College stars dreaded being drafted by the Packers. When veteran John Sandusky was traded from Cleveland to Green Bay during training camp in 1956, Bob Skoronski, the rookie tackle from Indiana University, greeted him with the words "John, welcome to the end of the earth." Misbehaving players on the other eleven NFL teams were threatened with trades to "the salt mines of Siberia," as Green Bay was known around the league. Commissioner Bert Bell was being pressured by big-city owners to fix the Packers or bounce them from the league. The long-running love affair between the people of Green Bay and its football team had also soured. The miracle that such a small town (population 62,888) could sustain a professional club was not enough; it had to win championships, as it had in the twenties, thirties and forties. Hang 'em high was now the prevailing attitude, best expressed by the effigy of Dominic Olejniczak (pronounced Oh-lah-KNEE-chick), president of the Packers board of directors, that swung from a lamppost outside the office a few nights before Scooter's departure.

Olejniczak had been president for only one year himself and was under scrutiny from all sides. He had arranged McLean's forced resignation, but many fans were still not satisfied. Ole, as he was called around town, was short and bulky, a self-made man with a florid complexion, watery eyes and a soft gravelly voice. A onetime disciple of Bob La Follette and the Progressives, he had recently completed five terms as mayor, but public office was nothing compared to the stress he felt running the Packers. The unencumbered communal judgment went like this: if the Packers stank, Ole stank. Whether it was an earnest committee or a bloodthirsty cabal of conspirators depended on one's perspective, but a group of men had been convening at the American Legion Sullivan-Wallen Post No. 11 for several months, secretly drafting plans for a massive reorganization of the Packers management. The legionnaires, with no real power to force the matter, nonetheless acted with a sense of entitlement, as did almost everyone in Green Bay when it came to the football team. The Packers were unique in professional sports as a publicly owned nonprofit corporation with 1,698 local shareholders, who had bought nondividend stock at $25 a share in 1949 when the team was on the brink of financial ruin. The largest share of stock was controlled by the legion post, to which all profits from the sale of the club would go in the improbable event that the team was put on the block. Around tables in the smoky legion hall, otherwise stoic men grumbled for Ole's head.

Although Olejniczak, like McLean, was a good-natured fellow, in that respect, he was not especially popular inside the Packers offices on the night of Scooter's wake. The revelers took out the effigy of him that had been cut down from the lamppost and carried it around as a prop of ridicule for their Christmas Eve merriment. At one point a woman picked up the sheeted broomstick and danced a wild polka with it, shouting, "Now, Ole, you be-have yourself!" Olejniczak was not the brightest figure in Green Bay; he was scorned by the social elite, who made him the butt of Polish jokes, embar-rassed by his rough and bumbling ways, but he had the scrappy survival in-stincts of a real estate developer, and he knew one thing above all else about his future and that of the Packers. For either to survive, they could not afford another coach like Scooter McLean. Not even the players and sportswriters wanted another Scooter, and they genuinely liked the man. Some people claimed that McLean's main problem was that he had been a Chicago Bear, as had Ronzani: how could a Bear coach the rival Packers? No more Bears! But McLean's deeper failing was that he acted like one of the guys.

Scooter chose to hang out with players, and sat down for poker games with them at training camp and on the road. He was carefree with the cards and his money, and usually lost. Owing money to players is not the best way for a coach to gain their respect. He thought Max McGee and Billy Howton were his gambling buddies, apparently unaware that they enjoyed playing with him because they "cleaned his clock all the time." One night three of the Packers—Gary Knafelc, Tom Bettis and Johnny Symank—walked by McLean's hotel room on their way to dinner on the eve of a road game in Washington and looked in on the scene, smoke curling toward the light above a card table, change jingling, bets going around, when the coach caught sight of them and told them to make sure they returned in time for bed check. They looked at each other in disbelief: "Imagine, Scooter telling us that!" Knafelc said later. "He was a great guy but he had no leadership qualities. He was not demanding. If you've been around ballplayers, you know they'll take you to the hilt every time. They'll drive you. They'll get everything they can out of you. And we took Scooter in every way."

In the locker room after losing to the Bears in Chicago, McGee and Paul Hornung told McLean that they wanted to stay overnight in the city rather than ride the train north with the team back to Green Bay. "Nah way," Scooter said to them in his New England accent, but after a bit more plead-ing he relented, cautioning that he did not want to read about them in the paper. "So Hornung and I go down and see Don Rickles at the Playboy Club, and he sees us and takes a shot at us in front of everybody, and then we go to Chez Paree and end up with a couple of those dancing girls, and we got back to Green Bay just in time for Tuesday morning practice," McGee said later.

"And there's Scooter sitting at his desk. 'Get in here, guys—look here!' and he points at 'Kup's Corner,' where Irv Kupcinet writes about how Hornung and McGee, after losing to the Bears, were seen dancing with Chez Paree adorables at two in the morning. And he tried to put his foot down. Never again! When he said he was fining us it pained him more than it pained us. It was hard for Scooter to get tough."

There were few rules in the McLean regime. Curfews were flexible and roundly ignored. No dress code. Players wore whatever they wanted on the road, sometimes sweatshirts. Scooter himself was rarely seen in coat and tie. Players skipped team meetings, often unnoticed by Scooter, who had a habit of drifting into daydreams when the film projector was running. The story— probably apocryphal, but representative of the way his old players remembered his era with equal parts pity and scorn—goes that once he fell asleep in the middle of a film session and awoke to find himself alone in the room, the projector whirring. Bart Starr, a young quarterback out of Alabama who had been raised in a military family, accustomed to discipline, felt lost and uncomfortable with Scooter. "Miserable, sickening, disappointing, testing," Starr said of the 1958 season. As the losses accumulated, Scooter lost confidence, and Starr saw no rational pattern to his selection of plays or use of players. "If you made an error you went out and if the other guy made an error you went back in. Not only does it test your resolve, it tests your reasoning, where you're going wrong. You're not accomplishing what you want to. It was a tough, terrible year." Hornung, the Heisman Trophy winner from Notre Dame, grew more dispirited as the season deteriorated, uncertain where Scooter would play him in the backfield (fullback? halfback? quarterback?) and unhappy with an atmosphere in which many players seemed more interested in their statistics than the team's success.

He wanted to be traded and thought about quitting. "It was very individual," Hornung said later. "Those guys in Green Bay that year didn't give a shit about winning or losing."

Scooter cared, but had no clue how to lift his team. On the way to work each morning, he stopped at Paul's Standard Service on South Broadway and commiserated with Paul Mazzoleni, the gas station owner, a longtime Packer fan who had been a water boy for Curly Lambeau's team back in the early 1920s. " 'Paul, what am I doing wrong? What's happening?' " Mazzoleni remembered McLean asking him. "He'd get very emotional. And he started to cry. He could see his job was on the line." Olejniczak and his executive board, a who's who of Green Bay merchants, bankers, lawyers and civic leaders, also cared about winning and losing; they had to, considering the pressure they were under from league owners and the demanding local citizenry. With funds raised through a municipal referendum, they had constructed a new 32,150-seat City Stadium on the west side of town—Vice President Richard Nixon had attended the opening ceremonies in 1957—and needed to fill it with fans if they were to remain solvent. With every loss the board interfered a bit more openly with Scooter's decision-making, demanding that he appear before them every Monday to explain what had gone wrong on the field the day before and outline his plans to correct the team's glaring mistakes.

One prominent member of the executive board was Tony Canadeo, the Gray Ghost, a former star Packers running back out of Gonzaga University. Canadeo landed a job selling steel after his playing days ended and stayed in Green Bay, one of some thirty Packers alumni still in the area and all embarrassed at the depths to which the team had fallen. The weekly grilling of McLean was humiliating and depressing but unavoidable, according to Canadeo. "When you haven't won a goldarn game, you want to know what's going on. If you don't ask, you're being a jackass. Scooter, hell, I knew Scooter and played against him and liked him. But Scooter had no control of the team. Deep down in his heart he knew things had to change." Ray Scott, the announcer from Pittsburgh who had launched pro football's national television debut on the Dumont network five years earlier, was broadcasting Packers games for CBS in 1958, and quickly discovered that players were manipulating McLean through the executive committee. "If you were a Packer who knew someone on the committee and you thought you should be getting more playing time, you'd go to a committee member, who'd go to the coach," Scott said. "Oh, it was awful."

The local sportswriters were easier on Scooter. He was close friends with some of them, played poker with them, too, in a weekly game that moved from house to house. When it was his turn to host the game, he asked Art Daley if he could borrow a poker table. It was a scene that Daley would not forget: the octagonal felt table wouldn't fit in Scooter's car, so the muscular coach held it with his left hand outside the driver's side window while steering the car with his right hand down the streets of Green Bay. For a softie, as Daley said, Scooter was "one strong little guy." Unlike many coaches, he never tried to keep the press away or snapped at reporters after a difficult loss. "When we got beat by Baltimore that year fifty-six to nothing, the feeling was, well, you know, what the hell," according to Daley. "It got away from him. There was a friendly, good feeling and we all felt bad for him." On New Year's Eve, his last night in Green Bay, Scooter ended up at Daley's house at two in the morning. No hard feelings by then about his brief dreary time at the top. "He took it all right. What the hell. Only won one game."

They cooked some eggs and drank a final round of toasts to auld lang syne and then Ray McLean scooted to Detroit.

LOMBARDI was in the kitchen at Lockwood Place, standing near the rose-colored cabinets, when he took the first call from Green Bay. On the other end of the line was Jack Vainisi, the young personnel manager for the Packers, who was conducting his own covert search for a new coach. "I don't have the authority to make this call, but I'm curious to know whether you're interested," Vainisi began. Lombardi had just started an off-season job as a public relations executive at Federation Bank and Trust, where the Giants kept their deposits. He was trying to overcome his annual postseason depression by taking to his new job as though he might someday coach a bank. First he had to learn all the plays and players, so he spent several hours during his first week interviewing tellers and loan officers to find out what they did and how they did it. He had even entertained the seditious notion of abandoning football for the banking life. More money, more time to golf. But there were only twelve head-coaching slots in the NFL, and those were the jobs he coveted most, even though he had already turned down one in Philadelphia. The Packers were offering something the Eagles could not—full control of the club as coach and general manager. Yes, he told Vainisi, he was interested.

Jack Vainisi was the bright light of the Packers staff: professional, energetic, with an uncanny ability to find football talent. His intention was to prevent Olejniczak and the executive board from making another hiring mistake, and in characteristically thorough fashion he had scouted Lombardi before calling him. He had studied Vince during the playoffs against the Browns and Colts, and interviewed the smartest football men he knew—Paul Brown of Cleveland, George Halas of Chicago, Bert Bell in the commissioner's office, Red Blaik at Army—all of whom said the same thing: Lombardi was their man, the best assistant in the country, ready to prove his merit as a head coach. Trying to steer the Packers president to the right choice while making him think it was his own, Vainisi told Olejniczak to consider talking to Brown, Halas, Bell and Blaik. Lombardi would be a tough sell: a New Yorker, Italian, from the other conference, unknown in the upper Midwest, with no head-coaching experience above the high school level. And there were as many job seekers as members of the Packers' forty-five-man board of directors. Top names being floated by different factions included Blanton Collier, coach at Kentucky; Otto Graham, the former Browns quarterback; Jim Trimble of the Hamilton Tiger-Cats in the Canadian Football League; and Forrest Evashevski, whose Iowa team had just won the Rose Bowl.

Even Earl Louis Lambeau, the inimitable Curly, founder of the Packers, who had moved to California when his thirty-year coaching career had ended, was seeking consideration, claiming he was the only one who could revive the fallen Pack. Days after Scooter's dismissal, Lambeau sent a wire from Palm Springs promoting himself for general manager, then flew back to Green Bay, met with Ole over the Christmas break and began drumming up a public relations campaign on his own behalf led by Fritz Van, a local radio announcer. Green Bay was susceptible to appeals from the past, especially from Lambeau. It was an inward-looking town whose culture was rooted in the rituals of church, family, neighborhood tavern and the Green Bay Packers, and Curly, the big, jovial Belgian, held the status of local patron saint. His rise had paralleled Green Bay's growing identification with football. He had starred at Green Bay East High, then played briefly with George Gipp in a Notre Dame backfield coached by the fabled Knute Rockne. When he dropped out of Notre Dame and returned home in 1919, he persuaded a local meatpacker, the Indian Packing Company, to sponsor a football team, and two years later brought the Packers into the American Professional Football Association, the predecessor of the NFL.

The history of Curly Lambeau and Green Bay football was as glorious as it was tenuous. His first team, which played against clubs in Wisconsin and Michigan's Upper Peninsula, was a powerhouse, winning ten straight and outscoring the opposition by a total of 565 points to 6. (Typical score: Green Bay 87, Sheboygan 0.) The Packers' specialty was the forward pass, with the freewheeling Lambeau once tossing forty-five in a game and completing thirty-seven. Matters on the financial side were less splendid. The team played its home games at an open field next to Hagemeister Brewery and did not charge for admission, collecting donations by passing the hat. By 1922 the Packers were on the verge of bankruptcy, and Andrew Turnbull, business manager for the *Press-Gazette,* stepped in to save them. With a group of businessmen known as the Hungry Five (always hungry for money), Turnbull turned the Packers into a stock corporation, selling shares at $5 each.

Lambeau brought in a series of colorful stars over the ensuing years, the rambunctious halfback John McNally, known as Johnny Blood, the quarterbacks Cecil Isbell and Arnie Herber, the fullback Clarke Hinkle and the greatest receiver of his era in professional football, Don Hutson of Alabama (the NFL record book had a page entitled "Records Held by Don Hutson"). With George B. Calhoun, sports editor of the *Press-Gazette,* cheering them on with daily stories, the Packers became one of the dominant teams in the NFL, winning six titles under Lambeau, including three straight from 1929 to 1931. But when the team started losing in the postwar years, the town's unlikely claim to a professional football franchise became endangered. In the old days, Lambeau had survived by his wits, once persuading a fan to auction his roadster to keep the team out of hock. By 1949 the team's debts had reached a point where that sort of improvisation would not help.

Professional football had long since left the other small towns where the game had got its start, places like Decatur, Illinois; Hammond, Indiana; Canton, Ohio. Green Bay, barely hanging on, turned to its citizens again for help, transforming the club into a nonprofit corporation and issuing $125,000 worth of stock, with no stockholder allowed to have more than two hundred shares. The move saved the city's team, for better and worse. On the plus side, by spreading the ownership to more than a thousand local share-holders and prohibiting a single majority owner, the Packers were assured of never being moved from Green Bay. On the negative side, there was no single wealthy owner who could dip into his own reserves to buy players, and the distribution of power among directors and executive directors made the administration of the team exceedingly contentious.

Now here came Curly Lambeau again, a decade later, seeking a second chance. In many respects, Lambeau *was* the Packers, but Olejniczak and his allies on the executive board, especially Canadeo and vice president Dick Bourguignon, a progressive-minded real estate man, were skeptical of Curly's resurrection effort. They remembered his hapless final two years as coach in 1948 and 1949, when he was burned out and the team faded into mediocrity. Curly, to them, was a remnant of the era when pro football was a minor sport populated by tramp players. In the spirit of the new, his days were done.

Following up on Vainisi's early scouting work, Ole and members of the executive committee called around the league to check on possible coaches, heard good comments about Lombardi and asked the Maras for permission to talk to him. Vince had a few years left on his Giants contract, and the Maras were torn between graciousness and self-interest. They had already persuaded Lombardi to reject one coaching offer and did not feel they could ask him for patience again. He remained the most likely candidate to be their next head coach, but Jim Lee Howell had given no indications that he was ready to retire. Yes, the Packers could talk to Lombardi, Wellington Mara said, while trying to divert his Green Bay suitors to another option: Wouldn't they rather have the other Giants assistant, Tom Landry? Ole said he wanted to talk to Lombardi first. It was agreed that he could interview Vince for the job at the second winter meetings in Philadelphia. But if the Packers hired Lombardi, there had to be one caveat, Mara insisted: if the Giants needed a head coach in the future, they could try to get Lombardi back.

Olejniczak said he had no problem with that.

WHO'S GOING to the Packers? That question was the buzz of the lobby at Philadelphia's Warwick Hotel when the league's owners and coaches gathered in late January to conduct the final twenty-six rounds of what was then a thirty-round college draft. Green Bay's quaint status as the smallest franchise in professional sports was wearing thin among many in the pro football community; there was a growing sense, especially now that the team was so inept, that the Packers were not just an oddity but a costly anachronism. One New York sportswriter angrily confronted Olejniczak near the hotel elevators and snapped: "You're nothing but parasites. You couldn't last in this league if not for the big checks you take away from other teams in the conference." Ole remained calm. "You just wait," he said. "We're going to get a man who'll impress you."

Early on the evening of January 22, he made his move, ambling up to the Giants' draft table and tapping Lombardi on the shoulder. The two men adjourned to Ole's room, where Canadeo was waiting. On the way through the lobby, they passed Ray Scott, the Packers television announcer, who caught Vince's eye and was overcome by a sensation that he would be "seeing more of that man." The sports department at the *Milwaukee Journal* believed differently, running with a scoop that the CFL's Trimble was about to take the Green Bay job. The most likely choice still seemed to be Evashevski, the big and glowering Evy, a proven leader and winner at Iowa. Could it have been mere coincidence that the Packers' top draft choice was Randy Duncan, the talented Iowa quarterback? Two assistants from Weeb Ewbank's championship Baltimore Colts were also getting late mention. But Lombardi exuded confidence in his meeting with Ole and the Gray Ghost. Though he would not commit to taking the job if it were offered to him, he talked about how he would run the team, what he expected from the players, the executive committee and himself. And he boldly broached the subject of salary, noting that he was the highest paid assistant in the league, that his wife did not want to leave the New York area but might be persuaded by a big new house and a higher standard of living, and that along with his positions with the Giants and Federation Bank and Trust he was a candidate to replace Colonel Blaik at West Point, where excellent housing was provided by the Army. "He grabbed our attention from the first minute," said Canadeo. "He knew where he was going. In football terminology, he knew his game plan."

On the Sunday morning after the draft, Evashevski made a secret visit to Green Bay to meet with Olejniczak and a few other directors. He left four hours later convinced that he did not want to relinquish his job at Iowa for the pros. That evening Lombardi learned that he was out of the running as Blaik's replacement at West Point, the Army brass having decided not to make an exception to their traditional practice of hiring only former cadets as head coaches. The news demoralized him. He grumbled to several friends that he suspected the real reason he was excluded from the job was that his "last name ended in a vowel." But events were unfolding so quickly that he had little time to brood. The next day he was flown to Green Bay for an interview with the Packers. Canadeo and Bourguignon met his private plane at the airport and rode with him to the H. C. Prange Department Store to meet with the company chairman, Jerry Atkinson, who was a Packers director. On the drive downtown Bourguignon asked Lombardi whether the Maras would release him from his contract. "Jack Mara told me, 'Let your good judgment and training be your guide,'" Lombardi answered. When he explained that Mara was referring to their shared Jesuit training at Fordham, Bourguignon noted that he had been trained by the Jesuits at Marquette. To which Canadeo added, "I graduated from Gonzaga and I've got that good judgment and training, too!" Lombardi broke into a huge grin, as Canadeo later remembered it, and said, "Between the three of us Jesuits here, we could kick the shit out of these non-Catholics!" He had found his first two friends in "godforsaken" Green Bay.

At the board meeting at Prange's, Lombardi listened more than he spoke. Atkinson took out a pen and scrawled the positives on the back of a paper place mat, making the case for coming to Green Bay: (1) More money. (2) Autonomy. He could be both coach and general manager, and the board was promising to stay out of his way. No more Monday morning quarterbacking. (3) Talent. Jack Vainisi had stocked the team with skilled young players. (4) Recognition. The Packers had nowhere to go but up, and Lombardi would get credit for their rise. (5) Living conditions. It was far cheaper to live in northeastern Wisconsin than in metropolitan New York. They would make sure he had a nice house. His children would attend fine Catholic schools. He and his wife would be welcome members at the Oneida Golf and Riding Club. After a brief but powerful statement by Lombardi, the executive board members asked him to wait in an anteroom while they held a private discussion. Twenty minutes later they called him back and made a concrete offer. As Lombardi later recounted the bargaining, "They told me the job was mine and I told them the salary was not enough. I gave them another figure, which they met." The two sides agreed on $36,000 per year for five years, handshakes all around. Lombardi had to take the proposal back to the Maras and Marie; Ole, Atkinson, Canadeo and Bourguignon had to present their choice to the full board of directors.

As usual, once he had made a tentative decision that would take his life in a new direction, Lombardi faltered, his normal air of certitude suddenly vanished, and he became a contradictory mess, torn between impulsiveness and introspection, hardheaded self-interest and sentimentality. The Jesuits' "good judgment and training" seemed of little use to him on these occasions; he could see all sides of an argument but no right side. Before leaving Green Bay that day, he impulsively found a suitable house. But when he returned to New York and stopped by the Columbus Circle office to tell the Mara brothers about the agreement, he seemed to be hoping that they would prevent him from leaving. Instead, Well Mara declared that Green Bay was just the right place for him because as coach and general manager he "could be the law unto himself out there." From New York, Lombardi drove down to Rumson, a town near his home in Fair Haven, and visited with one of his old friends, Jack Clark, a clothing store owner who loved football. Their families had been close since the days in Englewood. The Clarks were a loud and fun-loving clan, and it inevitably relaxed Lombardi to be around them. Once, when the Clarks held a "Pretty in Pink" baby shower at their house after having their first girl, DeDe, breaking a run of four boys, Lombardi rang the front doorbell dressed in a pink tutu, an incongruous vision that only the Clarks could inspire.

Should he really go to Green Bay? Vin and Jack sat in the formal living room of the Clarks' spacious new house and talked about it for hours, filling the ashtray with cigarettes. Clark was a Giants fan, but also Lombardi's friend. When Lombardi left, he drove home and found Marie waiting in the kitchen with his little brother, Joe. In what Joe described as a "very casual" manner, Vince announced that he had decided to take the job in Green Bay—and that, by the way, he had found a new house for them out there. Marie was also torn by conflicted feelings. She had always been the one pushing Vin—to get a better job, to fulfill his potential, to attain the prestige and money she thought he deserved. But now that the move to Green Bay seemed certain, she was distraught. The next night she and Vin drove back to New York for a dinner of Fordham alumni at the Waldorf-Astoria. Marie saw Wellington Mara there and drew him aside while her husband was talking to some old football pals from the Blocks of Granite era. She begged the owner to uphold the Giants contract and stop Vin from leaving. "She wanted me to stop it. She begged me not to let him go to Green Bay," Mara later recalled. "I could have stopped him. This was at a time when these contracts were sacrosanct. But I didn't. I said, 'Marie, I think Green Bay is the place for him.' "

The board of directors of the Green Bay Packers, Incorporated, a contentious group of forty-five know-it-alls, convened the next day at noon at the Hotel Northland. Their function was to approve or deny the decision of the executive committee, or "Supreme Soviet," as *Milwaukee Journal* sports columnist Oliver Kuechle derisively labeled the smaller but more powerful group. The full board met in the Italian Room, a name that caught the attention of one writer. There were seventeen reporters stuck in the makeshift press center, Room 173, lounging on the bed, in the chairs, sitting cross-legged on the floor, kneeling against the wall, resting on a turned-over wastebasket, coughing, cracking jokes and clouding the room with blue smoke as the hours dragged on with no word about a new coach. It was, one said, like waiting for the puffs of smoke that signaled the election of a new Pope in Rome. Inside the boardroom, every director had something to say about the future of the Packers. *Why couldn't we get Evy?* some wanted to know. *Did we try hard enough? Curly made this town, how can we turn away from him now? Why should we put so much trust in a guy from New York who's never run anything in his life?* But Ole and his allies had the votes, and when the directors had exhausted their complaints at last, the Packers hired a new coach and general manager. Ole came to the press room and, as the *Press-Gazette* reported, "read falteringly from a printed booklet which concerned the biography of a man named Lombardi."

Lombardi, by previous arrangement, was in New York awaiting the call at the Hotel Manhattan. Photographers from the wire services and New York newspapers came to his room to take shots of the new head coach as he talked by telephone with reporters in Green Bay. Yes, he had some ideas about who his assistants would be. No, he didn't know much about the Packers since they were in the other conference. His first task would be to review game pictures. No, he never played pro ball. "At 180 and a guard I was a little light." No, he was not looking back to New York. "I'm moving to Green Bay—lock, stock, and barrel." Yes, he would take the Giants offense with him, and only wished that he could bring Frank Gifford along, too. No, he did not expect the Packers to be as bad as last season. "I have never been associated with a loser and I don't expect to be now." As Lombardi talked, the cameras clicked. One photo showed him smiling broadly as he held the white telephone up to his left ear, his nose crinkled, eyes squinting, a large gap appearing between his two front teeth. In another picture, taken after he had hung up, he was gazing into the mirror as he straightened his tie—two images of the same man, real and reflected, past and future, going and coming.

The coming of Vince Lombardi to Green Bay completed a cycle of football mythology. Green Bay, where Curly Lambeau, founder of the Packers, taught football to Sleepy Jim Crowley, who became one of the Four Horsemen of Notre Dame, made famous by Grantland Rice, and went to New York to coach at Fordham, where he mentored the Seven Blocks of Granite, among them Vince Lombardi, who ventured out to Green Bay to reclaim the glory that began with Curly Lambeau. Lombardi's first impulse was to take another Block of Granite with him, but Tarzan Druze reluctantly turned down an offer to coach the ends; his coaching days at Notre Dame and Marquette were over and he planned to spend the rest of his life near the Jersey shore.

There were no round-the-clock radio sports shows in Green Bay then; the news of Lombardi's hiring spread through town that evening by word of mouth. Wayne Vander Patten, a local broadcaster, was sitting with his sports director, Bill Howard, at a basketball game at St. Norbert College when the word was announced. "Who the hell is Vince Lombardi?" he asked. Art Daley, the *Press-Gazette* sportswriter, went around town seeking reaction to the news. The most common response was, he reported, "Who's that? . . . Mary over at the coffee house or Joe over at the garage aren't quite sure who is this Mr. Vince Lombardi." At the Gazette Building, John B. Torinus, the publisher and a member of the Packer board, was personally overseeing an editorial welcoming the new man, relying on facts from Lombardi's résumé. "Over and beyond his coaching record is his scholastic record in college. He was a brilliant student." The editorial repeated the old Lombardi embellishments that he was on the dean's list at Fordham and had graduated cum laude, and concluded: "Everyone in Green Bay will wish him well, for we are all in this together."

At the breakfast shop the next morning, the men in Martha's Coffee Club were gossiping about the big news in the morning paper. There was a guest story in the *Press-Gazette* from a "New York writer," Joe King, who said the people of Green Bay "might mistake the new coach for a teacher of Romance languages who was about ready to earn his full professorship at an eminent college," with his "kindly, almost benign smile, his self-effacing manners, the horn-rimmed specs." But there was another side to him, King warned: "Lombardi is moody, Latinish, depressed, explosive from time to time."

This account made the Martha's gang more curious and anxious about the new head coach. Funeral director, plumber, insurance man, office supply merchant, sheet metal salesman—all the fellows in the coffee club lived and died for the Packers. For ten long years they mostly had been dying. After Scooter McLean, they were ready for a major change, but the naming of Lombardi took them by surprise. Green Bay was a city of Catholics— French, Belgian, Irish, German and Polish—but the number of Italians then could almost be counted on two hands: Canadeo, Mazzoleni, Vainisi, the Bilotti brothers over at the Forum Supper Club. There were none in Martha's Coffee Club. "It sounded as though we were getting a foreign-type person," said John Ebert, the office supply store owner. "He was from New York. We wondered how he would do in Green Bay, Wisconsin. There was desperation for anyone to come and succeed, and all of a sudden here comes this guy Vince Lombardi." The Green Bay Packers Alumni Association, less concerned about Lombardi's eastern background, issued a formal statement expressing its confidence that "the Lombardi plan for resurgence will pay dividends; and that the thrill of good, sound and representative football will again be a part of the everyday life of the citizens of Green Bay and Wisconsin."

When Bart Starr, the young Packers quarterback, first heard the news, he barely recognized the name and knew nothing about Lombardi beyond the fact that he had been a Giants assistant. Then Starr saw the picture in the morning newspaper: the glasses and the determined eyes and the gap-toothed smile. Yes, he did know something about this man, one moment etched in his memory. It hit him "like a lightning bolt" who this Lombardi was. His mind flashed back to a preseason game at Fenway Park in Boston where the Packers played the Giants. Green Bay had just scored and Starr, after holding for the extra point, was jogging off the field. Both teams were on the same side of the gridiron in the center field area. As Starr ran past the Giants bench, he saw "this person yelling and screaming at the defense" of the Giants. When he saw Lombardi's face in the paper, he realized—that was the same face! Here was the *offensive* coach screaming at the *defense* when they're coming off the field after allowing the Packers to score. That was his immediate reflection. It "jumped right out" at him. And it brought a smile to Starr's face. This Vince Lombardi, he thought to himself, is no Scooter McLean.

12

Packer Sweep

THE LOMBARDIS drove to Green Bay as a family, but only the father and son showed the slightest desire to go.

Marie could not suppress the tears when her husband steered their two-tone Chevy toward the turnpike to begin their long trek to Wisconsin. As she rode west on this dreary February day in 1959, she was separating from her family, friends, Fifth Avenue clothing stores, midtown restaurants, Monmouth racetrack, St. James Church, Atlantic Ocean, everything she had ever known. Her first impressions of Green Bay, which she had visited with Vince during a brief reconnaissance trip the previous week, had not made the leave-taking easier. She had told the local press then that Green Bay reminded her of Fair Haven, but in truth she found it to be a shudderingly alien place: sunshine glancing off blinding white snowdrifts when they had walked down the steps of the North Central Airlines plane onto the tarmac at Austin Straubel Airport, the temperature at zero, the landscape lunar and desolate, this little man known as Ole greeting them and escorting them in a car caravan along Ridge Road and Highland Avenue, past City Stadium and down to the neighborhoods of Allouez and De Pere, a trooper pulling them over for not coming to a complete stop at a stop sign! The people friendly, nosy, talking to her in singsong tones and slow rhythms as though they were reciting fairy tales to children.

Was this the beginning or end? Winnebago Indian legend held that humans first came to earth just north of modern-day Green Bay, brought by thunder and lightning. But Alexis de Tocqueville, paddling into the wilds of nearby Duck Creek River during his 1831 tour of America, declared that he had reached the perilous edge of Western civilization and was ready to turn back. Marie Lombardi was of a similar mind during the trip west, and as she cried in the front seat, her twelve-year-old daughter sobbed behind her. Green Bay was beyond Susie's imagination of the world. She remembered when her dad spread the map and tried to show the kids their new home, and he couldn't find it himself at first. Vincent bristled at his sister's sobbing and retaliated by battling over every inch of territory in the back seat. Not just Susie was back there, but also her favorite stuffed animal, a huge white bear. He would push the white bear down into the space below his sister's feet and she would start to cry again and the Old Man would get that look in the rearview mirror and order him to "stop it, mister."

Vincent was almost seventeen, midway through his junior year in high school, ready for an adventure away from the demanding Red Bank nuns. Football was his life almost as much as his father's, and he viewed Green Bay as an opportunity for both of them. His parents had already told him about the first question a reporter had asked at the airport earlier that month, a query that concerned not the new coach but his namesake kid. "Mr. Lombardi, what high school will your son enroll in?" the reporter had blurted out, and nervous laughter had filled the airport lounge because of the football subtext—what school would be lucky enough to get the bruising young fullback out of Red Bank Catholic?

On the morning of their third day on the road, the Lombardis rounded Chicago and crossed Wisconsin's southern border. As they approached Milwaukee, the scenery changed dramatically to white on white, and Vincent and Susan looked out in disbelief and despair at snowdrifts higher than car level lining both sides of the road. "The snow just blew your mind. It was right after a blizzard, and the roads were plowed, but the snow was piled up like I'd never seen it before," Vincent later remembered. Susan said that she "had no idea snow got that big and tall. When we drove around Chicago everything was fine and we were up and talking and then it got real silent in the car when we saw this snow, and my father was trying to do everything to get everybody up again. We were going into a depression here. I'm thinking, Where's he taking me? I don't think I want to do this."

Green Bay was more a blur of white. Fresh snow was falling by the time they turned down West Mission Road in Allouez and spotted No. 222, the two-story Georgian house on the corner. It snowed the rest of that afternoon and into the evening. They were invited to dinner at Dick and Lois Bourguignon's house two blocks away on Warren Court, and throughout the meal Vince and Marie and the children remarked on how unfailingly helpful and friendly the people of Green Bay had been. A man had already come down the street with a snowplow and cleared the drifts from the driveway and curb. A neighbor boy had shoveled the walk. The girl next door, Mary Jo Antil, had stopped by to see if Susan wanted to play. A clerk from the railroad station had brought out Ricky, the family dachshund, who had avoided the three-day car trip, riding west in a cage on a train. The little wiener dog was nearly frozen from the winter haul and seemed discombobulated by his new environment, his feet so stiff that he kept tumbling down the stairs. This was a strange new world for all of them.

On Monday morning the new life began. Susan went off to St. Matthew's parochial school. Vincent had decided to attend Green Bay Premontre, an all-male Catholic high school, where his first day was unlike anything he had experienced back east. He felt like a celebrity or circus freak. The papers had built him up as a New Jersey football wonder, a six-foot-two, 210-pound running machine—exaggerating his talent and his stature by about three inches and thirty pounds—even though his father had tried to present a more subdued assessment, telling the Green Bay press that his son was only "a fair to middling ballplayer." At lunch, when Vincent walked into the school cafeteria, he sensed "a thousand heads turn and two thousand eyes" focus on him and he could hear the buzz. Marie walked next door and visited with Mary Antil, Mary Jo's mother, and was fascinated by her antique silver collection. She decided that she would collect silver herself. Mary was equally fascinated by Marie, especially her voice, deep and smoky, not the stereotypical Jersey accent, with Jersey pronounced JOI-sey, but sharper, more like CHERH-zy.

THE OFFICES of the Green Bay Packers had been redecorated while Lombardi drove to Wisconsin with his family. During an earlier visit he had examined the quarters—peeling walls, creaky floor, old leather chairs with holes in them, discarded newspapers and magazines piled on chairs and in the corner—and pronounced the setting unworthy of a National Football League club. "This is a disgrace!" he had remarked to his new secretary, Ruth McKloskey. Walls were torn down, others repainted, desks shifted, cubicles and counters constructed, new furniture brought in, all to give it a more professional appearance. For Lombardi's own office, which he had appropriated from Verne Lewellen, he selected a wallpaper of tan burlap. McKloskey thought it looked strange and presented a health hazard, as she later remembered. "I almost died when they were putting it up because it was in great big rolls and lint was flying out all over the room. The men putting it up were groaning the whole time. When Mrs. Lombardi finally came in she said, 'Who in the world thought of this?' Mr. Lombardi was kind of sheepish about it. He thought it looked mannish."

The style of the remodeled office in this instance was less important than the message Lombardi meant to impart. The hapless losing ways of the old days were gone. The "Green Bay Packahs," as Lombardi called them, were starting over, in the spirit of the new. "We're not just going to start with a clean slate," he said. "We're going to throw the old slate away."

John Thurman Cochran and John Philip Bengtson, two of Lombardi's four new assistants, reported for work that Monday morning, walking from the downtown YMCA at Pine and Jefferson, where they had stayed overnight. Cochran, a feisty Alabaman who went by the nickname Red, had arrived from Detroit in what amounted to an informal swap, having been let go by Lions coach George Wilson to make room there for former Packer coach Scooter McLean. Bengtson, a soft-spoken Minnesotan who was brought in from the San Francisco 49ers to run the defense, had originally expressed greater ambitions; he had wired Olejniczak the day after Scooter's resignation to say that he was interested in the top job. Cochran and Bengtson, along with Bill Austin, a former New York Giants guard, the offensive line coach, and defensive backfield coach Norb Hecker, formerly of the Washington Redskins, all met Lombardi's first requirement for members of his staff—he wanted only assistants with professional experience. That standard would have precluded Lombardi himself from being hired by the Giants in 1954, but he remembered that his first year in New York had been a difficult adjustment and felt that there was no time for learning on the job now. He wanted to win immediately, and to do that he needed people who knew the pro athletes and the pro game.

In the job interviews, Lombardi focused intently on the arcane details of pro football, a variation of the pop quiz Red Blaik had thrown at him in the gym tower office at West Point a decade earlier—what offenses the assistants knew, how they taught the sweep, the option, the belly series, the trap, the audible, rule blocking, making cuts, the 4–3 defense, man-on-man coverage. After the interview (conducted in a lounge at Willow Run Airport in Detroit while Lombardi was changing planes from New York to Green Bay) Cochran felt as though he had endured an entrance exam for football graduate school. Still, Red and Phil were not the most confident fellows as they walked up Pine to Washington Street and took a left toward the Packer offices that first Monday morning. With the wind whipping across the Fox River into their faces, Cochran looked up at a bank building and noticed a below-zero temperature reading. Tucking his chin deeper into his inadequate winter coat, he muttered to his new colleague, "What in the hell are we doing here?"

Lombardi delivered no stirring speeches to his staff that first morning—"no ringing pronouncements" to define their mission, as Phil Bengtson later remembered it. This did not mean that Lombardi disdained pep talks, but rather that he rarely interacted with his assistants in that manner, then or thereafter. He viewed them largely as technicians and teachers; he did not expect them to be emotional leaders. He jealously guarded that role for himself, and saved his emotion for his players. He was not inclined to cede power to his assistants or anyone else. On the night before his first meeting with the executive board, he stayed late at the office and went over his contract again with secretary Ruth McKloskey, crossing out clauses that in any way appeared to limit his power. "One that I distinctly remember him cross-ing out is a paragraph that he couldn't drink in public places," McKloskey later recalled. "That was in the contract originally, and Mr. Lombardi said, 'No one's going to tell me where I'm going to drink!' "—an assertion of inde-pendence that he would not allow his players. At the board meeting, he an-nounced that in the unlikely event that he needed help, he would ask for it. "I want it understood that I am in complete command," he declared. If Pres-ident Olejniczak still harbored notions of being the overseer, Lombardi quickly disabused him of those by usurping his parking space.

His imperious leadership style was partly a manifestation of his innately bossy nature, shaped in childhood by his mother Matty's perfectionist per-sonality and his status as the oldest son and alpha wolf among the Izzo cousins; then refined at Fordham by Ignatius of Loyola, Father Cox and the Jesuits, from whom he learned the philosophy of sublimating individual de-sires for the common good; and further influenced by several strong leaders he encountered during his football career, from Harry Kane at St. Francis through Sleepy Jim Crowley and Frank Leahy at Fordham, Red Blaik, Red Reeder and Douglas MacArthur at West Point, and Paul Brown and George Halas in the National Football League. Past was prologue for Lombardi in all of those ways, but his present circumstances also played a role in determin-ing the coaching persona he assumed with the Packers. He felt that he had to be the antithesis of the happy-go-lucky Scooter McLean, and part of that necessarily meant distancing himself from the people in a small, busybody town. He had given "considerable thought" to the adjustment he would have to make, he mused aloud one day, not only the psychological transition from assistant to boss, but also the cultural shift from New York to Green Bay. "I realize it will be different here, where most everybody knows" everyone else, he said. "The coaches and players have an entirely different problem" com-pared to those in large cities "who can easily get lost."

The one matter that required the least adjustment from Lombardi's New York days was football itself. He brought the Giants offense with him and set about teaching it to his assistants that first week, using his football bible (the tan satchel) and a chalkboard as his pedagogical tools. "We knew Lombardi was going to be disciplined because he started with us on Day One," Cochran said later. "Every day Vince took a certain amount of time that we sat down and went through football just like we were learning it for the first time. He was on the blackboard teaching us with the same tech-niques that we eventually would use with players. He told us what plays we were going to run, how they were going to be blocked. We were making up our own notebooks at the time, putting all the plays on cards like he had—eight-and-a-half-by-eleven-inch notebook cards with holes in them, just like his bible. I'd call mine my brains. I'd say I left my brains somewhere if I didn't have my notebook. It was Lombardi's brains."

If Lombardi knew exactly the type of football he wanted to see on the field, he was less certain about the players he would put out there. His knowledge of the roster was limited. Since they came from different conferences, the Giants and Packers had rarely played against each other and had few common opponents. One was the Baltimore Colts; no heartening news there—the Colts split with the Giants in 1958, losing in the regular season before winning the dramatic sudden death game, but they obliterated the Packers on the most miserable afternoon of Scooter McLean's sadsack season, 56 to 0. Since his days with Red Blaik, Lombardi had been a true believer in the value of game films, and now he found them more important than ever. He set up a film room on the second floor of the Washington Street office and studied reels of old Packer films late into the night as he and his assistants graded the technique, speed and hustle of every player. It did not take him long to make his first crucial decision. His offense was built around the left halfback position, which in New York was filled by Frank Gifford, the triple-threat star who could run the sweep, throw the option pass and catch passes out in the flat. Could any Packer play Gifford's role?

In the dark hum of the film room, Lombardi found his answer. He was watching Paul Hornung, who had been an option quarterback in college and had been used by McLean at quarterback, fullback and halfback. Hornung loped out of the backfield at left halfback one game, followed his blockers perfectly, and cut upfield through the tackle slot with power and ease. "Run that play again!" Lombardi barked to Bill Austin, the line coach operating the projector. It was not raw speed that Lombardi was looking for—Gifford was not the fastest back around—but a combination of timing, grace, power and determination. He watched Hornung again. And again. The Heisman winner from Notre Dame, disappointing in his first two years, had what Lombardi sought. "There's my offense," he said. The next morning he placed a call to Hornung, who was home in Louisville, disillusioned with football, making money in real estate development with his family friend and patron, Henry Hoffmann, and thinking of retiring from the game. "I want you to know one thing, you're not going to be my quarterback," Lombardi told him. "Your quarterback days are over. You won't have to worry about playing three positions anymore. You are my left halfback. You're my Frank Gifford. You're either going to be my left halfback or you're not going to make it in pro football."

Hornung knew about Gifford and his success in New York, and hung up eager to give Green Bay one more chance. "I had been ready to bail out," he said years later. "And would have if Lombardi hadn't called."

It was easier for Lombardi to decide on a halfback than a quarterback. He had removed Hornung from consideration, and Randy Duncan, the first-round choice from Iowa, had decided to play in Canada. That left Lombardi with three choices from the remaining material: Vito "Babe" Parilli, who had been in the league since 1952, but had not yet been able to repeat the success he had at Kentucky; Joe Francis, a second-year man from Oregon State who had played mostly halfback in his rookie year; and Bart Starr, a late-round draft choice in his third year from Alabama. Starr had shown glimmers of talent—in one game film Lombardi studied, Starr attempted forty-six passes, completing twenty-six for 320 yards—but he seemed more mistake-prone than Parilli, with four times as many interceptions as touchdowns. Bengtson's analysis of Starr was that he might prove "adequate as a backup," but no more. "We've got a helluva problem," Lombardi agreed. "We've got to find somebody who can move this club."

The dominant figure in the Packers clubhouse during the long dry spell of the fifties was not a quarterback but an end, Billy Howton, who had been both a star receiver and a leader of the incipient National Football League Players Association. Howton was a tall Texan, quick and cocky, the sort who would return to the huddle and announce that he could get open on a deep fly pattern if only the quarterback could throw it that far. One night in February, Gary Knafelc, another Packers end who was Howton's roommate during the season and lived in Green Bay during the off-season, got a call from Howton, who was back in Dallas. "Vince called me," Howton began.

"Wait a minute, Billy. I sure wouldn't call him Vince," Knafelc cautioned his buddy. Knafelc had already had his first encounter with Lombardi—they had met in the stands at a Green Bay Bobcats minor league hockey game—and came away "scared to death" of him. Howton was undeterred, telling Knafelc that "Vince" wanted him to catch a flight to Green Bay and "talk about how we can make the Packers a winner." He asked Knafelc to pick him up at the airport. Knafelc had one last word of advice before hanging up. "Billy," he said, "I'm gonna tell you again—I would *not* call him Vince." The next day, when Knafelc picked up Howton at the airport, Howton said that he expected to spend several hours with Lombardi and made arrangements for dinner with the Knafelcs that night and for a return flight to Dallas the next morning. "So I dropped him off and my wife had some errands for me to run at Prange's," Knafelc later recalled. "I went there and got back home and my wife says, 'Bill wants you to pick him up right away. He's got to get back to Dallas.' And I say, 'I just dropped him off!' and she says, 'Well, he's waiting for you.' So I drove down to the office on Washington Street, and he's standing on the corner and gets in, and he's silent, and I say, 'What happened?' and he says, 'Nothing,' and wouldn't talk about it anymore."

What happened is that Lombardi had decided to get rid of Howton, who before long was traded to the Cleveland Browns for halfback Lew Carpenter and defensive end Bill Quinlan. Howton was among those who believed that he was shipped out of Green Bay because of his union position, which Lombardi might have perceived as a threat to his autocracy. That view appears to be half true at best. It is certain that Lombardi wanted nothing—certainly not a players organization—to get between him and his team. But Lombardi had no similar difficulties with Kyle Rote, who had been a players association activist with the Giants, nor with the Packers player representatives who succeeded Howton. His decision to trade Howton was triggered by their prickly meeting in Green Bay, at which the coach concluded that the wide receiver was a divisive force, but at bottom it resulted from a cold assessment of personnel. Lombardi was a skilled offensive coach, but he came to Green Bay realizing that he had to build a great defense to prevail in the NFL, just as the Giants had, and thought that Bill Quinlan—a free-wheeling defender from Michigan State who had a reputation for being every bit as rebellious as Howton—would be more valuable to him.

It was a talent appraisal that improved the team, as did most of the trades Lombardi made as general manager preparing for his first season as head coach. He acquired another lineman from Cleveland, Henry Jordan, a future all-star tackle, to fortify the defense, and also picked up Emlen Tunnell, the veteran all-star safety from the Giants—both for midround draft choices. For the offense he brought in guard Fred "Fuzzy" Thurston in a trade with Baltimore and quarterback Lamar McHan from the Chicago Cardinals. Quinlan and Jordan constituted half of the Packers front four. Em Tunnell, who had intercepted seventy-four passes during eleven years of ballhawking in New York, brought class and experience to the defensive backfield, along with an intimate knowledge of the defensive system Lombardi wanted to implement with his new team. Tunnell became an informal coach on the field, and as the first black star to play for the Packers, and a player who greatly respected the new coach, he also made it easier for Lombardi to bring in many more skilled black players over the next few years. Thurston, an agile basketball player in college at Valparaiso, fit perfectly at left guard in Lombardi's sweep offense. McHan, who had always played well for his underdog Cardinals when they had faced the Giants during Lombardi's New York years, was brought in as the favorite to be the starting quarterback.

Lombardi vacillated between optimism and despair during those early days in Green Bay. He was Mr. High-Low again. At times he was surprised by joy, the feeling that overtook him back at St. Francis Prep in Brooklyn when he first realized that he loved football. Now football in Green Bay was his whole world and he was the master of it, a sublime state of freedom that the Jesuits and Colonel Blaik, in different ways, had predicted would be his if he was disciplined, obedient, willing to pay the price. Now he was even free to relax and show some of the jovial Harry in him. One night during their first week in town, he stunned his son, Vincent, twice—first by asking if he wanted to go to a hockey game, then by picking up two hitchhikers on the way to the arena, something he had never done back in New Jersey. One of the hitchhikers became young Vincent's best friend at school.

Pat Cochran, the wife of assistant coach Red Cochran, was brought to tears late one Sunday morning as she struggled with the difficult conditions she found herself in—trapped by snow in an alien city, two toddlers, not enough room or furniture, her infant daughter sleeping in a dresser drawer. Red looked out the window and was shocked to see that Lombardi had stopped off on his way back from church and was now walking up their front steps. "Here comes the Old Man!" Red said, opening the door. After surmising that Pat was "not having any fun here," Lombardi invited the Cochrans over for dinner. "It was the best time I ever had with him," she said later. "We were all in the same boat. I remember Vince let their little dachshund out to piddle, and he laughed and laughed about the way it melted the snow."

A week later Lombardi invited the entire staff out to the house on Mission Street for a party—not just the football people, but also the secretaries and clerks and their spouses. Marie had the food catered and Vince played bartender. The guests were nervous and hesitant at first, uncertain about how to behave in an informal setting with Mr. Lombardi. After a few drinks Pat Cochran said her feet hurt. "Anyone mind if I take off my shoes?" she asked, flinging her high heels aside. The other women were startled, and a moment of awkward silence passed until Lombardi broke into his toothy grin and said, "That's a good idea. Let's all take our shoes off!" He untied his wingtips and lined them up at the side of the couch. "This feels good," he said, wiggling his toes. He was still in his stocking feet at the end of the night, standing at the door, saying goodbye.

But on other days Lombardi felt isolated and out of his element. Yes, he was master of this world, but what kind of world was it? There was more excitement on one block of midtown Manhattan, or the Grand Concourse in the Bronx, or Sheepshead Bay Road out in Brooklyn, than in all of this dark, snow-slushed, wide and empty place. In a strange environment, the most trivial deprivation can feed the largest worry. He couldn't find a hard breakfast roll anywhere in town; his team might not be any good—both thoughts jangled around in his mind, increasing his anxiety. Yes, he had freedom, but that meant freedom to fail. Late one afternoon, after being closeted in the film room since eight in the morning, he slumped down the stairs and sat behind his desk in brooding silence with his head in his hands. Ruth McKloskey had never seen him disconsolate before—she had known only the assertive side of his personality—and his melancholy alarmed her. When she looked closer from across the room it appeared that her new boss had tears in his eyes. She walked over to him and asked what was wrong. As McKloskey later recounted the scene, "He said, 'I think I've taken on more than I can handle. Will you pray for me and help me?' "

As the long northern winter persisted through February, March and April, Lombardi and his staff huddled inside the office on Washington Street, grading film and analyzing personnel. In May they finally took their first look at a few players, when the quarterbacks were flown in for a weekend minicamp, but even then there was no throwing; it was brains Lombardi wanted to deal with first, not arms. Lamar McHan, Bart Starr and Joe Francis, as well as a few receivers who happened to be in town, were taken up to the second-floor film area, where a classroom had been created for them. Lombardi handed out the playbooks and worked with them the first morning on the terminology of his offense. "We're going to take a giant step backward, gentlemen," he began. By that he meant that he was asking his quarterbacks to forget everything they knew about plays and play-calling, to empty their brains so that he could fill them up again with his system, his knowledge. He would teach it to them just as he had taught physics at St. Cecilia in the early forties, so that the slowest person in the room understood everything he said, writing it in chalk on a blackboard. A coach "must be a pedagogue," he once explained. "He has to pound the lessons into the players by rote, the same way you teach pupils in the classroom."

The quarterbacks had never experienced anything like this. Scooter McLean's playbook, based on a Clark Shaughnessy system that he had brought from the Bears, was more than four inches thick, as was the one McHan had used with the Chicago Cards. Lombardi's was an inch and a half. Scooter's plays were wordy and needlessly complicated, Lombardi's were clear and easy to remember. To call an end sweep in the old days, the quarterback had to recite a nonsensical rataplan of names and numbers—49 Bill O Grace Ed, or 49 MO Grace Pop. With Lombardi, the same play was just 49. The 4 signified the formation and 9 the hole—simple as that. In other systems, the quarterback called blocking patterns for offensive linemen. With Lombardi, blocking calls were left to the linemen themselves. There were fewer plays, but more options within each play, yet Lombardi taught the quarterbacks how to read the defense and select from the options in a rational way so that they did not feel overwhelmed. Freedom through discipline and simplicity. He also presented the logic of each play. "They call it coaching, but it is teaching," he once explained. "You do not just tell them it is so, but you show them the reasons why it is so and you repeat and repeat until they are convinced, until they know."

It might sound unimaginative, but there was in this a touch of Lombardi's genius. Even in his repetitive drills he had a way of making the mundane seem important, the football variation of a masterly novelist who could take the muddle of everyday life and bring clarity and sense to it, and allow readers to see, for the first time what was in front of their eyes all along. Bart Starr was on the edge of his seat, listening—*getting it* for the first time. All "the crap" was gone; this was "right to the bone," simple, yet "so refreshing and exciting," Starr thought. Everything was accounted for, labeled, identified, put in order, fundamental and sound. You could tell that the coach believed in what he was doing. His tone of voice, his posture, his manner, it all made you believe. It all made sense. Starr knew after the first twenty minutes that Lombardi was giving them a new world, and from then on he felt an insatiable hunger for more. When the players took their first break late that morning, Starr ran downstairs, found a pay phone and called his wife, Cherry, in Birmingham. "I think we're going to begin to win," he blurted into the phone.

THERE ARE two Green Bays, the city and the bay. The bay is part of Lake Michigan as it curls around the Door County peninsula, which sticks out from the coastline of northeastern Wisconsin like a disjointed pinky finger, or cursive lowercase *i,* if one thinks of Washington Island as the point that dots it. The city rests at the bottom of the namesake bay, yet the two seem only incidentally connected. Up through the Door County peninsula, the bay defines the life of artisans, merchants and the tourists who live and vacation in Wisconsin's summer resort mecca, a land of fish boils, cherry orchards, antique barns, gentle coves and radiant northern sunsets. But down at the bottom where the city meets the bay, the shoreline is blotted by an industrial scattering of warehouses, port facilities, and oil and gas storage terminals. The bay may have brought the city into being when French traders settled there three centuries ago, but it long since had stopped being central to the urban existence. A visitor could spend days in the city without seeing the bay; one New York sportswriter, in fact, traveled to Green Bay scores of times over four decades and never caught sight of it.

The city of Green Bay has always been defined by another body of water, the Fox River, which cuts through the middle of it, dividing the city equally east and west. In its culture, economy and civic architecture, Vince Lombardi's new hometown was in essence a river city. The low-lying downtown hugged the Fox River, and so did the huge mills operated by Charmin, Fort Howard, Nicolet and Northern that transformed pulpwood into paper towels, napkins and toilet paper for an entire nation. There was nothing beautiful about the Fox as it wended through town, two hundred yards across, vital and polluted; in the winter, fishermen built huts on the frozen sheet and dropped lines through holes in the ice, while dense gray and white plumes of factory smoke curled overhead. With all of Green Bay's comfortable old neighborhoods, there also came the transient underbelly of a river city, the railyards, empty lots and flophouses on the edge of downtown, the big-stakes all-night poker game at the Hotel Beaumont, the smoky gambling joint above a supper club called the Spot run by old man Wally Adamany. The river helped delineate Green Bay society: the upper class and working class tended to live in older neighborhoods east of the river, while the upwardly mobile middle class found more room to grow on the newer west side of town. Lombardi crossed the river bridges almost every day. His daughter attended school on the east side, his son on the west. His home on Mission Street and office on Washington Street were both east of the Fox. The stadium was across the river on the west side, as were the practice fields and airport. His country club, Oneida Golf and Riding, was west; his church, St. Willebrord, was on Adams Street in the east.

Only a few miles south of Green Bay sits De Pere, another bridge town split in half by the Fox, with an old downtown on the east side and St. Norbert College nestled above the western bank at one of the more scenic points along the river. The Norbertine priests who ran the small Catholic college in West De Pere wielded influence in the Green Bay area far beyond their numbers. They were casually known as the White Fathers, from the white robes that they wore. They were recruited from Holland by the bishop of Green Bay in 1893 because they were fluent in Flemish and Walloon, and it was hoped that they might counteract a heretic preacher who had been proselytizing among Belgian immigrant farmers in Door County. Over the decades they had established a small religious and academic empire in their new land, operating an elementary school, high school (Premontre, young Vincent's school) and parish church (St. Willebrord) in Green Bay, and an abbey and St. Norbert College in De Pere.

Like the Jesuits who had shaped Lombardi's life at Fordham, and the Carmelites he befriended at St. Cecilia in Englewood, the White Fathers tended to be gregarious fellows who played active roles in community life and held many of the same interests as the people they served. They could be seen hacking around the local golf courses and were fanatical about Packer football—and were delighted that Vince Lombardi, the new coach, who took daily communion at their church in downtown Green Bay, had agreed to keep preseason training camp at St. Norbert.

On Thursday evening, July 23, Lombardi stood at the front entrance of St. Norbert's Sensenbrenner Hall and shook hands with the first-year men, quarterbacks and centers—the first wave of players to report for 1959 training camp. A month earlier he had reached his forty-sixth birthday. He had waited since the summer of 1946, his last season as head coach at Saints, for a moment like this, when he could work with players from the first day of camp and have the power to shape them into a team in his image. As he described it later, those were "thirteen very long years, especially for a fellow with a naturally explosive temper and a seething impatience." But perhaps he was fortunate that he had to wait so long; when his time arrived, he was exuding a sense that he knew precisely what to do. And now here came the first troops, the rookies and handful of veterans moving through the receiving line of coaches that summer evening. Lombardi stood upright, all teeth and firm grip, with a friendly comment for each of them—*Good to see ya, welcome to the Packahs, look at those hands, Phil! heh! heh.*

Then he came across what he took to be an adolescent interloper.

"What the hell are you doing here? This line isn't for kids!" Lombardi snapped. To which Billy Butler, who was at least two inches and twenty pounds shorter and lighter than his program statistics of five foot ten and 180 pounds, replied: "Well, you drafted me. Ain't I supposed to show up?"

Butler was a Wisconsin boy, from the small town of Berlin, who had returned kicks and played defensive back at Chattanooga and was drafted by Jack Vainisi for the Packers in the nineteenth round. Had Black Jack lost his magic personnel touch? Not really. Butler was a tenacious athlete who became one of only three rookies to make the team; the others were Boyd Dowler, a rangy flanker from Colorado, and an offensive lineman from Northwestern named Andy Cvercko. It was not Vainisi's fault that Lombardi failed to find a place on the roster for an obscure running back from Ball State drafted in the twenty-seventh round named Timmy Brown, who went on to a sterling career with the Philadelphia Eagles, or that Lombardi did not like Alex Hawkins, another all-purpose back drafted in the second round out of South Carolina, who was picked up by the Colts and played in the league twelve years. Lombardi was operating in that first training camp with two assumptions that he carried with him for the next decade: first, he preferred veterans to rookies, even when starting from scratch; and second, he wanted only a certain type of athlete who was willing to play for him, even if the player disliked him. Lombardi might never have known that little Billy Butler couldn't stand him ("Lombardi was the biggest asshole I ever met in my life," Butler said later); but he did know that Butler went all out from the first day of camp.

The veterans were not due to report until Saturday night, but Max McGee, an end, and Howie Ferguson, a fullback, arrived in town late Friday morning and decided to stop by St. Norbert for lunch. After eating with the rookies, the two southern boys with Louisiana roots (Ferguson was from New Iberia; McGee was from East Texas but went to Tulane) took off again. They hit the local bars, partied late into the night, crashed at a downtown hotel and checked into camp the next day as scheduled. Lombardi was waiting for them, enraged. "He's ready to run us off and we've just met the guy," McGee remembered. Ferguson was in no mood for the tirade. "What the hell, we're not due till today!" he snapped. Irrelevant, said Lombardi—they had come under his watch by eating a meal at camp the previous day: "Once you do that you're part of this organization." McGee had the outward ease of a free spirit, but in fact hated confrontation, it upset his stomach, and he accepted Lombardi's dictate. Ferguson continued arguing, and soon enough, like Billy Howton before him, he was gone.

On Sunday evening Lombardi addressed the full squad inside Sensenbrenner Hall. He had been rehearsing riffs in the speech for months, turning it over in his mind from the time that he had driven up to Green Bay with his family that snowy day in February. He started with the practical: first the playbooks—they were important, the bible—here's what happens if you lose one. Then the practices—he would keep them tight and exact, an hour and a half, twice a day, the way Colonel Blaik had taught him, and the players would know exactly what they were supposed to be doing every minute. There was much to learn so he expected them to be on time, West Point time, hereafter known as Lombardi time, which meant ten minutes early. Meetings would start at nine, not five minutes after nine. Get there ahead of time, prepared. He promised to be relentless, driving constantly. *With every fiber of my body I've got to make you the best football player that I can make you. And I'll try. And I'll try. And if I don't succeed the first day. I'll try again. And I'll try again. And you've got to give everything that is in you. You've got to keep yourself in prime physical condition, because fatigue makes cowards of us all.*

He would have no tolerance for the halfhearted, the defeatist, the loser. The goal was to be the New York Yankees of football. World champions, every day, year-round. Admired everywhere. No more T-shirts on the road. Team blazers and ties for everyone. *Wherever you go, you represent the team. You will talk like, you will look like and you will act like the most dignified professional in your hometown.* Relentless in the pursuit of victory. Only winners. Anyone who didn't like it was perfectly free to get the hell out right now. *There are trains, planes and buses leaving here every day, and if you don't produce for me you're gonna find yourself on one of them.*

No one walked out. There was silence until Lombardi cleared his throat and smiled sheepishly and said, "Gentlemen," and gestured that the meeting was over. As the players filtered out, Lombardi caught Max McGee's glance and nudged him over to the corner, just the two of them. McGee had been in the league since 1954, the same year Lombardi joined the pro ranks. He had been through Ronzani and Blackbourn and Scooter McLean, and he had never witnessed anything quite like what Lombardi had just done. To him it was as though they had worked in the dark for five years and someone came in and "turned on the lights." Lombardi could not read McGee's face, but there was something about the veteran's open manner that softened him, allowing him to reveal uncertainties that he usually kept hidden.

"What'd you think?" Lombardi asked.

"Well, I'll tell ya, you got their attention, Coach!" McGee responded. "There's no doubt about that."

"You know, I wasn't sure," Lombardi confided. "Everybody could have gotten up and walked out for all I knew."

Some players might have considered walking out during the next week. The practice sessions seemed brutal compared to the lackadaisical training they had undertaken with Scooter a year earlier. Three laps around the goalposts at the start. Then twenty minutes of calisthenics, West Point style, ending with the up-down grass drill, running in place, Lombardi striding through the ranks, *Where is he?* "Get those knees up, Knafelc! Keep those legs moving! FRONT!" *Dive on your stomach.* "UP!" *Pop back up. Where is he now? Who's he looking at? Hawg's going down and he isn't coming up.* Hawg was Joel

David Hanner, the defensive tackle whose nickname perfectly captured his rural Arkansas roots and voracious appetite. Since joining the Packers in 1952, Hawg had made a habit of eating his way through the off-season and slowly working his way into shape. His blubber was deceptive. Even after Hawg had indulged at the trough, no one wanted to line up against him and discover once again that he was quicker and stronger. He checked into camp weighing 278 pounds, massive by the standards of that era, but after two days of Lombardi drills he had lost eighteen pounds, and at the end of the up-downs on the second afternoon he keeled over from sunstroke and ended up at the appropriately named St. Vincent Hospital, taking liquids intra-venously. He thought he was finished, but came back and found that "the toughest grind" he ever encountered became easier day by day as he lost weight, until he was down to playing shape at 250.

Young Vincent was there observing it all under the searing summer sun, attending his sixth training camp with his father, this time as an assistant to Dad Braisher, the equipment manager. He was the ball boy and water boy, though the Old Man barely believed in water. Players were discouraged from sipping water during most of practice; Vincent would sneak them ice cubes and towels soaked in ice water, which they could suck on. They were bitching and moaning under their breath. Guadalcanal, Billy Butler called it. *Bring us some goddamn vodka,* another muttered one afternoon. They weren't sure about the kid at first; he looked like Lombardi, had the same name, but Em Tunnell quickly spread the word: You don't have to worry about junior. The boy's not gonna tell any tales out of school. It was the same as with the Giants. Vincent worshiped the players, but had mixed feelings about the coach. When the father yelled, the son winced. He identified with players who were in the most trouble or most rebellious. The bond strengthened whenever Lombardi snapped at him, too, which was almost every day: "Get that ball over there! You know better than that, mister!"

When Ray Nitschke arrived in camp after finishing summer training with the Army, Dad Braisher sidled up to him with a warning for the ob-streperous young linebacker. "Ray, hey Ray, Ray, look, it's not like it used to be." First Hawg Hanner was taken to St. Vincent, then two rookies. "Geez, that first camp was tough. They were dropping like flies," said Vincent later. If someone dropped a pass, the Old Man shouted, "That's a lap!" and ran the offender around the goalposts again. One day Lombardi raged at Em Tun-nell, ordering him off the practice field twice to run punitive laps, but Vin-cent and Em were the only ones wise to the Old Man's trick. Lombardi was using Em, his old friend from the Giants, to demonstrate to the others that even a veteran all-star was not above discipline on his team. Tunnel knew the routine and could take it. But others who had never seen it before were stunned. Art Daley of the *Press-Gazette* witnessed it from the sidelines and later said he thought to himself, Vince Lombardi is a cruel bastard.

Controlled violence is what Lombardi called football, and he did not consider the phrase an oxymoron. The violence was as important to him as the control. He distinguished controlled violence from brutality, which he said "ultimately defeats itself," but he did not try to minimize the role of violence. To approach football any other way, he said, "would be idiotic." Every play began with a series of planned collisions, one man hitting, another hitting back, up and down the line. That was the pure element of the sport, the first Lombardi commandment: "Thou Shalt Hit." *Hit me!* He first heard those words as a freshman at Fordham during opening week of practice up on the scrimmage field at Rose Hill, with Frank Leahy, the line coach, standing across from him and demanding a thwack. *C'mon, hit me!* So Lombardi had ordered his little Saints in the twilight at MacKay Park in Englewood, taking them on one by one, man against manchild. For the Packers, Lombardi instituted a drill called the nutcracker that became his symbol of controlled violence. Two blocking dummies were placed horizontally on the field about five yards apart. The action had to take place within that confined space. The quarterback handed off to a running back, who ran for daylight between the dummies, but even the runner was incidental to the play. The violence was between an offensive lineman, blocking for the runner, and a defender who had to try to fight off the blocker and make the tackle. The defender's advantage was that he knew the play was a run. The blocker's only advantage was that he knew the snap count, allowing him to get in the first lick.

The nutcracker was Lombardi's "test of manhood" for offensive linemen, according to Bob Skoronski, the big left tackle from Indiana, who was returning to the pro game in 1959 after missing two years for military service. Skoronski knew that many factors could help him make a block during a game—the defensive formation, the uncertainty of the defender about pass or run, the double-teaming with another blocker—but with the nutcracker drill, there was nothing to make it easier, "no escaping it," as Skoronski said. If you "didn't have the courage to get your head in and get that guy out of there" the nutcracker would expose you. "Coach Lombardi loved it. He would be right in the midst of it, hovering over you, urging you on. He would get so excited about a good block." Most of the players, especially on offense, did not share their coach's enthusiasm. As Gary Knafelc, the tight end, waited in line for his turn, he gazed anxiously across the way to the corresponding line of defenders, counting back to see which one he would have to face. No one wanted Hanner, the immovable object, but Knafelc most feared Ray Nitschke, a second-year linebacker out of Illinois, who seemed to be salivating for his chance to slap and whack and "pound the hell" out of him.

And there stood Lombardi, pushing for more. The image lingers, for any examination of Lombardi as a leader inevitably leads to the subject of pain. The infliction of pain is an unavoidable part of professional football:

Pain is suffered by most players on almost every play. Football is hitting, and hitting causes pain. In other professions, pain is largely mental or symbolic, a word used to denote hard effort or the enduring of a difficult process. In football, pain is those things as well, but it begins with the physical: throbbing, aching, piercing, dizzying, screaming, vomiting, fear-inducing and fear-conquering pain. It is misleading to say that Lombardi was a sadistic coach who derived satisfaction from the pain of his players. Even if that were true on a superficial level, it misses a larger meaning of pain in Lombardi's view of the world. He operated from a philosophy of pain, complex and contradictory, woven from the geographic, cultural, religious and physical threads of his life.

Images of pain shaped his ancestral homeland of southern Italy, both the Neapolitan region of his father's Lombardis and the remote mountain village of Vietri di Potenza, home to his mother's Izzo clan. The people of southern Italy shared a history of pain on the largest scale fathomable: centuries of earthquakes, volcanic eruptions, mudslides, epidemics, revolts, famines, invasions, counterreformations, a communal memory of the works of man collapsing, crumbling, shaking, corpses burning, bodies thrown into the sea. In southern Italy pain was a constant of the human condition, the defining theme of religion and art. Paintings of flagellation, crucifixion, stigmata, biblical tragedies, luminous and muscular, with intimations of breathtaking pain. Pain was its own reward, to be endured, gloried, but not overcome. Of course that is not to say that anyone whose heritage traces back to southern Italy would have a propensity for pain, merely that in Lombardi's case the general historical thread connected to his specific family history.

During his life in the new world of Sheepshead Bay and Fordham, Saints and West Point, pain existed more within the reach and control of man. His mother disciplined him with pain, believing it could bring him closer to perfection. His father insisted to him that pain did not exist, that it was only in his mind, that it indeed could be overcome through persistence and denial. Pain was an aspect of Jesuitical free will, endured not with resignation but by choice, not from fear but out of hope. The penance of pain was accepted as a ritual leading to something more noble than individual desire. Paying the price, in Red Blaik's phrase, meant withstanding and conquering pain. Pain was a means to an end, not an end in itself. The art was not in the pain but in what pain created: tireless, fearless, unbeatable men. To succumb to pain for no greater purpose was to accept defeat. That is why Lombardi drove his men toward pain, and it is why he was so distraught during the first week of practice when he entered the Green Bay training room one morning and saw more than a dozen players seeking treatment for minor bumps and bruises and lounging in the whirlpool. Serious injuries were one thing, but this looked like malingering. "What is this, an emergency casualty ward?" he thundered, according to his later account. "This has got to stop. This is disgraceful. I have no patience with the small hurts that are bothering most of you." The next morning, the training room was virtually empty.

Lombardi's philosophy of pain was intensified by the contradictions of his own experience. He was constantly fighting his vulnerability to pain. He had a low pain threshold, and his athletic career was littered with injuries large and small that took him off the field. At his first high school, the pre-seminary Cathedral Prep, which did not even have a football team, the joke was that "Lombardi has more injuries than Hoover has commissions." At Fordham, he missed most of his freshman year, part of his sophomore year and three games in his junior year to injuries. His susceptibility to injury was matched only by his determination to recover. When he became a coach, the football trainers often treated Lombardi for minor complaints that he would not tolerate among his players: sore joint, headache, hangnail, nervous stomach—he always had something bothering him. It is a characteristic of many leaders that they confront their own weaknesses indirectly, by working to eliminate them in others, strengthened in that effort by their intimate knowledge of frailty. So it was with Lombardi and pain. It was in seeking a triumph of character and will both for himself and the team that he exhorted his Packers to confront pain and stood there, laughing, as Ray Nitschke pounded the hell out of another blocker in the nutcracker drill.

BEFORE THE START of the 1959 season, most pro football experts picked Green Bay to remain in the cellar of the Western Conference. "Last and probably least—that's the sad forecast for the once-proud Packers. They've got a good new coach in Vince Lombardi, but he might as well kiss this one off as a rebuilding year," declared a prognosticator in *Sport* magazine. But the team knew it was better than that. Through six preseason games, four of them victories, the players grew more convinced week by week that they could play with anyone in the league. In preparation for the opener against the rival Chicago Bears, Lombardi concentrated on building his new team's sense of family and community. He moved the entire club, including wives and children, to suburban Milwaukee for a final week of training and bonding on the grounds of a private boarding school in Pewaukee. This was a time of year that he came to relish. He had made the final cuts, the team was set, the playbooks had been studied and learned. Now they could go out to the practice field and drill the same play over and over until it was more than routine and familiar, it was in their blood, part of their reflexive being. This was not just any play, but *the* play, the power sweep, which came to be known as the Packer sweep.

Lombardi had used the sweep in New York, and had originally borrowed it from the playbook of the Los Angeles Rams, but once he arrived in Green Bay he transformed it into something that was singularly identified with him and his Packers. Since his days at West Point, he had based his coaching philosophy on Red Blaik's belief that perfection came with simplicity. The theory was to discard the immaterial and refine those few things that one did best. Years later, looking back on his development of the power sweep, Lombardi suggested that "every team arrives at a lead play, a No. 1 play, a bread and butter play. It is the play that the team knows it must make go and the one that opponents know they must stop. Continued success with it of course makes a No. 1 play because from that success stems your own team's confidence. And behind that is the basic truth that it expresses a coach as a coach and the players as a team. And they feel complete satisfaction when they execute it successfully."

The sweep was Lombardi's No. 1 play. His offense started with it and revolved around it. In his football lexicon, it was known as the 49—"Red Right 49 on 2," the quarterback might say. The 4 signified the formation, 9 was the hole farthest to the right sideline, and 2 was the snap count. "Red Right 49 on 2." Over and over again. Nothing could make Lombardi happier than the call of that play. He instructed his offensive linemen to take bigger splits, allowing slightly more distance than usual between each of them at the line of scrimmage. Usually they lined up thirty to thirty-six inches apart; Lombardi wanted them separated by forty inches. The tight end, the key blocker on the sweep, moved out wider from the right tackle, exactly nine feet to the tackle's right. Lombardi could sense immediately if it was eight feet or ten feet, and it had to be exactly nine feet.

The block of the tight end, Gary Knafelc or Ron Kramer, determined the entire shape of the play. Lombardi instructed the tight end not to leave his feet or smash into his opponent, but rather to calculate, in the split second after the snap, which direction the left outside linebacker could be pushed. If the linebacker was moving inside, the tight end had to stop him from penetrating the line of scrimmage and bump him toward the middle. If the linebacker was moving outside, the tight end's mission was to get in his way and keep bumping him farther outside, passively allowing the linebacker to beat on him during their contact. The point, said Lombardi, was to block the linebacker: "Whichever direction he takes, drive him in that direction."

The right tackle, Forrest Gregg, was taught to deliver what was called a slam on the left defensive end. From a three-point stance, Gregg drove into the end with his forearm or shoulder, a quick blow intended to set up the defender for a follow-up block, a cut below the knees delivered by the fullback, Jimmy Taylor, pounding at him from behind the scrimmage line. After slamming the defensive end, the right tackle sought out the middle linebacker and tried to seal him off from the flow of the play. This was what Gregg loved to do most, get beyond the line of scrimmage and rumble downfield, setting his radar on a linebacker to eliminate. In time, Lombardi would come to regard his square-jawed right tackle as the greatest downfield blocker he had ever seen.

One of the thrills of the sweep was the glory it provided the men who played offensive guard, Lombardi's old position. On most plays, the guards were hidden in a scrum at the line of scrimmage, the least noticed players on the field, indistinguishable in a tangle of feet, arms, bellies and sweat-soaked jerseys as they scrapped with the defensive interior linemen. But with the call of the sweep they were rendered majestic, a powerful and mobile matched set. At the snap of the ball, they swung their right arms back to begin the crossover step that Lombardi had learned from Frank Leahy decades earlier, then traced a precise arc behind the line of scrimmage and out toward the right sideline, ahead of the runner, serving as his proud body-guards, visible and essential. The right guard, Jerry Kramer, watched which way the tight end pushed the outside linebacker and rumbled toward the opening cleared by that block, inside or out, taking on whoever first appeared in his path—"the first color that isn't ours," as Lombardi put it. The left guard, Fuzzy Thurston, followed behind Kramer from a point deeper in the backfield, with the ball carrier, Paul Hornung, trailing directly behind him. They were so close sometimes that Hornung had his left hand on Thurston's hip. Fuzzy was looking for the next opposing color to come along after Kramer made his block.

Thurston and Kramer became the symbols of the Packer sweep, patrolling the turf ahead of Hornung, circling deep and around the corner, forearms out, ready to strike, Nos. 63 and 64 in green and gold.

The center, Jim Ringo, had to execute the most difficult block, moving quickly to his right after snapping the ball and hooking the left defensive tackle to prevent him from bolting into the backfield through the hole created when Kramer pulled out to lead the sweep. The left offensive tackle, Bob Skoronski, also pulled right, following Thurston, looking to hit anyone else who penetrated through the line, then turning upfield at the first hole. The flanker, rookie Boyd Dowler, who lined up outside the tight end, had to get inside position on the cornerback covering him and either push him to the outside or level him with a low block. The wide receiver on the other side, Max McGee, ran downfield looking to block the free safety. The play was made to order for Hornung, who lacked burning speed—his teammates teased that he was huffing just to keep up with Fuzzy—but had sharp eyes and powerful legs, and a knack of knowing just when to move off Thurston's block and slash upfield. And like Gifford before him, Hornung could transform the sweep into an option pass, a threat that made the defensive backs hesitate for a crucial few seconds.

The Packers first learned the sweep in their heads, with Lombardi at the chalkboard, instructing in the same fashion that he taught physics back at St. Cecilia, so that the dimmest pupil could comprehend. The beauty of the sweep, like all of Lombardi's teachings, was that it accommodated seemingly contradictory principles: It was at once simple yet subtle, direct yet flexible. Every player was taught not just what he should do under normal conditions, but how to respond to any unexpected defense. Position by position, Lombardi went through as many as twenty defensive possibilities, offering his players a logical response to each of them. Some coaches, considered innovative, might have twenty plays but no options for any of them; Lombardi, sometimes mischaracterized as unimaginative, preferred one play with twenty options. It was a variation of the Jesuit concept of freedom within discipline. The sweep again symbolized the philosophical lineage from Ignatius of Loyola to Vince Lombardi, both said to be limited to one great idea, but unrestrained in the incomparable realization of it. The sweep had another meaning in Lombardi's system: it was his definition of team, a play in which the offensive players had to think and react together, eleven brains and bodies working as one. "Everyone was important in the sweep," said Ron Kramer, recalling in his own lively language the message he took from Lombardi. "It's really all of life. We all have to do things together to make this thing we call America great. If we don't, we're fucked."

Like Lombardi's charges back at Saints, the Packers took in their lessons with some measure of fear, never knowing when he might order them to the front of the class to diagram a variation of the play. A fine balance between confidence and fear helped make the lessons stick. "You're watching this day after day, and it starts sinking in, becoming second nature," Bob Skoronski later explained. "And after a while you say, 'I don't care what happens, we can make this thing go.' "

Then came more repetition on the practice field. In Pewaukee during the week before the opener against the Bears, it seemed as though the sweep was all they did. The sweep dominated their thoughts and actions, the constant of their lives—Lombardi even injected it into their conditioning drills. For the wind sprints at the end of practice, they did not line up like most teams, toeing a line and chugging downfield in a track race; instead, Lombardi put them into the sweep formation and had them run out their assignments from that play, all dashing twenty yards to the end zone, again and again. The joke on the team was that they ran the sweep until *Lombardi* got tired. In that week before the Bears game, all the positions on offense seemed set except tight end, where Knafelc was fighting to hold on to his job against Ron Kramer, the huge and mobile end from Michigan who had just finished a military commitment, but had a knee injury and was struggling to regain his old form.

With his competition hobbled, Knafelc was at tight end most of the time that week. At the afternoon practice on Thursday, before the team left Pewaukee and headed back to Green Bay, Lombardi put the offense through a final half-hour drill, running sweep after sweep against the starting defensive unit. It was the modern equivalent of Bloody Wednesday for the Seven Blocks back on the practice field on Rose Hill, the smell of wet autumn leaves, smack and thud and up for more. "Again!" Lombardi shouted. Ron

Vincent Thomas Lombardi. Born in
Brooklyn, June 11, 1913.

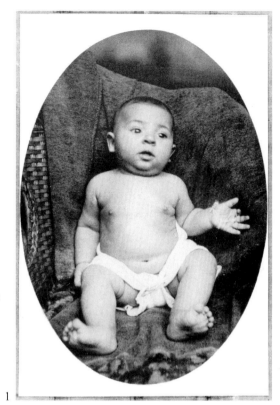

1

The family patriarch, Antonio Izzo,
known in Brooklyn as Tony the
Barber. Lombardi's maternal
grandfather was born in the southern
Italian town of Vietri di Potenza in
1864 and ran a barbershop in
Sheepshead Bay from 1890 to the
mid-1920s.

Laura Cavolo Izzo also emigrated
from Vietri di Potenza. She bore
thirteen children, including
Lombardi's mother, Matilda.

2

3

Harry and Matilda Lombardi in late middle age. Old Five by Five was a little strongman so powerful that he once loaded two kids on a coal shovel and lifted it with one hand. Matty, known as the Duchess for her perfectionist ways, was the disciplinarian of the family.

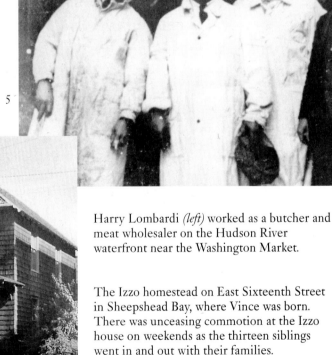

5

Harry Lombardi *(left)* worked as a butcher and meat wholesaler on the Hudson River waterfront near the Washington Market.

The Izzo homestead on East Sixteenth Street in Sheepshead Bay, where Vince was born. There was unceasing commotion at the Izzo house on weekends as the thirteen siblings went in and out with their families.

His mother's favorite picture of Vinnie as a child, standing in front of the East Fourteenth Street house on confirmation day.

The trinity of Lombardi's early years was religion, family and sports. Here he is *(third from right, top row)* with the priests of St. Mark's parish and neighborhood boys.

The thirteen Izzo siblings and their spouses. Matty and Harry Lombardi are fourth and third from the right in the front row. In the original picture, with a magnifier, one can read WORK and PLAY on Harry's knuckles.

Butch Lombardi as an undersized guard on Rose Hill. "There never was a more aggressive man who played for me," said Frank Leahy, Fordham's line coach.

Fordham's Seven Blocks of Granite lining up on the practice field. *(Left to right)* John Druze, Al Babartsky, Vinnie Lombardi, Alex Wojciechowicz, Natty Pierce, Ed Franco and Leo Paquin.

On graduation day for the Fordham class of 1937, Vinnie posed with the football lettermen, his white shoes glistening garishly in the sober congregation of black and maroon.

13

"I'm going to marry that man," Marie Planitz told her father the first time she brought Vince Lombardi home. "No you're not," Mortimer Planitz responded. "He's Italian."

At St. Cecilia High School in Englewood, New Jersey, Lombardi taught Latin and physics for eight years. The students regarded him with fear and respect. "When his eyes started to blink, you stayed away."

14

Lombardi's first head coaching job was as the basketball coach at Saints. He knew little about basketball, but eventually coached his team to a regional title.

15

It was at Saints, in the insular world of North Jersey schoolboy competition, that Lombardi developed many of the pedagogical skills that later allowed him to stand apart from the coaching multitudes.

"Vin" and "Rie" were married at the Church of Our Lady of Refuge on East 196th Street in the Bronx on August 31, 1940.

Vince and Vincent, coach and son, connected by football, at MacKay Park in Englewood.

The Lombardi family in Englewood, 1948: Marie with Susan on her lap, young Vincent and Vince.

20

Lombardi *(second from left, front row)* spent five years at West Point as an assistant to Col. Earl "Red" Blaik *(front row, center)*. Everything he knew about organizing a team and preparing it to play its best, he said later, he learned from Red Blaik.

Below left: Three men who helped shape Lombardi's life: Gen. Douglas MacArthur *(left)* loved Army football and declared that there was "no substitute for victory"; Colonel Blaik *(center)* said there was "a vast difference between a good sport and a good loser"; and Tim Cohane *(right)*, publicist and writer, promoted Lombardi from Fordham through his glory years in Green Bay.

Below right: Lombardi with Red Reeder at the Bear Mountain Inn. Reeder, who lost a leg at Normandy, taught Lombardi about leadership.

21

22

When Jim Lee Howell *(center)* served as head coach of the New York Giants, he left the defense to Tom Landry *(left)* and the offense to Lombardi *(right)*, perhaps the greatest assistant coaching duo ever in pro football.

Lombardi packs in his New York hotel room after being named head coach and general manager of the Green Bay Packers.

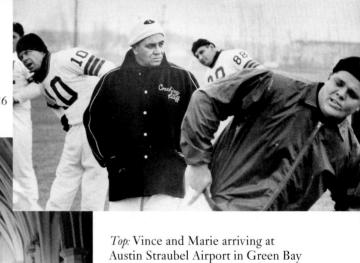

Top: Vince and Marie arriving at
Austin Straubel Airport in Green Bay
for the first time, greeted by Dominic
Olejniczak, the club president.

Above: Lombardi took over a team that
had gone 1–10–1 in 1958 under
Scooter McLean. "I have never been
associated with a loser and I don't
expect to be now," he said.

Left: Lombardi was a daily communicant. In Green Bay, before reaching
the office, he attended eight o'clock
mass at St. Willebrord, where he also
occasionally served as an altar boy.

28

After losing to the Philadelphia
Eagles in the 1960 championship
game, Lombardi told his players:
"This will never happen again.
You will never lose another
championship." In the
background is the young NFL
commissioner Pete Rozelle.

At a testimonial dinner in Sheepshead Bay, New York, on April 5, 1961. Lombardi,
led to the front by his Izzo relatives, overpowered people with his will as he
walked by.

29

OPPOSITE:

Top: There was a bitterly cold wind, and the game was brutal, but the Packers prevailed over the Giants to win the 1962 championship, 16–7. Fullback Jim Taylor explained his gutty performance by saying that you never know until you are faced with a hit how much pain you can endure, and then Lombardi steps in and pushes you beyond that point.

Bottom: "Boink!"—Jerry Kramer kicked three field goals that day, filling in for the injured Paul Hornung. Kramer later chronicled a season with Lombardi in *Instant Replay.*

Below: The Packer sweep was Lombardi's signature play, the one he practiced more than any other, refining it again and again until his players knew that they could run it anytime against any opponent. Guards Jerry Kramer (64) and Fuzzy Thurston (63) lead the way for Jimmy Taylor.

32

33

God, family and the Green Bay Packers. Lombardi believed that the wives were crucial to the team's success, and he rewarded them with presents after every championship. After Green Bay won the title in 1961, they all received fur stoles.

Lombardi with W. C. Heinz, his Boswell, who wrote *Run to Daylight!* from material he had gathered in six ten-cent Penrite memo books, filled from front to back with his legible notes.

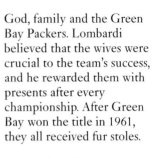

34

After every home game Vin and Marie invited friends to a postgame party in the basement rec room at their Sunset Circle home.

36

The Golden Boy. Paul Hornung was Lombardi's favorite son. At midfield, Hornung seemed like an ordinary runner, but near the goal line he was unstoppable.

Hornung's last great game came in the mud and muck of the 1965 championship win against the Browns. He scored the decisive touchdown in the 23 to 12 win on a classic Packer sweep, then walked off the field in Lombardi's embrace.

Bart Starr was the good son, Lombardi's brains on the field. He came to Green Bay as a seventeenth-round draft choice from Alabama and left as a Hall of Fame–bound quarterback, attributing his success to Lombardi.

Willie Wood (24), walking off the field with Herb Adderley (26) and Elijah Pitts (22). Wood wrote a letter to Lombardi asking for a tryout in 1960 and eventually became a Hall of Fame safety. He called his coach "perhaps the fairest person I ever met."

"Wherever you go, you represent the team," Lombardi told his players. "You will talk like, you will look like and you will act like the most dignified professional in your hometown."

The proudest day of his life, Lombardi said when he received Fordham University's Insignis Medal, honoring "Catholic leaders for extraordinary distinction." *(Left to right)* Marie's father, Mortimer Planitz; Marie; Vince and his parents, Matty and Harry Lombardi.

42

At the Ice Bowl, December 31, 1967: "There was this incredible haze of breath, tens of thousands of puffs coming out. Like seeing big buffaloes in an enormous herd on the winter plains. It was prehistoric."

Vernon Biever decided to leave his end zone position during the final drive and shoot pictures from the Packers sideline. He left it to his fifteen-year-old son, John, to take the iconic photograph of Starr (15) scoring the winning touchdown against the Cowboys.

43

Before a game, at halftime and after a game, his players thought of Lombardi as a football genius. But once the game started, the joke on the team was that he was the most useless guy on the sideline.

The Old Man's hands.

The difference between men, Lombardi said, "is in energy, in the strong will, in the settled purpose and in the invincible determination."

Lombardi was miserable in 1968, after he had left the playing field to serve as Green Bay's general manager.

48

The sentiment expressed at "An Evening with Vince Lombardi" in August 1968 was shared by politicians in both parties. Richard Nixon considered Lombardi as a possible running mate that year, until he learned that the coach was a Democrat and friend of the Kennedys'.

49

Marie found her dream house on Stanmore Drive in Potomac Falls, Maryland, but worrying constantly about her husband's health, she had little time to enjoy it.

Fathers and sons: Lombardi with his son, Vincent, and grandsons Vincent II *(left)* and John *(right)*. Vincent struggled to meet his father's expectations, eventually finding his calling as a motivational speaker drawing on the life and sayings of Vince Lombardi.

50

51

52

Top: There was an unfamiliar silence in midtown Manhattan on the morning of September 7, 1970, as Lombardi's casket was carried up the steps of St. Patrick's Cathedral.

Bottom: His football sons, Bart Starr and Paul Hornung *(center, left and right),* outside the funeral mass. They both said they felt as though they had lost a father.

Below: The Fordham wall still stands. The remaining six Blocks of Granite take their familiar positions along the line, with Marie and quarterback Handy Andy Palau among them. Lombardi's fame kept the Seven Blocks mythology alive, though he was the first to die.

Lombardi was an expressive man, his emotions never far from the surface. His front row of teeth took their positions in his mouth like Skoronski, Thurston, Ringo, Kramer and Gregg across the great Packers line.

Kramer was on the sideline, watching. Knafelc was in there for every play, sacrificial lamb, giving himself up to the linebackers, passively bumping them as they pounded him. This was too much like the nutcracker drill for Nitschke. He loved it. Blood spurting out from his knuckles, smeared on his pants, some his, some Knafelc's. He and Dan Currie just teeing off. Lombardi screaming: "Move! Knafelc! Seal it! Seal it! Again!" It seemed as if they had run the play twenty times, and Lombardi was never satisfied. *It's sticky,* he would say. *It doesn't look good.* Finally, Knafelc was so worn out that he lost his fear and said something sarcastic to Lombardi. "Coach," he said, "by this time I think even *Ray* knows it's a sweep!"

Lombardi turned his face to hide a smile.

"That's it!" he shouted. "Everybody in!"

As the players dragged off the field, one of Knafelc's young sons came running over to him and shouted, "Daddy, I still love you." Fine, but what about the seemingly displeased coach? The answer came the next morning, when Knafelc was eating breakfast with his wife and kids at the training table, and Lombardi walked up to him and said in his authoritative voice, softly but clear enough for the whole family to hear, "You're starting Sunday." Three simple words—that was all it took to erase the anxiety and fear that Knafelc had felt on the practice field when Lombardi was yelling at him. Now the ordeal seemed worth it. He was floating "nine feet high."

REPETITION, confidence and passion. The trinity of Lombardi's football success was established that Sunday afternoon, September 27, when he coached his first regular-season professional game. In the locker room beforehand, the players were overtaken by a sensation they had not felt in a long time. Something was transforming them; as they put on their Packers uniforms, they seemed surprisingly calm and self-assured. Lombardi worked the room, moving from locker to locker, shaking hands with his men, looking into their eyes, making sure they were ready. Then he gathered them around him for a pregame speech, and his will to win took on a physical manifestation. His body seemed to pulsate as he spoke, his words closing a circle of pride and emotion that began decades earlier, back when Sleepy Jim Crowley roused his Fordham Rams by evoking the image of his old mother listening to their game against St. Mary's on the radio as she sat in a rocking chair and counted her rosary beads out in Green Bay, a mythic place in the American heartland that Vinnie Lombardi, right guard among the Seven Blocks of Granite, had never seen . . . and now here he was, in that same faraway place, his coaching dream a reality at last, drawing on his memory of Crowley's ancient exhortation to the team manager to open the door and get out of the way, son, here comes my Fordham team!

Now go through that door and bring back a victory! Lombardi told his Packers, and with those words Bill "Bubba" Forester, a veteran linebacker, jumped up in a frenzied roar and banged his arm on a metal locker, his worst injury of the year, but not enough to stop him from leading his band of brothers, consumed by their mission, on a rampage out of the dressing room and into the darkening gloom and mist of City Stadium.

For all his obsession with offense, Lombardi arrived at his head coaching position realizing that he needed a fierce defense to win. He gave his defensive coach, Phil Bengtson, more freedom than his other assistants. Bengtson ran the defensive meetings and called the alignments during the game. With his phlegmatic demeanor, tall and pensive, a Camel dangling from his lips, he was a perfect counterpoint to his boss; the players found him a relief from the head coach's relentlessness. But even then, it was Lombardi's defense, in the end, still his fire that burned inside his players. And it was the defense that brought Lombardi victory in his professional debut.

The offense misplayed three easy touchdown opportunities in the first half, but Green Bay's linebackers swarmed over Chicago on the waterlogged field, limiting the Bears to two field goals, and the Packers finally put enough points on the board in the final seven minutes to win 9 to 6. Jim Taylor busted in for a five-yard touchdown run, and Hawg Hanner, the Razorback giant who had collapsed on the practice field during the first week of drills, now had enough stamina to tackle Bears quarterback Ed Brown in the end zone for a clinching safety—a play that had been set up by Max McGee's end-over-end sixty-one-yard punt that rolled out-of-bounds on the Chicago two.

There were 32,150 fans in the stadium that day, unaccustomed in recent years to football success, and they counted down the last fourteen seconds as if it was the end of a championship game. When the final gun sounded, Jim Ringo, the center, scooped up the ball and raced to the sidelines. "You deserve this more than anybody else," he said, handing the official "Duke" pigskin to Lombardi. A phalanx of Packers then swept the coach off his feet, shouting a victory chant as they bore him on their shoulders, and trotted off the muddy field, up the ramp to the delirium of a winner's locker room. His players had never seen a happier man than Lombardi after that game. He had "a grin that would not come off" as he spread praise all around until he found Max McGee and grabbed him by the cheeks, like Grandma Izzo might have done, and kissed him hard on the lips for that game-saving punt. How much did winning mean to this coach? McGee now knew the answer. They all liked to win, every player wants to win, but no one wanted to win as much as that "big smackeroo."

13

Trinity

Yes, strange things happened everywhere, but the Fordham wall still stands.

Here stood the Fordham wall one more time, aligned at midfield on the gridiron of Roosevelt Stadium in Jersey City before an exhibition game between Lombardi's Green Bay Packers and the New York Giants. It was the Monday evening of August 22, 1960, almost a quarter-century after Grantland Rice wrote "Old Gibraltar." The old left tackle, Ed Franco, had organized the reunion, assembling the Seven Blocks of Granite and their coach, Jim Crowley, for the first time since 1937. The Blocks were in their late forties now and had matured into increasingly irregular shapes, their fame fading with every year that distanced them from their storied accomplishments at Rose Hill, though the poetry and mythology of their nickname saved them from oblivion.

Devil Doll Franco operated a forty-two-lane bowling alley in Secaucus, New Jersey. Leo Paquin was still head football coach at Xavier Prep in Manhattan, where his charges had once competed against Lombardi's little Saints. Tarzan Druze had experienced a coaching rise and fall, working as an assistant for Frank Leahy at Boston College and Notre Dame before getting his chance as head coach at Marquette University, where he lasted only two losing seasons; he found a job with the Denver-Chicago Trucking Company in central New Jersey. Natty Pierce was in charge of physical rehabilitation at a veterans hospital on Long Island. Ali Baba Babartsky managed a plant for Fruehauf Trailer Company in Dayton. And Alex Wojciechowicz, the mighty Wojy, after an illustrious pro career as a linebacker for the Lions and Eagles, returned home to the Jersey shore to sell real estate. Sleepy Jim Crowley worked the rubber chicken circuit as a wisecracking toastmaster and served on the Pennsylvania Boxing Commission.

Lombardi had been the least publicized of Crowley's linemen during their glory days at Fordham, and he got the slowest career start after college. Three of the Blocks (Franco, Babartsky and Wojciechowicz) had played in the NFL, and the other three (Pierce, Druze and Paquin) had entered the coaching ranks before him. During those early days there was no certainty that Lombardi would go furthest in football. His apprenticeship had taken twenty years, but now suddenly he was a bright new national sports figure, being honored by his reunited friends for his selection as NFL coach of the year for his inaugural 1959 season in Green Bay.

Lombardi's triumphant return east brought Harry Lombardi down to Jersey City from Englewood, along with Father Tim Moore and his merry band of Carmelite Saints. A contingent of New York sportswriters crossed the Hudson, marking Lombardi as the coach to watch in a league that was rising along with the new decade. In the locker room after the game, which Green Bay won, 16 to 7, Tarzan Druze, who had been on the coaching staff at Notre Dame when Hornung played there, was shocked to see the Golden Boy sitting at his locker nursing a beer and a cigarette. Leahy would not have tolerated drinking and smoking in college, but this was the pros. "Yeah," Hornung said, catching Druze's surprised glance. "It's a little different here."

COACH OF THE YEAR. That 1959 rookie season in Green Bay had been an erratic one for Lombardi and his men. At first, this matter of winning seemed deceptively easy. The opening day triumph against the Bears was followed by two more home wins over the Detroit Lions and San Francisco 49ers, and by the middle of October the Packers were lodged in first place in the Western Conference. The turnaround coach was bathed in sporting press platitudes. Tom Miller, the team publicist, declared that Lombardi could have his choice of "being mayor of Green Bay or governor of Wisconsin." Headlines pronounced Lombardi a "Miracle Man." One New York newspaperman noted that "not since Napoleon's escape from Elba has such spirit been generated as the aroused hopes of Green Bay citizens over the comeback of their team." Tex Maule in *Sports Illustrated* found Lombardi's quick success as further proof of his theme that the modern professional game was becoming a sophisticated science. He wrote a column praising Lombardi's "cold, analytical mind" (and repeating the lore that the coach had a law degree).

The players themselves, when asked to account for their transformation, to a man attributed their success to Lombardi. Linebacker Tom Bettis admitted that he had shed twenty-five pounds in training camp and gained needed quickness because of Lombardi's conditioning program. Hawg Hanner, also in the best shape of his life, said the players were motivated by the fear that "if you goof off, somebody else will take your job." Gary Knafelc acknowledged that fear was a motivating factor, but said it made him play better. "We should have had Lombardi five years ago," he exclaimed. Lamar McHan, the rejuvenated quarterback, called Lombardi "a force" who radiated his "ability and desire" down to his men. He "knows what he is talking about," McHan added, "is very precise about it, and a lot of his orders work out." Lombardi, for his part, was not shy about accepting credit, telling one reporter: "You defeat defeatism with confidence, and confidence comes from the man who leads. You just have it. It is not something you get. You have to have it right here in your belly."

A test of that confidence came soon enough, along with a reminder that any coach, even one as effective as Lombardi, is not everything in football, that players also matter. By the time the Packers played their fourth game of the 1959 season against the Los Angeles Rams, they had lost their roughneck fullback, Jim Taylor, who had only just begun to show his great promise. A freak injury put him out of the lineup for several games. He had been lounging in the living room of his Green Bay apartment one weekday evening when his wife called out that a fire had started in the kitchen. She had been frying potatoes when the cooking grease burst into flames. Taylor dashed in, grabbed the frying pan and was trying to keep it balanced while carrying it outside, but spilled the hot grease, severely burning his right hand and bare feet. Three other starters were injured as well in more traditional football ways, and the Packers were outmatched by the Rams, losing 45 to 6. It was the start of a five-game losing streak, the longest of Lombardi's career.

There were a few moments of personal despair. Bart Starr became so despondent over his lack of playing time at quarterback behind McHan that he was spotted drinking several beers with Ron Kramer after a game in New York, a sighting as rare as a giraffe striding down Fifth Avenue. ("Bart had *four* beers. Miller High Lifes. It was the last time anyone saw him like that," Kramer later reported.) But for the most part the Packers maintained their confidence during the midseason losing streak. They felt like winners even as they were losing, so thoroughly had Lombardi rid them of the "defeatism" that had permeated the squad under Scooter McLean. Losing can have vastly disparate effects on athletes. Some teams learn nothing from a loss, but fall deeper into the abyss. The plays seem predictable, the squad grows selfish. Lombardi's team reacted in the opposite way. The players learned more about themselves with each loss—not only that they hated losing, but that they were close to winning and that, as McHan had said earlier, most of what Lombardi was teaching them actually worked and eventually would allow them to prevail. They learned something else equally important about their coach. As much as he ridiculed the notion of a good loser, he was not shortsighted in pursuit of victory. The truth was that he seemed more ornery after a game in which they had played poorly and won than after a loss in which they had played hard.

After five weeks of being battered and beaten, the Packers closed the season with four straight wins, finishing with a record of 7 and 5, good enough for third place in the west, the first Green Bay team in a dozen years to have more wins than losses. The offense began clicking during the winning streak. After McHan left the lineup with an injury, and Joe Francis was tried briefly, Lombardi finally called on Starr. The fourth-year man from Alabama still seemed tentative and prone to throwing interceptions, but he improved week by week, and by the final two games on the West Coast against the Rams and 49ers, which the Packers won convincingly, 38 to 20 and 36 to 14, he seemed to be operating the most explosive offense in the league. Taylor had returned to bang through the middle, Hornung had perfected the option sweep, throwing two touchdown passes in the final game, and Starr had begun to learn how to become Lombardi's quarterback, which is to say he was starting to think exactly like the coach.

It was during the San Francisco game that Starr had a quarterback's epiphany. He was poised at the line of scrimmage, bent over center waiting for the snap, and as he looked across the line he read the defense in a nanosecond and changed the play accordingly. What had once seemed rushed and confusing now seemed clear and obvious, as though it were all happening in slow motion. One quick look and everything that Lombardi had taught him snapped into order: read and react, freedom within discipline. It was also during the 49ers game that Starr began to assert himself with his teammates, at one point insisting that the garrulous Max McGee "hush up!" in the huddle. The order had a delayed effect: it seemed so out of character that Jim Ringo called a timeout so the offensive linemen could stop laughing; but from then on, Starr commanded his team's respect.

Soon after the season ended Lombardi appeared on Frank Gifford's "It's Sports Time" radio show in New York and was introduced by his former player as having overseen "the best reclamation project since the raising of the *Normandie.*" The Packers might not yet be the best club in the league, Lombardi told Gifford, "but in one quality there are few like it. We have great determination. And in Bart Starr we're going to have one of the great quarterbacks in football. In fact, Frank, with what we've already shown, it makes me want to look forward to next season." Later that week, while he was still on the East Coast, visiting with Harry and Matty and the rest of the Lombardi family, he was named NFL coach of the year in an Associated Press poll of sportswriters and sportscasters. "Vinnie, Vidi, Vici—NFL's Top Coach," read the headline in one New York paper. He won twenty-nine of thirty-seven first-place votes, with four going to Jim Lee Howell of the Giants and two to Weeb Ewbank of the Colts, whose teams were meeting for the second straight year in the championship game. "I was hoping to win five games— tops," he told the press that day. "Seven was a surprise. Determination made the difference. . . . I know it sounds corny, but that's the way it was."

When he got back to Green Bay, Ruth McKloskey, his secretary, noticed a certain bounce in his step as he "strutted around" the office, smiling broadly when someone mentioned the honor. Then Marie dropped by and decided that he seemed a little too proud of himself. "You may be coach of the year to everybody else," she said. "But you're still just Vince Lombardi to me." There were times when he responded to his wife's irritations by yelling at her, even in public—"Shut up, Marie!" was one of his familiar refrains. This time he turned silent until she left. "Boy, he didn't like that, because she said it in front of us," McKloskey later recounted. "He didn't say anything, but he got in his office and you could just tell."

NINETEEN SIXTY, the dawn of a new decade, a time to move up and out, and the Lombardis followed the crowd from city to suburb, from old house to new, heading farther south in Allouez past the massive stone State Reformatory out to a custom-built ranch house on Sunset Circle constructed to display the middle-class modern tastes that Marie shared with her husband. It was one level, long and low, with a narrow front portico, red brick with two front picture windows trimmed in white, wide driveway leading to side garage, sleek, elegant French furniture, custom drapes from H. C. Prange's (hung twice before Marie approved), built-in grill next to the kitchen stove, open counter leading from kitchen to the eating room, wall-to-wall carpeting, den and TV room around the back ell with wood paneling and console television in front of two big chairs, one the Old Man's recliner, a bedroom nearby, two more down the far hall, another guest bedroom in the basement behind the house-long rectangular party room and bar for entertaining friends after games. Three fireplaces went unused; Lombardi was afraid of fire, haunted by a childhood mishap in which he had burned his arm.

The setting seemed exotic then, so open and modern in contrast to the old streets of the east side that intersected Riverside on the way downtown: slightly humped in the middle and sloping to the curbs, darkened by overhanging oaks and elms, two-story wood-frame houses huddling close together, block after block of the same rectangular grid. Sunset Circle broke into daylight, a daring half-loop of quarter-acre lots with undeveloped land separating the four families inside the semicircle. Between the Lombardis and Riverside Drive stood vacant land that later served as an informal parking lot for Packers fans who drove out after Sunday victories to gaze at the coach's shrine. To the west and across the loop was a field of river brush and wild asparagus that grew down to the railroad bed running alongside the nearby Fox River. All this within easy commute of Lombardi's three primary workplaces: 3.8 miles up Riverside Drive and Monroe Street, then left at Crooks to reach the downtown Packer offices; about six miles up and across the river to City Stadium, and only 1.6 miles south to the training camp at St. Norbert in West De Pere. He could reach any of them within fifteen minutes.

It was not just the unused fireplaces that made the new Lombardi house feel cold. Inside, it seemed uncomfortably silent and somber much of the week. The halls were dark and uninviting. A friend of Susan's said that her lasting image of the home was "one of sadness. . . . It was a sad house as soon as you walked in, empty, you could feel the family void." The defining scene was at the dinner table: Vincent on one side, quiet and tense; Susan on the other, chatting away, oblivious, until she realized that no one was responding to her; Marie perched at the end nearest the kitchen, impeccably dressed, bony and uneasy, offering little visible motherly comfort to her children, barely showing interest in the events of their days, instead focusing her gaze on her husband across the way, looking at him with awe and adoration as he sat there, eyes on his plate, chewing his meat, thinking about . . . who knows what? Starr's sore ribs? The Bears linebackers? The Rams passing game? A new wrinkle in the belly series? When he cleared his throat, the others stiffened with anticipation: maybe, at last, the father would speak, his voice deep and resounding. *Pass the salt, Marie.*

Little Ricky was gone by then. The dachshund scrambled for daylight whenever the front door opened, even on the bleakest of northern Wisconsin days, and one morning he made a vain effort to flee across the street and was struck by a snowplow. Marie took him to the vet and had him put to sleep, then broke the news to Susan and Vincent, a more difficult task than the time back in New Jersey when she had to tell them that she had gassed their pet duck. The house would become even emptier with Vincent leaving— bound for college at St. Thomas, a small private school in St. Paul, Minnesota, where he could play football with minimum pressure. Vincent had matured during his year and a half at Green Bay Premontre, but his teenage life as the namesake of Vince Lombardi was still stressful. His father, preoccupied with coaching duties, did not find time to watch any of his football games, a paternal absence that was in dramatic contrast to the devotion with which old Harry had followed Vince's playing career at St. Francis and Fordham. Vince was Harry's life in a way that Vince could not repeat for Vincent. He did attend one meeting of the parents club, but Father Tom Dewane, then a teacher at Premontre, recalled that he appeared "bored to death and never came back." Vincent always felt the Old Man's stern judgment looming over him even when his father was not there physically.

The conflict between father and son worried Marie, who tried to ease the tension. She attended Vincent's games and cheered him on, believing that he could be a superior athlete, but "because of this thing with his father, he was too tense." Vincent's grades improved considerably at Premontre, but one time he received a deficiency slip, which was sent home to Lombardi, who resorted to his favorite disciplinary measure by grounding the son. Marie felt that Vincent was isolated enough in Wisconsin and did not deserve such harsh punishment. She called the Premontre principal and pleaded, "If my son ever gets in trouble again, please don't send it to Vince, send it to me."

Even when Vincent tried to emulate his father, it seemed to backfire. In his senior year at Premontre, he revealed to his dad that his ambition was to become a coach. Football was Vincent's world, like his father's. He could not imagine anything else. Yet when he announced that he intended to major in physical education in preparation for a coaching career, Lombardi reacted coldly, saying, "That's fine with me, but if you do, I'll not put one penny toward your education." It turned out that Lombardi wanted his son to be a lawyer, the same ambition his parents once had for him. In the summer before college, Vincent worked at a pickle factory, a job his father had arranged. His function on the assembly line was to take jars of pickles off a conveyor belt and load them into crates. If this was meant to toughen Vincent, he reacted the same way Lombardi had back when he was forced to haul huge slabs of frozen meat at Harry's wholesale butcher shop—he hated it. The one image Vincent carried with him decades later was of a bored worker "pissing into the vat" of pickle brine. It was a relief for him to quit that job and serve as a ball boy at training camp in late July, and even more of a relief to flee Green Bay for a new life at college.

One person unmoved by Vincent's departure was his younger sister. Susan and Vincent, separated by five years, were also distant emotionally and intellectually. They scrapped constantly. When their parents were out and Vincent was forced to babysit, he sent Susan to her room and imprisoned her there, chasing her back if she tried to escape. Seeking revenge once, she and Mary Jo Antil slipped into his room before he had returned from football practice and placed thumbtacks under the bedsheet. After plopping down on the bed and yelping in pain, he chased her out the back door with a baseball bat. Their differences were so evident that later in life Susan asked her brother in puzzlement, "How could you and I get raised in the same family?" Vincent was anxious, earnest, intelligent, with an outward appearance of arrogance that hid his inner struggle to understand himself and to overcome the guilt he felt for failing to live up to his father's image. Susan was carefree, loud, open, friendly, never a good student, struggling to hold down her weight, more frustrating to her parents than to herself. She was disarmingly candid about her shortcomings and her difficult position as the daughter of the coach in a town where football was everything. *I know the truth!* she would declare forthrightly. *I know they only like me because I'm Lombardi's daughter.* Yet she thirsted for affection and would take it any way she could get it. Her favorite place was not at home nor at school, but at the stables at Oneida Golf and Riding, where her horse, Captain Gladys, greeted her with unconditional love.

Marie at times seemed harsh in dealing with Susan's appearance. At social gatherings at Sunset Circle, Susan often served hors d'oeuvres to the guests. One evening, as she moved around the room with a tray, her mother blurted out, loud enough for all to hear, "God, I wish that girl could lose weight!" The grief Susan took from her father was louder but less personal. "What you saw on the field where he'd be yelling and screaming—he came home and did that. We never questioned it," Susan remembered. "My father was a great one for screaming and yelling at you, then turning around and saying, 'I'm sorry.' " When he yelled at Susan, it was usually over some trivial matter such as his socks. He maintained a precise order in his sock drawer— black, blue, brown, white—and took inventory every day or so, largely because he was color-blind and did not want to be embarrassed wearing an inappropriate color with his shoes and slacks. Susan often slipped into his room and filched a pair of white socks, but rarely got away with it. "He knew how many pairs he had. And he'd come out screaming and yelling until I coughed up the socks. It could be pretty explosive."

For the most part, though, Susan's relationship with her father was less tense than Vincent's. When Lombardi found time for her, he showed uncharacteristic patience. She long remembered the few times he brought her into the living room, where they sat together reverently listening to *Madame Butterfly* on a reel-to-reel tape, with her father narrating the story ("This is when she is going to try to kill herself"). Unlike his brother Harold, who was then working for an insurance company in San Francisco, Vince was unsophisticated in the arts, but he enjoyed opera, along with the popular music of Frank Sinatra, Tony Bennett, Dean Martin and Bobby Darin. "He thought he could sing," Susan later said of him, sarcastically. "He'd walk around the house trying to sing 'Mack the Knife.' " He was also entranced by modern contraptions: once he had appeared at the front door of the Antils' house holding a battery-operated, portable record player under his arm. "Listen to this," he said, when Mary Jo Antil answered the door, and he pushed a button and beamed as though he were witnessing a miracle as the tinny sound of his favorite song crackled out: ". . . and when that shark bites, with his teeth, babe . . ."

This autocrat of the football world found pleasure in unexpected diversions and habits. His favorite method of easing tension at home was cleaning closets. He also enjoyed reading mathematics books and was an ardent collector of cookbooks, accumulating scores of them, even though Marie preferred to eat out and his own culinary skills stopped at char-grilled steaks and wet scrambled eggs. It was an escape into fantasy for him; he would read a cookbook with the same narrative delight that he had long ago taken in the adventure tales of Richard Halliburton—not skipping around from the table of contents to favorite selections, but moving page by page, from front cover to back, engrossed in the plot line from tomatoes Provençal to Italian Parmesan and egg soup to braised rack of lamb to marzipan cake. "You know what, we really ought to make this," he declared now and then, but they never would. Another of his fantasies was that he was a magician. He took childlike delight in magic tricks, and practiced a few of the simplest ones involving strings, balls and handkerchiefs over and over, though never nearing mastery. "Mr. Lombardi, you blew it!" a neighborhood boy screamed one day when Lombardi tried to perform a trick making a cigarette move on the table while rubbing the youngster's head.

Everyone in town seemed to know the coach, but Lombardi's inner circle of Green Bay friends was relatively small. It included Canadeo and Bourguignon from the Packers board of directors, and several cronies from the foursomes at Oneida Golf and Riding, among them Jack Koeppler, an insurance man who underwrote the Packers' team policies; Ray Antil, Mary Antil's husband, a salesman who specialized in a line of Packers memorabilia; Jake Stathas, the auto dealer who provided Lombardi with his choice of Pontiac Bonnevilles and Catalinas every six months from Brown County Motors; and Harry Masse, who owned a local printing company. Father Dennis Burke, president of St. Norbert, and various other priests and doctors also were allowed into his coveted inner circle, along with old friends and sportswriters visiting from the East. The Green Bay press was decidedly not part of the group, nor were his assistant coaches or other members of the Packers front office. He socialized only on weekends during the season and followed a familiar routine.

Friday night began with cocktails at Dick and Lois Bourguignon's. Then down to the strip on Washington Street in a caravan of cars and inside Wally Proski's Food and Cocktail Lounge for the Green Bay Catholic ritual of Fish Fry Friday, the proprietor greeting Vince at the door, all smiles and pats on the back, the other regular patrons looking up, seeing the coach, murmuring, but allowing him his privacy, the party ushered into a back room, plates of fish and fries and slaw and pitchers of beer, then out into the dark northern night for the ride back to Allouez. Saturday found Vince relaxed, surprisingly at ease just at the time when most coaches would be unapproachable—which he seemed to be almost anytime *except* then. With preparations complete, the game plan set, for a few hours at least Mr. High-Low was demonstrably high, free and easy with his pals on the golf course in early autumn, playing gin in the clubhouse, treating himself and Marie to sixteen-ounce porterhouse steaks at the elegant Stratosphere Club out on County Trunk N.

There was more socializing on Sunday after the game. Friends, priests, visiting journalists thawing out, chatting, drinking whiskey and Budweiser and Hamm's in the wood-paneled basement rec room on Sunset Circle, smoke curling toward the low ceiling. Jake Stathas as bartender, pouring Lombardi's liquor into glass tumblers, bourbon for himself, scotch for the coach. Father Burke of St. Norbert munching away on the chips and Marie's hot crabmeat dip—cream cheese, crabmeat, mayo, mustard and a touch of wine, fresh from the oven. Lombardi leaning on the bar, sipping his drink, a

Salem burning away in the groove of his big glass ashtray, taking calls and greeting guests. You could tell how the game went without going to City Stadium; if Lombardi was booming, laughing, illuminating the room with his teeth, the Pack had played well, no doubt. Then off to another restaurant, alternately the Zuider Zee or Manci's Supper Club, Lombardi seated next to a priest, growing quieter by the minute, until finally Marie would look over and realize that he was gone, lost to the world, drained from the last game, anxious about the next one. This was his worst time, Sunday night around eight o'clock, when, as he once described it, "that deep, dull, indescribable weariness . . . began extracting the cork, or so it seemed, from my whole being." The only way he could overtake the weariness was by thinking about the next game. Marie could see precisely what was happening and thought to herself, she said later, "Oh, boy, he's coaching again. The curtain's come down." The change was so dramatic and predictable that she took to calling him Cinderella.

Marie fell into a depression after her son left for college, a mood for which her drinking was alternately cause and effect. She seemed to disappear occasionally during parties at her home; only her family knew that she had passed out in bed. She had conflicted feelings about her situation in Green Bay. She told friends that she felt it was her role to control her husband's pride and temper and to serve as a buffer between Vin and his players and the community. Yet the fact that he was becoming an esteemed public figure made her feel more worthy. Some in Green Bay saw this response as an expression of regal arrogance, and they found it offputting, particularly in combination with her sharp Jersey accent, her loud voice, direct manner, tailored clothes, and preference for long fur coats and jewelry. There were whispers around town about Marie's aloofness, an easterner who could not fit in. She in turn expressed puzzlement at what she considered the too-cozy behavior of the locals. In Green Bay "they would say, 'There's a new painting at the museum,' and collect forty people to go see it," she once explained. "I'd rather go by myself."

But she was not a recluse. She formed close friendships with a few women, including Lois Bourguignon, and became a presence in Green Bay social circles, participating in the Christian Mothers Society, the Antiquarian Society and the Republican Club, making dazzling ornaments, beaded flowers and crocheted tablecloths for church bazaars, instructing the younger wives of Lombardi's assistants in the ways of being a coach's wife. That last was the mission she took most seriously, bringing to it more devotion than she demonstrated as a mother. She became expert in the art of explaining her husband—which days he would be distant and distracted, which days she could talk to him. She studied the players, assessing which ones had talent, quietly soothing the feelings of those who had encountered Lombardi's wrath. *Can you get him off my back?* a player would ask her, to which she would reply, *How would you like to live with him?* The exchange was at once lighthearted and truthful. The players unavoidably caught a few uncomfortable glimpses of the tension within the Lombardi marriage. As much as Marie tried to adjust to her husband's life, sometimes it was not enough. At the training table one evening, Marie had ordered a special ice cream dessert for herself when the team was being served pie, and when Vince noticed it he banged his fist on the table and shouted, "Goddamn it, Marie! When you're with the team, you eat what the team eats!"

Yet no one could better interpret Lombardi's psyche than Marie. Many Packers came to accept his punishing style, or at least endure it, after Marie let them in on the secret she had learned after twenty years at his side: If Lombardi was on your case that meant he saw something in you. There was more reason to be concerned if he didn't yell at you; that usually meant you were a goner.

WILLIE WOOD seemed an exception to that rule. As a twenty-three-year-old rookie in 1960, he sprinted through training camp without encountering any disparaging words from the coach, or many words at all. After the first two weeks Lombardi walked past him on the way off the practice field and muttered, "Keep up the good work, Willie." Later, before the exhibition game in Jersey City honoring the Seven Blocks, the coach warned Wood that he should play through the pain of a strained ankle. "If you want to make this team, you can't make it being injured," Lombardi said tersely in the locker room, walking away before his young player could respond. "Well, I better get well," Wood thought to himself, according to his later account. "The first thing I can't do with this man is complain about injuries."

That William Verneli Wood was challenging for a place on the Packers at all was a measure of his mental strength and perseverance. It also underscored the determination of Lombardi and his personnel man, Jack Vainisi, to ignore the prejudices then prevalent in most NFL front offices in their search for the most talented players. Not that Wood came out of nowhere. For most of his junior year and all of his senior year, he had been the starting quarterback at the University of Southern California, one of the nation's leading programs, yet NFL scouts left him off their lists of prospects, partly on the advice of his college coaches, who claimed that he lacked the skills to make it at the next level. When the rookie draft was held before the 1960 season, 240 players were chosen, five from USC, but Wood was not among them. He was neglected, considered a man without a position, said to lack the arm of a quarterback or the speed of a running back. Left unstated, but influencing his situation as much as anything, was the fact that Wood was a black quarterback in an era when black athletes were seldom allowed the opportunity to play that position. Their numbers were slim in college and virtually nonexistent in the pros. (The Packers were among the few teams that had ever carried a black quarterback on their roster: Charlie Brackins from Prarie View A&M had been drafted in the seventeenth round in 1955 and made the roster briefly; he suited up for seven games and played once, but completed no passes and then was cut.)

Wood "looked raw failure in the face" and refused to accept it. After being shunned on draft day, he retreated to the cramped one-room studio apartment that he shared with his wife on the USC campus and typed a letter introducing himself, detailing his college record and stating that he could contribute to some team if only given the chance. Where should he send the letter? He had already made one painful but crucial decision, offering his services as a defensive back rather than quarterback. He studied the rosters of all thirteen NFL teams (the odd thirteenth club, added that year, was the Dallas Cowboys, originally named the Dallas Rangers), analyzing which ones might need a ballhawking safety. Wood had grown up in Washington, D.C., in the shadows of Union Station, and was a star athlete at Armstrong High near the corner of 1st and O Streets NW (from where a young USC assistant named Al Davis had recruited him to junior college and then to USC). But he never considered playing for the Washington Redskins, even though they were woefully in need of defensive talent. His hometown was still segregated, the most southern city in the league, and its owner, George Preston Marshall, was an unreconstructed racist who did not want black players on his team. Wood decided to send his letter to the Giants and 49ers, which had well-established traditions of hiring black players, and to the Packers. He "didn't know Lombardi from Adam," he said later, but he had heard that Green Bay had a new front office and surmised that they might be interested in him.

The Packers were in fact the only team to respond. First came a positive letter from Lombardi, followed shortly by a visit from Vainisi. At first glance, Wood was not the most impressive recruit. He stood just under five ten, weighed less than 175 pounds, and his sprint times were average. But he had broad shoulders and a thick neck, along with some unteachable traits: he was fearless, quick and agile, able to touch the top of the goalpost crossbar with his elbow from a standing leap. Vainisi offered him a $6,500 contract and sealed the agreement with a handshake. Wood was the last man to make the 1960 squad, and he was overwhelmed after it became clear that he had survived. When the Packers traded his rookie competitor for the final slot to the Dallas expansion team, he called his old high school coach, Ted McIntyre, who had also lobbied the Packers to sign Wood, and shouted into the phone, "Hey, I made it, Coach! I made it!" Thinking back on what he had endured, he realized it had been worth the pain and effort. "It was such a long shot. I was so pleased with myself." That lasted until the following Monday morning, when Wood attended his first meeting of the regular season squad. There stood Lombardi in the front of the room, glaring directly at the rookie, or so it seemed, and declaring that nobody really made his team until the second year, and even then they shouldn't feel too comfortable. "It was almost as though he was reading my mind," Wood said later. "He must have known that I might think the pressure was off, and it's never off. It was as though he was saying directly to me, 'You have to knock yourself out here every day.'"

Playing football, knocking himself out, was not the most trying task for Willie Wood during his rookie season with the Packers. He felt more pressure simply enduring the routines of daily life. He felt the blast heat of prejudice the first time he stepped off the bus as a Green Bay Packer before his first exhibition game, played against the Pittsburgh Steelers in New Orleans—a neutral site for everyone but the black athletes.

The scene remained vivid in Wood's memory: The team bus whines to a halt in front of a downtown hotel. Lombardi and the coaches march off, players clamber down and stream into the lobby, suitcases are unloaded from the belly of the coach and stacked near the registration desk. Emlen Tunnell, entering his thirteenth year in the league, dean of black ballplayers, knows the routine and hangs back. Whites only. The four black Packers must stay at a black hotel on the other side of town. But Tunnell forgets to tell the rookie about another Jim Crow edict: Stay outside. Don't even go in. Wood enters the lobby searching for his suitcase; a porter moves swiftly, intercepts him near the door and stiffly escorts him to the sidewalk. Four suitcases are finally hauled out for the four black players. There's a taxi by the curb. Wood opens the back door and starts to get in. No. Wrong cab. White cab. You can't get in a white cab. Have to catch a black one.

He has not played a game yet and he is "ready to explode." He is reminded inevitably of something worse that happened to him back during his first year in California, when he was playing for an otherwise all-white junior college out in the valley near Fresno, and his team arrived in the little town of Santa Maria. The local sheriff drove over to the hotel and announced that "the colored" player, Willie Wood, would be quarantined in his room that afternoon; no way he was going to be allowed to play on the same field with white boys.

Parched valley of California, river crescent of New Orleans, little difference. What about Green Bay? In the isolated province of northeastern Wisconsin, Wood and his black teammates—Tunnell, rookie receiver Paul Winslow and second-year defensive end Willie Davis, acquired from Cleveland—were strangers in a strange land. The four black Packers used to say that they constituted four-fifths of the permanent black population of the city, the fifth being the shoeshine man at the Hotel Northland. Now and then "you might see a black guy down near the train station or at the Y, just passing through," Wood said. This was a slight exaggeration: according to the 1960 U.S. Census, 128 blacks then lived in Brown County, but this was still only about .01 percent of the total population. Wood could not imagine that the racial homogeneity of Green Bay was happenstance. "There were no blacks there, and we just automatically assumed that none were there because nobody wanted them there, so you also automatically just assumed that your stay there would be unpleasant." Green Bay citizens did not seem hostile so much as uninformed on matters of race. During Wood's first month in town, he encountered a woman who remarked that she had "never met a Negro before" and that she was surprised he seemed so polite; she had only read about "you folks fightin' and fussin' in Chicago all the time."

The trailblazer for black players in Green Bay had been Bob Mann, a gifted end from the University of Michigan who arrived in 1950 (after playing briefly for the Lions) and stayed five seasons. During Mann's time in Green Bay the local newspaper referred to him as a "colored" athlete until he finally took sportswriter Art Daley aside one day and said, "We don't want to be called colored, we're Negroes." Daley pleaded ignorance. He had grown up in Fond du Lac without ever knowing a black person. "I don't know why I used 'colored'—dumb shit, I was. I wouldn't think of using that today," Daley reflected more than forty years later. Jim Crow segregation was not in effect in Green Bay, but private housing was largely unavailable to black players during the 1950s and at the beginning of Lombardi's tenure. Their living quarters were so inadequate that the married men among them chose to keep their families away during the season. Mann had lodged in a trailer. Davis and Winslow shared a rundown bungalow behind an industrial lot, and Wood spent his rookie year at the downtown YMCA, where his bill was a buck fifty per night, a modest rent that he reduced even further by checking out before road trips.

Em Tunnell, a bachelor who loved the high life of Harlem nightclubs, where he was as much a celebrity as Billy Eckstine, found a room at the Hotel Northland at the corner of Adams and Pine, one block from the Y. "Yes, Your Hotel Northland Has Kept Pace," boasted the establishment in its advertisements. The proof: two automatic elevators, the "most modern hotel desk in the Middle West," along with a new coffee shop, bay room and dining room. Despite these amenities Tunnell was excruciatingly bored in the dead old building in a ghostly white town, but at least the Old Man secretly picked up his tab; Lombardi respected and needed Tunnell's experience that much.

"I'd get out of this town if it wasn't for Vince," Tunnell told a visiting reporter from New York. "He's real brass, real arrogant. He's the kind of guy you have to cuss out once a week when you're alone. But nobody else can cuss him out to me. In my heart, I know what he is." Tunnell could offer no more impressive endorsement of his coach, and his black teammates felt the same way. Wood called him "perhaps the fairest person I ever met." Race was an issue that revealed the integrity of Lombardi's character. In later years he would try to explain his position on racial matters by saying that he viewed his athletes as neither black nor white, but Packer green. He insisted that there were "no barriers" on his team and all things were "equal, racially and socially." He was color-blind, he said. And though this was literally true—Lombardi *was* color-blind—there was more to it than that. It has always been easy for whites to claim color blindness in the United States since white is the dominant color in American society, but the claim often serves as a ruse for not recognizing the particular obstacles faced by non-whites. Lombardi might have seen only one color on the football field, but he was not blind to the discrimination that his black players encountered off the field, and he did everything he could to ease their way in an alien environment.

During his first year in Green Bay, Lombardi called his team together on the practice field and delivered a rare lecture on racism. "If I ever hear nigger or dago or kike or anything like that around here, regardless of who you are, you're through with me. You can't play for me if you have any kind of prejudice." His actions that year were more often quiet and behind the scenes, like paying Tunnell's hotel bill when it was hard to find suitable housing, or making sure the black players had enough money to go to Milwaukee or Chicago on off-days. But as his status and power increased in his second season, his sensitivity to racial inequities intensified as well, and his responses became more overt. Before the season began, Lombardi spread the word among Green Bay's tavern and restaurant owners that any establishment that did not welcome his black players would be declared off limits to the entire team. At Tunnell's suggestion, he allowed the black players to leave the St. Norbert training camp twice during the preseason for quick trips down to Milwaukee, the closest city where they could find barbers who knew how to cut their hair.

The Jim Crow discrimination that black Packers faced when the team played exhibition games in the South enraged Lombardi, and at the end of the 1960 preseason he decided that he would never again allow his team to be split by segregation; from then on, he said, any hotel that would not accommodate all Packers would get no Packers. The final preseason game that year was held in Winston-Salem, North Carolina, against the lily-white Washington Redskins. According to Lombardi lore, an event took place there that solidified the coach's decision to no longer submit his team to the segregation policies of the South. As the story goes, Lombardi, his naturally tawny skin further darkened by a month of practice sessions under the summer sun, entered a local restaurant the night before the game and was refused seating by a hostess who mistook him for a black man.

There is no documentation of the episode; decades later no one remaining from that team could remember precisely who was with him that night; and there are many apocrypha in the legend of St. Vincent of Green Bay—but this story nonetheless rings true. Lombardi told it to his family later, and to many of his players, and there was no reason for him to concoct it or exaggerate it. The black players often joked among themselves that by the end of summer camp their coach was a secret "brother." In any case, the all-for-one edict from Lombardi followed that trip to North Carolina. When he took the Packers into the Deep South the following summer for a game against the Redskins in Columbus, Georgia, he lodged the players at Fort Benning, the integrated army post, so that they could all stay together.

Lombardi had been keenly aware of the sting of prejudice long before his supposed *Black Like Me* experience in Winston-Salem. He had gone through life being called a dago and wop and guinea because of his dark skin and southern Italian heritage. Throughout his school years he had struggled to overcome the lower academic expectations that society seemed to have for Italian boys. In high school and college he had tried to dress more sharply, scrub cleaner, keep his hair trimmer and maintain a more businesslike appearance just so that he would not be defined by stereotypes. At Fordham, he had risked suspension from the football team by tackling and punching a teammate who had taunted him in the shower with ethnic epithets. At various points during his long apprenticeship in coaching, he had suspected that his advancement had been slowed by bias against Italians. But the world teems with people who are sensitive to prejudice only when it is against them, not when they are inflicting it on others. Lombardi's concern seemed universal, not merely self-centered.

There was evidence of this even when he moved in the most racially exclusive circles in Green Bay, such as his country club, Oneida Golf and Riding. Among the caddies at the all-white private club were several members of the Oneida Indian tribe who lived nearby on the western rim of Green Bay. Big Elroy and Ray Bear were legends at the course, said to know every blade of grass along Duck Creek, able to anticipate the slightest shift in wind. It was tradition for the Native Americans to caddy in the spring, when local teenagers were in school. "But the minute school let out, we'd take the white kids from school. Then when the kids went back to school, we'd take the Indians again," said Jack Koeppler, the insurance man who often played in the same foursome with his pal Lombardi. Koeppler said the men at the club followed that pattern, with one exception: Lombardi insisted on using Indian caddies year-round. "If they're good enough for spring and fall, they're good enough for summer," he once said. The first time he was greeted at the practice tee by a teenage boy, instead of Big Elroy, Lombardi stormed back to the clubhouse and "loudly berated" the club pro. He was a generous tipper to his caddies, and became a one-man interest-free lending institution as well. Indians in a financial pinch would appear behind the eighteenth green, taking a silent position down by the trees at the bottom of the hill, sometimes with wives and children, and wait for Lombardi to finish his round. Invariably, he would greet them, listen to their stories and provide the needed funds.

THE TRINITY OF LIFE, as Lombardi often described it, was God, family and the Green Bay Packers. He placed them in that order, though his family, in reality if not in his idealized image, usually came in third, unable to compete in his heart and mind with his dual passions of God and the Packers. There has been a tendency in recent decades to mix sport and religion in the most superficial, public ways, with athletes proclaiming that God healed an injury or guided the winning shot, that a comeback victory was the Lord's work, as though the Father and Son, if not the Holy Ghost, were taking sides and cared one whit about the outcome of games. It would be difficult to find someone who conjoined sport and religion more deeply than Lombardi, but as an old-line Catholic, trained by the Fordham Jesuits, he accomplished this in a more personal way, without proselytizing. He was not the sort to pray explicitly for victory over the Chicago Bears, but he could worry that his team might lose if he failed to pray before the Bears game. This was part raw superstition, part his sense that God cared not about the Packers or Bears but about the act of prayer itself.

Prayer was the essence of Lombardi's religious practice and the constant of his daily routine. Before he left Sunset Circle each morning, he fell to his knees in his bedroom and prayed to St. Anthony and St. Jude, their statue likenesses sitting atop his dresser above the sock drawer, icons he had carried with him since his days at Saints. Here was Lombardi, the winner, praying to saints of loss and miraculous recovery. Jude for the impossible, the lost cause. Anthony for finding what was lost, the lost key or lost emotion. "O Holy St. Anthony, gentlest of Saints, your love for God and Charity for His creatures made you worthy, when on earth, to possess miraculous powers. Miracles waited on your word, for which you were ever ready to speak for those in trouble or anxiety. Encouraged by this thought, I implore of you to obtain for me this request. The answer to my prayer may require a miracle, even so, you are the Saint of Miracles." The statues were ceramic, each a foot high, robed in green and blue paint, with the barefooted St. Jude revealing the holy spirit through the portal of an eternal flame burning atop his forehead.

In his coat pocket Lombardi carried old black wooden rosary beads. He had rubbed his long thick fingers over these same beads, uttering Hail Marys and Our Fathers, since studying for the seminary at Cathedral Prep. He even equipped his car for the purpose of prayer; snap-on rosary beads looped around the upper half of the steering wheel, allowing him to count off the decades while taking Susan to school or heading on to the office. The beads were fluorescent so that he could perform his prayerful obligations while driving at night. It was his usual practice to pray silently, but in the mornings during the six weeks of Lent, as he was driving Susan and her neighbor friend down to St. Joseph's Academy, he would recite the Rosary aloud all the way to town—and demand that the girls in the back stop gossiping and begin praying aloud along with him.

By his side in the car or at home were two religious books. The first was a new Holy Name Edition of the Catholic Bible, a treasured present he had received the previous spring, abundant in red leather, featuring full-color reproductions of masterpieces of religious art, photographs of the Vatican, the Sistine Chapel and the magnificent churches of Rome, and biographies of American cardinals. Inside were two black-and-white snapshots that his children had no idea he carried with him: one was of young Vincent and Susan playing in the backyard in Englewood at ages six and one; the other showed Susan as a pixie-faced six-year-old at West Point. Resting atop the Bible was a smaller book, a black leatherbound Maryknoll missal containing the prayers and responses for celebrating mass. Inside as book markers were two laminated holy cards. One featured a line from Ecclesiastes: "Be in peace with many but let one in a thousand be thy counselor." Another, hand-written, offered a prayer in case of unexpected death: "My God, if I am to die today, or suddenly at any time, I wish to receive this communion as my viaticum. I desire that my last food may be the body and blood of my savior and redeemer; my last words, of Jesus, Mary and Joseph; my last affection, an act of pure love of God and of perfect contrition for my sins; my last consolation, to die in the Holy Grace and in thy Holy Love. Amen."

That was among the prayers he whispered every day at his first stop, St. Willebrord, an old Dutch Catholic church near his office that was named for the patron saint of Holland and run by the Norbertines. St. Willebrord was a sturdy rectangle of orange brick and light stone dominating the corner of Adams and Doty, with a dark-shingled steeple rising to the low-slung northern sky. The church had taken on a new sheen at the time of Lombardi's arrival, its exterior sandblasted, thousands of bricks replaced, new plastic paint applied, and a six-foot statue of Christ the King, made from hard white Italian Carrara marble, erected on the south lawn. As a downtown institution convenient to urban professionals, St. Willebrord was among the more ethnically diverse churches in town. The French had St. John the Evangelist and St. John the Baptist, the Poles St. Mary of the Angels, the Belgians St. Peter and Paul and Holy Martyrs, the Irish St. Patrick, and the Germans St. Francis Xavier Cathedral. Lombardi was a daily communicant at St. Willebrord's eight o'clock mass, parking in the back lot, slipping in the side door and taking a pew near the white altar below an alignment of saints shining down from stained-glass windows. His daily ritual was so precise and predictable that Jim Huxford, who worked the sideline down-and-distance chains at Packers games, knew that if he drove by at 7:56 each day he could wave to the coach entering the church. Altar boys who regularly assisted when the priest served Lombardi wine and wafer noticed that his tongue was oddly serrated, bitten into jagged edges, perhaps from years of anxiety.

Lombardi fit comfortably into the religious culture of Green Bay, one of the most Catholic regions in the nation. Even Allouez, the suburb in which the Lombardis lived, had a Catholic origin; it was named for Claude Allouez, a Jesuit missionary and educator. Nearly three of every four residents of Green Bay identified themselves as Catholic. The parochial schools had as many students as the public school system. There were two Catholic high schools and ten Catholic elementary schools. Among the sixteen Catholic churches, worshipers could choose from forty-two masses during the week and ninety-four masses every Sunday, the earliest starting long before sunrise, at 4:30 a.m., the latest beginning at ten minutes past noon (only when the Packers were out of town or not playing). During the off-season or when the Packers were playing at home on Sundays, Lombardi attended mass at St. Matthew's parish church in Allouez (and later a new church there, Resurrection), taking a seat next to Marie near the center aisle about six rows back. The priests knew he was there, but tried not to look at him; one confessed later that if he made eye contact with Lombardi "the sermon was shot. Forget it. Just looking at him would throw you for a loop. He was so intense it was difficult to concentrate after catching his gaze." But for the most part, outside the church, priests and nuns were made to feel at ease around Lombardi, who had been accustomed to their presence in daily life since his Sheepshead Bay childhood.

There was no such thing as a practice session too secret for his friends in the clergy. Reporters would get the boot, but if Lombardi saw a priest hanging out on the other side of the gate, he was known to shout, "Hey, those are my agents, let them in." He was also a soft touch for nuns seeking tickets; they gobbled up a significant share of his fifty-seat allotment. Some priests had no need for tickets. Lombardi would give Father Burke game passes for himself and several fellow Norbertines. They stood on the sidelines near the bench; players joked on game day that it was hard to tell which Lombardi wanted more: to win or to get to heaven. He wanted both, of course. On rare occasions, he might introduce a touch of religion into his coaching by quoting a line from Scripture that he thought would inspire his troops, but he did not invoke God or Jesus in his locker-room pep talks. In a sense, there was no need for that—the currents of sports and spirituality within him converged at a deeper point than mere rhetoric. The fundamental principles that he used in coaching—repetition, discipline, clarity, faith, subsuming individual ego to a larger good—were merely extensions of the religious ethic he learned from the Jesuits. In that sense, he made no distinction between the practice of religion and the sport of football.

His religious side, in one sense, did serve as a necessary antidote to his football obsession. In order to be the best coach, to keep winning, to stand out from his peers, he understood that at some level he had to be imbalanced, to sacrifice his family, to use some of his darker characteristics, especially his volatility, to his advantage. His temper and impatience, he once said, were characteristics that he was "never able to subdue wholly." To some extent he regretted this, but he also feared that if he had been more in control of his emotions he "would not have coached effectively." His daily prayers were an effort to balance the tension between his will to succeed and his desire to be good. His son, Vincent, as he sought to understand his father's motivations over the years, later revealed perhaps the clearest appreciation of the contradiction at the center of Vince Lombardi. "He went to mass to repent for his anger," Vincent explained. "He thought, I've got this temper. I fly off the handle and offend people. I apologize. But it's this temper that keeps me on edge and allows me to get things done and people to do things. Life was a struggle for him. He knew he wasn't perfect. He had a lot of habits that were far from perfect. His strengths were his weaknesses, and vice versa. He fought it by taking the paradox to church. It went back to the Jesuits and the struggle between the shadow self and the real self—your humanity and your divinity. He saw that struggle in clear and concrete terms."

TODAY it requires an intricate computer program analyzing thousands of variables to construct a season schedule for the National Football League, but during Lombardi's early years with the Packers the task was simple and the pattern predictable—even in 1960 when the league expanded to Dallas and briefly became imbalanced with thirteen teams. Lombardi began every year knowing that he would open with four home games, three in Green Bay and one in Milwaukee, and that near the end of the year he would be competing mostly in enemy stadiums, with a traditional Thanksgiving Day contest against the Lions in Detroit and a December road trip finale to the West Coast for games against San Francisco and Los Angeles. The schedule seemed a reasonable adjustment to the weather, front-loading home games for the early fall and escaping to California for the harsh northern winter, but the lack of balance also meant that the Packers could not afford slow starts—they had to take advantage of the early run in Wisconsin—and could not falter down the stretch during pressure games on the road. The pattern of those early schedules seemed to shape the rhythm of Lombardi's teams: his rigorous training camps and pedagogical methods were designed to build teams that were mentally and physically strongest during the first quarter and the fourth, at the start of every season and at the end.

The Packers opened the 1960 season with the opposite rhythm, losing at home to Chicago, 17 to 14, when the Bears came back and scored all of their points in the fourth quarter. Disaster seemed possible, with the talented Detroit Lions and two-time champion Baltimore Colts visiting Green Bay for the following two Sundays, but the Packers won both games handily, launching a four-game winning streak that carried them to the top of the standings by early November. If the first humans were produced by Thunder and Lightning, as the Winnebago Indian tradition held, the same was being said of these Packers. Thunder was Jim Taylor, the bruising fullback, on his way to his first thousand-yard season, and Lightning was Paul Hornung, the left halfback, who had an uncanny knack for finding the end zone and lighting up the scoreboard, on his way to a record-shattering 176 points. Taylor and Hornung were about results, nothing more; other backfields around the league were bigger and faster, but none produced like Thunder and Lightning. It was said of Taylor that he loved contact so much that if no defensive backs were in his way he would go find one. To watch Hornung run at midfield was nothing special—he seemed a step slow and uninspired—but near the goal line he was the best, unstoppable.

The predictable midseason slump began at Baltimore in the sixth game. Lombardi knew it would be a trying day; the Colts, especially the passing combination of Johnny Unitas and Raymond Berry, had been all too familiar to him since the famous sudden-death championship game in 1958, his last as an assistant coach with the New York Giants. Unitas and Berry were at their prime now, each on his way to a record year, and the Packers secondary was hobbling. During pregame warmups Jesse Whittenton, the speedy left cornerback, pulled a leg muscle. In his fifth professional season out of Texas Western, Whittenton was the most talented of the Katzenjammer Kids, the nickname defensive coach Norb Hecker gave his devilish Lone Star backfield trio of Whittenton, Hank Gremminger and Johnny Symank. When the Colts game began, Whittenton tried to cover Berry, but he limped to the sidelines in pain halfway through the first quarter, and Lombardi instructed Hecker to "put Wood in there!" Willie Wood was a safety, being tutored to replace Em Tunnell, and had never played the corner before, but when Hecker asked him if he could handle it, he nodded yes and sprinted onto the field. As soon as he arrived, shouts of "Number 24! Number 24!" came from the Baltimore bench, signaling Unitas that an untested rookie was in the game.

Unitas immediately started flinging passes Berry's way, one hitch pattern after another, with the hesitant Wood arriving a second late every time. Finally, Wood said to himself, "If he runs another hitch, I'm gonna come up and be right there." Berry ran it, and Wood arrived quickly, only to discover that it was a fake. Unitas pumped and Berry took off deep, getting behind the Packers secondary for a long completion. They yanked Wood from the game after that and tried another young player, Dick Pesonen, who fared no better. Berry finished with ten catches for 137 yards, totals matched by the fleet flanker, Lenny Moore. At the airport after the game, as the team waited for the charter flight back to Wisconsin, Willie Davis and Jim Ringo and several other teammates started ribbing Wood. *You live in Dee-Cee, doncha? Ain't no need for you going back to Green Bay. Might as well stay here 'cause they're going to send your ass home anyway.*

Wood thought they had a point, until Lombardi overheard the conversation and took his rookie aside. "Don't you believe anything those fellows say. You're not going anywhere," Lombardi told him. "You're staying right with me. Every one of those guys making fun of you has had the same thing happen to them. You're going to be here as long as I'm here." It was the longest conversation Wood had ever had with his coach, and the most meaningful. Until then, he had not been sure where he stood with Lombardi. He was embarrassed, his confidence shaken, by the way Berry had beaten him. Were the NFL scouts right not to draft him? Lombardi waited until the precise moment when it would mean the most, when Wood was doubting himself, and then assured him that what had happened to him was no big deal, that there would be hundreds of other days of redemption, and that the coach believed in him. "He gave me confidence when he did that. I said, 'What I'm doing has got to be right because the man believes in me,'" Wood said later. "I think it made a hell of a better ballplayer out of me." Hell of a better ballplayer, indeed. When Lombardi bucked up his rookie that day at the airport in Baltimore, it might be said that Willie Wood started his long and improbable leap toward the Pro Football Hall of Fame.

The losing continued. The Packers dropped two of their next three games, and they headed home from Detroit on Thanksgiving evening after a 23 to 10 loss with a middling record of 5 wins and 4 losses. Taylor and Hornung were still going strong, but the quarterback position seemed uncertain again. Starr had been throwing too many interceptions, and Lamar McHan performed no better when given the chance. It might have been a dispiriting holiday, lonely and lost, but once again the coach showed a knack for pulling things together at the critical moment. Instead of lambasting his players for their mistakes (two fumbles and a punt blocked for a safety), he let them drink two beers on the flight home, spoke spiritedly to them about how they would right themselves for the rest of the season, and later that night brought them all downtown to the Elks Club with their families for a turkey dinner.

The Old Man could be gruff, awkward, unrelenting, but now he showed another side. All night long he moved from table to table, slapping backs, chatting with wives, joking with kids, inviting them to watch cartoons from a projector that had been set up downstairs, embracing everyone as part of his big happy brood. Watching him that night, Bob Skoronski thought of him as "the total father figure for the whole group." If only for a few hours, Lombardi was fulfilling a deep longing. Not on the football field, not yet, but here at dinner among his Packers he had closed the mystical gap between the hugeness of his desire and the smallness of reality. He might be silent and distant at the dinner table on Sunset Circle, but at this moment he seemed transported in time back to those childhood Sundays at the family homestead on East Sixteenth Street among the bountiful Izzos of Sheepshead Bay.

14

Remembering Jack

ON THE SUNDAY after Thanksgiving, shortly after ten in the morning, Jack Vainisi collapsed in the bathroom of his house at 1017 Reed Street two miles from City Stadium. By the time the rescue squad arrived, he was gone—dead at the age of thirty-three from a chronic rheumatic condition that had swelled his heart to twice its normal size. He left behind a pregnant wife and two young daughters and one of the most exceptional and underappreciated careers in professional football. While Lombardi lives on in American culture, Vainisi is lost in the oblivion of minor sports figures of the past. On the day that he died, the Packers were still recovering from their defeat in Detroit three days earlier. Most of the players spent the afternoon at home, watching the televised game in which conference-leading Baltimore was upset by San Francisco, a result that allowed Green Bay to slip back into the championship race, one game behind the Colts. In a sense it was then, on that cold November day in 1960, that Lombardi and his Packers began their long run to greatness, beginning an era of dominance that would not have been possible without the work of an accomplished young personnel man who had suffered through nine losing seasons and then died before he could witness the wonder of a team that he, almost as much as the famed Lombardi, had built.

It was Vainisi who had persuaded the Packers executive board to hire Lombardi in the first place, and he who had scouted and recommended most of the players on the 1960 team, going back to Hawg Hanner from Arkansas in 1952 and including seven future NFL Hall of Famers—halfback Paul Hornung from Notre Dame, quarterback Bart Starr from Alabama, Louisiana State fullback Jim Taylor, Illinois linebacker Ray Nitschke, offensive tackle Forrest Gregg from Southern Methodist, center Jim Ringo from Syracuse and free agent Willie Wood from Southern Cal. Other talented starters scouted by Vainisi were Idaho offensive guard Jerry Kramer, Michigan tight end Ron Kramer, offensive tackle Bob Skoronski from Indiana, receiver Max McGee from Tulane, flanker Boyd Dowler from Colorado, Southern Methodist linebacker Bill Forester, Michigan State linebacker Dan Currie, Purdue linebacker Tom Bettis, defensive back Hank Gremminger from Baylor and safety Johnny Symank from Florida.

Which is more important, the talent of the troops or the skill of the leader? That is one of the central questions of all group enterprises and can be debated forever, but remains essentially unresolvable. The fact that Vainisi's handpicked Packers had played on losing teams before Lombardi's arrival, including Scooter McLean's hapless 1958 squad, showed the profound difference a coach could make. But if Lombardi found the best in his players, their performance in the end was limited by what that best could be. Lombardi inherited an uncommonly talented collection of athletes when he came to Green Bay, and Jack Vainisi realized that before anyone else.

Even more than Lombardi, Vainisi was a creature of football. He grew up on the North Side of Chicago in the embrace of the Chicago Bears family. His classmate at St. Hillary's grammar school was George Halas Jr., known as Mugsy, the son of the Bears coach. Bears players would visit St. Hillary's to help a priest coach the eighth grade football team on which Jack played. One of the Bears, big George Musso, presented young Jack with a complete pro uniform, which he wore at every opportunity. Vainisi's father operated Tony's Fine Foods, a grocery and delicatessen that served as a hangout for many Bears who roomed across the street at the Sheraton Plaza Hotel during the season. At least once a year a carload of Bears would drive over to the Vainisi home for a five-course Italian meal cooked by Jack's mother. At St. George High School, Jack became an all-Chicagoland lineman on a powerhouse scholastic team that traveled to New York to play for the mythical Catholic schools championship. Notre Dame offered him an athletic scholarship in 1945, and he played as a freshman there under Hugh Devore, who had been among Lombardi's coaches at Fordham a decade earlier.

After one season at South Bend, Vainisi was drafted into the Army and sent to occupied Japan, where he worked at MacArthur's headquarters and played on a service team favored by the football-loving general. He became sick there with what doctors misdiagnosed as scarlet fever. Months later, after Vainisi had returned to the service team, he discovered that he had been suffering from the far more serious rheumatic fever and that the strain of playing football had permanently damaged his heart. He was brought back to Chicago, where he recuperated for several months at Hines military hospital near his home, then returned to Notre Dame and finished his studies. No longer able to play football, he devoted himself to the sport anyway

and decided that he would make his career in the front office. With his connections and enthusiasm, it took him only a few months after graduating in
1950 to land a job scouting for the Packers. The new head coach in Green
Bay was Gene Ronzani, one of the Bears who had dined at Mama Vainisi's,
and Ronzani's top assistant was the same Hugh Devore who had coached
him at Notre Dame.

As a scout, Vainisi was ebullient and innovative. He worked the telephones and traveled relentlessly in search of his "boys," developing contacts
with hundreds of high school and college coaches around the country, and
was so engaging that competing pro coaches—his favorites were Paul Brown
and George Halas—took his calls without fail and talked football talent with
him. For his honeymoon in 1952 he persuaded his wife, Jackie, to escort him
on a trip through Oklahoma, Texas and Alabama, where he spent most of his
time signing new players. He developed a network of informal tipsters as
well, many of them former Packers or friends from Notre Dame. His scouting reports, in eighteen thick blue canvas, three-ringed notebooks, ranked
and coded the statistics of nearly four thousand players. He became known
around the league as a boy wonder, lending Green Bay a measure of respect
that it could not gain on the football field. Head coaches came and went, first
Ronzani, then Blackbourn, then McLean—each more frustrating to him
than the last. He pushed especially hard for the Packers to take Paul Hornung, the Heisman Trophy winner from his alma mater, as the first bonus
pick in 1957, then fretted for two years as coaches played the Golden Boy at
the wrong positions and seemed unable to unleash his talent.

Lombardi was his salvation, a paisano who understood what he had been
doing. They had known each other for years through mutual friends, and they
shared the same passion for football and a desire to make the Packers a first-
class organization. When the Packers began recruiting Lombardi, he bluntly
informed the executive board that he would not have considered Green Bay
if Vainisi had not been there. He did not tell them the full reason: that Vainisi was already on his side. It was Vainisi who had warned Lombardi that he
had to demand full power as both coach and general manager or the board of
directors would persist with petty interference in the football operation.
"Jack was too much of a gentleman to ever say so, but he loathed most of the
board members," his wife said later. "They were small men." Most of the
board members were in Green Bay's social elite, members of Oneida Golf
and Riding, and despite their awe of Lombardi their attitudes tended to be
condescending toward Italians. "There's the Italian Mafia" was one of their
common salutations when Lombardi and Vainisi were seen together. They
smiled when they heard it, but considered the statement a slur, and after a
time made a point of being seen together less often in social settings.

Both men were in a hurry to win: Lombardi because he had waited so
long to get his chance; Vainisi because he feared he would not have much

longer. After every close game he would mutter only half jokingly that he did not know whether his heart could survive the tension. "I could go at any time," he said one morning during the 1960 preseason to his pal Art Daley, the beat reporter for the *Press-Gazette*. The two men were taking a stroll around Bear Mountain near West Point, where Lombardi had brought the team for a week of practice. Vainisi was always a hulk, standing six foot one with immense shoulders and hands, but by then he had become seriously overweight, busting the bathroom scale at the maximum reading of 250 pounds. He smiled at Daley and patted his weak spot, his huge and fragile heart. "I'd like to see something good happen to the club. You know how it's been for all these years." Months later, after the Thanksgiving Day drubbing by the Lions, he appeared more troubled than usual. The Packers had lost twice in five days. There were only three games remaining: the season-closing swing on the West Coast, but before that the Bears, the team of his childhood, at Wrigley Field in Chicago. With the rest of the coaching staff, he was working eighteen-hour days. "This is it!" he said that Friday at his desk at the Packers office on Washington Street. "We gotta win now."

That Sunday morning he and Jackie had returned from nine o'clock mass and were preparing to visit her parents' house in Green Bay for a late morning coffee. Jackie took their two girls upstairs to change clothes, and Jack went into the bathroom. He never came out. His heart stopped and he slumped to the tile, jamming the door with his massive body so Jackie could not get in. She went around the side of the house and looked through the small bathroom window to see her worst fear realized—her husband dead on the floor. She called the paramedics and her parents and then Lombardi, who came over with Marie. Word spread through the Packers team: Jack was dead. Vainisi was close to all of them. He was always doing something special for the players: finding circus tickets for Jim Taylor's family, giving Bob Skoronski a $500 bonus to pay off his furniture bill at Sears, arranging travel plans for the wives, finding off-season jobs for guys who wanted to stay in Green Bay, letting them know if they were in danger of being cut. "We're all deeply shocked," Lombardi said to the press. "I have lost a close personal friend. I had known [Jack] several years before I came here. It will be hard to do without him."

On Monday it began to snow and the weather turned colder, and the Packers scrimmaged inside City Stadium instead of at their normal outdoor practice field on Oneida Street. Their sessions preparing for the crucial Bears game, as Art Daley described them, were "grim and quiet" and conducted with a "heavy heart" for their lost scout. Lombardi seemed more determined than ever, but kept his voice down, offering soft words of encouragement. On Wednesday morning they practiced at eight-thirty and were finished in time to attend Vainisi's eleven o'clock funeral mass at the Church of the Annunciation. Players lined both sides of the entrance as the heavy casket was carried inside the church. The nuns at Annunciation's grammar school next door let their students watch, eager little faces pressed against cold windows, as the team escorted the coffin out to the hearse and on to Allouez Cemetery. Paul Hornung approached Jackie Vainisi and asked if there was anything he could do. "Yes," she said. "Become the kind of football player Jack knew you could be." He had been Jack's favorite, she said, the one who could make the Packers great.

Later that week Hornung vowed that the Packers would beat the Bears in Jack's honor. The year before in Chicago he had played his worst game as a pro, fumbling three times, but this time would be different, he promised. It certainly was. The Packers played their finest game under Lombardi that Sunday. It was the most lopsided Green Bay win to that point in their long history against the rival Bears—even more uneven than the 41 to 13 score. Willie Davis, the rangy defensive end, blocked a punt and pounced on the ball in the end zone for one score. Jimmy Taylor plowed for 140 yards. Bart Starr, back on target and feeling confident again, completed seventeen of twenty-three passes for 227 yards. And Hornung was incomparable, running for sixty-eight yards, catching three passes for thirty-two more, scoring two touchdowns on a ten-yard run and seventeen-yard pass, and kicking five extra points and two field goals for a total of twenty-three points, establishing a record season total of 152 points after only ten games. After his second touchdown Hornung casually tossed the ball into the stands, a gesture that infuriated Halas, a notorious penny-pincher and sore loser. Papa Bear threatened to seek a league fine against Hornung for the unusual gesture. "Don't worry," Lombardi said to Hornung. "If he tries to do something, I'll pay for it."

Lombardi had walked off Wrigley Field with a ball of his own, the one that had been in play when the game ended. He wrote the date and score on it, passed it around the locker room and asked all the Packers to sign it, and when he arrived back in Green Bay he gave the game ball to the widow of his fallen friend, Jack Vainisi.

THE COLTS lost again that Sunday, and suddenly Green Bay was in a three-way tie for first place with San Francisco and Baltimore, all with 6 and 4 records. The Western Conference title was within reach for Lombardi if his team could sweep the final two games on the West Coast. With the college regular season over and the pro schedule featuring the Packers and 49ers in a lone Saturday matchup on December 10, the game drew the attention of the national sportswriting corps, which would jump at any excuse to be in San Francisco. Football tends to be most exciting and poetic on either a crisp and radiant autumn afternoon or its opposite, a monsoon or snowstorm. San Francisco on that Saturday offered lousy conditions in full glory. A chill rain turned old Kezar Stadium into a muddy slop pile, the turf soft and slippery. Tex Maule was there for *Sports Illustrated,* and had brought along a New York illustrator and photographer named Robert Riger, who had been shooting pictures for a book with Maule titled *The Pros: A Documentary of Professional Football in America.*

The images Riger came away with that day were taken too late to appear in the book, but were among the most evocative he ever made. They had a mythic, ennobling quality to them, their character enhanced by the brutal conditions, each picture revealing another element of what it meant to be a pro, as the Packers under Lombardi were coming to define the term.

CLICK: Here comes "the Horn," Paul Hornung, "with the square toe of his kicking shoe flashing," looking for a hole behind the blocking of Jim Taylor and Fuzzy Thurston on a sweep.

CLICK: There stands quarterback Bart Starr "coldly watching" after making the handoff as Jim Taylor cuts back "and mighty Jerry Kramer crumples one man and looks downfield for more."

CLICK: Here looms Forrest Gregg, the square-jawed offensive tackle, his face and helmet smeared in mud, shouting from the bench as a Packer defender intercepts a pass. This photograph, entitled simply "Mud," became a classic on its own, winning the grand prize in *Look* magazine's sports photo contest.

CLICK: There paces Lombardi in his lucky camel's hair coat and brown fedora, as Riger describes him, "our friend the coach, the universal symbol stalking the sidelines—smoking his cigarette—his mind fixed on one idea alone—the next play."

Considering the field conditions, the Packers played their second near-perfect game in six days. With its high-flying passing game, San Francisco was stuck in the mud and never scored. Lombardi had Starr handing off the ball most of the day and throwing only one pass in the second half. Taylor bulled past the thousand-yard mark for the season with 161 yards on twenty-five carries ("You're as tough as a rat!" linebacker Ray Nitschke snarled at him after the game), and Hornung ran nineteen times for eighty-six more yards, including a classic sweep around the left end for a twenty-eight-yard touchdown in which his timing behind the blocks of his guardian angels, Thurston and Kramer, was so perfect that the 49ers never touched him. He scored all of Green Bay's points in the 13 to 0 win. On the bus after the game, Riger took a seat next to the coach and found him in an unusually chatty mood.

Lombardi talked with the photographer for nearly forty minutes, diagramming plays on the back of Riger's airline ticket, and praising his tandem of Thunder and Lightning. "Taylor has great balance and he can cut quickly, and our best play is a simple fullback slant," Lombardi said. "He can run it over tackle and if that hole closes he can come back over the center or he can swing wide outside. Three plays right there off one because Taylor makes them work." When it was noted that Hornung now had stretched his single-season scoring record to 165 points, Lombardi raved: "That Hornung is some ballplayer. That's an awful lot of points for one man to score in one season. I don't see how anyone will score more. It was just a simple sweep for the touchdown—the two guards pulled and gave him an alley, but the key was the flanker's [Dowler's] block on the safety. When he got that, he was in." When he was asked about the defense, Lombardi praised the play-calling of his old safety, Emlen Tunnell. He "roared that rough Lombardi laugh" and added: "Their shotgun offense backfired!" Then, as Riger later recounted it, the coach perfectly distilled his football philosophy into one statement: "You know I think that spread formation is a lot of junk. You play this game with your power. You do what you do best—and you do it again and again."

While Taylor and Hornung were running toward records at season's end, Lombardi realized that his Packers would rise only as high as their quarterback could take them. He would often tell his cronies at dinner that football was the perfect team game except for one glaring imbalance—the quarterback was too important. A pitcher might be more dominant in baseball, but a baseball team had a *staff* of pitchers; there was only one quarterback. A goalie was pivotal in hockey, but a goalie did not have to call plays or worry about much beyond his own performance. To win in the pros, Lombardi said, you needed a quarterback who could be a coach on the field, someone who was intelligent, rational, unflappable and occasionally daring, as well as a gifted passer.

Did Bart Starr have those characteristics? Lombardi had vacillated on that question for nearly two years. His first impression of Starr, he once acknowledged, was that "he was probably just a little too polite and maybe just a little too self-effacing to be the real bold tough quarterback that a quarterback must be in the National Football League." Starr felt otherwise, and was determined to prove himself to Lombardi no matter how long it took. "I could see in my own mind, day by day, week by week, that this was going to be a lengthy process because trust and respect should never just be handed out to somebody," Starr said later. "You have to earn it." If he lacked the raw talent of many other quarterbacks, he thought that he could compensate by working harder and overachieving. The more Starr studied Lombardi's system, the more convinced he became that he could flourish in it. Other players barely tolerated the classroom aspects of practice, endless hours of studying film and analyzing plays. Starr could not get enough of it: "I *loved* it. I loved the meetings. I never, ever was bored or tired at any meeting we were in with Lombardi. I appreciated what he was trying to teach. He was always raising the bar."

If anyone could have been prepared for Lombardi's methods, it was Bart Starr. After what Starr had endured at home with his father in Alabama, Lombardi's treatment of him seemed benign. Ben Starr was a stern military man who had drilled his sons, Bryan Bartlett "Bart" and Hilton "Bubba," in the practice of obedience and respect for elders. No differing points of view were allowed in the Starr household; everyone was expected to do and say exactly what the family "master sergeant" demanded. Bart, the oldest son, worried that he could never do quite enough. No matter how hard he tried, he felt that he could not win his father's love or respect. It was not Bart but his younger brother, Bubba, who was considered the vessel of his father's ambitions. Bubba was more athletic, stronger, decisive and fearless; Bart seemed too mediocre for Ben Starr. But Bubba died at age thirteen, before he could show the world much. The death of a child is devastating to any family; Bubba's death was particularly traumatic for the Starrs. He had been playing barefoot in a vacant field and was cut on the heel by an old dog bone and died of tetanus three days later. Bubba's mother had been reluctant to bring him in for the shot that would have saved his life, and she was plagued by guilt thereafter. And his father, believing that his dreams were lost with Bubba's death, did not turn to Bart as his new hope, but rather shunned or belittled him even more.

Ben Starr was not the only one who doubted Bart's talents; he always seemed to be struggling to prove himself to older men. During his high school years he had to grind his way past several more talented boys who were favored by the coaches to play quarterback. At the University of Alabama, he was sidelined by an injury during his junior year, just when he was starting to perform well, then had the misfortune of playing under a new coach who benched him for his senior season even as the team lost ten straight, the worst record in Crimson Tide history. As a local boy, he was put on the Gray roster for the Blue-Gray All-Star Game in Montgomery, but barely got in and cried in frustration afterwards. Somehow, Jack Vainisi had heard enough about Starr to recommend him to the Packers, who made him the 199th college player selected in the pro draft. He floundered in Green Bay under Coaches Liz Blackbourn and Scooter McLean until Lombardi arrived and detected the same glimmer of promise that Vainisi had seen.

Starr had flashes of brilliance when given an opportunity to play quarterback late in Lombardi's first year, but then seemed to regress and was benched again after the 1960 season-opening loss to the Bears. "That was a real wake-up call for me. A real punch in the side," Starr said of his benching. "I had let him down! Here's the man who had brought me along and given me the opportunity and I failed when I got the chance. So I was even more determined to get it back." Much as he had the first year, he used his time on the bench productively, studying the defenses and the best ways to respond to them. When his time came again, as the Packers began their drive for the conference crown, he was ready mentally and physically; ready even to stand up to his coach and prove that he had the toughness needed for the job. The change in their relationship came in practice one day when Starr threw an interception—one too many, as far as Lombardi was concerned. The coach exploded at Starr in front of his teammates. When practice was over Starr approached Lombardi in his office and asserted himself in a way that he had never done before.

The intercepted ball was tipped, he pointed out; it was not his fault. Furthermore, Starr said, the coach should change his habit of yelling at players in public and then, if necessary, making up with them in private. "You're asking me to be the leader of this team, and I'm challenged by that and I want to be the best leader I can be. But I can't be if you're chewing my butt out in front of the team you want me to lead," Starr explained to the coach. "You'll see later"—when the coaches watched film of the practice— "that the error was yours: the ball was *tipped* [by a defender] and intercepted. I can take any ass-chewing you want to deliver. And if you feel I have it coming, have at it. But please do it in the privacy of your office here where you make your apologies to me. I will be an even better leader for you if you do that." Lombardi listened quietly. "I hear you," he said contritely when his quarterback had finished his complaint. The challenge had worked. Lombardi never criticized him in front of the team again, Starr said later: "From then on we had a relationship that was just unbelievable. I don't think it had been that bad before, but now it just took off and went to another plane."

Starr and Lombardi were an odd pair—Deep South and New York City; they looked and talked like the geographic and cultural opposites that they were—but each in his own way was shaped by his experience with military discipline, and each understood how much he needed the other. Starr hungered for Lombardi's sense of order and keen football knowledge, and realized that it could make him excel. The full measure of respect that he had not yet won from his father came now instead from his coach. The good son found a father in the coach, and the coach found another son in the quarterback. Lombardi knew that if he told Starr to do something, it would get done. He did not have to worry about where Starr was at any time; he was always literally and figuratively within safe reach, which is not something that could be said about some other key players. If Lombardi fretted that the quarterback position was too important in football, at least he now had a quarterback who was loyal in every way, who would carry out his game plans flawlessly, who opened up his brain and let Lombardi pour his knowledge in. Murray Warmath, who had worked with Lombardi on Red Blaik's staff at West Point, came down from the University of Minnesota to watch the Packers and concluded that Starr was the perfect athlete to run Lombardi's huddle. "He and Vince," Warmath reflected decades later, "were hand and glove."

By the time the Packers reached Los Angeles for the final game, they were alone in first place with a 7 and 4 record, one game ahead of the Colts, who had lost three straight. They controlled their own fate at last; all they had to do was beat the Rams to win the Western Conference title. The Rams were out of the race and hobbling, with eight starters injured, but they had upset the Colts the week before and enjoyed being spoilers.

Bart Starr usually slept soundly the night before a game, just like Coach Lombardi, comforted by the thoroughness of his preparations, and "woke up refreshed." But he found no rest on the eve of the Rams game. All night long he flailed about uneasily, playing the next day's game in his subconscious, reviewing game situations that his roommate Gary Knafelc had been drilling him on the night before. ("It's second-and-three, we're on the far side against a 5–2 defense. What do you call?")

Knafelc could not sleep either, and shortly after dawn the two Packers climbed out of bed like brothers eager to scamper downstairs for Christmas. "I realized that the big day had finally arrived," Starr wrote in a diary he kept for that game. "We'd been aiming at it all week." He turned on the television and heard news of a massive midair collision over New York Harbor involving United Air Lines and TWA jets that killed 134 people, but he was so anxious about the game that even that stunning report could not hold his attention. He showered and dressed—without shaving; he never shaved on game day—and took the elevator down to the lobby of the Miramar Hotel. Jim Ringo and Hawg Hanner were already lounging in the lobby. Starr needed time alone. He walked across the street to the ocean front "and thought about the game—trying to adjust myself."

On the way back to his room, he stopped at a newsstand and bought a copy of Johnny Unitas's book. No subject interested Starr more than how to play quarterback, and Johnny U was the best, but even that seemed a bother now. The pregame meal began at nine, and Starr picked at his food. "Everything seemed so dry," he wrote, "even with all the butter on the baked potato and toast." After breakfast he and Knafelc went to the trainer's room to have their ankles taped. Lombardi believed in taping, every ankle, every game— an untaped ankle, if discovered, meant a certain fine, and injuring an untaped ankle meant a Lombardi eruption. All jokes and lightness in the taping room, as usual, "everybody laughing and cutting up" with equipment man Dad Braisher and trainer Bud Jorgenson, getting their "last-minute jokes out of the way." What next? Starr returned to his room one last time, losing himself briefly in a magazine story about a Seeing Eye dog. Then out the door and down the elevator to take the team bus to the stadium. What? Everybody was already on the bus, and there was Lombardi, in front, glaring at them.

That'll be fifty dollars, gentlemen! Starr thought they were seven minutes early, but they were eight minutes late; they had apparently missed an announcement at breakfast that the departure time had been changed. Starr was embarrassed. "It was," he wrote in his journal, "the first time I had ever been late for anything in my life." Bart Starr late for the bus for the most important game of his career—this did not go unnoticed by some of the more rambunctious players on the team, who had been fined many times already by the punctual Lombardi. Jim Taylor, an ornery individualist, would usually loiter around the side of the bus until the last possible second, just to get the Old Man teed off a little. Some of the team playboys might be seen hustling out the hotel door, tucking in their shirts, putting on their sport coats and clearing their pockets of extra condoms not used the night before. But never before was Bart Starr late. "Welcome to the club!" one shouted. A few giggles, then the bus grew quiet for the ride to the stadium.

It was Starr's habit to take a brief look at the field before going into the locker room to dress for the game, but he said that he didn't want to see the field this time. He and Knafelc dressed quietly in their cubicle. Starr read a game program, "trying to quiet the butterflies." He was struck by an open letter to the fans from Coach Bob Waterfield asking them to help keep Rams players in Los Angeles during the off-season. Starr had been thinking about that issue a lot in recent days; the closer his relationship became with Lombardi, the more sense he thought it made for him and his wife, Cherry, to live year-round in Green Bay. That thought was broken by Lombardi's booming voice—time for his pregame meeting with the quarterbacks. Starr and Lamar McHan and the coach went over the personnel of the Rams defense, the offensive game plan. Starr called his own plays, but Lombardi gave him the first few to start the game.

When Starr reached the field for the pregame warmups, his anxiety disappeared. Now he was feeling loose and easy. Max McGee, the team cutup, made a great catch in the drills, and everybody hooted and whistled at him. Then back in the dressing room one last time, heart pounding, adrenaline flowing. Starr rinsed his face and removed his jersey to put on the shoulder pads, and took a seat in the main squad room for the players' meeting. The old guys, Hawg Hanner and Em Tunnell, did most of the talking. "Em says the most intelligent things before the games," Starr noted in his diary. "He sizes up the situation perfectly. Only mistakes would beat us, he told the squad."

The players ended their session with the Lord's Prayer. Lombardi entered the room. "I was anxious to hear him," Starr wrote. "He said three weeks ago they had counted us out and now we were getting a second chance. He said he didn't have to tell us what this game meant but warned us about keying ourselves up too much. He told us how big the Rams are and kept reminding us that football is two things—blocking and tackling, plus running the ball. And play the game with abandon, because every time you played with abandon you won, the coach said. He always does an extremely fine job of getting us worked up. You could run through the wall when he lets you go. He doesn't plead. He just stands there telling us what to do in his very authoritative voice. We rushed out of the dressing room door with a shout and I felt well prepared to play the game."

The Packers threw only eleven passes all afternoon, nine by Starr, two by Hornung, yet they won the game with a spectacularly effective passing attack. Thunder and Lightning could go nowhere on the ground, gaining only sixty-six yards between them. But Starr completed eight of nine passes, including touchdown tosses of ninety-one yards to Boyd Dowler and fifty-seven yards to Max McGee, and Hornung completed a forty-yard halfback option pass to McGee for another touchdown. The Rams gained nearly twice as much yardage and accumulated twice as many first downs, but after scoring the first touchdown they were never again in the game. The final score was 35 to 21. The Packers had won their first conference title since 1944. In the locker room after the game, Fuzzy Thurston was a madman, grabbing people and shouting. A Hollywood contingent including Bing Crosby's sons and Gardner McKay came in to snap pictures and mingle with Hornung and his handsome young teammates. Starr and Knafelc were relatively quiet amid the celebration. Knafelc had been knocked cold in the second quarter and played the entire second half semiconscious, without memory. He was still in a trance when Coach Lombardi came around shaking hands, and when he reached their cubicle he said, "Great game, both of you. Forget the fine!"

"Thanks a lot, you sonofabitch!" mumbled the dazed Knafelc. The coach walked away smiling.

The team returned to Green Bay the following night, and as their charter plane rolled down the runway to the terminal, the players looked out into the frigid December blackness at an amazing scene. There were fans everywhere, roaring swells behind the cyclone fences at Austin Straubel Airport, eleven thousand Packer backers who had been waiting for hours, chanting and screaming for their team, holding signs that read "Eight and Four, Just One More!" and "It's a Cinch with Vince." With the team riding in two buses behind a police escort, and a mile-long line of cars behind the buses, a joyous caravan snaked through town from the airport, passing a fireworks display at City Stadium and crossing the Fox River to the Hotel Northland. At the homecoming ceremony, the players and coaches were given engraved wallets, each with a fifty-dollar bill. Lombardi was gracious in his comments, praising his players, his assistant coaches, the "wonderful fans of Green Bay"—and the scout with the oversized heart who died too soon. "A great part of this team is due to Jack Vainisi, who no longer is with us," he said. But nothing Lombardi said could diminish his own stature. He had earned a new nickname during the triumphant swing through the West. In restoring the Packers to their old glory, he was becoming not just a football coach but the stuff of myth, a transcendent figure. St. Vincent? No, more than that. Green Bay was an area with a bishop and a vicar-general, eight monsignors, fifty priests and 350 religious sisters, but there was only one Lombardi. *There he is!* people screamed. *The Pope! Look at the Pope!*

THE ODDSMAKERS favored Green Bay by two points in the title game against the eastern winners, the Philadelphia Eagles, but both teams were a surprise to be there. They had followed the same fast track, zooming from last to first in their conferences in two years. The Eagles had some talented young players, including running backs Tim Brown and Ted Dean, backup quarterback Sonny Jurgensen, receiver Tommy McDonald and linebacker Maxie Baughan, but for the most part their championship season was seen as a curtain call for three grand old pros: their coach, Buck Shaw; their quarterback, the fiery Norm Van Brocklin; and their indestructible throwback, Chuck Bednarik, who was playing not only his normal center position but also filling in for an injured linebacker. Concrete Charlie was the last real sixty-minute man in the league. The championship matchup in that sense contrasted two cultures: the Eagles were the old way, with gunslinging quarterbacks and two-way players, all grit and improvisation; the Packers were Lombardi's vision of the new professionals, methodical and relentless. They were also still a curiosity for much of the country.

"From Los Angeles to New York, from Green Bay to Dallas, pro football fans are wondering: 'How did Vince Lombardi do it? How did a 47-year-old Brooklynite become a hero to every native of a small midwestern city by leading the Green Bay Packers into next Monday's championship game with the Eagles?' " Frank Dolson, writing in the *Philadelphia Inquirer,* posed that question in his December 22 column and found one man, Colonel Red Blaik, who knew the answer. Blaik was retired from football by then. He had left the Army job two years earlier to work for a defense contractor, but he was thoroughly enjoying the success of his former assistant. "Surprised?" Blaik responded, when Dolson asked him about Lombardi's rise to the top of the coaching profession. "I was anything but surprised."

The only thing that puzzled Blaik was that it had taken so long for others to appreciate the qualities in Lombardi that he had seen during their time together at West Point. Lombardi was "a superior individual all the way around," he told Dolson—loyal, decent, inspiring, someone who "believes in winning" and never "rationalizes a defeat," and hates to lose "whether it's pinochle or cribbage or football," though he learns from every loss. Style rather than substance, Blaik said, allowed coaches of inferior character and talent to rise more quickly than Lombardi. "He doesn't look like a man of great intellect. But what do appearances mean? I deal with a lot of scientists today. You ought to see how little some of them look the part. Some fellows have that Madison Avenue smoothness. They get a coaching job and then they rattle around. Vince isn't that type of man. Oh, he has an extrovert side to him. He can be a dynamo when he has to be. But like a lot of men with ability, he's a man of moods."

Lombardi was in a generous mood in the days before the championship game. The weather in Green Bay plunged toward zero on Friday, so the coach limited outdoor practice to just ten minutes of loosening up. When he heard that Bob Skoronski's in-laws lived near Philadelphia, he invited the offensive tackle to bring his wife and three young sons along on the flight east. The Packers left Green Bay on Christmas Eve, taking a two-and-a-half-hour charter flight captained by Don Smith, a former Green Bay resident. Lombardi had a thousand little superstitions, and Smith was one of them, his "good luck pilot." As the delegation deplaned, an AP photographer captured Skoronski, loaded down with three kids, shouting for help, and Lombardi grinning broadly as he scooped one-year-old Steve Skoronski into his arms. "THE GANG'S ALL HERE," read the caption. Here was Lombardi, portrayed as the gregarious family man. Vincent and Susan could be excused for doing a double take when they saw the picture; he always seemed so loving with other people's kids. Lombardi and his troops arrived at their hotel at five that afternoon, greeted in the lobby by a band playing "On, Wisconsin," followed by Hornung's favorite, the Notre Dame victory march. It snowed in Philadelphia that night and the Packers woke up to a white Christmas.

The television sports industry had not yet cracked the sacrosanct Christmas barrier, so the championship game was held not on Sunday but Monday, December 26. And since the venue was venerable Franklin Field, which had no lights, the starting time was set at noon to assure that the final quarter would not be played in the winter gloaming. Monday noon was not exactly television prime time, but even placing the game that close to Christmas seemed excessive to many people, a sign of commercialism run amok. As the 1960s began, the writing press was still struggling with the new way, lamenting the fact that major sporting events were not just for the scribes in the press box and fans in the stands. "The sense of order, of propriety, has been offended," wrote New York columnist Jimmy Powers. "How far can commercials go? But with time we grow accustomed to a lot of things. It matters little now how many fans attend an event in person. Sports slowly are being beamed for the mass TV audience, the millions who sit comfortably at home. In effect, today's game between the Packers and Eagles is the World Series of football. It is reasonable to state that for every person who sits shivering in the stands to watch it in person, hundreds will be at home absorbing statistics and, through the magic of powerful lenses, actually seeing more of the intricate play."

The point clangs with absurd obviousness now, but it was fresh enough to seem worth making then, though in truth 1960 was not the best year for the NFL on television. This was through no fault of the new commissioner, Alvin Ray "Pete" Rozelle, the young publicity wizard who had made the Los Angeles Rams a glittering West Coast enterprise. Rozelle had revolutionary plans for promoting and selling his league on television, but it required what he called a "unity of purpose" among the set of cantankerous owners. He had to persuade them that they could have more power, and get richer, by negotiating collectively and pooling their resources, rather than operating each franchise like an individual business. They were in the process of reaching that unity in 1960—pushed along, to be sure, by the upstart American Football League, which had a league-wide contract with ABC—but they were not quite there yet. While ten teams were broadcast on CBS, the

Browns were under contract with the independent Sports Network in Cleveland, and the Baltimore Colts and Pittsburgh Steelers were broadcast on NBC, which also had rights to the championship game. The ratings drop in 1960—to 10.6, from 12.5 the previous year—was a one-year oddity, a result of the novelty of the AFL and the fact that teams in the NFL's three largest markets (New York, Chicago and Los Angeles) had mediocre seasons.

There were, in any case, enough people at Franklin Field that Monday noon to fill the stadium (67,325, the second-largest crowd in pro playoff history), and Powers need not have worried about their comfort—there was no shivering. The temperature soared to the upper forties, leaving the playing field in peculiar condition, with a thin layer of soggy grass over rock-hard earth in patches heated by the sun, but still icy spots in the shadows. From the opening play, when wild Bill Quinlan intercepted a Van Brocklin lateral pass on the Eagles fourteen-yard line, the Packers seemed relentless, but somehow kept coming up short. They ran Taylor, Hornung, Taylor, Taylor on the first four plays, but they could not grind out ten yards and the Eagles took over on downs. That was the first of two instances in the game when Lombardi chose to run on fourth down deep in Eagles territory—and failed—instead of taking the easy three points by kicking a field goal. When it happened the second time, during the opening drive of the third quarter, the Eagles were leading 10 to 6 even though the Packers had been controlling the ball and seemed to be dominating the line of scrimmage. The only Philadelphia touchdown to that point came when Hank Gremminger slipped on the ice and Tommy McDonald scooted by him to make a thirty-seven-yard touchdown catch.

It took a freelance scramble by Max McGee late in the third quarter to bring Green Bay back. Hornung was out of the game by then, a nerve in his left shoulder pinched from a ferocious hit by Tom Brookshier that would haunt him for the rest of his career. Starr had misfired on three consecutive passes (high to McGee, low to Taylor, high to Dowler), and McGee dropped back to punt from his nineteen-yard line. As he waited for the long snap, two thoughts ran through his mind. First were the words that Coach Lombardi had barked at him when he took over as coach: "McGee, you're gonna be my punter. You're not gonna run the football on fourth down!" Second was the vision in front of him. Wide open. "I catch this friggin' ball and all my instincts would not let me kick it," McGee recalled later. "I see these guys going back to set up their return. Normally, they keep one guy to make sure you kick it. They didn't. I could see the first down." Ignoring Lombardi's warning, the old Tulane halfback tucked the ball in and loped thirty-five yards downfield, taking the ball into Eagles territory. Seven plays later he caught a seven-yard touchdown pass from Starr to put the Packers ahead. When he trotted off the field after the extra point, even though his derring-do had given the Packers a 13 to 10 lead, he found a spot on the sidelines as far away from the coach as he could get.

Lombardi had little time to search out McGee. His eyes swung back to the field with alarm, as Ted Dean, Philadelphia's swift halfback, was busting loose and sprinting upfield, returning the kickoff fifty-seven yards, immediately putting the Eagles back in scoring position. Eight plays later Dean carried the ball on a sweep play around left end and scored from the five. With the extra point, Philadelphia led 17 to 13. Time was running out. After an exchange of punts the Packers took over for the last time with one minute and twenty seconds left in the game. Bart Starr trotted out to the huddle. He had struggled all day, but now as his teammates looked over at him, they noticed that he seemed eerily calm. There were sixty-three yards to the goal line, but every man in the huddle believed that they would get there. Starr five yards to Taylor. Starr four yards to Tom Moore, Hornung's replacement. Taylor on the Green Bay sweep for nine more, out-of-bounds just across the midfield stripe. Starr to Knafelc for seventeen. Incomplete to Dowler. Starr to Knafelc for eight more. The Packers are now at the Eagles twenty-two. Chuck Bednarik sits on Knafelc after the catch, letting precious seconds tick off the clock. Time for only one more play.

Red Smith of the *New York Herald Tribune*, Green Bay–born and Notre Dame–bred, a Lombardi man since Vince's West Point days, was watching from the press box. "For 59 minutes plus," he wrote, "the Philadelphia Eagles and Green Bay Packers, 1958 dogs of the National Football League, had heaved and hauled and grappled and threshed across the squashy turf for $2011.41 per Hessian, the difference between winning and losing the title of world's toughest mercenaries. From the Philadelphia 22 yard line, Bart Starr passed to Jim Taylor. That wonderful runner ducked his head like a charging bull, bolted like an enraged beer truck into Philadelphia's congested secondary, twisted, staggered, bucked and wrestled one step at a time . . ."

Photographer Robert Riger was watching the same scene from a more intimate angle. "I was the only camera in the end zone and wanted a picture of Taylor coming right at me for the touchdown," Riger said. " 'Come to Poppa. And I'll give you the whole town of Green Bay.' The play started and Starr shot the fullback a little nickel pass on the left side. He took it and cut back over center and had one man to beat, a rookie in a spanking clean uniform who had just been sent in—Bobby Jackson—and the kid made the stop. Bednarik came over and there was a big pileup, but had Taylor gotten by Jackson, Green Bay would have won and I would have had the picture."

The image that lingers is not the unheralded Bobby Jackson making the initial stop, but Bednarik pounding over to the scrum and sitting on Taylor as time ran out. "I was on top of him and I stayed there," Bednarik recalled. "You're darn right I was watching the clock. I made up my mind I was going to lay on him until it was over. That is known as stalling for time." Taylor remained sprawled on the ground for a half-minute after the gun had sounded. Philadelphia police rushed across the thawing field, "black buttons agleam on blue heroic abdomens," as Red Smith described them, in a vain effort to keep fans from tearing down the goalposts. Bednarik, a mess of mud and sweat, stood near the fallen Taylor. "Get up," he said. "This goddamn game is over!" Then he looked up to the roaring stands, lifted his gnarled fists high above his head in victory and unloosed a bloodcurdling shout of triumph. As Taylor made his way to his feet, the injured Hornung, shrouded in a warmup cape, walked out to console him. Thunder and Lightning—and old Concrete Charlie Bednarik stepped between them and embraced each of his young competitors and said they had a helluva football team and would be back in the championship the next year. Robert Riger never got the photograph of Taylor scoring the phantom winning touchdown, but he was nearby when this scene took place and shot a picture from behind the three athletes, exhausted and limping off the battlefield, arm in arm, that evoked emotions far deeper than winning or losing.

Dominic Olejniczak, president of the board of directors, wiped tears from his eyes as he entered the losing locker room after the game, but there were no tears among the players and coaches. To them, this was not a last, fleeting chance, but a first chance. The sense was that they did not lose, they just ran out of time. Lombardi said as much to the press. "If we could have added a couple of more seconds at the end of each half we would have been all right," he said. McGee chuckled to himself when he overheard his coach say that he was neither surprised nor bothered by Max's run off the fake punt. "With veterans like McGee, we give them the option," Lombardi said. Right, McGee thought to himself. And if I hadn't made the first down, it would have been my last option. With the press out of the room, Lombardi gathered his players around him and said there was a revelation in this loss. "Perhaps you didn't realize that you could have won this game," he said in a quiet, deliberate voice. "But I think there's no doubt in your minds now. And that's why you will win it all next year. This will never happen again. You will never lose another championship."

That night Lombardi took his family and a group of friends and team officials to dinner in downtown Philadelphia. At one point, he was sitting alone with Ray Scott, the voice of the Packers, and they replayed the game one last time. He was proud of his men, Lombardi said. They had given every ounce of effort. But that was more than he could say for himself. He had cost the team six points, the difference between winning and losing, by not going for easy field goals. "Coach," he said to Scott, using his all-purpose nickname, which he applied equally to people he admired and others whose name he had forgotten. "I learned my lesson today. When you get down there, come out with something. I lost the game, not my players. That was my fault."

AN IMPORTANT ASPECT of the mythology of Vince Lombardi is that his rise took place in Green Bay, not New York. For a New Yorker to succeed in

New York is a routine story. Even though it is an oft-told tale, there is a certain romance to someone coming from the provinces and making it in New York. But for the opposite to happen, for a New Yorker to leave the big city and head out to the middle of nowhere to become famous—that is an adventure story with something in it for everyone. New York, his hometown, the place where myths were conceived and written and broadcast and spread, was rooting for Lombardi as a favorite son, and the rest of the country found something magical and inspiring in the emergence of little Green Bay, the David among the Goliaths of professional football. As dissimilar as they were, this coach and town seemed the perfect combination: just as Green Bay could not have succeeded without Lombardi, Lombardi would not have become what he became without Green Bay.

It very nearly did not happen that way; the symbiosis of Lombardi and Green Bay almost ended before it had fully developed. At the end of the 1959 season, Jim Lee Howell had walked into Wellington Mara's office and announced that he was burned out. The thrill of winning, Howell said, no longer compensated for the deep anxiety he took from losing. He would coach the 1960 season, but that would be his last. Howell's surprise burnout did not come at the best time for the Maras. Not only had they let Lombardi go to Green Bay a year earlier, but they had just lost Tom Landry to the expansion team in Dallas. The brains in the New York coaching brain trust were employed elsewhere.

Would Lombardi come back? The Maras had reason to believe that he would. When they had released him from the final year of his contract back in January 1959 to go out to Green Bay, it was with the understanding that he "would have first chance at the Giants' coaching job should a vacancy ever occur." As soon as Howell told the Maras of his plans, they contacted Olejniczak in Green Bay and secured secret permission from him to talk to Lombardi about the Giants job. Lombardi met with the Maras during his winter trip to New York at the end of the 1959 season, when he was being anointed as coach of the year, and expressed an interest in returning. "However," as a Giants document on the issue later stated, "both parties recognized his obligations in Green Bay, and it was agreed that the matter would be tabled until the completion of the 1960 NFL season."

The Green Bay press spent the season concentrating on the stunning improvement of the Packers on the field, mostly trying to ignore rumors about Lombardi's departure, but sportswriters in New York devoted much of their energy to speculating about his return. It seemed that all of New York wanted Vinnie back. Ed Sullivan, the television host, who golfed at Westchester Country Club with Giants executives, was constantly promoting Lombardi for the job, sending clips about him to members of the New York press corps, who were eager to recount his glory and lay out the arguments as to why he should leave Green Bay.

Yes, he was hailed as the Pope in Green Bay and had performed a miracle there, but so what? they asked in print. In his columns from Green Bay, Red Smith never failed to write that Lombardi was pacing the wrong sidelines. "Lombardi has relished his success in Green Bay, has enjoyed being his own boss even though the double job makes heavy demands on his time," Smith wrote in a column after Thanksgiving, just before the season-changing Bears game. "But he doesn't try to hide his homesickness.... They love Vincent in Green Bay. They would love him in New York." Another Lombardi booster was Arthur Daley of the *New York Times,* a Fordham graduate and longtime Lombardi friend, not to be confused with Art Daley of the *Green Bay Press-Gazette.* Lombardi, he wrote in early December, was "a New Yorker at heart" and "always the Giants' boy." The venerable Stanley Woodward, who had known Lombardi since they shared a cabin together at Red Blaik's Bull Pond, pounded out the same theme: "Vincenzo, as every one knows, has about as much business being out in Green Bay as Mayor [Robert] Wagner. He is strictly New York–New Jersey and his playing-coaching career until he heard the jingle of Wisconsin shekels was on the line of Fordham–St. Cecilia's–West Point–New York Giants. He was Col. Earl H. Blaik's Tower of Pizza and the Giants have never attained the class they showed when he ran the offense. It's your move, Jack Mara."

These eastern writers watched with equal parts admiration and fear as Lombardi's Packers swept through the end of the season and headed toward Philadelphia for the championship. With every win, the *Times's* Daley wrote, it appeared that Lombardi was "tightening the chains anchoring him to Green Bay." It is clear that Lombardi was confiding in his pals in the New York press corps, and that their ambivalence reflected his own. Should he stay or leave? Marie had never fully adjusted to the small-town life and would gladly move back to New Jersey. Lombardi's attachment to the Packers board of directors could not match the personal bond he felt toward the Maras. Daley of the *Times* was right—Vince loved New York. During one of his trips back to Manhattan, as he was crossing Fifth Avenue in midtown, he looked up at the skyscrapers and announced, "This is *my* town!" New York was where he always thought he would coach, if not at Fordham, then with the Giants.

But there were compelling reasons to stay. He wielded more power in Green Bay than he could ever hope to have with the Giants. Wellington and Jack Mara admired him, but they were not willing to cede all authority. As much as he enjoyed many of the players he had coached as a Giants assistant, he felt equally close to the Packers—and in terms of talent they were younger and better. The people he admired most in the league, including George Halas of the rival Bears, urged him to remain in Green Bay. Part of the Halas argument, which was also made by Paul Brown and to a lesser extent by Commissioner Rozelle, was that Lombardi had in essence saved the

Green Bay franchise and that his leaving would endanger it again. Even more important to Halas was the fear that if Lombardi voided his contract in Green Bay and left for New York, it would weaken the NFL in its struggle with the AFL—if coaches could break their contracts, how could the league use moral pressure to keep players from doing the same?

With these factors to consider, Lombardi vacillated, as he had during most of his important career decisions. At times during that fall and winter he told friends that he could persuade the Packers to release him from his contract, at other times he said that they would not do it. Olejniczak made it clear that he did not want Lombardi to go. "I'd just as soon lose both legs as lose Lombardi," he said before the Eagles game. "But I know one thing, he's a man of integrity." There were reports later that the Packers board refused to release Lombardi. They might have, in the end, but it was never put to a final test. He met with Wellington Mara in Philadelphia before the championship game and told Mara that he had decided to stay in Green Bay. "He said that he had to fulfill his obligations there," Mara said later. "And he also knew that he had a darn good team coming back. He told me that." When reporters broached the subject after the game, Lombardi gave them an answer of sorts. "Let's have no more of that talk!" he barked.

SIX WEEKS after Jack Vainisi died, his wife suffered another heartbreak. The baby that she had been carrying was delivered stillborn on January 4, 1961. A few weeks later Lombardi called and asked Jackie to join him and Marie for dinner at the country club. Marie, who had suffered through two childbirth tragedies of her own, tried to console Jackie, and the three friends talked about football and children and old times through dinner, until finally Lombardi leaned across the table and lowered his voice to a rough whisper. "I have to ask you this or I will get no peace," he said. "Do you think I was at all the cause of Jack's death?"

Jackie Vainisi thought about how her husband would attempt to conceal the pain shooting down his left arm, how he would eat entire lemon meringue pies when she was not looking, how she had tried to change his diet, to give him vegetables, but he just kept gobbling up more desserts, despite his heart condition, and worked more, eighteen-hour days and nights, wanting to excel, to win, to find the best boys out there, agreeing with what Vince was doing, first-class all the way, nothing second-rate or halfhearted, the full measure of commitment, until that Sunday after Thanksgiving when he slumped dead on the bathroom floor at age thirty-three, before he could see all the great players he had scouted perform in their first championship game. "No," she said to Lombardi. "You didn't kill him. Of course not. Nobody could do that to Jack but Jack."

15

Golden

Time let me play and be
Golden in the mercy of his means
—Dylan Thomas, "Fern Hill"

H E STRUGGLED in obscurity for twenty years and then fame arrived, and it came to him in a rush. He had been in Green Bay for only two seasons. His Packers had won 15 games and lost 10. He had captured a conference crown but not a league championship. His achievements as a professional football coach were solid but not singular, not in the same class as those of George Halas, the Papa Bear who had been running things in Chicago since the league's creation forty years earlier, or Paul Brown, who had won an average of ten games a year over fourteen seasons with his Cleveland Browns, or even Weeb Ewbank, who had led the Baltimore Colts to consecutive championships at the end of the fifties. Yet by the first few months of 1961, Vince Lombardi was a transcendent figure in football, worshiped as the Pope in Green Bay, coveted by other teams, held up by national sportswriters as the model of leadership. He was so hot that John F. Kennedy, the new president, who had first met him on the steps of St. Willebrord during the 1960 Wisconsin primary, talked about him admiringly and wrote notes to him and invited him to the inauguration in Washington (missed it; league meetings to attend), and Robert F. Kennedy, the attorney general, made plans to see the Packers the next time they came east.

What was it about Lombardi that set him apart? It could not have been style over substance in any conventional sense. He was innately shy, sometimes painfully so, according to Marie. He had to screw up his courage every day to be a public figure; the witty chatter and glad-handing did not come naturally to him. He was literal, not subtle. If you invited him to a six-thirty cocktail party, peer out the window at 6:25 and you would see him pulling up in his Pontiac, ignoring Marie's plea that they drive around the block a few times to avoid being the first guests ringing the doorbell. Straight ahead with Vince. He did not fake or seduce or charm his way into celebrity. Nothing flashy about his looks: squat and sturdy build, gap-toothed smile, broad and fleshy nose, thick-lens glasses, short wavy dark hair, salted with whitish gray, always fresh from the barber's chair. In dress he was indistinguishable from the State Farm agent on Monroe Street or the cheese broker over at the Bellin Building or the floor manager at H. C. Prange's Department Store: invariably neat, with his big class ring and wristwatch and tie clasp and button-down short-sleeved white shirt.

The furthest thing from Kennedy cool. He wore hats and galoshes and rain slickers made of translucent plastic, and played golf and gin rummy and cried and screamed and smoked and sweated and watched *Tom and Jerry* cartoons and laughed so hard that tears squirted out of his eyes like windshield wiper spray. He fell asleep in the recliner chair in his den and snored away until supper.

No way around it, Lombardi was a square. And yet look again and something else emerges. Here he is, on the Wednesday evening of April 5, 1961, making his way through the banquet hall of Tappen's Restaurant at the corner of Ocean and Voorhies in Sheepshead Bay, guest of honor at a testimonial dinner-dance sponsored by his hometown board of trade. Chris Schenkel, the network sportscaster, has just introduced him. Sellout crowd, the place buzzing. Frank Gifford is there, and the Maras, and Father Tim, and Harry and Matty and all the Izzos. Uncle Pete and Uncle Frank, in black tie and tails, lead him up to the front, this way, this way, past the Kiwanis Club table and the Knights of Columbus table, band playing the Fordham Ram fight song, Lombardi walking with his left fist clenched in triumph, a white carnation shining in the lapel of his dark gray suit, the suggestion of a smile creasing his face—his confirmation day smile, four decades later.

These are his people, yes, and he is their favorite son, former altar boy at St. Mark's, grandson of Tony the Barber. His homecoming harks back to a Sheepshead Bay that is fading from view, like Brooklyn, stores closing, families moving out to Jersey and Staten Island, Dodgers gone to the California sun. Like any aging small town now, a departure place, not a destination. As the program for the evening states: "Since we cannot root for a home team, we root for home talent. We are grateful, Vince, your deeds have done us proud." But if there is, unavoidably, a touch of sentimentalism to the occasion, there is more to Lombardi as he strides through the room. Square and awkward he might be, yet he overpowers people with his will as he walks by. Character is the will in action, his Fordham tutors used to say, and here it is, embodied, magnetism of the will, asserting that life is not merely fleeting luck or chance, that discipline and persistence can prevail, even if it takes twenty years, and as he presses forward the crowd seems certain that he knows the way, the right way, that even if he has not won everything, he will, that he is beyond Sheepshead Bay and Green Bay, and the applause wells up in the hall, deafening now, and it lifts them out of their seats as he goes by and they want to follow him.

IT WAS A SNAP to draw the organizational chart of the Green Bay Packers then: Vince Lombardi in a box at the top, alone, everyone else below him at about the same level. If he was the Pope, there was no College of Cardinals. Assistant coaches, ticket office clerks, players, members of the executive committee—they were all equally afraid of him. As one assistant later explained, "It became a reciprocal thing: Don't tell on me and I won't tell on you. Sooner or later you knew you were going to screw up in a way he wouldn't like if he found out. That bonded everyone together." When Dominic Olejniczak confided that he would rather have his legs amputated than lose Lombardi, the sentiment was one-sided. "No other club had given a coach as much authority as we gave Vince," the Packers president said. Lombardi seized the opportunity and wanted as little to do with the executive committee as possible. "He'd let a few on the plane with us, but they were more like the players," according to Bob Skoronski. "If we lost they wanted to sit in the back with us."

During the off-season, grateful that Lombardi had not fled to New York, Ole and his executive committee rewarded him with a new five-year contract, tearing up his original pact, which still had three years to run. His salary was not revealed at the time, but records indicate the raise pushed it above $50,000. The new contract only strengthened his iron rule. Even his closest pals on the committee, Tony "the Gray Ghost" Canadeo and Dick Bourguignon, understood the imbalance in the relationship. "If you don't agree with me, I'll take away your vote," Lombardi once said to them. It was a joke, but he meant it; he expected a rubber stamp from the board of directors. At league meetings he and attorney Fred Trowbridge did most of the talking for the club, with one notable exception; at sessions limited to owners, Olejniczak stayed in the room and Vince was asked to leave. It always "bothered the hell out of him" to face this reminder that he was not complete master of his universe.

Lombardi was not the sort of boss who slipped into the office unnoticed. People sensed him coming before he arrived, like a meteorological phenomenon, a weather front rolling into Green Bay from Saskatchewan.

His mood, high pressure or low, was going to define their day. If he smiled as he hung his camel's hair coat on the rack near the Crooks Street entrance, and began with a pleasant "Good morning, Ruth," to Ruth McKloskey, the staff responded in kind, with great relief. If he tramped in with a scowl, they tried to steer clear of him until the storm passed. The storm in most cases featured a sudden tirade, often directed at Tom Miller, the mild-mannered publicist. If Lombardi strolled over to the duplicating machine and told one of his corny jokes and laughed loudly, they all laughed with him. Although he seemed to have a one-track mind, the track was long and wide—anything to do with his football operation. Lorraine Keck had been working at H. C. Prange's that year when she was told that "the Packers needed a girl" to help with secretarial duties. She walked over to the team's downtown office—and there was Lombardi, waiting to ask her how fast she typed and whether she could take shorthand.

Keck quickly learned Lombardi's philosophy of perfecting the little things, a trait that he had acquired from Colonel Blaik at West Point. When he spoke into the dictaphone, he meticulously included all punctuation. After letters were typed they went back to him so that he could double-check the spelling. He demanded precision—letters answered quickly, documents neatly filed, no unfinished tasks lingering at the end of the day. The office hours were nine to five, but anyone arriving at nine was considered fifteen minutes late—the same Lombardi Standard Time that his players had encountered. One morning, before leaving for an off-season vacation with Marie, he called the staff into his office. "While I'm gone, I don't want any slovenly work around here. Do what you're supposed to do!" he said. A few days later he called from the Caribbean to check on them.

One young receptionist was "scared to death" of Lombardi. Whenever she got near him, her hands shook uncontrollably. She could not speak when she saw him coming. At night she dreamed about him, all nightmares. Finally, after a few weeks of torment, she went to Ruth McKloskey and said she had to quit. For the most part, though, Lombardi knew when to pull back. After lecturing McKloskey one morning on the proper way to list assets and liabilities—a subject she knew more about than he did—he approached her at the mail counter later and poked her on the arm. "Still mad at me?" he asked, breaking into a grin. She laughed and said no. There were other saving graces that counterbalanced his autocratic bearing. He was a "softie at heart," according to Keck, and would not hesitate to send people home to attend to sick relatives. Though it was impossible not to hear him swearing in the film room, he was courteous around the women. McKloskey approached his desk once when he was screaming into his phone at a league official—"What the hell is going on, goddamn it!"—until he saw his secretary, covered the receiver, turned to her and said, "Excuse me, Ruth." Keck discovered that the more outspoken she was around Lombardi, the more he seemed to enjoy it, as long as she did her work. "I was dumb enough and green enough that if I thought something was not right, I would tell him. He got so little of that pushing back. Everyone was 'Yes, sir. Yes, sir.' He liked a little 'No, sir.'"

That was true only when it served his purposes. Lombardi was decidedly less open to argument when it came time to negotiate new contracts with his players, and he would thwart their efforts by any means necessary. The players union was not yet a bargaining force, there were no agents to haggle with and players had little freedom or security. Along with these advantages, Lombardi brought to the negotiations the skills of a psychologist. He knew just when to stroke and when to intimidate. When Bob Skoronski began making a case for a raise, Lombardi pulled a piece of paper from his drawer and said, "You had a pretty good year, but, heh, heh, against the Rams we had a third and one and we ran a 36 and you didn't get the job done, did you, Bob?" As Skoronski tried to counter by citing a crucial block he had made against San Francisco, Lombardi rose from his chair, walked around the desk and affectionately rubbed his tackle's crew-cut scalp. The tactic silenced Skoronski and settled the debate—a preemptive strike that compelled Skoronski the following year to open by saying, "Coach, I want you to sit in that chair and not come over and touch me during these negotiations."

Gary Knafelc was so certain that he would be tongue-tied that he came in with a typed sheet of accomplishments. As Knafelc later recounted: "I walked in and he acted like he was on the phone and left me just standing there. I was just perspiring. He looked at me and said, 'Sit down!' I sat down. I said, 'Coach, I have this . . .' He stopped me and said, 'Just a minute.' He had to make another call. I knew I was dead already. He hung up and said, 'Yes?' And I said, 'Please read this.' It listed my passes caught to passes thrown, blocking awards, grasping anything I could. He didn't look at it a second and a half and then threw it back to me and with that big finger he had he pointed clear across the table at me and said, 'Gary, all you played was offense. You were not on the kickoff team. You were not on the punt return team. All you played was offense!' He said he would give me two thousand instead of four. And I got up and left the room. I was so happy just to be invited back to training camp. But that's the kind of guy he was. He would build you up, but never to the point too high where you thought you could tell him what to do. He was still the master and you were the slaves."

"I'M SCARED," Lombardi said on the first day of training camp in July 1961. Coaches are notorious worrywarts, constantly underrating their squad and inflating the opposition, but in this case his apprehension was more informed. During his first two seasons in Green Bay, Lombardi had been concerned about the team's talent and whether it knew how to win. Now his fear was different—a fear not to lose. The will to win became not just a positive goal but a neurosis, an obsessive hatred of losing. The Packers had not won it all, they had not established the winning tradition of the New York Yankees, his sporting model, yet they were being portrayed as sure winners. On the schedule of every other team in the league, he said, there would be a circle around the date of their game against Green Bay.

Lombardi carried this dread with him to St. Norbert that summer. In an effort to overcome it, he took nothing for granted. He began a tradition of starting from scratch, assuming that the players were blank slates who carried over no knowledge from the year before. He reviewed the fundamentals of blocking and tackling, the basic plays, how to study the playbook. He began with the most elemental statement of all. "Gentlemen," he said, holding a pigskin in his right hand, "this is a football."

To which Max McGee, from the rear of the squad, delivered the immortal retort, "Uh, Coach, could you slow down a little. You're going too fast for us." McGee's line had even Lombardi chuckling, but not for long. He seemed more intense than ever at the daily workouts. "This guy was full of piss and vinegar from the first day of camp," remembered Willie Wood. "I mean he was *hot!* You had to work your tail off. He took no nonsense from anybody. He knew that he had a big challenge and he was determined not to lose again." Lombardi was right, of course. The other teams were gunning for the Packers, making winning more difficult than before. The coach who never wanted to lose drove his team through an undefeated preseason, then lost the season opener to the Lions in Milwaukee.

There were two major changes in the starting lineup. Ron Kramer took over for the veteran Gary Knafelc at tight end. It was not that Knafelc played only offense, as Lombardi had complained during negotiations, but that Kramer was bigger and a ferocious blocker who could add another dimension to the offense. And Willie Wood replaced Em Tunnell at free safety. In his final year, Tunnell had taught Wood the lessons learned during a long career. "I used to sit around and quiz Em all the time. What do you do in this situation? How do you know when your man's coming inside? He taught me how to anticipate what would happen," Wood said later. "Em was a very bright guy who helped me tremendously. He had been around so long, one of the first black stars in the league, and for me just to have the opportunity to hang around him, I was awed by that. Em was so cool."

Wood looked rather cool himself back at free safety, though he was anything but relaxed in the locker room beforehand. His pregame routine was to sit alone at his cubicle, chewing worriedly on a fresh white towel, then another one, before he traipsed over to the bathroom and threw up. But once he took the field, he was all intuition and grace: No. 24 in green and gold, closing ground in a sudden burst to knock away a pass or upend a runner with his unorthodox tackle, flinging his body at the ballcarrier's ankles, cutting the feet out from under him so that he flipped wildly into the air, cleats over helmet. It looked effortless, but no one could tackle low like Willie Wood. He and Herb Adderley, a fleet rookie from Michigan State, brought another weapon to the Packers that year, the threat of returning any punt or kickoff for a touchdown. In the first game after the disquieting loss to the Lions, it was Wood's score on a punt runback that led the Packers to a 30 to 10 win over the 49ers, restoring the hint of a smile to Lombardi's face.

THE MYTHMAKERS were finding their way to Green Bay, and none of the coach's fears about losing could stop them. The first to arrive that autumn was Tim Cohane. Ever since his days as Fordham's publicity man, Cohane had been Lombardi's Great Mentioner, praising his talent in almost any discussion of football coaches. Lombardi's success could be traced back to his old college promoter, in a sense. It was Cohane who had persuaded Colonel Blaik to hire Lombardi as an assistant at West Point, and it was Blaik who then shaped Lombardi's coaching persona. As sports editor of *Look,* Cohane decided that now was the time to write a piece about Lombardi and the rise of professional football. He reached Green Bay during the week of practice for the third game of the season, against the Bears, and settled into the guest bedroom at Sunset Circle, bringing with him a passel of books and opinions, which he shared freely in his booming voice, lighting up the house.

In their discussions, Lombardi presented a case as to "why the pros play better football" to Cohane, who dutifully recorded it. There was no nostalgia in the coach's perspective. He said that football had improved so much since his days at Fordham that "today, I couldn't even make the team." The pro game, he said, had improved most of all. Once he had experienced it, he was hooked on its sophistication, two platoons of specialists, the swiftest and biggest athletes in the country, every team with a first-rate quarterback and receiving corps. He came to appreciate that "full-time concentration, and the opportunity to play for several more years, make a better player." His ambition once had been to lead a revived Fordham team, but now he doubted that he could ever be satisfied in college. "In fact, I think I'd be unhappy if I didn't have the added duties of Green Bay's general manager. Tickets, salaries, TV and radio contracts all pose headaches beyond the migraine of trying to win games, but I thrive on work. I'm restless, demanding, sometimes impatient and hot-tempered. For these characteristics, a full schedule is the best antidote."

That Sunday morning, as Cohane and Marie were driving to City Stadium for the Bears game, the sportswriter could see that Lombardi's wife also had a deep understanding of Vince's needs and motivations. Her observations were offered with detachment and objectivity. "That beating by the Lions two weeks ago was a good thing. Lombardi needed to be taken down a few pegs. Did he ever!" she told Cohane. "But you're going to see quite a football team today." She could tell by the way Vince had moved spiritedly around the house that week. She anticipated that both he and his players had tasted just enough defeat to drive them through the season.

Pro or college, the spirit was there, and from his vantage point in the press box before the game Cohane had a moment of sweet serendipity that left him "deeply stirred." He looked down on the field and saw Lombardi in his camel's hair coat and fedora stepping gingerly around the field, testing the wet turf, and just then the loudspeaker began playing a familiar tune— the old Fordham Ram fight song. "The impact was weird," Cohane said later. "Almost as if a faded dream—that Fordham would restore itself to football power under Vince Lombardi—had come true vicariously there in Green Bay, far from Rose Hill in the Bronx." And what a power it was. The Packers, as Marie had predicted, were quite a football team that day. Bart Starr threw two touchdown passes in the 24 to 0 win, one to his favorite new target, the big bull at tight end, Ron Kramer. The defense shut out the Bears for the first time since 1935. In the first series of the game, the Bears had the ball on the Packers one but could not score, and the thunderous roar in the stands after the fourth-down stop transported Cohane back through the years—back to the tumult in the Polo Grounds on that afternoon in 1936 when the Seven Blocks, with Butch Lombardi at right guard, stopped the Pitt Panthers at the two and secured a scoreless tie.

That evening at Manci's Supper Club, past and present merged again as the two old Fordham Rams, in boisterous and throaty voice, with Cohane doing harmony, belted out the fight song for Ole, the Gray Ghost, Father Burke and the other dinner companions: "Once more the old Maroon, wave on high; We'll sing our battle song: WE DO, OR DIE!"

After his return to New York, Cohane began spinning the new Lombardi myth. The headline for his photo essay tied past and present again, evoking Colonel Blaik's favorite phrase. It read:

Vince Lombardi . . .
Under this Green Bay Gridiron Genius,
the Packers Pay the Price

The praise continued with a caption under a photograph of Lombardi on the sidelines, pondering the action: "Profound as an ocean depth, yet voluble as a summer cloudburst, Lombardi had to learn to modify his explosive temper." And a closing sentence in the story's lead paragraph lifted Lombardi above the coaching crowd: "Brilliant and tough-minded, a driving perfectionist, natural leader and born teacher, Vince Lombardi seems certain to become one of the greatest coaches of all time, if, indeed, he is not that already."

The following week Lombardi's men played as though no praise could be too purple. Johnny Unitas and his Colts came to Green Bay and left in

disarray after a 45 to 7 loss. Willie Wood returned a punt seventy-two yards
for a touchdown, and the rest was left to the one-man scoring gang, Paul
Hornung. He ran for three touchdowns, took in an eight-yard pass for another, and kicked a thirty-eight-yard field goal and six extra points—scoring
thirty-three points by himself. And it could have been more; on the option
play, he threw a forty-yard touchdown pass that was nullified by a penalty.
Tony Canadeo, the color man in the television booth next to Ray Scott, and
himself the leading ground gainer in Packers history, watched Hornung's
performance with his jaw agape. The majesty of No. 5, the way he glanced
inside, saw a Colts linebacker plugging the hole, so cut outside to daylight
and glided down the left sideline fifty-four yards for a score; then, later, how
he plowed through three Colts, carrying them with him into the end zone on
a ten-yard sweep. It was, in the estimation of the Gray Ghost, "the greatest
day ever by a backfield man."

   And out came more writers from the East to see the genius coach and
his prodigious left halfback. One of them was Dick Schaap, at age twenty-
seven the sports editor at *Newsweek* and frequent contributor to *Sport*. The
lone problem with the Packers story as far as Schaap and other New Yorkers
were concerned was its travel requirement. "You had to be brave to go to
Green Bay," Schaap once declared, advancing a theme articulated earlier by
Alexis de Tocqueville of France and Marie Lombardi of New Jersey. "You
had to fly the route of the Blue Goose, North Central Airlines, which gave
out free beer on its flights." The first time an editor at *Sport* asked Schaap to
visit Green Bay to gauge whether Hornung was reality or myth, Schaap responded jokingly, "Can't we check on the phone?" As a rule, he noted, "out-
of-town sportswriters go to Milwaukee only under threat of torture; the
thought of going a hundred miles farther north is unthinkable."

   To remote Green Bay Schaap ventured nonetheless, arriving in town
between Hornung's spectacular performance against the Colts and the first
road game in Cleveland. What struck him immediately in Green Bay was
how open the players were. They welcomed him as a brother, inviting him to
hang out at the rambling brick house near the stadium on the west side that
Hornung shared that year with Ron Kramer and Jesse Whittenton. (Max
McGee, Hornung's usual bachelor pad pal, was married then, briefly—"a
six-month tryout-type deal," as Hornung put it.) They were all about the
same age. Wealth or fame had not set them totally out of reach. They were
narcissists, as most athletes tend to be, Schaap thought, but there was none of
the maddening condescension of millionaire athletes of a later era. The
Packers seemed honored that an eastern sportswriter would come see them.

   Lombardi was not what drew Schaap to Green Bay, but the broad
shadow of the coach was palpable everywhere. "I remember being frightened of him," Schaap recalled of his first impression. "But I was probably
frightened of all authority figures. He looked tough. Even when he said

hello, he sounded tough. He had that bulldog bark along with the bulldog face." The players were equally intimidated by Lombardi, Schaap noticed, though their feelings were complex, at once irreverent and awed. They joked about his "martinet tendencies"—when he was not around to hear. Hornung and McGee once hid a tape recorder outside his office before traipsing in for one of his bawling-out sessions. All that could be heard on the tape was Lombardi yelling. Later, they re-recorded it, inserting obscene retorts between the coach's rants. "Yeah, sure. Yeah. Go fuck yourself, Vince! Yeah, who do you think you're talking to, you asshole." All the things that they would never dare say to his face, and as they replayed the spliced version they laughed with hilarity and glee and terror. The players needed that private release from the pressure Lombardi imposed, but as Schaap noted in an article that autumn in *Sport*, "to a man they respect him and what he has done for them."

Much of what Schaap saw and heard in Green Bay found expression in his writing, but not all of it. Along with his interview notes, he kept separate mental note of Hornung's off-hours existence during that first trip, a chronicle of youthful saturnalia. "Each morning Paul would get up about quarter to nine and be at the field by nine o'clock. They would practice until twelve and there would be meetings to three. At three he'd come home, mix a pitcher of martinis and drink martinis until six o'clock with Kramer and the others. Then they'd go out to dinner, a group of players. Scotch before dinner. Wine with dinner. Brandy after dinner. Then back on scotch. Every day. I lost count by the time it had reached more than sixty just how many drinks he had in that week leading up to the Browns game. Also, he never went to bed before four in the morning, he never went to bed alone, and he never repeated himself. Paul by that time had become such a sex symbol that he had lost the power to differentiate. All women looked the same to him. They could be tall, short, fat, beautiful. It was part of his image that he was supposed to get laid every night. And therefore to live up to this image he would get laid every night." And run and block and pass and catch and kick like hell on Sunday afternoons.

Myth or reality? Hornung seemed both. It was said that half the world wanted to be with him and the other half wanted to be him. The yearning he stirred in others is evoked in one Saturday afternoon scene in early fall. A young boy named Gary Van Ness is sent by his mother to pick up a bag of hamburgers at Sneezer's takeout place near the corner of Highland and Ashland on the west side. As Gary approaches on his bike, he sees a cream-colored 1959 Cadillac convertible in the driveway. A beautiful girl sits in the front, her head tilted to the sky. And out from the storefront steps Hornung, his wavy locks shining above his brilliant high forehead. He is wearing light slacks and a fresh T-shirt, and he is carrying a case of Hamm's beer under his right arm. He puts the beer in the back, eases into the Caddy, glances at the kid, smiles, winks and drives away.

To trade places for a moment with the Golden Boy—among those who made such a wish might have been none other than his straight-arrow coach. "I don't know what it is about Hornung that gets me," Lombardi confided to a visiting friend one day. "Maybe," came the reply, "he is the other side of Vince Lombardi."

"Maybe," Lombardi said.

A significant part of it was that Hornung was so skilled at football. He was a money player, the one Lombardi knew would somehow find a way to score when they were near the goal line, that rare gifted runner who was not too proud to block, a charismatic leader who wanted to be one of the boys yet lifted the hearts of his teammates just by being among them. But the free and easy side of Hornung also attracted Lombardi. Ruth McKloskey thought her boss "got a kick out of some of the things Paul did—what he wanted to do and couldn't do." Lombardi needed daily prayer and relentless discipline to make it; with Hornung it seemed effortless. Jack Koeppler, Vince's golfing buddy at Oneida, concluded that "given a different time and place, the Old Man would have loved to have stepped out with Paul and those guys." The coach's son, the collegiate Vincent, also felt that his father wanted to live vicariously through Hornung. "I always suspected he had an affinity with Paul. He was a bit of a hell-raiser in college. He liked to have fun, he liked his scotch, but he felt that he had to be so responsible all the time."

There were, in a sense, three Lombardi sons, not one.

First Vincent Henry Lombardi, the conflicted son, who looked like the Old Man and talked like the Old Man and blinked his eyes like the Old Man but struggled to live up to his expectations. No flesh and blood son could, perhaps. Vincent was a good kid, smart, bottled up, tense, but his father thought he was soft, too much like his mother, not ready to pay the price, a decent athlete, but he got hurt too easily—a genetic trait? an unwanted reminder of Lombardi's own injury-prone past?—and he ran awkwardly at fullback, lifted his legs wrong. No way he could compete. It was always complicated with Vince and Vincent.

Then Bryan Bartlett Starr, the dependable son, his opposite in culture and demeanor, yet the one who did everything that Lombardi wanted, who believed in him and sought only to please him. Bart alone among the players seemed actually to want to be with Lombardi. He looked forward to their meetings, yearned to hear him explain football and life, and appreciated—while it was happening—how much the Old Man had shaped him. Lombardi knew that he would always be there, clearly and soberly and rationally acting as his surrogate on the field. It was a relationship of trust between Vince and Bart.

And finally Paul Vernon Hornung, the prodigal son, talented and wasteful. All the bona fides that Lombardi coveted: Notre Dame, Heisman

Trophy, good Catholic boy, polite to his mother and Marie. How could Vincent—or even Bart—compete with that? Here was the son who moved Lombardi. "He loved Hornung, *loved* him," said Tony Canadeo. Marie often told this story: Late at night the telephone rang at Sunset Circle, and she stirred, and Vince grumbled, "Don't pick it up! Hornung's in trouble!"

"What?" Marie asked.

"Don't pick it up. I know something's happened to Paul."

"Well, don't you think we ought to pick it up and see if it's one of our kids?"

"Oh."

Hornung, for better or worse, was often the first thing on his mind.

PAUL HORNUNG never enjoyed much of a relationship with his own namesake father. His mother, Loretta, was pregnant with Paul when she separated from her husband, an insurance executive on Long Island, who had begun a long downward spiral brought on by excessive drinking and carousing. Loretta Hornung moved home to Louisville, where she and little Paul, born in 1935, stayed with her parents, who ran a grocery on the blue-collar west side. His dissolute father eventually returned to Louisville and bounced from job to job as his drinking worsened. When Paul was nine his grandmother died, and he and his mother set off on their own. "You'll have to be a man now, Paul," she said to him. For a time they shared a room in another family's house, sleeping on two army cots. "I was very close to my mother," he said later. "She was the only person I had."

Despite the hardship Hornung would look back on his early years as idyllic. He lived "a perfect athletic childhood," playing football, baseball and basketball with ease. "Back in those days you didn't lift weights. You were either an athlete or you weren't. You couldn't artificially chisel it. I was always the best athlete on the block." When he was in sixth grade he starred on the eighth grade basketball team. At Flaget High, where he played quarterback, he became the most sought-after scholastic star in Kentucky history. Paul Bryant, then head coach at Kentucky, tried everything to lure Hornung to the state school. He brought the governor to visit Loretta. He promised that he would offer scholarships to every senior player on Flaget's squad if Paul signed with him. A Kentucky booster showed him a shiny new Cadillac. But his mother loved Notre Dame, and nothing Bryant did could turn Paul away from the Irish after he visited South Bend and walked into Frank Leahy's office, and the coach who had once taught blocking to Vinnie Lombardi and the fabled Fordham wall put his arms around Hornung and said, "I think I can make you the greatest football player in the country."

Leahy was sparing with praise, but remained effusive during his prize recruit's freshman year. He predicted that Hornung would be the best quarterback in Notre Dame history and offered an unerring metaphor to describe his running style. Hornung cut through a defense, the coach said, "like a lawnmower going through grass." Leahy left Notre Dame later that year, and the program slumped into a dim era brightened mainly by Hornung. To be the Irish quarterback was to hold the most glamorous job in college football, and Paul fit the role. He became known as the Golden Boy, playing under the Golden Dome. Looks, talent and Notre Dame's prestige combined to create a global athletic idol. He had fan clubs everywhere; thirty teenage girls sent pictures from the south of France. One of Paul's friends, a shy but eloquent classmate, the Irish equivalent of Cyrano de Bergerac, answered letters to Paul from strange women, sending out romantic missives under Hornung's signature. He was a "205 pound Adonis," wrote John M. Ross in *America Weekly*, who "constantly runs the risk of becoming the first player in history to be carried triumphantly from the field on the soft shoulders of a shrieking female horde."

Hornung had his own agent in college, Julius Tucker, who lent him a Studebaker and set up speaking engagements. During the summer before his junior year, he was flown out to speak at a Catholic high school in Pueblo, Colorado. Pueblo was the hometown of Gary Knafelc, then finishing his second year with the Packers, and the pro was stunned to see a banner hanging across a downtown street welcoming the college kid. "I was in town, too," Knafelc said. "And nobody cared. I wasn't even invited. He was the Golden Boy." Flashy sportsmen who rooted for Notre Dame became Paul's newfound friends; one of them, Abe Samuels, introduced him to the high life in Chicago, where he began dating dancers from the Chez Paree. "It was carte blanche for me all over Chicago," Hornung said.

His legend on the playing field grew during his junior season, when he played his first two classic Hornung games, compiling 354 total yards against Southern Cal and displaying all his skills in beating Iowa. In that game, during a crucial late drive, he completed four passes, including one for a touchdown, kicked the extra point, boomed a deep kickoff and made the tackle himself, and finally kicked the game-winning field goal. It was all the material Notre Dame's sports publicist needed to push him for the Heisman the following season. Hornung essentially had the trophy won even before his senior year started, luckily, since he was occasionally injured and his team was pathetic, winning only two and losing eight. The national class of seniors was amazing that year, with Johnny Majors at Tennessee, Tommy McDonald at Oklahoma, John Brodie at Stanford and Jim Brown at Syracuse. Majors later insisted that he should have won the Heisman. Hornung confided that he thought McDonald deserved it. History might favor Jim Brown. "But Brown didn't get the publicity," Hornung said. "We had the best publicity guy in the world. Everybody loved Charley Callahan. All the sportswriters knew him." And they voted for Paul Hornung.

Jack Vainisi, the Packers scout and Notre Dame alumnus, considered

Hornung the best of the group, too, persuading Green Bay to select him as the bonus pick, the No. 1 choice, in the pro draft. After playing in the College All-Star Game the following summer, Hornung and his newfound pal and teammate, Ron Kramer of Michigan, drove north together to the Packers training camp, then held in Stevens Point. The Golden Boy's reputation had preceded him. As soon as they reached the dormitory "this girl came up to Paul and grabbed him around the neck and screamed, 'I've been waiting hours for you!' " Kramer recounted. "I thought she was going to kill him. She looked like a Purdue guard—a big girl. He finally got her off him and we go into the dorm, and the coach, Liz Blackbourn, comes up to Paul and yells, 'You're here five seconds and you've got a girl on your arm!' " The young woman had reason to think Hornung would greet her affectionately; she had been among those who received romantic notes from his ghostwriter back at Notre Dame. This odd first impression became a symbol of Hornung's precarious early standing in Green Bay. Until Lombardi came along, it appeared that the Golden Boy was simply the hyped creation of the Irish publicity machine. Blackbourn sarcastically called him "Golden Dome."

HIS TEAMMATES in Green Bay had other nicknames for Hornung. They called him the Horn, or Goat (because of his drooping shoulders), or Eileen (during the off-season, he had gone to Hollywood for a role in the television show *My Sister Eileen*). All were uttered with affection. Hornung "could be an asshole at times," Ron Kramer said, "but he was a lovable asshole." There was nothing stingy about him; he was as willing to pick up the check at the bar as he was to throw the block to spring Jim Taylor. He treated rookies with respect, and was especially generous in that summer and fall of 1961 with halfback Elijah Pitts, a thirteenth-round draft choice from tiny Philander Smith College in Arkansas. Pitts, the son of a sharecropper, went to camp with the attitude that he was "as good as anyone," telling friends back in the little town of Mayflower that he would not see them until the end of his rookie season. But he was overtaken by anxiety at times at St. Norbert, fearful that he would be overlooked, and never forgot how the Golden Boy believed in him. "I gotta make it. I gotta make it," Pitts kept saying softly. "You're gonna make it. Believe it. You'll be playing here longer than I will," Hornung replied.

Another aspect of Hornung's generosity involved Lombardi. He served as a buffer between the fiery coach and the other players. Lombardi could rant at Hornung, blister him with criticism, fine him if necessary, and Hornung would accept it with equanimity. "Coach could whip him and Paul would take it. He wouldn't break. He could handle it," said Ron Kramer. Most of the other prominent players could not. Starr felt that practice field criticism undermined him with his teammates. Taylor sulked, certain that Lombardi was picking on him. Even the seemingly unflappable McGee

churned inside whenever Lombardi singled him out. Hornung's willingness
to absorb the heat made it easier for less talented players. They knew Lombardi adored Hornung, so they thought, as Gary Knafelc put it, "Jeez, if Paul
can take it, we all can."

The Horn was larger than life in some ways, yet always one of the boys.
As a team, around Lombardi, the Packers were models of discipline and professionalism, but on their own they were closer in disposition and lifestyle to
the left halfback than they were to the quarterback or the coach. Many of
them were what Ron Kramer called "jerk-off young kids, swearing all the
time, bullshitting all the time"—and smoking and drinking incessantly as
well. Cartons of Marlboros were stacked on the floor at Hornung's house,
freebies that he received from the tobacco company for advertising them.
The boys often took little giveaway four-packs downtown to hand out to
young women in the bars. They smoked the rest themselves. Before every
game Hornung sat alone on his stool, puffing away, gathering his thoughts.
There would be time for two cigarettes during halftime, when the clubhouse
was dense with smoke: Marlboros passed around (none for Starr, who never
smoked), Lombardi dragging on his Salem, Henry Jordan bumming a Camel
from Phil Bengtson, Jimmy Taylor pulling out a cigar.

The sixty-odd drinks that Hornung consumed during the week before
the Browns game, by Dick Schaap's calculation, were nowhere near a club
record. Fuzzy Thurston was the undisputed drinking champion. Dan Currie
dared to challenge the buoyant left guard once in San Francisco: after a
night-long martini marathon, Currie was carried from the bar on the shoulders of a cordon of pallbearing teammates, semiconscious, an ice pack on his
head, while the unfazed Fuzzy performed push-ups on top of the piano.

It seemed that the only establishments that outnumbered churches in
Green Bay were bars. Candlestick. King's X. Piccadilly. The Spot. Cin-
derella's Glass Slipper. Buzz Inn. Chatterbox. First and Last Club. Green
Arrow. Harvey and Aileen's. Gail's. Hank's. Helen's Tiny Tap. Howard's.
Harold's. Josie and Murph's. Johnnie's. Jerry and Irene's. Lucille and
Whitey's. Marie and Harv's. The culture of Green Bay had always been wet.
During Prohibition the town overflowed with speakeasies that closed whenever federal agents ventured north from Milwaukee, then reopened as soon
as they left. In 1928 the *Milwaukee Journal* wrote of Green Bay: "Wine,
women, and song, all to be had in variety." At the same time, the society had
always been closed and inward-looking, creating a claustrophobic atmosphere for the town's football celebrities. Rumors about the players served as
a prime form of entertainment. John Ebert, who ran an office supply store,
once "tested how fast a rumor would spread through town" by inventing a
tale that Marie Lombardi had been made pregnant by Hornung. The next
morning a man walked into Ebert's favorite coffee shop and said, "Hey, anyone here hear about this Hornung and Marie story?" The residents of

Brown County considered themselves owners of the team, and were thus perpetually concerned with the whereabouts of their precious property, the players. Lombardi was regularly fed unsolicited information from citizen spies: The Katzenjammer Kids are breaking curfew. McGee and Hornung are out at the off-limits place. Fuzzy's here. Kramer's there. Nitschke's over there.

Lombardi had rules about drinking. He allowed only two beers on flights home after road games. Any player caught standing at a bar received an automatic fine. They could sit at a table and drink, but not stand at the bar—that sullied the professional image he wanted to convey. He declared certain bars off-limits. But for all of his discipline, Lombardi was more flexible than he seemed. When presented with reports of wild goings-on involving Packers, he gave the benefit of the doubt to his players. He accepted their explanations at face value unless he had hard facts to the contrary. He believed it was better to build trust that way than to impose discipline with a pack of town snitches. He also allowed emissaries to warn the players. During road trips, when he was returning from dinner, he often sent broadcaster Tony Canadeo ahead to walk through the hotel bar and spread the word, "The Old Man's coming, boys. The Old Man's on his way"—allowing those standing at the bar to scatter and avoid a fine.

THE PACKERS defeated the Browns in Cleveland in the fifth game of the season, 49 to 17, and held first place in the Western Conference with a 4 and 1 record. They looked unstoppable on the field, as close to perfection as Lombardi could get them, no obvious weaknesses on offense or defense. When Hornung wasn't scoring, Taylor was; he busted loose for four touchdowns against the Browns. But there was a sense of uncertainty shadowing the team that had nothing to do with football. World events threatened Lombardi's drive to his first championship. In response to the construction of the Berlin wall by the Soviets late that summer, President Kennedy and the Department of Defense had activated thousands of military reservists and national guardsmen. Three Packers were among the two dozen professional football players who received call-up notices in October. They happened to be three of his best players: Paul Hornung, Boyd Dowler and Ray Nitschke. Hornung was designated to report to Fort Riley in Kansas by the end of the month.

Lombardi was openly distraught about the prospect of losing key players during the decisive final stretch of the season. He bemoaned his fate in the press, saying that he felt the Packers were hit harder than other teams. "We can't afford to lose anybody," he said. Which came first, Packers or country? In this case, it seemed, he felt the country could wait until the end of the football season, at least. Behind the scenes, according to Army documents, Lombardi personally contacted officials at the Pentagon in an effort to keep Hornung and Nitschke. "On 11 October, 1961, Coach Lombardi of the Green Bay Packers requested that both men be deferred from being recalled to active duty on the basis of their being critical members of the team," stated a confidential memorandum to the Army chief of staff. A panel of four colonels considered Lombardi's request and disapproved it. Another appeal was filed a week later, this time by Hornung and Nitschke individually, though with the assistance of team lawyers, "their basis being primarily financial loss, the fact that they are paid by the game, and there are no job rehiring rights."

If this had been a real war, perhaps the sentiment would have been different, but for many Wisconsin residents the Cold War confrontation in Berlin did not seem worth depleting their beloved squad for the weekly football battles of the Western Conference. In a bipartisan display of Packers fever, Republican senator Alexander Wiley and Democratic congressman Clement J. Zablocki requested deferments for the players. Packers fans launched letter-writing campaigns to the White House. From fraternity row at the University of Wisconsin–Whitewater came a petition to President Kennedy signed by "staunch backers of the Green Bay Packers." The three activated players, it declared, "are idols to the people of Wisconsin—especially the youth of Wisconsin. They are perfect specimens of physical fitness. If we recall correctly, you want the youth of America to become more physically fit. How do you expect these youths to increase their interest in physical fitness when you take away idols such as these?"

In considering the Green Bay situation, Army officials acknowledged that deferring the players through December would have "no impact on the units to which they are presently assigned." They were not regular members of their units, but "filler personnel," of which there was an abundant supply. But since the players did not meet the established deferment criteria of personal or community hardship, Army officials feared that "an inequity would be created by not granting delays to equally deserving individuals for professional or business hardships." The final word arrived from Washington on October 18: the Packers had to serve. Lombardi accepted the decision with resignation. "They are going to have to go and there is not much I can do about it," he said.

One alternative remained for Hornung: he might fail the Army physical. Lou Cordileone, a defensive lineman for San Francisco, had just been granted a deferment because he needed knee surgery. Was Hornung, with his injured shoulder and pinched nerve, any more fit than Cordileone? His first examination came at the induction center in Milwaukee. "Am I Four-F?" Hornung asked the doctor, after his various ailments were noted on the chart. "Basically, you are," he was told. "But not bad enough. If I flunk you, they're going to send you somewhere else until you pass." It was a political issue as much as a medical question, so the Milwaukee officers sent Hornung on for another examination at the Great Lakes Naval Station in Illinois. When Hornung arrived at the hospital there, a military orderly told him that his examination would be conducted the next morning, and that in the meantime he would be confined to base. "I had looked at it like a three-day vacation," Hornung said later. "My man Rick Casares [fullback for the rival Bears, but a Hornung pal] was going to pick me up and we had dates for dinner in Chicago that night. So I asked the orderly, 'Am I in the goddamn service?' He said no. So I said, 'Well, then, I'm not confined to base. I'm out of here.' He said, 'You can't do that, Mr. Hornung.' I said, 'Yes, I can.' And I did."

A two-day physical began the next morning. Same story. A Navy doctor—"a captain who was likable as hell," as Hornung recalled—explained the dilemma. "He said, 'We've got to pass you. You're going in.' So I went in." After the results of the physical were announced, Hornung released a statement to the *Milwaukee Sentinel* in which he said: "I hate leaving the best football team in America, but I have no regrets. I have a duty to the United States which is above all the rest." Hornung also told the *Sentinel* that he was sorry "outsiders meddled" in the situation and asserted that "at no time" did he or "any member of the Packer organization make a request for a deferment through a congressman or anyone else"—a claim that he may have believed to be true, but that was directly contradicted by Army documents.

Hornung arrived at Fort Riley on November 14 and was assigned to the 896th Engineer Floating Bridge Company, a National Guard unit from the Bismarck region of North Dakota. As a rule, men in that company were restricted to within twenty miles of camp when off duty. Even if Hornung could get weekend passes, was there any way he could play in the remaining games? Perhaps no private in Fort Riley history was better situated for exceptional treatment than the Golden Boy in that fall of 1961. The connections between the Green Bay Packers and the U.S. Army ran long and deep. From his days at West Point, Lombardi knew colonels and generals in the Pentagon and all around the country. His chief scout in the East, Lewis B. Anderson, worked for the U.S. Army Corps of Engineers in Washington. In a confidential report to Lombardi and Packer personnel director Dick Voris, Anderson suggested that his boss, Brigadier General Robert G. MacDonnell, might prove helpful. "He told me that he knew Vince while at West Point. . . . He was not certain if Coach Lombardi would remember him or not. Further I might add that the general is an ardent Packers fan."

Anderson proved to be as thorough scouting the military as he was in his football reports. He provided Voris and Lombardi with inside information on Hornung's situation at Fort Riley, where the commanding officer was Major General John F. Ruggles of the First Infantry Division. "Gen. Ruggles, I am informed, is very athletically inclined. He was assigned to West Point a few years ago and quite possibly could have been there at the time Coach Lombardi was at the Point," Anderson wrote. "In checking with the Public

Information Office, they feel certain that there will be no difficulty encountered in obtaining approval for Paul to play with the Packers. . . . It is my suggestion, and I base this on my discussions with the PIO as well as military personnel in this office, that Coach Lombardi place a telephone call to Gen. Ruggles on an informal basis and advise Gen. Ruggles that he is forwarding a request to the commanding officer of Paul's unit requesting that Paul be allowed to play ball on Sunday, providing it did not interfere with his military obligations." In a final instruction to Voris, Anderson requested that his letter be closely held. "I would appreciate it very much if you would destroy this letter by burning same after it has been read by yourself and Coach Lombardi."

Perhaps equally helpful was the fact that Lombardi had just persuaded a recently retired friend from his West Point days to move to Wisconsin and run the Packers operation in Milwaukee. Colonel O. C. Krueger had carved out a special niche as an operator on the jock side of the military. Ockie, as he was known, considered himself a "valet" to the powerful. At West Point he served Red Blaik's interests, and later, as commander at Fort Meade, he became accustomed to "taking care of the brass." On sunny summer days, Pentagon officials would say they were going to "visit an installation"—which meant they were driving up to Fort Meade to play golf. "I had lockers for all of them," Krueger said later. "I knew everybody in the Pentagon." He also, as it turned out, had an intimate acquaintance with Major General Ruggles at Fort Riley; they had been in the West Point class of 1931. Their contact increased as soon as Hornung reached Kansas. "I would call out there and say, 'Johnny, I don't want any favors or anything else,' " Krueger recounted later. " 'All I want to find out is—is Hornung going to have duty on the weekend? That's all I want to know.' "

Even before Krueger first called, Ruggles had already received word from the Pentagon that he should let Hornung play, according to his later account. "That arrangement was approved all the way up. It came down to me," Ruggles said. "To bait Ockie a bit," he gave Krueger the same answer every time—"We're going to handle this just like any other soldier"—and would then hang up on his old classmate.

Hornung in fact did miss the November 19 game against the Rams. He had been on active duty for less than a week by then and had not finished his orientation. Furthermore, the Packers were playing Detroit the following Thursday in the traditional Thanksgiving Day game, and it would have required too much elasticity in the already well-stretched military rules for him to be granted leave for two games in five days. Detroit was in second place, chasing Green Bay. Los Angeles was in last place. Lombardi wanted Hornung for the Lions. He was flown from Fort Riley to Detroit and back in a Cessna 310 piloted by Pat Martin, a Notre Dame alumnus and Packer backer who lived in Green Bay and had married into one of the big paper-mill families. Although it was not one of Hornung's better games, he kicked one field goal and two extra points as the Packers prevailed, 17 to 9, solidifying their hold on first place in the conference with 9 wins and 2 losses. The next week Martin flew Hornung to Milwaukee for a game against the Giants. They left Fort Riley at Saturday noon and had to be back by midnight Sunday. The Giants game was a bruiser, Hornung seemed sluggish again, and the Packers played barely well enough to win, 20 to 17.

Even though the win clinched the Western Conference title, the coach was grumpy and anxious after the game. His team had appeared invincible at midseason, before the call-up. Now it seemed less imposing.

"Are you working out down there?" he asked Hornung pointedly.

"Yeah, I'm working out," Hornung said.

"Well, we're going to send you the offense," Lombardi said. Every week from then on, amid the pile of love letters sent to Private Hornung, was a manila folder from Green Bay, a copy of Lombardi's offensive plans for the next game.

Hornung had fibbed to his coach, he said later. He was not working out in the way Lombardi expected. When reporters inquired about Hornung's activities at Fort Riley, eager to do feature stories on "the Army's most famous jeep driver," they were told that he was following the routine of all the men in his company—here waking up for kitchen duty at 4:30 a.m., there walking guard on a cold winter night. He was described as the jeep driver for a lieutenant of the 896th Engineer Floating Bridge Company, Duane Dinius of Bismarck. Dinius was quoted as calling Hornung "a real fine boy." All of which, except for the lieutenant's feelings about Hornung, were stretches. "He was assigned as a jeep driver, but he never drove my jeep," Dinius said in an interview decades later. "They got a picture of him in the jeep but he never drove it. Never drove me. He never went out in the field with us at all. We were out in the field practicing building bridges out by the Kansas River. We only saw him back at the fort for morning formation. He spent the rest of his time in the sauna." As Hornung explained: "I had that injury showing up on the X-ray so I could go every day for treatment. So I went every day."

By the time the Packers flew west on December 9 for their annual season-ending games with the 49ers and Rams, Green Bay was agog over its two-time Western Conference champions. Local merchants coined a community nickname—Titletown USA—capturing the spirit of this unlikely success story. The capital of professional football in America now was not New York or Chicago or Cleveland or Baltimore, but little Green Bay, a place where the people owned the franchise, where the boys in Martha's Coffee Club (who convened each morning to tell tall tales and talk Packers; fines were imposed on anyone mentioning politics, religion or business) felt as empowered as Wellington Mara or Art Modell; where sheet metal contractor Howie Blindauer printed hundreds of training camp rosters every summer so that his fellow citizen-owners could pretend they were general managers—as powerful as the Pope!—and check CUT or STAY in the margins as they observed the seventeenth-round tackle from North Carolina Central; where these same fans would stand patiently behind the fence in subzero weather to watch their Packers practice on December mornings; where Whitey Klicka, a local movie theater operator, arranged a babysitting service of sorts for Packer-crazed parents: he screened matinees for children that ran from before the kickoff till after the final gun of every Packers game. At least one person disliked the Titletown nickname: Vince Lombardi knew that his team had not won a title yet, and he fretted about overconfidence.

The squad seemed unusually tight in the dank Kezar Stadium locker room before the San Francisco game. Lombardi had been driving his boys as hard as ever, even though the West Coast trip was meaningless, in a sense, nothing more than a long tune-up before the league championship game against the Giants, who were winning the Eastern Conference. Before Lombardi gave the team his final instructions, he and the assistants left the locker room briefly so the players could talk among themselves. "Anybody got anything to say?" asked Jim Ringo, a captain. "Yeah, I've got something to say" came a voice from the side. It was Private Hornung. "Let me tell you something," he said. "There are three of us here from the service, me and Nitschke and Boydie. And we're real happy to be here and we needed this weekend a helluva lot more than you guys. And I want to tell you something. I came here for two things. I took care of the first thing last night. Now let's take care of the second and kick the shit out of the Forty Niners!"

The room exploded in laughter, which brought Lombardi storming through the door. "What's so funny, for Chrissakes? What the hell's going on in here?" he bellowed.

Ah, nothing, Coach, they said. *Nothing. Just Paul.*

The Packers lost that day by one point. Perhaps it was just coincidence that Hornung missed the final game against the Rams, but he was not needed in any case. Better for him to rest his sore shoulder in preparation for the championship game, which was to be held in Titletown on New Year's Eve. But when Hornung was told of the Christmas leave policy at Fort Riley, he realized that he had another problem. Furloughs had been divided into two sections by the alphabet. Surnames A through L were off the week leading up to Christmas, M through Z the week after. Hornung called Lombardi. "Coach," he said. "I can't make the game. I've gotta be back the week of the game." Lombardi was upset, Hornung recalled, but said that he had one more card to play. The coach had seen President Kennedy that month at the National Football Foundation Hall of Fame dinner in New York; they had sat together on the dais and chatted and joked about the Army coaching job, which was opening again with the firing of Dale Hall. Kennedy had given Lombardi the number to his private phone line at the White House and said to call if he ever needed anything. "I'm going to call him," Lombardi told Hornung. "You be ready to go."

As Hornung later told the story, "I go back and pack and Kennedy calls Fort Riley and asks to speak to the camp commander, who is not there, so he finally gets the company commander. And he says, 'This is President Kennedy and I'm calling on behalf of Paul Hornung,' and the guy says, 'Yeah, and I'm Donald Duck.' But he got me out. A major came down and told me I could leave." The details of the story most likely were enriched in the retelling, part of Hornung's good-natured bluster, but there is one document that confirms the essence of the transaction. Lombardi later wrote a letter to Kenneth O'Donnell, special assistant to the president, thanking him for two things: First, an autographed picture of Kennedy and Lombardi at the football banquet, which the coach said he was "completely thrilled to have." And second: "I would like to take this opportunity to thank you for your help in obtaining leave for Paul Hornung so he could participate in the Championship game. . . ."

ONLY THE GIANTS stood between Lombardi and the world championship. With the reservists Hornung, Nitschke and Dowler all there in preparation for the title game, the Packers had their full team on the practice field for the first time in eight weeks. That is not to say that the team appeared in prime shape. Starr had been playing with a stomach pull since midyear, an injury that he kept from Lombardi. Jerry Kramer had been sidelined with a broken ankle. Jim Taylor was hobbling from a leg injury he had suffered in the Rams game. Hornung, with his sore shoulder and military duties, seemed to have lost something since that fabled game against the Colts. Ron Kramer and Fuzzy Thurston had conditioned themselves over the holidays in their inimitable style. "We were dissolute for two weeks," Kramer said later. "We drank and ate every night. I went from 248 pounds to 264 in two weeks." The weather in Green Bay was biting cold, almost as stinging as Lombardi. With his full ski cap drawn down to his brow and up to his lips, Lombardi was obscured yet unmistakable as he worked his boys on the frigid practice field. "Occasionally you'd hear his muffled voice through the ski cap," noted Bob Kurland of the *Bergen Record* of New Jersey. "One player said, 'It's bad enough working out and seeing the man's face, but it's worse when you can't see it.' "

How could Lombardi not be driven? Winning it all, beating the Giants, two obsessions converging. Marie told the story about their first flight to Green Bay, back in February 1959: Vince had been silent for the first leg, not a word. Then as they were making the turn in Chicago, boarding the Blue Goose for the flight north, he turned to her and declared, "The New York Giants will never beat my Packers!" He was determined that they would never outwork them or outclass them, either. Giants Week for Lombardi's teams was different from the rest: sharper workouts, cleaner locker room, new practice uniforms. "It meant a lot to Lombardi when the New York people came out to Green Bay," said Willie Wood. "Coach Lombardi wanted them to see a pretty picture up there." It was more cold than pretty when the New York delegation arrived at the airport on the western edge of town and rode the bus to the Hotel Northland. Ten degrees. Safety Em Tunnell, who lived at the hotel, greeted his old teammates with cutting humor. "You guys got here for the heat wave," he said, and he was right. It had been subzero earlier.

The Giants thought they had a chance, even though Gifford had been out all year with an injury. Their rookie coach, Allie Sherman, had kept the old defensive gang together and reenergized the offense with one key addition: Y. A. Tittle, acquired that year from San Francisco, got most of the playing time at quarterback, ahead of Charlie Conerly. At a banquet in Connecticut, Andy Robustelli, the defensive end, stood on a chair and vowed that his Giants would clobber the Packers. The two teams seemed about even in New York's narrow loss earlier in Milwaukee. There was nothing Lombardi could do to surprise them, they felt, since he ran the old Giants plays and even used the same terminology. But no one knew the two teams better than Lombardi, and he sensed something else. Two nights before the game, at Fish Fry Friday at Proski's, he stunned his friend Jack Koeppler. "It was the only time he talked like that before a game," Koeppler remembered. "He said, 'You know, I hope that ball doesn't bounce funny on Sunday.' I said, 'What do you mean?' He said, 'If it just bounces straight for both of us, if nobody gets lucky, we'll kill them. They don't have anything left. If it bounces bad for us and good for them, we'll still beat them. If it bounces for us and not them, they can't score.' "

On Saturday night, Vince and Marie invited a group of New York friends to dinner at the Stratosphere Club north of town in the snow-covered farm fields. The Moore brothers from Englewood were there, Father Tim and Father Ken, along with the Fordham-trained Giants contingent, led by Wellington Mara, Vic Del Guercio and Ray Walsh—all from Lombardi's class of 1937—and their wives. "There were four or five couples and a few priests and we had a great time," recalled Mara. "And then at the end of the meal, Vinnie got up and said, 'Well, that's it. You're on your own now!' He made it sound like we'd have to get our own cabs into town." The title match was looming, the courtesies were over, and these dear old friends were now the opposition.

In the predawn darkness of New Year's Eve, starting at five o'clock that Sunday morning, the ground crew began clearing the field at City Stadium, first shoveling off a layer of snow, then removing a covering of straw and finally rolling back a canvas tarp that had protected the grass since the last home game in November. The field was just as Lombardi had hoped: hard but not frozen, with sure footing for his running attack. No real break in the weather; by the one o'clock kickoff the temperature would still be in the teens. The stadium filled to the last seat, with the final tickets selling on the street for five dollars. Orange jumpsuits, red and black hunting coats, ski jackets and snow pants, raccoon coats, minks and heels, blankets, sleeping bags, flasks of brandy, bourbon and scotch—the citizen-owners of Title-town were ready to claim their due. There was no need for Lombardi to say much to his troops in the locker room beforehand. They had waited a year for this chance. Never again, he had promised after losing the 1960 championship to Philadelphia. "Usually," Bob Skoronski reflected later, "players don't realize what is happening to them when they are playing in a big game like that. They are sort of in a daze. We realized everything. We knew it did no good to get that far and lose. We had been so infused with Lombardi's philosophy. We were loose and focused at the same time. It was a bit frightening."

For the Giants, it certainly was. As a record-breaking 55 million viewers watched on television, the Packers came as close to perfection as Lombardi could take them. Hornung was at his best again, running for eighty-nine yards, scoring the first touchdown from six yards out, and booting three field goals and four extra points for a championship record nineteen points. His housemate, Ron Kramer, showed no signs of his two-week holiday binge, instead playing the most dominating game of his career, blasting the way for Hornung and Taylor on sweeps, and bulling into the end zone on touchdown passes of fourteen and thirteen yards. Bart Starr did nothing to hurt the team. He called Lombardi's game from beginning to end, threw three touchdown passes despite his sore stomach muscle and had no interceptions. Nitschke made one of the defense's four interceptions. The Giants went nowhere all day, picking up only six first downs, one by penalty. They knew they had lost by halftime, when they were trailing 24 to 0. They were silent, dazed, eager to go home already. Sherman did not even try to change or fix anything. The New York sportswriters were tapping out their obituary columns.

"The poisonous polish of the Packers was equaled only by the fortitude of the natives, who turtled down into their mackinaws and buffalo robes and parkas, and stayed into the bitter dusk, yelping and bawling for blood," wrote Red Smith in the *Herald Tribune*. There would have been more blood, according to Hornung, "if Vince didn't have a soft spot. They'd still be talking about the game if not for that. We could have scored a hundred points. We called off the dogs early. We could have set every record. But Vince loved the Maras and didn't want to rub it in. They didn't want to play. We wanted to play. It was too cold for them. Not too cold for us. And everything went right."

In the final series, with the Packers leading 37 to 0, Lombardi began pulling his starters from the field one by one, each for a standing ovation. Hornung, Taylor, Starr, Ron Kramer, McGee, Dowler, Ringo . . . "One helluva thing," said the *Press-Gazette's* Art Daley in the press box. Red Smith took note of it in his column. At the final gun, Hawg Hanner and Dan Currie lifted Lombardi onto their shoulders and a swarm of Packers gathered around and ran joyously toward the clubhouse on the stadium's south end, the coach's bright yellow knit wool cap bobbing above the crowd. Fans swarmed the field and raced toward the goalposts, rocking, swaying until the heavy metal posts gave way to the weight of this gang of spectators drunk on the elixir of winning. The Packers Band strutted out and played "Auld Lang Syne." Cheerleaders in gold sweaters and green skirts joined fans in party hats doing the peppermint twist on the fifty-yard line. Horns, noisemakers, confetti, streamers. The story had come full circle: little Green Bay had humiliated mighty New York. Titletown USA.

The Giants dressed hurriedly and fled to their charter plane. They "beat the New Year east," wrote a columnist in the *Times*. "It was the only thing they beat today." Ben Starr, the stern military taskmaster who had always told his son that he was too soft, found the quarterback lingering in the locker room after the game and hugged him and uttered words of redemptive apology that Bart never thought he would hear. "I was wrong, son," said his old man. The other old man, Lombardi, declared that his team was the best ever. He called the title game the biggest thrill of his life. He said he was the only emotional one on the team. "I laugh, I cry, everything." And he laughed and cried. Fuzzy Thurston had promised that if they won he would eat the sports page. So he did. "He ate it, I mean ate it!" said Ron Kramer. "Ate it. Aaarrgghh!" He and the boys were downtown, drinking the night away at the Spot and the Candlestick and across the river at the King's X, while out on Washington and Adams a parade of honking cars kept inching by, a station wagon loaded down with fifteen celebrants dragging one of the goalposts behind, sparks flying in the winter night.

Lombardi's society crowd congregated in the party room in his basement, smoke drifting to the ceiling, glasses clinking, the coach's grin lighting the room. Hornung was invited, Private Paul, one of the few times a player was allowed to mingle with this crowd. "Anything I can do for you, Paul?" Lombardi asked. "Yes," came the reply, "a scotch and soda, please." The coach's smile momentarily disappeared. "Mix your own damn drink," he huffed. But he loved Hornung. Red Smith was there and remembered how Lombardi would look across the room at the Golden Boy "with a great big grin pasted on his face that would not come off." The phone never stopped ringing. One call was placed from Washington to EDison-61695. It was for Vin. He tossed his pack of Salems on the bar counter, put down his scotch, took a drag, picked up the receiver of his red telephone. It was President Kennedy, calling to offer congratulations. Later a telegram arrived that

Lombardi cherished as much as his trophies: "Congratulations on a great game. It was a fine victory for a great coach, a great team, a great town. Best regards, President Kennedy." It was almost as if Kennedy had been part of the victory himself.

Later that night the Lombardis and Bourguignons and Canadeos and a few other couples and priests went to a New Year's Eve dinner-dance at the Neighborly Club. They were seated at a long table and served a champagne brunch as midnight approached. The Pope sat at the end, and in the midst of the revelry a door flew open and a drunk stumbled in and collapsed to the floor. He staggered to his feet, turned around and strained to focus on the imposing figure glaring at him from a few feet away. "Oh, my God!" he announced, pointing at the vision. "It's Lombardi!" Then, lights out, he keeled over again.

16

A Night
at the Elks

MYTH BECOMES MYTH not in the living but in the retelling. The Lombardi myth grew less on the field of City Stadium when his Packers won the NFL championship than at Elks Lodge No. 259 four months later, when Green Bay toasted its most celebrated citizen at a testimonial banquet. On the Monday evening of April 30, 1962, as patches of fog drifted from the warming Fox River across the flat streets and parking lots of downtown, more than seven hundred people gathered inside the cavernous new Elks hall near the corner of Crooks and Adams for what was billed as a tribute to Vincent Thomas Lombardi. Placed on the table at each setting was a souvenir program made from textured white card-stock paper and designed with regal simplicity. An elegant golden cord with a tassel at the bottom served as the binding. On the cover there was only a small Mercator globe in dark green ink set under a triple-pointed gold crown. Below and slightly to the right of the globe, and barely perceptible depending upon the angle and light, the letters VINCE were embossed in subtle white on white, like gentle lines of snow neatly arranged to spell his name on unswept winter ice. Nothing more was needed to make the point that from his little northern outpost Lombardi ruled the football world.

This was a night for tales, and the dais was arrayed with storytellers, foremost among them Jim and the two Tims: Sleepy Jim Crowley, Lombardi's old coach at Fordham, Father Tim Moore, the priest from St. Cecilia, and Tim Cohane, sports editor of *Look* and historian of the Lombardi myth. Also up front were native son the Reverend Ben Masse, now an academic at Fordham; George Halas, coach and owner of the rival Chicago Bears; and

Pete Rozelle, commissioner of the NFL, who had flown in through a noon-day rainstorm. Cohane served as toastmaster, his sharp Connecticut Yankee voice rising above the background din of clinking dinnerware and china. He opened the evening with his favorite theme of circular football fate.

"The threads of the quill of life, so to speak, run in some very strange repetitive patterns," Cohane said. "And I'm thinking of the fact that Curly Lambeau in 1918 went to Notre Dame. Came back. Coached East High in 1919 and 1920. Founded . . . the Packers in 1920. Was instrumental in sending Jim Crowley down to Notre Dame. Where Crowley was for four years, becoming a member of the Four Horsemen, of course. And after that Crowley went to coach at Fordham. And he was to deliver as his most famous pupil the man who came back to save the old homestead, Vince Lombardi. And that's a story that hasn't been emphasized as much as it should be. It's surely a romantic story—and a true one."

Cohane then introduced Father Tim and stepped aside to let the jocular Carmelite priest take the stage. Moore began, "Mr. Toastmaster Tim, it's a real distinct pleasure to come from the East and the New Jersey–New York section where we have second-rate pro football teams"—the hall rocked with hoots and cheers—"and come to a city that has the world's best football team, the world's best coach and the world's best fans. Yeh. Heh, heh. If I wanted to tell you tonight what I really did to help Vince it would take two and a half hours. And that would be the preface to my talk. Vince coached football at St. Cecilia when I was athletic director. We won six state championships in a row. He always goes down two hundred, but he was making seventeen hundred a year. He coached football with my help. I was an assistant coach and gave him all those plays. He taught chemistry, physics, Latin. We had a baseball team. We won a state championship in basketball. And off and on when I had something else to do, he would hear confessions. . . ."

An explosion of laughter, starting with Lombardi and rolling through the hall, the sounds of men wishing life could always feel like this, suddenly contented, warm, tingling from the confluence of alcohol and hail-fellow bonhomie.

Soon Cohane moved to the mike again, introducing Father Ben Masse, a Green Bay native who edited *America* magazine and taught at Fordham. On cue, the Elks Orchestra fired up a round of the Ram fight song and the Fordham men at the head table—Masse, Cohane, Crowley and Lombardi—belted out the final refrain, vigorously, if off-key . . . "We do, or die!"

"Tim, Vince and fellow citizens of the greatest small town not merely in the United States but in the whole world," said Masse. "This is a painful experience for me, because coming back as a native son on such a glorious occasion a man would have to have a soul of putty if he couldn't strike from it a few sparks of inspiration. . . . I saw a picture of Vinnie in the *New York Daily News* some time ago. This photograph made the mistake of showing him shoveling snow. This might have fooled the people living along the Gowanus Canal in Brooklyn, but it couldn't fool an old native of Green Bay who shoveled. And I'll say this, Vince's stroke was all wrong. He was too stiff in the knees and there was no follow-through."

The guffaws of men who had shoveled through a long winter and could not be sure that it was over, even though midnight ushered in the first of May. It had rained all morning, clearing away a lingering crust of snow, and temperatures by three o'clock had soared into the sixties. Spring might be here at last. The smelt were running on the shores of Lake Michigan.

Cohane came forward again with his long and serious face. "For perhaps forty-two years, Green Bay children upon reaching the age of speech and reason were taught that the devil himself walks the world in many forms. . . ." A few chortles on the dais, where they knew the order of speakers, then peals of laughter bouncing from table to table, growing louder with the momentum of recognition of the track down which Cohane's train of thought was rolling. "The most evil form in which he walks it is vested in the person who is known as the Papa Bear. The Papa Bear in [the] fairy tale connotes something entirely different than that image connoted to the children of Green Bay. I have always felt that it is an unfair attitude. My perspective of Uncle George, admittedly from the distance of New York most of the time, is that I have never felt he was particularly concerned with the scoreboard in football, nor with the box office. I have always felt that he was impelled primarily by his very deep aesthetic appreciation of the game."

Nervous laughter. The titters of small-town men who had been subordinate to Chicago for decades, whose wives shopped in Chicago at Marshall Field's and Carson Pirie Scott & Co. as soon as they had enough money. Now, amazingly, they were on top.

"That was never underscored more emphatically than a year ago last fall when the Packers were playing the Bears in Wrigley Field, when the Horn went into the end zone for a touchdown and flipped the ball gaily and gallantly into the stands. Of course, even the Packer coaching staff is laboring under an illusion about that. They feel Paul was tossing the ball to a lady. Which shows that despite the fact that they coached him for three seasons, they don't understand him very well, because he certainly would have no lady sitting in the end zone. She would be on the fifty-yard line."

Hornung sat at a table in the back of the hall with several teammates, and they all laughed, but not as loudly as many other men of the community whose lives were further separated from the glow of the Golden Boy. Hornung was still stuck down at Fort Riley most of the time; they had let him come north on leave for the ceremony. His military life, with two months of active service remaining, was cushier than ever. Now he was living in what amounted to a bachelor pad on the second floor of the First Cavalry museum, and General Ruggles was using him as a show horse, flying him around Kansas, Oklahoma and Texas to give speeches. He and Lombardi had visited earlier that spring, when the Old Man drove to Hot Springs, Arkansas, with Jack Koeppler and Ockie Krueger for a golfing vacation. One morning the coach called Hornung and ordered him to come over for a visit. "I don't have to call that guy again, do I?" Lombardi joked, alluding to the call he had made to President Kennedy to free Hornung for the championship game. Hornung received a weekend pass and drove to Arkansas. Midway through a round of golf with Lombardi he found himself negotiating his next contract, or having it settled for him by the Old Man. There was a minor squabble over his bonus. Vince usually gave him a $10,000 to $15,000 bonus, but he seemed reluctant this time.

"Paul, you didn't have *that* good a year," he informed Hornung as he steered their golf cart from tee to green. "You were hurt. You missed four games." To which Hornung replied, "Well, I was MVP of the league. Doesn't that count for anything?"

Now here was Halas, the mortal enemy, moving to the microphone. Strange how it worked: Halas had created this league with Jim Thorpe and a few others. He had been the pilot light of professional football for four decades, but now the flame was burning bright and it was Lombardi's flame and even Papa Bear knew it.

"It's a pleasure to be back in Green Bay to see so many familiar smiling faces," Halas said. "I wonder, are you, uh, thinking of what you did last year?" (Laughs all around. Green Bay had won both games against Chicago, 24 to 0 and 31 to 28.) "Or in smiling anticipation of what you expect to do to us next fall." (Cheers. Yes!) "We're delighted to be a part of this richly deserved tribute to Vince Lombardi. Although my role is out of character. In the past when we have come to Green Bay it was not to praise Caesar. It was to bury him. But due to our notable lack of success in arranging the football demise of Vince Lombardi and the, uh, Packers, we know that his record will continue for quite some time."

Lombardi could imagine no greater compliment than to be toasted by George Halas. Their relationship had an odd balance. Halas hated to lose to Lombardi. As soon as Babe Parilli was cut by the Packers in 1959, his first call came from Halas, who was less interested in his quarterbacking abilities than in debriefing him on whatever he had picked up during training camp with Lombardi. In the privacy of his film room in Chicago, Halas was heard more than once snarling, "Look at that sonofabitch" at the sight of Lombardi stalking the opposing sidelines. As one journalist wrote of Halas, he "had all the warmth of breaking bones." Yet he was loyal not only to his team, but also to his league, and to him the strength of the NFL was its durability, symbolized by the rivalry between his Bears and the Packers. It was that deeper bond that led him to advise Ole and the Packers board to hire Lombardi in the first place, and that inspired him to work behind the scenes to prevent Vince from leaving vulnerable Green Bay for New York after the 1960 season—even if it meant more drubbings administered by Lombardi's team.

Cohane was back, first explaining how he had exhumed the name Seven Blocks of Granite from an old AP cutline from 1930, then offering to recite Grantland Rice's "Old Gibraltar"—the sportswriter's ode to the Fordham wall of 1936. "In those days, when Rice wrote a poem about your football team in his Monday column, believe me, you had arrived," Cohane said. "I have recited 'Old Gibraltar' so many times, drunk and sober, I believe I can do it one more time."

And he did. And the wall still stood.

Next came telegrams from Red Reeder, the buoyant one-legged colonel, and the other Red of West Point, Colonel Red Blaik. Both had been invited to participate in the testimonial, but could not attend. Blaik called Lombardi "America's finest coach" and described him as "volatile, imaginative and highly intelligent." Reeder wrote a line of doggerel and asked Cohane to compose the rest. Lombardi had always thought that he learned more about leadership at the Military Academy from Blaik and Reeder than anywhere else in his life. But Lombardi had moved beyond West Point now, and there was no going back, no matter how enticing the offer.

A few weeks after the championship win over the Giants, he had received another call from the White House. "Hello, Coach, how are you?" Kennedy had asked. Lombardi said he was fine. Why would the president be looking for him again so soon after the congratulatory call on New Year's Eve? The answer came directly. "Good," Kennedy responded. "Now, Coach, I've got three generals standing in front of me, and they want me to ask you if you would come back to West Point and coach Army again." Lombardi was puzzled, unsure what to say. He would have taken the job in a second back in 1959, when Blaik retired, but Army was not willing to give it to a non-cadet then. Now, after a few mediocre seasons under Dale Hall, and with Lombardi's rise to the top of the coaching world, they had reconsidered the policy. The job no longer interested Lombardi, but how could he politely refuse the president of the United States? With no answer coming directly to mind, Lombardi merely laughed, nervously. Kennedy understood. "I thought that would be your answer, and I told the generals so before I called," he said. "Good luck next season, and if you get here, stop by and we'll have lunch. Goodbye, Coach." It was a grace note that Lombardi never forgot.

The testimonial rolled on. Now it was time for Lombardi's top assistant coach, Phil Bengtson, mentor of the defense, who said that Vince was "due all the accolades" he had been given.

"One incident during the season stands out to me," Bengtson said. "We had our problems, injuries and other things that hurt our efficiency. We had the military call-up of three fine football players hanging over our heads for so long. We worried about it every day. The more optimistic of us felt that they would not be called. But one Tuesday we reported for practice and they were all gone. Hornung. Nitschke. Dowler. None present. Taking three integral cogs out of our lineup. And I will never forget: Vince pointed out that these boys now are gone. We must get along without them; and it was not a question of getting along without them, we were still going to win! With or without them, we were going to win! Vince, to me, that was great."

Sleepy Jim Crowley was up next, introduced with knowing precision by Cohane, his old publicist at Fordham. During the nine years that Crowley coached on Rose Hill, Cohane said, he had the third best college record in the country, behind only Minnesota and Alabama. He was the son of Agnes Sweeney Crowley, who taught dance to youngsters in Green Bay, and on the banquet circuit he still showed his dancing Irish wit.

"I was in the Navy and it was the war," Crowley began. "I was very proud of the outfit I was with. We leveled four bridges, blew up six ammunition dumps and captured seven cities."

Pause.

"And then we went overseas."

Lombardi no doubt had heard that one before—it was part of Crowley's rubber chicken repertoire. It was the sort of joke that Lombardi wanted to tell, but he never could get the timing down. He would start laughing too soon, long before the punch line. Crowley was master of the deadpan.

"When you are coaching football, there are only two ways to keep your job," Sleepy Jim continued. "The first is win games. But if you can't do that, you must become a character builder."

With that single sardonic stroke, Crowley had punctured one of the swollen claims of football: that it was, by its very nature, a molder of human character. People inside the game knew better than anyone else that there was an uneven line between myth and reality here, between the *characters* of the game and the *character* of the game. The team that Lombardi had put together in Green Bay had its share of narcissists and roustabouts who in other professions might not be candidates for citizen of the year. Football was a violent sport, Lombardi insisted, and he had known from his earliest experiences that many of the boys with a natural affinity for the game came from troubled backgrounds. Crowley and Red Blaik had recruited heavily from the coal mines of Pennsylvania and mill towns of Massachusetts. Even at little Saints, Lombardi often used the Englewood police as informal scouts, asking them to point out borderline juvenile delinquents who might be football prospects. He did not tolerate rebellion, he shaped the team in his image on the field, and the positive effect that he had on his players off the field was undeniable, but even with Lombardi there was a direct correlation between the amount of time he would put into character building and the talent of the character in need of building.

Crowley ended by dedicating a Gaelic toast—"Not bad when it's for an Italian"—to his former player:

> *May the roads rise to meet you,*
> *May the wind always be at your back,*
> *And may the good Lord forever hold*
> *You and yours in the palms of his hands.*

"Well," said Cohane. "It's ten o'clock and we're getting to the home stretch. It must have been the handiwork of fate for Vince to coach here and no place else. When he was at St. Cecilia, he might have been picked as Fordham coach. If he had been, the school today would be a first-rank eastern power. He might have been selected as head coach of the Giants at the end of 1953. He was not. In 1954 there was an attempt to restore football at Fordham with Vince as head coach. It didn't work. In 1959, Army went looking for a coach, but it was not ready to break with the tradition of cadet coaches. So fate fingered him for Green Bay. In 1956, after the Rose Bowl game, he and I took a ride out Wilshire Boulevard and drove out to Coldwater Canyon to the Tail of the Cock restaurant. He had been offered some jobs, but not the right ones, and he was wondering whether the right one would ever come along. Now we know the answer to why he did not become a head coach until he was forty-five years old. When God has reserved real greatness for somebody, God makes sure he is ready for it."

The time had arrived for Pete Rozelle to present Lombardi with the two-foot-high Jim Thorpe Memorial Trophy for winning the NFL championship. "This trophy has a great deal of history behind it," Rozelle said. "In passing it on, I'd like to say that as commissioner I'm not concerned with individual records or individual team efforts. I am concerned with the high caliber of players we have in the league, and the owners, and coaches, who have that indefinable something called class. And the gentleman I'm handing this to personifies it—Vince Lombardi."

More presentations came Lombardi's way—a new gold-plated putter, a life-scale portrait, a plaque from the city. Finally it was the coach's time. As Lombardi reached the microphone, people nearby could see that he was starting to choke up, tears forming at the corner of his eyes. "I planned to say many things this evening in appreciation and gratitude, and maybe be even a bit witty. But I'm afraid I'm so filled with emotion that regardless of what I would say I could not express myself adequately," he began. "Ahem. Ahm. However, I would like to thank the Elks, the committee, all of you who made this a wonderful night. I've received many tributes since I came to Green Bay, but none, I don't believe, would ever replace or compare with this great tribute here"—he lowered his deep voice further and spoke even more deliberately to make the point—"in . . . my . . . home . . . town."

From the side of the hall came a loud yelp—*Yeah!*—and more cheers. Lombardi cleared his throat again.

"I would like to thank in particular some of our guests who traveled many miles: Father Tim Moore, who's been a very close friend and adviser to me for many years; Jim Crowley, my first coach and a great coach; Tim Cohane, who has been a close personal friend of mine for many years; George Halas, for taking his time, the dean of all coaches and one of the most respected, believe me, of all time; Commissioner, and Father Masse and all of you out there. I am proud and happy of course to have been able to bring a championship to Green Bay. I don't know of any city more deserving of a championship than this city for its loyalty and cooperation and support for many, many years before I came here. Green Bay has been good to me, good to my family. And I am proud and happy to call it my home."

He could not accept the tribute, Lombardi said, without mentioning the people who were "every bit as important" as he was in bringing home the title, all of whom, he said, should have been up there with him sharing the honor. "In particular, a very—"

For a moment it seemed that he could not go on, but he struggled to regain his composure. No one else in the room knew what Marie had endured for twenty years because of his obsession with football: the silent meals, the flashes of temper, the demands for perfection, the Mr. High-Low, on top of the world here, sulking in gloom there. Nor could they know his share of the burden as the husband of a woman who numbed herself with alcohol. Yet despite their troubles, she had devoted herself to his cause and become a coach's wife. He finished the thought.

". . . ehmmm . . . patient . . . wonderful . . . wife."

Another pause.

"And the Packer executive board and its directors. And a fine group of assistant coaches. A great group of players without whom none of this would be possible. . . ."

Wild applause from Hornung and Fuzzy and Jesse Whittenton and the rest of the boys at the back table. As despotic and unfeeling as he could seem sometimes on the practice field, the coach had taught them how to win, lifted their self-image, challenged them to accomplish things that they had thought might be beyond their reach. And recently he had won the hearts of their wives as well, presenting every Packer woman with a luxurious fur stole in celebration of the title. The Golden Boy did not get one to give away to a girlfriend; Lombardi sent it directly to his mother. That made it one fine year for Loretta Hornung; her son also gave her the Corvette sports car he had won as the outstanding player in the championship game.

". . . And to the good Lord for His help and understanding. And I pray to Him each day to give me enough of a sense of humor to be serious, yet never allow me to take myself too seriously. Thank you, again."

Cheers, whistles, pounding applause. After a benediction delivered by the Reverend Dean Kilgust, the men in the audience moved toward the head table with the reverence of parishioners waiting to receive communion. The Pope signed autographs, showed off his new putter, traded gibes with Rozelle and Sleepy Jim and the two Tims. The high of the evening was wearing off, the same transition from elation to exhaustion that overtook Lombardi after a big win. He stepped out into the downtown mist, found his car in the darkened lot behind the Elks Lodge and headed home to Marie.

17

Daylight

THE CALL CAME one Sunday afternoon during the 1961 Christmas break. "Bill, Red wants to talk to you," Betty Heinz hollered down to her husband, W. C. Heinz, who was ice-skating on a neighborhood pond at the end of their property in Stamford, Connecticut. Heinz crunched his way home through the snow, removed his skates at the door, walked inside and took the phone.

"What are you doing?" asked Red Smith, the columnist for the *New York Herald Tribune*, who lived nearby.

"I'm doing what you should be doing," Heinz responded, in the sarcastic manner that defined the friendship of two eloquent sportswriters. "I'm skating around on the pond with *your* son." True enough: Heinz had been skating with Terry Smith, Red's son, home from college for the holidays.

"Well, are you going to be there for a while?" Smith asked. "I've got something I want to talk to you about."

"Sure," said Heinz. "Come on over."

Smith arrived with a proposition. He had entered into an agreement with Prentice-Hall to serve as general editor of what would be called Red Smith's Sports Series, as-told-to memoirs in which prominent sports figures would give readers an inside look into their lives and professions. Robert Riger had signed on to do illustrations and photographs, and Smith would select an established author to write each book. "They want to start with a book on Lombardi, and we think you should do it," Smith said. He acknowledged that Heinz was a replacement choice; their first thought was Lombardi's old Fordham pal, Tim Cohane, but Cohane had declined, saying he was too busy. "So, when are you going to get finished with that *doctor* book?" Smith asked. The question came with a tone of disdain. Heinz had devoted himself recently to writing *The Surgeon,* a true-to-life fictional account of the pressure-filled days of a doctor, and he thought that Smith "always kind of looked down on" that project because it broke up their relationship in sports. The doctor book would be finished by July, Heinz said. Soon enough.

"But there's gonna be trouble with that Lombardi book," Heinz added. "You remember it, Red. Up there at St. Michael's. The Five O'Clock Club." He was referring to the New York Giants training camp in Vermont, which Heinz and Smith and Frank Graham, now working for the *Journal American,* had visited every summer during the mid-1950s when Lombardi was a Giants assistant coach. At the daily Five O'Clock Club, the Maras, the coaching staff and visiting sportswriters would gather late in the afternoon to drink and tell off-the-record stories, usually in Doc Sweeney's dormitory room. "Here's the problem," Heinz continued. "Did you ever hear Lombardi tell a story up there?"

"No, now that you mention it. I never did," Smith acknowledged.

"He's got a great laugh," Heinz said. "But he doesn't contribute. That's gonna be a problem."

Heinz agreed to take the work nonetheless, signing up for a $7,500 advance. A few weeks later, in the middle of January 1962, he and Smith drove down from Connecticut to Manhattan to meet Lombardi, Riger and George Flynn, the Prentice-Hall editor overseeing the project, at the Penthouse Club, a top-story restaurant and bar overlooking the south end of Central Park. In keeping with Lombardi Standard Time, the coach was the first one there, a half hour early, and sat at the bar nursing a scotch (flouting his own Packer prohibition against bar-sitting) as he waited for the others to arrive. The five men talked for several hours that night, and Lombardi was amiable throughout. These were *his* writers, New York guys, and Heinz could tell that Lombardi "respected Red tremendously" and that the feelings were mutual. At ten that night, as Smith and Heinz rode north along the West Side Highway on the way back to Stamford, Smith expressed delight with the way things went. "Gee, that was a good meeting," he said. Heinz was less fervid. "You know what this sounds like to me, Red," he said. "It sounds like Bill Heinz punchin' that same ole Remington typewriter again as he has since he was seventeen. The whole load gets dumped on me."

Wilfred Charles Heinz was then a lean and crisp man of forty-six who saw the world with uncommon clarity through his black-rimmed glasses. He was a perfectionist with a clean and unencumbered style, always seeking the precise word, phrase, metaphor, that would convey his meaning perfectly. He had covered sports most of his writing career, though at the start of World War II he served as a war correspondent with distinction for the *New York Sun.* After that, he wrote a sports column, then turned to books and freelance magazine articles when the *Sun* folded. He was a favorite of Grantland Rice and Damon Runyon, and a close friend of Red Smith, who was ten years his senior. His writing models were Ernest Hemingway for novels and Frank Graham for newspapers. Graham, he thought, was a "classical stylist with prose so pure that you could always learn from it." He also thoroughly enjoyed Smith's writing, but considered him "more of a dancer and mover, with a style that you couldn't imitate." At the horse tracks during racing season, Graham and Smith were so inseparable that they became known as an entry, "1 and 1a." While Smith was more celebrated outside the profession, within the sportswriting tribe it was clear that Graham was 1 and Smith 1a.

Graham not only taught Heinz the purest way to construct an English sentence, but also deepened his reportorial skills. He had a way of being un-obtrusive, the proverbial fly on the wall, to catch athletes and coaches at their most authentic moments and then use their dialogue verbatim to re-create a scene. And he did it without a tape recorder—without even pulling out a notebook. "Frank never took notes, so Red and I learned how to do that too, how to look and listen," Heinz recalled later. "The first time I tried it, Frank and I were both interviewing Rocky Graziano at Stillman's gym. He wasn't taking notes, so I didn't either. When we came out I said, 'You jerk! I don't think I'll remember.' He said, 'You will. When you get home tonight and Betty asks you where you were and what you did, you'll tell her who said what and where you were and what you did.'" Graham was right, and the powers of memory that Heinz developed then stayed with him thereafter, so four decades later he could remember the smell in the air and the color of a tie. Still, as a backup, he continued to take copious notes in unhurried and, for a journalist, remarkably legible handwriting.

ON THE THIRTIETH of June, with *The Surgeon* completed, Heinz began his new life as Lombardi's Boswell. He traveled the usual route west through Chicago and up to Green Bay on the flight of the Blue Goose, arriving at Austin Straubel Airport shortly before six that summer evening. He brought with him $130 for travel expenses, his old portable Remington and a brief-case holding the deceptively simple tools of his trade: a mechanical pencil and a supply of pocket-size Penrite memo books, sturdy and wirebound from the top for easy notetaking, each costing ten cents. As he strolled across the tarmac in the warm and gentle Wisconsin air, he was struck first by an aroma: heavy acid smells wafting over from the paper mills along the Fox River. And there stood Lombardi, neatly dressed in black slacks, white short-sleeved shirt and striped tie, waving at him from behind the Page outdoor fence. The coach seemed cheerful and eager, even offering to assist the visit-ing writer with his bags as they walked out to the Pontiac. Marie was waiting in the front passenger seat. Heinz slid in back, and Lombardi drove them to a restaurant in an old Victorian house that reminded the writer of an 1890s funeral parlor.

"So," said Marie, as they relaxed with a drink in the bar before dinner, "what kind of book is this going to be?"

"I don't know," said Heinz.

"Don't look at me," said Lombardi.

"Well," Marie concluded sarcastically, "it's going to be some great book!"

After dinner they drove Heinz to his new living quarters, not a downtown hotel but the spare bedroom near the TV room at the Lombardi house on Sunset Circle. The Lombardis enjoyed housing guests, even writers, anything to change the often tense atmosphere. Heinz was keen for the idea, too. It gave him more time with his subject, more chance to penetrate Lombardi's public persona and find the real man. Furthermore, he intended to stay in Green Bay for several weeks, and a room at the Northland or Downtowner would have used up most of the advance. Both children were there—Susan was entering high school and Vincent was preparing for his junior year at the College of St. Thomas—but they were rarely home and the house did not seem overcrowded. Heinz and Lombardi agreed on a work schedule: for the two weeks between then and the opening of training camp, they would meet every morning at nine o'clock, after Vince had returned from mass at St. Willebrord's, and go at it, Heinz asking questions, Lombardi answering, until they grew tired.

The interviews began the next morning in the basement rec room. Lombardi sat on the couch, Heinz at a chair on the side of the coffee table. He pulled out one of his Penrite memo books, wrote the numeral I on the front and launched the first question. It was not his favorite approach, too open-ended, suggesting to him "the start of a long, arduous journey," but he felt compelled to begin this way. "So," he said, "give me the date of your birth."

"June 11, 1913," Lombardi answered.

Nothing came so easily after that. Heinz was a veteran interviewer, but Lombardi was a problematic subject, just as he had feared. No matter how shapely the question, the answer came back flat. The Day One session went on with all the depth of a hospital clerk taking information for an insurance form.

> *Page 1 of Notebook 1:*
> 6-11-13
> 2 brothers & 2 sisters
> wholesale beef—father came
> few months old, mother born
> here—

Resort area—charter boat
fishing—flounder, snappers
Sunny Jim took me to Saratoga
each August—8th grade
No wants
Father stern
Came in 2 a.m.—took shoes off
at top stairs—got whacked—
mother—she went to bed & I
did too
Both parents perfectionist
2 story wooden frame
house—gray
Cathedral Prep—complete 4 yrs.
Atlantic Ave—Brooklyn

Heinz was not the sort to miss evocative details. They just were not there. On the second morning, Lombardi seemed anxious. He had things to do: players to sign, rounds of golf to play at Oneida before training camp. This sitting around talking was frustrating him. "How we doing?" he asked Heinz.

"All right," Heinz answered halfheartedly.

"What do you mean, 'all right'?" Lombardi asked.

"Well," Heinz said, "you don't have any audiovisual recall."

"What the hell is that?" Lombardi asked.

"Well, I just made it up," Heinz responded. "But you don't remember what anybody said or what they sounded like. You don't remember what anything looked like."

"Whadaya mean?"

"Well, you told me that you decided that football was what you wanted to do in your life when you had a great game at St. Francis Prep."

"You already got that!" said Lombardi proudly.

"I know I have it, Coach," Heinz said patiently. "Now, as you pulled your jersey over your head . . . I asked you what color the jersey was and you said you didn't know."

"That's right. I didn't know."

"That's what I mean!" said Heinz.

Lombardi even forgot to offer a revealing explanation for why he could not recall the jersey color. He was color-blind. On the third day, Heinz could tell that "the romance of being an author" had clearly worn off on his collaborator. The interview was cut short when Lombardi said he had to leave to play golf with Don Hutson, the former star Packers receiver. Heinz was left alone in the house with Marie, who promised to be a far better source of information. She was not only able to remember details from her husband's life, but also, as Heinz discovered, "was extremely sensitive to the ballplayers and their families," and understood Lombardi's football psychology, how he assessed and related to each of his players. Heinz realized that the book would be nearly impossible without Marie, but even with her he was uncertain about its potential. On the night after his fourth halting interview session with Lombardi, he retired to the guest bedroom and struggled through a long bout of sleeplessness brought on by anxieties over the project. I'm getting out of this! he said to himself that night. This is impossible. But how in the hell do I get out of it? These are nice people. I like them. How am I going to tell them, You don't shape up, in my estimation?

Finally, late that night, a solution came to him. There's one way to do it, he said to himself. And that's the way I've done it before. It was the progressive narrative technique he used for the first major magazine piece he wrote back in 1946, when a dying Damon Runyon recommended him to the editors at Hearst's *Cosmopolitan.* The article was on boxing, the day a prizefighter goes into the ring. He chose Rocky Graziano as his subject, and followed him from the break of dawn on the day that he fought Tony Zale at Yankee Stadium and was knocked out in the sixth round. The story later won the E. P. Dutton award for sportswriting, the first of five for Heinz. The beauty of the progressive narrative was that it provided a natural plot, established by the second, the minute, the hour, the day. Maybe this is the way I can do Lombardi, Heinz decided. I'll start the Monday after a game and take it through the next game. I'll get all the background material I need now, and then come back in the fall for a couple of games until I get a good game.

With his plan set, Heinz worried less about the limited amount of time Lombardi was devoting to the book. During his two weeks at Sunset Circle, he turned increasingly to Marie for tips that he could then use in sporadic follow-up interviews with her husband. Marie would tell him how Vince viewed Hornung or Jerry Kramer and he would then ask Lombardi about Hornung and Kramer, eventually gleaning the coach's insights into all of his key players, which later could be fitted into the narrative. Inevitably during that period he also came to know about the Lombardis' relationship. Once, when Lombardi was out of the house, Heinz talked to Marie about her husband's temper, a subject about which he was sensitive because of his own father's unpredictable disposition, which had made life difficult for his mother. Marie surprised him with a confession. "She said, 'I wasn't married to him a week when I said to myself, Marie Planitz, you have made the greatest mistake of your life.' And she said, 'But I found out what to do. When it gets so bad that I can't stand it, I stand right up to him and he backs off.' " Another night, when he was at dinner with the Lombardis, Heinz listened as they talked about their marriage difficulties until Vince declared, "But when I love you, I really do!" And Marie responded, "Yes, you do!"

In the middle of July, Heinz followed Lombardi across the river to St.

Norbert College, the two occupying the commodious dean's suite where the coach lived during training camp. Heinz went to practice, interviewed players in their dorms, attended Lombardi's version of the Five O'Clock Club, and sat in on film sessions with the coaches. He was at once unobtrusive and omnipresent, just as Frank Graham had taught him to be. Bill Austin, the line coach, called him the Shadow. It was at training camp that Heinz reached a conclusion on why Lombardi had such limited recall of his own past: Details of the past were not material to his mission. Discard the immaterial, Red Blaik had taught him at West Point, in the context of preparing for a football game, and Vince had become the master of discard. He purged from his life and mind as much as he could that did not have a direct bearing on the success of his Green Bay Packers. If it did not help the cause, it was a distraction. There were a few exceptions to the rule—daily mass at St. Willebrord's, golf at Oneida, an hour of mindless television late in the day— but those were to relax his soul or clear his head or settle his nerves, and as such they could be considered necessary for the making of a successful coach.

THE BOOK with Heinz was granted a partial exemption from Lombardi's policy of eliminating irrelevancies; the idea came from his New York pals, after all, and it stroked his ego. When the distinction could be made, he was driven by a will to prevail more than a desire to be famous, but he nonetheless enjoyed the notion of being a celebrity author. The Green Bay media were an altogether different matter. Lombardi considered the local press 95 percent immaterial, 5 percent public relations tool. He tended to treat Wisconsin sportswriters with indifference or cruel condescension. One morning after preseason practice, as Lombardi was changing his clothes in the coach's dressing room on the south end of City Stadium, Lee Remmel, a writer for the *Green Bay Press-Gazette*, approached Heinz, who was standing outside the room.

"Bill, is the coach in there?" Remmel asked.

"Yes," Heinz said. "You want to talk to him?"

Heinz entered the coach's room and caught Lombardi's attention.

"Lee Remmel's out there," Heinz said.

"What about it?" Lombardi muttered.

"He wants to see you."

"What does he want?"

"Coach," Heinz answered with a hint of exasperation. "He's a reporter. He wants to ask you some questions."

"All right," Lombardi said gruffly. "Send him in."

Heinz felt embarrassed. He and Remmel were brothers in the trade, and he was the interloper and Remmel was on his home turf. It bothered him to see any reporter feel compelled to so humble himself just to talk to a coach. With Lombardi driving them to lunch that noon, he decided to try to instruct him on the demands of journalism.

"I want to tell you something about Lee Remmel," he said.

"What about him?" Lombardi growled.

"He's a good writer."

"He is?"

"Yes," Heinz said. "He writes well enough to work for the *New York Times,* the *Herald Tribune,* the *Kansas City Star, Chicago Tribune*—you name it. And I'll tell you something else about him. He's a married man. He has to make a living. And you make life awfully tough for him. You make it so tough that you're giving him an inferiority complex. And that's not right, Vince."

As Heinz later recalled the scene, Lombardi responded with a noncommittal grunt.

Later that afternoon, at the end of the second practice session, Lombardi and Heinz walked off the field together. Remmel was about six paces ahead, and when Lombardi noticed him he shouted, "Lee! Got any questions?" The next day at the Five O'Clock Club in the basement lounge of Sensenbrenner Hall, Lombardi sat at his usual corner spot, reading the *Green Bay Press-Gazette.* Tom Miller, the team publicist, was at the bar getting some drinks, and other coaches were milling around. The door opened slowly and there stood Remmel, looking in. Lombardi perked up immediately. "Oh, Lee! Come in! Good. Good. Tom, get'm a drink...."

"Well, I..." Remmel seemed uncomfortable with the attention.

"No. No. Tom, get'm a drink. Get'm a drink," Lombardi insisted. "Lee, come over here!"

What was going on? Had Heinz truly softened the Old Man? A few days later the answer came. The co-authors were driving to lunch again, and Lombardi had had enough.

"You and your Lee Remmel!" he harrumphed.

"What do you mean?" Heinz asked.

"I'm getting an inferiority complex worrying about *his* inferiority complex!"

From the beginning the relationship of Lombardi and the Wisconsin press was a curious one. During his years in New York, Lombardi was known to the big-city writers as Vin or Vinnie. They sought him out for explications of the Giants offense, for analyses of the opposition, for quotes before and after games. They drank with him in the midtown restaurants and saloons. He was by turns gregarious or earnest, playful or professorial. This was the largest sporting press tribe in the world, hard to control, fiercely competitive—yet Lombardi had few problems. It was only after he arrived in Wisconsin, where the press corps was thin, unassuming and generally compliant, and where reporters deferred to his title, calling him Coach or Coach Lombardi, that the relationship gradually soured. The transformation could be explained by the change in jobs as well as settings. As an assistant coach, Lombardi acted as aides traditionally act, serving as a liaison between the head man and the players and the press. His friendship with many New York journalists was authentic, but his demeanor might also have been shaped by an appreciation of the balance of power. Certainly the writers needed him for tips and insight, but he needed them, too—to promote him as a brilliant assistant who deserved a head coaching position.

But did he need the Wisconsin press? Perhaps to help fill the seats every Sunday, at least in the wake of the Ronzani-Blackbourn-McLean era, when City Stadium and Milwaukee County Stadium were far from sold out. Lombardi was so eager for publicity about the team then that he persuaded the Milwaukee papers to cover the Packers training camp full-time, something they had not done before. "He said if you wanted to cover the team you had to come up and stay at camp," recalled Bud Lea, the beat reporter for the *Milwaukee Sentinel.* "I think he must have done that because he felt he was up in the boonies. Not that he liked us one single bit, but going to Green Bay was said to be like falling off the cliff at the end of the earth—and he needed some coverage to prove he existed and to generate ticket sales." Even with the Milwaukee writers on hand, it was a slim journalism brigade: Daley and Remmel from the *Press-Gazette,* AP and UPI, usually the three sports directors from Green Bay television, no radio. The whole group of regulars totaled ten at most.

Local writers tended to view Lombardi as a mixed blessing. Yes, he brought winning to Green Bay and winning made their jobs glamorous, but something was lost in the bargain. Life had been relaxed before, and now, as Bud Lea said, "this guy came in and suddenly all the rules were changed. Actually, there *were* no rules under Scooter." In the old days Art Daley could amble into the office and get the coach to say whatever was needed. Lombardi put up barriers, verbal when not physical. Once Daley was in Lombardi's office "fishing for a story" and getting terse non-answers. "Damn it," he finally blurted out in frustration. "If I stay here long enough I'll get a story out of you." Lombardi promptly rose from his chair and left the room and disappeared. When the coach deigned to answer questions, it was rarely an easygoing process. Chuck Johnson of the *Milwaukee Journal* wrote many of the main Packers stories and also edited the sports section. Every Tuesday morning after a game, while sitting in the slot laying out the afternoon paper, he was allowed to call Lombardi at nine o'clock sharp for a follow-up story. If he phoned a few minutes late, Lombardi might not take the call. Johnson wrote out his questions in advance, and he knew that he had to read fast and could not pause to collect his thoughts or Lombardi would say, "That's enough, gotta go," and hang up on him.

Terry Bledsoe was the *Journal's* cub reporter on the Packers in 1962, assigned to write postgame locker room features. He would never forget the first time he was assigned to get some quotes from the coach. "I walk into the shower room and here's this little short, fat guy toweling himself off, and he sees me and snarls, 'Who the hell are you?' He answered a few questions, but it was clear I was on borrowed time, so I got the hell out of there." Sometimes subjects who appear surly to writers soften up around photographers. Not this coach. When word spread that Lombardi had received a congratulatory telegram from President Kennedy after the title win, the *Press-Gazette* dispatched photographer Russ Kriwanek to shoot a picture of him sitting at his desk holding the prized memento. "He was gruff as hell when I got there," Kriwanek said later. "He kept saying, 'Let's get this over with!' Then, just when I took the picture, he broke into a beautiful smile. And it was a beautiful picture."

He was the Pope and he made the local media genuflect. The sports directors at the three television stations in Green Bay were allowed to travel to away games on the team charter, but they had to ask the coach individually every week whether there was room. "You can't imagine how difficult and demeaning it was to go to his office, wait until he would see you and humbly ask, 'Is there any room?' Sometimes he would drag it out and say, 'I don't know. We'll have to wait and see later in the week,' " recalled Jim Irwin, who later became the radio voice of the Packers. Al Sampson, as the producer of Lombardi's weekly television show, had the strongest connection to the coach, but even he waited to find a seat in the back of the plane. On occasion during flights home he was invited up to first class, where they served liquor instead of beer, but this was no bargain. The invitation would come from Marie Lombardi, who wanted to change seats with Sampson because her husband was in a particularly surly mood.

When entertaining the press, Lombardi often took on the role of benevolent despot. He hosted an annual off-season party for the media at Oneida Golf and Riding, but according to secretary Ruth McKloskey, after he stood for a few minutes of pleasantries with his guests, she might find him hiding off in a far corner playing gin with his country club cronies. At gatherings of the Five O'Clock Club, whether in the lounge at St. Norbert during training camp or in the coach's hotel suite for road games once the season began, reporters lived by Lombardi's rules. Drinks started at five and stopped exactly at six, no lingering. "At five of six, when you saw the hands on the clock getting around to there, you were preparing to depart," said Remmel. While sipping scotch and water, reading the waiver wires that his personnel man brought in, or the newspaper, or even occasionally watching cartoons on television, Lombardi would lead an off-the-record discussion. He controlled the topic, whether football, politics or the latest corny jokes. "He was friendly in that atmosphere," according to Jim Irwin. "But you were always wary of saying the wrong thing. I did a lot more listening than talking."

Bud Lea came to think of the Five O'Clock Club not just as a jocular gathering of sportsmen, but as another way for Lombardi to control his domain. "It was almost like checking in," Lea said decades later. "You had to go to that damn thing whether you wanted to or not. What power he had then! The power was about as one-sided as anything I've seen in my reporting life." Now and then on the road, Lombardi would announce that everyone was going to dinner after the Five O'Clock Club. Reporters who had made separate plans rearranged them. Lombardi chose the restaurant, usually Italian, and sometimes ordered the meals all around as well. Heinz watched with bemusement once as Lombardi raved about the linguine with clam sauce, and commanded everyone in his party to get it—which they did— and then ordered antipasto for himself.

There was a method to Lombardi's often brusque or domineering approach to reporters. He cut them off or tried to control them in part because he feared that rather than simply being immaterial to his mission, they could harm him by providing valuable material to the opposition. In a locker room where the walls were plastered with aphorisms on winning and effort, one of the largest signs instructed the players on their bond of silence. It read:

What You See Here
What You Say Here
What You Hear Here
Let It Stay Here
When You Leave Here

Al Del Greco, a writer for the *Bergen Record* who had followed Lombardi's career since his days in Englewood, New Jersey, said little had changed over the years in that respect: "He just can't lay it on the line to writers because he thinks giving out information is helpful to the enemy." What sorts of information? Injuries, first and foremost. Lombardi was obsessed with keeping news on the condition of his key players away from the press and the opposition—and he could do it rather successfully before the era of twenty-four-hour radio sports shows and strict league requirements on reporting injuries. Not only did he pressure reporters not to write about certain injuries, but he also tried when possible to keep the news from them in the first place.

Robert Strom, then an X-ray technician at St. Vincent Hospital on Van Buren Street, later related a story revealing the lengths to which Lombardi went in that regard. Strom once got a call from Dr. James Nellen, one of the two team physicians, after a home game. "Our X-ray department had a fire door in the back that you could get out, but it was not supposed to be an entrance," Strom recalled. "Nellen called and said, 'Bob, meet us at the back door in exactly thirty minutes. Be there!' Thirty minutes later a car pulls up by the back door. Nellen, Vince Lombardi and Bart Starr get out. Bart had an injured finger. Vince wanted to hide all his injuries from the media and the league. Nellen said to me, 'This is not to be recorded.' Every patient had to have a number and a file. 'No number, Bob,' he said. So I didn't record it in the book. I took the picture. They waited for it to be developed. And before anyone else saw it, Dr. Nellen took it. Lombardi came along to make sure none of the media saw it. It was a cloak-and-dagger thing. When they left, Nellen said, 'If anyone calls and asks, any Packers here? You know what the answer is.'"

Journalists sometimes mistakenly assumed that Lombardi was oblivious, so preoccupied with coaching that he had no idea who they were or what they wrote. In fact, he read almost everything, and paid more attention to them than he let on. With the flinty eyes of a censor, he edited every press release and game program that his publicity department published. He combed the papers looking for stories that might distract his players from the mission of winning the next game. He studied the power and influence of various sportswriters. When he brought his West Point ally Ockie Krueger to Wisconsin to run the Milwaukee ticket office, he gave him one bit of advice: "The only man you've got to get along with in Milwaukee is Ollie Kuechle." Krueger made a point of befriending Kuechle, the lead columnist of the *Milwaukee Journal*. Bud Lea of the *Sentinel* grew close to Krueger, too, but never felt the same about Lombardi. "Honest to God, I wanted to get along with the guy," Lea said later. "It was a great opportunity. He was a great leader. But I never felt at ease with him." Once, after having a few drinks at the Five O'Clock Club on the road and screwing up his nerve, Lea confronted Lombardi—almost.

"I'll take this stuff, but only one thing," Lea said.

"What's that?" Lombardi asked.

"Don't lose!"

"Mister," said Lombardi, "I don't intend to."

HE VERY NEARLY kept his word in 1962. The Packers were so talented and prepared in Lombardi's fourth year that they barely needed the multiple skills of their left halfback. Paul Hornung was out of the service. "HORNUNG ARRIVES IN PACKERS CAMP!" shouted the headline in the *Chicago Tribune* when he joined his teammates on July 24 to prepare for the College All-Star Game, a reflection of how big he had become. The Golden Boy returned to the Packers with a new glow, having snubbed a $250,000 offer to switch leagues and play for the New York Jets of the American Football League. Players were worth more than they were getting, Hornung said. But a quarter-million dollars? "Nobody is worth that much." Besides, leaving the Packers for the Jets would be like "leaving the New York Yankees for the Louisville Colonels." Hornung stayed, but in the fifth game he was slowed by a knee injury that sidelined him for several games and forced him to relinquish his kicking duties for the rest of the year. Tom Moore, Elijah Pitts and the rookie Earl Gros filled in nicely when needed in the backfield, and Jerry Kramer, the strapping offensive guard, took over the placekicking, booting thirty-eight extra points and nine field goals in eleven attempts. Bart Starr, also ailing, had an average year, throwing nearly as many interceptions (nine) as touchdown passes (twelve). Most of the offensive load was carried by Jim Taylor, who had been improving every season and now had the best year of his career, pounding for 1,474 yards and nineteen touchdowns, surpassing the totals that year of the immortal Jim Brown.

The Packers amassed more than thirty points eight times that season, outscoring their opponents by a total of 415 to 148 and compiling the highest point spread of the postwar era—19.1 points more than their opponents per game. It was their defense that made them nearly invincible. Ray Nitschke had tamed his self-destructive off-the-field behavior and channeled his aggression into playing a ferocious middle linebacker on Sunday afternoons. He had always seemed like an angry man, especially when he had drunk too much, when even his teammates were afraid of him. Nitschke had grown up virtually parentless on the West Side of Chicago. His father had died when Ray was three, his mother when he was thirteen. He lived with an older brother and roamed the streets feeling that the world had been unfair to him and that he wanted to even the score. "I took it out on everybody else," he said later. "A day didn't go by that I didn't belt some other kid in the neighborhood. I was like that right through high school and college and even after I joined the Packers. Didn't take anything from anybody." Now he was married, and calming down, six days a week at least. In front of Nitschke, Willie Davis and Henry Jordan were having dominating years on the front line. And behind him, Herb Adderley at cornerback and Willie Wood at safety lifted the play at those key positions to unparalleled heights, combining to stifle the opposition's passing game every week. Wood intercepted nine passes and Adderley seven, returning them an average 18.8 yards. "We were a great, great team in 1962," Wood said later. "We were well oiled. We had talent everyplace. Every guy knew what he was supposed to be doing. We were veterans then. And I thought we were awesome."

Bill Heinz had circled the date back when he left training camp in early August. He would return to Wisconsin for the September 30 game against the Chicago Bears. It was the third game of the regular season. Green Bay by then had swept through six exhibition games and the opening two against Minnesota and St. Louis without a blemish. Chicago had started on the coast with wins over San Francisco and Los Angeles. Packers versus Bears seemed to offer everything Heinz needed to lend character and depth to his progressive narrative: the longest-running rivalry in the league, Halas and Lombardi, Papa Bear and the Pope. Casares and Taylor, Bill George and

Nitschke, Doug Atkins and Willie Davis, J. C. Caroline and Adderley. It sounded dramatic in theory, but it did not turn out that way. Taylor scored three touchdowns, Starr, Ron Kramer and Pitts one apiece, and Adderley returned an interception for another score. The Packers were nearly perfect, which was fine, but the game was utterly without suspense—a 49 to 0 shutout would not do for Heinz's purposes. Heinz knew he had to stay for at least another week. The Detroit Lions were coming to Green Bay next. "I'm hoping they win this one and it's a good game," Heinz said later. "I can't stay there forever waiting for a game I can use."

He got the game of a writer's dream, or at least the ending. The Packers are trailing 7 to 6 with less than two minutes remaining. The game has been draining, grudging, alternately brutal and sloppy. The same offense that humbled the Bears cannot cross the goal line, scoring only on Hornung field goals. The Lions have the ball near midfield. Terry Bledsoe of the *Milwaukee Journal* is on the Packers sidelines, plotting in his head the lead to a story about the team's first loss. There is no way for the Packers to win, he is thinking. Detroit is in full control. And then . . . Milt Plum, the Lions quarterback, decides to throw a pass, down and out to the flanker. But the receiver slips. "I see the ball pass his outstretched hands and then I hear the thop-sound it makes as it hits Herb Adderley's hands, and he's got it," Lombardi recalled later. "He's got it, and he's racing right by me now, down our sideline." Adderley glides all the way down to the Lions eighteen. After two running plays, Lombardi calls for a field goal on third down, and Hornung boots the three points that win the game, 9 to 7.

The Lions leave the field in disarray: big Alex Karras, the defensive tackle, throws his helmet in disgust in the direction of his errant quarterback, Plum. Lombardi chokes up in the dressing room as his troops chant "Herb! Herb!" Bledsoe is amazed by what he has witnessed. He calls it an "absolutely illogical result" brought on by only one thing: "I attribute it to Lombardi's will." And Heinz has his book. He is a pro and knows how it works. "Sometimes," he says, "it just drops in like that."

After a final day of wrap-up reporting, Heinz bade farewell to Green Bay and returned home to Stamford to begin writing the Lombardi book. He spent several days organizing his notes, a process of remarkable precision and simplicity. All of his material was contained in six of his little ten-cent memo books. They were filled in pencil from top line to bottom, both sides of the paper, from the first page to the last, with legible and orderly notes. On the right margin of every page, he drew a bracket down from the top line of a specific subject to its last line, and on the outside of the line wrote in vertical letters a simple subject heading. When he finished this task for all six books, he created a master index, listing all the subjects and the notebooks in which they appeared. No computer of later generations could be more efficient than W. C. Heinz and his sixty cents' worth of indexed notes.

The Packers and Heinz worked on nearly parallel schedules through the rest of the season. They practiced at nine. He began writing at nine. They broke for lunch and worked into the afternoon. He did the same. They were led by Lombardi. So was he. In fact, for the purposes of the book he had become Lombardi. In the end, after all, this was Lombardi's book, written in the first person. The first word on the first page would be "I," meaning Lombardi. For the book to work, he had to capture how Lombardi thought, talked and felt. Heinz had the proper disposition for the task. He was not as obsessed or temperamental as his subject, but he got along with Lombardi and thought he understood the coach and appreciated his greatness, despite the apparent flaws. "The thing that hit me with Lombardi and that we agreed on right away is that if you are gifted you have a moral responsibility to fulfill that gift as best you can," Heinz reflected later. "I always believed it. And Lombardi believed it all the way." The book would be straightforward narrative, not a philosophical treatise, yet driven by that single overarching idea: the moral imperative of paying the price to be great.

Heinz wrote the book in his makeshift den, a bantam-size office that he had constructed off the TV room in a corner of his garage. A radiator warmed him as winter approached. The cement floors were softened by cork tiles, the walls by Philippine mahogany paneling. There was just enough room for a desk and chair and small daybed for naps. With his notebooks and index laid out before him, he rolled two sheets of yellow copy paper around the platen of his Remington portable and began tap-tapping away. He wrote every day from September through Thanksgiving without taking a day off. On Sundays he paused to watch football on television and track the remarkable progress of the Packers. The wins kept coming after the close call against the Lions: Minnesota, San Francisco, Baltimore, Chicago, Philadelphia (49 to 0, payback for the title defeat in 1960) and Baltimore again. Lombardi and his Packers had ten wins and no losses—unbeaten and seemingly unbeatable.

The astounding team in the heartland was luring more eastern writers to Green Bay along the route of the Blue Goose. Herbert Warren Wind of *The New Yorker* blew into the Northland for stays in October and November, arriving the second time to witness the rematch with the Colts. Wind paid homage to football particulars, calling the Packers perhaps "one of the authentically great teams of all time," but his true function seemed to be that of an anthropologist relating the practices of an exotic aboriginal tribe to the sophisticates of New York City. He described the airport limo driver who had blurted out "Real great! Real great!" in response to one of Wind's dry jokes. "I mention this because it soon became evident that a second addiction of the people in Green Bay is the phrase 'real great,' which they use as frequently and with as many shades of intonation and meaning as the French do with '*Ça va.*'" When Wind arrived at the stadium an hour before the Colts game, he took note that "several thousand people were already on hand, milling around the food concessions and taking on frankfurters, bratwurst and coffee as reserve fuel against the sharp, cold air. With a food counter tucked under the stands at nearly every portal, City Stadium is as beautifully designed for eating as it is for football. The field itself, like that at the Yale Bowl, is sunk well below ground level."

After watching the Packers defeat the Colts, 17 to 13, aided by a 103-yard kickoff return by Adderley and two stirring goal line stands, Wind signed off with this summation of Green Bay culture: "According to our native folklore, Green Bay, all wrapped up in football, epitomizes the sort of Midwestern community that drives its gentler spirits out of town—to Chicago, to New York, to Paris, to anyplace where their alien talents have a chance to flower. It is hard to know about these things, but my own feeling is that Green Bay would be an excellent place for any boy or girl to grow up in. Of course, I wouldn't go so far as to recommend that a visitor launch into a long disquisition on the *coureurs de bois* for the benefit of the gang at the Packer Playdium, but if he did, there would be no bother about it. The chances are that they would simply think he was running on about some new quarterback who had just come up with the Montreal Allouettes." One can see the gang at the Playdium reading that line and muttering in various shades of intonation "Real great! Real great!"

Which is not what they would have been saying in the early afternoon of November 22 during the Thanksgiving Day game against the Lions. Detroit had a defense as tenacious as Green Bay's—and on that day a demonstrably better one, with Joe Schmidt and Wayne Walker battering away at linebacker, and Night Train Lane, Yale Lary and Dick LeBeau closing off the passing lanes. The scariest Lions were in the middle: rarely did two defensive tackles dominate the way Roger Brown and Alex Karras did for those few hours in chilly Detroit. Brown stood six foot five and weighed three hundred pounds, and he looked even larger as he tossed aside Packer blockers and lumbered into the backfield in pursuit of Bart Starr. The lasting image of the game is of No. 15 disappearing into the turf as Brown smothered him in the end zone for a safety. Karras was three inches shorter and fifty pounds lighter than Brown, but played just as large, harassing Starr all day. Jim Ringo, Fuzzy Thurston and Jerry Kramer seemed at a loss on how to stop the mad rush. Thurston joked later that it was during the first half of that game that he perfected the lookout block, a maneuver in which he would look over his shoulder and yell, "Look out, Bart!"

Bill Austin, Green Bay's line coach, later acknowledged that he had a copy of Detroit's defensive game plan—a scout had slipped it to him before the game—but that it made no difference. "We deciphered as much as we could, but we couldn't understand some of the words, I guess," Austin said. Starr ended up being sacked eleven times. With the Lions leading 26 to 0 as the fourth quarter began, the Packers knew they were beaten. The players seemed ready to head back to Green Bay; this did not promise to be the most joyous turkey dinner at the Elks Club, but anything was better than getting knocked around for another fifteen minutes. During an offensive huddle the bloodied Starr asked his bruised receivers if any of them believed they could get open. One after another these usually ball-grubbing athletes demurred, until Max McGee finally broke up his teammates by advising, "Bart, why don't you throw an incomplete pass and nobody'll get hurt." With that single joke it was as though all the weight of the afternoon was lifted, and the Packers regained a small measure of pride with two last-quarter touchdowns, making the final score a less humiliating 26 to 14.

As he watched the Turkey Day debacle on television back in Connecticut, Bill Heinz grew increasingly glum. He was a realist, but nonetheless had harbored some hope of a perfect season, the sort of year that would make Lombardi and his Packers even larger in the national imagination and in so doing "help the sale of the book." Lombardi, however, was not as dismayed as his co-author. He was even seen laughing in the dressing room after the game as he told the press, "You didn't think we were going to win them all, did you?" It was the psychology of the moment that mattered to Lombardi. After chatting warmly with Frank Mautte, an old Fordham teammate who lived in Detroit, he went around the locker room and quietly talked to his players. Fuzzy Thurston had lost his mother that week and was preoccupied; Lombardi said he understood. Starr seemed too hurried; Lombardi told him to maintain his normal patience. Then he gathered the team around him and said that the true challenge was now before them. "Let it be an example to all of us. The Green Bay Packers are no better than anyone else when they aren't ready, when they play as individuals and not as one. . . . Our greatest glory is not in never falling, but in rising every time we fall."

Everyone had been too confident, he said—his team, the press, but mostly himself. In the week before the game, he had allowed a television crew inside squad meetings for a report on the making of an undefeated team. No more of that. Now the press would stop writing about how invincible his team was. And he could whip the players again, reminding them that football was not easy, that they had to pay the price. "I wouldn't go so far as to say he was in favor of losing that game," said Terry Bledsoe. "But he seemed delighted the next week because he could scare everybody about what they had to do. He was always figuring that we were trying to get him to say they were a great team. He didn't want his players to think that unless he told them." The loss, said Willie Davis, the defensive end, "did more than remove the pressure. From that point on we never again got shook by losing." And they returned to their winning ways.

By late December, Heinz had written six chapters: Monday, Tuesday, Wednesday, Thursday, Friday and Saturday. He waited until the season was over to write Sunday. Lombardi traveled to New York again for league meetings, and he and Heinz met one morning at the Prentice-Hall offices in Englewood Cliffs, where editor George Flynn set up a projector and they watched the film of the first Lions game. Lombardi offered more thoughts on each play and Heinz asked questions and took notes. With details he gleaned from that film session, Heinz returned to Stamford and continued pecking away in his cork-bottomed room. He was Lombardi again, and one afternoon in February, before he packed up his Remington and took the children on a holiday to Washington, D.C., he typed the final few paragraphs as though he were inside the coach's head driving home from City Stadium in Green Bay on the October evening after the Lions game:

> I've got to make them believers, I'm thinking, and then the problem all week will be to get them up again, all of them, for next Sunday. After this, how will I ever get them up again for next Sunday? That's what I'm thinking now, turning off Oneida Avenue in the traffic. Then for the first time I feel the fatigue coming, the tiredness coming all over me.

The book came out the following September. Heinz had wanted to title it *Six Days and Sunday,* but Red Smith vetoed that idea. "With that title it'll end up in the bookstores with the biblical tracts," Smith said. What phrase did Lombardi use that might capture his personality? "How about, 'Shut up, Marie!' " George Flynn suggested wryly. But of course Marie would not shut up. As Heinz realized better than most, the fact that she kept talking made the book possible. It was only fitting, in the end, that Marie came up with the title. She said she loved Vin's phrase describing his philosophy of offensive football. Perfect, the others realized, and here at last was the title for a book that became a sports classic, with twenty-three printings over the ensuing decades. They called it *Run to Daylight!*

18

The End
of Something

MARIE HAD TRAVELED to nearly every road game since the end of their first year in Green Bay. She sat at her husband's side in the front row of the plane and bus, shopped on Saturday in whatever city they visited, attended the Five O'Clock Club late that afternoon, accompanied Vin to mass Sunday morning, and watched the game from a seat in the stands with Ockie Krueger and his wife, who supplied her with coffee and cigarettes and warm blankets. She was an essential part of the team's winning dynamic. As contentious as her relationship with Vince could be, it was never more clear how much he needed her than when the Packers were on the road. Marie could take Lombardi and give it to Lombardi like no one else, serving as both release valve and governor for his temper. Once she skipped a game in Texas and Lombardi turned so surly that the players beseeched her never to do that again. No problem: she truly enjoyed the traveling life and any opportunity to leave her remote northern outpost.

The touchier part was Vince's insistence that their daughter, Susan, come along. One variation of God, family and the Green Bay Packers was that wherever God and the schedule took the Packers, the Lombardis followed as a family. In explaining her father's motives, Susan later concluded that "he felt that his job wasn't going to entitle him to be home at five o'clock every night like any normal father, so one way to keep the family together was to bring it along." Susan stayed home only for the West Coast swing at season's end, which would have taken her out of school for two weeks. The rest of the time there was a seat reserved for her on the charter. And she hated it. "You look back and say how lucky you are, but at the age I was then, a teenager, I was involved with my friends and I wanted to stay home," she said later. "I never put away my suitcase from weekend to weekend. I packed clothes, washed them, put them back in. My father made me go."

The entire family, including Vincent on break from college, boarded the flight three days after Christmas carrying the Packers to New York for the 1962 championship game, a rematch with the Giants. The Lombardis were national celebrities now. One week earlier, in the December 21 issue of *Time,* on page 60, there was a picture of "Lombardi & Family" near a paragraph extolling Vince's proud home life: "He lives in a comfortable $35,000 home whose den is filled with trophies won by Daughter Susan, 15, an accomplished horsewoman, and Son Vince, 20, a 195-lb. fullback for Minnesota's College of St. Thomas." And there was Lombardi, with his oversized hands around both children, teeth shining; Marie to the side, her neck ringed with pearls, laughing at the joke; Susan staring straight at the camera; Vincent stiff at attention in sport coat and tie, hands clasped politely in front of him, head tilted up with eyes closed, as though humoring his father's public joviality.

Why wouldn't the Old Man be happy? His team had finished the regular season 13 and 1. The photograph was part of a huge cover story on Lombardi and his team and his sport. His bespectacled face dominated the cover, a color portrait of the coach in lucky camel's hair coat and fedora, with two indistinct Packers behind him in uniforms, winter capes and helmets with the simple G, and beyond them twelve rows of anonymous fans in the City Stadium stands. The identifying slash across the upper-left corner promoted *Time's* trendy contention that professional football had reached a new place in American life. "The Sport of the '60s," it declared, correctly, two years into the decade. The story ran under a familiar headline, "Vinnie, Vidi, Vici," and it seemed that every word was aimed at constructing a new mythology with Lombardi at the center. He was called "the world's greatest football coach." His Packers were labeled "the current wonder team of football, a group of superstars romantically molded out of a gang of has-beens." And the game they played was defined in Tex Maule style, as the ultimate modern spectator sport and best expression of athletic professionalism and specialization:

> Football, as the pros go at it, is a game of special brilliance, played by brilliant specialists.... So precise is the teamwork that a single mistake by one man can destroy the handiwork of ten. So many are the complexities that connoisseurs argue endlessly in a mysterious lingo over slotbacks, stunters and buttonhooks. Even the innocent are mesmerized. Action piles upon action, thrill upon guaranteed thrill, and all with such bewildering speed that at the end the fans are literally limp.... No other sport offers so much to

so many. Boxing's heroes are papier-mâché champions. Hockey is gang warfare, basketball is for gamblers, and Australia is too far to travel to see a decent tennis match. Even baseball, the sportswriters' "national pastime," can be a slow-motion bore. . . .

The *Time* article was well received not only in Wisconsin but also at the league office in New York, where Pete Rozelle, the aggressive commissioner, had been striving for three seasons to make the NFL anything but a bore. He could not have created a more effective cover himself. As a former publicity man in Los Angeles, he had paid special attention to creating the right buzz, and took notice at league meetings whenever magazines focused on the pro game. *Life, Look, The New Yorker, The New York Times Magazine* and *Time* had all done big spreads that year. The word was out among advertising agencies, publishers and corporate executives that pro football was hot. One of Rozelle's missions was to make the NFL outrageously rich, and he had taken a crucial step toward that goal, convincing the owners to adopt his "unity of purpose" plan on television rights by signing a single network contract for 1962. The plan strengthened the league all around, according to the commissioner, giving it more bargaining leverage with networks and more clout with blue-chip oil, beer and cigarette advertisers, while also distributing revenues evenly to the benefit of small-market clubs. Lombardi and his Packers perhaps benefited most of all, as the joint venture meant that they earned as much from television as the New York Giants, where previously they were earning less than half as much.

By the end of the 1962 season, it was apparent that pro football and television were made for one another. Baseball might be the national pastime, but its wide field, slow pace and long summer season worked against it on the tube, whereas pro football was a weekend sport with fewer than twenty games a year, most of them played in fall and winter when more people were indoors. The game also seemed to benefit more from television technology: the zoom lens, slow motion, isolated cameras (and later, instant replay) all made it easier for the average fan to pick up nuances of the action that were hard to see from a seat in the stands. Baseball was a long novel whose story grew in complexity and richness over the course of months; pro football offered a discrete live drama every week, with an uncertain ending. The sport had a new cliché, that any team could win on any given Sunday, and the Lions had proved it once again on Thanksgiving Day with their defeat of the otherwise unbeaten Packers.

Of the 54.9 million homes in the United States then, 49.8 million had television sets, and nearly 12 million of them had been tuned to that Packers-Lions game, a record number for a regular-season contest. The overall viewing audience for pro football had grown every year since 1956, with the exception of 1960. The ratings had gone up 10 percent in 1962 alone, a rise that made pro football attractively cost effective for advertisers, according to Philip Morris Inc., one of its major sponsors. Using a formula that took into account the expense of a minute of advertising and the number of homes reached, Philip Morris determined that its advertising on an NFL game cost $4.56 to reach a single home, compared with $5.45 for college football. To reach adult males, advertising an NFL game was even more cost effective than sponsoring the average prime-time show—$4.21 to $6.33. Efficient advertising made the NFL more alluring to sponsors, which made it possible for Rozelle to get more money from the networks and put more into the pockets of his owners.

The commissioner's other mission was to make the league seem endlessly exciting, and he believed that this also could be accomplished as much off the field as on, by accommodating and ingratiating the television and print media, encouraging them to promote the new professional ideology.

There would be a seamless web between playing the game and selling the game, conjoining life and art. Publicity efforts were coordinated by the league office. There were standard rules for press releases, statistics, press conferences. Story lines were conceived in New York and pushed around the country. To the extent that Lombardi had become the symbol of modern pro football, Rozelle hoped to use him in that effort. This was one of many instances during the 1960s when others would try to enlist Lombardi in some larger cause—financial, cultural or ideological—and though he usually obliged them, it was rarely a perfect match. At times Lombardi was seen as a remnant from the old school, but he could no more be assigned to the past than considered a product of Rozelle's new publicity machine. He was a transitional figure between old and new, but more than that he was singular, with his own distinct philosophy and mythology.

Rozelle had not yet turned the championship game into a week-long extravaganza, but he had wished that Lombardi would put more into the selling of the 1962 title match than he did. The Packers practiced in Green Bay until noon Friday, then flew to New York and rode the bus into midtown to their quarters at the Hotel Manhattan. Vince had made plans to take the family across the river that night to visit his parents in Englewood. He had prepared his team for Sunday, even installed a surprise passing attack if conditions were suitable, and his pregame duties were mostly done, or so he thought. New York City newspapers were not publishing again, the second time in four years they had been silenced by labor strikes while the NFL Championship Game was in town. Lombardi assumed that he would not have to do much with the depleted press corps until Sunday. But shortly before five o'clock he received a call from Jim Kensil, Rozelle's chief publicist, who said the league had set up a big press conference at another hotel. It was about to start, but everyone was waiting for the *Time* cover boy to appear.

Lombardi started arguing with Kensil. He said no one had told him about the press conference and that he could not attend because his parents were expecting him. Rozelle took the phone from his aide. Lombardi was still angry, but he would not openly defy the league. After a short discussion the commissioner hung up and said, "He's on his way."

Whether Lombardi served any use was another matter. He uttered a string of yeps and nopes, disparaged a few questions and left with his image as a temperamental grouch intact with some reporters. Lombardi considered himself "a city man"—there were times during the off-season when he would escape from Green Bay just to take a room at the Waldorf "and sit, surrounded by the city." He would go to Toots Shor's, where the proprietor greeted him as a beloved "crumb bum." Then over to Mike Manuche's with his friends Eddie Breslin, William O'Hara and Jim Lawlor and his little brother, Joe, and a group of writers. Jerry Izenberg of the *Newark Star-Ledger* described Lombardi as never happier than in that setting, standing amid his friends, "first among equals, not emperor as he was in Green Bay," stationed so that he could see everyone in the place, unloosened by a few scotch and waters, talking about Fordham or his favorite singer or place on the road. "At times like this his laughter would fill the room and everybody would smile no matter where you were in the room."

Yet nothing could make him laugh or relax now. By Saturday he seemed agitated to a state of exhaustion. Red Blaik, who sat at his table for dinner that night at the Metropolitan Club, was struck by Lombardi's anxiety. Lombardi talked about how difficult the game would be, and how beat-up his team was, and how the stress of success was starting to eat at him and drive him harder than ever. This was not about television revenues, magazine covers, publicity plans, sexy new ways of selling the game on Madison Avenue—it was about overcoming fate and temptation and paying the price and becoming immortal. "We're going to win!" he finally blurted out, and then abruptly departed.

He and Marie had left their daughter back at the hotel with the usual instructions. She was not to open the door for anyone except the waiter delivering dinner, and she was not to leave the suite for any reason. When she was done, she should place the tray in the hall and lock the door and go to bed. This was fine with Susan: she could eat in private and not have to worry about performing in front of her parents' friends. As soon as they left to meet Colonel Blaik's dinner party, she put on a bathrobe, turned on the television, picked up the phone and ordered room service. When the knock at the door came, she hurried to her suitcase and threw on a dress, a bright red one that her mother and Aunt Marge had helped her pick out that day, then let the waiter in and watched him set up her food. After eating she did as her father said and set the tray outside.

Slam. Click. The heavy hotel door closed and there she stood, alone in the hall, without a key, locked out, wearing only a little red dress, no stockings, no shoes, stuck on the top floor of a big hotel. What now? She had to make her way down to the lobby for a new key, but she was at the age where the last thing she wanted was to be noticed, and she was too embarrassed to get in the elevator in her bare feet, so she took the stairs. "I went down flight after flight. I was crying. I was in a panic," she said later. "I finally got out of the stairwell at an exit on the mezzanine level and all I could do was look down and there was this huge crowd of people in the lobby and I hoped I would see somebody I knew. What were my chances?"

In the swirling sea of faces, she spotted her brother. He was talking to Paul Hornung. She started waving and shouting his name, "Vincent! Vincent!" He looked up, right at her, then turned his gaze. It appeared that he did not want to acknowledge her. He was a college man, hanging out with the Golden Boy, the coolest guy in the world. This was humiliating. Susan kept yelling and waving, until finally Vincent relented and walked up to the mezzanine and asked, "What's your problem?"

She tried to explain. "He was mad at me because I was always a little rat. But he goes down and gets me a key. I think he's going to take me back up. But he pushes the button, the elevator opens, he hands me the key and says, 'Go back to your room.' And I'm standing there in the elevator with these people and no shoes and the red dress and all the way up I'm saying to myself, Someday, I'm going to kill him. I get back into the room and get in bed and I'm a wreck. My parents finally come in. They always come in to kiss me good night. And my dad looked at me and knew that something was wrong. I started to cry and told him what happened and he thought it was funny, and I said, 'I don't think this is very funny, Daddy! I was stuck and I was trying to do what you told me to do!' He was laughing because knowing me he thought that would be par for the course that I'd lock myself out like that and walk down twenty-six flights of stairs. I thought he was going to get mad at me and he just laughed and laughed." Perhaps, if only for those few moments, his daughter's human foibles had settled the churning in Vince Lombardi's gut and provided a welcome relief from his life's burden of needing to be perfect and to win and win and win.

BY GOD it was thrilling to be part of this, even if the coach made the job uncomfortable at times, the *Milwaukee Sentinel*'s Bud Lea noted to himself as he looked around the bus carrying the proud Packers from the Hotel Manhattan up to Yankee Stadium that Sunday morning. Before Lombardi came to Green Bay, covering the football team "never amounted to a hill of beans." Now, the talent and sense of purpose the players exuded made Lea feel as though he were part of Patton's Third Army moving across Europe. Tex Maule had the same sensation. He was almost one of the boys now. "He loved the Packers, and we liked him because he knew something about football," Hornung said later of the *Sports Illustrated* writer. "He was always with us. We'd go out with him. Get him smashed." The team had seemed sleepy during the final few games of the season, but their last few practices had grown more intense day by day, and now, on the ride to the showdown in the Bronx, Maule sensed that the Packers "were imbued with a furious professional determination to prove that the licking they had given the Giants a year ago was no fluke."

Lombardi was in his pregame trance, saying nothing, looking straight ahead. Phil Bengtson sat in the next row, reviewing his plans for containing Yelberton Abraham Tittle, the bald poet who played quarterback for the Giants and had ripened wondrously in his old age, throwing for 3,224 yards and thirty-three touchdowns in his thirteenth professional season. Bengtson had watched the films so much he thought he had Yat figured out. Likes to throw on first down on the first series. If he calls a running play and it goes six yards or more, he'll come right back with it. If the last running play doesn't work, he'll throw twice. If it's long, it's to Del Shofner. Short to Frank Gifford or Joe Walton. Red Cochran, the offensive assistant, was heartened by what he saw out the window: bitterly cold winds whipping paper trash through the city streets. In his hotel room late the night before, he had listened to gale-force winds whistle through the midtown skyscraper canyon and said softly, "Blow, winds, blow. The worse it is, the better for us." The Giants were a passing team. The Packers had Taylor and Hornung. Cochran liked their chances. Jesse Whittenton, the defensive back, looked over at Maule and said, "It's cold as hell right now, but my hands are sweating!"

When the bus stopped and the players lumbered out, Jerry Kramer felt overwhelmed as he walked into Yankee Stadium to defend the championship. It was a "huge thrill" just to be there, he said later. "The House That Ruth Built, all the legends of the place. Playing against Katcavage and Robustelli and Huff. I'm going, 'Legends! What are you doing going out there against those guys?' " Replacing one legend with another is what he and his Packers were doing. That's what the Old Man said. Back in Green Bay earlier that week, Lombardi had installed a sign above the locker room door:

HOME OF THE GREEN BAY PACKERS

THE YANKEES OF FOOTBALL

But were the Yankees this beat up? The Horn sat at his cubicle, dragging on a Marlboro, his shoulder sore, his knee still tender. He was determined to run and pass and block, just couldn't kick. Jim Ringo was concerned about his right arm. A nerve problem made it feel numb, hard to snap the ball. He didn't want to hurt the team. Should he play? Lombardi came by and said, "We've come this far, Jim, you have to play," and that settled that. Ron Kramer, the Big Oof, as Vikings coach Norm Van Brocklin called him, was getting taped up again. It took the trainer twenty minutes:

white tape around the ankles, elastic around both knees, elastic around the back—a tight end mummy wrapped from head to ribs. And Jimmy Taylor was looking gaunt. It was a mystery then what was draining him of fifteen pounds in a few weeks. It would not be until many days later that doctors realized he had hepatitis. Taylor was wrapped and ready to go.

Red, white and blue bunting ringed the second deck of the stadium, filled to capacity with 64,892 frigid, breath-blowing fans, most of them rooting for Giant revenge. "OK, Y.A., Make Green Bay Pay," read one bedsheet banner. Inside Madison Square Garden earlier that week, New Yorkers at basketball and hockey games had been chanting, "Beat Green Bay! Beat Green Bay!"—and the call was picked up again now. News flashes on the transistor radios announced bumper-to-bumper traffic on the Jersey Turnpike, a mass of steel and humanity inching in the other direction, toward Philadelphia, beyond the blackout zone, where people could watch the game on television. Others mobbed a few enterprising motels in Westchester County that had erected tall antennas to bring in the game from a station in Hartford. NBC had the broadcast rights for the championship, and fielded a bipartisan announcing team of Ray Scott and Chris Schenkel for the play-by-play. But CBS, which broadcast the Giants during the year, held jealously to its booth, forcing Scott and Schenkel to work in an open photography platform down the right-field line. Sportswriters filed into the press box. Red Smith gazed around the stadium to conjure the images that might evoke the scene. When the teams came out for warmups, it was clear that this game would be decided by the basic elements.

Earth and air, each in harshest form. Hornung ran a practice sprint and pronounced the field "atrocious." It was hard, frozen in large swatches, with holes and ruts everywhere. "Better suited to ice hockey than football," wrote Maule. When you fell, Ron Kramer noticed, there were sharp pieces of dirt that cut like glass. Vincent, the college fullback, examined the field with his sidelines pass and thought it would be "like playing in a parking lot." Bart Starr likened it to "a slag pile." The Packers and Giants both came out in cleatless, ripple-soled football shoes, not unlike the ones Lombardi always wore at games, though his had blinding white laces. Frank Gifford alone chose sneakers. The wind was as unforgiving as the field. During warmups Tittle threw one pass that was pushed to the ground after five yards and another that soared and flailed up and away toward the first row of stands. "We just lost our passing game," an assistant lamented to Allie Sherman, the Giants head coach. Red Smith devoted much of his column to meteorology. "Polar gales clawed topseed off the barren playground and whipped it into whirlwinds about the great concrete chasm of Yankee Stadium," he wrote. "The winds snatched up tattered newspapers, more newspapers than people can find in all New York these days, and flung the shreds aloft where they danced and swirled in a Shubert blizzard. . . ."

Once, when all the Packers arose from their wooden bench, it was blown over and onto the field. The temperature at game time was 18 degrees and dropping. This was before the era of wind chill factors, but the winds were 25 to 40 miles per hour, and the athletes remembered it as the single coldest game they had ever played in—colder even, many Packers insisted, than a more famous game five years later in subzero Green Bay. So cold that Lombardi gave up his lucky camel's hair coat for a thick-lined winter parka. Some of the fiercest scrums were around the heating drums on the sidelines. "There'd be flames shooting out and we'd all be fighting to get closest to them," said Gary Knafelc. Lombardi had invited Tom Brown, a talented athlete from Maryland whom he had just selected in the second round of the college draft, to join the Packers on the sidelines for the game. An unwise invitation, it turned out. As Brown shivered and looked around at the frigid and foreboding scene, he decided then and there to skip football and sign a contract to play baseball, the summer game, for the Washington Senators.

Up in the auxiliary press box, an uncovered ledge on the second deck, Red Cochran lost control of his frosted writing hand and was unable to chart the game. Ray Scott, in his makeshift broadcast booth nearby, with his spotting boards resting on his quaking knees, found his face stiffening minute by minute. "We ended up taalllkking . . . liiiike . . . thiiis," he said later. "For years afterward people accused me of being drunk." He was warmed by a few swigs of brandy from fellow announcer Bud Palmer's flask, but his paper cup of coffee froze when he poured in the liquor.

There were eight extra cameras at the game that day, filming not for television but for the league to use in publicity game films. The contract for the job had been won by Blair Motion Pictures Inc., a small outfit in suburban Philadelphia owned by Ed Sabol, who had never before shot a professional game. When Sabol got the job, he called his son Steve, who was then in college, and said, "I just bought the film rights and I can see from your grades that all you've been doing is going to movies and playing football and that makes you uniquely qualified for this job." Steve signed on as assistant producer, launching a family partnership that would later become known as NFL Films, an enterprise that more than any other would be responsible for creating the films and television shows that shaped the new mythology of professional football for the rest of the century. Ed Sabol's start was inauspicious enough. He was so nervous before the game that he spent most of the next two hours in the restroom.

Willie Wood kicked off for the Packers. He had the strongest leg, and Lombardi liked to have him back there as a sure-tackling last resort in case the returner broke clear. Wood placed the ball on a tee, and it blew off twice. Finally, he called a teammate over to hold the ball, and the game began.

The Packers realized immediately that Tittle would keep passing despite the conditions, but he could only pass short. The long ball, his specialty, would dip and float aimlessly in the wind. He ended up throwing forty-one passes, but none near the end zone. Lombardi scrapped his surprise aerial attack plan and put the game in the hands of Taylor and Hornung and his defense, led by Ray Nitschke, who recovered two fumbles, forced an interception with a blitz on Tittle and would have had an interception of his own if his hands had not been so cold. Taylor gained eighty-five yards running the ball thirty-one times, almost every effort ending with a smack and thud and sprawling legs, three Giants piling on, Sam Huff, the aggressive middle linebacker, occasionally giving Taylor an extra push into the icy turf or knee in the groin and telling Taylor that he stunk.

"Did everything I could to that sonofabitch," Huff said later. And Taylor just looked at him and spit and said, "That your best shot?" Taylor was never considered the brightest Packer—Dick Schaap had once written of him in a *Saturday Evening Post* article: "Jimmy Taylor, the great fullback of the Green Bay Packers, spent four years in college and emerged unscarred by education"—and some of his teammates found him prickly off the field, but when it counted, in games like this, they were all thankful that he was on their team.

It is part of football tradition that gridiron violence in the retelling takes on the form of comedy more often than of tragedy. And so it was with the defining story of that game, apocryphal or not, when Taylor groaned at the bottom of a pile and saw an exposed calf and bit it and Giant tackle Dick Modzelewski screamed "Ow!" and Taylor looked up and said, "Sorry, Mo, I thought you were Sam." But it was not funny then. In the first quarter, Taylor was smacked in the helmet by Huff and cut his elbow and bit his tongue and was swallowing blood for the rest of the half. Dr. Eugene Brusky sewed him up at the break. His teammates could hear his moans of pain, stitch by stitch, as they sat in the locker room silent and freezing, rubbing their bodies trying to get warm, before heading out for the second half. "You wondered if he'd be ready to go in the second half and be the football player he was in the first half," recalled Nitschke. Taylor did play, and he played just as hard, pushed on by Lombardi. He later explained his gutty performance by saying you never know until you are faced with it how much pain you can endure, how much effort you have left, and then the coach steps in and pushes you even beyond that point. He never held it against Lombardi, though: the push made the difference.

Before a game, at halftime and after a game, his players thought of Lombardi as a football genius. He always seemed able to anticipate what the other team was going to do. Although his game plans seemed simple, it was because of the dozens of plays that he had eliminated—following Blaik's dictum of discarding the immaterial—to get to the fifteen or twenty that he was certain would work. But once the game started, the joke on the team was that Lombardi was the most useless guy on the sideline. Starr called the plays for the offense. Bengtson called them for the defense. Lombardi never wore a headset. Red Cochran, the offensive coach in the press box, was afraid to call down to Lombardi for fear he would snap at him on the phone. "All Lombardi would do," said Gary Knafelc, "was stand there and holler. Hornung thought his coach "wasn't worth a crap during the game. He was an observer. A kibbitzer. All you'd hear is, 'What the hell's goin' on out there?' " He was always on the go, striding up and down the sideline, watching the down markers, yapping away at the officials, correcting every call. The game itself was the superficial part of coaching for Lombardi. He had already done his work getting his team prepared.

This title game in New York drew on all the lessons he had learned from the Jesuits and Colonel Blaik: simplicity, subsuming individual desire for the needs of the group, second effort, enduring pain as a means to an end, paying the price. The Giants played ferociously and the Packers held on with their will: Ringo playing through the numbness in his arm, Whittenton with his rib cage bruised in the first quarter, Jordan hobbling on a sprained ankle, Taylor bleeding. They lost Willie Wood in the third quarter when he was ejected for bumping a referee—unintentionally, the game films indicate—while protesting a pass interference call. Hornung, his knee banged again, limped from the lineup soon thereafter.

Their kicking situation was a mess. Boyd Dowler could not punt, so Lombardi told Max McGee to return to his old job. "Jesus Christ, thanks a lot, Coach!" he muttered to himself. The winds made punting a horrible chore, as McGee later described his predicament. "You either had to lay the ball on your foot or throw it hard at your foot. If you dropped it to your foot like you normally did, the wind would blow it off path." He never had a punt blocked in his life until the third quarter of that game. The Packers were ahead 10 to 0 when McGee stood at his end zone and took the snap. Usually, he would look to see if someone was coming, but this time he stared down at his foot as he threw the ball at his shoe and began his kicking motion . . . and there was Erich Barnes, the swift Giants defensive back, on top of him, thump, and the ball was rolling on the hard parking lot of a playing field toward the end zone and Jim Collier was falling on it for a touchdown.

It was the lone New York score, less than the output of Green Bay's unorthodox scoring machine, Jerry Kramer, the placekicking right guard. Since Hornung's bad knee forced him to stop kicking after the fifth game of the year, Kramer had substituted for him with equal parts efficiency and good humor. He had missed only one extra point and two field goals during the last nine games of the season, though every kick was an adventure. He was a lock-legged straight-ahead kicker, as they all were in that era, but Kramer's signature was that he had no follow-through with his right leg. His teammates did a locker room routine—"Sports quiz! Who's this? Boink." That was the description of Kramer's kick. Boink. He boinked three field goals and one extra point against the Giants. "I was a little nervous about kicking in Yankee Stadium," Kramer said later. "What you do when kicking is keep your head down. The first one, when I looked up, it looked like the ball was outside the goalposts, yet the official was going like this [good], and I was saying, 'What the . . . what did. . . ?' and Bart Starr [the holder] said, 'Shut up and get off the field.' "

The last boink came from thirty yards out with less than two minutes left in the game. It made the score 16 to 7, clinching the win. As Kramer gazed in stunned disbelief at his glorious achievement, the pigskin knuckle-balling through the damp air up and over the crossbar and through the uprights, his partner at guard, Fuzzy Thurston, wrapped him in a bear hug, and the two big lugs, No. 64 and No. 63, four-legged it off the field in a giddy embrace, Kramer still shaking his head as he reached the sidelines and vanished in a huddle of backslapping Packers.

THE MOOD in the locker room after the victory had a sharp edge. Lombardi was Mr. High-Low: Hugging Jimmy and Ray and Jerry; then snarling at a reporter for asking about the violence of the game, then taking Pete Rozelle into a corner and yelling at him briefly (the subject no one could remember—the Friday press conference snafu? the Giants' dirty play?), then not recognizing one of his old New Jersey friends and booting him from the locker room, then smiling again in the embrace of his gritty players.

The press upset him because they were asking questions that had nothing to do with what he was feeling. He could not fully express it himself yet. It would take a few days before he could address a New Year's letter to his players and their wives. He would tell them that the victory in the championship game "was particularly pleasing" because of his old connections with New York and the "very trying conditions" the team had endured. The Giants had tried to intimidate them physically, but had failed because "in the final analysis, we were mentally tougher than they were and that same mental toughness made them crack. Character is the perfectly disciplined will, and you are men of character." In his letter he would also reflect on the burden of success. "I believe you realize now that success is much more difficult to live with than failure. I don't think anyone realizes, except ourselves, the obstacles we had to face week after week." And he would sign off with the motto he had learned from General MacArthur. "Best wishes to you both and remember, 'There is no substitute for victory.' "

Back to the locker room. The official who had ejected Willie Wood came in and said that he might have reacted too abruptly, maybe it was an accident. Ray Scott made his way through the room, deicing from his frosty broadcast perch. He was shocked to see Taylor's stripped body—"all black and blue and purple and yellow." Nitschke was dressed. With his turtleneck sweater and sport coat and bald head and horn-rimmed glasses, the ravaging middle linebacker known as Wildman departed in the professorial disguise that made it possible for him—what a different world it was then—to be named the game's most valuable player and yet appear on the television quiz show *What's My Line?* afterwards and not immediately be recognized by the panelists.

Hornung said he had never seen "a team up so high" as the Giants were that day. "Man, that first series of plays, that leather was really poppin'," he said. "They were really up. We just had a better football team, that's all." Ed Sabol heard someone in the locker room mutter, "Boy, this is the longest day I've ever played football." Sabol had just seen the war movie by that name, and the phrase clicked. He had the title for the championship film. "We're going to call this 'Pro Football's Longest Day,' " he told his son Steve. (After six weeks of editing, they premiered it at Toots Shor's on West Fifty-second Street, setting up a projector amid the cocktail tables—there was no cable sports network then to run it, not even a half-hour pregame show. The premiere viewing was interrupted when a waiter tripped over the cord and knocked the projector from its stand.

Ken Kavanaugh, a Giants assistant who had worked alongside Lombardi during his New York days, eventually left his bone-tired colleagues and went over to congratulate the winners. As he was walking underneath the stadium, he ran into Marie and Susan, who were waiting outside the visitors' dressing room. Susan had endured another rough day. Marie by habit never left her seat, but at halftime she had retreated under the stands to escape the bitter wind. Susan asked to use the ladies' room, but got lost on her way out and wandered through the stadium until she found her mother. Now they were waiting for Lombardi. Kavanaugh went inside. The place was cleared out. Where's Green Bay? he asked an attendant. Gone. On the way to the airport. "I had the coach's wife and she was supposed to be with him," Kavanaugh said later. "Vince had just gone off and forgot about her. Just flat forgot." Marie and Susan took a cab and arrived in plenty of time, the flight delayed anyway by the weather.

The winds were still blowing strong, but as Paul Hornung said, "We were young and happy and we'd had a few bottles of champagne and we wanted to get out of there, and we did." And that was it—the end of something. They rolled down the long runway, champagne corks popping, the plane shaking and bumping and rising uneasily and dipping and rising again into the whirling winter dusk, and they were headed home to Green Bay, Lombardi and his family and his Packers, champions once more, best ever, and none of them knew at that moment how much could be lost so soon, a president and a Golden Boy and even a way of life. Perhaps the past was not so innocent, but it seemed that way once it was gone, and it was gone the moment that plane left the ground.

19

Foot
of the Cross

NOT LONG AFTER the Packers returned to Green Bay with their second consecutive NFL championship, Max McGee was contacted by investigators and asked to report to their Chicago office for questioning. He had a notion about the general subject. Rumors had been spreading for months, and bits of the story were now breaking in the press in these first days of 1963. Pete Rozelle had brought in a team of sixteen former FBI agents to investigate reports that some players had associated with gamblers and bet on games. The same leads were being pursued by federal gumshoes working for Senator John McClellan's investigations subcommittee. Were games being thrown? Were players missing tackles or fumbling the ball on purpose to meet point spreads? Were they betting against their own teams? Troubling questions. But of the few names mentioned in accounts so far, McGee's had not been among them, and no Packers at all. He wondered, Why the hell do they want me?

Then it hit him. *The punt!* He had never had a punt blocked in his career until the third quarter of the Giants game. "We're ahead ten to nothing and the betting line is six and a half and I get one blocked and it goes under the point spread. Maybe they think I had something to do with it." It was a stretch to make that case, of course. The punt was blocked because Erich Barnes was fast and had a clear path to the ball and McGee had been so concerned about the wind that he was not looking at the rush. And Jerry Kramer's final field goal pushed the score above the point spread anyway. But that is what McGee decided the investigators wanted to quiz him about, and even though the punt was a hapless flub he went into the meeting with some measure of trepidation. As he said later, "Somebody says FBI and it kind of scares the shit out of you."

As it turned out, they were not interested in the blocked punt at all, nor anything specifically involving McGee. They only asked him questions about Paul Hornung: what telephone calls Hornung got, when the calls came, what the conversations were about. They wanted to talk to McGee because he was Hornung's roommate. The session was quick, tense, but not hostile. "They already had Paul on tape," McGee said. He told them little, and nothing that they did not already know.

Hornung's other roommate, Ron Kramer, was interviewed by investigators in Detroit, who ushered suspected players in and out of interrogation rooms at a motel near the Willow Run Airport. They asked him about a Las Vegas bettor named Barney Shapiro, and Kramer said, "Yeah, I know him, what about it?" And little more. Kramer had grown up in East Detroit. He knew a lot of characters whom law enforcement officials might call unsavory. "I came from this life," Kramer said later. "I learned how to say, 'I don't know.' Even if I do know. 'I don't know.' If they asked something, I'd say, 'Why do you want to know this?' I'm not some kid on a street corner. You tell me why you want to know this and I'll tell you. But if you don't have any explanation for your question, I ain't telling you. I had some very dear friends who were the best lawyers in town. They said, 'Tell the truth, but don't add anything to it.' As far as I was concerned, I didn't do anything."

The investigation seemed petty and political to Kramer. Truth be told, the guys had placed a few bets on football, but they had wagered more money on one race at the Kentucky Derby than they had on any game. And almost everybody bet, he believed, one way or another. "What about the owners? Carroll Rosenbloom of the Colts never bet? Wasn't the Maras' old man a bookie?" Even the Coach liked gambling, in his own way. Not on football, but Lombardi enjoyed the racetracks and he went to the gambling parlors in Hot Springs, Arkansas, and put in his five-dollar ante for the cribbage tournament at training camp every summer and exchanged cash in gin games at the country club.

The Big Oof did not intend to take the rap, and he urged Hornung not to, either. "I said, 'Horn, I don't know what you're going to do.' It wasn't like he was betting four million dollars and throwing a game. I told him, 'Jesus Christ! Don't say nothin'! Don't say nothin'!' "

But Hornung did say something. "Why he did, I don't know," Kramer said later. "I guess because he's an honorable man."

THE STORY of how Paul Hornung reached this tenuous position began six years earlier, at the end of his senior season at Notre Dame. The Golden Boy was in San Francisco to play in one of the annual showcase bowls for future pros, the East-West Shrine Game. At dinner one night on the coast, he was introduced to Bernard "Barney" Shapiro, a big, suave man in his early thirties. They became "fast friends" that week, and saw each other every year thereafter when the Packers went to San Francisco on their December swing. Shapiro split his time between San Francisco and Las Vegas, where he owned United Coin Machine, a pinball and slot company. He had a stake in a Vegas hotel and made large profits from the patent on a blackjack slot. He often encouraged Hornung to go into real estate with him, but Hornung never did. Instead, Shapiro used Hornung for his betting. Once or twice a week during the football season, he would place a call to the house on the west side of Green Bay for a chat with the star halfback.

One of his questions was always the same: *How do you think the Packers will do this week?* There was no deception in the query and Shapiro was breaking no laws. He wanted to know how he should place his legal bets. "I knew he bet and he knew I knew," Hornung said later. "I would tell Barney to bet on us, what the hell." Perhaps it was inside information, but Hornung did not think of it that way. The Packers were so good that they consistently beat the point spread. The nature of their telephone conversations had changed back in 1959, coincidentally Lombardi's first year in Green Bay. Along with making recommendations to Shapiro, Hornung began asking the gambler to place bets for him. Barney became his betting angel. He'd say, "Barney, bet me three hundred dollars" or "Barney, bet me five hundred." His first bet was on an exhibition game, and from then on he bet on college and pro games, often on the Packers. "Not once did I ever bet against us," he said. "But if I chose not to place a bet on us one week, there was a reason why. Just too tough a game or something."

Hornung had grown up around gambling and bettors. In Louisville, home of Churchill Downs and its Kentucky Derby, the local customs and idioms were shaped by the culture of betting. Even decades after the 1963 investigation, Hornung would walk into a lunchroom on Walnut Street and casually introduce an out-of-town visitor to his bookie. But if betting was in his blood, football was his livelihood, and he understood then that he was living dangerously, even though he was using Shapiro, not a bookie, to place his bets, and doing it in Las Vegas, where betting was legal. The standard NFL player contract specifically prohibited betting on league games, with penalty of suspension. Hornung also seemed to appreciate the larger dangers of betting. As he later acknowledged, there were times when he was on the field late in Packers games and would consciously "think about the action"— meaning the point spread and whether it had been met. "I'd know we weren't leading by enough points to make my bet a winner." There was a possibility in that situation that he might try something foolish to fatten the margin; or that through losing bets he could fall into debt and do something reckless. Nothing of either sort happened, by all accounts, but Hornung was aware of how he could have been made vulnerable.

Late in the summer of 1962, Commissioner Rozelle toured the league to warn each team that betting was strictly forbidden. He met with the Packers at the dining room of the Pfister Hotel in Milwaukee on the eve of a preseason game at County Stadium. There would be severe penalties for anyone caught gambling, Rozelle said that day. The severest penalty was banishment from the sport. Hornung left the meeting saying to himself, I've placed my last bet. Not that he thought betting was wrong, but it "was silly to risk a pro career for it."

Rozelle in fact had been receiving reports on the Golden Boy's behavior since the previous spring, and though he did not have proof yet, he was concerned enough to look into them. Hornung had not been one of the players mentioned during early press accounts, but he was always at the center of the investigation. Lombardi appeared mildly concerned, but not obsessed with the issue. He stopped visiting a restaurant in Green Bay that he feared might have gambling connections and placed it off limits to his players. He asked Hornung once whether he bet, and Hornung strongly denied that he did. Lombardi maintained his normal policy of believing what his players told him unless presented with incontrovertible proof to the contrary. His Packers were professionals, winners, men of character, and Paul was his boy.

After the championship game Hornung was in Los Angeles on off-season business when Rozelle reached him and summoned him to New York. It was what Hornung would call "a real bullshit clandestine operation"—meaning that the league tried to house him in a seedy hotel under an alias the night before he was to be questioned. Hornung barely played along. He left the flophouse immediately, checked into the Plaza Hotel, and then went over to Toots Shor's saloon and had dinner with Shor and Frank Gifford and "got completely smashed." The next morning he was taken to an office where Rozelle's agents had set up a lie detector test. It appeared obvious to Hornung that they knew what he had been doing. He suspected that they had wiretapped his phone when he was living with McGee and Kramer. At least the conversations weren't dull, he joked. But he told Rozelle he did not want to take the lie detector test.

"I said to Pete, 'Let me tell you something, I'm not the only sumbitch that's gambling. But I'll never say that publicly, because that's none of my business. But I know who has bet. I know the guys. Forget the lie detector test. I'm not answering any questions about anybody else.' I said to Pete, 'I'll be honest with you. You know I did bet. I did. I admit it. That's all the farther I'm going.'" If Rozelle pushed him further, Hornung said, he might go down to Washington and appear before the McClellan subcommittee. "'If we go down to Washington your ass is in trouble if I talk about how many guys I know who are betting. Don't have me go to Washington and raise my right hand.'" He was bluffing, but Rozelle agreed he did not want that, and urged

Hornung to keep their meeting confidential. "I'm going to have to make a decision on this and get back to you," Rozelle said. "I want you to swear that you won't tell a soul."

At the end of January, at the Kenilworth Hotel in Bal Harbour, Florida, Rozelle convened a meeting of the NFL executive committee. Owners only—Lombardi was excluded, Olejniczak represented the Packers. According to minutes of the meeting, Rozelle announced that he was investigating several players for betting on games, that the investigation "had been underway for some time," and that he would give no publicity to it until he had concluded what he considered an adequate investigation. He said it was not his intention to "minimize or in any way 'whitewash' the cases." He said that he had enlisted a team of former FBI agents and was reserving the right to request lie detector tests. And he chastised some owners for being "too liberal" in not laying down "sensible and mature" rules governing the private lives of their players.

Hornung was home in Louisville then, staying with his mother, enduring the most anxious period of his life. Every phone call jangled his nerves as he awaited word from Rozelle. His nervous behavior made his mother suspicious, so he told her what had happened, and she began offering special novenas for her only son at church every morning. He returned to Green Bay a few times to play on the Packers' winter basketball team. Bob Skoronski remembered that after one game Hornung said his ambition for 1963 was to make the comeback of the year. It was a curious statement, Skoronski thought, but maybe Hornung meant coming back from his knee injury. Milton Gross, a sportswriter for the NEA syndicate, spent a half hour with Hornung late that winter and brought up the rumors of gambling. Hornung confided to him that Rozelle "had him on the griddle," but as he related the story to Gross, he had merely had a telephone conversation with the commissioner, nothing more, and he made it sound like a trifling matter, no more troublesome than deciding what shirt to wear on a date that night.

On the first of April, the league office sent out a bulletin instructing each team to have "No Gambling" signs placed in their dressing rooms at training camp. That same week Rozelle invited Lombardi to his office in New York. They met on April 6 and Rozelle showed him the findings of his investigation, including Hornung's signed statement. Lombardi was shocked. He was "outraged, saddened, disillusioned." He was upset with Hornung in every way: that Paul had been foolish enough to bet on games, that he had lied about it when Lombardi first asked him, and that he had not later told the coach about his confession to Rozelle. The evidence was overwhelming. When Rozelle stated that he believed his only choice was to suspend Hornung indefinitely, Lombardi responded: "You've got to do what you've got to do." Then the two men left the office and "wandered around" Manhattan until one in the morning, commiserating. "I warned him time after time not to bet," Lombardi kept saying. "How could he look me in the eye and keep lying?"

Life was circling back on Lombardi again. The Packers had reached the top through talent and diligence. They had become the definition of first-class professionalism—and now this. The cadets of West Point were in the same position twelve years earlier, the very best, the model of collegiate prowess and class, and then it all collapsed in a cribbing scandal. A bewildered father asks his son, How could you? It was the question Colonel Blaik had asked his son Bob when the mess broke at West Point and the football team was about to be expelled, and now Lombardi was asking it of his boy Paul. *How could he?* Why did some of the Fordham Rams play illegally in semipro contests that autumn of 1936 and come back lame for the crucial NYU game and thus ruin the team's chances of going to the Rose Bowl? Why did the cadets pass the poop and destroy one of the finest squads Red Blaik had ever built? Why did Paul Hornung place bets on the Packers and endanger Lombardi's awesome team? The answers are as complex and varying as human nature itself: Hubris. A sense of invincibility. Reckless youth. Thrill of winning. Peer pressure. Boredom. Temptation.

AS OFTEN HAPPENS with people awaiting painful news, Hornung was hoping that the telephone would never ring. But the call he dreaded was inevitable, and it came at last on the morning of April 17. On the line from New York, Rozelle informed him that he was being indefinitely suspended. The commissioner said it was "the hardest decision" he would ever have to make. There was more punishment to be meted out that day. Hours later Rozelle told the press that his investigators had conducted fifty-two interviews "relating to individuals connected with eight clubs." Along with Hornung, he was also indefinitely suspending Alex Karras, the obstreperous tackle for Detroit, for placing several bets over the years, and fining five other Lions $2,000 each for betting on the 1962 title game. The Detroit club was also fined $2,000 for ignoring reports of gambling by players.

The suspension of Hornung and Karras, two of the league's premier players, was dramatic, but Rozelle seemed relieved that it was not worse. "There is no evidence that any NFL player has given less than his best in playing any game," he said. "There is no evidence that any player has ever bet against his own team. There is no evidence that any NFL player has sold information to gamblers. There is clear evidence that some NFL players knowingly carried on undesirable associations which in some instances led to their betting on their own team to win and/or other National Football League games."

Hornung was on the seventh hole at Audubon Country Club that afternoon when a swarm of reporters and photographers arrived at the clubhouse asking for his response to Rozelle's announcement. Karras had reacted immediately, asserting that he had done nothing wrong and was not guilty of anything. Hornung retreated to the club's locker room and drafted a statement. He knew many other players who bet on games. But that's life, he said to himself. If they got away with it, fine. Others could argue that he was being made a scapegoat because he was the Golden Boy, but he did not feel that way himself. He had gained far more as the Golden Boy than he had lost over the years. As he once put it, he felt as though he had lived "a whole life on scholarship." Now he felt terrible, but he knew that he had erred. There was no question about right and wrong: It was there in the contract, in black and white. No betting on NFL games. Hornung emerged with red, watery eyes and offered words of contrition. "I made a terrible mistake. I realize that now. I am truly sorry. What else is there to say?"

The story was on the front page of every major newspaper in the country, jolting much of the sporting world. Senator McClellan praised Rozelle for "taking effective action to clean up conditions in professional football." Hornung's teammates reacted with words of support. Skoronski said that the Horn "had great heart" and that the Packers all respected him. "We all thought the world of Paul," added Jerry Kramer. "You hate to see a good guy like him get fouled up." Fans in Green Bay responded as though there had been a death in the family. John Holzer, a local pharmacist, wore a black armband and said of Hornung's relationship with Barney Shapiro: "Anyone who watches practice could pass along information as Hornung did. Just about everybody in the United States gambles. He makes more money. His five hundred dollar bet is like a dime bet for most of us."

Dick Schaap, the New York sportswriter who had spent considerable time hanging out with Hornung and his Packer pals in 1961, was among those not surprised by the news. The gambling story, Schaap wrote in *Sport* magazine, evoked the Golden Boy as he really was—not perfect but endearing and in no way malicious. "To anyone who knows Paul Hornung, who knows his taste for the grand gesture and his thirst for the sweet life, the size of his bets could have been the only legitimate shock," Schaap wrote. "Within Hornung's circle, the fact that he had gambled was surely not news; that he had been caught—and suspended—was hardly startling. Paul Hornung is many things, not all of which would qualify him for sainthood, but the one thing he has never been, and probably never will be, is sneaky." Schaap revealed that Hornung was so trusting that he once placed a football bet in front of writers. "I saw him back the Packers, and when his team won by more than the point spread, he earned $100." Schaap was reporting the incident now only to "help set in perspective" the relatively benign nature of what Hornung had done. He said that he could have written about it earlier, and gained notice for a scoop, but chose not to because it would have violated "the trust and friendship [Hornung] thrusts upon so many people."

The essential relationship threatened by the scandal was not that of the

Golden Boy and the press, but of the prodigal son and his father-figure coach. Warned by Rozelle that the announcement was coming, Lombardi, like Hornung, had fled to the sanctuary of a golf course. Marie took the flood of calls at Sunset Circle and said she was not sure where he went. Ockie Krueger finally tracked him down at Oneida. Lombardi's public statements later that day were utterly without sentiment. The indefinite suspension, he said, was fully warranted and necessary. "One, it will preserve public confidence in this league. And two, it will keep things like this from getting more serious." As for Hornung's future, he added: "He's through for now. We won't look ahead to the future. Football is too risky to look ahead that far." When pressed further, Lombardi finally said that Hornung's return depended on two factors—how the Packers did without him and whether his teammates forgave him.

It was only in private that Lombardi revealed how devastated he was by Hornung's fall. He told Rozelle that he wanted to quit, and said the same thing to Marie and many of his friends, who talked him out of it. "It hurt the Old Man more than anything that happened to him in Green Bay," said Jack Koeppler, his golfing buddy. To Ray Scott, the Packers broadcaster, Lombardi lamented, "You know, Coach, I think he thought he was pulling something on the Old Man." He expanded on that theme in a discussion with Tim Cohane. "Hornung bet for the thrill of it," he concluded. "The thrill lay in the fact that it was forbidden. I was fond of Paul and I'm sure he was fond of me. Yet he still liked to feel that there was something he could put over on me." Lombardi accepted the suspension, he believed in rules and obedience to authority, but still he wished that Hornung had confided in him earlier, especially after he had confessed to Rozelle. Colonel Blaik had always thought that he could have resolved the cribbing scandal without losing his players if only they had come to him earlier, and now Lombardi was thinking the same about Hornung.

"I wish you would have told me," he said to Hornung when they first discussed the matter by telephone. "You should have told me. I think I could have rectified it." This was probably wishful thinking; there was little Lombardi could have done. Maybe it was a way of redirecting his distress, or of absolving himself of responsibility for his player's actions. In any case, Hornung certainly felt the sting of Lombardi's anger. He also finished his first painful discussion with the coach sensing that he might work his way back into grace. "You stay at the foot of the cross," Lombardi told him, using the idiom of their shared Catholicism. "I don't want to see you go to the racetrack. I don't want to hear about you going to the Derby. I don't want to hear about you doing anything. Keep your nose clean and I'll do my best to get you back. But, mister, stay at the foot of the cross."

20

Coming in Second

Only two of Harry Lombardi's three sons cared about football. Vince had become the dominant symbol of the NFL by 1963. Little Joe, once an all-county guard at St. Cecilia, had long since stopped playing, but worked at the edges of the game as a regional salesman for a sporting goods company. Harold, the middle brother, never played football, considered it a waste of time to watch on television, and on the rare occasions that he attended games did so primarily to visit with his sister-in-law Marie when the Packers were playing at Kezar Stadium in San Francisco. It had been more than a decade since Harold had left the family compound in Englewood and given up teaching for a new life on the West Coast. He had intended to study for a doctorate at Stanford, but dropped that plan and took a job as an underwriter for Northwestern National insurance company.

Harold looked much like his brother Vince, though heavier, and shared his perfectionism and religious devotion, but at heart he was an artist. Opera, not football, was his passion. He much preferred the stirring world of Richard Wagner's *Lohengrin* and *Der Ring des Nibelungen* to the vision of Fuzzy and Jerry pulling out on the sweep or Ray Nitschke crunching another blocker in the nutcracker drill. For many years after he left Englewood, his parents pestered him with the same question each time they spoke on the phone: Harold, when are you going to get married? After years of dodging the question, he decided to write a letter providing the answer and the reason for it. The words were not so direct, but the message was this: He would never get married because he was a homosexual. From the moment he put the letter in the mail, Harold wondered what would happen next. Would

Harry and Matty disown him? "I was very nervous waiting for a response," he said. His father was not a letter writer, but one day Harold picked up his mail and there was the envelope from Englewood, and his father's handwritten note inside, and a line that he would never forget: "I don't care. You are my son."

During his years in San Francisco, Harold lived on Ashbury Street on a block that later would become the epicenter of the counterculture, but he was no flower child. Since the days when he and Marie had attended an "America First" rally at Madison Square Garden, he shared Marie's Republican politics. He spent his days examining applications for automobile and casualty insurance, checking credit reports, working out math tables for rating and pricing, and drafting mock-ups of policies for the secretary to type. He found the work interesting and he excelled in it, and at the start of 1963 the company promoted him to a new job at their larger office in Milwaukee.

He moved to an apartment on North Prospect Avenue one block from Lake Michigan and near the Northwestern office, to which he walked. One consolation for leaving San Francisco was the chance to see his brother's family in Green Bay. He visited Sunset Circle for holidays and many home games, largely because he enjoyed being around Marie, whom he regarded as "the greatest woman" he had met in his life. His brother tended to be a one-track conversationalist, all football, but he was amazed to discover the transformation in Marie since their New Jersey days. "At Fordham and St. Cecilia she sat in the background surrounded by all these people talking football," he remembered. "Then she decided she was going to get in the middle of it and she learned football, and now she was able to compete with anyone." The subject of Harold's lifestyle was not discussed when he was with Vince. "I never said, he never asked, sort of like the military," Harold reflected decades later. "I don't know if Vince knew, to tell the truth. He was my brother."

Vince did know that Harold was gay, and here was an area where the coach showed an open mind, according to friends and family. He ignored Catholic teaching against homosexuality and instead considered gays another group deserving respect, like blacks and American Indians, and Italians. In later years he would have players who were gay, and quietly root for them at training camp, hoping they could show they were good enough to make his team.

If there was any awkwardness in the relationship between Vince and Harold, it was because of Vince's fame and its ripple effects. As an expert underwriter, Harold had every reason to believe that he was promoted to Milwaukee because of the superior quality of his work. But from the moment he started at the home office, it was impossible for him not to be aware also of the company's ulterior motive. He was assigned a desk in the middle of the second floor, the first person a visitor saw coming off the elevator. Other underwriters worked in another part of the building. "There was nothing around me. I had this great big space and this great big desk and I was all alone," Harold said later. "And whoever came in the building was escorted right to me and was told, 'This is Vince Lombardi's brother!' "

To see and perhaps shake hands with Vince Lombardi's brother was regarded as a memorable event for businessmen—another indication of how the coach had become larger-than-life by 1963. Marie by then had developed the habit of walking behind him in airports to watch people stare as he strutted by. He had attained such godly status that Dave Robinson, the Packers' first-round draft choice that year, a marvelous two-way end and future linebacker from Penn State, was shocked the first time he visited Green Bay and laid eyes on his new boss. "My first impression of Lombardi was that he was smaller than I thought he should be," Robinson said later. "I had heard that he was a guard on the Seven Blocks of Granite. I thought I would see a guard. Instead I shake hands with this little squatty dude. I said to myself, What is this? He's kind of short to be Lombardi. You envision a big man ranting and raving."

Bigness is relative in all things. Robinson thought he had signed a huge contract to play for the Packers, and perhaps he had by the standards of the day. He had been the beneficiary of a bidding war between the Packers and San Diego Chargers of the AFL. The new league would have loved nothing more than to have stolen the first-round pick of the world-champion Packers. But San Diego dropped out when the asking price reached $38,000, and there was talk that the Chargers would sell Robinson's draft rights to the Buffalo Bills. Robinson's wife had been intrigued by the prospect of living in the warm California sun, but with the choice narrowed to Green Bay or Buffalo, the sun was no longer a factor, and Robinson quickly signed with the Packers. He agreed to a two-year $45,000 package, including a $15,000 bonus and the use of a new Bonneville convertible from Lombardi's car dealer friend, Jake Stathas of Brown County Motors.

A big deal, or so it seemed—so lucrative that Lombardi felt compelled to give Ray Nitschke a raise to match it. Pete Rozelle might have been hell-bent on making the league rich, and the war with the AFL was increasing the cost of top draft choices, but the true salary explosion for football players remained a few years distant. Football was still regarded as a part-time job in 1963, so much so that every player on the Green Bay roster found the off-season employment that he needed to supplement his football income. Willie Davis was a sales representative for Schlitz Brewing Company. Willie Wood taught at a junior high in the District of Columbia. Bob Skoronski was in sales for Josten, the jewelry company that designed the championship rings. Bart Starr managed the Edlo Arcade in Green Bay. Jesse Whittenton ran the King's X restaurant and bar in Green Bay. Fuzzy Thurston had just opened the Left Guard Steak House in Menasha. And Hawg Hanner worked on the cotton crop control program for the U.S. Department of Agriculture in Arkansas. Max McGee was hired by T. E. Mercer Trucking Company in Fort Worth.

MCGEE WAS COMING BACK, but not his buddy. Dad Braisher hung No. 5 above Hornung's old locker every day, but old Goat Shoulders would not slip the jersey on that year. How much would the Packers miss Hornung? In terms of talent, the combination of Tom Moore and Elijah Pitts seemed nearly his equal. Moore was just as big with more speed, and both Moore and Pitts could throw the option pass. Taylor was in his prime, the next best fullback to Jim Brown, and Green Bay's talent at most other positions was deeper than ever. But there was something about Hornung that Lombardi and his veterans knew they would dearly miss. No. 5 had a way of loping onto the field and lifting the confidence of everyone around him. "Hornung was one hundred percent football player. He is a winner and a tremendous leader on the field," Lombardi said at the Packers stockholders' meeting in Green Bay that spring. "He was one hundred percent football player even when he was injured. But I believe we can make up the slack somehow, somewhere."

How and where was not made immediately clear in the first contest of the year, the annual preseason game at Soldier Field in Chicago between the NFL champions and the college all-stars. On paper, the game was always a mismatch: men against boys, a fluid veteran team against a collection of novice players. The all-stars had Penn State's Robinson and Bobby Bell of Minnesota on defense, Ed Budde of Michigan State anchoring the offensive line, and the pass-and-catch duo of Ron VanderKelen and Pat Richter of Wisconsin, but it was not the most talented group of college seniors ever assembled. Richter remembered how he and his teammates watched in silent awe as the Packers bus "pulled up across the way and these guys got out—Ron Kramer and Willie Wood and Herb Adderley. Wow!" In the all-star locker room before the game, Dave Robinson sensed that "everybody was nervous, worried about getting blown away," though as a Packers draftee he considered himself in a no-lose situation. "Hey, if we win, I celebrate with you guys. If the Packers win, I go celebrate with them," he told his teammates.

The evening was humid and draining, the Packers were not yet in playing shape, and no one on the Green Bay side seemed engaged until it was too late. VanderKelen, a Green Bay kid from Preble High, hit Richter for a touchdown, giving the collegians a ten-point lead late in the game, and they held on to win 20 to 17. Pat Peppler, Lombardi's new director of player personnel, had invited the three all-stars who were Green Bay draft choices to attend a team buffet at the Drake Hotel after the game. Tony Liscio of Tulsa and Chuck Morris of Ole Miss showed up, along with Robinson, conquering heroes. They received a decidedly cool reception. "Lombardi wouldn't even speak to me. He was so mad because of the game he wouldn't speak with any of us," Robinson said. "He looked at us, turned and walked away. We were like lepers, sitting all by ourselves. A couple of players came over and said welcome to the team, but they weren't real happy. They knew we had created havoc and there would be hell to pay next week."

Finally Ockie Krueger, the former West Point colonel, came over to ask the rookies about their military draft status, what he could do to help them get into the reserves or National Guard if need be, anything to make their football lives uninterrupted. As Krueger was conducting his interview, a woman approached and said, "Well, you beat us, but you're part of the team now."

"Who the hell are you?" Chuck Morris asked.

"Young man, if you stay in Green Bay long enough, you'll find out who I am," she replied.

Morris stayed in camp only long enough to find out that it was Marie Lombardi. Soon enough he was cut and sent back to Mississippi.

Perhaps it was a meaningless game, but Lombardi was deeply embarrassed by the loss. He hated to lose, period. *Winning is not a sometime thing; it's an all the time thing,* he was fond of saying. Before the all-star fiasco, his Green Bay teams in fact had won seventeen straight preseason exhibition games, going back to a loss to the Giants in 1959. At his office the day after the game, he broke his usual policy of never talking about games with his secretarial staff and broached the subject with Ruth McKloskey. "I don't blame the players a single bit," he told her. "I didn't impress on them that the all-stars had something to prove and would play hard. It was all my fault."

Of course the way he would demonstrate that it was all his fault was by taking it out on his players, just as they suspected. Pat Peppler had warned Dave Robinson about Lombardi time—everything starts fifteen minutes ahead of schedule—so he arrived early for the first team meeting a few days after the game. When he entered the room Lombardi was already there, "and his game face was on." They were to review film of the all-star debacle. This should be good, Robinson thought. After all, he had excelled, at one point slipping by tight end Ron Kramer to throw Tom Moore for a loss. So there they all were, proud rookie, embarrassed veterans, angry coach, watching the film, and it came to that play and Lombardi stopped the projector and Robinson said to himself, Coach is going to give me a compliment now. And instead Lombardi bellowed, "KRAMER! Look at that rookie get rid of you! That kid probably won't even make the team that drafted him!" Robinson slouched lower in his seat. Whoa, this is tough. What have I done? he wondered. Didn't Lombardi even know who he was? Willie Wood, seated next to him, chuckled.

Practice was hell that week. Every time the players came off the field,

Lombardi ran them more, and the vets looked over at the big rookie and said, "Thanks a lot, Robinson!"

Lombardi was consumed with the idea of winning three NFL championships in a row. It had been on his mind since that windy December evening when he and his Packers had flown home from New York after their second triumph over the Giants. Bill Forester had made a surprise stop at Sunset Circle late that night to say goodbye to the coach before going home to Texas for the off-season, and Lombardi had pulled him aside and said, "Bubba, it's never been done three times in a row before." Even aside from the loss of Hornung, Lombardi knew the third time would be more difficult. As he said in his letter to the players and their wives that winter, living with success is more difficult than living with failure: the pressure relentless for more and more. Success, Lombardi told W. C. Heinz in *Run to Daylight!*, is "like a habit-forming drug that in victory saps your elation and in defeat deepens your despair. Once you have sampled it, you are hooked." When you are successful, he thought, everyone else is jealous and every game becomes a grudge match.

The burden of past success was evident from the first play of the regular season, when J. C. Caroline of Chicago sprinted downfield on kickoff coverage and smacked returner Herb Adderley to the ground before he reached the twenty-yard line. George Halas and his players and hordes of Bears fans who made the traditional journey north by car and train were all in a spirited and vengeful mood. The Packers had beaten them five straight times, the last two in 1962 by humbling scores. Desperate to find an edge, Halas had signed a former Green Bay player during the off-season, linebacker Tom Bettis, who had fallen out with Lombardi and was eager to divulge details of the Packers offense. The Bears also had a new defensive coordinator, George Allen, who had figured out Green Bay's offensive tendencies and devised a series of novel defenses to thwart them. In an ugly game that saw both teams flailing in the September sun, the Bears prevailed, 10 to 3. Pat Peppler remembered that Lombardi was "beside himself, like a man possessed" after the game.

He pushed harder, and while his players responded, his body did not. As the Packers launched a winning streak, Lombardi grew increasingly fatigued. He was chain-smoking Salems at a furious pace, three cartons a week. Ruth McKloskey emptied his big round ashtray "at least two or three times a day." His tongue felt sore and bloated, and he had trouble eating. The team had moved its administrative quarters that year from downtown to a new addition at the stadium, and he had to climb a flight of stairs to reach his office, a trek that at times left him panting. One morning he came in, cast a stern glance at McKloskey and muttered, "Don't talk to me." She obeyed, and watched him enter his office and close the door, only to emerge a minute later.

"I quit smoking last night and I'm not fit to talk to anybody," Lombardi explained.

"Oh?"

He had long talked about quitting. He considered smoking an indica-tion of personal weakness and a bad example for children. But it was fear that made him finally give up cigarettes. "I've been getting dizzy spells," he told McKloskey. At the postgame party in his basement rec room the night before, he had struck a deal with his friend Jack Koeppler to entice them both to quit cold turkey: if either man found the other with a cigarette, the smoker would have to buy dinner. When Red Cochran heard that Vince had quit, he joked with the other assistant coaches, "Vince didn't quit, he offered them up to God to put an extra strong deal on Him." The staff kept smoking, Bengtson dragging away on his nonfilter Camels, and they were none too happy that their boss had quit. "He *would* have to do it during the football season, when we have to put up with him," Cochran lamented. It was not easy for Lombardi; he quickly gained twenty pounds and yearned for ciga-rettes for years thereafter, but never smoked again.

As Lombardi paced the sidelines, dying for a smoke, his hands clasped behind him, fidgeting with two small steel balls, his Packers ran off eight straight wins. They prevailed without Hornung, with Jerry Kramer kicking and Tom Moore and Elijah Pitts running, and finally even with John Roach passing instead of Bart Starr. In the sixth game in St. Louis, Starr was tum-bling out-of-bounds when a defensive back hit him and broke his right wrist. Lombardi at first tried to hide the injury, but word leaked out to Al Sampson, a local sportscaster, who shot film of Starr trying to throw with his left hand. That night Sampson received an angry phone call from Marie. "It was the angriest I ever heard Marie. It turns out they were trying to get Zeke Bratkowski as a backup in a trade with the Rams and were afraid the Rams would screw them if they knew how hurt Bart really was," Sampson recalled. "So Marie called me up at home and said I wasn't loyal to the Packers." The trade went through in any case and Bratkowski arrived in Green Bay, but he was unfamiliar with the Packers system and not ready to play. Lombardi faced the ultimate test of his theory that football's central flaw is that one player, the quarterback, is too important.

Could the Packers win with a substitute who had thrown only sixteen passes, completing a mere three, in the last two seasons? They beat St. Louis, Baltimore, Pittsburgh, and Minnesota with Roach at quarterback, backed up by Bratkowski, and approached the rematch in Chicago tied with the Bears, each with 8 wins and 1 loss. The Packers returned to the Drake Hotel, scene of the dreary postmortem after the all-star embarrassment, but there were few signs of concern now. Eight straight wins had restored Lombardi's men. There was a sense, Max McGee felt, that nothing could stop them—not scandal, not injury, certainly not the Bears. On the eve of the game, a

Chicago player strolled through the Drake's lobby and saw Lombardi smiling hugely, all teeth, exuding confidence, and it upset him so much that he told his teammates about it before the game the next day to fire them up. It didn't take much; they hated the cocksure Packers. The game drew a sellout crowd, with fans huddling in line overnight for standing-room-only tickets. Illinois residents without tickets flooded across the Wisconsin border to watch the game on television in the bars and bowling alleys of Monroe and New Glarus and Janesville and Kenosha.

Angry fans spat on Lombardi as he walked under a pedestrian ramp at Wrigley Field to reach the locker room, and the game was equally nasty, if one-sided. The Packers were flat, Roach was no match for George Allen's shifting defense, and the Bears dominated from the beginning, winning 26 to 7. With the game out of reach, Phil Bengtson inserted Dave Robinson at linebacker in the fourth quarter, giving him his first regular season playing time. Nothing in his football life had prepared Robbie for what he experienced during those last few feeble minutes of the loss against the Bears. He ran onto the field and was stunned by the hubbub and commotion. Even from the sidelines you could not truly hear or feel the explosive verbal intensity near the line of scrimmage: players cursing and screaming at the top of their lungs, the foulest language he had ever heard. And it was all coming from the same team, from his team. They were swearing at each other, even at themselves. Willie Davis cursing a blue streak at Dan Currie. Currie giving it back. Willie Wood chewing out the whole line. Nitschke never shutting up. All of them now swearing at Robinson.

What was that all about? Robinson asked the defensive coach after the game. Just the way the guys fire up each other, Bengtson told him. He said he would tell Willie Davis not to swear so much at the rookie the next time. But in fact Robinson had seen them at their mildest. They really weren't up for the Bears game the way they should have been. Broadcaster Ray Scott came into the dressing room after the game just when Bengtson turned to Lombardi and said, "Vince, we were flat out there." Lombardi "turned on him like a tiger," as Scott remembered, "and shouted, 'How could you be flat for a game like this?'" It was the only time Scott had seen a Lombardi team that did not seem mentally ready for an important game.

This was the first time the Packers had flown to Chicago; in past years they had taken the train. The bus ride back to the airport seemed to take longer than any flight, and Lombardi was steaming all the way. He boarded the plane without uttering a word. "Like a man in a trance," recalled Ruth McKloskey. "He wouldn't talk. Never talked to Mrs. Lombardi. Nobody said anything. It was real quiet." Finally, as the plane passed high over the twinkling lights of a city, Lombardi rose from his seat and found McKloskey, who had not flown before. "Look over there, Ruth, isn't that a beautiful sight, the lights of Milwaukee? How are you enjoying your first flight?"

"Fine. Just fine," McKloskey replied. She didn't dare say what she was thinking: too bad they lost.

Lombardi returned to his seat and started talking with Marie. Jack Koeppler sat nearby and watched his friend transformed before his eyes. Lombardi had been sullen, uncommunicative, and now he was lighting up. He left his seat again and ambled back to the coach section and got the attention of his players. "I really got outcoached today," he said. "We all got outplayed, but I got outcoached. Next year, we'll be ready for them in no uncertain terms." Then he went back row by row and patted each player on the back, and beers were passed out and the plane was alive with chatter as it left the city lights behind and passed over Lake Winnebago on the way north through the November night.

"What the hell was that all about?" Koeppler asked Lombardi when he returned to his seat.

"They're down enough already," Lombardi said.

If he was not sure of it before, Koeppler at that moment realized that "the Old Man was one shrewd psychologist."

PRESIDENT KENNEDY was killed five days later. Lombardi was in his office that Friday, making final preparations for the next game against the 49ers in Milwaukee, when news reached him of the assassination. The next game, which had always been the center of his universe, now seemed meaningless. Lombardi was a loud and emotional man, but this report numbed him. His players were just leaving the building after their weekly awards meeting. Many of them were in the parking lot, gathered around car radios. Others wandered back inside to listen together in the training room. Lombardi came down and said a few words—"no big speech, nothing emotional, no tears," Bob Skoronski remembered—and then left to pray for the fallen president at St. Willebrord, the church where he had first met JFK during the early days of the 1960 Wisconsin primary, when the senator and the coach were beginning their brilliant ascents. Among his most cherished mementos were the telegram Kennedy had sent him on New Year's Eve 1961 after their first championship victory and the program from the Jefferson-Jackson Day Dinner in Milwaukee on May 12, 1962, when the president was the main speaker and Lombardi was an invited guest. Now he would add another bittersweet memento, a laminated prayer card for John F. Kennedy that he carried thereafter in his Bible.

Most sporting events were canceled that weekend, but not the seven games of the NFL. Commissioner Rozelle issued a statement defending his decision to proceed. "It has been traditional in sports for athletes to perform in times of great personal tragedy," Rozelle claimed. "Football was Mr. Kennedy's game. He thrived on competition." At eight-thirty Saturday morning, Lombardi and his team boarded the North Western train in Green Bay for the trip to Milwaukee. On the way down, the players talked mostly about the assassination. Five of the Packers were from Dallas, ashamed of what had happened in their city. The game seemed to be the last thing on their minds. Lombardi tried to focus on football, calling his coaches together to analyze the upcoming college draft. The next day's game was an eerily contained and somber affair. There was no pregame introduction of the starting lineups. There were no commercial announcements on the scoreboard. The television booth was shut down; the only broadcast was on radio. The only music was the national anthem. No halftime band. The players were equally subdued. The normally raucous Willie Davis played in dazed silence at his defensive end position, no swearing that day. Davis said that "the whole team was lackluster" and he played "the worst game" of his career, but San Francisco was worse and the Packers won easily.

It was the sort of sloppy win that normally sent Lombardi into a rage, but instead he "hardly said a word" afterwards, according to Davis. "He did not chew us out."

The year was essentially over. Starr had returned to the lineup, only to see Nitschke break his arm in the Thanksgiving Day game against Detroit, a 13 to 13 tie. The middle linebacker had been the MVP of the previous year's championship game, but there was no doubt that Lombardi's axiom was correct—his quarterback was always most valuable, and the Packers did not lose again that season. Still, it was no use. The Bears never lost again either, and though they were tied twice, the Chicago club finished first, a half-game ahead of the Packers. Second place. It might have seemed sweet back in 1959, but not now. There were no wildcard teams in the playoffs, only the winners of the two conferences playing for the world championship. The league had instituted a Playoff Bowl in Miami for the runners-up, but Lombardi viewed it largely as an exhibition, a place to experiment by trying defensive backs at wide receiver. The game presented him with a psychological conflict. On the one hand, he believed that you could not win the runner-up bowl and call yourself a winner. On the other hand, winning was not a sometime thing. The Packers played to win and beat the Cleveland Browns 40 to 23.

Lombardi later would place the 1963 squad in a special category when he thought back on his career. He had lost Hornung that year, and then Starr, and then Nitschke, and his friend the president was killed, and there was no third consecutive championship, yet the team persisted and nearly prevailed. "As far as the Packers are concerned, as someone once said, 'We are not slain, just wounded. Let me lay awhile and bleed a little and I will rise to fight again.' So will the Packers," Lombardi declared during a speech to the First Friday Club after the season. "While this has been a very frustrating season, for many reasons, this team will always have a soft spot in my heart because of the many adversities and the many frustrations it had to meet. The one big lesson it had to learn, which we all have to learn, is that a team, like men, must be brought to its knees before it can rise again."

• •

PAUL HORNUNG, on his knees for a year, at the foot of the cross, was on vacation in Miami Beach in early March 1964 when he was summoned to New York again to see Commissioner Rozelle. They met for an hour; Rozelle talked, Hornung mostly listened. Hornung was reminded of the troubles that could result from keeping the wrong company and told to be more careful in the future. At the end of the lecture Rozelle asked him if he had any questions. "Yes, I have one," Hornung said. "Am I going to be reinstated?" Rozelle declined to answer, but Hornung left the meeting convinced that he would get another chance. One week later, on the morning of March 16, the league office released a five-paragraph statement announcing that both Hornung and Karras had been reinstated. Headlines throughout the country proclaimed "The Return of the Golden Boy." Hornung was so eager to return to the field that he called Lombardi and volunteered to report to Green Bay immediately after the Kentucky Derby in early May, two months before training camp. He was ten pounds above his playing weight and wanted to begin a strenuous off-season exercise program under the coach's direction.

There had been rumors all year that Lombardi was disillusioned with Hornung. Their father-son bond had been broken by Paul's betrayal, it was said, and Lombardi would remove him from the team for good as soon as possible. Stories circulated about Hornung being traded to Pittsburgh or New York, or being released to play in the AFL. Lombardi had rarely hesitated to rid the team of players he thought would undermine him. Billy Howton and Howie Ferguson were sent packing when they challenged him before the first training camp. Bill Quinlan was traded after the 1962 championship, when Lombardi concluded that his on-field talents were not worth his erratic off-field behavior. One could argue that Hornung did more to hurt the team than anyone else by behaving so recklessly that he lost a full season of play, but Lombardi did not view it that way. He was disappointed, but not willing to give up on his favorite player. Every time he was asked, he said no, he did not intend to trade Hornung, he wanted him back. And now he said it again. When Hornung told him that he intended to come to Green Bay in early May to start getting in shape, Lombardi revealed how much he still needed him with the eager reply, "Mid-April would be better." And so they "compromised," as Hornung later joked, and the Golden Boy reported in mid-April.

Bart Starr and Boyd Dowler were in Green Bay that spring and worked out with Hornung. They ran wind sprints—four at one hundred yards and then four at fifty yards, over and over. Then Hornung, alone, jogged up the stadium steps, again and again. "There are sixty steps, in case you're interested. I've counted them a few times," he told Dick Young, the sports columnist for the *New York Daily News*. "I think I'm in great shape. I pulled a groin muscle the other day, but that's nothing. What is important is that my right knee, the one I hurt in '62, was given a year's rest. It feels better than ever. I want to have a great year."

No sooner did Lombardi welcome back his prodigal son than he sent another of his key players away, trading Jim Ringo (and fullback Earl Gros) to the Philadelphia Eagles for linebacker Lee Roy Caffey and a first-round draft choice. The manner of Ringo's departure later became one of the familiar fables of the Lombardi mythology. As the story would be told through the years, Ringo visited Lombardi's office that spring seeking a substantial raise, and to help negotiate he brought along a newfangled creature in the sporting world, a player agent. Ringo had been a Green Bay stalwart, a perennial all-pro who had not missed a game in ten seasons, captain of the offense, smart and swift, his blocking agility essential to the success of their signature play, the Packer sweep. Lombardi knew all of that and admired Ringo, but was insulted by the presence of the agent. He could not tolerate anything or anyone getting between him and his players, making the process seem mercenary, less personal. The presence of an agent made it harder for him to get up from his desk and rub the player's head and get him to relent, as he had done with Bob Skoronski. It interfered with his concept of team, the subordination of individual desire for the greater good of the group. And so, as the story went, when Ringo and his agent demanded a raise, Lombardi excused himself, went into the next room and returned a few minutes later saying, "Go talk to the Eagles about it. Mr. Ringo has been traded to Philadelphia."

The story became ever more popular in later years when agents emerged as central figures in the sports world and the public grew increasingly disillusioned with multimillionaire athletes. Lombardi never would put up with that stuff. Remember what he did to Ringo? Traded him as soon as he walked in with an agent. But it did not happen that way. Ringo did have an agent that year, and he demanded a $25,000 salary, but the negotiating was done with Pat Peppler, the personnel director, not Lombardi. And both the player and coach had other motives. Ringo was interested in moving back to the Philadelphia area, his home. Lombardi had spent weeks studying his team's strengths and weaknesses, and concluded that Ringo was slowing down and that he needed another young linebacker and more draft choices. (He used the Eagles pick to draft Donny Anderson, the running back from Texas Tech who would not be eligible to play professionally for another year.) It was not an impulsive act, but a carefully calculated maneuver. "Vince had been thinking about this and working on it quietly for a long time," Peppler recalled. "Most of the story was not true. It was all done on the telephone." It did happen suddenly enough, however, that Lombardi had to scramble for a center. Within minutes of trading Ringo, Lombardi was in the locker room with Bob Skoronski, working him on the snap, knowing that he would have to use his left tackle at center until an untested rookie came along.

The apocryphal story of Ringo's quick exit was perpetuated largely because Lombardi wanted it to be believed. Rather than correct the tale, he spread it himself, Peppler said, in the hope that it might discourage players from hiring agents or making difficult contract demands. His bark, for the most part, was worse than his bite, and like all general managers, Lombardi out of necessity found himself dealing with agents and lawyers during the latter half of the sixties.

IF THERE WAS anything in Lombardi's life that approached his obsession with football during his time in Green Bay, it was golf. He attended mass every morning out of a combination of habit and spiritual need, but he would have played golf 365 days a year if it had been possible, wholly out of love. He kept several of his gift putters at work and at odd hours dropped a few balls on the floor and practiced putting them at one of those light aluminum golf-hole contraptions with the clinking hinges. Marie often caught him doing the same at home, lagging balls at a plastic tumbler. The golf season was cruelly short in northeastern Wisconsin, but he and his cronies hit the Oneida links at the first sign of survivable weather: he and Ray Antil once played two days after Christmas, wearing long underwear and warmers and flap-eared hats, although the club did not officially open until April 1. "My father's life was golf," Susan reflected. "He loved golf. My mother hated to go to some vacation spots like Bermuda and Puerto Rico and the Bahamas with him because she knew he just wanted to golf."

His off-season schedule was arranged around golf opportunities. First there was a late-winter trip with Marie, but not Susan, who spent most of her teens home alone with a babysitter on her birthday, February 13. That trip often coincided with a league meeting set in a warm golf course–rich locale. Then came a stag holiday with Harry Masse, Ockie Krueger and Jack Koeppler, a four-day southern swing every March to Gulfport, Biloxi and New Orleans, or once, Hot Springs. Lombardi fed his golfing addiction by insisting that they play on the afternoon they arrived and the morning they left, and gambling was fit into the trip as well. Krueger's lasting memory is of Lombardi heading straight for the craps table—the game he had learned long ago from his Izzo uncles on the green felt of the pool table in the basement at the family homestead in Sheepshead Bay. "He'd sit at the craps table and, Christ, everyone stopped in the casino because he was making so much noise, shouting 'C'mon! C'mon!'" Krueger recalled. Marie tolerated that trip, barely, rationalizing that her husband needed it to relieve the stress, but she always held it against Koeppler for taking her husband away from her. Finally there was a two-day outing in May in which the Green Bay coaches played against their counterparts from Detroit and Cleveland, rotating cities and country clubs every year.

From April through the opening of training camp in mid-July, Lombardi golfed three or four times a week, including Tuesday and Thursday afternoons, a welcome relief for his overworked assistants, who would create "a traffic jam on the steps getting out of the office" as soon as Lombardi left, according to Pat Peppler. Lombardi reduced his trips to the golf course once the football season began, but continued playing, slipping out to Oneida after the morning practice on Saturdays when the team was at home the next day. "It was a form of relaxation for him," said team physician Eugene Brusky, perhaps Oneida's longest driver. If Lombardi relaxed on the course, his body language failed to show it. There was nothing graceful about his game. He had a bulky frame with little suppleness. His swing was stiff and jerky, and he had a short follow-through, the golfing equivalent, perhaps, of Jerry Kramer's placekicking. "He looked ugly out there," said Max McGee, who played with him occasionally on Mondays, when the players were allowed on Oneida. "You'd play a round with him and think he'd shot a hundred and ten." But in fact he was far better. Bob Milward, the pro at Oneida, who gave Lombardi lessons, called him "a pretty straight shooter" whose average was in the mid-80s.

It seemed that Lombardi willed the ball, or sought to intimidate it, into the cup. He was "an intense competitor," said Koeppler, a regular in Lombardi's foursome. Koeppler, who carried a three-handicap, ten strokes better than Lombardi, enjoyed being the coach's partner in best-ball contests, where a team played the superior shot hit by either player. "It was amazing how well he could play if I happened to miss a shot. If I was playing well, he would just play along. But if I happened to knock it somewhere not as good as it should be, he could just focus on making that thing do what he wanted it to do. Some guys go the other way. When playing with a low-handicap player, and that guy gets stuck somewhere, they get it stuck worse. Vince may hit only three or four good shots a round, but they were the ones that saved us. Of course we would win quite a few matches before they started; the other team would be three or four down before they got over the fact that they were playing against Vince Lombardi."

When Lombardi was playing golf, it rarely could be kept secret. He brought his booming voice and volcanic temper with him. "You could hear him anywhere on the course when he missed a shot," said Tom Hallion, who occasionally caddied for him at Oneida. "It was very R-rated and guttural—'Goddamn it! Sonofabitch!' Several Oneida golfers would later tell variations of a story of Lombardi furiously tossing his putter into Duck Creek as he walked across the bridge at the fourth hole. Bob Maahs, another teenage caddy at Oneida during that era, said he was carrying Lombardi's bags one day when the foursome got stuck behind a group of slow-playing women, including the wife of the owner of Nicolet Sporting Goods. "He would scream obscenities and hit the ball; he was hitting when she was marking her scorecard on the green," Maahs said. "Everyone was afraid of him." Once

Lombardi got back in the clubhouse, the young caddy noticed, "he was all smiles and grins, just like you would see on TV. His whole personality would change."

If golf was a needed outlet for Lombardi, a place to smack a ball around and curse and hang out with his cronies, it also revealed a deeper insight into his personality as a leader. He once told Mitch Fromstein, a Milwaukee businessman, that "the toughest single battle he had in life was his golf game." Fromstein thought he was joking. "But Vince said, 'I'm going to tell you why. Because I have the toughest opponent in my golf game. ME. I'm trying to improve my score, and it's just me. I'm always fighting to get better against myself. That is tough.' "

Lombardi understood that he was not the perfect vessel for the sporting life. He was short, stocky, slow, color-blind, awkward, injury-prone and emotional. He could not excel at any athletic endeavor that depended on his own primary skills, whether it was running or blocking or hitting a baseball or shooting a basketball or craps or playing hands of gin or rounds of golf. All were difficult for him. He could make himself better, but never the best. But he had a sharp mind, keen memory and overpowering will. He knew what perfection looked like and what was required to approach it; all he needed was the material with which to work. In football, as a coach, he had it—in the arm of Bart Starr, the agility of Willie Wood, the fluid grace of Paul Hornung and Herb Adderley, the muscled abandon of Jimmy Taylor and Ray Nitschke, the rugged perseverance of Forrest Gregg and Henry Jordan, the savvy of his captains, Bob Skoronski and Willie Davis. They provided the talent that he lacked; he provided the will and the way, pushing them to levels of performance that he knew were possible for them but that he could never attain himself, closing the gap between the hugeness of his desire and the smallness of reality.

ON THE FIRST DAY of 1964 training camp, Paul Hornung unpacked his suitcase on the brown-blanketed bed in Room 120 at Sensenbrenner Hall at St. Norbert College. It was the same compact dorm room that he used to stay in, with the same old wisecracking roommate. "I don't know if I should be rooming with you," Max McGee said upon greeting him. "I'm not supposed to associate with gamblers." The Golden Boy's comeback had begun, and it seemed as though half the sports journalists in America were on hand to chronicle it. Articles on Hornung were commissioned by magazines ranging from *Sports Illustrated* to *Parade. Sport* ran two pieces, one by Dick Schaap and another by *New York Journal American* writer Dave Anderson ("His name isn't Paul Hornung this season. It's Paul Hornung Returning from a Suspension for Gambling," Anderson began). W. C. Heinz also wrote a piece for *Life* while he was back in town to ease the way for the production of a television documentary version of *Run to Daylight!*

The documentary borrowed the name of the book more than the dramatic concept. It did not follow the coach's life hour by hour and day by day through a week leading up to a game, but rather took the viewer on a tour of training camp, beginning with a juxtaposition of the profane and divine: dark and chaotic frames of violent contact at the line of scrimmage followed by a bright and bucolic scene of Lombardi strolling down the sidewalk outside Sensenbrenner Hall on a July morning, birds chirping, sun shining through the trees, the first day of camp.

"Good morning, sisters!" he says cheerily as he encounters two young nuns walking in the other direction.

"Good afternoon, Mr. Lombardi!" they respond in unison.

"It's nice . . ." (he has stepped on their lines)

"Nice to see you back," they go on.

"Well, thank you. It's nice to be back here at St. Norbert. It's a beautiful day, too, by the way, isn't it?"

There are scenes of Hawg Hanner driving to camp from Arkansas in his pickup truck, of Willie Davis and Ray Nitschke toting a football as they lumber down the practice field in wind sprints, of a quartet of rookies singing an earnest if painful version of "Hello, Dolly!" for the veterans in an after-dinner ritual, of Jimmy Taylor talking about how football is a contact sport and how much he and his coach love contact. There are two interviews with right guard Jerry Kramer, whose accounts of the inner game reveal an honest and articulate sensibility that will be put to profitable use years later in his own books, and a multitude of scenes involving Hornung, the man of the hour: sipping soup, stepping on the scale, running the stadium steps, gliding behind Jerry and Fuzzy on the sweep, talking into the camera about getting in shape, reminiscing on the fears he felt as a rookie, and to some extent was feeling again now, hoping that the other players would accept him "as a football player and as a man"—and finally, in the last frame of the film, the Horn steps toward the ball and kicks a field goal, straight and true.

Lombardi is the film's main character. In many scenes he seems painfully conscious of the camera and microphone recording him for posterity. Even when he is stationed at his favorite practice field post, riding on the back of the blocking sled, imploring his troops to hit harder and drive him farther, there is a sense that he is not so much an obsessed coach lost in work as Lombardi trying to play Lombardi. Perhaps the camera captured something that otherwise would have gone undetected: there was always an element of performance in his coaching routine. Through the years several of his assistants and his son, Vincent, at various times entered his dressing quarters and found him in unguarded moments standing in front of the mirror rehearsing the facial expressions—sober, grimacing, intense, inspiring—that he would use minutes later in the locker room as he exhorted his players.

The most authentic Lombardi moment was also the most planned, though scripted by him, not the producers. Every year, on the opening Sunday night of training camp, he delivered a speech to the players in which he defined what it meant to be a member of the Green Bay *Packehs*. Lombardi is standing behind a lectern; his players are seated at classroom desks in the lecture hall, some taking notes, all appearing to give him their undivided attention. The theme of his oration is pride and how much it matters. "I'd like to welcome you all, of course, and tell you how proud we are to have you as part of the Packers, just as you should be proud to be here with this team," Lombardi begins. "Now, one thing about the Packers, it's a team with a great tradition. A great and wonderful tradition. And that tradition, or that whatever you want to call it—that glory that is the Packers—has been developed from one thing only, and that's pride. Everybody has ability, but pride in performance is what makes the difference. Now how do you develop pride? Pride is developed from a winning tradition."

While Lombardi's speech is timeless, the documentary as a whole, which ran for an hour on prime time on ABC, did not transcend its time and place, although it got good reviews. From the remove of decades it has the feel of a quaint period piece, an innocent narrative set to tinkly music, produced before the era of quick-cut action accompanied by jazz riffs and slow-motion montages set to uplifting pop ballads. But it holds a special place in the Lombardi mythology for several reasons. It introduced him to a larger television audience beyond those who watched the Packers on autumn Sunday afternoons, and it also marked his first association with Howard Cosell, who was beginning his rise as the dominant mythmaker of the modern television sports era.

Cosell's nasal voice was nowhere to be heard, his declarative ego not yet fully unleashed in front of the camera. The narrator was Horace McMahon, whose deep, rumbling delivery bore a haunting similarity to Lombardi's, and who was best known for his iconic introduction to a popular television show: "There are seven million stories in the Naked City. . . ." Lou Volpicelli was the director, and Cosell, who had read *Run to Daylight!* and considered Heinz a "great writer," produced the show in partnership with ABC, putting up half the money. Cosell and Lombardi had been casual acquaintances for decades. Each grew up in Brooklyn and attended college in New York, Lombardi at Fordham and Cosell at NYU. Cosell followed Lombardi's rise from West Point to the Giants to Green Bay with increasing interest. He admired Lombardi's straightforward style, his will to win, and his ability as a leader to see beyond race, class and culture to build a loyal and dependable team out of disparate characters. While others viewed Lombardi as the archetypal opposite of another Cosell favorite, the young boxer Cassius Clay, one symbolizing authority, the other freedom, Cosell saw them as singular personalities with compelling stories.

What Lombardi thought of Cosell is less clear. According to Heinz, the coach was not enthralled by the prospect of having the sportscaster lurking around training camp that summer. "He said Cosell was a pain in the neck," according to Heinz. "I said, 'C'mon, Coach, he's putting up half the money. This is a good thing. It's good for you. It's good for the Packers. It's good for football.'" Lombardi was playing golf in Neenah the day that Cosell arrived. He had lent his Pontiac to Heinz, who picked up Cosell at the airport and drove him to meet the coach. "Listen, tread lightly with Vince," Heinz warned, fearing that Cosell's overbearing nature might antagonize the over-bearing coach. "I know, I know," Cosell said. Lombardi was sitting in the clubhouse in Neenah, and when he saw Cosell he shouted, "How are ya, Coach?"

Cosell was struck dumb. "He called me Coach," he whispered excitedly to Heinz. Cosell thought it was a sign of intimacy. Coach was Cosell's own nickname for himself. "Raymond," Cosell could be heard announcing to the bartender at Les Artistes, his hangout near the ABC studios in Manhattan, "keep the martini chilled for the Coach. I'll be back in ten minutes." Heinz did not feel like telling Cosell that Lombardi was indiscriminate with the nickname; to him everyone and anyone might be Coach. Two days later Heinz entered Lombardi's office and found the real coach in a foul mood.

"Out!" Lombardi growled.

"What?"

"You know who! Cosell! I don't want him around anymore!"

"He's going home tonight, Coach. Relax," Heinz said.

Cosell had been asking questions nonstop, propounding his own theories on football, beating Lombardi at gin, using words that Lombardi only vaguely knew, exhibiting no apparent fear of the coach, showing an ego just as large. Cosell might have thought he was bonding, but Lombardi considered it too much. The story went around the locker room that Cosell once said to Lombardi, "Coach, how many great sportscasters do you think there are?" and Lombardi responded, "One less than you think, Howard!" It sounded unlikely, Lombardi rarely displayed such wit, but it might have ac-curately expressed his exasperation with his fellow New Yorker. "You had to play Lombardi carefully. Don't interrupt him and push him too far at any time," Heinz said. "Howard was always so aggressive. But he was a great re-porter. You've got to give him that. A great reporter." And from then on Cosell considered himself the coach's close friend and the world's leading expert on the genius of the great Vince Lombardi.

MUCH WAS AT STAKE in the season opener in Green Bay. It was not only Hornung's first game since 1962, but also an opportunity for the Packers to gain revenge against the world-champion Bears. None of that seemed to faze the Golden Boy, who remained easygoing in the days leading up to the game. He declared himself in the best condition of his life, down to 212 pounds, and ready for a season that would make everyone forget about his forced year off. After practice on Friday, he picked up his mother at the airport, then drove over to the Northland for a haircut. Lombardi was already there, and they took their trims two chairs apart. Just having Hornung in the lineup reassured the coach; he had felt better since the first intrasquad game, when Hornung had made his patented cutback on the sweep and found his way to the end zone. "Hornung's back! Hornung's back! The Golden Boy is back!" Lombardi had yelled on the sidelines that day. Now he was silent, dozing in the barber's chair, and soon enough, so was his halfback. Like father, like son. "You put on the clippers and he goes to sleep," the barber explained to Tex Maule, who was spending the week with his favorite team.

As Sunday broke bright and cool, there was a sense in Green Bay that everything was right with the world, restored to the way it was supposed to be. Lombardi had his boy back and played him for nearly the entire game. Hornung remained on the field for all but two offensive plays, completing an option pass, kicking three field goals and gaining seventy-seven yards on fifteen carries, including one classic Packer sweep, the Horn gliding to the right, then cutting back sharply and loping downfield for forty yards. As if to show off the renewed dynamism of the Lombardi-Hornung partnership, the coach drew on his daring and rulebook expertise to send Hornung in for a rare free-kick fifty-two-yard field goal with eight seconds remaining in the first half. Elijah Pitts had received a punt near midfield with a fair catch, which according to an obscure rule allowed the Packers to place the ball on the line of scrimmage for an uncontested free-kick field goal. Hornung's boot was low and unpretty, but with no Bears rushing in for the block, it sailed over the crossbar. Green Bay won, 23 to 12, and Maule had the headline he wanted: "Shining Hour for Golden Boy."

It was, as it turned out, the last shining hour of the season for Hornung, Lombardi and the Packers. Jerry Kramer played in the opener despite a piercing pain in his abdomen, and that was the last time he suited up all year. Doctors feared that he might be suffering from life-threatening cancer, until they belatedly discovered that he had been infected by a seven-and-a-half-inch sliver of wood that had been lodged in his body undetected for years, going back to an incident in his Idaho teens when he was chasing a calf and slammed into a fencepost. With Ringo traded and Kramer out, Lombardi's offensive line, the key to his running attack, was not the same. Kramer was missed even more in another way. The difference between winning and losing that season was so narrow that the major problem turned out to be the inaccuracy of Hornung's toe, and the unavailability of Kramer to replace him as the kicker. The Packers lost the second game of the year to the eventual conference champions, the Baltimore Colts, 21 to 20, and the difference in the game was a missed Hornung extra point. In the fourth game, the

Vikings blocked an extra point that proved decisive in a 24 to 23 Green Bay loss. In the sixth game, Hornung missed four field goals and had another blocked as the Packers lost to the Colts for a second time, 24 to 21.

Green Bay outgained its opponents all year, and played vigorous defense, but won 8 games, lost 5, and tied 1 as Hornung missed twenty-six of thirty-eight field goal attempts. It was a measure of the respect with which he was held by his teammates and coach that they refused to blame him for another second-place season. Lombardi said he might have put Kramer in to kick if he had been available, but always believed that Hornung would regain his rhythm. He likened Hornung's kicking woes to "a .300 hitter who gets in a slump, except we can't bench him." For the second straight year, Lombardi took his team to the Playoff Bowl in Miami, but this time he did not even feign interest in the game against the St. Louis Cardinals. In private meetings with his squad, he disparaged the whole notion of such a game. "He called it the 'Shit Bowl,' " according to Bob Skoronski. "That's the word he used. He said it was a losers' bowl for losers." The Packers lost to the Cardinals, and afterwards Lombardi fumed about "a hinky-dink football game, held in a hinky-dink town, played by hinky-dink players. That's all second place is—hinky-dink." He said that he would never come back and had no intention of ever finishing second again.

It was an uncertain time for Lombardi, the most confusing period for him since he had reached Green Bay. He had thought about leaving the year before, when the 49ers made a covert inquiry and then the AFL's Jets presented him with a lucrative offer to return to New York. But none of that had worked out, Olejniczak and the league would not let him go, nor would his pride; he wanted those three in a row, so he had stayed and appeared committed to Green Bay for several more seasons. Two years of losing, or not winning, had taken a toll, and Sunset Circle was a particularly depressed place after the season. Mr. High-Low was low and his wife was lower as the long Green Bay winter continued through the first months of 1965. The dark, dreary days, the agitated condition of her husband, her own psychological need to be the center of attention—all apparently combined to send Marie into a depression.

On the afternoon of February 12 she apparently drank too much, swallowed too many prescription pills intended for headaches and depression, and passed out in bed. Susan found her, holding a bottle of pills in her hand. It was not the first time. Susan yelled to her father, who came into the room and shook Marie awake. They drove her to St. Vincent Hospital, where she was watched overnight. Her depression and pleas for help were obvious, but the family did its best to avoid the subject. Susan said that she and her father acted as though Marie had a bout with the flu. Vincent coincidentally arrived from St. Paul the next day, unaware of the trouble, and was looking forward to celebrating the most joyous event of his life. He had proposed to his girlfriend, Jill Butz, a senior at the College of St. Catherine, and was bringing her home so that they could both tell the family. They arrived at Sunset Circle only to discover that everyone was at the hospital. Marie was recovering by then, but news of her son's engagement did not cheer her up. Jill showed her the engagement ring, which did not satisfy Marie. Perhaps nothing could then. The ring was a band of sapphires, not a diamond, and not big enough, Marie complained.

That night Vince and Susan, Vincent and Jill went to dinner, leaving Marie at the hospital. It was also Susan's eighteenth birthday, an event nearly lost in the commotion. There was no mention of Marie's illness at the restaurant. Lombardi tried to act festive for his children, but appeared distracted. He spent much of the time talking about a new high-protein diet that Marie had put him on, limiting his carbohydrate intake: steak and salad, no bread. For Vincent, here was another bittersweet instance when he and his dad were not quite connecting. He was announcing his engagement and his father was going on about a new diet. The problem was not an absence of love. Love was there; the problem was how to show it.

There was the time in Vincent's junior year when the Packers were playing in Minnesota and Lombardi made a rare appearance at a St. Thomas football game. Vincent ran for sixty-four yards and scored two touchdowns against Gustavus Adolphus—and the only thing the father said to his proud son after the game was that he should lift his feet up higher when he ran. Or the time in his freshman year when he hurt his knee and was "limping around, not playing, feeling sorry" for himself. The Packers were in town, so he went over to the hotel to visit his father. "I walk in the lobby and there are a lot of players there and they're all saying, 'That's too bad'—lots of sympathy and pats on the back," Vincent said later. "I go up to Dad's suite and he says come in here, and he's got Dr. Nellen there, who looks at it and says it's loose but there's nothing serious. And Dad lights into me. Just rips me up one side and down the other. 'You're going to be running on that tomorrow,' he says." Vincent left the hotel with tears running down his cheeks, certain that his father did not understand him. Two weeks later he was starting.

The Old Man had been right, and perhaps he had acted out of love, but it came out in uncomfortable ways. For the most part, Lombardi's transference of ambition had been to his players, not his son, and perhaps that was lucky, otherwise the pressure might have been wholly intolerable. With thirty-eight other young men to work with every day, Lombardi did not need so much to live through his son, try to attain success through his son and ruin his son, like Willy Loman and his son Biff in Arthur Miller's *Death of a Salesman*. Lombardi was the successful salesman that Loman could never be, but there nonetheless are faint echoes of Willy and Biff in the frustrating scenes between Vince and Vincent. "When you hit, hit low and hit hard, because it's important, boy," Willy says to Biff in a dream sequence near the end of the play. They are on a football field, and it is a final yearning, plaintive, empty offering of advice on how to succeed and win in modern America. "Lift your legs up when you run," Vince said to Vincent, and the meaning was almost the same.

The wedding was scheduled for June 26 in Minot, North Dakota, Jill's hometown. Marie arrived three days early for a series of luncheons and a society page interview with the *Minot Daily News.* Vince flew in through a summer squall in time to play golf with the Butz brothers and the club pro at Minot Country Club the morning before the wedding. At the rehearsal dinner that night, Vince and Marie received word that one of their old friends, Jack Mara, who ran the Giants with brother Wellington, was dying of colon cancer at age fifty-seven. Marie dabbed at tears the rest of the night. When asked why she was crying, she said it was for Jack. The wedding was held at noon the next day, a grand social event, drawing more than four hundred people to the Church of the Little Flower, many of them awestruck at the sight of the famous father of the groom. After a reception at the country club, dinner was offered at the Butz house; the gathering spread out from the patio onto their spacious back lawn. The rains came before dusk, and as guests traipsed into the house, their soiled footprints blackened Mrs. Butz's white carpeting. After Vincent and Jill left for their honeymoon, Marie found a seat on the front porch and sat motionless for hours, rarely speaking, lost in the darkness of the northern plains, sobbing softly late into the night.

She was confronting the same emotion that her husband had been facing in a very different realm: the unbearable pain of coming in second, again.

21

Winning Isn't Everything

THE COMPULSION TO WIN, Bertolt Brecht once wrote, is "the black addiction of the brain." The Marxist playwright and the Jesuit football coach were philosophical opposites, but on this matter they were not far apart, and there is no doubt that Lombardi had the addiction by 1965. After coming in second two years in a row, he vowed never to lose again, and redoubled his efforts to assure that he would not. He papered the locker room walls with motivational aphorisms, all variations on the themes of competition and success. One of those maxims later came to be regarded as the essence of his philosophy: "Winning isn't everything, it's the only thing."

What exactly he meant by that, indeed whether he believed it or even said it, has been a matter of debate ever since. His critics blamed Lombardi for promoting a win-at-all-cost competitive pathology that led inevitably to Richard Nixon's dirty tricksters at the Committee to Re-elect the President, whose 1972 headquarters featured a sign that read "Winning in Politics Isn't Everything, It's the Only Thing." Lombardi's supporters insisted through the years that he was misinterpreted. What he said, or meant to say, they claimed, was that winning isn't everything, it's the only thing *worth striving for*, or winning isn't everything, but *making the effort to win* is.

His philosophy of winning was more complex and contradictory than either side would allow. The precise words—"Winning isn't everything, it's the only thing"—were indisputably part of the Lombardi phrase book and did appear in bold letters once on the locker room wall, but to say that he believed them is true yet meaningless out of context. Every year Lombardi told his players that professional football was a cruel business. His job and theirs, he would say, depended on only one thing, winning, and the only way to win was to accept nothing less. To that extent, his statement was an articulation of the obvious, the reality faced by any professional athlete or coach, and not necessarily relevant in a broader sense. But to say that winning was merely a practical necessity for Lombardi would be misleading. He considered it a matter of personal as well as national definition—"the American zeal," he once called it, "that is to be first in what we do and to win, to win, to win." He was obsessed with winning, and that obsession led to unfortunate imbalances in other aspects of his life.

Still, there was a crucial distinction in his philosophy between paying the price to win and winning at any price. He did not believe in cheating to win, and he showed no interest in winning the wrong way, without heart, brains and sportsmanship. Although he never shied away from the violence of the game, insisting that football was "not a contact sport, but a collision sport," he did not encourage dirty play. "Piling on, cheap shots, clotheslining people—that wasn't our style of play," said Tom Brown, the former baseball player who took over as strong safety in the mid-sixties. When one of Lombardi's defensive backs tripped a receiver in frustration, he immediately yanked him from the game, even though the referees did not see the violation. Winning in and of itself was not enough for him. His players knew that he was more likely to drive them mercilessly after they had played sloppily but won than when they had played hard but lost.

"After games, Henry Jordan would always get this look on his face and say, 'Who won?'—because we always won but you wouldn't know it from Vince," said Red Cochran. "Vince would be chewing everybody out. He would be most like what everyone probably thought of Lombardi—a tyrant, more volatile—after a close win where we screwed up than any other time." Carroll Dale, a receiver who came to the Packers in 1965 from Los Angeles, said that it was "human nature, when you win, to overlook mistakes." But Lombardi was different. "He would not overlook them. He would correct them, immediately. Winning wasn't everything for him, he wanted excellence. There's a difference." For years afterwards, his players spoke with amazement at the recollection of Lombardi's behavior after an exhibition game they had played in Jacksonville against St. Louis. The Packers thoroughly whipped the Cardinals that day, 41 to 14. After the final gun, Bob Skoronski was strolling casually back to the dressing room, talking to some friends who had come down for the game. "Suddenly the door opened and an assistant coach grabbed me and said, 'You better get in here.' And I walked in—and there was Coach Lombardi standing on a chair, screaming at the top of his lungs. I thought I was in the wrong locker room. I thought we had won." He was furious with the way they had played in the second half. Winning was not enough.

The signature phrase itself—"Winning isn't everything, it's the only thing"—was not coined by Lombardi, and in fact the first time it was recorded for posterity, it was uttered not by Lombardi or by any other football coach but by an eleven-year-old actress. Its etymology goes back decades before the philosopher coach reached his rhetorical apogee in Green Bay in the mid-1960s, but the best place to start is in Hollywood in 1953 with the screenwriter Melville Shavelson. Warner Brothers had optioned a piece of short fiction from the *Saturday Evening Post* about a football coach at a small Catholic college, and recruited Shavelson to write the screenplay, which he agreed to do after also being made producer. He sent the script to John Wayne, who surprised everyone by taking the starring role, even though, as Shavelson said, the football coach "didn't ride a horse or shoot a gun."

The script became the movie *Trouble Along the Way*, which was a box-office flop and quickly assigned to the dustiest bins of celluloid obscurity, yet takes on a rich subtext when viewed in parallel with the life and mythology of Vince Lombardi. The story involves a fictional college in New York named St. Anthony's, which bears a certain resemblance to Fordham. The school has fallen into debt and is to be closed by the diocese, but the old rector, Father Burke, is determined to save it. His scheme to stay afloat is to create a big-time football team that can draw sellout crowds at the Polo Grounds. In search of someone to resurrect the program, he finds Steve Williams, the John Wayne character, a winning coach with a checkered past who has lost jobs in several conferences already. Steve also happens to be a down-on-his-luck father. He lives above a pool hall with his tomboy daughter, Carol, who calls him Steve and knows how to cure his hangovers and loves football as much as he does. Her mother, Steve's ex-wife, has run off with a Manhattan dandy. Miss Singleton, a social worker played by Donna Reed, comes in to examine the home life of young Carol, and is almost deceived by the manipulative ex-wife into believing that Steve should lose parental rights, but eventually falls in love with him despite his outrageously sexist behavior, and also becomes best pals with his daughter.

Steve in the meantime goes about the business of bringing winning football to St. Anthony's. At first he seems like no one more than Vince Lombardi when he replaced the hapless Scooter McLean in Green Bay. "We gotta get back to fundamentals," Steve says, swaggering cockily around the practice field in sweatpants and a letter jacket, exhorting his players to hit him, teaching them by example how to block and tackle. But soon enough he is doing whatever it takes to win. He recruits a quarterback from the Canadian professional league, brings in more ringers by promising them a share of concession and gate receipts, and holds workouts all summer in violation of collegiate rules. His schemes, as Shavelson lets them unfold, come in the context of society's larger hypocrisy. Why shouldn't his players get the money instead of some rich alumni? Steve asks at one point. He exacts free equipment from a sporting goods store by reminding the salesman of kick-backs he had taken in the past, and forces the Polo Grounds to book St. Anthony's by threatening to organize a religious protest against the professional contests held there every Sunday.

Before the opening game of the year, Steve's ringers show up at mass wearing their letter jackets and pray for victory. The crowd at the Polo Grounds is standing room only. Father Burke is there amidst a covey of giddy religious fathers who suddenly worship football. Miss Singleton and Carol arrive at halftime after escaping a hideous society party for rich young people at Carol's mother's penthouse suite, a phony event that contrasts sharply with the vigor of football. And a huge upset is in the offing. St. Anthony's is ahead 13 to 0. Carol chomps on a hot dog, delighted with her father's success. But the virtuous social worker seems concerned. She has learned about Steve's illegal recruiting methods.

Carol wonders why she isn't cheering.

"I'm not getting paid," Miss Singleton says. Then she asks, "Is winning so important?"

And from the mouth of an eleven-year-old girl comes the immortal answer. "Listen," she responds. "Like Steve says, 'Winning isn't everything, it's the only thing!' "

In the end, of course, it is neither everything nor the only thing. Father Burke learns about Steve's underhanded methods and temporarily suspends the football program. Then he decides that Steve was just doing what he knew how to do, and that it was his own desperation to save the school that led to trouble. He brings Steve back on better terms, and the final scene shows Steve, Miss Singleton and Carol, hand in hand, leaving church.

The drama behind the scenes surpassed anything on the set. Wayne, the symbol of American manhood, was cheating on his second wife, and had brought his latest lover, Pilar, who would later become his third wife, to Hollywood to be with him during the filming. His second wife had hired a detective, however, so Wayne occasionally disappeared, once for a week, trying to lose the gumshoe's tail. When he was on the set, he demanded that in every scene with Donna Reed she had to make a play for him. Machismo wasn't everything, it was the only thing. This would have ruined the Miss Singleton character, so Shavelson pretended to adhere to Wayne's wishes, then reshot many of the scenes without him to restore them to their original intent. It was from this milieu of Hollywood mythology and deceit that Lombardi's trademark phrase arose.

Shavelson had only a passing knowledge of football when he wrote the script. Decades earlier he had covered the sport one year for the student newspaper at Cornell, from which he had graduated in 1937, making him a contemporary of Lombardi, who was playing guard at Fordham during that same era. In contrast to the formidable Fordham team of the Seven Blocks of

Granite, Cornell stumbled through the season without winning a game. But Shavelson saw enough to develop what he later called "a troubled take" on football, aware that "a helluva lot of players on other teams were too big and driving big cars and something was wrong." The coach at Cornell then was Gil Dobie, known as Gloomy Gil, who once warned Shavelson never to bet on college football games because of their unpredictability—"The outcome depends on whether the quarterback got laid last night." As to the famous phrase, Shavelson said that it came from his Hollywood agent, who also happened to represent the colorful UCLA football coach Henry "Red" Sanders. "The agent quoted me the line once and said that he had heard Sanders say it," Shavelson recalled. "That's how it got in the script."

If Red Sanders coined the phrase, as it appears he did, it would be appropriate. Before heading for UCLA and the West Coast in 1949, Sanders had been at Vanderbilt. He was the best friend of the most revered sportswriter in Nashville, Fred Russell of the *Nashville Banner,* and by extension also close to Russell's mentor, Grantland Rice, who had gone on from Vanderbilt and Nashville to become the great mythmaker of sports in New York. Herb Rich, who played for Sanders at Vanderbilt and for Lombardi in New York, said they were equally intimidating. Sanders, he said, "was one of those coaches who, if he walked by, you would start jogging in place, just to show that you were active. He had a cutting tongue, and we feared him." His cutting tongue meant something different to the press. He was known for his sardonic wit and frequent use of sayings. Sometimes he would throw out a series of clichés just to exasperate the sportswriters. "With malice aforethought," Russell once wrote, Sanders would answer questions "with such moth-eaten phrases as 'I hope Dame Fortune is with us.' . . . Then, after he's had his fun, Red will talk so articulately and with such a sense of what is news that he practically writes the lead paragraph."

According to Russell, who continued writing his column into his nineties in the late 1990s, Sanders first uttered the winning isn't everything phrase long before he reached UCLA, indeed before he began at Vanderbilt. "I remember hearing him saying it back in the mid-1930s when he was coaching at the Columbia Military Academy," Russell recalled. It is likely that Sanders meant it literally, yet with a touch of sarcasm. Three years after Sanders passed the phrase along to his agent and his agent passed it along to Melville Shavelson, Sanders got in trouble at UCLA for recruiting violations. He gave a speech at a prison shortly thereafter to a group of lifers, and began by saying, "Men, we've all got our problems. You all are mighty lucky you're not in the Pacific Coast Conference."

How did the saying get from Sanders to Hollywood to Lombardi? It is possible that Lombardi watched *Trouble Along the Way* in New York during his West Point years. His friends said that he would seek out any movie that had football in it, and that he liked John Wayne. But even if he saw the movie, the phrase might not have stuck. Although his dream in 1953, when the movie came out, was to revive a dormant football program at a small Catholic college, Fordham, he would have taken issue with the dark interpretation of the movie, and thus the context of the phrase. Like most aphorisms, it seems to have found its way gradually and ineluctably into the national consciousness. Before Lombardi put it on his locker room wall, it had already appeared in the yearbook of the 1961 San Diego Chargers, then coached by Sid Gillman, who decades earlier had preceded Lombardi as Colonel Blaik's line coach back when MacArthur was declaring that there was no substitute for victory. Perhaps the lineage traces back through West Point. "Winning isn't everything to Coach Sid Gillman," the Chargers yearbook biography began. "It's the only thing."

22

It's the Only Thing

WHADAYA THINK OF THAT, ya big fat wop!" Alex Karras shouted at Lombardi as he ran off the field at halftime of the Packers game in Detroit on October 17, 1965, with the Lions ahead by eighteen points. Karras appeared to love nothing more than beating Green Bay and Lombardi. For years the Packers had been the better team, but their games were always waged with ferocity by players as familiar with one another as brothers on opposite sides of a civil war. When Detroit had beaten Green Bay on Thanksgiving Day 1962, handing the Packers their only loss of that season, the victory nearly validated the Lions' ultimately disappointing year, and that single defeat was so distasteful in Green Bay that not even the championship win over the Giants completely erased it.

Now the Packers seemed on a roll again. They had won their first four games, two of critical importance over the Colts and Bears, teams that had won the conference title the previous two years. The feeling was that this team did not have the flair of the championship years, but had a more aggressive defense. In each of the first two games, Herb Adderley had returned interceptions for touchdowns, and linebacker Lee Roy Caffey, the "big turkey," as Lombardi called him, who came over in the Ringo trade, scored on an interception in the third. But at halftime at Detroit, Karras had reason to roar. His Lions were ahead, 21 to 3. They had won three of their first four games, and would be tied with Green Bay if they held the lead that afternoon. The season could turn right there.

Lombardi's players were furious as they clattered into the dressing room at halftime. Surprisingly, they were more upset than their coach.

Rather than vent his frustration on his players, Lombardi stepped atop a foot locker and delivered an oration on pride and loyalty. "Win, lose or draw, you are my football team," he said in closing. "You are the Green Bay *Packehs*. And you have your pride!" Pat Peppler, the personnel man, found himself misting up, and realized that he was not alone. The second half was no contest: Bart Starr at his best, three long touchdown passes and a four-yard run for another score, and the Packers had their belated response to the loud-mouthed Karras, winning 31 to 21.

The fact that Alex Karras was the one who had taunted Lombardi had a special meaning for the Green Bay players. They knew the Detroit tackle with the sort of intimacy that comes with playing against someone twice a year for half a decade and studying him on film for countless hours. At times Karras seemed like the best defensive lineman ever, but in films they noticed that he might play hard for one down, then rest for three. His coach could not get him to play consistently, every snap. In that sense, Karras reminded the Packers players of the edge they had over other teams. It was not that they were of superior character, but that they were pushed to overcome human nature in a way that Karras was not.

Most professional football players, explained Tom Brown, the Packers safety, "are basically lazy guys. We want to take the easy way out. We are so far superior. We've always been better. As nine-year-olds. Ten-year-olds. We were always the best athletes on the field. We probably got preferential treatment from youth coaches and all the way up. So we never really had to give one hundred percent effort. Because if we gave seventy-five percent we were better than all the other kids." If Karras had played for Green Bay, Brown and his teammates were convinced, he would have been unstoppable. Lombardi would have found a way to bring out that unused 25 percent.

The comeback against Karras and the Lions marked the beginning of another amazing run for Lombardi and Green Bay. No more second place. Other teams could go to the Shit Bowl. His favorite players grew creaky and slower, some were disabled and some left. The culture of the 1960s changed around him, challenging him and everything he believed in. Winning, the black addiction of the brain, left him depleted, mentally and physically, and his disposition became increasingly edgy. His distrusting relationship with the press devolved into occasional paranoia. The stakes seemed to increase exponentially, so that any slip threatened to erase all that he had already accomplished. Yet he persevered and won and won and won—and that made all the difference. The early championships of 1961 and 1962 had a sweet innocence that could not be duplicated, but it was in 1965 that Lombardi and his Packers began separating from the rest, lifting the team to a singular place in NFL history and turning the philosopher coach into a figure who transcended his sport.

• •

"THERE'S AN OLD FABLE that a guard is a fullback with his brains knocked out—but it's only a fable," Lombardi once told Tim Cohane. "I'm not saying guards are smarter than fullbacks or other ballcarriers, but their blocking assignments lead them to see more of what makes a play succeed or fail. More linemen and quarterbacks than fullbacks or halfbacks become good coaches." For a quarter of a century, since he took his first job at St. Cecilia in 1939 and worked alongside Handy Andy Palau, his old Fordham teammate, Lombardi had been outcoaching former backs. What made him better than the rest?

The fact that he had played guard, and from that position saw how plays worked, could only be a small part of it. After all, he also had outcoached many former linemen. One of his friends, Jack Koeppler, tried to explain Lombardi by saying that he was not the best at anything—not the most intelligent, innovative, disciplined, organized, energetic or inspiring—but far above average at everything. Herbert Warren Wind of *The New Yorker* concluded that what set Lombardi apart was his purposefulness. "He really means to do the job, and there isn't a moment when he isn't working at it." Others attributed Lombardi's success to something more mystical, an ineffable spirit that he radiated. The coach himself seemed skeptical on that score.

"What's charisma?" he once asked W. C. Heinz.

"What?"

"You're the writer. I keep reading that I have charisma. What the hell is it?"

"Relax," Heinz said. "It's not a disease."

To Steve Sabol, the young producer for NFL Films, the secret of Lombardi was not so much what he said but the sound of it. "It was all the voice," Sabol said. "The great leaders in history—Kennedy, Martin Luther King Jr., Roosevelt, Hitler—all had these really unique voices. And Lombardi's voice was so unique, so strident, so resonant, it could cut through anything. He could be on the other side of a room and talking in his regular tone and everyone would hear him." The story of the little dog, in Sabol's opinion, revealed the power of Lombardi's voice. The Sabols were in Green Bay filming the Packers preparing for a season. As Willie Davis and Ray Nitschke led the team in drills, a little dog darted around the field, rubbing up to the players, a sideshow that brought gales of laughter from fans. Then Lombardi appeared, bellowing, "Get that dog off the field," and the dog scampered away. "It was the power of that voice," Sabol said. "Any animal would respond."

To others, Lombardi's brilliance was his simplicity and dependability. Straight ahead all the way. Tell everyone what you are doing and do it better. That undeniably was an important aspect of his coaching character, yet it might also be the most misleading explanation of all, according to Lombardi's son, Vincent. "People say the only constant in life is change. I say the only constant in life is paradox. My father's life was a paradox. Everything about him." A paradox is something that seems self-contradictory but in reality is possibly true, and by that definition Vincent was right. It is only by looking at Lombardi as a paradox that one can fully appreciate him as a leader and coach.

Was it love or hate, confidence or fear, that drove Lombardi and his players? All—at the same time.

Lombardi confessed in *Look* that he considered football "a game for madmen" and that he once pounded on a huge lineman with his fists to get him to "hate me enough to take it out on the opposition." He struck the player, the coach said, because he believed that to play football well you had to have "that fire in you," and there was "nothing that stokes that fire" like hate. Hit or be hit, that was the reality of football, Lombardi believed. He had coached much the same way since his days at Saints, when he had ordered his adolescent charges to hit him until they felt a surge of emotion that approached hate. In Green Bay, he strutted around the practice field screaming "Defy me! Defy me!"—at once testing his players' resolve and fueling their anger. Jerry Kramer, Fuzzy Thurston, Henry Jordan, Jimmy Taylor—many of Lombardi's best players at one time or another felt intense hatred for him and came close to throwing a punch. "There were times," according to Max McGee, "when a lot of those guys would say 'I hate this sonofabitch!' "

And yet Lombardi simultaneously believed in love and said that love made the difference. "On this team, there is great love," he declared of his Packers. He "had a tremendous amount of love in him," thought Tim Cohane. "He loved his players and his teams." He even gave sermons to his Packers about the meaning of love. "I remember once he began a speech to us by asking 'What is the meaning of love?' " recalled Bob Skoronski. "And this is what he said. He said, 'Anybody can love something that is beautiful or smart or agile. You will never know love until you can love something that isn't beautiful, isn't bright, isn't glamorous. It takes a special person to love something unattractive, someone unknown. That is the test of love. Everybody can love someone's strengths and somebody's good looks. But can you accept someone for his inabilities?' And he drew a parallel that day to football. You might have a guy playing next to you who maybe isn't perfect, but you've got to love him, and maybe that love would enable you to help him. And maybe you will do something more to overcome a difficult situation in football because of that love. He didn't want us to be picking on each other, but thinking, What can I do to make it easier for my teammate? It was more than football, but crucial to our football success. When I got home that day, I said to my wife, 'That should have come from a pulpit somewhere.' "

From the outside, Lombardi tended to be seen in stark terms, an avatar of love or hate. Francis Stann, writing in Washington's *Evening Star*, called Lombardi's *Look* article a "hymn of hate" that was unnecessary and dangerous. "Just because Lombardi vows that it is essential to hate in order to win doesn't make it so. Certainly not on a level as relatively unimportant as athletics," Stann wrote. "But he will be believed, alas, mostly by kids who regard Vince as a genius and put his Packers on a pedestal." From the other side, hearing a different hymn, the *Catholic Herald Citizen,* the weekly newspaper of the Milwaukee Roman Catholic Archdiocese, extolled Lombardi as a theologian. "What better practical theology could there be" the *Citizen* asked, than Lombardi's theology of team love? Stann was no more right or wrong in his assessment than the archdiocese: neither saw the larger picture that with Lombardi hate and love coexisted.

There was a similar paradox in Lombardi's emphasis on confidence and its opposite, fear. He instilled confidence in his players in many ways, beginning with appearances. His insistence that his players wear blazers on the road was based largely on a belief in the old saw that clothes make the man. Once when the Jets were playing in Oakland on the same weekend that the Packers were in San Francisco, the squads arrived at the airport at the same time. Most of the Jets were in faded T-shirts, and Lombardi pointed at them and said, "Take a look at them! We don't look like that. That's not us. We're professionals." Lombardi also encouraged his players to provide generous tips to clubhouse men at every stadium, believing that they would then get more towels, after-shave talc, better treatment all around, further instilling in them a sense of professional confidence.

On the bulletin board of the locker room, Lombardi tacked a fan's note as a reminder of the correlation between professionalism and confidence. "I have begun to notice something just as important as your winning games," the letter stated. "Self-respect! The attitude you have instilled in your players is amazing. Too often conceit and a boisterous personality are symbols of stardom. If so, you have no 'stars' on your team. I think the quiet performance of the Packers shows confidence and respect for the other members of the team and is just an extension of the attitude you have instilled in them. You are doing more than just winning football games; you are teaching many more to compete in the game of life." It was one more way, said Bob Skoronski, that Lombardi made the players "feel that we were something special."

If there is a fine line between exuding confidence and feeling comfortable, Lombardi intuitively found it. He used fear to make sure that his players never felt too comfortable. This happened in two ways. One was indirect: a fear arising from the unpredictability of his reactions. "He kept the players off balance," said Pat Peppler. "When they thought he was going to raise hell, he might, but often didn't. When they thought he'd be pleased, he'd raise hell. They were always trying to read him: How is the Old Man going to react?" If his use of fear had involved only fear of the uncertain, however, it might not have worked; his players would have considered him unfair and eventually that could have led to a loss of respect. And so beneath his volatile personality he constructed a foundation that was predictable and objective. He made sure that his players understood the standards by which they would be judged—and one way he did this was by quantifying every block and tackle they attempted on the field. This created a different fear: fear of the certain. It is why Tom Brown could look over at Forrest Gregg on the plane returning from a game in Dallas and see the square-jawed right tackle quietly muttering to himself. The Packers had won, the all-pro Gregg had played his usual dominant game, and yet all he could think about was a block he had missed in the third quarter, muttering, "Jesus Christ, I'm gonna dread films on Tuesday."

Nothing went ungraded each Monday when the coaches studied the previous day's game: every play, every player. On offense, scores of zero, one or two were assigned, depending on the effectiveness of a block. Different positions had to meet slightly different standards, but the standards were immutable. The players became so familiar with the system that as they returned to the huddle after a play, they would think to themselves: that was a one or a two or, God forbid, a zero. On Tuesday they watched the film with the coaches. "When the movies come, you know about how many times you might have zeros, you've been thinking about it since the game," said Skoronski. "And everybody's gonna see it and Lombardi's running that film back and forth and you're deathly afraid that he's going to dwell on your mistakes. He rarely passes over that zero performance." Sometimes Lombardi directed the projectionist to run a play back and forward, no one saying a word, until that familiar guttural voice broke the silence with the dreaded "Mister. . . ."

The grades were posted in the locker room on Thursday, when Lombardi assembled his Packers for an awards ceremony. Players whose grades met the highest standard were called to the front. Lombardi presented the awards himself, pulling them from his fat wallet—crisp bills (fives in the early years, tens later). Here was the other side of fear, the confidence that came with meeting or surpassing the Old Man's expectations. "It was amazing how prideful you would become," recalled Gary Knafelc, the first of Lombardi's tight ends. Knafelc's blocking skills never matched those of his successors, Ron Kramer and Marv Fleming, but his experience with the grades was typical. With every bill he received from Lombardi, Knafelc's confidence grew, and he found himself blocking better than he thought he could. "He gave you that five or ten in cash, and when he did that it meant more than anything. It could have been five thousand dollars, it meant so much."

Lombardi's weekly grading system revealed another apparent contradiction. His coaching philosophy stressed the sublimation of ego for the good of the group, yet the weekly grades placed the emphasis on individual rather than team performance. This seeming paradox can be explained in part by his concept of individual striving, which was shaped by his Catholicism. Individual will and pride, the need to be better—all of this was not a selfish assertion of ego, it was what God wanted, the sincerest expression of holiness. "We have God-given talents and are expected to use them to our fullest whenever we play," Lombardi once said. By relating individual performance to a higher calling, according to the *Catholic Herald Citizen,* Lombardi was offering "the profound, but often ignored admonition that everything we do should glorify God, and we glorify God the most when we 'put out' the most in whatever occupation or profession we have chosen."

There was a more practical explanation. According to assistant coach Phil Bengtson, Lombardi understood that team pride and his patriarchal family approach were not enough to motivate athletes. "I don't really believe that a pro player does well 'for the coach,' even when he believes he is," Bengtson once argued. "The player produces for himself and for the team as an extension of himself. That's what made Lombardi's approach so successful. He pushed each player to push himself, reward himself. Even when he spoke of team pride and performance, the basic appeal was to individual pride and performance." And here was the essence of Lombardi's coaching genius. It was once said by Henry Jordan, the defensive tackle, that "Lombardi treats us all alike. Like dogs!"—and though the phrase was a telling bit of gallows humor, it was not the truth. Lombardi studied each player on his team and constantly calibrated his use of love and hate, confidence and fear, until he found what worked.

"There are other coaches who know more about X's and O's," Lombardi once told Jack Koeppler. "But I've got an edge. I know more about football players than they do." He knew that his quarterbacks, Starr and Bratkowski, were not to be yelled at: Bart took it as an affront to his leadership and Zeke was too nervous. Hornung could handle anything, absorbed all of the Old Man's heat and kept going. Marv Fleming, the new tight end, was hugely talented, but Lombardi thought he required constant riding to play at his best. Taylor played better when he was mad at the coach, if not the world. Willie Davis was above reproach; Lombardi shrieked at him once, then explained the next day that he was only "trying to prove nobody is beyond chewing out." Skoronski was sensitive to criticism and best left alone. Fuzzy would yell at himself, deflecting Lombardi's wrath with premeditated self-flagellation. Forrest Gregg was such a monster by Wednesday afternoon that even Lombardi seemed afraid of him and stayed away for the rest of the week.

Max McGee, the seemingly carefree receiver who was notorious for challenging Lombardi's curfews, required special treatment. "If I got caught with a curfew violation during the season, Lombardi would chew my ass out. But he knew that I was the kind of player who couldn't play with that over my head. I couldn't play with people screaming at me," McGee explained. "He'd scream at me early in the week, but it would get to be Friday and practice was over and we'd be walking up the hill and he'd come over and nudge me and say, 'Hey, Maxie, how ya doin' there, heh, heh.' I hadn't talked to him for three days because he'd embarrassed me, but he was afraid it was getting close to game time and I was a big play kind of guy and he didn't want me going into the game mad at him, so the next two days he'd be making up to me for chewing my ass out in front of my buddies. It worked every time. He was the greatest psychologist."

Lombardi also calculated how his treatment of a player affected the rest of the team, a consideration that closed the circle, bringing his leadership approach back around to the precept that the group came first. He once told Dave Robinson that whenever he fined a player, he realized that the act of discipline could divide the team into three groups: those who thought he was right, those who thought he was too harsh and those who thought he was too lenient. How could he clearly demonstrate the consequences of breaking rules and yet not fragment the team? McGee was his foil. "Max was the type of guy Lombardi could fine and the entire team would accept it as no big thing," Robinson said. "Everybody knew how much he liked Max. Guys like me would think, If he's gonna fine Max a thousand dollars, what's he gonna do to me? So actually he ended up fining fewer people less money than any coach I played for. He didn't have to fine them. And when he did, he put it in a fund and used it for a postseason party. One year we were drinking champagne at the party and Max said, 'Y'all have me to thank for this!' " When McGee negotiated his next contract, Lombardi gave him back the money that he had been fined.

IN THE ELEVENTH GAME of the season, the Packers were soundly defeated by the Rams, 21 to 10, dropping their record to 8 wins and 3 losses. On the airplane returning from the coast, defensive end Lionel Aldridge started singing a carefree tune. Lombardi was infuriated by this apparent lack of concern over their dismal showing. At the morning meeting the next Tuesday, he ordered his assistant coaches to leave the room and then excoriated his players. "Dammit, you guys don't care if you win or lose. I'm the only one that cares. I'm the only one that puts his blood and guts and his heart into the game! You guys show up, you listen a little bit, you concentrate . . . you've got the concentration of three-year-olds. You're nothing! I'm the only guy that gives a damn if we win or lose."

What happened next was recounted deliciously by offensive lineman Bill Curry in *One More July,* a memoir he later wrote with George Plimpton:

> Suddenly there was a rustle of chairs in the back of the room. I
> turned around and there was Forrest Gregg, on his feet, bright red,

with a player on either side holding him back by each arm, and he was straining forward. Gregg was a real gentlemanly guy, very quiet. Great football player. Lombardi looked at him and stopped. Forrest said, "Goddammit, Coach … excuse me for the profanity"—even at his moment of rage, he was still both respectful enough and intimidated enough that he stopped and apologized— "Scuse the language, Coach, but, Goddammit, it makes me sick to hear you say something like that. We lay our ass on the line for you every Sunday. We live and die the same way you do, and it hurts." Then he began straining forward again, trying to get up there to punch Lombardi out. Players were holding him back. Then Bob Skoronski stood up, very articulate. "That's right," he said. "Dammit, don't you tell us that we don't care about winning. That makes me sick. Makes me want to puke. We care about it every bit as much as you do. It's our knees and our bodies out there that we're throwing around."

There was an awkward silence after the offensive captain sat down, and then Lombardi harrumphed, "All right! Now that's the kind of attitude I want to see. Who else feels that way?" Willie Davis, the defensive captain, had been leaning back in his folding chair, and as he came forward again the momentum propelled him unexpectedly to his feet, and there he was, rising at Lombardi's call. "Yeah, me too. I feel that way, man," he said, and after that the whole room of Packers came alive—all standing and vowing that they wanted to win as much as Lombardi did.

If Lombardi had regained the heart of his team, he knew that the soul was still missing. Paul Hornung had disappointed him game after game, even though some of the pressure had been eased with the acquisition of Don Chandler from the Giants to do the placekicking. The once-prolific Golden Boy had made it to the end zone only three times all season. In the loss to the Rams, he had gained nine yards in five carries, his third single-digit rushing effort of the year. For the past five weeks, Elijah Pitts and Tom Moore had been getting more playing time at halfback, and now, against the Vikings the week after the Rams loss, Lombardi did the unthinkable, benching Hornung for an entire game. The Packers won, narrowly, then traveled to the Washington suburbs to spend a week preparing for the key game of the season, a rematch with the Baltimore Colts, defending conference champions, now a half-game ahead of Green Bay with two games remaining.

Hornung seemed rejuvenated in practice that week, and uncommonly tame during his off-hours. He spent his nights in the motel room watching TV and drinking nothing stronger than Coca-Cola. It all worked—Lombardi's decision to bench him, Hornung's solitary nights of atonement—and on Sunday against the Colts he was restored. He scored five touchdowns, three on short runs and two on long passes from Starr, including one in which he caught the ball over the middle and sprinted away with an unexpected burst of speed. If Hornung had still been kicking, he certainly would have broken his own single-game scoring record, but even so, it was the sort of performance that reminded people of his unmatched versatility, a virtual replay of the thirty-three-point effort in 1961 that left Tony Canadeo sputtering about "the greatest day ever by a backfield man."

The play that set Hornung apart this time was not a run or a catch or a block, not even a kick, but a tackle, and it changed the game. The Packers were leading by a point, 14 to 13, with a minute left in the half when Baltimore defensive back Bob Boyd stole the ball from Taylor and raced for the end zone. Boyd would have scored if not for Hornung, who pursued him from an angle and knocked him out-of-bounds at the four. Two plays later, Dave Robinson intercepted a Baltimore pass and rumbled eighty-seven yards for a touchdown, and the rout was on, with Hornung's three second-half touchdowns leading Green Bay to its final 42 to 27 victory. Lombardi was jubilant in the locker room afterwards. It was all about pride for Vince and his boy. "This was the big one and no one on the squad reacts to pressure better than Hornung," Lombardi said, repeating his favorite words of praise. "The bigger the game, the better he plays."

The next big game came two weeks later against the Colts again, this time back in Wisconsin. The game was scheduled for December 26. The Colts arrived in Green Bay on Christmas Day with nothing to lose. Already that season they had lost through injuries not only the superb Johnny Unitas but also his backup, Gary Cuozzo, and were now playing with Tom Matte, a converted halfback, at quarterback. Matte was a gutsy player but could barely throw and remembered the plays by wearing a cheat sheet on his wrist. Passing from the pocket was unknown to him; his basic play was a college-style rollout. Even so, he led the Colts to a final game victory over the same resurgent Rams who had defeated the Packers. Anything was possible, Lombardi feared.

Searching for ways to motivate his team before the game, Lombardi turned to the signature phrase of his mentor, Red Blaik. Above each locker he had Dad Braisher post a sign that read: "ANYTHING IS OURS . . . PROVIDING WE ARE WILLING TO PAY THE PRICE." It always came back to Blaik: how Lombardi taught the game, how he motivated players. "My football is your football," he wrote in a letter to Blaik from Green Bay. "My approach to a problem is the way I think you would approach it. I just hope and pray I can do justice to it and you." Paying the price meant that talent alone would not suffice. Lombardi could not have chosen a more appropriate message for a game in which neither team had much to offer beyond endurance and will.

Hornung was hobbling again, in and out. The first play was a disaster: Starr completes a pass, the tight end fumbles, Colts linebacker Don Shinnick scoops up the ball and heads toward the end zone, Starr tries to knock over one of Shinnick's blockers but is smacked in the ribs and carried off the field, not to return. No beauty now, not much offense, just pounding and punting and waiting for breaks on a long afternoon. A field goal put the Colts up 10 to 0 at the half. The mistakes started to even out in the third quarter when Baltimore's punter bobbled a snap and was tackled trying to make a run for it. A short drive led to a Hornung touchdown plunge. In the fourth quarter, with the Packers trailing 10 to 7, they got another break. Zeke Bratkowski, in for Starr, was tackled for a loss on third down, apparently ending a crucial drive—but Billy Ray Smith was called for roughing the passer and Green Bay kept the ball.

With 1:58 left, Don Chandler kicked a twenty-seven-yard field goal to tie the game. Colts players and fans would argue forever that it was wide of the post. "Wide by three feet," said tackle Lou Michaels. The Baltimore newspapers ran a picture showing the ball in the air just after it had passed the goalpost, and from the angle of the shot it looked as if it might have missed. The problem was that the uprights in that era were extremely short. Although Chandler did not hit the ball solidly, it soared high and near the imaginary line rising straight above the upright. Two members of the officiating crew were well positioned and considered it good. Ray Scott was on the field behind the other goalpost, waiting to do interviews with the winning team when the game ended. He had a straight-on view of the ball's trajectory. "I had the best view of it, and it was good, for Chrissakes it was good!" Scott insisted.

Overtime and sudden death, the first for Lombardi since the championship match between the Giants and Colts in 1958, when he was New York's offensive assistant. There was nothing as stirring in this one. No long drive with Johnny U hitting Raymond Berry, no Ameche bursts up the middle. Just one ferocious block and tackle after another and twenty-eight plays and punts back and forth and Lou Michaels lining up for a forty-seven yarder, Lombardi on the sidelines thinking his team has played so well that it will be no disgrace to lose, a game that reminds him of the old Fordham-Pitt scoreless ties, but Michaels misses, and the battle goes for thirteen minutes and thirty-nine seconds of overtime until the Packers field goal team trots out, rookie center Bill Curry praying to God for a good snap, all-pro cornerback Herb Adderley closing his eyes and turning away, listening to a scratchy sidelines radio, Chandler lining up from twenty-five yards out and kicking and—it is good, indisputably. The Packers had paid the price, winning what Henry Jordan called the toughest game he had ever been in. "Well, gentlemen," Lombardi said to newsmen crowded around him in his dressing room after the game. "You can't say we don't give the world a thrill."

The world championship was played in Green Bay the following Sunday, the Packers against the Eastern Division's Cleveland Browns. It began snowing before dawn that morning and five inches covered the ground by noon. Dozens of cars slid off the Buttes des Morts bridge near Oshkosh, causing a major bottleneck on the road up from Milwaukee. The Browns were staying in a hotel in Appleton and it took their bus nearly two hours to reach the stadium from thirty miles away. When Jim Brown and his teammates stepped onto the field less than an hour before kickoff, the turf was soft from the snow and protective hay that had just been removed, and a cold rain made the footing treacherous. Henry Jordan had joked before the game that he had a plan to stop the great Cleveland runner: step aside and let Willie Davis get at him. Now the Packers had a better defender—the weather held Jim Brown to fifty yards.

In time, this game would be nearly forgotten, lost in the middle of Lombardi's great triumphs. It was the last title game played before the era of Super Bowls, and though it was attached to the two Packers championships that followed in a remarkable string of three straight titles, the fact that it was not hyped as Super in retrospect made it seem oddly apart. This was both unfair and fitting in a sense, because the game was best considered on its own, a faded dream played in the mist and slop, a transitory moment between football past and future. It was, as it turned out, the last great game for Lombardi's glorious running back tandem of Taylor and Hornung, No. 31 plowing for ninety-six yards despite a sore groin, No. 5 stepping his way to 105 with his ailing shoulder, their jerseys and faces caked in mud.

The decisive touchdown in the 23 to 12 win came on a Packer sweep: Starr taking the snap at the thirteen-yard line, handing off to Hornung who follows left behind his linemen, Kramer and Skoronski, making textbook blocks, sealing an alley, the Horn cutting at precisely the right moment up the alley, one more time, gliding through the mud to the end zone. The image of that perfect Packer sweep endured even as the game itself diminished with time. Ed and Steve Sabol were at the stadium that day and captured it on camera for NFL Films, and from then on when they went into their film archive for a classic piece of pro football footage, they often turned to those few timeless seconds of the Golden Boy sweeping through the mud and snow to beat the Browns.

With ten seconds remaining, Lombardi honored his stars just as he had done the last time he won a title at home, bringing them out one by one—Starr, Taylor, Hornung—to standing ovations from the exuberant home fans. The gun sounded and Green Bay was Titletown USA once more. Hornung and Taylor, their faces smudged with the grime of a day's work, hoisted Lombardi to their shoulders and carried him onto the field, and he rode atop them in his rain hat and slicker, one arm around each, teeth flashing, winning the only thing. In the locker room he said that his 1965 Packers were not the best team he had ever coached, but the one with the most character, and he lifted a champagne glass to his boys and to the new year.

• •

THE GAME on the field no longer seemed the most demanding part of football. Year by year the competition between the NFL and AFL had grown fiercer and more expensive, requiring more of Lombardi's attention as general manager. The Packers had never lost a first-round draft choice to the new league, but that now seemed possible. Only a year before, Joe Willie Namath, the AFL's first pick, had signed with the New York Jets for a record $427,000, giving them an enormous public relations boost. For 1966 the first pick in the AFL was Jim Grabowski, a fullback from Illinois, chosen by the expansion Miami Dolphins. He had also been Lombardi's first selection. With Taylor nearing the end of his career, Lombardi intended to groom Grabowski as his successor, the same way that he hoped to bring in Donny Anderson, the lanky halfback from Texas Tech, as Hornung's eventual replacement. Anderson, Green Bay's top choice in 1965, had been redshirted a year in college and was only now eligible to play for the Packers.

The war against the AFL forced rival teams in the older league to form odd alliances of collusion. An informal group of "concerned citizens" with ties to the NFL had been recruited to babysit coveted draft choices. Grabowski's babysitter was Vern Buol, who was not a Packers fan but an associate of George Halas's son Mugsy in Chicago. Buol, the vice president of a meatpacking company, was assigned by the league to befriend Grabowski and keep him from the AFL's clutches. When the young fullback traveled to New York to be honored on *The Ed Sullivan Show* as part of an All-America team, Buol came along and took his wife and Grabowski's fiancée, Kathy— the three of them staying at the Plaza Hotel while Grabowski was put up at the Waldorf-Astoria with the players. Grabowski had grown up in northwest Chicago, the son of a butcher (just like Lombardi), and was stunned by the lucrative professional world now awaiting him. The Dolphins kept offering more money, but he considered it an honor to be drafted by the world-champion Packers and expressed little interest in the enticements of the newer league.

In an effort to keep Grabowski away from the Packers, the Dolphins gave Jets owner Sonny Werblin permission to talk to him. Werblin asked Grabowski whether he would be interested in signing with the Jets if they acquired his rights. He could run in the same backfield with Namath and have a wallet just as thick. Grabowski remained noncommittal; his heart was with the NFL. When his attorney, Arthur Morse, called Lombardi and pointed out that the AFL was offering more money than the Packers, Lombardi summoned the player and his agent to Green Bay. As Grabowski later recounted:

"So they send a private plane down to pick us up in Chicago, and we're flying up to Green Bay and Arthur is whispering to me because he's afraid the pilot might be a spy, one of their guys, and he whispers, 'Jim, no matter what Lombardi offers, say you need twenty-four hours to think about it.' And I say, 'Of course, twenty-four hours.' We get to Green Bay and a car picks us up and takes us over to Lombardi's office in the stadium. We walk in there: championship trophies, pictures of all these great players as you are walking down the hall. And for a twenty-one-year-old kid who would have played for a hamburger and a shake, it's pretty impressive. So we sit down in his office. It's huge, with a boardroom table on one end. More pictures and trophies. We sit down at one end of the board table, across from Lombardi. I'm looking across at a legend. My attorney is trying to keep me calm. Remember. Twenty-four hours. And Arthur starts by saying, 'Mr. Lombardi, we told you we wouldn't go back and forth, but you must know that the Miami Dolphins offer is considerably more than yours.'

"Lombardi, without hesitation, looked me right in the eye and said, 'Here's what we'll offer you. We'll give you a three-year contract. The amount is four hundred thousand. You can split it however you want. The only thing is your salary can't be higher than forty thousand because that's the highest salary on the team right now.' He looked me right in the eye and said, 'What do you think, son?' And I, without thinking, shook my head yes and said, 'Sure.' My attorney is hitting me under the table to remind me of the twenty-four hours. But I couldn't help but say yes. That's it. Let's get it over with. The instructions to me went right out the window. It was the way Lombardi looked at me and said, 'What do you think, son?' The look, the trophies, the pictures of the team, the legend, how can you not be influenced by this? I should have known then this was the first sign of the great psychologist that he was."

Anderson also signed with the Packers, though for more money, more than a half-million-dollar package, and Lombardi had his next backfield. Grabo and Donny: was this the making of another legend? *Sports Illustrated* put them on the cover. The press labeled them "The Gold Dust Twins." As a general manager, Lombardi bragged about them, proud that he had acquired such talented players, though he had paid far more money than he had wanted to, and was pushed by the league to sign his draft choices at whatever cost. As the philosopher coach, he could not celebrate. He had won the war with the AFL, but that did not matter most; what he cared about was his own team, its mental and financial balance. How would the veterans take it, the ones who had paid the price and won for him season after season? Most of them responded surprisingly well, offering variations of the words Henry Jordan said to Grabowski the first time they met: "Kid, I don't care what you make just so long as you help me win. If you help us win you'll fit in fine." Hornung was a prince to them, and so was Elijah Pitts. But one Packer was furious and determined to get his due: Jim Taylor looked at the salaries Anderson and Grabowski were getting and decided that he would play in Green Bay one last year, finishing his contract, then get some big money of his own.

Money was coming, freedom was here, the world was changing. Lombardi struggled with it himself. The expansion Atlanta Falcons had made him a tremendous financial offer to leave Green Bay that year, but he had resisted, largely because he coveted power more than money. "I just turned down being a potential millionaire," he told his aide-de-camp, Ockie Krueger. He urged the Falcons instead to hire one of his assistants, Norb Hecker, while he stayed with his Packers, wringing from the executive board another raise and contract extension through 1973. If he was tempted, imagine how his players felt. This all meant nothing but trouble for his football family.

ON THE ELEVENTH of June, Lombardi turned fifty-three, and the next day he became a grandfather. Another namesake, this one with even the same middle name—Vincent Thomas Lombardi II. The Old Man sounded ecstatic when his son called from the hospital with the vital statistics. Baby Vincent was a big one. "I have a grandson and he weighs ten pounds and is thirty-one inches long!" Lombardi boasted at the office, until Boyd Dowler said to him, "Uh, Coach, I was a long baby and I was only twenty-two inches." No matter. God, family and the Green Bay Packers. Vince and Marie went to St. Paul for the baptism. He brought a Polaroid with an electronic flash, his latest contraption, and kept forgetting to plug it in, and every time he snapped a picture the flash fizzled and he had to try again. Jill and Vincent soon came out to Sunset Circle with their toddler. Lombardi arrived home and saw his grandson in the family room. "Look at that!" he boomed in amazement—and it was all over. He had traumatized the baby with his voice, and Vincent II started to cry and wriggle unhappily. For months thereafter, much to Lombardi's dismay, Baby Vincent cried every time his Poppop came into sight.

Once, at a postgame cocktail party in the basement at Sunset Circle, Lombardi and broadcaster Ray Scott entered into a discussion about the consequences of their busy lives. Scott said he regretted not spending more time with his children, and Lombardi concurred. "You know what, Coach? I was a terrible father," he told Scott. He tried to be a family man. The speech he gave to his players about loving someone who did not have outward beauty or overwhelming talent—in a sense that theme came from his feelings about Susan. She was a senior in high school that year, already nineteen, barely getting by in school, constantly testing her father's rules. Once he asked her when she was going to take the SAT's and she said, "What the heck are those?" Had no clue, and when he told her they were the tests to get into college, she said she had no intention of going to school again after high school. Susan had won several equestrian awards, but was not competitive. Her mother sent her to weight clinics but she kept eating. "She accepted herself for what she was," said Mary Jo Antil, her classmate at St. Joseph's.

Susan had a yellow Mustang convertible and a fake ID card. On spring weekends she and her friends gathered at Sunset Circle before going out. Lombardi would be in the recliner in the back room, drinking a Budweiser and eating apples and cheese, dozing on and off as he watched television. As Susan was leaving, he would yell, "Susan, where are you going?" She would lie and he would tell her to be home by midnight. Like his players, she always had a curfew.

Sometimes after a few beers at the Prom off Highway 41, she lamented to friends that it was no fun being the daughter of a famous man. If she did not often break curfew, she loved to nip it. "I was nineteen and my friends could stay out till one and I had to be in by midnight, so I took it right down to the last minute. I had it timed from the moment I left wherever I was to getting home by twelve o'clock sharp." Her dad invariably was asleep by then. Before graduation, Lombardi and Ray Antil took their daughters, Susan and Mary Jo, to the father-daughter banquet at the academy. The girls asked if they could go out on the town afterwards, and their fathers agreed. "They took us to all the bars," said Mary Jo Antil. "We went to Speed's on Monroe Street and ended the night at Tropics. It had all these palm trees. I danced with Mr. Lombardi. I can still see him doing the locomotion and the watusi. He was totally out of his realm, and he enjoyed it immensely."

LOMBARDI'S PACKERS seemed unstoppable again in 1966. They lost only twice by a total of four points. The defense, anchored by big Ron Kostelnik, the underrated left tackle, was dominant. Six touchdowns came on interceptions, two by Bob Jeter, who had combined with Herb Adderley to form the best cornerback duo in the league. Starr had blossomed into the league's most valuable player, enjoying a career year in which he completed nearly two-thirds of his passes for fourteen touchdowns and only three interceptions. The backfield was not as fearsome as it once had been, but more diverse, with Elijah Pitts scoring ten touchdowns, the sturdy rock between fading stars Taylor and Hornung and the untested Gold Dust twins. There did not seem much to complain about all year, but Lombardi found it—at the most unlikely time. On October 23, the expansion Atlanta Falcons visited Milwaukee and were beaten 56 to 3. It was the sort of game where everyone contributed: the defense scored two touchdowns, Anderson ran a punt back seventy-seven yards, and both he and Grabowski got some playing time in the backfield.

After the game Ken Hartnett, a sports reporter for the AP in Milwaukee, found Jim Taylor at his locker. Taylor seemed upset that Lombardi had not played him more. Hartnett asked Taylor about a rumor that had been going around: Was he playing out his option with the Packers? *Yeah,* Taylor said, adding that the large salaries paid to Anderson and Grabowski had been an affront to his pride. Hartnett wrote the story. In a different time and place, this would have been no big deal. In Wisconsin during the Lombardi era it was. So big, in fact, that Bud Lea of the *Milwaukee Sentinel* had had the same story and had been eager to write it, but his editor, Lloyd Larson, instructed him not to. "We don't want to upset that guy up in Green Bay," Lea later remembered Larson telling him. Larson was an unabashed cheerleader for the Packers, but there was another reason he was afraid to upset Lombardi. "He accepted a ton of complimentary tickets," said Chuck Lane, then the team's junior publicity man. "I'd go down to advance a game and Larson would shake me down. He was one of the biggest ticket brokers in the city of Milwaukee."

In any event, Lombardi erupted when he saw the story in Monday's papers and ordered Tom Miller, another of his publicists, to find Taylor pronto and bring him in for an explanation. Taylor was asleep at his apartment above an east side tavern. "Put your clothes on. Coach wants to talk to you," Miller told him. When Taylor reached the office, Lombardi held up a copy of the paper and bellowed, "Explain this!" Taylor claimed that he had been misquoted.

Lombardi then announced that he was banning Hartnett from all pregame and postgame press conferences. The reporter would not be allowed in the Packers locker room or offices. Wisconsin sportswriters had taken a lot from Lombardi over the years, but this was too much. By that afternoon they had drafted a petition to Commissioner Rozelle protesting the coach's action. The AP's Milwaukee bureau chief, Austin Bealmear, called Lombardi and urged him to change his mind. It soon became clear that Lombardi had a rebellion on his hands, and that even he, the Pope of Green Bay, could not do anything he wanted unilaterally. Rozelle called to remind him of the NFL policy: accredited writers could not be banned from clubhouses, dressing rooms or press boxes. Lombardi was forced to retreat. On Wednesday he called Hartnett's boss and rescinded the order.

The most revealing aspect of Lombardi's botched effort to punish the press was that he knew Hartnett had written an accurate story. Taylor had not signed his contract and was privately threatening to leave at the end of the year. The truth is what had infuriated Lombardi, and the fact that someone in the press would print it. If his only concern had been the spirit of the team, one could see why he would be distressed that Taylor had raised the salary issue in public. But taking it out on Hartnett revealed a sense of grandiosity. "He didn't want it publicly known that Taylor wanted out of Green Bay because that challenged his total control," Bud Lea explained later. "It was going to be Lombardi's decision. Lombardi tells guys when to quit here. Lombardi tells guys who's going to play and who isn't. Nobody makes decisions but him, not Jimmy Taylor or Kenny Hartnett. Everyone had feared the guy up here—and he wanted it to stay that way."

It was one thing for Lombardi to cut or trade a player when he wanted to, but quite another for someone to try to leave Lombardi, even his assistant coaches. When Bill Austin announced after the 1964 season that he was leaving for the Rams, explaining that his wife could no longer tolerate Wisconsin winters, Lombardi tried to stop him. "You can't leave," Lombardi said, and Austin was forced to go to the commissioner's office to win his freedom.

Lombardi had a need to prevail. Back when Curley Lambeau died in June 1965, the founder of the Packers had been duly honored in his hometown, and Lombardi seethed. When Art Daley decided to switch covers of the team yearbook, replacing a picture of a player with one of Lambeau and Lombardi shaking hands, Lombardi threw a fit. "That's the worst book you ever put out! Terrible!" he complained. It was the picture with Curly that had bothered him so much. He disliked Lambeau, a colorful philanderer, but more than that he wanted to be regarded separately and better. He refused to talk to Daley for nearly a year after that, and when he finally gave up the grudge, Daley saw him at Oneida Golf and Riding and asked politely, "What the hell was that all about last season?" In a rare acknowledgment of his oversized ego, Lombardi answered, "Let me tell you something. I don't like to have the spotlight taken away from me and my team." Even worse than the yearbook picture was the Packer board's decision to rename the stadium. He was now coaching at Lambeau Field.

The black addiction of the brain had overtaken Lombardi, as it did so often during those middle years in Green Bay. There were times when every question from the press seemed to be taken as an affront or dismissed as stupid, every photographer, even the team's official photographer, the skilled and unobtrusive Vernon Biever, was regarded with suspicion as a possible spy ("Get him off the field!"), and the mildest stories were considered seditious scouting reports for the enemy. The always-faithful Lee Remmel was watching practice once and noted that Zeke Bratkowski had thrown two interceptions in successive series. "I took it down thinking it might be a sentence or two in my notes," Remmel recalled. "And I hear this roar, 'KEEP THAT CRAP OUT OF THE PAPER!' Lombardi was yelling in front of hundreds of people. I was stunned. 'Me?' 'Yeah, keep that crap out of the paper. Be original!' " When Remmel confronted Lombardi, saying he was especially insulted that the coach considered him unoriginal, he was afraid that he would be barred from the team plane. Lombardi backed down, as he often did when he was directly challenged. The sporting press was in transition during the middle sixties, in many places just starting to assert its independence from teams and coaches.

Even his favored New York reporters riled Lombardi then. Tim Cohane came out for a Bears game and was shocked to see how "paranoid" his old friend had become. "Arthur, how can you ask a stupid question like that!" Cohane heard Lombardi growl at the other Arthur Daley, the one from Fordham and the *Times*. "That's a very stupid question, mister," Lombardi snapped another time at columnist Jerry Izenberg—to which Izenberg responded, "I don't think you coached such a brilliant game, mister!" The insults went on from there, with Lombardi saying Izenberg didn't know a goddamn thing about football and Izenberg retorting that Lombardi didn't know a goddamn thing about journalism—and the Wisconsin writers in the room, according to Bud Lea, "enjoyed the absolute hell out it, somebody finally standing up to Lombardi like that." But it was a bitter joy. The atmosphere in almost any room that included the coach and members of the press was tense and uneasy.

Not even paperboys were immune from Lombardi's intimidation. Mike Gourlie, who rode his bike around Allouez with a cloth bag over his shoulder, delivering the *Milwaukee Journal,* spent two years rehearsing an admiring speech he would give if Lombardi ever answered the door at Sunset Circle when he was collecting. For two years it was always Marie who gave him a generous quarter tip. Finally, one night he knocked and there was the Pope himself, and Gourlie looked at him and "nothing would come out." Lombardi shot him an angry look and growled, "Spit it out, boy!" No speech. "Collecting, sir." Gourlie forgot everything else he was going to say.

The pressure of success seemed to weaken Lombardi's health as the 1966 season progressed. He had given up smoking three years earlier, but he still suffered occasional dizzy spells and found himself nearly blacking out in the locker room a few times. He had always napped in the evening; now he needed another in the early afternoon. Every workday at quarter to one, after checking his mail, he closed the door to his office and settled on the green leather couch. "No sooner would his head hit the davenport than he was asleep," according to Ruth McKloskey. She was under strict instructions to block all calls, putting off Pete Rozelle and Art Modell if need be. At exactly quarter to two, she would ring him from her office and say, "Wake-up call. Time to get up, Mr. Lombardi."

He struggled with diarrhea and constipation. Dr. Eugene Brusky, who conducted a physical on Lombardi every year, wanted to do a proctoscopic exam, but Lombardi said no, asserting that there was no way he would let anyone "stick that goddamn thing up my ass." He had several confidential talks with Father Burke, the Norbertine priest who had befriended him at St. Norbert. Once, "in the sanctity of the chapel," Burke later recalled, the coach "confided that something bothered him a lot in his stomach." Lombardi consumed bottles of antacid medicine to try to ease the churning. What Burke noticed, more than physical pain, was mental anguish. "The pressure for constant wins had gnawed on his nerves. He wanted to win, it is true, but he was disturbed over the tactics he had to use to effect his record. He told me quite confidentially that he knew he would have to give up coaching to get away from the tensions that plagued him."

Lombardi broached the subject in public at the end of the regular season. After winning the Western Conference, the Packers left for Tulsa for a week of training in preparation for the NFL Championship Game. The title match was in Dallas against the Cowboys, who had won the Eastern Conference in their sixth year under Coach Tom Landry. For more than three decades, the NFL title game had been the ultimate in pro football. But this year it had a penultimate feel. If Lombardi's team beat Dallas, there would be one more game. The NFL and AFL had ended their war and agreed to a gradual merger. The symbol of football peace would be a first-ever playoff between the two leagues for the world championship.

"LAST GO FOR LOMBARDI?" asked a headline in the *Dallas Times-Herald* five days before the NFL title game. In an interview with sportswriter Steve Perkins on the Tulsa practice field, the coach intimated that the answer might be yes. "Lombardi himself brought the subject of retirement up when he was told of a remark by linebacker Ray Nitschke, who said that this game against the Cowboys was the 'biggest' for Lombardi since he came to Green Bay," Perkins wrote. Lombardi "instinctively bristled at the presumption of a player deciding what was 'biggest' for his coach." When Perkins explained that Nitschke meant this was the first NFL title game where the winner went on to something more, Lombardi relaxed somewhat. "Oh, well. That's very true," he said. "And another thing that makes it a big one is that it could be my last one." Why would he quit now? "The job has become too much to handle. I think it's time I gave somebody else a chance. There used to be an offseason. For that matter, there used to be some time off during the season. I remember when I was in college I used to drop in on the Giants meetings. They had one reel of film and they'd show it to the team one time, and that was it."

Perhaps Lombardi wanted to relax but could not bring himself to, just as he sometimes longed to be more like his carefree playboys, Hornung and McGee. But more likely his concern was that the nature of his job had changed. Once, it was hard for him to distinguish between work and play; they fit together like the tattoos etched into his father's knuckles. Now it was WORK on one hand and more WORK on the other. This week he had to work harder than ever. It would be painful for him to lose to Landry. Even when they were on the same side, as the top assistants for Jim Lee Howell in New York, they had been competitors—the explosive Vinnie's offense against cool Tom's defense. Lombardi had set himself apart in the years since, but people were starting to write about Landry as the mind of a new age. Landry and his multiple offense and flex defense, making football seem robotic and complicated—enough to goad Lombardi into devising a new offense for one game, which is just what he did in shockingly cold Tulsa that week.

Lombardi's schemes worked well enough when it counted in Dallas. On the first play from scrimmage, Elijah Pitts popped through a hole in the flex for thirty-four yards, and a few plays later Starr connected with him for a seventeen-yard touchdown. Pitts had the same nose for the goal line as his mentor, Hornung, who had been out since the second Bears game, his shoulder inflamed again by a hit from Doug Buffone. On the next kickoff, Mel Renfro fumbled and Jim Grabowski scooped up the ball and galloped in for another score. "My feet never touched the ground after I reached the end zone," Grabowski said later. "I floated back to the sidelines." Starr threw four touchdown passes before the day was over and Lombardi's offense had thirty-four points, but the game was in doubt until the last play.

Tom Brown, the strong safety, was having as much trouble with Cowboys tight end Frank Clarke as he once had with the curveball during his cup of coffee with the Washington Senators. In the fourth quarter, with the Packers leading 34 to 20, Clarke ran a pattern straight at Brown, turned him the wrong way and broke clear to catch a sixty-eight-yard touchdown pass from Don Meredith. Dallas got the ball back in the final minutes and Clarke "ran the same damn play to beat me again," Brown recalled. This time Brown grabbed Clarke as he was going by, and the referee called interference. Ball on the Packers two, a touchdown to tie, and it seemed almost inevitable. But an offensive lineman moved before the snap, a critical penalty that cost the Cowboys five yards. On fourth down, Meredith tried to roll right, and there was big Dave Robinson hunting him down, and Meredith in desperation tossed the ball high and gentle into the end zone—and there was the prayerful Tom Brown, waiting for redemption. "God, yeah," he said to himself as he cradled the ball.

In the locker room after the game, Dave Robinson was sitting on his stool, receiving congratulations from teammates. Lombardi came by and stared at him, unsmiling. Later, in private, Lombardi would hug Robbie and praise him for the game-winning play, but now he wanted to make another point. "You weren't supposed to be blitzing," he growled, and walked away, thinking already about more WORK—now he had to make sure he didn't lose it all to the Kansas City Chiefs.

THE GAME was a lowercase phenomenon that first year at the Los Angeles Coliseum—super bowl, no Roman numerals attached. Lamar Hunt, owner of the Chiefs, took the name from his grandson's toy, a high-bouncing super ball. The official name on the game programs was World Championship Game AFL vs. NFL. The Packers went to Santa Barbara for a week of training (the superstitious Lombardi considered it good luck to stay in cities named for saints) and were of two minds about how seriously to take the Chiefs. Much of what they saw on film made them dismissive of the other league. Sherman Plunkett, an offensive tackle for the New York Jets, his prodigious gut sprawling over his belt, became their symbol of the sloppy AFL. Every time he appeared on film, Henry Jordan shouted, "Hey, roll that back! Look at Plunkett!" and the Packers all laughed. Plunkett did not play for the Chiefs, of course, but the films also revealed plenty of ways to exploit Kansas City on offense and defense. Particularly noticeable was the way their linebackers would stay near the line of scrimmage and not drop back into pass defense. "We had them checked," said Willie Wood. "It was just a matter of how emotionally involved we were gonna get."

That was Lombardi's job, and he took to it with manic intensity. The practice sessions in Santa Barbara were unforgiving. "He was miserable that week, he liked to have killed us," said Bob Skoronski. "I personally thought he was going to leave the game on the practice field, the only time I ever thought that." Lombardi was so obsessed that Marie left for Las Vegas for two days and he barely noticed she was gone. ("You mean you flew over the mountains?" he said to her when she got back. "No, dummy," she replied. "I flew under them.") No relaxation for his men, no distractions. He raised the fines for curfew violations to record amounts. "Vince made it very clear from our first day out there that we had to win that game and that he didn't want to make a squeaker out of it," said Red Cochran, his offensive assistant. Lombardi had nothing to gain. One loss and all was lost, he said. If he lost, it would diminish everything that he had accomplished since he got to Green Bay: the championships of 1961, 1962 and 1965, the NFL title win over Dallas in 1966—if he could not beat the Kansas City Chiefs, what would any of that mean now?

There were other reasons they had to win. Not just for his legacy and theirs, but for the NFL. Tony Canadeo said Lombardi felt that he was carrying the league on his shoulders. "If we'd have dumped that game, God! Everyone would have blamed the Packers!" Even before they reached Santa Barbara, the pressure had started. "We were getting all kinds of telegrams and telephone calls from all these millionaires who owned teams," said Ruth McKloskey. " 'Go get it. Go get 'em, Vince!' And over the league Teletype. Everyone giving advice. Watch this. Watch that. Every time something came in, you could see this grim look on Mr. Lombardi's face. The NFL was all uptight about it. So he was very upset." What the owners said to Lombardi, Lombardi said to his players. "He told us this was for a way of life, a game of survival, a test of manhood," remembered Willie Davis. Lombardi received a letter from Wellington Mara of the Giants that moved him so much he read it to his team. Like other owners, Mara reminded Lombardi how essential it was that the NFL team win, but he ended his note with the ultimate compliment. He was happy, Mara said, that it was Lombardi and his Packers, among all the league's teams, carrying the NFL standard.

Before dinner on the eve of the game, Max McGee spotted Ray Scott in the lobby of the Packers' hotel in Los Angeles. McGee was nearing the end of his career and had not played much that season. He had caught four passes all year, playing behind Boyd Dowler and Carroll Dale. But Dowler had been hurt while scoring a touchdown against Dallas, so McGee paid more attention than he might have to the game films. Scott, the Packers' regular season play-by-play man, was working the game for CBS. The competition in the television world was as fierce as the one between the leagues. CBS was the NFL network, NBC had the AFL, and both had rights to the game. McGee motioned to Scott to come with him to a corner of the lobby, behind a potted tree. He had a scoop.

"Scotty," he said. "I don't know if I'm gonna get in that game tomorrow, but if I do, they'll never get old Max out."

"What do you mean?" Scott asked.

"I've been studying film and I've found me a cornerback. I'm gonna have him for breakfast, lunch and dinner."

Then McGee went back to his room to see if Paul Hornung wanted to go out on the town with him. The week in Santa Barbara had been frustrating for McGee—not Lombardi's practices, but the fact that there was nothing to do at night. He was wired and ready for action by the time he reached Los Angeles. Before conspiring with Scott behind the lobby tree, he had met a few stewardesses in the bar, and they had agreed to meet later that night. "Horn," he said to Hornung back in their room. "I made a little deal. Gonna meet a coupla girls." But Hornung declined. He knew that he was not likely to play the next day, the nerve in his shoulder was still bothering him, but the notion of paying thousands of dollars to break curfew did not appeal to him. "He had a little more value of money than I did," McGee explained later. Hawg Hanner, who had retired and was now an assistant coach, was in charge of the curfew bed checks that night. McGee and Hanner had snuck out together many a night in the old days. The night before the Chiefs game, Hanner went to Max and Paul's room first. They were always checked first on the theory that if they were in, everybody was in.

Hawg stuck his head in the door and saw McGee under the blankets, covered to his neck. "Okay you guys, you're here now," Hanner said.

"Hawg, you gonna check us again?" McGee asked.

"Yeah, gol dang, I'm gonna check you guys every hour," Hanner responded. As he closed the door, he looked back one last time and shook his head no.

Minutes later McGee was on his way. He returned to the hotel the next morning just as Bart Starr was walking through the lobby to buy a paper and get breakfast. Starr noticed that Max was wearing the same sport coat and shirt he had on the night before. When McGee got back to the room, he asked Hornung, "Am I safe?"

"No," said Hornung. "They caught your ass."

"You're shittin' me."

"Ah, nothing happened."

McGee was so relaxed he napped for an hour and looked refreshed boarding the bus for the stadium. Lombardi was the last man on. He took his seat, front right, and the driver shut the door and started to pull out. "Just a minute," Lombardi said. "Stop a minute." He rose to his feet, stepped into the aisle, got the attention of his players and danced a soft shoe. The players started screaming, "Go, Coach, Go!"

When he sat down, Jack Koeppler asked him, "What the hell was that?"

"They were too tight," Lombardi said.

The game would be watched by the largest television audience ever to view a sports event, more than 65 million people, but in person it did not feel historic. There were 61,946 people inside the Memorial Coliseum, more than enough to fill Lambeau Field, but they seemed lost inside that monstrous stadium. The most expensive ticket was twelve dollars, and still more than a third of the seats went empty. Pete Rozelle saw Ed Sabol in the locker room before the game and handed him fifteen complimentary tickets. Sabol passed them along to one of his cameramen, who went outside with the freebies; he returned later with five tickets that he could not even give away. Steve Sabol took his NFL Films camera out for the coin toss and had the strange sensation that there was a bigger crowd at midfield, with the officials, the two networks, the still photographers, the team captains, than there was in the stands. A band played the national anthem and virtually no one in the audience sang.

As the game began, McGee and Hornung were sitting on the bench together, not paying attention. They were making plans for an unlikely event—the marriage of the Golden Boy later that month to Patricia Roeder, a Green Bay native now in Hollywood. Max was throwing a bachelor party for him in Las Vegas and then they would come back to Beverly Hills for the wedding—they were getting all of that lined up, just two guys talking on a Sunday afternoon, could have been anywhere, and then a single word pierced their consciousness—"McGEEEEE!"

Hornung looked at McGee and McGee looked at Hornung, and the first thing that passed through McGee's mind was that Lombardi was going to fire him right there in front of a full stadium and sixty-some million people watching on television.

"McGEEE! Get in there!" Lombardi was screaming.

Dowler had tried to play, but his shoulder was still hurting from the Dallas game. Lombardi needed an end. He could have gone with someone younger, but he trusted McGee in big games. Max was eager, he had watched the films, but still this was unexpected. He didn't even know where he had put his helmet and grabbed the first one he could find. It belonged to a lineman. "He looked like Ned the third grader going out there," Hornung said. No passes came his way during the first series, but when he came back to the bench he told Hornung, "If Bart'll throw me the ball I'll win the car. They're not even covering me." The car was the '67 silver Corvette convertible that

Sport was giving to the game's most valuable player. He passed the same message along to Starr. In the next series, he slipped past the cornerback, broke into the clear over the middle and reached back effortlessly to bring in Starr's slightly errant pass for a thirty-seven-yard touchdown.

Perhaps there was something to be said for ignoring Lombardi and staying out all night. McGee was among the few Packers playing free and easy. Willie Wood had two interception chances, but was too anxious and dropped them. Ray Nitschke was so keyed up he forgot his assignment on several plays. The Packers were playing hard, but just missing, and took a precarious 14 to 10 lead to the locker room at halftime. Lombardi told his men that they were "too tight." Nitschke muttered to his defensive pals, *Well, who the hell does he think got us so nervous in the first place?* In the first half, Lombardi continued, they adjusted to Kansas City. "Now I want you to go out there and make Kansas City adjust to you."

That was all it took, not a change in the game plan but a subtle adjustment of attitude: Don't worry, you're the best, make them respond, go after them. The key play of the game came early in the third quarter. Third-and-five for the Chiefs near midfield. Quarterback Len Dawson tried his patented rollout pass, but Lee Roy Caffey, the big turkey, was blitzing from outside linebacker and forced Dawson to throw hurriedly toward his tight end, Fred Arbanas. Willie Wood, loose at last, stepped in, made the interception and raced down to the five-yard line. Elijah Pitts scored on the next play, and the game was theirs. McGee came back to the huddle after every play urging Starr to throw to him. He caught seven passes for 138 yards and thought he could have had twice as many if the ball had come his way more often. Winning wasn't everything to Lombardi this time, winning big was. When it got to 35 to 10 he started feeling good, and when Donny Anderson smacked Kansas City's boastful defensive back, Fred Williamson, with a churning knee, he felt even better.

Williamson wore white cleats like Joe Namath and was a trash talker long before the phrase entered the sporting lexicon. He had been boasting all week about his tackling technique, which he claimed had busted open the helmets of thirty opponents over the years. Hence his nickname, The Hammer. And how exactly did The Hammer do it? With "a blow delivered with great velocity perpendicular to the earth's latitudes. I grab the guy with one arm anywhere from his waist up—preferably around the neck—and slam him to the ground, and boy, it smarts." During film sessions in preparation for the game, Lombardi concluded that Williamson was the dirtiest player he had seen. "If he hits one of our men in the back or head or throws one dirty elbow, he's out of there," Lombardi told his team before the game. And now Anderson had knocked him out accidentally, just by lifting a gangly leg into Williamson's chin. When he went down, unconscious, the Green Bay bench erupted with noise. Who was it? Who got hit? "That's The Hammer!" Willie

Wood yelled out, "They just nailed The Hammer!" The Packers had made the Chiefs adjust; The Hammer was carried out on a stretcher.

After the game Steve Sabol sought out Lombardi for a brief interview for NFL Films. The locker room was relatively quiet; no yelping or spraying champagne. After the awards ceremony, Sabol found the coach in his dressing quarters struggling to take off his tie. Long ago, in another locker room, Vinnie Lombardi had been overtaken by joy when the young and outmatched Cadets of Army had stunned Duke at the Polo Grounds, and he had moved triumphantly among his players that afternoon with a pair of scissors, cutting off their sweat-soaked T-shirts, the symbols of hard-won victory. Now, in the moments after winning his fourth pro championship in six years, the symbol was not a player's sweat-soaked shirt but a coach's knotted necktie. The tie said everything about Lombardi and the pressure he was under to win. He had cinched a Windsor knot so tight that he could not undo it, no matter how vigorously he yanked and pulled. The tie was his noose and he was hanging himself, until finally, in exasperation, he asked the equipment man for a pair of scissors and cut it loose from his straining neck.

23

In Search of Meaning

Fox River, frozen. The bay, frozen. Christmas and the cheer of a new year, long gone. The glow of a new spring, impossibly far away. Green Bay took on a bleak and empty cast in late January and early February. The setting was colorless and without relief. Gray plumes of paper-mill smoke lingered in a cold gray sky. The subzero temperatures and dirt-encrusted snowbanks were nothing new, but earlier they had provided local atmosphere for the stretch run of the champion Packers. By the end of January football memories had faded and even a Super Bowl season seemed as old and flat as a half-drunk bottle of last night's Blatz.

The doldrums of 1967 could have been worse. Lombardi might have stopped coaching, but instead he said that his comments in Tulsa before the Cowboys game were the idle musings of an exhausted man. He would not retire, not with the possibility of winning an unprecedented three straight titles. The Pope's reign would continue, though there was one new casualty. Red Cochran, the offensive assistant, quit even before the team plane got back from the Super Bowl. Seven seasons with an obsessed boss were enough. "The pressure to win just got to Red," reported his wife, Pat. "Vince was hard to live with day after day."

It is human nature that famous people can become more difficult to live with in direct proportion to their rising public esteem. Lombardi was more celebrated than ever that winter as he continued the transition from winning football coach to national icon. He had become especially popular in the business world, where his sayings on leadership were admired by a growing legion. That crossover process had begun in a small way years earlier when a pharmaceutical company bought several boxes of *Run to Daylight!* and assigned its sales force to read the book during a convention in Florida. Bill Heinz had noticed then that his co-author was "fascinated by the guys who were big business executives," and now it amazed Lombardi that they were also fascinated by him. With pride and nervousness, he accepted an invitation from the American Management Association to speak on February 8 at its annual personnel conference in New York. What would he say? In his rhetoric he made it sound easy to transfer football lessons to business, but to friends he confided that he was not all that sure.

When responding to letters, Lombardi's habit was to write his answers in a long, looping script on the back of the correspondence and have them typed by his office assistant, Lorraine Keck. But for speeches he used a different process. The ideas for his New York speech came to him as he paced his stadium office and spoke into a dictaphone in rhythmic cadences, slowly spelling each difficult word and instructing Keck on punctuation. Although, as Heinz once told him, Lombardi was virtually useless when it came to recalling vivid anecdotes from his own life, he had a powerful memory for rhetorical phrases. He could remember a speech almost verbatim after reading it twice and deliver it relying on note cards with a few key words.

Lombardi was not a creative thinker, but he was a methodical gatherer and organizer. For years he had been collecting philosophical thoughts and sayings in paragraph chunks, filing them away like football plays in his brown leather satchel, and for a speech he would take them out and reshape them neatly in his own style, then fit them together one on top of another as if they were little square blocks of granite. Some of his ideas were taken from popular culture, magazine essays and motivational books, but more were mined from the lessons of his own past. They came from Harry's tattoos and Matty's scoldings, from the exercises of Ignatius of Loyola, the lectures of Father Cox, the halftime orations of Sleepy Jim Crowley, the leadership psychology of Red Reeder, the pronouncements of General MacArthur and the axioms of Colonel Blaik. That was how he constructed his New York speech, and from then on, rather than create something new, he mostly rearranged the same familiar blocks.

The Great Lakes region below Green Bay was buried in snow that February, record amounts from central Wisconsin down through Chicago and around to Detroit. The paralyzing weather began with what *Life* described as "a preposterously uncivilized blizzard" that struck Chicago in late January, dumping twenty-four inches in twenty-nine hours, 24 million tons of snow on the city alone, closing O'Hare International Airport for three days. Another storm arrived on February 2 and yet another four days later, silencing Milwaukee under a foot of snow. The storms then moved east and pounded New York with a double blow, first three inches of snow and a forty-degree temperature drop, then the full force of a blizzard. More than a foot of snow fell overnight and into the morning of February 7, closing La Guardia and Kennedy Airports. The New York Stock Exchange and Macy's shut down early, and the lobbies of midtown Manhattan hotels overflowed with men in galoshes carrying attaché cases, stranded commuters desperately seeking overnight lodging.

It was in the midst of this storm that Lombardi made his way from Green Bay to New York to deliver his speech at the personnel conference. With major airports on both ends socked in by snow, he traveled by rail, his first long train ride since his days as an assistant at West Point. He sat in the parlor car most of the journey from Chicago eastward, talking, drinking and playing cards with two judges, Christ Seraphim of Milwaukee and John Pappas of Boston. Pappas had been an owner of Suffolk Downs racetrack and a major importer of Spanish olives. Seraphim, known for dispensing a harsh brand of justice, was a casual acquaintance of Lombardi's and had dined with him several times before Packers games in Milwaukee. Once, years earlier, as Lombardi's party sat around a table at a Bayside restaurant, Seraphim and the coach had argued passionately over the roots of crime. The judge blamed crime on the bad character of individuals; Lombardi insisted that society shared responsibility for allowing desperate conditions to exist. Now, according to Seraphim, Lombardi's views were edging closer to his. As the train rolled east, Seraphim recalled, they bemoaned a society "where people thought they could break the law with impunity."

At several stops along the route, Lombardi had been calling conference officials in New York to update them on his progress. It was slow going, he told them, but not to worry, he was on his way. By early Wednesday morning he had reached Philadelphia and called again. There were more delays on the corridor, he reported, and he feared it was now "touch and go" whether he could make it on time. Lawrence A. Appley, president of the American Management Association, suggested that Lombardi might consider staying in Philadelphia. He could deliver his speech from there over a speakerphone piped into the conference hall at the Americana Hotel. Calling it in—no way Lombardi would agree to that. He had worked too hard on the speech, he had gone through too much already, and phoning from Philadelphia would have drained the power from his message on strong leadership. "I've gotten this far," he said, rejecting Appley's offer. "I'll get there. Hold them if you can." Appley turned to his director of conference arrangements, George Disegni, and said, "Look, I don't know if he's going to make it for lunch, so we'll have to delay a bit. Let's put on a big cocktail party for our guests."

As the twelve hundred executives sipped cocktails in the hallway outside the grand ballroom, Appley announced that Lombardi was slowed by the snowstorm and that lunch would be delayed an hour. Since this was the final session of a three-day conference, anyone who had to leave would be excused and reimbursed for lunch. Virtually no one left. This was a predominantly male huddle, hopped up about seeing the famous football coach, and by one o'clock it was a decidedly well-lubricated crowd as well. Still no speaker. Jim Cabrera, an assistant program director, was sent down to Penn Station to greet the slow-moving train. He kept a taxi idling outside for the trip back to the hotel at Seventh Avenue and Fifty-third Street.

Cabrera knew the car and compartment number, and was there ready to grab a suitcase as soon as Lombardi stepped onto the platform. "He's here! We're on the way!" he reported back to Disegni from the nearest phone, and the personnel executives were ushered into the ballroom for lunch. They were finishing the salad course when a murmuring began, and suddenly the crowd was on its feet and the large ballroom exploded with applause. "An unbelievable standing ovation," as Disegni recalled it. "Vince had made it!" Lombardi strode to the podium in a dark suit, his hair freshly trimmed, a championship ring shining from his left hand (he loved to wear rings and had just designed the Super Bowl version, which had the word CHARACTER etched on one side and LOVE on the other). For someone who had been rushed to the Americana after enduring an exhausting overnight journey, he looked amazingly fresh and neat.

William D. Smith, who covered the event for the *Times,* wrote in his story the next day that the audience "listened almost spellbound" as Lombardi lectured them on leadership. Joe Lombardi, the coach's youngest brother, was in the audience as a special guest, and remembered that when Vince finished the room was silent. Joe looked up to the lectern and noticed a startled look on his brother's face. "There was a moment of almost panic— did they like it? what's going on?" Then the silence broke, another rousing standing ovation. As Smith described it, "The mostly paunchy and out-of-shape audience" seemed ready to "carry Lombardi out on their shoulders" and then "go out and take on the Kansas City Chiefs."

The speech itself was not recorded beyond a few snippets in Smith's article and the AP, and the prepared text seems to have been lost to history. Lombardi's hosts did not receive a copy. His secretaries in Green Bay maintained an archive of his speeches for posterity, but that one was not among them. In many of his later speeches, however, Lombardi referred to the American Management Association address as the first of its kind. He considered it a seminal moment in his emergence as a public figure known for more than winning football games. Virtually every major speech that he delivered in later months and years was a variation of what he said that snowy Ash Wednesday in 1967.

LOMBARDI STRUCTURED his standard speech around seven themes, his seven square blocks of granite that fit one atop the other. These themes went deeper than his mentor Red Blaik's axioms, which did not seem to cohere into a larger philosophy (Axiom: Inches make the champion, and a champion makes his own luck), but it was nonetheless clear that Lombardi lifted some of his thoughts and words from Blaik. This was especially true for his first theme: the meaning of football itself.

Many of Blaik's long-held thoughts on football were contained in his autobiography, *You Have to Pay the Price,* first published in 1960. In it he described football as "the game most like life." In Lombardi's speech it was "a game very much like life." Blaik said it was "a game that is 100 per cent fun when you win and that exacts 100 per cent resolution when you lose." Lombardi called it "a game which gives 100 per cent elation, 100 per cent fun, when you win, yet demands and extracts a 100 per cent resolution, 100 per cent determination when you lose." Blaik described it as "a game of violent body contact." Lombardi characterized it as "a violent game and to play it any other way but violently would be imbecilic." To Blaik it was a game "played in some form by over a million young Americans, a game uninhibited by social barriers." Lombardi said it was "a game played by millions of Americans, yet is completely uninhibited by racial or social barriers." Blaik called football "a Spartan game" that required "sacrifice, selflessness, competitive drive, and perseverance." Lombardi said it demanded "the Spartan qualities of sacrifice, self-denial, dedication and fearlessness."

That this was some minor form of unattributed borrowing is beside the point. It is even possible that the precise words came originally from neither man but from Tim Cohane, the erstwhile Fordham publicist who collaborated on Blaik's autobiography and wrote several articles with Lombardi for *Look.* Lombardi, in his speech, said that he had been in football all his life, and that although he sometimes wondered why he "stayed in an occupation as precarious as football coaching," he did not feel "particularly qualified to be part of anything else." The point is that he was a Blaikian in football in the same way that he was a Catholic in religion. It was what he knew and what he believed in without question, and if he recited verbatim from the colonel's football missal, it was only as an expression of true devotion.

Lombardi's second theme, a block fitting onto the first, concerned the value of competition, what he called "the American zeal" to compete and win. Over the years he had grown increasingly "worried about the lack of interest in competition, particularly athletic competition among our young people." He took particular note when the trend away from competition hit close to home, when small Catholic colleges like his own Fordham deemphasized sports, for instance, or when Admiral Hyman Rickover complained that the military academies stressed competitive sports too much. Men needed the test of competition to find their better selves, Lombardi insisted, whether it was in sports, politics or business.

Fifteen years earlier, as an assistant at West Point, he had traveled to New York to show Army game films to General MacArthur, and he had listened attentively as the old soldier, in his tattered gray bathrobe, lectured him on the merits of competitive sports. Although he had coached for five years at West Point, Lombardi was not a military man. He knew little about the military controversies of MacArthur's career: leaving the Philippines in World War II, driving his men to a bloody Red Chinese ambush at the Yalu River in Korea a decade later. He knew that Red Blaik adored MacArthur and that MacArthur had a stirring rhetorical style, which he could not help drawing on in his speech. "I need no greater authority than the great General MacArthur, and I would like to quote some of the things he said to me. Namely: 'Competitive sports keeps alive in all of us a spirit of vitality and enterprise. It teaches the strong to know when they are weak and the brave to face themselves when they are afraid. To be proud and unbending in defeat, yet humble and gentle in victory. To master ourselves before we attempt to master others. To learn to laugh, yet never forget how to weep, and it gives a predominance of courage over timidity.' "

The third block in Lombardi's speech was about striving for perfection, what he called "a man's personal commitment to excellence and victory." Perfection was to be considered on a more ethereal realm than mere competition. Winning was part of it, but not all of it. His mother, Matilda, had instilled in Lombardi an anxious perfectionism. The Jesuits had taught him that human perfection was unattainable, but that all human beings should still work toward it by using their God-given capacities to the fullest. While "complete victory can never be won," Lombardi said, "it must be pursued, it must be wooed with all of one's might. Each week there is a new encounter, each year there is a new challenge. But all of the display, all of the noise, all of the glamour, and all of the color and excitement, they exist only in the memory. But the spirit, the will to excel, the will to win, they endure, they last forever. These are the qualities, I think, that are larger and more important than any of the events that occasion them."

In the sixties, Lombardi feared, more people were turning away from competition and fewer were striving for perfection. Why? His answer was the theme of the fourth block: too much freedom, not enough authority. Though his speech addressed the changing world of that decade, his words here echoed the lessons he had learned thirty years earlier in the ethics class of Father Ignatius Cox. For most of the twentieth century, Lombardi said, "we as individuals have struggled to liberate ourselves from ancient traditions, congealed creeds and despotic states. Therefore, freedom was necessarily idealized against order, the new against the old, and genius against discipline. Everything was done to strengthen the rights of the individual and weaken the state, and weaken the church, and weaken all authority. I think we all shared in this rebellion, but maybe the battle was too completely won, maybe we have too much freedom. Maybe we have so long ridiculed authority in the family, discipline in education, and decency in conduct and law that our freedom has brought us close to chaos."

When Father Cox was teaching young Vinnie Lombardi from his text-book, *Liberty: Its Use and Abuse,* back in the mid-thirties, he feared that liberty already had taken a dangerous turn. "The evidence for this lies all around us," Cox wrote. "Such liberty unrestrained by law, which ultimately proceeds from the Supreme Lawgiver, God, has eventuated in license. Disintegralization has become the characteristic of modern life in morals, in science, in education, in government, and in international relations.... The vaunted liberty which was to make us free has eventuated in a more galling servitude to man's lower nature—especially to sex on the one hand, and to autocratic political power on the other. It is only the truth which can make us free and the truth is that liberty unchecked by law, the Natural Law of God and human law in accordance with the law of God, leads to license and thence to servitude."

In his lament against license, Father Cox drew on the 1888 encyclical of Pope Leo XIII attacking the doctrines of liberalism. Lombardi could not turn to his church now for the same traditionalist material. U.S. Catholicism was in the throes of liberalization itself in the aftermath of Vatican Council II. English was replacing Latin in most services, parochial schools were turning away from the rote memorizing of dogma, abstinence was no longer required on Fridays, and a majority of American Catholics were telling pollsters that they disagreed with church policy on birth control and divorce. Lombardi had mixed feelings about the reforms, according to his friend Jack Koeppler, who attended several religious retreats with him at St. Norbert during that period. He welcomed the ecumenical spirit and the church's renewed emphasis on solving secular issues such as poverty and racial discrimination, but on the rituals of the mass, Koeppler said, Lombardi was "essentially a pre–Vatican II type of Catholic." He knew Latin and liked the old traditions. During an era when some young Catholic clerics were shedding their collars to work in experimental urban ministries, Lombardi was turning the other way, retreating in his mind to the days when he had trained at the preseminary Cathedral Prep and a father had led the boys in a chant: "I want to be a priest!"

Father Lombardi? His secretary Ruth McKloskey walked up the stairs at work one morning and noticed that the door between their offices was shut. It was never closed; this made her curious. "And all of a sudden the door opened and there he stood in the doorway with all these priest robes on, and he had a miter with a tassel, everything. He stood there and I said, 'My God!' He said, 'How do I look?' I said, 'I'm afraid to say. You look like a bishop or something.' Then he heard somebody else coming up the steps and closed the door and reopened it five minutes later wearing his regular suit. Mr. Lombardi never mentioned it to me again and I never brought it up."

Lombardi could adjust to some of the reforms within the modern church in 1967, but he was surprised and alarmed by the larger counterculture movement emerging in America. As he acknowledged later, he had been "so wrapped up" in his own world, in his God and family and especially the Green Bay Packers, that he had not seen it coming, and then "all of a sudden there it was"—all around him. As he was embarking on his journey to deliver the speech in New York, students at the University of Wisconsin were burning draft cards to protest the war in Vietnam. The U.S. troop buildup in Southeast Asia had recently doubled to 400,000. The number of young American men who had fled to Canada to avoid military induction had exceeded five thousand. At a national gathering of student body presidents in Ann Arbor, a letter was being drafted attacking President Lyndon Johnson for his handling of the war. Plans were being set for a massive antiwar march on Washington in April. Noam Chomsky, an influential radical intellectual, was announcing in the *New York Review of Books* that he was withholding half his income taxes to protest the war, arguing that the time had come to resist authority.

The February 6 edition of *Newsweek* featured a story on the other side of the movement, the disengaged hippies. The article described a "Human Be-In" staged at Golden Gate Park on January 14—the day before the Super Bowl—at which "10,000 long-tressed hippies of both sexes and various fellow-trippers" gathered around a psychedelic maypole, burned incense, played recorders, chanted Hare Krishnas with Allen Ginsberg, and were encouraged by Timothy Leary to "turn on, tune in and drop out." Hendrik Hertzberg, a *Newsweek* writer, visited a "pad" in the Haight-Ashbury district of San Francisco, near where Harold Lombardi had lived a few years earlier. The hippies there told him that repetitive work was "blasphemy" and that God intended for people to play. They lived cooperatively in reaction to the competitiveness around them. "You're brought up in a competitive society and you're taught to grab first because if you don't everyone else will," one said.

All of this was deplored by Lombardi as a dangerous disregard for authority and an abuse of liberty. In his speech he put it this way: "I am sure you are disturbed like I am by what seems to be a complete breakdown of law and order and the moral code which is almost beyond belief. Unhappily, our youth, the most gifted segment of our population, the heirs to scientific advances and freedom's breath, the beneficiaries of their elders' sacrifices and achievements, seem, in too large numbers, to have disregard for the law's authority, for its meaning, for its indispensability to their enjoyment of the fullness of life, and have conjoined with certain of their elders, who should know better, to seek a development of a new right, the right to violate the law with impunity. The prevailing sentiment seems to be if you don't like the rule, break it."

This led to Lombardi's next theme, block five of his speech: discipline. It was not just an abuse of liberty but a lack of disciplined leadership that had brought disarray to modern society, he maintained. "It could be that our leaders no longer understand the relationship between themselves and the people they lead." To properly understand that relationship, Lombardi believed, a leader had to appreciate a paradox. "That is, while most shout to be independent, [they] at the same time wish to be dependent, and while most shout to assert themselves, [they] at the same time wish to be told what to do."

In that sense, Lombardi thought the youth rebellion was not a reaction to stifling authority so much as a response to ineffectual leaders. This line of thinking went back directly to Colonel Blaik. In December 1950, during Lombardi's second season at West Point, Blaik made a similar argument in a letter to Dwight D. Eisenhower. "I have been closely associated with youngsters for the past 20 years and am convinced that our youth is more bewildered than at any time in our history," Blaik wrote. "As for the training of these youngsters, I hope it is realized as in football any course of training which envisions softness will not win the respect of the youngster. After he once gets into a system of training, all a young boy needs is understanding, fair treatment, and a two-fisted approach to the objective."

What makes a great leader? This was Lombardi's next theme, block six of his speech. Here again, one could hear the echoes of the Jesuits and West Point. "Leaders are made, not born," he said. "They are made by hard effort, which is the price all of us must pay to achieve any goal that is worthwhile." In those two sentences he combined the free will of Ignatius of Loyola and the price-paying of Colonel Blaik.

From there, however, Lombardi became less reliant on his mentors. As he described a great leader, he was describing himself as coach of the Green Bay Packers. "A leader must identify himself with the group, must back up the group, even at the risk of displeasing his superiors. He must believe that the group wants from him a sense of approval. If this feeling prevails, production, discipline and morale will be high, and in return he can demand the cooperation to promote the goals of the company. He must believe in teamwork through participation. As a result, the contact must be close and informal. He must be sensitive to the emotional needs and expectations of others. In return, the attitude toward him should be one of confidence and, possibly, affection. The leader, in spite of what was said above, can never close the gap between himself and the group. If he does, he is no longer what he must be. He must walk, as it were, a tightrope between the consent he must win and the control that he must exert."

To walk this tightrope, a leader had to find the precise balance between mental toughness and love, Lombardi said. The toughness came from Blaik's notion of spartanism. The love was Lombardi's concept of team. "The love I'm speaking of is loyalty, which is the greatest of loves. Teamwork, the love that one man has for another and that he respects the dignity of another. The love that I am speaking of is charity. I am not speaking of detraction. You show me a man who belittles another and I will show you a man who is not a leader; or one who is not charitable, who has no respect for the dignity of another, is not loyal, and I will show you a man who is not a leader. I am not advocating that love is the answer to everything. I am not speaking of a love which forces everyone to love everybody else, that you must love the white man because he is white or the black man because he is black or the poor because he is poor or your enemy because he is your enemy, but rather of a love that one man has for another human being. . . . Heart power is the strength of your company. Heart power is the strength of the Green Bay Packers. Heart power is the strength of America and hate power is the weakness of the world."

The contradictions of Lombardi all came out in that long ode to love. He had belittled players time and again on the practice field. He had shown little charity or heart power for some who could not help him win, especially journalists covering the Packers. He sometimes incited hate power in players for the very purpose of spurring them on to victory. But if there was an obvious contradiction here, it was not necessarily duplicitous. Lombardi believed what he was saying, and most of the people closest to him, all of whom had suffered at various times—his players, his wife, his children, his assistants, his friends—believed him when he said it. He was "such a forceful personality," said W. C. Heinz, "that if he hadn't been a good guy, he could have been a terrible danger."

Lombardi's final theme, the seventh block of granite in his speech, concerned two inseparable qualities that he believed distinguish great leaders: character and will. All the men who took Father Cox's ethics class in the mid-thirties had the intertwining definitions pounded into them day after day. *Character is an integration of habits of conduct superimposed on temperament. It is the will exercised on disposition, thought, emotion and action. Will is the character in action.* Character in action, Lombardi asserted at the end of his speech, was the great hope of society. "The character, rather than education, is man's greatest need and man's greatest safeguard, because character is higher than intellect. While it is true the difference between men is in energy, in the strong will, in the settled purpose and in the invincible determination, the new leadership is in sacrifice, it is in self-denial, it is in love and loyalty, it is in fearlessness, it is in humility, and it is in the perfectly disciplined will. This, gentlemen, is the distinction between great and little men."

LOVE AND LOYALTY. What did they really mean? Where did they end and practicality begin? In the real world, apart from the rhetoric, those were difficult issues for Lombardi, and he had to face them immediately in his football life. Two days after the New York speech, a special draft was held for the newest NFL expansion team, the New Orleans Saints. Each team had to make eleven players available to the Saints, who would pick three from that group. Lombardi included Paul Hornung on the list. He figured that Hornung was injured and at the end of his career, and assumed that New Orleans would not take him. He wanted his Golden Boy to stay in Green Bay, for personal and inspirational purposes, if not to start at left halfback. Jerry Kramer, the inquisitive right guard, who had just begun keeping a diary of the 1967 season, came by the Packers offices on that afternoon of February 10 to pick up his mail. He met Lombardi walking out of the building, and used the scene as the opening anecdote of *Instant Replay*, the extraordinary best-selling book he later wrote with sportswriter Dick Schaap.

> I just stood there and Lombardi started to speak again and again he opened his mouth and still he didn't say anything. I could see he was upset, really shaken.
> "What is it, Coach?" I said. "What's the matter?"
> Finally, he managed to say, "I had to put Paul"—he was almost stuttering. "I had to put Paul on that list," he said. "And they took him."

The loss of Hornung "hurt Lombardi more than anything I ever saw," said Max McGee. "He didn't put him on the list to lose him. It didn't make any sense for the Saints to take him." How did this mesh with his philosophy of love and loyalty? Had he been disloyal to Paul? For days afterwards, whenever Lombardi tried to talk about it, his reaction was the same as when he encountered Jerry Kramer. He choked and stuttered and sometimes cried. It was as though a son had been ripped from his arms. But there was more to it than Lombardi realized, more than love, loyalty and family. The son wanted to leave for a better deal.

"I kind of orchestrated that, unbeknown to Lombardi," Hornung revealed later. He had placed a secret call to Tom Fears, the Saints coach, who had been an assistant in Green Bay. "I called him. I knew my neck was bad. I said to him, 'Vince is going to put me on the list.' He said, 'Oh, he wouldn't do that. How's the shoulder?' I said, 'To tell you the truth, I don't know. I need to get it checked.' He said, 'Tell you one thing. If he puts you on that list, I'm going to take you. You'll make lots of money down here. You'll sell a lot of tickets.' "

When the draft was held and the Saints selected him, Hornung expressed surprise. He told the press that he "held no animosity" against the Packers for putting him on the list, never letting on that he had wanted to go and had eased his own way, realizing that he could get far more money in New Orleans and his own television show in a big market. "No way I'd tell Lombardi what I'd done. I was thinking money then," he explained later. "The Saints took me, Lombardi was pissed and hurt. But that was business."

It was big business in New Orleans. The Saints had the Golden Boy, and soon enough they had his old backfield mate, Jim Taylor, a Louisiana native who took the money and fled Green Bay after his contract option expired that spring. Lombardi's relationship with Taylor had been complicated. Their negotiations every year were nothing more than tests of stubborn will. Once they sat in the room saying nothing, refusing to budge from their positions, until Taylor finally just got up and left. Paul was soft and easy; Jimmy was rock-hard and difficult. Lombardi had insisted all year that Taylor was a great player and that the Packers could not afford to lose him. He believed it. And yet the day Taylor left, Lombardi had an appointment with his dentist, Bert Turek, and while sitting in the chair confided that as much as he admired his fullback's toughness, his leaving had brought "a sense of relief."

Taylor went to New Orleans in pursuit of liberty and money, as much money as he had seen the young Packers Anderson and Grabowski receive. He played there one frustrating season, the worst since his rookie year at Green Bay under Scooter McLean, and then his career was over. Hornung did not play at all. In July, he underwent tests at the Mayo Clinic and in Houston that seemed inconclusive, but a third examination at Scripps Clinic in California found that he had a severing of the fifth, sixth and seventh vertebrae and damaged nerve roots in his spinal cord. Another hard blow on the football field, he was told, and he might be crippled for life. Hornung immediately retired. "I've had ten beautiful years," he said.

AT SEVEN O'CLOCK on the eighth of May, the people of Lombardi's life gathered in the faculty lounge at Fordham University in the Bronx for a special dinner marking another step in his apotheosis from football coach to patron saint of discipline. Harry and Matty were there, along with Marie, Vincent and Susan. From Fordham came Sleepy Jim Crowley, Tim Cohane, Jim Lawlor, Handy Andy Palau and the six other Blocks of Granite: Druze, Franco, Babartsky (now known as Al Bart), Wojciechowicz, Pierce and Paquin. From Saints came the merry Carmelite fathers, Tim Moore and his brother Ken. Red Blaik and Red Reeder represented West Point. Wellington Mara was there for the Giants, along with Jim Lee Howell and Frank Gifford. From his Green Bay years came Paul Hornung, the would-be Saint, Bart Starr, Bob Skoronski, Ole, the Gray Ghost, Dick Bourguignon and Jack Koeppler.

Earlier that day Lombardi had received Fordham's highest honor, the Insignis Medal, awarded to "Catholic leaders for extraordinary distinction in the service of God through excellent performance in their professions." The name was taken from *The Spiritual Exercises of St. Ignatius of Loyola*. The founder of the Jesuits had used the Latin word *insignis* to describe someone whose service to God was ardent and unstinting. Past winners had included Francis Cardinal Spellman and Nobel physicist Victor Hess, but it had never before been presented to someone in the world of sports. Father Leo

McLaughlin, S.J., president of Fordham, had "pulled a little rank" so that he could read the citation himself.

"In honoring Vincent Lombardi of the class of 1937, Fordham faces an embarrassment of riches," McLaughlin said. "On which of the many men who are Vincent Lombardi should its Insignis Medal be pinned? On the master planner, the fearsome strategist of attack and defense—Alexander in a football jersey? Or rather on the field tactician capitalizing on his enemies' mistakes and shrewdly covering his own—Napoleon without the hat? Or the merciless opponent but gracious victor? Or simply as the ablest, most respected, and most successful coach in football's brief history? All of these he is, as surely as he is Fordham's." Yet Fordham was honoring him for none of that, McLaughlin said. Lombardi was receiving the medal for being a great teacher.

Lombardi considered being honored in the tradition of St. Ignatius "the finest moment" of his life. After dinner he took a party of family members and pals to Toots Shor's saloon. As they were celebrating there, Arnold Palmer, the swashbuckling golfer, came by and said hello and planted a kiss on Marie's cheek. And that, according to Marie, was the finest moment of *her* life. So what if her husband was being treated like a saint; Arnie Palmer had kissed her. "She won't wash her cheek for a month," Lombardi said, and he exploded in laughter, and everyone at his table laughed with him.

24

Ice

Ed Sabol could not sleep the night before a title game. He and his son Steve had been working pro football championships for NFL Films since 1962, and every year he was nervous, as if he had never done this before. Were his cameras in the right locations? Would there be a dramatic story line? Would the weather create problems again? By seven on the morning of December 31, 1967, he already had been awake for two hours, and now he was standing at the window of his hotel room, staring out into the northern darkness. Friday seemed unforgiving in Green Bay, with heavy snow and a fierce wind, but on Saturday there was a brilliant winter sun and the temperature had soared toward thirty. Local forecasters had predicted more of the same for today's one o'clock game.

The telephone rang. Steve, who had been asleep in the other bed, fumbled for the receiver.

"Good morning, Mr. Sabol."

The wake-up message came in a gentle singsong voice.

"It is sixteen degrees below zero and the wind is out of the north. Now have a nice day."

"Dad," Steve said. "You're not going to believe this!"

The same words of disbelief were being uttered all over town. The phone at Paul's Standard station on South Broadway had started ringing at five that morning, and the overnight man couldn't handle it, so Paul Mazzoleni went in himself and took to the streets with his tow truck and jumper cables. One of his first stops was at Willie Wood's. The free safety was standing next to his dead car, shivering, convinced that even when Mazzoleni brought his frozen battery back to life he was not going anywhere. "It's just too cold to play," Wood said. "They're gonna call this game off. They're not going to play in this." Chuck Mercein, the new man on the Packers, brought in at midseason to help fortify the depleted backfield, was alone in his apartment, semiconscious; his clock radio had just gone off. Had he really just heard someone say it was thirteen below? He must have misunderstood. Wasn't it near thirty when he went to bed? He called the airport weather station to see if he had been dreaming. "You heard it right. It's thirteen below and it may get colder."

Lee Remmel of the *Press-Gazette* had arranged a ride to the stadium with a cityside writer, one of eleven reporters the home paper had assigned to the game. His colleague called at seven with the question, "Lee, do you know what the temperature is?" Remmel guessed twenty. No. Twenty-five? Go look at the thermometer. "I was aghast," he recalled. "The weatherman had been predicting twenty." Chuck Lane, the Packers' young publicist, had grown up in Minnesota and was familiar with the telltale sounds of severe winter in the northland. As soon as he stepped out of his downtown apartment on Washington Street, he knew this was serious. "You can tell when it's cold by the sound of your foot in the snow. I could tell by the first stride that this was damn cold. The sound has got a different crunch to it." By his second stride he could feel something else—"the fuzz in your nose froze up."

Dick Schaap led a foursome of New Yorkers out to Green Bay for the big game, which he hoped would provide a narrative climax for the book he was writing with Jerry Kramer. As he and his editor, Bob Gutwillig, and their wives were driving downtown for breakfast, Schaap noticed the temperature reading on the side of a bank. It was -13. "Look, it's broken," he said. He had never before seen a negative temperature and assumed that the bank got it wrong. Dave Robinson was in his kitchen, eating his traditional pregame meal: scrambled eggs, the filet of a twenty-ounce T-bone steak, toast, tea with honey. His little twin boys hovered in the next room, waiting for their dad to leave so they could eat the rest of the steak. His wife came in and gave him a kiss. "It's twenty below out there," she said. "Twenty above, you mean," Robinson said. "Can't be twenty below."

There was a full house at Sunset Circle. Susan lived at home again after a short and unhappy stint at a Dominican-run secretarial school in Boca Raton. Vincent and Jill came down from St. Paul, and now they had two boys, Vincent II and John. Vincent was working days and going to law school at night. The father-son relationship had developed another odd twist. Vince rarely had time to watch Vincent play in college, but now he insisted that Vincent attend as many Packers games as possible. Lombardi the family man? Partly, no doubt, but there was also a measure of superstition involved. The Packers had won a key game the year before when Vincent was there, and ever since the Old Man thought of him as a talisman. Vincent loved football, he had grown up standing on the sidelines, but sometimes this good-luck business seemed more for his dad's benefit than his own.

At his father's request, he had once boarded a flight in St. Paul during a heavy storm to attend a game in Green Bay. The plane was diverted to Milwaukee and he ended up studying his law books and watching the Packers on television at the airport. Another time he brought Jill along for a preseason game in Milwaukee. They had left the boys with a babysitter and were excited about having a night alone at the Pfister Hotel. At dinner after the game, Vincent and Jill were startled to hear the Old Man suddenly announce "We're going home!"

"Jeez, Dad, it's kind of late," Vincent pleaded.

"I'll drive halfway and you drive halfway," Lombardi said, and that was that. Vincent and Jill packed up, and soon they were in the car with Vince and Marie, heading north to Green Bay. Five miles up the highway, Lombardi pulled over. "My knees are killing me," he said to Vincent. "You drive."

Maybe it had all done some good. The Packers had finished in first place again. They had finished first in the newfangled Central Division of the Western Conference with a 9–4–1 record, and then whipped the Los Angeles Rams in the playoff game for the western title. Critics were saying that the Packers were too old and slow aside from their one breathtaking rookie, Travis Williams, known as The Roadrunner, a return specialist who had run four kickoffs back for touchdowns, including two against the Browns in one game. Yet here they were, back in the championship, playing for their record third straight NFL title against the Dallas Cowboys. If standing on the sideline in subzero weather this afternoon could help them win one more time, Vincent was game.

Not much was said about the temperature in the Lombardi house. There was little talking about the game at all that morning. "Everybody was very uptight," Susan recalled. Vincent II had been up all night with a fever, distracting everyone, including the coach, who patted his grandson on the head before leaving for church. The cars were in the heated garage; Vince's Pontiac started right up. Silence on the way to mass. The priest prayed for the Packers. All quiet on the way back. Then Vince and Vincent left, driving clockwise south to the bridge crossing the Fox in downtown De Pere, then west to Highway 41, north to the Highland Avenue exit and east to Lambeau Field.

The Sabols were already there, positioning eleven cameramen around the stadium. They sent a technician up to the scoreboard to place a microphone near a camera that peeked through one of the number holes. When it came time for a pregame group meeting, one member of the crew was missing. What happened? He had brought a flask with him and had taken a few shots of bourbon to stay warm—a few too many, it seemed. He had passed out cold and might have frozen to death behind the scoreboard had they not gone looking for him. The parking lots were starting to fill up by 11 a.m., two hours before game time, with many Packers fans insisting on going through their pregame rituals as though it was just another winter day in paradise. Not as many tailgaters as usual, but they were still out there. Folding chairs, card tables, brats and beer. One concession to the weather: more of them than usual were huddled around fires. Jim Irwin, a local TV sports director, arrived at the press box two hours before kickoff, and looked out and saw hundreds of people already stationed at their seats. "They didn't have to be in the stands," he noted. "They had reserved tickets. They *chose* to be out there when it was thirteen below."

Chuck Lane was heading out from the locker room to check the field when he met a group of assistants coming the other way. They had a message for the coach, an unwelcome one, the sort of news they would rather have Lane tell him. "Tell Lombardi that his field is frozen," one said. *Tell Lombardi that his field was frozen?* That, Lane thought, would be like "telling him that his wife had been unfaithful or that his dog couldn't hunt." But that was his job, so he turned around and found Lombardi, who was leaving the locker room to check the field himself when Lane intercepted him. Lombardi seemed crestfallen, then angry and disbelieving. "What the hell are you talking about?" he thundered.

The field could not be frozen. The previous spring, in his role as general manager, Lombardi had paid $80,000 for a gigantic electric blanket devised by General Electric. He had bought it from George S. Halas, Papa Bear's nephew, who was the central district sales representative for GE's wiring services department. The fact that the Bears did not have an electric blanket themselves, even though young Halas was also a Bears scout, did not make Lombardi suspicious; it just showed that he was less tight with his team's money than old George. Lombardi loved modern inventions, and this electric blanket seemed to mean more to him than any play he had ever devised. Only the day before, he had taken a group of writers on a science field trip of sorts, first giving them a lecture on the underground magic, telling them how electric coils were laid in a grid the length of the turf, six inches below the surface and a foot apart, with another six inches of pea gravel below the coils and a drain below that. Then he led them back to a tiny control room off the tunnel below the stands.

Bud Lea of the *Milwaukee Sentinel* was in the group. "He goes in that little room and all these lights are blinking, and he's like a mad scientist in there, showing these writers from New York and Dallas how it all works," Lea recalled. "All these bulbs are going on and off, and I don't think Lombardi understood one thing about it, but, by God, he thought it was working."

It seemed to be working on Saturday when the grounds crew pulled the tarp off the field to let the Cowboys practice. Puffs of steam came out like a low rolling fog. The ground was cool but not cold, the turf soft but not soggy.

Lombardi had been so satisfied then that he yelled over to the project engineer and gave him the okay sign with his thumb and forefinger. Even Tom Landry, the skeptical Dallas coach, who hated to play in Green Bay, had deemed the field "excellent" though a little damp. No dampness now. Parts of the field were frozen "as hard as a rock," reported Jim Tunney, the alternate referee. It seemed that the coil system had malfunctioned. Heat might rise here and there and thaw parts of the field, drawing out moisture, but then the turf would quickly freeze again. George S. Halas insisted afterwards that there was nothing wrong with the system, but the controls had been mishandled. In any case, those who paced the sidelines that day were struck by the juxtaposition of a wide patch of frozen turf next to a sign warning: THIS FIELD IS ELECTRIFIED.

In the locker room, Willie Wood took off his street clothes slowly, reluctantly, still convinced that the game would be canceled. "Man, it's too damn cold," he said to his teammates. "They ain't going to play in this shit." The room was full of smoke, cigarettes burning from the built-in ashtrays on almost every locker. Dad Braisher passed out long underwear to everybody, even Lombardi. Coach said it was okay to wear it today, but he didn't want them stuffing too much underneath the uniforms; he had a thing about players feeling loose and easy. Lee Roy Caffey and Tom Brown wanted to wear gloves, but Lombardi vetoed that request. Linemen could wear them, but no gloves for anyone who handled the ball. Dave Robinson walked over to the equipment man as soon as Lombardi left the room. "Give me a pair of those brown gloves and he'll never know the difference. I'm the only linebacker with brown hands anyway." Braisher agreed to the conspiracy, and Robinson wore gloves the rest of the day.

When the players took the field for warmups, most of them kept their hands tucked inside their pants. Every deep breath was an arrow shooting into their lungs. Donny Anderson, a Texan, had never played in weather like this before, but he had no choice because Elijah Pitts, the other halfback, was out for the year. Pitts had been enjoying his best season until the game in Baltimore, when he suffered a severe ankle injury. Jim Grabowski had been hurt during that same game when Bobby Boyd smacked him in the right knee. Grabo was making his way back and thought he might play against the Cowboys; the knee had felt good all week in practice. Then, during warmups, he went out on a pass pattern, a little fullback hook, and he planted his right foot and felt something pop, and his comeback was over before it started. Chuck Mercein would get most of the action at fullback.

Of all the major characters in this game, Mercein was the unlikeliest. The former Yale star had begun the year feeling "humiliated, embarrassed" when Allie Sherman, coach of the New York Giants, had cut him from his squad. He practiced several weeks with the semipro Westchester Bulls, then was recalled by the Giants and cut again. After a tryout in Washington, Redskins coach Otto Graham agreed to sign him, and Mercein returned to Scarsdale and told his wife to start packing for Washington. Then, as they were loading the car that Sunday night, Giants owner Wellington Mara called. "Listen, Chuck, if you haven't signed yet, I've been on the phone with Vince Lombardi and he inquired about your availability," Mara said. Mara and Lombardi talked every Sunday night during the season; they'd been doing it for seven years. "I've recommended you to Lombardi, Chuck. Stay by the phone."

A few seconds later Lombardi rang him. "Chuck, I understand you're available," Lombardi said, according to Mercein's recollection. "I want you to come out here and play for me. I don't want you to play for the Redskins. We're going to the Super Bowl, Chuck. You're going to help us get the world championship. You're going to be part of this team. We need you. We want you. If you want to be part of a championship, come out here and play for us." That was it. "Absolutely, instinctively and intuitively I knew this was where I was going to play," Mercein recounted. "I said, 'Yes, sir. I'll be on the next flight.' I hung up the phone and turned to my wife and said, 'Unpack the car.' She said, 'What?' 'Yeah, I'm going to the Packers.' It was great. I was thrilled. Playing for the great Vince Lombardi!" He took the flight of the Blue Goose to Green Bay that Monday, and personnel man Pat Peppler picked him up at the airport. And now, with Grabowski hurting again, here he was starting in the NFL Championship Game.

When the team returned to the locker room after warmups, the reality finally hit Willie Wood. "Well, it looks like we are going to play this game," he said to Bob Jeter. Then came another thought. If we're gonna play, we gotta make sure we're gonna win. We don't want to come out in these kinds of conditions and lose a damn ball game. Lombardi was of a similar mind, of course. He never wanted to lose any game, but especially not a game to Landry and the Cowboys. He had a thing about the Cowboys, according to Willie Davis. "Even in preseason he didn't want Dallas to beat us." Lombardi had always stayed one step ahead of his old Giants colleague and rival. He became a head coach in 1959, Landry in 1960. He turned a losing team around in one year, it took Landry six years before he could get his expansion Cowboys to a winning record. But now the Cowboys were being cited as the team of the future, with the flex and the Doomsday Defense and multiple offense, their flashy uniforms and speedy receivers.

In his heart of hearts, Max McGee thought Dallas had the better team. "Not that they could beat us," McGee said. "We had their number. Lombardi had the hex on Landry."

GARY KNAFELC, the old tight end, was in the press box that day. His playing career done, he could not stay away and signed on as Lambeau Field's public address announcer. Looking out from his perspective atop the stadium, he was overwhelmed by the panorama. The players were the story, perhaps, and as the game went along they would rivet his and everyone else's attention, but at first it was hard to take one's eyes off the crowd in the stands. "There was this incredible haze of breath, tens of thousands of puffs coming out. Like seeing big buffaloes in an enormous herd on the winter plains. It was prehistoric."

To many fans, attending this game was a test of their resourcefulness. Carol Schmidt and her husband, who worked in the oil business, sat in Section 24 near the twenty-yard line, where they snuggled inside a makeshift double sleeping bag made from the heavy mill felt used at the local paper mills. To warm their feet they turned a three-pound coffee can upside down, punched holes in the top and placed a large candle inside on a pie plate. Bob Kaminsky arrived from Two Rivers with his wife's twin brothers and took his seat in the end zone, oblivious of the weather. "This is what I wore," he reported. "Longjohns. Work shoes. Over the work shoes I put those heavy gray woolen socks that came over the knees. Pair of galoshes over that. Flannel pajamas over the longjohns. Work overalls. A T-shirt. Flannel shirt. Insulated sweatsuit. Heavy parka. Face mask with holes for mouth and eyes. Wool tassel cap. And then I climbed into a sleeping bag. I had foam on the ground and seat for my feet and butt. I was not cold."

Lombardi's golfing pal Jack Koeppler and his son wore deer hunting outfits (red and black in that era, not yet the glaring orange). Two layers warmed their hands, first deer hunting gloves, then huge mittens. At their seats near the forty-yard line they zipped two sleeping bags together and slipped inside for the extra warmth generated by two bodies. Jerry Van, owner of the Downtowner Motel, where Hornung and McGee once lived, wore "two of everything." He cut up several thick cardboard boxes into twelve-inch squares and put three layers on the concrete floor to keep his feet warm. Lois Bourguignon, the wife of Packers executive board member Dick Bourguignon, wore a plastic garment bag under her winter coat to keep the heat in. Red Cochran, the former assistant coach who had quit the year before, watched the title game in the stands with his six-year-old son, both wearing bulky snowmobile suits. Teenager Gary Van Ness, who had come to the stadium planning to sneak in, was given a ticket near midfield by a doctor who had decided to leave, and found himself amid a group of rich folks; he had never before seen so many fur coats.

Fur coats? They were plentiful at Lambeau Field, even in arctic weather. The games were *the* social events of the year in Green Bay. Many women bought their fall and winter wardrobes with Sunday football games in mind and wore different outfits to every game. Mary Turek, Lombardi's dentist's wife, sat in prestigious Section 20, just above the players' wives, in her heavy fur coat with fur-lined stadium boots that extended over her calves. Around her she saw women in less practical attire, many of them exposing their legs to the weather in nylons and high heels. They tended not to last long. Tom Olejniczak, the team president's son, took a date to the game who left for the women's room midway through the first quarter and didn't come back until the game was over. Lorraine Keck, Lombardi's assistant secretary, got stuck in a restroom for more than a quarter, the door blocked by paramedics treating a girl who had passed out. Throughout the game bathrooms and passageways underneath the stands were jammed with people trying to get warm. When Red Cochran took his young son to the men's room, they got stuck in the human flow. It "was so mobbed," he said, "you had to go with the crowd, wherever it took you."

The temperature on the field as kickoff approached was thirteen below, with an estimated wind chill of minus forty-six. The leather ball felt heavy and airless. The field had already been rendered more dangerous from the warmups. Players said it was as if someone had taken a stucco wall and laid it on the ground. Clumps of mud had coagulated and stuck to the rock-hard ground. Blowers on both sides of the field shot warm air in the direction of the benches, but you had to be right next to one to feel it. Some players huddled in makeshift dugouts constructed from wood and canvas, like duck blinds. Lombardi paced the sidelines in his long winter coat and black fuzzy hat with muffs. No matter how cold the Packers felt, one look across to the other side made them feel superior. The Cowboys, said Chuck Mercein, "looked like earthmen on Mars. The outfits they wore. Most of them had hooded sweatshirts on underneath their helmets, which looked silly as hell. And a kind of scarf thing around their faces with their eyes cut out. They looked like monsters in a grade B movie."

For the first quarter and most of the second, the Cowboys played like anything but monsters. Their main receiving threat, Bob Hayes, known as the world's fastest human, also seemed to be the world's coldest, and unwittingly gave away every offensive play. If it was a run, he tucked his frigid hands into his pants as he lined up; if Cowboys quarterback Don Meredith called a pass play, Hayes pulled out his hands. "You can't catch a pass with your hands in your pants," said Tom Brown, the Packers strong safety. "We played eleven guys against ten whenever he did that. He was just stone cold."

The first time the Packers got the ball, Bart Starr led them on an eighty-two-yard drive that culminated in a touchdown pass to Boyd Dowler from eight yards out. In the second quarter he hit Dowler for another touchdown, this one of forty-three yards, and the score was 14 to 0. If a blowout seemed to be in progress, lingering in the back of everyone's mind was the memory of the previous year in Dallas, when the Packers had also bolted to a quick two-touchdown lead, then barely hung on to win the championship game on Tom Brown's last-second interception in the end zone. Could Dallas come back again? The weather seemed to argue no; conventional wisdom dictated that these Cowboys just didn't know how to play in subzero weather.

Four minutes left in the half. Green Bay holds the ball on its own twenty-six, first down. Starr drops back to pass. There is no protection, the entire Doomsday front line is roaring after him; he drops farther, turns away from Bob Lilly, retreating nineteen yards the wrong way, back to the seven, where Willie Townes hits him. Starr's hands are nearly numb, and he fumbles and George Andrie picks it up and plows into the end zone as he is being tackled by Forrest Gregg and Jerry Kramer—and suddenly a seemingly secure lead is cut in half. Two minutes later Willie Wood drops back to receive a Dallas punt. Wood has the surest hands in the league. In eight seasons as a return man, he has fumbled only once, during a rainstorm in San Francisco, and that time he recovered his own fumble. Now he is standing near his own twenty, looking up, and Danny Villanueva's punt is fading on him. Wood is thinking too much: about how cold his hands are, about field position. Should he try to run it back or call for a fair catch? He puts his hand up, fair catch, and the ball fades away and when it hits his hands he can't really feel it. Fumble—Frank Clarke recovers for Dallas. Four plays later the Cowboys get a field goal, and they race for the warmth of the locker room at halftime back in the game, trailing 14 to 10.

The Packers are supposed to be winter's team, yet ten points can be attributed to the weather and all ten are for Dallas.

LOMBARDI HAD LITTLE to say at halftime. His assistant coaches did most of the talking. Ray Wietecha, the offensive line coach, was distraught over the way Dallas's front line was breaking in on Starr. Another assistant pointed out to Starr that Dallas's linebackers were dropping straight back on pass plays, so deep that he should be able to complete short passes to the backs—something to keep in mind. But mostly it was quiet, the urgency on getting warm, having a smoke, a Coke, a section of orange.

Paul Hornung was in the locker room, another of Lombardi's talismans. The coach had missed him all year, the good and the bad. He had missed having Paul to yell at, and he had missed having Paul to give the ball to in the clutch. On Friday, when Hornung entered the room during a press conference, Lombardi stopped in midsentence and put his arm around the Golden Boy, and the press corps watched the man who at times tried to bully them turn soft and sentimental. "Gentlemen," he had said. "This man is like a son to me." Perhaps a bit too much like a son, as far as Hornung was concerned. He had hoped to watch the title game from the press box, in relative warmth and comfort, but Lombardi insisted that he stand near him on the sidelines. Hornung and his buddy Max McGee, still in uniform, playing his last game in Green Bay, tried to position themselves in front of the blowers, but Lombardi kept looking around for them and calling them back to his side. Hornung was scheduled to be on national television at halftime, talking to Pat Summerall here in the locker room for CBS, but by then he was so cold that his mouth couldn't move and Summerall decided against the interview.

The wives of Dick Schaap and Jerry Kramer left at halftime and listened to the rest of the game on the radio. Schaap stayed in the press box, still uncertain how the final chapter of his book with Kramer would end. All season long Kramer had been talking into a tape recorder, providing daily material for the sportswriter to mold into a diary-style memoir. To this point, the story looked rich. Kramer had a poet's eye for detail and was a natural storyteller, making his rough draft more in need of cutting than reshaping. For every five minutes of Kramer on tape, it seemed, four minutes were usable. Schaap had suspected that might be the case. When a publisher had first asked him if he could recommend a football player to keep a diary the way Jim Brosnan had for baseball, Schaap had answered immediately, "Sure, Jerry Kramer." He barely knew Kramer at the time, but was basing his answer largely on an unforgettable first impression. It was at training camp in 1962, when Schaap was in West De Pere reporting a story on Jim Taylor. Kramer was then Taylor's roommate, and when Schaap entered their dorm room he saw Taylor on one bed sleeping and Kramer on the other reading Wallace Stevens poetry aloud to himself.

Six weeks after the first inquiry about a football diarist, the publisher called again, asking Schaap to find out if Kramer was interested. Kramer said he was, as long as Schaap would help him. The next day Kramer flew to New York to meet with his co-author and a literary agent, Sterling Lord. As the three men were walking down a street in midtown Manhattan after lunch, a stranger yelled out "Jerry Kramer!" The stunning realization that an offensive lineman for a team in Green Bay was recognizable in New York City, Schaap would say later, "raised the contract price of the book." Now he needed a similar exclamation point for an ending to raise the sales of the book.

THE THIRD QUARTER was nothing but frustration. Neither team scored. Bill Schliebaum, the line judge, had his whistle freeze to his lips and lost a layer of skin yanking it loose. Jim Huxford, working the chains, had to pull off his ski mask after part of it froze to his mouth. Ray Nitschke refused to go near the blowers—he had a tradition of kneeling on one knee near the coach when the defense was off the field—and now he was starting to get frostbite in his toes. Chuck Mercein's left tricep felt numb after a tough hit in the second quarter. Steve Sabol, stationed on the ledge above the end zone stands, and shivering in his cowboy boots, discovered that his camera had broken, the focus wheel on his telephoto lens frozen at a thirty-yard distance. Pat Summerall, whose assignment for the second half was to work the Green Bay sideline, was getting blistered every time he went near Lombardi. The fact that he had once played for the coach in New York made no difference. "Get the hell away from my bench," Lombardi barked. "This is my office!"

The press box had its own share of discontent. Reporters stationed in the front row found that their portable typewriters were freezing on the ledge. The game was down there somewhere, but the writers and broadcasters were having an increasingly hard time seeing it through the big picture windows, which were either too steamed or too frosted. Writers took to scraping small patches of visibility in the window with their credit cards. Chuck Lane had zipped across the street at halftime to buy some deicer at the service station, and one press box attendant was squirting deicer on the windows like lighter fluid while another used a squeegee to clear away the condensation. Every time someone opened the side door letting in a blast of cold air, Bud Lea called out, "Holy God, shut the door!" Ray Scott, calling the game for CBS with Jack Buck and Frank Gifford, insisted on having a window open in their booth. "You don't have the feel of the game, otherwise," he said. Gifford was losing his feel for anything. "I think I'll take another bite of my coffee," he muttered famously on the air.

As the third quarter ended, Dallas had possession at midfield. The Cowboys were now dominating the game. Twice in the third quarter, they had threatened to score, but one drive was thwarted when Lee Roy Caffey made Meredith fumble on the Green Bay thirteen, and another ended with a missed field goal attempt. The Packers seemed hapless, having gained only ten yards in the quarter. On the first play of the fourth quarter, Dan Reeves took the handoff from Meredith and ran wide to the left. Green Bay's defensive backfield played it as a run, and by the time they realized it was an option and Reeves was passing, receiver Lance Rentzel had slipped behind everyone, and Tom Brown could only chase him into the end zone. Dallas held the lead, 17 to 14.

Over the next ten minutes Green Bay got the ball twice but failed to score. Their one chance to tie the game fizzled when Don Chandler missed a field goal from the forty, wide to the left. Dallas picked up two first downs on its next possession and held the ball for nearly five minutes before they were forced to punt. Willie Wood thought of nothing but catching the ball this time. He cradled it safely at his twenty-three then burst nine yards upfield. The Packers were on their thirty-two, first down, sixty-eight yards to go for the winning touchdown, four minutes and fifty seconds remaining in the game.

Ray Scott had left the broadcast booth to work his way to the winner's dressing room. The quickest way to get there was to walk down through the stands to the field. He reached the Green Bay sideline just after Wood was tackled. The return team was running off the field and the offense was heading out to the huddle. Ray Nitschke, the emotional leader of the defense and special teams, had lost his voice. His toes were numb. Scott watched him as he rumbled off the field this one last time, his fist clenched, and yelled hoarsely but fiercely to the offense, "Don't let me down! Don't let me down!"

Dick Schaap had also left the press box with five minutes left, following a crowd of reporters to the field. He figured the game was over. Kramer had told him about one of Lombardi's favorite sayings: The Packers never lose, but sometimes the clock runs out. That's what would happen now, Schaap thought. At long last the clock would run out on the Packers. Run out for this championship game, but also for the whole incredible run the team had been on since Lombardi came to Green Bay. The game was changing, these Packers were old, time was moving on. That was it, Schaap thought. He had the title for the book: *The Year the Clock Ran Out.* Great title, he said to himself as he walked down the aisle, through the primordial scene in the stands, the huge buffalo herd, fifty thousand puffs of breath, fifty thousand fans warmed by four quarters of brandy, bourbon and beer. Still buzzing. Didn't they realize this was over?

Vincent realized it and had begun inching toward the dressing room a few minutes earlier. For most of the game he had been with the doctors, trainers and priests on the far right end of the bench, freezing in his green and yellow Packer jacket. Now he was on the far left end, near the end zone and the tunnel. He could not wait to warm up in the locker room. His sister, Susan, was also pessimistic. When Wood fielded the punt, she turned to her boyfriend, Paul Bickham, and said, "We're not going to win this!" Out in Sheepshead Bay, Harry and Matty were watching on television in the living room of the original Izzo homestead on East Sixteenth Street, now the home of Matty's younger sister Millie. Harry and Matty had moved back from Englewood and taken an apartment across the street, restored to the embrace of the vast Izzo family. Ten or twelve of them were here now, watching Vince's team. Harry was almost deaf; the volume was turned all the way up. "We were all scared to death," said Matty's niece Clara Parvin. "Especially Uncle Harry." He had survived two heart attacks, but these final five minutes were intolerable.

On the sideline at Lambeau Field, Doc Brusky was called over to help Jim Huxford on the chains crew. Huxford was recovering from a heart attack and the tension was getting to him. He needed another nitroglycerin pill. Ockie Krueger left his seat next to Marie Lombardi and started for the exit. He had driven Marie to the game in her car and wanted to make sure that it would start and be warmed up for her when the game ended. Paul Mazzoleni, after his busy morning jump-starting stalled cars, had watched the game from a seat in the south end zone, sharing a thermos of brandy with four guys from Kenosha. He, too, was heading for the exit, preparing for another long night of work ahead. Steve Sabol, his camera completely useless now, came down from his end zone perch to take a position near the Packers bench, as close to Lombardi as he could get. Sabol worshiped pro football and considered Lombardi the game's patron saint, the main character in the romantic story that he and his father were telling. The young filmmaker was among those who believed. He thought he was in a great spot to witness football history.

Before trotting onto the field, Starr had talked to Lombardi about what they would try to do. They had decided not to go for the quick score, but rather "just try to keep moving the ball." In the huddle, Starr seemed inordinately calm. "This is it," he said, looking directly at his teammates. "We're going in." Bob Skoronski had struggled all day to keep George Andrie out of the backfield. Earlier in the game Lombardi had lit into him on the bench, accusing him of falling asleep during this critical game. But now Starr's demeanor had a transformational effect. Ski was fully awake and confident. He looked at Starr and saw Lombardi, the reminder of everything they had learned in nine seasons with their coach. All of Lombardi's schooling was for precisely this moment, all the hundreds of times that he had run them through the sweep, convincing them that they could respond to anything, that no matter what the defense tried, they had the answer. There is nothing they can do to stop us, Skoronski thought to himself.

Chuck Mercein, the fullback, had played only six games with the Packers, yet he felt the same way. "The feeling I had was that we are going to score. I felt calm. I felt that everyone in the huddle was calm. I didn't sense any anxiety or desperation. Determination, yes, but not desperation. Bart just said a few words, 'We're going in,' but he had this tremendous presence. He was the on-field personification of Lombardi." Donny Anderson, the halfback, was more composed than any of his teammates had seen him before. He had tried to present himself as a latter-day Hornung, but before now the similarity had been most noticeable in his playboy persona off the field. Now it seemed as though he had grown up in one long cold afternoon. "If you dump me the ball, I can get eight or ten yards every play," he told Starr. The play had been there all afternoon, but as important as the sagacity of his observation was its fearless message: with the game on the line, he wanted the ball, just like the Golden Boy once had.

On first down it worked: Starr dumped a little pass to Anderson good for six yards. Then Mercein ran around right end for seven more and Starr hit Dowler for thirteen, and with those three successful plays the Packers had taken the ball into Dallas territory, forty-two yards from the end zone. Anderson lost nine on the next play, caught in the backfield by Willie Townes on a busted sweep, but he came back with two consecutive little gems, taking dump passes from Starr and picking his way cautiously down the ice-slicked field, eluding the linebackers for twelve yards and then nine more. The clock was down to two minutes. Mercein had noticed something during those plays and felt confident enough to bring it up with Starr. "I'm open on the left side if you need me." The ball was on the Dallas thirty, only one minute and thirty-five seconds left. Starr went back to pass, Mercein swung to his left, Starr looked for Dowler and Anderson, then saw Mercein in the clear and went to him, the ball floating in the wind, behind Mercein and high, but he snared it on the run and slipped by the linebacker and was moving past the cornerback, nineteen yards and out-of-bounds at the Dallas eleven. Gil Brandt, the Dallas personnel man, called that catch a killer, one of the best he had ever seen, considering the conditions.

Then came what Starr considered the best call of the game. All week Lombardi had told him to look for the perfect spot and use it only when he really needed it. Now was the time. It was known as GIVE 54, an influence play. It looked like a variation of the Green Bay sweep, run from what was called the Brown formation, with the fullback lined up directly behind the quarterback, instead of Lombardi's preferred red formation, in which the halfback and fullback were spread. On the sweep from this formation, the left guard pulled and the fullback was assigned to block the guard's man, which in this case would be Dallas's Hall of Fame tackle Bob Lilly. Lilly was so quick and smart that he could shoot through the hole and bring down the runner from behind before the sweep unfolded.

The GIVE 54 was designed to take advantage of Lilly's aggressiveness. Starr would fake the sweep and hand the ball to Mercein, who would run through the hole vacated by Lilly. It could be a dangerous play. If Lilly held his ground there was no one to block him. But when the guard pulled, Lilly followed, and Mercein came busting through. Skoronski made a clean block on the left end, sealing an alley, and a linebacker went the wrong way, and as Mercein came through he saw "a helluva great hole there." He thought that if he could only get behind Forrest Gregg for one more block he might take it in, but the field was almost all ice down in the shadows of the scoreboard, no footing at all, "like a marble tabletop," according to Starr. Mercein picked up eight crucial yards. "I can still hear the sound of his feet clicking on that ice," linesman Jim Huxford said three decades later. "You could hear it on the ice. He was slipping but he kept going." All the way to the three, where he stumbled into Gregg and fell to the ground.

On the next play Anderson barely picks up the one yard needed for a first down. The Packers are one yard from the goal line. Anderson again, no gain. Twenty seconds left. Timeout. Anderson again. This time he slips on the ice as Starr hands him the ball, almost fumbling. Again, no gain. Green Bay calls its last timeout with sixteen seconds remaining, and Starr jogs to the sideline to talk to Lombardi.

A field goal would tie the game and send it into sudden death overtime, but bringing in the field goal team is not even discussed. Nothing needs to be said about a field goal. After playing for Lombardi for nine seasons, Starr knows exactly what his coach is thinking. He is conservative, he goes by the book, but he's a winner. *Run to win.* Lombardi had been preaching that motto to his team all through the final difficult weeks of this season, quoting St. Paul's exhortation to the Corinthians: *All the runners at the stadium are trying to win, but only one of them gets the prize. You must run in the same way, run to win."* Also, Lombardi is freezing his tail off, like everybody else in the place.

Hornung, in his street clothes standing near the coach, thinks they should try a rollout pass; that way even if it falls incomplete the clock stops and they can get in another play. He wonders whether Lombardi knows there are no timeouts left. Lombardi doesn't seem to be listening. Starr says he wants to go with the wedge play, where the runner pounds between the center and guard, but he wants to be certain that Jerry Kramer, who has to make a key block, can get good footing. It looks like an ice rink down there at the one. Watching films of the Cowboys earlier that week, they had noticed that Kramer's man, Dallas tackle Jethro Pugh, stood the highest in goal line situations, making him the easiest defender to cut down. Mercein is out on the field, he can't hear the discussion, but he's thinking the same thing, "one hundred percent certain" that they're going to give him the ball on the wedge, the simplest play in football.

"Run it!" Lombardi says. "And let's get the hell out of here." Starr trots back to the huddle.

Pat Peppler rarely stands anywhere near Lombardi during a game, but now he can't help himself. He moves closer to the coach and asks, "What's he gonna call?"

"Damned if I know," Lombardi says.

Starr asks Kramer if he can get good footing.

"Hell, yes," Kramer says.

"Huddle up," Starr says. He calls the play. Brown right. 31 wedge. That's the 3 back (fullback) through the 1 hole (between center and guard). Mercein hears it and thinks, This is it. I'm going to score. But as Starr is calling the play, a thought flashes through the quarterback's mind: No matter how good the block is, if Mercein should slip, he won't be able to reach the hole in time. Starr remembers a game against the 49ers in Milwaukee in 1966: an icy field, at the end of a long drive, he called the wedge, then kept the ball himself and scored on a sneak. The Packers didn't even have a quarterback sneak in their playbook. Never practiced it. But the improvisation had worked once, why not now? I can just hug the block in there, just get one step and go right in, Starr thinks to himself. He doesn't tell anyone. All his teammates think Mercein is getting the ball.

The Packers break from the huddle. The Doomsday linemen—Lilly, Pugh, Townes and Andrie—are kicking the ice at the goal line, desperate to find a patch of unfrozen turf so they can get a quick start off the ball. Jerry Kramer takes his position next to center Ken Bowman—and there it is, a soft spot in the ground, just for him. He digs in with his right foot, certain that he can cut Pugh at the snap. On the Packers bench, Willie Davis is "thinking of all the possibilities, a bad snap or whatever." Aw, hell, he says to himself, and turns his head away. He can't watch. Willie Wood puts his head down. Looks hard at the ground. "Sometimes you don't want to see bad things," he explains later. Lombardi wonders whether they'll have enough time to bring in the field goal team if they don't make it.

Vincent has worked his way back down the field to this end, standing in the shadows. Steve Sabol is nearby, thinking to himself, *Here I am watching history.* Ockie Krueger never made it to Marie's car; he's standing atop a seat down near the field, shouting like everyone around him. Paul Mazzoleni is in a crowd that has jammed one of the exit ramps, on his tiptoes trying to get a better view. Dick Schaap is still on the far end of the field, nearly a hundred yards away. He has no clue that his co-author is expected to make the crucial block on the season's most important play. Vernon Biever, the Packers' official photographer, has been standing behind the end zone with his son John, his fifteen-year-old assistant. It makes no sense for them both to be shooting from the same spot, so he says to John, "You stay here. I'll change film and go to the bench area, so if they score I'll get the emotion over there." John Biever stays in the end zone and lifts his Nikon motorized camera, anticipating the final play coming his way.

One year earlier, in Dallas, the Cowboys were down near the goal line, threatening to score in the final seconds, and one of their offensive linemen was penalized for moving before the snap. Now the Packers are in the same situation, and Kramer is coming off the ball fast and hard, and Jethro Pugh thinks it is too fast, that Kramer is offside, but no call is made, and Kramer cuts Pugh off his feet and then Kenny Bowman knocks him back into a linebacker and Pugh falls on top of Kramer, and the wedge opening is there. Mercein gets a good start, no slips. "I'm psyched, I want this thing to go right," Mercein recalled later. "I'm taking off and—lo and behold, Bart's not giving me the ball. He's kept it and he's in the end zone." Mercein is coming right behind him, and he doesn't want the officials to think he's pushing Starr forward, which would be a penalty, so he throws his hands above his head, trying to say, see, I'm not assisting him, and it looks as though Mercein is signaling the touchdown in midair.

John Biever clicks his Nikon and captures the moment for history: Kramer's block, Starr's sneak, Mercein's dive. Vernon Biever is near the bench and gets a shot of Lombardi lifting his hands jubilantly: touchdown. Victory. Dick Schaap knows that he has to change the title of his book. The clock did not run out. Harry Lombardi is whooping and screaming at the television set in Sheepshead Bay. Henry Jordan turns to Phil Bengtson and says in a deadpan, "Whadaya say, Coach. Another day, another dollar, huh?" Mercein is surprised, but not disappointed. He might have scored and been the hero, but he knew that he had done more in that one game than he ever could have dreamed. He was lucky enough to be in the right spot at the right time. Bart Starr had been in the right place doing the right things for nine years. With Hornung no longer in uniform, Starr had to be the one to go in for the winning score.

The coach, it could be said, had nothing to do with that final drive in a game that would be remembered thereafter as the Ice Bowl. Starr called the plays and scored the touchdown, Anderson and Mercein offered helpful advice and made the key runs and catches, Kramer and Bowman threw crucial blocks. Yet to every Packer on the field, and to many of those watching from the sidelines and in the press box, that final drive, more than anything else, was the perfect expression of Vince Lombardi. The conditions were miserable, the pressure enormous, and there were no fumbles, no dropped passes, no mistakes, just a group of determined men moving confidently downfield toward a certain goal. In his speeches Lombardi talked about character in action, and here it was, in real life. "Of all the games I've done," said Ray Scott, "that final drive was the greatest triumph of will over adversity I'd ever seen. It was a thing of beauty."

THE LOCKER ROOM was a jangle of cameras and lights when Lombardi got there after the game. He evicted the press and talked to his men alone, telling them how proud he was: for running to win, for persevering and meeting their greatest challenge, winning three straight championships. He barely stifled the tears that came so easily to him, then fell to his knees and led the team in the Lord's Prayer. When he returned to his dressing room and began taking questions from the press, he could not stop fidgeting in his chair. He rose, sat down, got up again. He claimed with a touch of whimsy that the decision to gamble for the touchdown was dictated largely by the weather. "I didn't figure those fans in the stands wanted to sit through a sudden death," he said. "You can't say I'm without compassion, although I've been accused of it." But the story was "out there, not here," he told the media, nodding in the direction of the outer locker room from which only minutes before he had evicted these same reporters.

Glacial tears burned the cheeks of Ray Nitschke. The offense had not let him down, and now he said he felt a deep sense of satisfaction. He was also cold and numb and had frostbite on both feet. He and several teammates were soaking their feet in a bucket of lukewarm water. The hot water in the showers disappeared quickly, and Tom Brown and Willie Wood came yelping out of the shower room when it turned cold. They decided to take their showers at home. Jim Grabowski, who had watched the game from the bench, wishing he could have contributed, now took in the postgame scene with feelings of loneliness and separation as injured players always do, even in the midst of their teammates' joy. Grabo nonetheless sought out his replacement for congratulations. "Chuck, you just did a great job," he said to Mercein. "As good a job as I possibly could have done. Better, maybe."

Jerry Kramer could not stop talking. As Dick Schaap observed from the edge of the crowd, Kramer told one huddle of reporters after another about the last drive and the block, which CBS replayed in slow motion over and over. It was only then that Schaap was struck by the serendipity of the day's events. The last play of the biggest game, and his colleague had made the block, and now an enormous television audience was listening to him talk about it, and also about this special team and its uncommon coach. Kramer was the narrator of his diary, but he shared the role of main character with Lombardi, a looming presence in almost every scene. Kramer hated Lombardi and loved Lombardi, but he thought that he and his teammates knew him in a way that no outsider could. Weeks earlier, *Esquire* had published an article by Leonard Shecter that had portrayed Lombardi as a bully and tyrant. "Many things have been said about Coach," Kramer now told his TV interviewers. "And he is not always understood by those who quote him. The players understand. This is one beautiful man."

Red Blaik was watching the postgame interviews on television, and when he heard Kramer's remark he picked up the phone and called the Green Bay dressing room, getting through right away, much to his surprise. "Vince," he said to his former assistant. "A great victory, but greater were the remarks of Kramer, who has stilled those who were skeptical about you as a person."

Vince and Vincent drove home together, retracing the route they had taken hours earlier. As Lombardi steered the Pontiac out of the parking lot, he turned to Vincent and sighed. "You've just seen me coach my next to last game," he said. They rode in silence the rest of the way. That evening, in the basement party room at Sunset Circle, "everyone was floating on the ceiling," according to Jill Lombardi, Vincent's wife. The Old Man was so excited amid the hubbub of toasts and congratulatory phone calls and New Year's Eve jollity that he even kissed a few journalists. At one point he put his arm around Marie, and called for quiet and loudly thanked his wife for "making it all possible," a public declaration that made Marie squirm and shudder with embarrassment. Ed Sabol had been invited to the cocktail party with his son Steve, and entered the basement shouldering a small Bell & Howell camera to capture the scene. Lombardi was taken aback when he saw the lights. "What are you doing?" he barked. Just taking a few shots, Ed Sabol said. A few shots for history.

A FEW DAYS LATER Chuck Mercein's parents called him. "Chuck," said his mother. "Guess who's on the cover of *Sports Illustrated?*" Starr, he guessed. No, his mother said. *You.* Mercein thought back to sitting in the barber's chair when he was a child in suburban Chicago, reading *SI*'s "Faces in the Crowd" column and hoping maybe he could get in there someday. Now he was on the cover.

A few weeks later Jerry Kramer was in New York as a guest at Schaap's journalism class at Columbia. He was describing his block on the final play of the Ice Bowl and how the television kept showing the play over and over. "Thank God for instant replay," Kramer said.

Aha, Schaap thought. There's our title.

Instant Replay would become one of the best-selling sports books of all time.

A few months later the crowd that had gathered in Lombardi's basement on the night of the game reassembled there, now to watch the highlight film of Green Bay's championship season produced by Ed and Steve Sabol. They draped a bedsheet against the wall to serve as a makeshift screen, then turned off the lights. The film, titled *The Greatest Challenge,* was narrated by John Facenda, who was being phased out as a newscaster at Channel 10 in Philadelphia when Ed Sabol asked him to be the voice of NFL Films. With his deep and melodramatic tone, Facenda became known as "the voice of God." He read his scripts without ever looking at the pictures that accompanied them.

At the climax of the film about the 1967 Packers, Jerry Kramer said that he played pro football because of all the men who had been his teammates during the Lombardi era in Green Bay. "I'll tell you in a nutshell, if you can understand this: I play pro football because of Emlen Tunnell, Bill Quinlan, Dan Currie, Paul Hornung, Fuzzy Thurston, Max McGee, Henry Jordan, Herb Adderley, Ray Nitschke, Dave Robinson, Bart Starr." Then came Facenda's voice: deep, reverberating, sentimental. "They will be remembered as the faces of victory," he said. "They will be remembered for their coach, whose iron discipline was the foundation on which they built a fortress. And most of all, they will be remembered as a group of men who faced the greatest challenge their sport has ever produced—and conquered."

When it was over, the room stayed dark and the projector ran on and on, the film flapping noisily over the reel. Someone belatedly turned the light switch, and there stood Lombardi. He had been watching football film for decades, and he had run this projector himself, the old pro. But this time he was not grading the blocking technique of his players with ones or twos or zeros. He had a handkerchief out, and he was crying.

25

Until Lombardi
Loves You

SUSAN LOMBARDI had suspected something at Christmas, and fretted about it more as she shivered in the stands at the Ice Bowl. Finally, in the middle of January, when her parents were in Florida, she turned to a friendly doctor, the father of a former classmate, who agreed to sneak her into St. Vincent Hospital. One of the nurses there, an older nun who seemed gentle and protective, discreetly conducted the test. Susan was twenty, living at home on Sunset Circle, working part-time at H. C. Prange's and going steady with Paul Bickham, a young man who attended St. Norbert College. When the results came back, the doctor gave her the news that she was pregnant.

What now? Susan and Paul agreed to get married, but they did not want her parents to know that she was pregnant, at least not yet. Her father often teased her about her infallible sense of timing, how she got into trouble at the worst possible moments, and here was another example. The Packers had just won Super Bowl II, defeating the Oakland Raiders 33 to 14. Lombardi, who had become a national symbol of old-fashioned discipline and moral rectitude, was taking a much-needed rest with Marie in Miami Beach. He was exhausted and pondering his future amid rumors that he would step down as coach. The last news he wanted to hear was that his unwed daughter was pregnant. The young couple decided instead to explain their dilemma to Father William Spalding, a parish priest at the Church of the Resurrection in Allouez. At first he seemed to agree to marry them in secret, but then reconsidered and called back a few hours later saying that in good conscience he could not do it without her parents' knowledge, even though both Paul and Susan were of legal age. Susan did not want to make the call to Florida. Father Spalding said he would.

Marie answered the phone at the hotel just as Vince was walking into the room, and when he heard her moan, "Oh, no! Oh, my God!" he demanded to know what was going on. *Susie's pregnant.* He took the phone and grilled the priest for details. At first Lombardi was "extremely angry, of course," according to Spalding, but then calmed down and began drafting a game plan. Later that day he called his daughter and presented it to her. Susan and Paul were to get married as soon as possible, while her parents were still in Florida. It would be a Catholic wedding, blessed by the church, but not in Green Bay. If they applied for a marriage license in Brown County, the story would appear on the front page the next day, and this had to be kept quiet. They should go to Michigan, where it was less likely to draw attention. Father Spalding would work out the details. When they returned, they should say that they had eloped.

On the morning of January 24, Susan, Paul and the Lombardi's housekeeper, Lois Mack, drove north in Marie's Thunderbird to Escanaba in Michigan's Upper Peninsula, carrying marriage papers that Father Spalding had prepared. Mack and the Catholic priest who performed the ceremony were the only witnesses to the concealed marriage at St. Anne's Church. The trio drove back to Green Bay that afternoon, and Susan and Paul moved into a first-floor flat on Fourth Street in West De Pere, a former bachelor pad with windows painted shut and without a shower, but within walking distance of St. Norbert. As soon as Vince and Marie returned to Green Bay, they paid a visit to the newlyweds. "My father was pretty cool about it," Susan said later. "He stuck out his hand to Paul and said welcome to the family and asked him about his education and his plans. He wanted to have a party to celebrate. It was my mother who was a basket case. She just glared at me like, What are we going to do with her now? My dad looked around and told her to make sure we had enough furniture."

A few days later Lombardi came home from work and prepared to settle into his favorite brown chair. It was time for his late-afternoon off-season ritual: beer, cheddar cheese, slices of an apple and a half hour of belly laughs watching his favorite television show, *McHale's Navy.* But the comfortable old chair was gone, replaced by an unfamiliar new model. *Marie!* Well, she explained, he told her to find Susan decent furniture, so she gave the kids the family room set and bought several new pieces. The Old Man decided he could adjust. That was the least of the changes he faced.

THE FIRST REPORT of Lombardi's imminent retirement broke not even twenty-four hours after the dramatic end of the Ice Bowl. On New Year's Day, Minneapolis sportscaster Hal Scott, the brother of Packers play-by-play man Ray Scott, reported that Lombardi intended to step down as coach after Super Bowl II, but would remain as general manager and anoint Phil Bengtson as his successor. Lombardi had been dropping hints about relinquishing the coaching post since that week in Tulsa a year earlier. In various informal settings, he had told trusted friends, including some journalists, that the two jobs were too much for him. He was not the world's best keeper of secrets. He had confided to several priests, including Father Burke at St. Norbert and Father Spalding at Resurrection, that this would be his final season. Marie and Vincent knew, as did Red Blaik.

When Hal Scott came out with his report, the team publicist issued an oblique response. "There were rumors to this effect last year and rumors of the same sort this year," Chuck Lane said. "But Coach Lombardi has made no official comment about it." The following day Lombardi issued his own statement with stronger wording. Scott's report "could be upsetting to everybody in Green Bay," he said. "It's completely without verification. I haven't talked to anyone about any such thing. I repeat: I have no plans either for tomorrow or for the next year. Who knows, I may even be dead by then."

In fact he had privately revealed his decision to retire, but did not want it publicized for two reasons. First, he feared it would distract his players as they prepared for the Super Bowl in Miami. He also knew that he might change his mind after the season. As a result, he received Scott's report crankily, much as he had responded to Ken Hartnett's equally accurate report on Jim Taylor playing out his contract in 1966. He instructed his assistant, Tom Miller, to find Ray Scott, whom he suspected of leaking the story to his brother. Ray Scott was playing gin at a country club in suburban Minneapolis when Miller reached him, and took offense at Lombardi's accusation that he had broken a confidence. "Tom, I had nothing to do with the report on television," he told Miller. "I didn't see it. I didn't talk to my brother. And I'll let Lombardi know how I feel about this directly." Scott then wrote Lombardi an irate letter noting that over the years there had been "a thousand times" when he could have broken the coach's confidence, but never did. The two men did not speak for several months thereafter.

Lombardi's fear that retirement talk would distract his players from their final mission, winning Super Bowl II, was inconsistent and ultimately misplaced. It was inconsistent because he was the one who kept dropping hints about it, not only to his friends but to the press and even to his players. At the final film session with his team on the Friday before the Raiders game, he choked back tears as he told them, "This may be the last time we'll be together, so . . ." Some of the players didn't get it; they thought he just meant it was the last meeting of that year, but others, including Bart Starr and Jerry Kramer, deduced precisely what he meant. Rather than diminishing the team's concentration, the possibility that this was Lombardi's last game helped spur Green Bay to victory. Much like the game against Kansas City the year before, the Packers were relatively unimpressive in the first half, leading Oakland this time by only 16 to 7. It was after Kramer's halftime exhortation to "win this for the Old Man" that they put the game away, scoring the first seventeen points of the second half.

Two and a half weeks after that victory, and one week after his daughter's secret out-of-town wedding, Lombardi hosted an affair at Oneida Golf and Riding Club. The dinner and press conference on the Thursday evening of February 1 was staged and scripted by Lombardi. He was uncharacteristically chatty and nervous beforehand, constantly sipping water as though he had an unquenchable thirst. Twice he left the room to pull himself together. Then he sat down next to his top assistant, Phil Bengtson, and read a statement in front of twenty-four microphones, fourteen cameras and more than a hundred newsmen, the largest press delegation ever to assemble at a sports announcement in Green Bay. "What I have to say, gentlemen, is not completely without emotion," he began. "And a decision arrived at only after a great deal of thought and study." The statement that followed, on paper, seemed impersonal and devoid of sentiment. He said that because of "the nature of the business and the growth of the business" he had concluded that it was "impractical" for him to serve as both coach and general manager, but he was fortunate to have "a very capable and a very loyal assistant" to succeed him. "Gentlemen," he concluded, "let me introduce to you now the new head coach of the Green Bay Packers, Mr. Phil Bengtson."

There was no poetry or romance about five championships in nine years as coach. Lombardi refrained from calling the roll of players who stayed with him from the opening day win over the Bears in 1959 to the victory in Super Bowl II (nine of them: Starr, Thurston, Skoronski, Jerry Kramer, Gregg, McGee, Jordan, Dowler and Nitschke). He chose not to revisit the glorious moments, from the perfection of the 37 to 0 trouncing of the Giants in the first championship to the block and sneak in the arctic darkness at the Ice Bowl. No rhetoric about pride, character and will. All of that was in the tremor of his voice, but not in the words—and soon after he made it official, turning the attention to the new coach, he left the room to compose himself again.

Why did Lombardi quit? Not even his aides accepted at face value the pragmatic answer he gave about simply not having the time to do both jobs. "I guess all of us were sitting back and trying to read between the lines," Chuck Lane said later. Lombardi's claim that he would be satisfied doing only the work of a general manager, Lane thought, was "like a great racehorse saying it would be content plowing." Despite his assertion that he was in "excellent health" and that "any rumors to the contrary" were "completely false," it was indeed Lombardi's health, physical and mental, that more than anything drove his decision.

After leading his aging team to its third straight title, Lombardi was spent. For years he had suffered from digestive problems and heartburn, and over the past season those symptoms had worsened. Players became accustomed to seeing him with a bottle of antacid medicine in his hand. He had traumatic arthritis in his left hip, and it hobbled him more than ever during the 1967 season. Carroll Dale, the receiver, remembered once that season when "the team was fogged in somewhere waiting for a plane, and Lombardi talked about the weather and how much it hurt him. How tough it was to be out on the field with that pain in his hip." He took indomethacin daily for the arthritis, which had an ulceric side effect on his stomach, creating a vicious cycle of pain. He tried various other treatments, delving into folklore remedies to wear a copper bracelet on his wrist. The pain did not go away.

Father Spalding had reason to believe that the arthritic hip alone was enough to force Lombardi off the field. The priest had been visiting Marie at Sunset Circle one afternoon in December, a few weeks before the Ice Bowl. "We were sitting in the living room talking when Vince came in and said, 'Well, that's it. I'm done.' He had just been to his doctor's about the hip. He said, 'I've got to quit coaching.'"

Marie worried that he would drop dead of a heart attack, a fear that seemed all too possible several times that year. He blacked out in the dressing room twice, according to Chuck Lane, and several times complained about shortness of breath and chest pains. Friends thought that he looked more fatigued than ever before. "He didn't look too good after the game in Baltimore this year" were Father Tim Moore's first words after hearing that Lombardi had retired as coach. "And he seemed tired and low after the win over the Giants. Many of us were concerned. But if you know Vince, you know you don't harp on things with him." Lombardi "at fifty-four is a lot older than coaches older than he, if you follow me," Moore added. "The intensity he puts into his coaching is almost unbelievable. He left nothing undone to win a game." By the time Lombardi met with the Packers executive board to discuss his future, Tony Canadeo thought that he looked awful. "He said he was tired, and he looked tired," Canadeo said. "You don't want someone dying on you."

Lombardi's physical exhaustion was exacerbated by mental strain. Here was the familiar cycle from success to anguish: The more he won, the more famous he became; the more famous he was, the more a target of criticism he became; the more he was criticized, the more he felt misunderstood; the more misunderstood he felt, the more anguish he carried. All of this had come to a climax with the publication of Leonard Shecter's "The Toughest Man" piece in the January 1968 issue of *Esquire*, in which Lombardi was described as swearing at his players, casually dismissing their pain and injury, arguing with Marie and generally acting bellicose if not abusive.

When considered from the remove of decades, Shecter's piece seems relatively tame. Lombardi's reported curses were nothing more than "dammit" and "shit" and "for Chrissakes." His players described his excesses on the practice field, but the details were accurate and most of the anecdotes were familiar to any journalist who had spent time in Green Bay. In addition, the players were quoted by name; this was not a deliberate hatchet job in which the writer attacked his subject with blind quotes. Dick Schaap, who read the piece as he was editing the manuscript of *Instant Replay*, thought Shecter was off mostly in tone. There was almost nothing in the magazine article that did not echo something in Jerry Kramer's diary, but Kramer's assessment of Lombardi was more complex and forgiving. "There were a lot of truths in it, but it was too far one way," Schaap said of Shecter's story. "It may have been one hundred percent truthful, but one hundred percent truthful isn't always the truth. It may have been accurate, but it wasn't fair."

Whatever its merits, the story had a profound effect on Lombardi. He was a New Yorker and Shecter was a New Yorker, and he had assumed that Shecter would intuitively understand him. During the week that Shecter was at training camp, in fact, Lombardi had noted with hometown pride that the writer was "a real New Yorker" because he read the newspaper by folding it in eighths, the style perfected by subway riders. But he told aides and friends that he did not recognize himself in Shecter's portrait. He had always been forthright in acknowledging his explosive temper, realizing that it was a difficult aspect of his personality, but he did not think, as he thought the story implied, that his temper defined his character. "It absolutely destroyed him. He thought he was being compared to a Bavarian beast who drank blood from his victims," said Chuck Lane. Lombardi often recounted the scene of his mother calling him in tears from Sheepshead Bay after reading the story. The other side of that anecdote is that he was nearly reduced to tears by his mother's lament: *Is my son really like that?*

The story diminished him, Lombardi said, reducing him to nothing more than another brutal football coach. He preferred to be known as a teacher, leader, bearer of the Insignis Medal, the man who had preached the nobility of sport. Instead, Shecter described him almost pathetically as a self-important little man who has "a little bit of a weight problem and walks with his belly sucked in and his chest expanded like a pigeon's. Even so, the waistband of his beltless (but pleated) slacks sometimes folds over to show the lining. . . ." Years later, in an interview with Howard Cosell, one of his sympathetic chroniclers, Lombardi dismissed the criticism he had faced in late 1967. Yet, he said, "that kind of talk, I think, was one of the reasons for my retirement. . . . I think it had a great deal to do with it."

Two other reasons were mentioned by others as factors in Lombardi's decision, although he was hesitant to acknowledge them. He had pushed his Packers as long and far as they could go, many believed, and it was becoming obvious that their era was over. "He was a very smart guy. He knew. The

Packers were dead," said Gary Knafelc, who had played on Green Bay's early championship teams. "He didn't do Phil [Bengtson] any favors. To win the Ice Bowl and that last Super Bowl was amazing. The Packers were old and dead. He didn't want to go down a loser." Even if that judgment was too harsh, perhaps the relationship between Lombardi and his players had reached a point of diminishing returns. He had said it all; they had heard it all. That was the assessment of Lombardi's son, Vincent. "Anybody who motivates and gets people going sooner or later runs out of things to say. You've got to take your act to a new venue. What's he going to tell these guys to get them to reach down and do it one more time? They'd done it five times now. I think he saw that coming. I don't think he bailed out because he saw the inevitable decline so much as he just figured, what's the point?"

On the Friday morning of February 2, the morning after he announced his retirement from coaching, Lombardi took the same route to work, walked up the same stairs, said hello to the same secretary, Ruth McKloskey, entered the same door with the same nameplate, MR. LOMBARDI, on it. "I feel about the same," he said, smiling. "I don't feel any different. I don't know whether the impact has hit me yet." On his desk was a stack of telegrams. He picked through the names: Red Blaik, Jim Ringo, Bobby Kennedy, Bob Jeter. Pete Rozelle ("VINNIE VENI VIDI VICI I AM HAPPY FOR YOU PETE"). Mailbags full of letters were on the way.

One came from W. C. Heinz, who said that he had stayed near the radio all day at his home in rural Vermont listening to hourly news reports from a station in Schenectady until finally, late at night, Lombardi's voice "came booming through the static." Another came from Father Burke of St. Norbert, who noted proudly that he had kept the secret of Lombardi's desire to quit for more than a year. From Oliver Kuechle, sports editor of the *Milwaukee Journal,* came a note congratulating him on "the greatest coaching era" in the history of pro football and adding: "I don't believe there would be a Packer football team today except for you." Barbara Hecker, wife of Lombardi's former assistant Norb Hecker, recalled in her letter that her youngest daughter had trouble saying the letter *l,* so that, appropriately, " 'Lombardi' somehow always came out 'Somebody.' " She and Norb were "filled with emotion" when they got word of Lombardi's retirement, she said. "You are a great man, yes, but a good and gentle man also."

"It's about time you got the hell out of coaching," wrote Carroll Rosenbloom, owner of the Baltimore Colts. "Now I can put away my sign—Break Up Lombardi." Don McIlhenny, by then a real estate agent in Dallas, recalled the 1959 season, the one year he had played halfback for Lombardi: "During that season you paid me a compliment that I am sure you have since long forgotten, but it will always be remembered as the highlight of my football career." Bob Voloninno, who played for Lombardi at West Point, wrote that he would "always be grateful as to what you, Colonel Blaik and Murray

Warmath taught me at West Point. Not only from the technical aspect of football, but also in helping me become a better individual. I will always remain an ardent admirer and a loyal fan of yours."

The most touching letter was written on a broken typewriter whose *d* key jumped a half line each time it was punched. It came from Ben Starr, the father of Bart, who wrote from his home on Biscayne Drive in Montgomery, Alabama.

> It is with a feeling of deep gratitude that we say "thank you" for all you have done for Bart since he has been associated with you. He gives you the entire credit for any and all success that he has had and we know he is going to miss the meetings he has shared with you, but we are thankful that you will, at least, still be associated with the Packer organization. I and my wife both feel that Bart will probably rely on you to still offer him advice. It is not only because you are the finest coach in football, but the type of religious man you are also that has made us so happy for Bart to be associated with you. He admires you in so many ways that you have had a far deeper impact on him in more ways than you will probably ever know.

Lombardi's own father was less sentimental, more succinct. "You made the biggest mistake of your life," Harry Lombardi told his oldest son. "You gave up the best job in the world."

FOR SEVERAL YEARS Jack Koeppler had been making the three-hour drive from Green Bay down to Madison to attend board meetings of a mortgage guarantee company owned by David Carley, a prominent businessman and political activist who had run for governor of Wisconsin in 1966 and served on the Democratic National Committee. At every meeting, it seemed, Koeppler greeted Carley with the same offer: "I'd like to introduce you to my golfing buddy, Vince Lombardi." Carley invariably declined. He knew who Lombardi was—it was nearly impossible to live in Wisconsin and not know—but Carley was completely absorbed in commerce, politics and public policy, and unlike many businessmen was not awed by the winning ways of a football coach. "Until, one day, driving to Milwaukee in my car, all of a sudden it hit me," Carley recalled later. "I'll get Koeppler to introduce me to Lombardi for this new company I had going."

The company was Public Facilities Associates, Inc.—a name that Carley's wife disliked, believing it sounded as though they made toilets. In fact, they had entered the field of what were known as turnkey projects, building apartment complexes for the elderly and poor and selling them to local public housing authorities. Carley considered this the first stage of his ambitious development plans, which involved redeveloping downtowns with

a mix of housing and sports facilities. "As soon as I saw that correlation between housing and stadia, I thought, I've got to get Lombardi interested in
this," Carley said. "I thought he would make some money at it. And, unques-
tionably, he would give me access or entrée." Polls were listing Lombardi as
the sports figure most respected by American industrialists. "And he was no
less respected in Wisconsin by city councils," Carley noted. "That name in
Wisconsin! I always found it unbelievable."

Carley and Lombardi met at Oneida Golf and Riding Club early in the
spring of 1968, soon after Lombardi's retirement from coaching. Koeppler,
serving as the go-between, had personal and business connections to both
men. He not only played golf with Lombardi, but also handled the pension
plan for Green Bay's administrative personnel. In addition to serving on the
board of Carley's mortgage company, he was an ardent Democrat who kept
Carley abreast of politics in the Fox River valley. Politics also bonded him to
Lombardi; they were among the few Democrats at the country club. When
the three men gathered for lunch at Oneida, Carley outlined his plans for
Public Facilities and said that he wanted Lombardi to serve as chairman of
the board. Lombardi's manner swung from taciturn to gregarious over the
course of the meal. Though it became apparent to Carley that Lombardi was
"certainly not knowledgeable about business" he found him interesting and
surprisingly generous with his time.

From Lombardi's perspective, the business offer could not have come at
a more propitious moment. During his nine years in Green Bay, he had devoted himself almost exclusively to the cause of winning football games,
something he did better than any other coach in the world. To that end, he
had become expert in the art of power, gaining it and wielding it, but as to
power's frequent companion—money—he had not accumulated much beyond his generous near-six-figure salary and knew little about it. His financial ventures in Green Bay had been modest and sporadic. With Dick
Bourguignon, he had invested in a cherry orchard in Door County, and at
the suggestion of golfing friends at Oneida, he had bought various stocks.
"But it was just five shares here or eight shares there," recalled Ockie
Krueger, his aide-de-camp. "He got a lot of tips from guys, but he never invested much money in them. He'd have all these little checks coming in."

As he became more famous, Lombardi associated more frequently with
wealthy businessmen and professionals, and though his celebrity status allowed him to meet them as equals, he was still and always the Brooklyn
butcher's son. At league meetings he spent much of his time in closed rooms
with the owners, and listened to this collection of egocentric multimillion-
aires talk about private jets, real estate deals, penthouse apartments in Miami
Beach and Manhattan. They spoke a language that he did not quite know
and wanted to learn. He told friends that no matter how much power he accumulated in Green Bay, he would never have as much power as an owner.

As his son, Vincent, later explained, "You don't have to be around the NFL long to understand that if you're not an owner, you're zip. You're fungible. You're a dime a dozen, no matter how great a coach you are." Lombardi saw that football was changing, becoming more a business, in which authority meant less without money to back it up. The league was richer than ever, television advertising revenues and network contracts had doubled in five years, and in a sense the fight over the spoils had only just begun, as players hired agents and strengthened their union.

Lombardi now equated money with power, and he wanted more of it. On May 1 he signed on with Carley, agreeing to a sweetheart deal in which he received 12.5 percent of Public Facilities stock by putting down $6,000. It was the only money that he ever invested in the enterprise, and within less than two years, after the company was sold twice, the second time to Inland Steel, he came out with more than a million dollars. His involvement with Carley's firm was announced on May 10 at a press conference at Milwaukee's Pfister Hotel. Carley had brought in public relations man Mitchell Fromstein to help develop the coach's business persona. An hour before the press conference, Fromstein handed Lombardi a page of notes on how the company hoped to serve the public by providing low-income housing for the poor and elderly. "He read it once and walked up there and delivered a speech like he had prepared it carefully the night before," Fromstein said. "It struck me immediately that he had a near-photographic memory. And he had a presence that was very, very strong. His voice made people respond to him."

At the press conference, Carley said that he intended to draw on Lombardi's planning skills to help shape the company, but that was a public relations ruse. Lombardi did attend all the board meetings, but his role was limited. "David never expected that Vince was going to contribute something to the business that was technically important," Fromstein said, nor did Lombardi expect it. His value to the company was obvious. His name alone could get Public Facilities a hearing anywhere. "We wanted to build housing for the elderly in Sheboygan, and we had tried to see Carl Prange from H. C. Prange's several times," Koeppler recalled. "We were up there talking to Vince, and Vince said, 'I'll call him.' Soon he puts his hand over the phone and says, 'Want to meet for lunch tomorrow or the next day?' When we met the next day, they both knew why they were there. Prange ran Sheboygan. Vince ran Green Bay."

Carley was surprised by the way "other people in business and politics were awed" by Lombardi. His own opinion was that the coach's worldview seemed limited. "Everybody kissed his ass so he didn't learn things in the way most people learn things," Carley concluded. Although Carley had heard that Lombardi was a football intellectual who read books, he was suspicious. Whenever he mentioned a book, it seemed that Lombardi could not engage in a discussion about it. "I wasn't all that impressed with Lombardi," he said later. "But I was impressed with the fact that other people were impressed. I caught on early to that." He caught on late, too. Inland Steel might never have been interested in buying his company had the company president not been infatuated with the famous football coach.

If Public Facilities made Lombardi rich, it was not at the center of his new pursuit of money and power. Year by year, as more teams approached him with lucrative offers, he became more certain about what he wanted. His ideal situation would be to have his money and power in the same place, as part-owner of a professional football team, and he pursued that goal in a frenzied, if oddly diffuse, manner.

He had tried to persuade the Packers executive board to allow him part-ownership of the Packers, but Olejniczak and the team lawyer, Fred Trowbridge Sr., rejected his private queries on that subject. They and the other wealthy board members owned no more than single shares themselves, and they insisted that the club's nonprofit status and its unique relationship to the people of Green Bay precluded private accumulation of stock. Not even the Pope could rewrite the bylaws of the Packers. For four years he had been affiliated with a syndicate that had made sporadic and underfinanced efforts to buy a professional team. Red Blaik was part of the group, while the money came from New Jersey financiers led by Joseph McCrane Jr., a former racetrack operator, who had played football at West Point. The syndicate twice made overtures to the Jets and Eagles, with no results.

Lombardi had been invited to join the Jets management independent of that syndicate, but backed away in part because of Wellington Mara's distaste for any such deal. The only veto power Mara had was the result of his longtime friendship with Lombardi, and he gently used it, saying he did not want a charismatic New York–born Italian-American owning and coaching his crosstown rivals. Mara remained interested in bringing Lombardi back to coach the Giants, but was not willing to give him part-ownership. Even as all these discussions were going on, Lombardi was being courted by a trucking magnate who wanted to buy the Philadelphia Eagles, and he had secretly signed on with a partnership making a bid for the San Francisco 49ers. McCrane was on the edge of that group, though Blaik was not. The lead figure now was R. B. "Bud" Levitas, president of Juillard Inc., a wholesale liquor distributor in northern California. In an April 22, 1968, letter to Pete Rozelle, marked "personal and confidential," Levitas informed the commissioner of his and Lombardi's intentions, which seemed close to being realized.

"Dear Pete," he wrote. "I know you are aware of the fact that Vince Lombardi and I have had some conversations with Marshall Leahy and the two major owners of the San Francisco 49ers. We have come to a tentative understanding with a couple of qualifications, one of which, of course, is approval of any transaction by the League." Levitas said his entity would buy 51 percent of the 49ers, and that he and Lombardi would be the major stockholders. There "possibly could be one, or at the most 2 additional minor stockholders"—identified as Joe McCrane and Don Pritzker, who ran the Hyatt Hotel chain. "If this transaction is finalized, which I sincerely hope it is," Levitas concluded, "Vince Lombardi will be the Chief Executive Officer of the new corporation and would be empowered to act and speak for the 49ers in all matters."

The bartering in San Francisco continued all year, and Levitas made frequent visits to Wisconsin without a word leaking to the press. It finally fell apart after the rejection of a final $13 million offer. There was, in the end, perhaps one small benefit for Lombardi—from his friendship with Pritzker he later arranged a postgraduation job for his young son-in-law, Paul Bickham, with the Hyatt chain in Chicago.

SIDES WERE being taken that spring, players versus owners, and the very idea troubled Lombardi. The only side he believed in was the Packers side, the side that united him, his coaches and his players. But a dozen years after its inception in 1956, the National Football League Players Association had awakened from a long somnolence, its leaders insisting that the players deserved a larger proportion of the wealth in Pete Rozelle's rich new world of pro football. They presented the owners with a list of demands and insisted on real, not sham negotiations. In the old days, talks between players and owners were so cordial that each player representative sat side by side with his owner. Now players sat on one side of the table, owners on the other.

Lombardi was assigned to the management negotiating team, joining Wellington Mara of the Giants, Rankin Smith of the Falcons, and Mugsy Halas of the Bears. On the players' side of the table were Dave Robinson of the Packers, John Gordy of the Lions, Ernie Green of the Browns, Jim Marshall of the Vikings, Dick Butkus of the Bears, Bob Vogel of the Colts, and their Chicago lawyers, Dan Shulman and his partner Bernie Baum, with help from Baum's brother, Robert.

The owners had grown accustomed to dominating the meetings and assumed a superior posture from the start again this time, an attitude that infuriated Shulman. At the first session, Lombardi addressed his questions to the players in a way that made Shulman believe that he was trying to drive a wedge between the players and their lawyers. It was a variation, in this different setting, of the friendly but distracting head rubs Lombardi would give Bob Skoronski during their contract talks.

"Mr. Lombardi," Shulman said, trying to change the atmosphere, "any questions you have should be addressed to me."

This relatively mild statement struck a raw nerve in Lombardi. How dare someone tell him not to talk to the players! He turned on Shulman and responded, "You'll get down on your belly and crawl in the gutter before I'll address anything to you!"

In late May, during a negotiating session at the Palmer House in Chicago, Shulman and Baum decided that Lombardi and the owners were still pushing the players around too much. They took the players to an anteroom for a caucus, seeking to stiffen their resolve. "Go in there and tell them to go fuck themselves," Shulman instructed John Gordy, the union president. "Use some swear words. Shake them up." When they returned to the table, Gordy started the attack, or tried to. "We've got to, we've got to get these . . ." he stammered. "We've got to get these negotiations . . . these"—finally, it burst loose—"these FUCKING negotiations off center."

"Mister, I don't like that language, and you could never play for me if you talked like that," Lombardi thundered.

Was Lombardi going to get the dominant position again? Shulman was determined not to let it happen. He rose from his chair, leaned his thin, five-eight frame across the table toward Lombardi and said, "FUCK! FUCK! FUCK! FUCK! Vince, the word is FUCK!"

Lombardi, seemingly enraged, bounded from his chair and moved toward Shulman, as men on both sides scrambled to hold them back and prevent a brawl.

"Well," Mara said, smiling, as Lombardi settled down. "I see both teams were up for the game today."

The owners then called a caucus. As Lombardi rose from his chair, he caught the eye of Robert Baum—and winked. It was a sign that he was in full control and knew exactly what he was doing. "With Vince you had to show that you were not afraid of him," Bernie Baum explained later. "That's why we were goosing the players. He was an amazing guy. Very tough. Very gruff. But if you showed him you weren't afraid, he would respect you. He loved football players."

Along with salary and pension concerns, the labor talks had a racial subtheme that spring in the aftermath of Martin Luther King Jr.'s assassination. The union pushed for a nondiscrimination clause in the contract, asserting that many teams were purposely drafting poor black players from the South and paying them less than anyone else. Lombardi opposed the nondiscrimination clause, saying it implied that there was a race problem in the league. He was so certain of his own fair treatment of athletes that it blinded him to the larger situation. Dave Robinson was among three black players Lombardi had drafted in the first round and paid hefty salaries. "We don't have a problem, do we, Robby?" he asked. He was certain that Robinson would say no, but instead the linebacker offered a measured response that decades later proved true: "Coach, we don't have a problem, but we're winning. If we weren't winning, very possibly we could have a problem."

The negotiations sputtered through May and June, and as July approached a strike seemed inevitable. Lombardi's frustration turned away from the players and toward his fellow owners. In Baum's opinion "he became the heart of the negotiations." At a session at a country club in Detroit, Lombardi called a caucus of his management team and laced into them, urging them to "start negotiating and stop playing games." When management threatened to bring replacement players, or scabs, in for the season, Lombardi balked. Wellington Mara noticed that just as Lombardi hated the union getting between him and his players, he also felt resentful when the owners tried to disrupt his sense of team. "You can do what you want, but I'm not having scabs on my team," he said. "I spent nine years making a unit in Green Bay. They're either going to all play together or all walk together." The owners backed down, instead voting to lock out the veterans and open training camp to rookies and free agents until the strike was settled.

On July 9 the negotiations were close to being resolved, but stalled over a pension plan. Shulman and Baum realized that they had nearly everything they wanted, but felt that a short strike would help emphasize the point that "we'd not take it in the future," as Baum later described their reasoning. When the players announced their intentions to strike, the owners responded with a lockout, and veteran players who tried to report to camps were barred. Bart Starr and several Green Bay veterans showed up at the Packers training fields on July 10, but were intercepted by Lombardi, who politely asked them to leave. "I'm very unhappy about this," Lombardi said. "I didn't put thirty years into this business to have it come to this. But I always have hope." The next day, as Starr and his teammates practiced at a high school in Green Bay, Lombardi left for New York and another round of negotiations.

An agreement was finally reached on the evening of July 14 after a five-hour session at the Waldorf-Astoria. The players won a substantial increase in their pension benefits, retroactive to 1959, a boost in major medical insurance, as well as increases in minimum salaries and exhibition game pay. The new minimum salary would seem impossibly modest decades later, but it was a victory for the players then. Second-year players were assured of at least $12,000, minus exhibition pay. When the deal was struck, Lombardi came up behind John Gordy and Dave Robinson and patted them on the back. "Good job," he said. The assumption in Green Bay was that Robinson might as well forget trying to get a raise from his boss after sitting across the table from him all spring and summer. Not so, according to Robinson. "I had less trouble negotiating a raise from Lombardi that year than any of the previous years. All he said was, 'No hard feelings.' Our negotiations lasted about half an hour."

IN THE OLD DAYS, when he was driving his Packers to five championships, Lombardi at times could seem callous, obsessed, self-inflated, but now the people around him almost longed for any of those qualities in place of what they encountered. Training camp opened, Phil Bengtson was in charge, and

Lombardi seemed miserable, lifeless, confused, bored. For the first day or two, he lurked around the edges of the field, standing alone, rubbing the rosary beads in his pocket or sitting on the blocking dummies, watching everything but saying nothing, restraining his urge to bark out directions. "For him to be quiet on a football field was just unheard of," said Chuck Lane. "But he had such discipline that he wouldn't step in." Soon the strain of silence became too much, and he stopped attending practice—and it was as though his life had lost its meaning.

His routine started the same way each morning: St. Willebrord for early mass, in the office before nine, but then it quickly fell apart. The staff had everything under control—contracts, stadium accounts, tickets, vendors, scouting reports, press releases—and he was just getting in the way. In almost the tone of a volunteer intern, he would ask Ruth McKloskey what she thought he should do. He tried to discipline himself to sit down at his desk and push papers, but inevitably bounced up and paced the room. He had often complained about not having enough time; now he had a vast ocean of it. He slipped over to Oneida to golf in the early afternoons, added more speaking engagements to take him out of town, attended hearings and business meetings with Dave Carley, continued his private maneuverings with the 49ers, took a bit part in the movie version of George Plimpton's *Paper Lion* ("Have you tried the AFL?" he ad-libbed to Alan Alda, who played Plimpton, turning him down for a tryout with the Packers), signed up to star in *Second Effort,* a best-selling promotional film for salesmen, as well as a less successful instructional film for football coaches. None of it was enough. "He didn't know what to do with himself," said his daughter, Susan. "He started to come home early. He was driving my mother nuts. She had handled all the household things, and now he was around questioning her."

The players at first expressed relief about the new regime. Bengtson was tall, calm, gentle, laconic, the opposite of Lombardi. Hawg Hanner, his defensive assistant, had advised him to run the players to the point of exhaustion during the first week, reminding them that the Lombardi tradition still lived, but Bengtson declined, saying he had to establish his own style. Where Lombardi conducted his practices with metronomic discipline, Bengtson was easily distracted and might pass the whole day dragging on his Camels and discussing the intricacies of a zone defense. The players called him Phil, an informality they rarely dared with Coach Lombardi. Willie Wood sat on his helmet one morning at camp and joked that he could never do that when the Old Man was around. Bob Skoronski, like most of his teammates, considered Bengtson "just a fantastic guy." And yet by the second week of camp, Skoronski said, it was obvious that Bengtson "didn't have a chance in hell of succeeding."

Under Lombardi, the players were motivated, instructed in philosophy, always on the edge between love and hate. Bengtson's team meetings were boring. There was no inflection in his voice and no message in his speech. "You would go to sleep. He was a monotone," said Skoronski. "And you knew if you didn't play well it wasn't a threat on your life as it was with Lombardi." While the simplest detail seemed endowed by Lombardi with a grander purpose, the players could see no larger scheme in Bengtson's details and dismissed them as trivial. "He was interested in how we lined up for the national anthem before the game," recalled Chuck Mercein. "Lombardi would get us ready to go through a wall, and this guy would be telling you to make sure to put your helmet in your right hand and tuck your shirt in."

There was an odd sensation of afterlife, as though Lombardi had died and his ghost had returned to see how everyone was getting along without him. On August 7 the city staged "A Salute to Vince Lombardi"—yet another ceremony honoring him, this one with the trappings of a state funeral. Three of his Izzo cousins, Buddy, Eddie and Dorothy, came out for the daylong affair, along with Marie's sister, Marge, Vinnie's college chums Jim Lawlor, William O'Hara and Pete Carlesimo, writer W. C. Heinz, Paul Hornung and several other retired Packers, and ten NFL owners. Many of the out-of-town guests gathered the night before in the basement rec room at Sunset Circle for a traditional Lombardi cocktail hour. Lombardi, to borrow the image of his writing nemesis Leonard Shecter, was in full pigeon strut that evening. As much as he professed not to deserve the honor, it temporarily lifted his spirits. He was standing at the bar, chatting with his cousins, when Bill Heinz approached. "Bill Heinz, wait'll you hear this!" he bellowed. The room hushed. "I got a letter the other day and the only thing on the envelope was my picture and a stamp—and it came right here!"

Heinz gave him a blank look.

"You're not impressed?" Lombardi asked.

"Coach," Heinz said. "I'd be more impressed if your picture was on the stamp."

Lombardi roared. Heinz had a way of pricking his ego without wounding him. Eddie Izzo seemed to derive special pleasure from the irreverent comeback. "Thanks for doing that, Bill," he whispered to Heinz. "Vin was just like that when we were kids in the neighborhood in Sheepshead Bay."

At 7:10 the next morning, courtesy cars arrived at the Beaumont Motor Inn to take guests and members of the press out to Resurrection Church in Allouez for an invitation-only seven-thirty mass celebrated by the bishop of Green Bay. "At least some good is going to come of this—I got you all up for early mass," Lombardi joked to the bleary-eyed contingent. After mass and breakfast Lombardi rode in an open convertible out to the stadium for a formal dedication of Lombardi Avenue—the former Highland Avenue. "Most of these are usually named for dead presidents," he said to friends on the way there, a theme that he repeated in his public remarks. "I hope this is not ... I just want you to know that I'm not dead," he said. When a reporter asked if, as a boy, he had ever wanted a street named after him, he answered quickly, "Yes, Broadway."

More than five thousand people filed into the Brown County Arena that night for the closing ceremony, or wake, "An Evening with Vince Lombardi." Fuzzy Thurston, Max McGee and Paul Hornung bleated off-key to a musical rendition of "Run to Daylight!" Travis Williams wowed everyone with a stirring performance of "That's Life." And Lombardi, delivering his own benediction, gave a shorter version of his leadership speech. He reminded his audience of the difference between freedom and license, toasted the American zeal to be first, and praised football for providing the lessons of perseverance, competitive drive and respect for authority. At the close, he thanked his friends and family for their love and support, then turned to his deepest passion, borrowing the cadence of MacArthur, the old soldier who had faded away with memories of West Point "and the corps, the corps, the corps"—but now it was the old coach "and the team, the team, the team."

SINCE THAT SNOWY DAY in February 1967 when Lombardi addressed the management conference in New York, he had delivered the same speech dozens of times around the country. His message in one sense was political, a reaction against a culture that he feared was coming undone because of the excesses of freedom. But it was also in essence personal. He acknowledged that he knew little about the antiwar movement, the black power movement, hippies, sex, drugs and rock and roll, but he tended to think of them all as a single entity that challenged what he believed in and what he had accomplished. His life could be defined by three simple notions: he had led, he had built a team, and he had won. To him, the movements of the sixties seemed to prefer rebellion over authority, separatism and factionalism over teamwork, and losing, or sympathy for losers, over winning and admiration for winners. He could not see the hypocrisy or the inequities (with the exception of racism) that these movements were rebelling against, but focused only on their tone, which he considered negative or defeatist. As a football coach, when he encountered a negative ballplayer, he sent him packing on one of the planes, trains and buses that left Green Bay every day.

As Lombardi's audience grew, his message inevitably took on larger dimensions, and he came to be seen as an important voice in the national cultural debate. The personal was transformed into the political, and people began talking about a football coach as a political leader. The suggestion was raised publicly in an editorial in the *Milwaukee Sentinel* at the start of the 1968 election season. "If Hollywood movie stars can sit in the California statehouse and the United States Senate, what bar exists to the election of a good football coach?" the editorial asked. Lombardi's speeches, the paper said, were "a cut above some pronouncements made in the halls of government" and demonstrated that "he is articulate in matters of national concern as well as in athletics." At the evening ceremony on Vince Lombardi Day in Green Bay, when the lights were dimmed in the Brown County Arena, a bright white banner could be seen in the dark: Vince for President.

This was not merely the wistful speculation of home state boosters. In his search for a vice presidential running mate on the Republican ticket that year, Richard Nixon apparently became intrigued by Lombardi. Nixon loved football and was a student of strong leadership. He was impressed by Lombardi's charisma and old-fashioned philosophy, and assigned one of his counselors, John Mitchell, to conduct a background check on the coach. By Mitchell's later account, he returned with disheartening news—they had the affections of the wrong Lombardi. Marie Lombardi was a conservative Republican and longtime Nixon supporter, but Vince Lombardi was aligned with the Kennedys, too much of a Democrat, and had little regard for Nixon. They had misread Lombardi, mistaking his conservative cultural rhetoric as a signal that he was on their team. In fact, he had been an ardent supporter of Robert F. Kennedy, and the affection was mutual. "Vince, now would you come and be my coach?" Kennedy had cabled him after his resignation announcement in February. When Kennedy was assassinated in June on the night of the California primary, Lombardi lamented "a complete breakdown of discipline in this country." The next month he joined a group of sports figures pushing for strict gun control legislation, which was not Nixon's favorite issue as he strategized to capture the South.

During that turbulent summer of 1968, many Democrats were as intrigued by Lombardi as Nixon had been. Despite his private doubts about Lombardi's depth, David Carley, from his position on the Democratic National Committee, promoted his business partner as a possible vice presidential candidate. "This might sound like the craziest idea you've ever heard, but it isn't crazy," Carley said to the Democratic presidential nominee, Hubert H. Humphrey, at a private meeting. "Think about Lombardi." At the Democratic convention in Chicago late that August, before the clash between young protesters and Mayor Richard Daley's riotous police overwhelmed the scene, the hotel lobby gossip included rumors about Lombardi, as reported by Miles McMillin, an iconoclastic editor and columnist of the *Capital Times* of Madison.

"In this town where rumors of sensational events to come are born every second and shot down the next, there is one speculation that persists and it concerns Wisconsin and one of its most famous citizens," McMillin wrote from Chicago. "It is the talk of Vince Lombardi's developing fascination for politics. His name is sometimes even connected with the speculation about who will be the candidate for vice president. This speculation made the papers in Texas recently after he delivered a speech there. When he was recently asked by the sports writers during the All-Star game festivities about his political intentions he replied cagily, 'I'm too much of an idealist.

Those fellows would eat me up.' One political pro . . . remarked when he heard Lombardi's response, 'He sounds like a pro already.' "

Nothing came of this talk, though both parties continued to court Lombardi, nationally and within Wisconsin. Gaylord Nelson, the Democratic senator who was seeking reelection that fall, asked Carley if he could "get Lombardi to say something nice about me anywhere at any time of his choosing." Lombardi was reluctant. He had avoided the endorsement game with the exception of the Kennedys. But he admired Nelson and eventually agreed to attend a banquet in Oshkosh. Nelson could not have wished for a better endorsement. Lombardi praised him as "the nation's No. 1 conservationist"—and the scene was so good that Nelson's campaign staff swiftly turned it into a commercial and began playing it around the state. The next time Carley saw Lombardi was at a postgame party in the Sunset Circle rec room. "He called me aside and said, 'You sonofabitch. Who gave you the right to have Gaylord Nelson use my name like that?' " Carley recalled. "He knew chapter and verse about it. The Republicans had called him, furious. Marie was angry. He was very upset with me. He thought he had been used and set up."

THE LOMBARDIS had a favorite new hangout in 1968, Alex's Crown Restaurant on the south side of Appleton, operated by Milton and Marge Arps. It was plush in a quasi-Victorian style, dimly lit with deep red walls, gold-cushioned chairs, elegant continental cuisine and soft music provided by Frank Ripple, a pianist studying at Lawrence University's music conservatory. The Crown was thirty-two miles from Green Bay, still deep inside Packer country, yet far enough away from the local haunts that reminded Lombardi of things past and a team he no longer coached.

The first time he and Marie went to Alex's Crown, it was with the Canadeos and W. C. Heinz, and they took two cars. Canadeo had been selling steel in the Fox River valley for years and recommended the restaurant. "I knew Appleton like the back of my hand," he recalled, so when Lombardi asked him how to get there from Sunset Circle, Canadeo gave him the fastest route, taking Highway 47 and turning left and coming in the back way. "Nah," said Lombardi, "I'll come in the other way." Canadeo knew that Lombardi was going ten miles out of his way, but he also understood how stubborn the Old Man was, and how insistent he was about being right. "Jeez, let's let him win," Canadeo said to his wife as he started the trip south. "He'll be so much more sociable tonight if he wins." Canadeo drove slowly, imagining Lombardi in the other car burning down the highway. Winning wasn't everything, but what else was there to compete over during that long teamless year?

Lombardi developed a routine at Alex's Crown. He wore the same outfit every time: powder blue sports coat and navy blue pants. Before leading his party to a back table for dinner, he would stroll over to the piano on the left side of the room near the bar and make the same request—a *My Fair Lady* medley. "He would eat it up," Ripple said. "Just sitting there at the bar, beaming." Marie sat nearby, drinking scotch stingers, mouthing the words to "I Could Have Danced All Night."

It was not only his football celebrity that made "Mr. Lombardi" so welcome at Alex's Crown. He was also a grand tipper, matched only by one of the Kelloggs of the cereal fortune who would come over from Michigan to court a local woman. Everyone who attended to Lombardi's table received a $10 tip—maître d'hotel, waiter, salad server, coat and hat check girl, bartender, piano player. He had one peculiar rule, however, a variation of a concept he had first used with Red Blaik when they golfed at West Point and Red Reeder's son served as their caddy. They had tipped young Reeder handsomely, but deducted a dollar for every lost ball. At Alex's Crown, it was not lost balls but interruptions that resulted in a penalty. If anyone on the restaurant staff asked Lombardi for an autograph or allowed a customer to get to the table, he deducted a dollar from every tip. When a new waitress unwittingly requested two autographs, he signed them graciously, then at the end of the night got $80 in ones from the bartender and distributed $8 tips.

Before leaving Alex's Crown and heading back to Green Bay, Lombardi and his party always returned to the bar, and Marie, loosened by her night's libations, took the microphone at the piano. This was an elegant bar, singing by customers was against house policy, but Marie was exempted. Ripple knew what to play without being asked. It was the tune of "You're Nobody 'Til Somebody Loves You"—but Marie had her own words, and with her husband looking on proudly, in her deep, throaty voice, she crooned, "You're Nobody 'Til Lombardi Loves You."

The trips to Alex's Crown ended that fall, abruptly and loudly. Lombardi had made reservations for a party of fifteen to celebrate an anniversary, but was distraught when he arrived to find an unfamiliar piano player. "Where's Ripple!" he demanded of Milton Arps. It happened to be Ripple's night off, but that was unacceptable to Lombardi. He walked over to the reservation book, pointed his thick finger at his name and time, and bellowed, "You knew I was coming! Why isn't he here?" He eventually calmed down and proceeded with the meal, but the Arpses were offended by the public display of petulance and were not upset that their famous guest never came back. "He was God around here," Ripple said later. "Only a god could be that fussy about a piano player. Celebrities pay a price."

You've got to pay a price, Red Blaik always said. But he was not talking about paying the price of fame, nor was he talking about paying the price of a regrettable decision. Yet those were the prices Lombardi was paying now. For the first time since 1938, a football season was beginning without him on the sideline. He had never been more a part of the popular culture as the quintessential coach—with his speeches, with a prime-time documentary on CBS produced by Ed and Steve Sabol, with the *Second Effort* motivational film being gobbled up by insurance companies and sales organizations, and yet he wasn't even coaching. "I miss the fire on Sunday," he told Bill Heinz, who came out to Green Bay for the home opener that September. Doing a piece for *Life* on Lombardi's first game out of coaching, Heinz observed Vince's perspective of the world of pro football widening. Lombardi noticed, for the first time, that fans actually held tailgate parties outside Lambeau Field before games—"Look at these people!" he shouted, motioning out his window to the ritualistic scene of middle-aged men in Packer jackets grilling bratwurst over charcoal fires. It fascinated him for a minute, but then he lost interest. Now what?

At Lombardi's direction, Chuck Lane had overseen the construction of a special booth for Lombardi on the left-hand side of the second level of Lambeau Field's press box. It was furnished with a small refrigerator and a television monitor, and soundproofed so that Lombardi's commentary could not be overheard as he watched his old team put on one hapless display after another. When the Vikings visited Milwaukee County Stadium early in the year, Mitchell Fromstein sat next to Lombardi, who seemed more animated than the losing Packers on the field. "He was pissed," said Fromstein. "He was fidgeting and walking back and forth in the box. He never sat down. I don't think he was happy with somebody else coaching." But that early-season anger at times gave way to something else, an expression of ego that Max McGee, who had retired, noticed when he sat in Lombardi's box one Sunday. "I think it's human nature that he didn't think just anybody could take this team and win a championship. He wanted the feeling that he was the reason. And he was. But I caught that once when the Packers scored on a lucky play, and he said, 'Those lucky sonsofbitches!' I got the feeling he would rather Bengtson lost every game he coached. That may be too harsh, but I got that impression."

As difficult as this new life seemed for Lombardi, the consequences for Marie were worse. She had a new granddaughter to brighten her days, Susan's daughter, Margaret Ann, had arrived in August, but family never seemed enough. Earlier that summer Marie had traveled east with Jill Lombardi and Jill and Vincent's two sons, Vincent II and John, showing off her grandsons to East Coast relatives, but from what Jill saw, the trip brought as much pain as joy. After spending a few days with Harry and Matty and the Izzo clan in Sheepshead Bay, they drove through a blinding rainstorm across the Verrazano Narrows Bridge from Brooklyn to Staten Island and down to New Jersey, where they visited Marie's father in Fair Haven. Marie could not see her father without also encountering Cass, her aunt and virtual step-mother, the woman who had broken up her parents' marriage. She refused to acknowledge Cass the entire visit, Jill remembered, "except to tell her to get out of the pictures. It was very awkward." But Marie loved the East Coast, and longed for it again the moment she returned to Green Bay, where she was no longer the center of attention. She had relished her role as the coach's wife, and now that had been taken from her. "I don't think she could handle it," Susan said. "She had a hard time dealing with the fact that Dad was no longer the coach. Plus, he wasn't handling it so well himself."

That fall Marie slipped into another depression. Jack and Ethel Clark, old friends from New Jersey, paid a visit for a home game and brought along their daughter DeDe, who had just returned from Europe. Marie drank too much at the game and had to be helped from the stadium by Doris Krueger and another friend. Ockie Krueger was already at Sunset Circle, setting up the bar for the postgame cocktail party, when Marie was carried in and taken to her bedroom. "I have one ear out and I hear Vince's car come in," Krueger later recalled. "So I go out and get Vince and I say, 'Coach, it ain't good.' He didn't ask what happened. He just said immediately, 'Where is she?' I said, 'She's in the bedroom with Doris.' And he said, 'I've got to get her out of here.' " That night Susan and Paul went out with DeDe Clark and a date. Susan called home during dinner and came back to the table with frightful news: her mother was in the hospital again after taking tranquilizer pills mixed with the alcohol.

It was a mild overdose, not life-threatening, but enough to draw her husband's attention. "I think my dad was stunned by it," Susan said later. "He had been living in a little denial."

As the season entered its final stretch, the Packers had sunk below .500, but with their 4–5–1 record they were still mathematically alive in the mediocre Central Division's playoff race. Lombardi's mailbag was now over-flowing with letters and telegrams from Packers fans deploring his decision to quit coaching. ("What are you doing to my Packers?" implored Bruce Bouche, an "ex-resident" of Green Bay, in a telegram from Rialto, California. "Dear Mr. Lombardi. I am from Chicago and I am a Packer fan. You never should have went to management. The Packers need you at coaching," wrote Richard Menke, age eleven.) Lombardi could stay away from his boys no longer and entered the dressing room at midweek before a game against the Redskins in Washington, reminding his players in an emotional plea that they were defending world champions, that it was time to show they could still win, and that he would "despise" anyone who quit now. After the speech he retreated to a side room, where Pat Peppler was working, pulled a chair close to the wall and broke down in tears. "There were so many damn things I wanted to say to them," he said. "So many things."

Lombardi traveled to Washington with the team, accompanied by Marie, and stayed in a suite at the DuPont Plaza Hotel. After covering Lombardi for a decade, Lee Remmel of the *Press-Gazette* had become accustomed to his routines. He knew that Lombardi traditionally ate breakfast with

Marie on the morning of a game. But this time, when Remmel entered the dining room, he noticed someone else at Lombardi's table—Edward Bennett Williams, the president of the Redskins. "I noted it," Remmel said later. "But at the time I didn't think too much of it, except that it wasn't Marie." Later that day Lombardi viewed part of the game from Williams's box, and though much of their conversation was in hushed tones, he was overheard gushing about the nation's capital, "Washington is really a great place, isn't it? This is where it all happens." Chuck Lane, who sat near Lombardi for part of the game, noticed that he appeared unusually relaxed. It might have been that the Packers were winning easily that day, but Lane thought there was more to it than that. "It was like two guys sitting in a bar and having a beer together. He's talking about the players analytically. He's relaxed but his mind is clicking."

To what end, Lane did not then know, though he did notice the banner several fans had carried around the stadium that day: "Save Our Skins— Hire Lombardi." Not long after his return from Washington, Lombardi started quietly laying the groundwork for his next move. "How long would it take you to get ready to move to Washington?" he asked Ockie Krueger, his aide-de-camp. "About ten minutes," Krueger replied. "And my wife about ten seconds." Pleased with the answer, Lombardi urged Krueger to keep quiet but stay on the ready. The following Sunday, before the Packers played in San Francisco, he addressed the team once more, rekindling the old spirit, but Starr and Zeke Bratkowski both got hurt, an early lead over the 49ers slipped away, and with it the season. All that was left was a final home game against the Baltimore Colts and then a road game in Chicago.

Over the years Lombardi had ordered the world around him so willfully that he had virtually forced life to make sense to him: his soul cleansed at daily mass, short hair, crisp clothes, clean desk, everything in its place, reduced to its basic elements, nothing more complicated than the Packer sweep, authority respected, hard work rewarded, God, family, Green Bay Packers. He insisted in his public speeches that there was a clear purpose to life, that one's daily efforts added up to something great and enduring, that with the will to excel one could prevail "not only now, but in time and, hopefully, in eternity." Yet life intruded, chaotic and ambiguous, overpowering his perfectly disciplined will. As general manager and not coach, he had chosen the wrong job, and nothing in his daily efforts now satisfied him. His supportive but brittle wife was depressed and desperately seeking attention, and nothing he had done eased her suffering. Where was the full reward of family when his daughter was married in secret, without him there, without a ceremony, in a faraway church by an unfamiliar priest? Where was order, discipline and respect for authority when players went on strike against his game of football and young men burned draft cards and berated his beloved country?

In his search for the old order, Lombardi turned to symbols. He enthusiastically embraced a proposal by a group of Green Bay women to stage a Pride in Patriotism Day ceremony at Lambeau Field for the December 7 nationally televised game against the Colts. It was to be a flag-waving answer to young antiwar demonstrators and draft card burners. NFL team banners ringing the stadium were taken down and replaced by American flags. Before the game, the St. Norbert choir sang "This Is My Country" and "God Bless America." More than fifty thousand miniature flags were distributed to the sellout crowd, and after the Pledge of Allegiance by the Boy Scouts the swelling sea of fans waved little flags in the brilliant winter afternoon sunshine. The scene brought tears to the eyes of Ruth McKloskey, whose son Neil was fighting in Vietnam. It reminded Lombardi of boys he had lost to war over the years, the fallen quarterbacks whose mass cards he carried in his Bible: Billy White from Saints, killed in Korea more than a decade earlier, and Don Holleder of West Point, shot in an ambush a year ago in Vietnam. At halftime, Lombardi received a one-word cable from the league office: wonderful. Then the Packers lost again, and finished the season with a losing record, something they had never done when Lombardi was the coach.

SUPER BOWL III was held in Miami that January, the first Super Bowl without the Packers. This time the Baltimore Colts represented the old league, favored by eighteen points over the AFL's New York Jets. Lombardi had thought about coaching the Jets off and on since 1963, when David "Sonny" Werblin first tried to lure him back to New York, but the deal had never been struck. He was intrigued by this team, which seemed utterly unlike a Lombardi team. The Jets had an unassuming coach, Weeb Ewbank, and a daring quarterback, Joe Namath, who was from Alabama like Bart Starr, but Starr's opposite in demeanor, with his long hair and white shoes and cocksure boasting. Broadway Joe was wild, in need of taming, but he had the quickest release Lombardi had ever seen and he was a winner, like the Golden Boy. When Lombardi spoke of the Colts, he used the pronoun "we," a term of loyalty to the old league, but he had a hunch about the Jets. "They're going to beat us," he told several friends.

In the press frenzy before the game, word spread about other jobs for Lombardi. He was going to the Eagles, the Patriots, the Redskins. There were so many reports of his secretly buying real estate here or there that Pete Rozelle came up to him and said jokingly, "Congratulations, Vinnie, on your real estate holdings." And another rumor: He would become the next baseball commissioner. Howard Cosell asked him about it. The *Times* promoted him for the job. "But do the diamond fathers really want a strong man?" asked New York's Arthur Daley. "Or do they prefer to watch their life blood drain away with stooges? Can they subordinate individual selfishness for what's best for the game?" Lombardi roared when Daley mentioned the baseball job, and said he had not heard anything about it, but added: "I'll tell you one thing. I love baseball."

If he loved baseball, he was committed to football. On the Friday night before the game, in the bar of the Kenilworth, where he and many of the NFL brass were staying, he ran into George Dickson, a lifelong assistant coach who shared dozens of mutual friends with Lombardi, including Johnny Druze, one of the Seven Blocks. "Are you committed for next year?" Lombardi asked him. Dickson knew the insider jargon. That meant Lombardi was surreptitiously putting together a staff, getting ready to head back into coaching. The next night Lombardi went to dinner at Tony Sweet's restaurant. At the table with him was Edward Bennett Williams, who by one account appeared practically lovesick. The Redskins had not had a winning season in a dozen years, a streak that Williams was determined to bring to an end. He had first met Lombardi in Miami six years earlier, after Green Bay's second straight NFL title win over the Giants. He had tried to hire the coach before the 1966 season but had no stock to offer then, and settled on Otto Graham. Since the Packers game in Washington in November, their meetings had become more productive, though not always as clandestine as Williams wished. Their last dinner meeting, at Joe and Rose's restaurant in Manhattan, had been interrupted when Commissioner Rozelle and a party of league officials came in and stumbled upon Lombardi and Williams. It was, Williams said later, like being caught with another woman.

Whenever the two men met, along with practical discussions of what it would take to bring Lombardi to Washington, they talked about their shared obsession for competition, what Williams called "contest living." Williams lived life and practiced law that way, ferociously, going for the win. He loved boxers and ballplayers, jocks of all sorts, and in his pantheon of sports figures, Lombardi stood at the top. Ben Bradlee, executive editor of the *Washington Post* and Williams's close friend, said, "Lombardi was the first guy Eddie loved." He courted Lombardi with everything he had: stock in the team, unlimited power as general manager and coach, the biggest office, his own driver, access to the most powerful people in the world.

Lombardi was listening. He had to get his wife out of Wisconsin, he wanted the stock, he dearly missed the players, he needed to be needed, he longed for a cause. And he was addicted to success, just as the president of the Redskins was addicted to him. When Edward Bennett Williams set his sights on Vincent Thomas Lombardi, he was sure that he had found the best man for the contest of life. "You know," Williams said to him that night in Miami, "you're the only one I want."

26

The Empty Room

NOT SINCE THE DAYS of Scooter McLean had there been such disarray in the leadership ranks of the Green Bay Packers. The team's brain trust had gathered in the coaches room across from Lombardi's office on the Tuesday morning of January 28, 1969, for the annual rite of selecting players in the college draft. Scouting reports were spread across tables, several phone lines were buzzing, one large magnetic board ranked four hundred players by position, another kept track of the twenty-five other teams and players they had selected, and a chalkboard listed the select group of athletes coveted by the Packers. After a disappointing season Green Bay held the twelfth pick in the first round. O. J. Simpson went first to Buffalo, then Atlanta took big George Kunz of Notre Dame. There were plenty of high-profile players left when it came around to the Packers, including running backs Calvin Hill and Ron Johnson, quarterback Terry Hanratty, and linemen Dave Foley, Ted Hendricks and Fred Dryer. Phil Bengtson passed them up and instead drafted Rich Moore, an unheralded defensive tackle from Villanova.

As soon as Bengtson made the choice, unilaterally, personnel director Pat Peppler left the room in dismay. Moore was an interesting prospect, but Peppler and several scouts had him listed lower, and they thought they had persuaded Bengtson to wait until a later round to pick him. As Peppler fumed in the hallway, Lombardi, still the general manager, stepped out to talk to him. Peppler said he was upset about the way Bengtson had made the selection. "Pat, I'm sorry, but I've got to stay out of it," Lombardi responded. "It's Phil's team."

A short time later Lombardi emerged from his office again and saw a familiar figure walking toward him. W. C. Heinz had arrived to oversee more work on *The Science and Art of Football,* an instructional film series on how to play football the Lombardi way. Heinz had written new material for Lombardi to narrate, but the coach did not seem eager to see him. "You came at the wrong time," Lombardi said. No surprise in that response: Heinz had heard similar words often enough over the years from his preoccupied friend, but this time Lombardi motioned him into the office, closed the door and confided, "Bill, don't tell anyone about this, but I'm going to the Redskins." The rumor had been around for weeks, but it was still just a rumor, not confirmed fact, and Heinz would tell no one, not even his close friend Red Smith. He understood why his old collaborator had to leave. Expecting Lombardi to stay in Green Bay would be like asking someone who had written a great novel to do it again without changing the setting or many of the characters. It could not be done, Heinz thought, "and he couldn't make anything of that ball club after that."

Stuck in Green Bay with no chance of getting work done, Heinz accompanied Lombardi across the hall to watch the draft. As the selection process continued at its slow pace, Heinz could barely repress his amusement at the way Lombardi was reacting. No one on the coaching staff had been told yet that Lombardi was leaving, or where he was going, but his refusal to interfere in the first-round selection was only one piece of evidence that something had changed. He seemed to be following Washington's selections with more interest than Green Bay's, and was becoming increasingly annoyed. Washington had traded away its first, second, fourth, ninth and tenth choices. "My God," Lombardi said at one point, "the Redskins are getting nothing!" A thousand miles away in the Redskins draft room, Otto Graham was feeling the same way, and his nervousness over a lack of draft picks was compounded by fear that he might soon be displaced as head coach. "I think I'll call Lombardi in Green Bay and see if he wants to trade Donny Anderson and Jim Grabowski for A. D. Whitfield," Graham said sarcastically to his staff. "If he says yes, I might as well go home."

That weekend Lombardi traveled to New York, where he met privately with Williams and completed their deal, and by the time he returned to Green Bay late Sunday the story had broken, once in a speculative report by a Detroit television sportscaster and then with more authority in the *Washington Post.* "Vincent Lombardi on Monday will ask the Green Bay Packers to release him from the remaining five years of his contract so that he may become the head coach and general manager of the Washington Redskins," the *Post* story began. It was written under the byline of sports editor Martie Zad with utter certainty, even though it said that Williams "had turned aside" all press inquiries involving Lombardi and there was no mention of other sources. In fact, while the Redskins president was not answering calls from sportswriters that week, he had spilled the beans to the *Post'*s Ben Bradlee.

Williams, Bradlee and Art Buchwald, the humor columnist, were best pals and regular lunch partners at Sans Souci and Duke Zeibert's restaurant in downtown Washington. Their lunches were ostensibly off-the-record, but Williams seemed to have inside information on everybody in town, and Bradlee would return to the paper with a week's full of delicious tips. Sometimes he would dish them out indirectly by asking a reporter a pointed question. Other times he would hold them until a reporter or editor came into his office knowing that he might have the scoop on a rumor that they could not pin down. Zad's pro football writer, Dave Brady, had picked up the Lombardi-to-Washington speculation but could not confirm it. "Know anything about it?" Zad asked Bradlee that Saturday at the office. "If I tell you Williams'll kill me. You sons of bitches are gonna get me in trouble," Bradlee responded at first, smiling. Then he confirmed the report, ending with the warning, "Whatever you do, don't quote Ed."

Lombardi's mind and spirit were already in Washington, but breaking the news in Green Bay was not easy for him. After getting home on Sunday evening, he called Dick Bourguignon, his closest ally on the Packers executive board, and invited Bourguignon and his wife, Lois, to come over to Sunset Circle at nine o'clock. "Dick had a sense of what Vin was going to say and told him he didn't want to hear it," according to his wife, who had become Marie's best friend in Green Bay. "But Vin persuaded us to come over. When we arrived, he and Marie were waiting in the living room, and Vin took Dick into his study. They were there a long time, and when they came out, Vin walked over to where I was sitting, kneeled down and draped an arm around the chair. He said, 'This is so hard.' Tears welled in his eyes and he started to sob. We told him that he went with our good wishes." Lombardi left it to Bourguignon to pass the word to other key members of the executive board.

At his stadium office the next morning, Lombardi called in secretary Lorraine Keck to take down a letter. He sat at his desk and began dictating:

> To Dominic Olejniczak, president, and the Board of Directors of the Green Bay Packers:
> It is with sincere regret and after many hours of deliberations that I am requesting a release from my contract with the Green Bay Packers.

Keck had heard rumors, but had held out hope that they were not true. Now, as she took down Lombardi's words in shorthand, it began to sink in that he was leaving. "I started crying," she recalled. "Then the phone rang and it was a call he had to take, so I went into the bathroom and composed myself. When I came back in he started dictating again."

> This was not only a difficult decision, but a highly emotional one. I have made many close friends in Green Bay and in Wiscon-

sin. Many of those are among the board of directors and the executive committee. I sincerely hope we will continue in that friendship.

My decision was based upon a number of factors. One was the equity position with the Washington Redskins and I do not believe I need to go into the advantages of a capital gain position under today's tax laws.

The ability of Lombardi to better himself as a shareholder in the Redskins is what would allow him to break his Green Bay contract, which still had five years to run. The NFL's policy was to allow coaches and general managers to break contracts only if they were moving to higher positions. Lombardi was by no means a business expert, but he had made the capital gains argument earlier to Olejniczak when he sought a share of ownership in the Packers. Early reports indicated that Lombardi might get a 13 percent share of the Redskins, which was the amount held by the estate of C. Leo DeOrsey, who had been team president before Williams. In fact, Lombardi was offered less than half the DeOrsey shares, totaling 5 percent of the team stock, worth about half a million dollars, and with a provision that his shares could be bought back at any time. When his business friends, Jack Koeppler and David Carley, looked over the contract and told him he was getting into a weak position, Lombardi brushed aside their concerns. "He grabbed the paper right out of my hand and said, 'Oh, hell with that!' " Carley recalled later. "He was so eager to go to Washington and a new life."

The other factor was really altruistic in that I need a challenge and I have found the satisfaction of a challenge is not in maintaining a position but rather in attaining it. I can no more walk away from this challenge than I could have walked away from the one ten years ago. I am the same man today I was ten years ago.

This was the most disingenuous paragraph in the letter. Perhaps Lombardi was using the term "altruistic" to separate his need for a challenge from his desire to make himself rich, but altruism involves the unselfish concern for others instead of oneself, and his reasoning here was self-centered. It was typical of Lombardi that he would try to soften perceptions of his outsized ego by explaining his actions in the rhetoric of his public speeches: here he was not bailing out of Green Bay for a better deal, but bravely meeting a challenge. For obvious reasons, he did not mention what might have been his one altruistic motive: his desire to move his troubled wife back to the East Coast.

The future of the Packers is in good hands; the front office, ticket office and the football field. The Packers have a good football coach, who will be a better one without the pressure of having

Vince Lombardi looking over his shoulder and without the players wondering how the man upstairs might have done it.

It was in Lombardi's interest to leave the team in good hands, but there was increasing concern that the Packers were on a downward slide that would only worsen when and if he left. Many citizens remembered the bleak decade before his arrival and feared that the losing season in 1968 was the first sign of a significant relapse. It was. Bengtson coached three years, and was fired with a losing record. The Packers without Lombardi fell into a dark age that lasted for more than a quarter-century. After winning Super Bowls I and II, they would not win again until Super Bowl XXXI.

Each of us, if we would grow, must be committed to excellence and to victory, even though we know complete victory cannot be attained, it must be pursued with all one's might. The championships, the money, the color; all of these things linger only in the memory. It is the spirit, the will to excel, the will to win; these are the things that endure. These are the important things and they will always remain in Green Bay.

This riff came straight out of Lombardi's standard speech, but who wanted to stay in Green Bay to find out if he was right? Keck, with tears still streaming down her face, interrupted the dictation to ask whether she could go with him to Washington. The same question was asked in ensuing days by Pat Peppler, the personnel director, and Forrest Gregg, the offensive tackle (who had just retired and wanted to get into coaching), as well as several other players. Lombardi's answer was that as part of his contract obligation he could not steal anyone from Green Bay for at least one year.

There has never been a question of remuneration. After making a decision a year ago not to coach, I think you can all well understand the impossibility of my returning to the field in Green Bay. It would be totally unfair to coaches and players alike.

I have spent ten happy years in Green Bay. I know I will miss the city, the team, but most of all, my friends.

Sincerely,

Vince Lombardi

That morning Olejniczak called a meeting of the executive board across the river in the downtown law office of Fred Trowbridge Sr. on the fifth floor of the Bellin Building. Ole and Bourguignon were there, both realtors, along with lawyer Trowbridge, *Press-Gazette* editor John Torinus, H. C. Prange's executive Jerry Atkinson, industrialist Les Kelly and steel salesman and former Packers great Tony Canadeo, the Gray Ghost. Ole had received news that Edward Bennett Williams had scheduled a news conference for one o'clock that afternoon (noon Green Bay time), but he felt several matters still needed to be resolved before the Packers could release Lombardi from his contract. The local press corps learned about the meeting and began a vigil outside Trowbridge's office. Ole stuck his head out at one point and said somewhat obliquely, "The matter is under consideration." Trowbridge emerged later to instruct his secretary to place a call to Commissioner Rozelle, a request that stirred more curiosity among the sportswriters, whose number was increasing by the hour as more arrived from Milwaukee and Chicago.

After returning from lunch, Olejniczak announced that he doubted anything would be resolved that day. His discussions with Rozelle had achieved the desired result, forcing Williams to delay any announcement from Washington until the issues in Green Bay had been settled. Just then the elevator door down the hall from Trowbridge's office opened and out stepped Lombardi, his cheeks rosy from the near-zero temperature outside. He spent less than an hour in the room with Ole and the directors, then came out and held an impromptu press conference in the hallway, jumping the gun on his once and future bosses. "I might as well say it," he began, unable to repress a smile. He said that he had asked the Packers to release him from his contract so that he could accept "a position as executive officer and coach—with equity—with the Washington Redskins." He would be executive vice president of the Redskins, in "complete charge," even though Williams would retain his title as president.

Someone asked him whether he worried that he might be risking his reputation by getting back into coaching after achieving such legendary status during his first round of coaching in Green Bay. "Reputation, schweputation," he said with a thunderous laugh, then turned and walked toward the waiting elevator.

Nothing definitive happened on Tuesday. Lombardi returned to New York in the afternoon, this time to accept the Jack Mara sportsman of the year award from the Catholic Youth Organization. Williams waited anxiously in Washington, embarrassed that twice already he had had to postpone the press conference at which he could lay claim to bringing in the legendary coach. Olejniczak spent the day taking a census of his contentious forty-five-member board of directors and determined that an emergency meeting of the full board was needed to answer all the concerns.

They convened at 6:10 on Wednesday evening at the Forum Supper Club, in a room the Bilotti brothers had transformed into a Lombardi shrine, with a vast mural on the wall depicting St. Vince between the Roman Coliseum and Lambeau Field. Ten years earlier, in the last emergency session of this same group, directors had convened in the Italian Room of the Hotel Northland and argued vehemently about whether to hire Lombardi. Now they were in the Lombardi Room, debating about how to let him go—an un-

forgettable decade seemingly gone in an instant. Some directors were furious that Williams had never contacted Olejniczak to ask for permission to
talk to Lombardi, but rather had gone through Rozelle. Others pointed out
that Lombardi was not only breaking his contract but defying it, since one
paragraph in the agreement stated that he could not coach any team other
than the Packers for five years. They told Ole that he should demand heavy
compensation from Williams and the Redskins, perhaps top draft choices for
the next two years.

The discussion raged for three hours, and when it was over, Ole got in
his car and drove across the lot to Lambeau, where he met with reporters inside the team dressing room. He sat under the locker of Chuck Mercein,
hero of the Ice Bowl. He was uncomfortable and sweating, running a finger
under his tight collar. His socks drooped, revealing his bare ankles. He was
tired and distraught and almost incoherent. Yet this was Dominic Olejniczak's finest hour, a moment when he showed a humility and grace that ennobled him as much as the man he was praising. He said that there had been
much discussion at the Forum about getting compensation from the Redskins, but in the end he could not put a price tag on greatness. "Very seriously, I think if anyone would have offered me fifteen players on any one
club for Vince Lombardi, I would have turned him down," he said. "If I had
been offered a million dollars for Vince Lombardi, I would have turned it
down. I would not cheapen this deal by measuring his worth to us in dollars
or in a couple of players."

Word of Lombardi's departure curdled like sour milk in some parts of
America's Dairyland. For all the recognition of what he had brought to Wisconsin, there was an underlying feeling of being jilted. Fans who once saw
Lombardi as the symbol of loyalty and discipline now whispered that he was
as greedy as anyone else. It was impossible for him to leave without appearing hypocritical. He had railed against Jim Taylor and any player who dared
play out his option, he had tried to stop Bill Austin from leaving for another
assistant coaching position, he had blasted the players union for splitting
player from coach and putting money before team, and now he was breaking
a contract, abandoning a struggling team, drawn away by nothing nobler
than the scent of more power and money.

"It is true that our hero has treated us rather shabbily at the end. Vince
Lombardi has gone off, without asking us about it, and made himself a deal
in a foreign land to the east. He has cast us aside, rather roughly at that,"
wrote Glenn Miller, sports editor of the *Wisconsin State Journal.* "It is probably true that our former idol has been crafty, calculating, even a little deceit-
ful with us."

"He didn't leave the city with a very good taste," said Paul Mazzoleni,
the service station operator who had greeted Lombardi as a paisano a decade
earlier. Howie Blindauer, a leading Packers fan and member of Martha's

Coffee Club, was so angry at Lombardi that he slapped a lien on his Sunset Circle house and demanded immediate payment of an overdue $500 air-conditioning bill. When Lombardi finally paid it, after a shouting match in his office, Blindauer proudly refused to cash the check. "You couldn't blame Lombardi for leaving, but people sure did," said Lois Bourguignon. "Some people thought he was terrible. They directed some anger at me, a few of the women, because I was close to Marie. They complained that Vince left this washed-up team and handed it over to Phil."

Lombardi realized that many members of the Packers board were angrier than they showed in public, and he warned some of his assistants that they might take the brunt of that frustration. He told Pat Peppler that he had suggested to the board that they split up the coaching and general manager's duties again and make Peppler the general manager. "But I haven't done you any favor," Peppler recalled Lombardi saying to him. "They aren't going to pay any attention to what I've said. They're mad at me." (Soon after Lombardi left, his prediction was proved right; both jobs went to Bengtson.)

During a drive to the airport Lombardi had a long "heart-to-heart" talk with Chuck Lane, his young publicist, warning him "who to look out for in Green Bay." There was more contention between the board and him than anyone could see on the outside, Lombardi said. Even as directors enjoyed the prestige his winning ways brought to Green Bay, they resented him for stripping away their power, and now they would move quickly to regain it. "He told me that it was a very, very political organization and that Bourguignon and Canadeo would now be virtually isolated by other members of the executive committee, whose power would grow," Lane recalled. "And he was right on the money."

Even the *Press-Gazette*, traditionally loyal to the head man, offered a hint of criticism in its farewell editorial, noting that "there are those who felt that his participation in civic affairs could have been broader." Lee Remmel, who had covered the breadth of Lombardi's Green Bay era for the paper, wrote that it was human nature for the average fan to feel some resentment, but argued that "a calmer appraisal suggests another approach. Admittedly, he has prospered greatly, both artistically and financially, since coming here. But, by the same token, Green Bay has been fortunate to have had a man of his unique talents for as long as it has." There were more huzzahs in the press. "In saying goodbye, we may feel free at last to call the great man Vince," the *Milwaukee Journal* offered humbly, while the *Chicago Tribune* promoted him on a larger stage, declaring: "If Lombardi can repeat the miracle of Green Bay, there is only one place left for him to go. You guessed it: the White House."

Lombardi was obsessing again, but not in that direction. He was returning to football. For several weeks Al Treml, the team film coordinator, had been following up on his request to duplicate the composite films of spliced footage they had compiled over the years. Lombardi had used the composites for teaching his style of football: one composite went back to Hornung and Taylor running the trademark sweep, again and again, behind Kramer and Thurston; another showed traps and off-tackle runs, another short-yardage situations, another his favorite pass plays. Now Treml knew why Lombardi wanted them. He would take his greatest hits to Washington to show to his new team. Lombardi made another football request when he called in Bart Starr to explain his decision to leave. "He wanted all my game notes," Starr said later. "All my team game plans for the teams we'd played over the years. I had my own detailed notes, in folders, filed by teams in a cabinet, and I gave them to him and he copied them all and sent them back. It was the nicest tribute he ever paid me."

PERHAPS HE HAD BEEN LEAVING, slowly, for a year, but in the end it did not seem like a long goodbye. There was a farewell party at the office. The secretaries ordered cake and coffee. Not many send-off jokes, nor much talking at all. Ten years of brilliance gone in a flash. As Lombardi often told everyone in his speeches, all of the color, and all of the glamour, and all of the excitement, and all of the rings, and all of the rewards were now limited to memory. He had promised that the will to excel and the will to win would endure in Green Bay, but there was a sense that he was taking that will with him, leaving behind only an overwhelming sense of loss. Good luck in Washington, someone would say, then more silence. "I gotta get out of here," he said to Ruth McKloskey at one point, his eyes brimming with tears. Bart Starr stopped by and handed him a handwritten note of thanks.

> The shoutings, encouragements, inspirational messages, and vindictive assault on mistakes transcended the walls of our dressing rooms but in the privacy of those same rooms to have known the bigger man, kneeling in tearful prayer with his players, after both triumph and defeat, was a strengthening experience that only your squads can ever fully appreciate. From one of those kids who became a poised, confident, unrelenting man come his heartfelt thanks and best wishes for even greater heights for his Coach.

McKloskey gave Lombardi a perpetual calendar. He promised to keep it forever, and then he left.

A few days later Vernon Biever, the team photographer, drove up from his home in Port Washington to take pictures. McKloskey let him inside Lombardi's office for the first and only time. The nameplate was still on the door: MR. LOMBARDI. Framed photographs and awards sat on the desk, others had been packed in boxes. Biever felt excited to be in the office even though there was little to shoot. As he aimed his camera around the room, he realized that he was documenting not just the desk of a winner but also an aura of irreplaceable loss. No one else could fill this room, Biever thought to himself, clicking away at the emptiness. There would never be another Lombardi.

27

Taking Charge
in Washington

Washington, at last. The patron saint of American competition
and success had finally reached a town where winners were everything. After
napping for two hours in a Mayflower Hotel suite and attending a prayer
breakfast on Capitol Hill, he arrived at his new job on Connecticut Avenue a
few blocks north of the White House at ten o'clock and immediately
snapped into his routine. This was what Edward Bennett Williams had hired
him for, what people were expecting of him, what he knew how to do better
than any politician here, including Richard Nixon, who had been sworn in as
president a few weeks earlier. Vince Lombardi was taking charge.

His title was executive vice president of the Washington Redskins, but
his function was boss. Just as he had done in Green Bay ten years earlier, he
began by rearranging furniture and personnel. The big office that had belonged to Williams was now his. Pictures were coming off the walls and into
a box marked EBW. "Why don't you go back to your law practice?" Lombardi told Williams, half jokingly, and the proud lawyer took it in good
humor. He was still president, but had abandoned any pretense of running
the club, something that was hard to imagine him doing for anyone but his
beloved Lombardi. The very idea that he had landed "the Coach!" was said
to make Williams quiver with boyish excitement.

One was the son of an Irish night watchman, the other of an Italian
butcher, and now here they were, Williams and Lombardi, strolling down
the sidewalk to lunch in the nation's capital, and it seemed as though they
sucked up all the power in the city as they walked by. The noontime crowd
turned and stared at Lombardi as he waited for the walk light at the corner

of Connecticut and L. Inside Duke Zeibert's, the regular table up front awaited Williams and his guest. Red meat, martinis, sports pictures on the wall, ephemeral clatter of boasting, dealing, lying, all suspended momentarily as patrons gawked and then pushed back their chairs for a standing ovation, like the one Grant received from victory-starved Washingtonians in 1864. After lunch the pair went to the Sheraton-Carlton, marching through the bright lights and television cables to the front of two hundred cameramen and reporters in the Chandelier Room. Over at the White House, President Nixon had just finished a press conference, but that was a mere warmup act for this announcement of the coming of Lombardi. "Gentlemen," the coach said, after Williams had introduced him by calling this the proudest day of his life, "it is not true that I can walk across the Potomac. Not even when it is frozen."

Perhaps not, but who was listening? Washington was agog over its new leader and the prospect of a football revival. The Redskins had not won a championship since 1942 and seemed in worse shape than even lowly Green Bay had been when Lombardi took control there a decade earlier. Four unsuccessful Redskins coaches had come and gone through a dozen straight seasons without a winning record, from Joe Kuharich (26–32–2) to Mike Nixon (4–18–2) to Bill McPeak (21–46–3) to Otto Graham (17–22–3). If Graham, once a great quarterback for the Cleveland Browns, was not as ineffectual as Scooter McLean, Lombardi's predecessor at Green Bay, he suffered from some of the same unfortunate perceptions. Nice guy, not a leader. Players called him Toot (Otto, inside out). During his final losing season, they once took bets before practice on how many times he would slap his clipboard, a nervous habit, and they chattered and cheered with every slap. He never knew what his men were cheering about, that they were making fun of him, and the deception took on a touch of pathos when he told the press afterwards that he was encouraged by the team spirit that day. Goodbye, Toot.

The fact that the home team was a loser did not seem to diminish the sports fascination of Washington's power elite. Earl Warren and Richard Nixon, the departing chief justice and arriving president, might have had nothing else in common by that point in their careers, but both still read the sports section first. Football meant a lot to Washington even then, and Lombardi meant more; not just as a coach but as what Williams called the philosopher king, someone who knew what he believed in and could get things done. David Broder of the *Post* offered a similar assessment. "The Lombardi administration seems certain to revolutionize life in official Washington," he wrote. "For one thing, he is dedicated to winning. He defines happiness as the achievement of one's objectives. This is radical doctrine in a government and a city where most jobs depend on seeing that no problem is ever really solved." It was "bad luck for Mr. Nixon," Broder said, that "fate has made him only a bit player in this momentous drama, but the Lombardi era has begun."

THE MOVE to Washington was as much for Marie's well-being as for Vince's restoration. She had braved ten snowy winters in Green Bay, and though she had tried to put the best public face on it she dearly missed the East Coast and metropolitan life. During the previous year, after her husband retired to the front office, she had longed for the action of being a coach's wife as much as he had yearned to return to the sideline. Her occasional overuse of alcohol and prescription drugs to numb her pain had become more frequent and alarming to her family. "I've got to get her out of here," Vince had said one winter's day in Green Bay when she had drunk too much at a game. Now he had kept his word, got her out of there, with the promise of a new life and new home. The outside world knew none of this internal trauma. In social settings Marie seemed optimistic and vibrant, and in her first public comments in Washington she sounded as certain of her role as her husband was. "I feel sorry for the women who have to find their niche in life, and can't," she said. "I never wanted to be anything but be married to Vin."

The Lombardis stayed in Suite 675 at the Mayflower Hotel for most of February 1969. Vince walked to work from there, while Marie went out looking for a new house with Jackie Anderson, a longtime friend from Arlington who was the wife of Packer scout Lew Anderson, and Connie Boyle, a young real estate agent who worked for W. C. & A. N. Miller Company. On the afternoon of February 18, Marie and Jackie returned to the hotel in late afternoon after house-hunting and were surprised to find Lombardi already there. He had left the Redskins office early with what the newspapers the next day—reporting what the team publicist told them—called a heavy cold. "He said he didn't feel good and needed a doctor," said Anderson. She called her husband the scout, who quickly found Dr. Phil James at the Washington Clinic and asked him to make a house call at the Mayflower. From a few preliminary questions, Dr. James determined that this was far worse than a cold. Lombardi was feverish, urinating frequently, and had a sore lower back near the kidneys. Dr. James contacted a urologist at his clinic, Dr. Landon Banfield, and asked him to come to the hotel.

Dr. Banfield, a Redskins fan who had played football through his freshman year at Princeton, was thrilled at first "to be called to see Vince Lombardi." When he arrived at the suite at 8 p.m., Marie and Jackie were waiting in the outer living room, along with Lew Anderson and a few assistant coaches. And there sat the coach, still dressed in shirt and loosened tie; he had refused to go to bed. Dr. Banfield took him into the bedroom for an examination. Lombardi was shaking, had chills, and his temperature was 102 degrees. The diagnosis: he had "a roaring urinary tract problem," probably prostatitis, an infection of the prostate. Dr. Banfield treated him with ampicillin and said he would check on him again in a few days. When they emerged from the bedroom, Dr. Banfield recalled later, Marie gave him a look "like, 'Oh, God, what have you done to my husband?' " Three days later Lombardi visited Dr. Banfield's office. He was sweating profusely, but the kidney pain had diminished and his fever was gone. One week later Dr. Banfield brought him in for a third checkup and performed a more thorough examination. Lombardi's blood pressure was 120 over 60. He told the doctor that he had had no serious ailments in his life, glossing over a long line of problems going back to his sophomore year at Fordham when he had been knocked unconscious and was hospitalized with internal bleeding in his lower intestinal tract.

Urine tests indicated that the infection had improved, and a rectal exam revealed no noticeable mass in Lombardi's prostate. But his reaction to the rectal exam was one that Dr. Banfield would long remember. "He *hated* the rectal exam," Dr. Banfield said later. "He screamed so loudly the nurses came running into the room. He was very unhappy about it." That was the last time Lombardi would see Dr. Banfield. After he recovered from that "bad spell," as Marie later called it, he still seemed tired all the time, especially in private when only she was around. This renewed her nagging concerns about his overall health, reminding her once again of how exhausted he had been during his final year coaching the Packers. She pleaded with him to go in for a complete physical, including a proctoscopy to check for tumors in his colon, but he ignored all such entreaties from Marie and Dr. James, just as he had in Green Bay. No way he would let any doctor do that, he said. This was part of Lombardi's squeamishness and stubbornness that Marie knew all too well. Her husband had just arrived in Washington, his first game with the Redskins was still a long way off, and as she noted later in a letter to their son, Vincent, "of course he couldn't quit."

Marie's outlook brightened somewhat when Connie Boyle showed her a house that had just been constructed at 11013 Stanmore Drive in Potomac Falls, an upscale development in suburban Maryland beyond the Beltway, about forty-five minutes by car from downtown. It was a spacious four-bedroom colonial made of orangish tan brick with yellow cream trim, designed on the slope of a hill so that the paneled family room in the basement opened out to an expansive two-acre yard. Stone steps led up a manicured terrace from the two-car garage on the side to the front portico. "This is my dream house. This is what I want!" Marie said, and though Lombardi had preferred an old house closer to town, in the Somerset neighborhood, he deferred to his wife, saying, "I promised her she could have whatever she wanted." Edward Bennett Williams called Boyle to see if he could get the price down—another contest, what he thought life was all about—but the young widow with five children held firm, kept the price at $125,000 and made the deal of her lifetime. When the contract was signed, she came home with an autographed picture of the coach for one of her boys.

Lombardi would not be home much in any case. There was a football team to turn around, and he went about it the same way he had in Green Bay a decade earlier. Repetition had always been his mantra, so there was no reason for him not to repeat what had worked for him before. Again he assembled a coaching staff of loyalists, looking not for innovative young football minds or future head coaches but seasoned pros who understood his methods and could carry out his directives. From his early Green Bay days he brought back Lew Carpenter, one of his first halfbacks, and Bill Austin, his first line coach, recently fired as head coach of the Steelers. He wanted to hire two of his retired players, Forrest Gregg and Zeke Bratkowski, but the Packers would not allow it. For the defense he turned to Harland Svare, who had played for him with the Giants. George Dickson was hired to coach the backfield with a glowing recommendation from Bob Blaik, the colonel's son. Don Doll and Mike McCormack were retained from the Graham regime.

What kind of material did they have? Lombardi had been studying game films every night, and assigned each of his assistants to assess the players at each position. He took the quarterbacks himself, by far the easiest task. Sonny Jurgensen had been in the league for a dozen years, and Lombardi had always loved the way he passed. The films confirmed his impressions: Jurgensen was the best pure thrower he had ever seen, with a quick release and unerring accuracy. "My God," he was heard muttering in the darkness of the film room one day, "if we'd had him in Green Bay ..." His voice trailed off. Bart Starr had been his brain on the field, the most committed and disciplined of his ballplayers, but in terms of pure talent he was not in the same category as Jurgensen.

Jurgensen's reputation as a playboy did not bother Lombardi. If anything, it reminded him of his favorite son in Green Bay, Paul Hornung. The Golden Boy might break curfew, but he had uncommon talent and did not waste it; he was the best money player Lombardi had coached. People who did not know Lombardi often held the misimpression that he expected his players to be as conservative in their private lives as he appeared to be. That is what Jurgensen feared at first. When he heard that the Old Man was coming to Washington, he called Hornung and asked, "Jesus, Paul, what am I to expect?" Hornung chuckled and said, "Sonny, you're gonna love the guy." Lombardi announced at his opening press conference that he was giving Jurgensen a "clean slate" and noted that despite his autocratic image he had never been obsessed with rules. "The city of Washington may have a lot of bars but I assure you Green Bay has fifteen times more," he said. "We will have as few rules as we can get away with." After his first meeting with Lombardi, Christian Adolph Jurgensen came away saying he wished the season could start the next day.

Who would carry the ball? George Dickson studied films of the returning running backs and presented Lombardi with a pessimistic assessment,
the last line of which read: "If we are going to win here, none of these guys
will be here when we do." Lombardi was a realist. He knew that Dickson was
probably right, but the report angered him nonetheless. "He came in after he
read my assessment, threw that paper on my desk and said, 'Goddamn it! But
you've gotta coach 'em! Maybe you don't think these men are any good, but
you've gotta coach 'em!' " Dickson recalled. "I said, 'I know I gotta coach 'em,
but you only asked me what I thought of 'em!' "

It was typical of Lombardi to expect the world to bend his way. He established the expectations, the routine, and people adjusted. The barber at
the Mayflower knew when to expect him for his weekly haircut. The administrative staff quickly learned about Lombardi time and arrived at meetings
ten to fifteen minutes early. His assistant coaches knew that they would be
expected to work late on Monday nights and go to Duke Zeibert's for dinner.
He had been a daily early-morning communicant at St. Willebrord during
his years in Green Bay and wanted to establish the same pattern in Washington. One morning, a priest answered a knock at the door of St. Matthew's
Cathedral, and there stood a man who introduced himself as Vince Lombardi. What time was the first daily mass? Lombardi wanted to know. At 7:30
a.m., came the reply. "Why don't you change it to seven; it would fit my
schedule better," Lombardi said. The priest was a kind man; it amused him
that a football coach would try to reschedule his mass, but that was asking a
bit much. Lombardi might be bigger than the president, but there was still a
higher order.

Devoting endless hours to the film room, watching, rewinding, grading,
was second nature to Lombardi; he had been doing it for twenty years, since
he joined Red Blaik's staff in 1949, but it could never replace the thrill he felt
being around players. Even this off-season, during which he had far more
than usual to do as he analyzed what it would take to make winners of the
Redskins, seemed far too long for him. He visited relatives in New York,
played golf with Ockie Krueger at Congressional and Burning Tree, attended more social functions in Georgetown in a few months than he had in
Green Bay in years, but still he was itching to get on with it. Marie saw the
telltale sign; they had been in their new home only two months when he
started cleaning the closets.

ON THE EVENING of June 9, the Lombardis sat in the steamy armory at the
College of St. Thomas in St. Paul and watched their son receive his law degree from William C. Mitchell Law School. Vincent was twenty-seven, and
he and Jill now had three young children: three-year-old Vincent II, two-
year-old John and Baby Gina, five months. As his father said of him that day,
"it was a long, hard pull for the young man." He had entered the University

of Minnesota law school after graduating from St. Thomas, but dropped out, uncertain that he wanted to be a lawyer. He reconsidered and attended Mitchell at night, while working several jobs, first at a bank, then an insurance company, then a law office. Newspapers in the Twin Cities, which published feature articles about his graduation, noted that in getting his law degree he was following in the footsteps of his famous father. It was reported that Lombardi received a law degree from Fordham but never used it, choosing instead to go into coaching. Of course this was one of the old Lombardi myths. He had dropped out of Fordham Law during his first unimpressive year there.

In his rhetoric, Lombardi had little use for quitters or losers. Success, he liked to say, is "not a sometime thing—it is an all-the-time thing." He called it "a matter not so much of talent and not so much of opportunity but rather of concentration and perseverance." Vincent had struggled with this philosophy for most of his life, fearing that he could never live up to his father's expectations. But here was one time when he had persevered when his father had quit. He went back to law school, he said, because he did not think he could compete with his dad in the world of sports. He had been as uncertain about whether he truly wanted to be a lawyer as his father had been—he had a family to support during law school, while his father had still been single—and yet he kept going and got the degree.

Vincent, as his dad and Colonel Blaik would put it, had paid the price. "I think maybe I appreciate the degree more because I had to work for it," he said. Lombardi never seemed prouder. "My son the lawyer," he boasted. God, family and the Washington Redskins. After mass the next morning, before rushing back to D.C. to make final preparations for the season, Lombardi announced to the press that Vincent and Jill and their children would be moving to Washington later that summer, arriving in time for the first exhibition game.

On June 16, Lombardi was finally with his football players, taking his first look at candidates for the Redskins roster at a four-day minicamp of skull sessions and drills on Kehoe Field at Georgetown University. The first practice was scheduled for 2 p.m. and most of the players were there twenty minutes before, revealing an early appreciation of Lombardi time. Tom Brown, the former strong safety of the Packers, showed up, having been acquired in a trade for a draft choice. He sensed the beginning of another era, convinced that players who stuck around Lombardi would "someday feel on top of the world." As passers and receivers went through basic drills, Lombardi was back in his element. No signs of physical exhaustion, no outward indications of worry, just pure football again. "I missed it more than I can say," he said. "It feels good to be back."

That night in the dressing room with his assistants, Lombardi expressed his private hopes and concerns about one of the running backs. Ray McDonald had been the team's No. 1 draft choice in 1967 from the University of Idaho. On paper, he was an incredible talent—huge, fast and powerful, six four and 248 pounds. Edward Bennett Williams, in his most conspicuous intrusion into the realm of player personnel, had selected McDonald himself, and had been disappointed by his choice's performance during his rookie year. Surely Lombardi could get the best out of him. It so happened that McDonald was gay. All the players and coaches knew it; some felt uncomfortable about it and talked about him behind his back. Lombardi knew and did not care. His brother Harold was gay. He had made it a point throughout his coaching career that he would not tolerate discrimination of any sort on his teams. "George," he said to Dickson. "I want you to get on McDonald and work on him and work on him—and if I hear one of you people make reference to his manhood you'll be out of here before your ass hits the ground."

Confidence and fear, that was how Lombardi coached the game. He needed his quarterback to be confident, not afraid, and from the first day treated Jurgensen like a leader, something other coaches had been reluctant to do. They had considered Sonny talented but self-oriented. Lombardi saw more. "Take 'em down to the goalpost, Sonny," he said at the start of practice on the third day. Jurgensen running ahead of the pack—an unheard-of thought before, but there he went, holding the lead for several strides. Sonny was Lombardi's man, and after only a few days he realized what that meant. Jurgensen had been around great quarterbacks much of his career, including Norm Van Brocklin in Philadelphia and Otto Graham in Washington. Yet it was not until he hooked up with the undersized guard from Fordham that he understood the best way to play his position. Lombardi's system, he said, was "completely different" from anything he had seen before. It placed the emphasis on reading the defense and giving the quarterback fewer plays but more options. As had happened to Bart Starr earlier, as soon as Jurgensen got into Lombardi's system, the game seemed to slow down. What had been chaotic suddenly made sense; everything became clear and comprehensible.

When training camp opened at Dickinson College in Carlisle, Pennsylvania, at high noon on July 9, Lombardi was surrounded by old friends and familiar faces. Not just Austin and Carpenter, Brown, Bob Long and Krueger from his Green Bay days, but also Sam Huff, who had played for him in New York and now came out of retirement for one last year, and his traditional army of priests, this time led by Father Guy McPartland, who had played fullback for him at St. Cecilia, and Father Tim Moore, the jovial Carmelite who had been the athletic director there. Father Guy, who had been known as Iggy in high school, said mass for Lombardi in the morning and heard confession in the afternoon, then went to the traditional Five O'Clock Club in shorts and T-shirt and knocked down scotches with everyone else. Father Tim preferred to go out on the field to run under Charlie Gogolak's kicks, then chatter on the sidelines with Joe Paterno, the onetime Brooklyn Prep halfback visiting from the Penn State coaching staff, and Mike Manuche, the Manhattan restaurateur.

Ed Williams came up from Washington, along with his pals Art Buchwald and Ben Bradlee, whose young son Dino was a ball boy. Lombardi took one look at the shaggy-haired adolescent and compulsively barked out, "Get a haircut!" as though he was talking to his own son or one of the ballplayers. Dino showed up the next day with a crew cut. It was the same for Sam Huff as it was for the young ball boy: Lombardi ruled as the voice of authority. On the first night of camp, he gathered the squad together for his opening speech, similar to the one he had delivered for nine straight years in Green Bay, and though it was always effective, in this case it hardly mattered what he said. All he had to do was gesture with his big hand and let his Super Bowl ring glisten in the light and the message was clear. "He was like God himself to these players," George Dickson said. "This was the be-all and end-all of knowing how to win." He told the Redskins that night that he did not have many rules. "But, gentlemen, there is just one thing that I want you to understand. If you do anything to embarrass me or the organization, in any way, you will answer to me and me alone."

Lombardi talked himself hoarse, riding the seven-man blocking sled, daring his linemen to knock him off, hollering at his troops during grass drills. He was a perfect gentleman in social settings and loved a good joke, but in the film room and on the football field he could not stop cursing and yelling. His voice was so loud, and his language so purple, that a college official called David Slattery, Lombardi's administrative assistant, and asked whether he could tell the coach to calm down. When Slattery broached the subject with him, Lombardi seemed contrite. "You know, David, I don't understand it. I go to mass, I never use bad language in my life, until I get to the football season." Then he laughed and said, "I'll try to watch it."

Many of the Redskins were not accustomed to Lombardi's style and had as hard a time with it as the college secretaries who had complained to the dean. Within a week three rookie draft choices from Ohio had bolted camp. Once, fifteen years earlier when two rookies named Sam Huff and Don Chandler had packed up and headed for the airport at the Giants camp in Vermont, it was Lombardi who had talked them back. This time he let the rookies go, berating the "moral code," or lack of one, that would allow them to take signing bonuses and then go home. In some ways he seemed as gruff as ever, especially when he was lost in thought on the football field. Joe Lombardi, his little brother, who was then a regional salesman for Rawlings Sporting Goods, visited camp with two company executives and approached the coach at afternoon practice to see if he had time to meet them.

"Get the hell out of here and get those goddamn people out of here!" Lombardi snapped.

"But c'mon, Vince, these are my bosses!" Joe pleaded.

"I don't give a damn who they are," Lombardi said.

It was not that he did not love Joe or did not want to help him. In fact, Lombardi bought new uniforms from Joe that year and sparked a minor controversy by clothing his team in a color that he insisted was the traditional burgundy but actually was a variation of rose. It was just a matter of habit; he had been kicking people off his field indiscriminately ever since he became a coach. Despite his bluster at Carlisle, in fact, some people who had been around him for years thought Lombardi had actually mellowed that summer. "To me he was not as aggressive, and I figured, well, he's just trying to feel his way around," Tom Brown recalled. "But maybe he didn't have the energy, the enthusiasm, to do what he did in Green Bay. The other guys thought he was pushing them like crazy, but I'm thinking he doesn't have the same intensity."

Brown's observation was discerning. Lombardi had lowered his intensity a notch and was struggling in private with his decision to come back to coach, something he would never admit in public. When Howard Cosell visited camp to do another piece on his favorite coach, Lombardi told him that he had no regrets. "I want to say that I'm very, very happy that I am back," he declared. But with a few confidants he talked about feeling older and tiring more easily, and questioned whether his desire to coach had overpowered the common sense that led him to retire. "I don't know if I made the right decision," he told Father McPartland one night as the two men sat on the back porch of the house he had made his training camp headquarters. "I think I made the wrong decision." The priest at first thought he was talking about the prospects of a winning season, and tried to encourage him by recalling how he had turned the Packers around the first year in Green Bay.

But Lombardi was also still hurting from the harshest portraits of him during his final years in Green Bay, and the criticism of him as a bully continued even now. George Wilson, coach of the Miami Dolphins, was quoted that summer insisting that he was just as good as Lombardi, but more humane. "I'm tired of all this Lombardi business. Everyone makes him out to be such a great coach," Wilson harrumphed. "Given the same material, I'll beat him every time. I can get a team up on the day of a game. I bawl guys out as much as Lombardi does, but I don't holler at a fellow in front of his teammates. I don't want to embarrass him. That's just a big show and I'm not going to do it." (Wilson finished 3–10–1 that year and was fired, ending a twelve-year coaching career with 68 wins and 84 losses; in ten years Lombardi won 96 and lost 34.)

As training camp progressed, Dickson and Lombardi found their runner, though it was not McDonald or any of the other veterans but an unheralded rookie from Kansas State named Larry Brown. From the scouting reports, there did not seem to be much promise in Brown; he was relatively slow and small, had few moves and little experience catching passes out of the backfield. But he was fearless, with uncommon leg strength and terrific explosion off the ball. Dickson considered him the toughest runner he had ever seen. Lombardi needed convincing. "You're always looking for tough guys," he said to Dickson early on. "Give me talent, I'll make them tough." He was also concerned about Brown's mental errors; he had a tendency to miss the snap count and go too early or too late.

"Does that Brown hear?" Lombardi asked Dickson one night at a coaches' meeting.

"I don't know; he always turns his head one way when I'm talking," Dickson said.

"Goddamn it, he must be deaf!" Lombardi said.

They fitted an earpiece in his helmet, and suddenly the errors stopped. Brown played impressively in the exhibition opener at RFK Stadium, pounding through the mud and rain on two short touchdown runs, and when Dickson walked out to the practice field a few days later he saw Lombardi standing with his arm draped around the rookie. "Son," Dickson said to him later during drills, realizing what the Lombardi drape meant, "you've got this ball club made."

LOMBARDI WAS STILL at training camp when his son came out from St. Paul to begin a new life in Washington. Vincent and the boys flew out first, while Jill stayed with Baby Gina until the movers loaded their furniture. By the middle of August they were all staying in Marie's dream house on Stanmore Drive. In his few public comments, Vincent politely made it seem that he wanted to move to Washington, that it was his idea, or at least that he understood and agreed with his father's expressed desire to have the family close together. In fact, he did not feel especially close to his parents then, and from the moment he arrived was uncertain about what he was doing there. Was this going to be another time when he could not meet his father's expectations? Lombardi had mentioned helping Vincent get a job at the Justice Department, but the talk seemed to evaporate when he finally got to town, and there were few contacts for Vincent to pursue. The Old Man was unavoidably too busy with the football team to spend much time with family. Vincent understood this. He did not blame his father, but merely felt awkward about it. He took his boys to Carlisle for a few days, and Lombardi enjoyed his limited time with his grandchildren, toting them around in his golf cart. Then what?

Marie found a house that she wanted Vincent and Jill to buy, a few miles away from hers in Potomac, but to the young couple it seemed unreasonably expensive. They had just bought Marie's station wagon, and between paying her and taking care of the moving van bill they were out of money. Lombardi was a millionaire now, not from his Redskins holdings but from the sale of Public Facilities, the housing company that David Carley had brought him into in Wisconsin. When Scholz Homes bought the company on August 17, it was estimated that he had made $1.7 million from the sale. He was accumulating wealth at last, enough, he said, to take care of his family for the rest of their lives.

The Old Man had good intentions; he wanted to create one big happy family, but it never quite seemed to work. Little John banged his head on the bathtub at Stanmore Drive and had to be taken to the hospital. Jill suffered a miscarriage during a troubled early pregnancy. She and Vincent decided to rent the house Marie had found for them rather than buy it, and Vincent finally found a job in a downtown law firm, but during the long drive into town every morning he asked himself, Do I need this commute? I could be working for a law firm in Minnesota and life would be easier. The season had started and Lombardi was back from training camp, preoccupied with his players and the next game. Marie seemed to love her house and the social whirl. She spent much of her time shopping in Georgetown with her friend Jackie Anderson. There were catered postgame parties at Stanmore Drive, the family room filled with celebrities: Joe DiMaggio, singer Martha Wright, Frank Gifford, television newswoman Nancy Dickerson, Ethel Kennedy.

It was a wonderful life, or so it seemed. One day Lombardi and his son were in the car together and Vince said, "You think I've made a big mistake coming back, don't you?" Vincent took this remark as an indirect way for his father to express his own misgivings, and the implication surprised him. He never considered the possibility that his father doubted himself. It was he, not his dad, who had made the mistake in coming to Washington, he thought. A few weeks later he and Jill decided to move back to St. Paul. When Vincent broke the news to his parents, not much was said. Vince was preoccupied; Marie expressed herself largely through body language, according to Jill, who could sense that her mother-in-law was "extremely upset."

Not long after Vincent and his family left, Lombardi wrote a note to his daughter, Susan, who had moved to Chicago Heights, Illinois, with her husband and daughter, Margaret Ann, and was pregnant again. Lombardi was an emotional man—he could cry while giving a speech to his football team—yet he had rarely been able to express that same level of feeling with his own family. The letter to Susan was about as expressive as he got. "Dear Susan," he wrote. "Enclosed please find $100. Buy yourself something and something for Margaret Ann from her grandfather. I'm looking forward to seeing you at Thanksgiving. Regards to Paul and give Margaret a kiss and remember I love you."

His football team was winning that fall, never easily or impressively, but enough to maintain his status as the quintessential winner. Just having him there raised the public expectations, perhaps unreasonably, but there was a growing sense in Washington that Lombardi was creating another dynasty. After defeating the Giants 20 to 14 at RFK in the fifth game, the Redskins record stood at 3–1–1, in second place in the East behind the Dallas Cowboys, and the postgame party at Stanmore Drive was especially festive. A band of Izzo cousins came down from New York and Baltimore, mixing with the Washington elite. A few days later Ethel Kennedy wrote Lombardi a note on her Hickory Hill stationery.

> Dear Coach,
> Many thanks for an exciting afternoon watching our favorite team. And also for the after game victory celebration in your delightful home. I didn't think anybody had as many relatives as the Kennedys. I guess you know the greatest asset to the team is living right in the house with you. Basically you realize it isn't Sonny's arm but Marie's Hail Marys that pull us through every Sunday. The children and I are grateful to you both for sharing your box with us. With continued admiration and affection,
>
> Ethel Kennedy
>
> P.S.—Is it true you fired up the team at halftime by telling them it's only a game!

For a year after Robert Kennedy's death Ethel Kennedy had been in mourning, staying away from Washington's social life. When she had begun appearing in public again that June, a year after the assassination, she immediately found comfort in Lombardi's presence. She first sat next to him at a party at Ben Bradlee's house, and though he made her nervous at first, he quickly put her at ease, talking about his friendships with Jack Kennedy and her husband and how they both had the qualities of great athletes. "His presence was so overwhelming," she said later, "that I forgot who else was in the room." Over time, as she saw more of the coach, in her prayers she thanked Bobby for sending Vince Lombardi to Washington to look after her. He was invariably polite in her presence, as was Marie, though in private Marie could be dismissive of the Kennedys. As a conservative Republican, she found President Nixon and Vice President Spiro Agnew more to her taste.

Lombardi was moving that way himself, pushed away from his Democratic roots by what he saw as the excesses of the counterculture, and pulled toward conservative Republicans by their growing hero worship of him. The Lombardi Creed on discipline, respect for authority and the American zeal to win had become the anthem of the business world. His *Second Effort* motivational film was then the best-selling film of its kind, pushed by insurance companies and corporations as the positive capitalist answer to Arthur Miller's dark *Death of a Salesman*. Patriotic groups reprinted his speeches and recruited him to join their causes. William O'Hara, a friend and classmate from Fordham, persuaded him to join a list of conservative figures supporting the Nixon administration's policies in Vietnam and development of the ABM defense system. O'Hara considered Lombardi by then "very much to the right." In fact, he was not so much to the right as disturbed and confused by the cultural choices, and in an era of symbols, he became a symbol of old-fashioned conservatism.

During his years in Green Bay, as he developed his strong rhetoric challenging the behavior of young antiwar protesters, Lombardi was speaking from a removed perspective. Green Bay, with its heavily Catholic working-class population, was largely isolated from the movement, its sons more likely to fight in Vietnam than march on the streets of Madison or Washington. But now that he was in Washington, he could see it all firsthand. Hundreds of thousands of antiwar protesters flooded into the city twice that fall, first for an October 15 demonstration sponsored by the Vietnam Moratorium Committee, then a month later for what was called "the Mobe." The November 15 event, organized by a more confrontational wing of the peace movement, drew an enormous crowd, estimated by police at 250,000 and by others at twice that number. When the speeches ended at the Washington Monument, a few thousand young militants scrambled over to the Justice Department and incited a rocks-and-bottles versus tear gas melee with police. Attorney General John N. Mitchell looked down on the confrontation from his office and seized the opportunity to portray the antiwar movement as anarchistic, even though all but a small fraction of the demonstrators were peaceful.

Lombardi's reaction was not precisely like Mitchell's, but he also worried about anarchy. Before and after the demonstrations, thousands of peace marchers had filled the sidewalks of Connecticut Avenue on their way to and from the Mall, and the coach had watched them from his office window, lamenting the sight—the long hair, the seeming disregard for authority. What kind of courage did it take to be a college rebel? he wondered aloud. "It's easy to break the law if there's impunity. I'd like to go out there and throw a rock through that window, if I knew the only thing I'm going to have is a reprimand." As a band of protesters passed below, he shook his head and said, "Look at that!" George Dickson, his backfield assistant, snarled sarcastically that he would like to turn a machine gun on the crowd. "Goddamn it, that's *your* generation!" Lombardi responded. In fact, Dickson was only eight years younger than Lombardi, and unlike the coach, had served in the military. He had been a paratrooper in World War II and still had his helmet with a bullet hole in it. But Dickson knew better than to argue with Lombardi when he thought he was right.

The Sunday before the Mobe, Lombardi staged a patriotic counter-demonstration of sorts, a ceremony at halftime of the Redskins-Eagles game called "The Flag Story." It was much like the patriotic show he had put on at Lambeau Field the previous December. This one brought a letter of thanks from President Nixon. After first offering condolences that "the game didn't turn out better for you and your Redskins" (it was a 28 to 28 tie; the would-be coach in the White House was down on the defense), Nixon wrote: "You have always demonstrated on the field and off the qualities of faith and determination which are at the heart of true patriotism. I am very happy to know that the fans got to see such a wonderful and inspiring show of this kind at a time when it can do the most good."

Lombardi received the letter at work and took it home to show his wife, the Nixon fan, who filed it away for posterity. Marie had other things on her mind that November—worries about her husband's health, her future, family relationships—and decided to share them with her son, who was back in St. Paul, starting a new job in the investment field. The following Friday, on her old Green Bay stationery, she wrote a letter that jolted Vincent and Jill with its tone, which vacillated between intense love, coldness and despair, and its message, which indicated that Vince's dad was far sicker than anybody realized and that she was more afraid than she had ever let on.

> Dear Son,
> The time has come to write this to clear the air, and tell it like it is.
> First chalk one up for mom. I said all along you would wind up in the investment business. Good for you. You'll enjoy it. You'll be successful, and it will reward you with the excitement you need. Bravo.
> Now let me explain my get tough policy. I tried to tell you a few times that Dad is not well. Last spring he had a bad spell while we were at the Mayflower, kidney infection, he pulled out of it but was tired all the time and of course he couldn't quit. After that he took his physical for insurance, he flunked, heart.
> About two weeks ago, he became ill again, ran a high temperature and was feeling generally lousy, but again he couldn't quit. Over last weekend he started bleeding from his kidney, bladder and prostate, who knows? He went into the hospital for some tests. He checks out fine but they don't know what's causing the bleeding. Of course they are looking for cancer.
> I have been absolutely frantic. Knew for a long time he just wasn't right. Now we're in a bind, and we all get into these binds, and all we can do is grin and bear it and mostly pray.
> Believe me son, if anything happens to him I will fold up my tent and go with him cause there is no way I could live without him. I suddenly realized what a price I had paid for fame and fortune. I would have nothing. I could never end up like Nanna and Pop Pop [Matty and Harry Lombardi], sick, poor, unwanted and unloved.

It was always enough for me that Dad and I loved each other so much that everything else I had missed was all right, but the thought that I could lose him staggered me. So now I am going to get tough and try to protect him from anyone or anything else that might pressure him—no speaking or public appearances, no books or anything. It's just Dad and I cause in the end that's all we have.

I am writing you this in absolute confidence, you are the only one who knows, please don't even tell Jill, especially Sue cause she worries so.

I gathered from our talk you're in the usual bind that comes from being young. You'll pull out of it. We always do. You've been a good son and for that I'm grateful, but there has been one sorrow in my life and that is you and your father were always so far apart.

The one thing you didn't understand is that he is a very shy and lonely man, believe it or not. He is a very great, generous wonderful man and his whole life has been giving and doing things for me, you and Sue. He sure didn't want anything for himself. All he ever asked was a thank you and that's a word you never learned to say. I have been trying forever it seems to bring you two together cause again believe it or not he really needs you. Oh, how he needs you.

And you have made damn little effort to care to love or to understand him. So now I have to give up and face the fact that it can never be. All these years I have fought your battles, softened him up so to speak and you let me and now I know I was wrong.

I also realize it was good you went back to Minneapolis cause out of sight out of mind and that way no one gets hurt.

We all thought that Dad would endure forever—at least I thought he was so strong. I can't tell you how frightened I am, but with lots of prayers and if he takes it easy and believe me he <u>will</u> take it easy if I have my way, he will be okay. The next thing they want to do is X-ray his kidneys cause his urine is cloudy and has a heavy odor, also the prostate is enlarged.

This letter has rambled on but that's my state of mind. I repeat please keep this down to a roar. I have written this cause I think you should know so you will understand a lot of things.

So now I'll end this and ask you to pray. Just phone or write if you get time.

All my love,
Mom

Vincent had a more complicated perspective on the struggle between father and son and his mother's role in it. He tended not to think of his mother as a unifying force, but rather as an insecure figure who jealously guarded her relationships, subtly turning one family member against another so that she would be the center of attention, needed by everyone. And

Vincent suspected something that she acknowledged to him later—that she could never love her children nearly as much as she loved her husband.

As a medical report, Marie's letter is more revealing than the minimal documentary evidence concerning Lombardi's condition that fall. He had not gone back to Drs. James and Banfield since they treated him the previous February, but instead relied on the team physician, Dr. George Resta, who treated patients at Doctors Hospital downtown. Resta died in 1977, the hospital closed in 1979, and any records that might have shown Lombardi's treatment that November are gone with them. Lombardi's administrative aides on the Redskins staff, including Ockie Krueger and David Slattery, remember that he did pass his team physical. Later records indicate that a minor heart problem—moderate atherosclerosis of the aorta—was discovered only after his death, during a pathology report. But there is no reason to doubt the essential accuracy of Marie's account. She knew her husband better than anyone else, and the letter shows remarkable and tragic prescience, her intuition taking her to a fearful place that doctors could not yet reach.

Lombardi did not slow his busy schedule despite Marie's vows to protect him from outside interests. He gave speeches, accepted awards, made frequent jaunts up to New York and continued his coaching duties without showing a hint of trouble to his assistants. Not long after Marie wrote the letter, Vince called two of his favorite old Packers, Paul Hornung and Max McGee, and asked them to come to Washington and hang out with his team. "I want these guys to see some winners," he told McGee. Lombardi invited them to stay at his house, and McGee almost accepted until Hornung talked him out of it. "No, no, no, Max, we're not gonna stay three nights at Lombardi's. Shit, no way! Get us a suite." The trip probably meant more to Lombardi than to his players. McGee and Hornung visited the dressing room, but stood around joshing with a few friends, nothing more than that. Vince and Marie took them to dinner, and when they walked into Duke's the patrons again gave Lombardi a standing ovation. "He pretended he was embarrassed as hell, but down deep he loved it," Hornung recalled. When it reached eleven o'clock, McGee started checking his watch, and Lombardi knew what that meant. "McGee, you guys haven't changed a bit. You want to get the hell out of here, don't you. Get the hell out of here."

Perhaps Max and the Golden Boy made no difference, but the Redskins won that week, defeating Pittsburgh. Their offense, led by Jurgensen's accurate passing (completing 62 percent) and Larry Brown's toughness (gaining 888 yards), was explosive all year, but the defense remained inconsistent. In the next-to-last game against New Orleans, the Redskins broke out to a quick 17 to 0 lead, then held on to win, 17 to 14, and the players gave Lombardi the game ball. Twelve years of losing were done and gone; the club had assured itself of a winning record, finishing 7–5–2. It was the same winning percentage that Lombardi had during his first year in Green Bay, but he was disappointed. "I thought we could have had a better won-lost record," he said. "I hope we can find some better people. That's what we're going to have to do—find them." In Green Bay, the talent was already there, and by his second year he was taking the Packers to the championship game. That seemed less likely now; it was a more competitive league, with smarter coaches, better scouting and twenty-six teams instead of the old dozen.

He went to Super Bowl IV in New Orleans that year, watching in the stands as the Kansas City Chiefs beat the Minnesota Vikings, the second straight loss for old NFL teams. Sonny Jurgensen was also there. They were too far apart to consult during the game, but every now and then they looked at each other and made hand gestures indicating what play they would have run against the Chiefs, nodding in agreement, the coach and his quarterback, both certain that soon enough they would be down on the field—playing for a championship and winning it.

28

Run to Win

LOMBARDI'S STOMACH was troubling him again, and he was taking pills to ease his gastric distress, but he was just where he wanted to be on a sunny day in paradise, hacking away on a Hawaiian golf course with Wellington Mara, Tex Schramm and friends. The work of the NFL league meeting was over for March 26, 1970, and it was time to play. They were well into the back nine when Lombardi noticed a golf cart hurtling their way, and a woman waving her arms and screaming at them. "Who the hell is that?" he muttered. "Uh, Vinnie, it's your wife," said Mara. And so it was. Marie had commandeered a cart and gone driving all over the course looking for him. "She's having twins! She's having twins!" she shouted breathlessly. "Who's having twins?" Lombardi asked. "Your daughter, dummy! Susan! She's having twins!" Paul Bickham, their son-in-law, had just called to report that Susan was in the delivery room and the doctor had discovered that she was giving birth to twins.

Lombardi did what any golf addict might do. He smiled and kissed his wife, and told her that he would meet her back at the clubhouse when the round was over, then teed one up and, as Schramm later recalled, "just whammed it, he was so proud."

When he returned to the clubhouse, Marie was there—nothing yet. While they waited, they drank and giddily warbled silly nursery rhymes. "Georgie Porgie puddin'n pie, had a set of twins and made 'em cry." Georgie was Paul's nickname. Finally the good news arrived. Susan had delivered two healthy babies, a five-pound, fourteen-ounce girl named Marie Ann and a six-pound, ten-ounce boy named Paul. Susan was back in her hospital room when her parents reached her on the phone. "My father was absolutely elated," she said later. "He said, 'Well, Susan, you have been unpredictable for twenty-four years and damned if you haven't kept true to your word.' Because nobody knew I was having twins. And he said, 'Congratulations. I'll be there as soon as I can get there.' " Marie flew directly to Chicago to help out—Susan had three infants in diapers then, and no cribs—but Lombardi had other obligations, speeches, business seminars, contract negotiations, and could not make the trip.

In the second week of May, he and Marie went to New York for his induction into the Fordham Hall of Fame, and stayed through the Mother's Day weekend. Their son, Vincent, was in Manhattan for a training program for stockbrokers, and Jill had come out to visit. The foursome met on the evening of May 9 at the Waldorf-Astoria, then continued their evening at P. J. Clarke's saloon, where they were joined by little brother, Joe, and his wife, Betty. Jill sat next to her father-in-law most of the night and had an unusually intimate discussion with him. It was a tumultuous spring. Only ten days earlier Nixon had ordered the bombing of Cambodia, a decision that sparked protests across the country, culminating in the tragedy at Kent State University in Ohio, where National Guardsmen shot and killed four young people on May 4. Just trying to make her way around New York, Jill had been caught in a series of protests and counterprotests, a demonstration near the United Nations decrying the Kent State killings, then a patriotic showing of hard hats near Wall Street. Lombardi talked to her about those events and the effect that parents can have on children.

He gushed about Vincent II, his grandson, what a sensitive child he was, how understanding and patient Vincent and Jill were with him, and how perhaps he might grow up to be less alienated than the current student generation. Lombardi was in a rare self-reflective mood, bittersweet as he looked back on his own role as a parent. "I made so many mistakes with my kids," he confided to Jill. "I was too hard. You can't be too hard on them. You have to be more understanding." When the group finally emerged from P. J. Clarke's, they encountered a street woman selling flowers. Jill thought the flowers looked old, as though they had been taken from a graveyard, but Lombardi pulled a wad of bills out of his pocket and bought them all, handing some to Jill, some to Marie and some to Betty.

The next day they all drove out to Sheepshead Bay to visit Harry and Matty for a Mother's Day dinner. As everyone sat around talking, Vince fell asleep on his mother's sofa.

"You're tired," Matty said when he woke up.

"I'm getting old," Vince said.

"I'm getting old," his mother responded.

"Yeah," he said. "But I'm always tired. More tired than usual."

Lombardi had been named salesman of the year that spring by the Direct Selling Association, and was in more demand than ever as an after-dinner speaker. His standard fee was $5,000; sometimes he kept the money, other times he donated it to charity. Two days after his New York visit, on May 12, the Independent Insurance Agents of Wisconsin brought him to Milwaukee for a luncheon address. He gave his standard speech about the zeal to win and the need for discipline, but the events of the last few weeks had clearly affected him. In recent months his speeches had become increasingly strident as he complained that protesters were breaking the law with no recrimination, but the killings at Kent State jolted him. "The way to treat violence is not with violence," he said in Milwaukee. "That only snowballs it." While issuing his traditional call for discipline, he began acknowledging that the voices of the young protesters should be heard. "I think the students have a great deal to say, but I don't think violence, disruptions and burning are the right way to do it."

From Milwaukee, Lombardi traveled north to Green Bay, which still seemed almost lost in time, removed from the turmoil of the big cities and major college towns. He arrived in time for a three-thirty golf match with Jack Koeppler at Oneida Golf and Riding, his old course. This was his first visit to Green Bay since he had left for Washington more than a year earlier, and there was some concern about lingering hard feelings, but he was welcomed back by old friends and journalists who wished he had never left. Koeppler had called Lee Remmel of the *Post-Gazette* the day before and alerted him that the Old Man was coming. "Would you like to interview him?" Koeppler asked, to which Remmel responded, "Is the Pope Catholic?" Remmel arrived at Oneida just after Lombardi had finished a round of 84, about his norm. He was in the locker room, getting ready to head upstairs to the Calcutta Room to play gin, when Remmel laid eyes on him. He was naked to the waist, wearing a pair of light blue slacks, and Remmel was struck by what he took to be the coach's trim, tan, vibrant appearance.

"Coach, you look great!" Remmel said.

"I feel wonderful," Lombardi said, breaking into his toothy smile.

Later, as Lombardi and his cronies were playing gin, the *Press-Gazette*'s Art Daley approached the table. "Jack and all those guys were sitting around and I went in and saw Vince, and knelt down beside him and said, 'Vince, you never should have left here,'" Daley recalled. "And those eyes of his, they bubbled up like crazy." Daley, too, came away thinking Lombardi looked "good and tan."

Lombardi visited all of his stations of the cross during his two days in Green Bay. He stayed at the home of Dick and Lois Bourguignon, visited with the Gray Ghost and Ole, and they both gave him big hugs, no hard feelings, drove out to his old house on Sunset Circle, paid a visit to Father Spalding at Resurrection and Father Burke at St. Norbert, went to mass at St. Willebrord and swung by Lambeau Field, where he walked up to the second floor and surprised Ruth McKloskey and the other secretaries. There was another round of golf the second day down at North Shore in Neenah with Koeppler, Doc Brusky and Judge Robert Parins, known to his pals as the one-armed bandit (he had lost his right arm and played a mean round of golf with his left hand). Parins showed up in a pair of fake muttonchop sideburns, teasing Lombardi about the mod hairstyle sported by a few of his Redskins. That night the same gang that used to gather in the basement rec room at Sunset Circle reassembled on a boathouse on the Fox River and toasted Vince. It was only when he was alone with Dick Bourguignon during the final hours of the visit that Lombardi confided his troubles.

He did not want to alarm anyone, so he told the others that he was feeling good, Lombardi said, but in fact he was not. He was having problems with his stomach, kidneys and bowels, he said. According to Lois Bourguignon's later recollection, her husband told her that Lombardi had said "he'd had a physical but wouldn't have a proctoscopy. Dick bawled him out and told him don't be foolish and go in there and do something about it."

A few weeks later he at last reached Chicago to see his daughter and her infant twins. He had come to town for a Boy Scouts of America awards luncheon at the Conrad Hilton Hotel, where he was joined by David Carley, his old business partner. Carley noticed that Lombardi did not want to eat his meal that day, and was so tired later that he insisted on taking a cab to travel three blocks. Carley's last memory of Lombardi was of the two men standing on the sidewalk arguing about Bobby Kennedy and Spiro Agnew. Lombardi said he liked them both, a notion that infuriated Carley. "That's impossible! You cannot like both of those men except on a purely personal basis, because they stand for things that are completely different," Carley said. But Lombardi meant it: he liked the way Agnew stood up for his country, but he also loved Bobby Kennedy's energy and his urgency to solve problems.

Marie had accompanied her husband to Chicago, but avoided the banquet. She rejoined him at the hotel and they drove together to Chicago Heights. A wrong turn sent them into an unfamiliar South Side neighborhood, and they wandered around for more than an hour before regaining their bearings, sniping at each other all the while. It was part of their routine, Vin and Rie, they could hardly go anywhere in the car without fighting. By the time they reached Susan's apartment, the twins were asleep in a bassinet. Vince was awed by the sight and stood above them whispering, "One baby, two babies," the miracle of birth compounded. He wanted to hold them, but Marie insisted that he not wake them up, so after a brief time chatting on the couch, he started fidgeting. They could not stay the night; from Susan's they were heading to the airport and back to Washington. Marie could sense her husband's discomfort. "You know something, Vin, why don't you take Susan to the store and buy her some groceries," she suggested. He jumped at the idea, and soon Susan and her father were strolling down the aisles of her local supermarket.

It was as though Lombardi was on a game show where he had five minutes to throw as much as he could into the shopping cart. The more exotic the better as far as he was concerned. Caviar, canned hams and chickens, anchovies, Brie, delicate crackers, all piling up in the cart as he moved down the gourmet row, then on to the baby formula section. *Here's a case, that enough?* He was reading labels, but no price was too steep. Susan could not help laughing; her dad let loose in a grocery, showering her with gifts for this one brief moment, as though each little package could make up for a week spent without her. It was not that he had to buy her love, the love was there, but time was not. He rang up a bill of more than $200—"and in 1970, that was a lot of money," Susan said. When they got back to the apartment, the prospect of lugging all those bags up the stairs was too daunting for him, so he found two neighborhood boys and paid them with a dollar and his autograph. They betrayed no hint of knowing who he was.

PATRIOTISM AND GOLF occupied most of Lombardi's time in early June. He had been asked by J. Willard Marriott to serve as honorary vice chairman of an Honor America Day program schedule for July 4, and accepted enthusiastically. When skeptical journalists asked if he was being used by the Nixon administration, he noted that former presidents Johnson and Truman were also on the committee as well as AFL-CIO chief George Meany. "This is not pro-administration, not pro-Nixon, not pro-anything, except one thing—America," he said. "We'd like to show the world and maybe a lot of our own people that we are Americans and we are proud of what we have here." Gordon Peterson, a local television and radio reporter, visited Lombardi at his Connecticut Avenue office to conduct an interview on Honor America Day. Peterson said that he had come in "prepared to shrink the legend," expecting to be disappointed by Lombardi, but came away "taken by him." Some of his rhetoric could sound harsh, Peterson said later. "But in person he seemed very open-minded, more so than I expected him to be. The protests were raging, and he said these people have a constitutional right to protest, but that the country had been very good to him. And he said the racial thing is a disgrace. He said that very forcefully."

Lombardi had acquired a new group of golfing partners in Washington. He played several courses, including Burning Tree and the Army-Navy Club, but most of his rounds were at Congressional Country Club in Potomac. One of his frequent partners there was Ralph Guglielmi, a former quarterback at Notre Dame (preceding Hornung), who played nine seasons in the NFL. They played for two-dollar nassaus, which Lombardi fought to win with the same determination he would put into a Super Bowl. During one round Guglielmi told Lombardi that a friend of his in the computer business in Dayton had asked whether he could persuade the coach to come out to Ohio in mid-June for a speech to salesmen. "Goddamn it, Ralph, that's the time I'm having camp," Lombardi said. "You oughta know better than asking me then." Guglielmi said he had already told his friend that there was not much chance of it, but that he had to ask.

A few days later Lombardi called Guglielmi. "What about that thing out there, the banquet?" he began. "Would it help you out any if I did it?" That was the generous side of Lombardi; he had felt guilty about not helping a friend. "Tell them I want five thousand, and you come with me and you get fifteen hundred," he went on. "You emcee the ceremonies. I don't want any stranger introducing me." Guglielmi readily consented.

Lombardi had felt tired and constipated for several days before the trip. In preparation for the season, he had tried running up the hill behind his Stanmore Drive home, and the simple exercise exhausted him. He went to Dayton nonetheless, catching a plane with Guglielmi late on the Sunday afternoon of June 21. They arrived in time to have dinner at an Italian restaurant, and by Guglielmi's account Lombardi ordered a huge meal. The sales seminar, sponsored by the SCM-Allied-Egry company, was held the next afternoon. Guglielmi did his job, making the introductions, then sat dumbstruck as Lombardi took the podium and began by announcing that both he and Ralph would donate their honoraria to the local boys' club. "I say to myself, You sonofabitch!" Guglielmi recalled. Then he sat spellbound with the rest of the audience as the coach gave them the full Lombardi, all seven blocks of his standard speech—football, competition, perfection, authority, discipline, leadership and character. He even had a new introduction explaining what he meant by the well-known phrase "Winning isn't everything, it's the only thing":

> You know being a part of a football team is no different than being a part of any other organization—being a part of any army, being a part of a political party. The objective is to win—the objective is to beat the other guy. Some may think this is a little bit hard and a little bit cruel. I don't think so. I do think that is the reality of life. I do think that men are competitive, and the more competitive the business the more competitive the men. They know the rules when they get into the game, they know the objective when they get into the game—and the objective is to win: fairly, squarely, decently, win by the rules, but still win. In truth, gentlemen, I've never really known a successful man who deep in his heart did not appreciate the discipline it takes to win.

When the speech was over Lombardi received a standing ovation, then fielded questions, most of which, to his apparent relief, were about football. He said that Bart Starr was the greatest quarterback he had ever seen, but that Sonny Jurgensen was a better athlete. "Jurgensen is so important in my plans that if he were to leave, I'd follow him the next morning." He dismissed Kansas City coach Hank Stram's claim that the era of rollout quarterbacks was coming. Quarterbacks were too special to be endangered that way, he said. In fact, Lombardi insisted, there were no new trends in football that impressed him. "If there were, I'd put 'em in." In taking the last question, Lombardi said that this would be his final nonfootball speech of the year. "There are 365 days in a year, and I get at least five hundred invitations to speak," he said. "I don't take many, but I think this will be all."

At the hotel late that night, Lombardi placed a call to Guglielmi's room. "C'mon down, Ralph," he said. "I'm having some problems I have to talk to you about." When Lombardi opened the door, Guglielmi could see that he was in pain. "He said, 'I haven't taken a crap in three days,'" Guglielmi later recalled. "I said, 'Well, that's not normal, Coach. But you've been kind of on the go a bit. You had a big meal last night. Maybe you're just constipated.' And he said, 'Can you go out and get me a Fleet enema?' I said, 'I don't know, Coach, it's eleven at night. But I'll try.'" Guglielmi went down to the front desk, learned the location of a late-night pharmacy, called a cab and returned to Lombardi's room with three Fleet enemas.

The next morning, at breakfast, Lombardi said that he did not feel like eating. Did the enemas work? No, he said. He had ended up taking all three of them, but no luck.

The flight to Washington was to leave shortly after noon. Lombardi and Guglielmi reached the terminal just as an airport bar was opening. "He says, 'I want to stop in here,'" Guglielmi recalled. "So we stop. A waitress comes over. Lombardi says, 'Give me a double vodka on the rocks, please. You want anything, Ralph?' I get a glass of tomato juice. Now he gets one, two, three double vodkas. It's too early to drink, I'm thinking. Lombardi isn't an imbiber. He likes a scotch or two. I don't know why he's doing this, but you don't question the Coach. When we get back to the airport, his driver is there to pick him up and take him home. The next thing I know, he's in the hospital."

GEORGETOWN UNIVERSITY HOSPITAL.
Admission Date: June 24, 1970. *Time:* 2:30 P.M.
Name: Lombardi, Vincent T.
Room Number: 6316
Rate: $80
Occupation: Football Coach

He returned from Dayton on the twenty-third and was in the hospital by the next afternoon. In between, he had told Dr. Resta, the Redskins team physician, that he had been unable to defecate for several days, and Resta sent him to Georgetown after a barium enema revealed a lesion in his left colon. Marie was in the room with her husband when he received his first visitor, Father Edward Bunn, S.J., Georgetown's chancellor. The two men had known each other for more than three decades, since Lombardi was an undergraduate at Fordham and Bunn was a professor there who taught him philosophy and psychology. "You know, Father, I've never been in a hospital before in my life," Lombardi said, discounting the weeks he spent in the Fordham infirmary after a football injury. "I didn't even bring any extra clothes with me." Father Bunn said he would pray for him and began a daily vigil at his old student's bedside.

Later that afternoon, Dr. Robert Coffey, a specialist in colon surgery, conducted a preliminary examination that found Lombardi in "no distress." His prostate was slightly enlarged, according to the medical report, and he had tenderness and fullness in his lower left abdomen, a small internal hemorrhoid, but no rectal mass. But further tests the next morning brought grim news. The biopsy from a proctoscopy revealed anaplastic carcinoma in the rectal area of his colon—a fast-growing malignant cancer in which the cells barely resemble their normal appearance.

Marie had suspected it long before anyone else, and had confessed to a haunting fear that he had cancer in the letter she had written to Vincent the previous November. Now here was the reality. She tried to keep the news from some people. When she called Susan in Chicago Heights, it was only to say that he was in the hospital, but there was nothing much to worry about, it might be a hernia. She passed along the same message to Vince's parents in Sheepshead Bay, afraid that the truth might kill Harry, the tough Old Five by Five who had plugged on past several heart attacks but might not survive bad news about his oldest son. Vincent had been on vacation with his family in Wisconsin that week and discovered that his father was in the hospital from a news report while watching television in their motel room. He immediately called his mother, who said she had been frantically looking for him. Why? he wondered. The report made it sound as if his father had the flu. "It's worse than that," Marie told him. "You better come on out."

Exploratory abdominal surgery was performed on Lombardi at eight-thirty on that Saturday morning, June 27. During a two-hour and fifteen-minute operation, a team of surgeons led by Dr. Coffey removed a two-foot section of the rectosigmoid colon, the part of the colon closest to the rectum, where they had discovered a polypoid tumor. Tests revealed that the tumor was malignant, just as the earlier biopsy had indicated. But at Marie's request, when Dr. Coffey met the press later that day, he left the opposite impression. He said that preliminary findings indicated the tumor was non-malignant. They would not know for certain until tests came back in four days, he said, but most similar tumors turned out to be benign. Decades later this sort of deception would be rare and controversial, but at the time it was common and accepted.

Edward Bennett Williams continued the public deception, telling reporters that Lombardi's prognosis appeared "excellent" and that he would "resume normal activities" within four weeks. While Williams and Marie both knew that Lombardi's condition was worse than the public diagnosis, they did have some reason to hope for the best. The doctors had told them that the cancer had not spread to the liver or lymph nodes. Losing part of his colon could not stop Lombardi, Williams told friends. "Vince has so much guts they could take out fifty feet and he'd still have more than the rest of us."

Four days after the operation a hospital spokesman said there would be no update on Lombardi's condition. The test results were in, but they would not be made public. "Members of Lombardi's family have instructed us that they have given out all the information they want released on the case," the spokesman said. This inevitably created an air of mystery around the ailing coach. The Honor America Day celebration on July 4 came and went with Lombardi still in the hospital. On July 6 he missed his annual golf outing with the sporting press, this one held at Congressional. Williams was there, pounded with questions about who would run the Redskins training camp when it opened in two weeks. Would there be an interim coach? Williams offered an even more optimistic timetable than his earlier back-in-four-weeks prediction, now insisting that Lombardi would return in time for the first day of camp, July 19.

On the day Williams made that optimistic statement, Lombardi's temperature spiked to 102 because of an infection in his surgical incision, but it appeared to be only a minor setback. By July 10 he was ready for release. The wound was considered "healed and strong" and his temperature was back to normal. He was sent home with instructions to follow a low residue diet and to take Darvon and chloral hydrate for pain and sleep. "At that point," said Vincent, "we thought the prospects seemed good."

Back at home, Lombardi felt alternately restless and fatigued. He was supposed to be recuperating, but he seemed to be losing weight and strength every day. His brother Joe came down to stay that first weekend. For all of Joe's life, Vince had been the quintessential older brother, dictating, demanding, expecting, challenging. Now he seemed helpless. "I remember tying his shoelaces for him," Joe said later. "He would sit on the bed and I would go up and tie his shoes. Then we'd go for a walk around the property a little bit, and he'd talk." They discussed everything: wives, children, regrets and the Washington Redskins. "I have a big job to do here," Vince said, listing what it would take to lift the Redskins up to a championship-caliber team. But Joe thought Vince knew he would never get that chance. "It was never said, but I got that feeling."

His outlook seemed to change depending on the day or the company he was with. When Wellington and Ann Mara came down from New York for a two-day visit, Lombardi was tired but optimistic. He had to excuse himself after dinner to rest, but he also told Mara with a determined voice that he intended to go to training camp. "I'm gonna beat this!" he said. He and Marie drove downtown for lunch at Duke's with Ed Williams and Ben Bradlee, and if Lombardi was strong enough to get in a spat with Marie and tell her to shut up, part of their routine patter, he showed little other energy. "He was very quiet," Bradlee recalled. "I remember him appearing to be uncomfortable, and not well." The next visitor at Stanmore Drive was Jack Koeppler, who came out from Green Bay with his son Kevin. Koeppler's first impression was that his old friend "looked smaller, his face had gotten smaller." At one point Marie took Kevin to the trophy room in the basement to show him Vince's mementos, and after they had left the room Lombardi told Koeppler that he was dying. "I said, 'Ah, you've fought through a lot worse,' and he said, 'No, I know I'm dying.' I asked, 'How do you know?' and he said there were three doctors working on him and he found the weakest of the three and asked him how soon it would be before he could resume coaching. And the guy says, 'I don't think you'll be coaching again.' Vince knew. He knew."

As concerned as Lombardi was about his health, he was also troubled by the game he loved. For the second time in three years the preseason was being delayed by a confrontation between players and owners over salary and pension issues. The NFL and AFL Players Associations had merged that year under the leadership of a new executive director, Ed Garvey. When the players threatened to strike, management preempted them by locking them out, opening the camps only to rookies. The day before Redskins camp was to open, Lombardi summoned his coaching staff out to Stanmore Drive. It was clear that he would not make it to Carlisle then, if ever. "Well, boys, Bill's going to run training camp," he said, referring to Bill Austin. "He's been with me the longest. He knows how to run it. Operate for him as you would for me." He never uttered the word "cancer," but as they were all leaving, he said obliquely, "You can all make your own opinion about this."

The labor dispute infuriated him so much that he decided to travel to New York on July 21 for a meeting of NFL club owners. Marie was worried about his fragile health and tried to talk him out of it, as did Dr. Coffey, but Lombardi was insistent. Marie ended up accompanying him on the trip, and asked Joe to meet them at the airport and drive them to the midtown session. It all jumbled together for Lombardi now: long hair, rebellion, student protests, anarchy, unions, strikes—all of it to him reflected what Father Cox had been talking about back at Fordham a third of a century earlier, the abuse of freedom. The only answer was to be fair but firm, he told the owners. He did not believe in football strikes, but he hated the idea of opening up camps to veterans who might cross the picket line, an act that he insisted would destroy team unity. He was equally repulsed by the notion of giving in to the union. It was up to the owners, he said, to maintain "the structure and the discipline" of pro football. "Gentlemen, you must not give away your game to a bunch of twenty-two-year-old kids." Redskins aide David Slattery entered the room as Lombardi was speaking those lines. "His voice was almost a whisper. He was fading out on them, and I think he finished before he intended to," Slattery said. "He looked absolutely terrible, like death warmed over. He told me he had to get back to Washington immediately."

The trip home was a disaster. On the ride to the airport Lombardi became dizzy and his heart started beating rapidly. Marie was afraid that he was having a heart attack. (It was later diagnosed as paroxysmal atrial tachycardia, an arrhythmia caused when the heartbeat begins at an abnormal place.) They were in a taxi, with no one to help them. Marie lugged their two bags through the terminal, her husband leaning on her as they walked. There was a long line at the ticket counter. She pleaded with the airlines clerk to let Vin on the plane ahead of everyone else so that he could relax, but she was rebuffed. The stewardesses seemed rude, unconcerned with her plight. Marie got to her seat and started crying. When they arrived at Washington National, Lombardi was struggling to carry his own bag when "a nice young man" asked if he could help. "Vin never would ask for help," Marie said later. "But this time, he said, 'Help me, please.' I almost cried right there."

When he got home, doctors treated his rapid heartbeat with digitalis. The next day he asked Leroy Washington, the chauffeur he shared with Ed Williams, to drive him to Georgetown—not to reenter the hospital, but to watch his veteran players, who were working out on their own at Kehoe Field. These were his boys. Even if he didn't like them as a union, he loved them as individuals and as a team. And there they were, paying silent tribute to the Old Man by going through his conditioning drills, even without him hovering over them and driving them to do more, push harder, get those feet moving. Pat Richter, the player representative, was leading the grass drills when he looked up and saw in the distance a frail figure struggling to get out of a black sedan. Who was that man, now leaning against the car? My God, Richter said to himself, that's Coach Lombardi.

There was a game the next day, the Redskins rookies against the Colts rookies at Memorial Stadium in Baltimore. Lombardi could not stay away, and sat in the owner's enclosure with Marie and Edward Bennett Williams. He visited the locker room after the game, shuffling slowly amid the players, offering quiet words of encouragement. Just standing there for a few minutes tired him out, so he found a training table and leaned against it. George Dickson approached him looking for a scouting report. "Coach, anything you want to tell me about the running backs?" Lombardi was a shadow of his old self, but his football mind was still keen. He stared at Dickson and said bluntly, "You haven't got any running backs."

•   •

ON JULY 27, exactly one month from the day of his first operation, Lombardi was readmitted to Georgetown and immediately sent back into surgery. His preoperation symptoms pointed to trouble. He had not had a bowel movement in three days, and an X-ray showed a partial bowel obstruction. This time the exploratory surgery found that the cancer had spread massively to his liver, peritoneum and lymph nodes. Dr. Coffey was stunned, calling it one of the most voracious cancers he had ever seen. There was nothing they could do except sew him back up, bombard him with cobalt irradiation and chemotherapy, and pray. He was a terminal case. Ockie Krueger would never forget Marie's wail of despair when Dr. Coffey delivered the fatal prognosis.

Again, there was no public announcement of his condition. He was said to be "resting comfortably," but beyond that, at the family's request, there would be no comment. His fatal condition was an open secret among journalists in Washington, yet it was never reported. The most famous coach in America, the head coach of the local pro football team, was dying in a nearby hospital, and not one word of it in the newspapers or on the airwaves. "It was getting more and more rampant around town that he was dying," said Martie Zad, sports editor at the *Post*, but those were still the days when the media would respect the wishes of family and friends, and self-censor the news.

The cobalt irradiation began on July 30, blasting away at his entire abdomen. That same day, when he was wheeled back to his room, Lombardi noticed a large bouquet of flowers. The card read: "YOU ARE A GREAT COACH AND A GREAT INDIVIDUAL TO ALL OF US." "Look at those flowers in the corner," Lombardi said later to Ockie Krueger. "Now look at who they're from."

The card was signed by the National Football League Players Association. Lombardi could lambaste the union all he wanted, the players still loved him. In absentia, in fact, he had been crucial to their solidarity that year. At a key meeting in Chicago, several big-name players were talking about bailing out of the strike and going back to camp, and it was Bart Starr, one of the most conservative members of the group, who put a stop to it, and he did it by evoking Lombardi. "I just want to say that two years ago, Coach Lombardi called me in and said, 'I don't like unions and I sure don't like players associations, but if I were quarterback of the Packers, I'd sure as hell be a leader of the union,'" Starr said. The message was that Lombardi had taught Starr the meaning of teamwork and loyalty. "Starr became sort of a legend from that speech," said Ed Garvey, the NFLPA director. Added Pat Richter of the Redskins: "That's one great thing Coach Lombardi preached —singleness of purpose. He wants to keep a whole team together."

The coach was fading, and priests, nuns and football players streamed up to the sixth floor and waited in Marie's side room for permission to see him on his deathbed. Boxes of letters came in, five hundred a day, and more flowers than Marie could find room for. Lombardi seemed haunted, embarrassed by his helpless condition, a relentlessly proud man whose body was giving up, forty pounds lost already in the struggle against cancer. IVs in his arm. A Cantor tube leading out through his nose evicted a copious flow of dry blood and gastric juices. His heart was beating too rapidly, his blood pressure was dropping. His face was so gaunt that he might have been unrecognizable if not for his top front row of teeth, appearing larger than ever within his shrinking face, taking their gaps from left to right like Skoronski, Thurston, Ringo, Kramer and Gregg at the line of scrimmage. His fingers—long, fleshy digits that were unforgettable to anybody who had ever been on the other side of one of his pointed lectures—now looked bent and withdrawn. The only part of him growing along with his cancer was his hair, despite the radiation treatment, untrimmed and free at last, as if to mock the myth of the Old Man. He had cut his hair every week of his life. "Vin a long hair, that's beautiful," said his wife.

Even his eyebrows were growing wild.

Father Bunn stopped by every day, praying for a miracle. Father McPartland drove down from New Jersey and gave his old coach a blessing. Little Joe made Washington a twice-weekly stop on his sales rounds for Rawlings, and stopped by Room 6100 so often that Lombardi gave him a double take once and, tough big brother to the last, muttered sternly, "Don't you ever work?" Ed Williams came by every day and often left crying. Wellington Mara called Lombardi every afternoon at two, right before he went out for the Giants practice. When he forgot one day, Lombardi groused, "What the hell's the matter with Well?" Howard Cosell and Toots Shor rang up Marie at night seeking medical updates. Jackie Anderson devoted herself to Marie, spending her days in the waiting room and nights in the large and lonely house in Potomac Falls. Marie virtually lived at the hospital, drinking endless cups of black coffee and chain-smoking Salems as she accepted condolences and directed traffic in and out of her husband's room.

His boys make the pilgrimage in August. Frank Gifford leans over the bed, feeling an urge to kiss him, thinking about the pasta dinners in New Jersey, hearing Vinnie tell him "God, Frank, it hurts!" In comes Bill Curry, played center for the Packers for two years, left hating the Old Man, now realizing that he resented him because he forced him to grow when he didn't want to, and he tries to explain that change of heart and the coach looks up at him and says, "If you want to help me, Bill, pray for me." Chuck Mercein, hero of the Ice Bowl, comes in, doesn't know what to say and leaves crying. Sonny Jurgensen stops by and the coach is briefly alert, has a new idea for a pass play against the 3–4 defense, a way to fool the weakside linebacker, it's got to work. Willie Davis makes the red-eye flight from San Diego. He had played for great coaches all his career, first Eddie Robinson at Grambling and then Paul Brown at Cleveland, but it was Lombardi, he says, who changed his life. He walks into the room and sees a ghost of his old coach and says if you'll come back to Green Bay, I'll come out of retirement, and Lombardi growls, "You're a helluva man, Willie. Now get out of here!" In for maybe a minute and half, and even now he does what the coach says and leaves.

Willie Wood is working in his hometown that summer. He thinks he owes his career to Lombardi, a black quarterback undrafted out of USC, but the Old Man "was all merit, straight down the line, and gave me a chance." He thinks he will visit Lombardi in the hospital every week, but after one visit leaves so distraught that he cannot return, saying he doesn't want to remember Coach like that. Jimmy Taylor, the roughneck fullback who had played out his option and jilted Green Bay for New Orleans in 1966, surprises Marie by showing up. She accompanies him into the room and "Vince takes his hand and holds it, and holds it, for such a long time." Jerry Kramer, working on a book of recollections, visits the hospital on August 4, arriving as the coach is being brought back from cobalt treatment. Lombardi is tired and apologizes to his old right guard, saying they'll have to wait for another time to do an interview, "until I get this thing licked." Fuzzy Thurston and Bob Skoronski show up together and chat with Marie first. They can see that "she is losing the only thing she had in her life," and after a while they ask if they can go in to see the coach. When they enter his room, he reaches out a feeble hand and they both grab it. His eyes start to flutter and the nurse says they had better leave.

Paul is here, Marie tells Vince, and his eyes light up. The Golden Boy walks in alone. He looks at Lombardi but can't think of what to say and leaves regretting that he cannot find the words to convey how much the Old Man means to him. (Lombardi already knows. Hornung found the words once before and put them in a letter he wrote on February 23, 1967, as he was leaving Green Bay for New Orleans. "I want you to know that I have always felt closer to you than any coach I have ever had or ever hope to have. I believe the greatest thing I have learned from your 'Football' has not only been the idea of winning but WHY you want to win! Each and every ballplayer who has had the opportunity of playing under your guidance in some ways will always try to mirror some part of your personality.")

The prodigal son is followed by the good son, Bart Starr, who comes in with Zeke Bratkowski and has the same experience, all words inadequate. A minute or two and they are out of the room, riding back to the airport in the back of a taxi, silent.

On August 8 the Redskins played the Bengals in Cincinnati. Marie watched the game in Vince's room. He seemed lively at first, chewing out players as though he were down on the field. When Marie told him that Charley Taylor dropped a pass, he growled, "I can see." But he was exhausted before halftime, and when Marie noticed that he had fallen asleep, she turned off the television and left him alone. Curtis Wilkie, a young journalist, was staying on the same floor, recovering from gall bladder surgery. He looked across the hall when the sportscasters declared that Vince Lombardi was watching the game in his hospital room. Not really, not anymore, Wilkie noticed. Lombardi's room was dark and silent.

Everyone in Washington now knew Lombardi was dying. President Nixon called on the night of August 11, wishing him well and saying that the whole country was rooting for him. "You are very kind," Lombardi said. "What you have said is very flattering." Both houses of Congress took time out to praise him two days later. "Mr. President," said Senator William Proxmire of Wisconsin, "a remarkable man lies ill." In a sense, said Representative Hugh Carey of New York, "he is the coach of our generation." Lombardi was being eulogized before his death. The word of his condition had finally reached Harry and Matty in Sheepshead Bay, despite Marie's efforts to keep it from them, and one of Vince's Izzo cousins drove them down to Washington, where they stayed for two days, preparing for the blow that was soon to come. Susan also paid a visit, and though Marie warned her beforehand about how much her father had changed, the sight still shocked her. "It just wasn't my father lying in that bed," she said. He was strong enough to talk and asked about his grandchildren, and as Susan was leaving he turned to Marie and said, "Well, I guess everything is going to be fine."

By the twentieth his white blood cell count had dropped to 2100. He was having continuous heart palpitations. He began to have periods of disorientation. One night, as Marie sat nearby in the stillness of the room, he startled her by barking out a stern warning in his sleep. "Joe Namath!" he shouted. "You're not bigger than football! Remember that!" Lombardi respected Namath's talent; before the opening kickoff of the 1969 Super Bowl he had seconded the white-shoed quarterback's bold prediction that the insurgent Jets would upset the Baltimore Colts. But Namath, a relatively tame character compared with what was to follow, nonetheless might have evoked something deeply troubling to the Old Man. It was as though, in his dying vision, he saw Michael Irvin and Brian Bosworth and Deion Sanders coming along behind Broadway Joe.

Marie told friends that she thought she understood what her husband was expressing in his semiconscious state. As difficult as it was for her to accept the fact that he was dying, she tried to console herself with the idea that perhaps he was meant to die now because the world was changing in ways that he could not accept. He loved the players above all else, yet circumstances might force him to turn away from them, as his sleep-talking warning to Joe Namath suggested. She predicted that he would plead with the owners to hold the line but that they would be incapable of doing so and the players would end up with too much freedom, tearing away at the order that held his world together and destroying his concept of team. "In the end," Marie told friends, "I think football will break his heart."

It could be argued that Lombardi was dying at the appropriate time. He was in danger of being reduced to a convenient symbol by then, his philosophy misused by all sides in the political debates of that war-torn era. The establishment had turned him to stone even while he was alive, hoisting him up as a monument to righteousness, patriotism and free enterprise. Counterculturists smashed him as a relic of old-line authoritarianism and a dangerous win-at-all-costs philosophy. Both were wrong—he was more complicated, his philosophy more authentic, than either side could then appreciate. But if he had lived for another two decades, he might have faced more frustrations. The age of skepticism was coming with Watergate, combining with a long era celebrating the self. Lombardi was meant for none of that, and leaving the scene was a way for him to survive in memory as a mythic symbol, the block of granite and steadfast coach of the glorious Packers, rather than staying around to become an increasingly frustrated coach fighting for relevance in the fickle modern American culture.

Lombardi might have disagreed with that line of thinking. "I'm not afraid to die," he told Father Tim Moore one day in the hospital room. "But there's so much yet to be done in the world."

Vincent visited his father's hospital room several times that month, coming from his home in St. Paul. He was twenty-eight, and for all of his life he and his father had never talked much. How many times had they driven to the stadium and back in silence? It was the same now. No deathbed reconciliation, at least not a verbal one. "My dad and I never made conversations, so this wasn't much different," Vincent said later. "I was just there." He would not blame his father for this, and in time would blame himself. "There were things that could have been said that were not said. The time never seemed quite right. But we were getting there. I think you had to grow to my dad's level. Having kids and graduating from law school helped. I was getting there." There was one expression of love between father and son in those final days. Vince was strapped to tubes, his hair mussed and wild, and in came Vincent, short sideburns, hair neatly trimmed, wearing a conservative business suit. The Old Man smiled with approval. "You look like a lawyer," he said.

By August 31, Lombardi was slipping in and out of consciousness, but he remembered that this was a special day, their thirtieth wedding anniversary. "Happy anniversary, Rie," he said to Marie. "Remember, I love you." Earlier in the month, when he was more coherent, he had tried to start a conversation with Marie about what she should do when he died. "I don't want to talk about it," she had said. Now it was too late. On September 1 his liver and kidneys started to fail, clots formed in his lungs, his blood pressure dropped, and he became unresponsive. His organs were shutting down. Vincent was called again to come out from St. Paul, and Ockie Krueger arranged tickets for Susan and Paul to fly in from Chicago on United. The doctors suggested to Marie that she should stay by her husband overnight. The loyal communicant received last rites. The press was finally alerted to his condition. On September 2 the *Post* ran a small item saying that Lombardi was near death. Hours later a hospital spokesman announced that Lombardi had an "extraordinarily virulent" form of cancer. Vincent and Marie took turns napping and sitting by his side. At 7:20 on the morning of September 3, a nurse shook Vincent awake and told him that his father had died.

Paul Hornung, who happened to be in nearby College Park, where he was to open a restaurant later that day, was jolted awake with an odd sensation. "It was freaky," he said later. "I woke up and said to myself, We lost him. We lost him." Tom Brown, who was in Minnesota trying out for the Vikings, bolted out of bed at the same moment with a similar foreboding. "I looked at the clock and it was six-thirty and all I could think of was Lombardi. Just Lombardi. That's all I could see."

Susan was still packing her bags at her apartment, getting ready to leave for the airport. She zipped her suitcase and took it to the car, then said that she had forgotten something and went back inside. The phone rang and it was her mother telling her that her father had died. "I passed out. Fainted. Paul picks me up from the floor. My father-in-law is there. They're shoving me out the door because now I can't miss the flight. Get to the airport and Paul is guiding me. I'm totally lost. My father has died. We get on the plane and the stewardess comes down the aisle and says, 'Mr. and Mrs. Bickham, the captain would like to move you to first class. We have two seats up there for you.' The captain comes out of the cockpit and tells me how sorry he is that my father has died. My father flew United with the Packers for all those years. We get to Washington and they let me and Paul off first, and my father's limousine is waiting for us, with my brother and Leroy Washington, and we drive out to the house and I'm just dazed. We get there and my mother is in another world."

Marie called her friend Jackie Anderson and asked her to come over to Stanmore Drive. They left the family inside and went out to the patio, where Marie collapsed into a chair. "I don't know what I'm going to do," she said. "I can't go on." Vincent and Ockie Krueger and old Fordham friends in New York began making all the calls and the arrangements. There were viewings at Joseph Gawler's Sons funeral home in Washington and the Abbey Funeral Home in New York, open casket for the family only, the closed casket viewed by thousands of strangers, young men with long hair, blacks in high Afros, nuns in black drape, boys in uniform carrying helmets and footballs.

Four days after his death, at ten on the morning of Labor Day, September 7, the funeral was held at St. Patrick's Cathedral. There was an unfamiliar silence in midtown Manhattan that holiday morning, not the normal blare and pound of taxi horns and construction drills. Fifth Avenue between Fiftieth and Thirty-ninth Streets was closed to traffic. A late summer sun heated thousands of onlookers who stood somberly behind the police barricades across the avenue from the cathedral. On a side street a long fleet of black limousines waited to ferry family and friends to the burial site at Mount Olivet Cemetery in Middletown Township, New Jersey, not far from the Lombardis' old home in Fair Haven. The casket was shouldered up the steps through a cordon of priests in white vestments and dark-suited honorary pallbearers, including Paul Hornung, Bart Starr and Willie Davis, Wellington Mara, Tony Canadeo, Dick Bourguignon and Edward Bennett Williams.

Marie, in black dress and veil, took a seat up front with Vincent and Susan. Nearby were Harry and Matty and brothers Joe and Harold and sisters Madeline and Claire, protected by scores of Izzos. Cousin Anthony Izzo thought of all the years that had led up to this moment, all the games they had gone to see at the Polo Grounds and Yankee Stadium and Michie Stadium up at West Point, all of the honor that cousin Vince had brought the family—"and now it's all over." To the side sat the team owners and Commissioner Rozelle, who three days later would name the Super Bowl Trophy after Lombardi. And behind them were row upon row of square-cut football players. The entire Packers squad flew out on a chartered flight from Green Bay. The Redskins came from Tampa, where they were playing an exhibition game. Most of the New York Giants were there. Retired Packers from the title years came on their own, as did former students from Saints, colleagues from the Giants and West Point, and classmates from Fordham, including the remaining Blocks of Granite.

Vincent was called to the podium to read from Scripture to honor his father. Dave Robinson, the Packers linebacker, had lost his own father when he was young, and witnessing this seemed almost as traumatic. The tears started rolling down his cheeks. It was, he said, meaning it not as a sign of race consciousness but as honest feeling, the only time he ever cried at the funeral of a white man. Bob Skoronski, seated nearby, had the speeches of Lombardi resounding in his head, and realized that he would hear the coach's voice for the rest of his life.

Terence Cardinal Cooke delivered the eulogy, basing his homily on the Epistles of St. Paul. He knew that Lombardi was drawn to St. Paul because "it was not uncommon for St. Paul, faced with the mysteries of life and death and eternal life, to describe them in terms of an athletic contest with victory or defeat as the outcome and with a prize as the reward for the victors." It was St. Paul, in his letter to the Corinthians, who had given Coach Lombardi his favorite quote from Scripture, the one he kept repeating to his Packers during their final drive to football greatness in 1967, the saying that hung, framed and illuminated, on the wall of his den back home. "Brethren: Don't you know that while all the runners in the stadium take part in the race, only one wins the prize. Run to win."

Epilogue

WINNING IS NOT a sometime thing, it is an all the time thing, Vince Lombardi often said, and his wife believed it. Marie believed almost all of his maxims at least as much as he did. Believing in the Coach was a matter of survival for her, even now that he was long dead. That explains why she was following his advice here in the solitude of her oceanside condominium and practicing a speech until she got it right.

"Oh, yecch!" she said to herself with smoky disdain. She turned the tape recorder off again. This was her third rehearsal. It had gone smoothly until the end, when she momentarily lost her train of thought. If she wanted to do it right when it counted, at the NFL Hall of Fame in Canton, she had to perfect it here first. This one was important to her: the introduction of Jimmy Taylor, the roughneck fullback, first of their boys, the Green Bay Packers of the 1960s, to be immortalized in bronze alongside her husband. She searched for descriptive words and memories, revising and reciting over and over again. She even used that refrain in the speech, quoting her husband: You do what you do best, again and again and again.

She turned the tape recorder on for another take:

Thank you. This is my third trip to what is known as football's greatest weekend. I'm thrilled and I'm honored to be here. About six weeks ago, I wasn't certain that I was going to be here, because I was in the hospital having a nerve block on my face. And it's a terrible thing because it numbs one whole side of your face. And your mouth doesn't work too well. What's worse for a woman than your mouth doesn't work? If I seem nervous or I seem to slur my words a little bit, please bear with me. Now, this thing shattered me pretty badly, and I wasn't sure I could be here, as much as I really wanted to do this for Jimmy. So I called my son in Seattle and said, "Vincent, you better call Jimmy and tell him I can't go to Canton, because I can't speak." And he said, "All right, Mother, if that's what you want."

An hour later I called him back and I said, "Don't call Jimmy." Because a big VOICE up there said to me, "You better be in Canton and you better do a good job." So here I am, and I better do a good job because if I don't he'll probably trade me. And I suspect that I am pinch-hitting for that Italian with the big voice who can't be here. So I'll try to do a good job.

This was the summer of 1976, six years after his death, and the Italian with the big voice was still telling Marie Lombardi what to do. It seemed that she lived in another world. Her penthouse suite occupied the top floor of a three-story condo on Ocean Boulevard in Manalapan, just south of Palm Beach. The decor was Florida provincial, white on white, with splotches of color provided by her needlepoints. Looking out the sliding glass door from her living room, she watched cruise ships ease past and storms amass at sea. From the picture window of her back bedroom, facing west, she followed luxury yachts and cabin cruisers up and down the Intercoastal Waterway. Within easy reach were the exclusive shops of Worth Avenue, and she made a habit of strolling there; in almost every shop the clerks knew her name. Although it had become more difficult for her recently, because of illness and depression, she still attended the local charity balls and found her picture in the shiny sheet, Palm Beach's celebrity paper. People thought she wanted to go out and that she hungered for publicity; she certainly seemed to long for the reflected fame that had been hers back in the days when she entered restaurants at the side of the dominant figure in pro football.

But her daily outings and frequent visits from friends and relatives seemed to be diversions from her single great preoccupation. Lombardi was dead and she was not sure that left her with much reason to live. She retreated into what her family called her dream world, ushered into this ethereal realm by alcohol, pills, endless cups of coffee, black with sugar, at least one lighted Salem, often two going at once. Cigarettes were her best friends, she said, the room enshrouded in smoke, her ashtray looking like a sea anemone with its jumble of red lipstick–smeared butts. She sat there and let memories wash over her. With few appointments to keep, she set her clocks and watches on Lombardi time, ten minutes fast. She still wore the bracelet with the little gold footballs on it, counting the gridiron Hail Marys of her life with Vin: two from Fordham, two from St. Cecilia, two from Army, six from Green Bay. When the lights dimmed, his words still shone on the side wall, the biblical passage from Corinthians. Run to Win.

In her single-mindedness, Marie was like the Coach during football season, when life was a distraction from the game. Now, to her, it often seemed that anything but Vince Lombardi was a distraction. When a friend asked if she ever thought of remarrying, she said only if she could find a man who wouldn't mind staying up until two in the morning listening to her talk about Lombardi.

She continued rehearsing the speech.

> Everybody knows about all those marvelous records that Jimmy Taylor made in Green Bay. Especially those five magnificent years when he gained a thousand yards. But I suspect that tonight, this weekend, this honor, will be the thing he will take most pride in because, you see, he is the first person of the great Packer players of what is popularly known as the Lombardi era to be enshrined in this great hall. And there's something about being enshrined... it's like being crowned or canonized... that is truly awesome. And I go up to the Hall of Fame and I cry. It occurs to me that the era of the sixties was professional football's finest hour. And I think the Packer players of the sixties dominated professional football at its finest hour.

Marie still watched pro football, well past its finest hour. She even took Vincent and Susan to a game at RFK a week after the funeral. Then, for a time, she became furious at the game that had consumed Lombardi. But she came back, and now she never missed a Sunday, watching all day long, two sets going at once, rooting for old Packers wherever they played. When the games were over she retreated back into her dream world, looking at the scrapbooks and listening to his voice on tape. Things have changed, she would say. There's no one like Vince saying those things today. And she would bring out the tape of Lombardi's own induction into the Hall, with young Vincent saying that his mother, more than any other, was responsible for the success that his father had, and Well Mara saying that Vince Lombardi did not invent professional football, and he did not found the NFL, "but he embellished them both to a degree never surpassed and seldom if ever equalled." And then the tape of Richard Nixon at the Knights of Columbus convention at the Waldorf-Astoria saying that he called Lombardi days before he died and said, "Coach, you've had millions of people rooting for your teams, but there have never been so many rooting for you as there are tonight."

Then she would listen to the voice of Howard Cosell, narrating Lombardi's biography on the night of his funeral:

Vincent Thomas Lombardi ...
Born ... Nineteen thirteen ...
Principal occupation ... FOOTball coach.

Her favorite tapes were of Lombardi himself talking to his players and to business conventions. She memorized his speeches about pride, country, freedom and discipline, quoting him verbatim, incessantly—to the hairdresser, Joanne, who made house calls at the condo to give her a perm, to the attendants in the basement garage who parked and delivered her silver Lincoln Continental, to her daughter, Susan, who lived nearby and would visit with her three children, to friends from Green Bay and New Jersey, who stopped by during their winters in Florida. When not quoting Lombardi, she lionized him. It was her mission, she said, to protect his image. She said that he was bigger than life, that she was the envy of everyone who knew him, that she would walk behind him in airports and people would stare at him, but he never saw it, he was so terribly shy. That he was the symbol of everything this country once stood for and was now losing. That he would never die. And one more thing, something she inserted into the final draft of her Hall of Fame speech for Jimmy Taylor. She said it right near the end: "... And we have a need in our country today for heroes. We don't have any heroes."

When her son, Vincent, visited and heard her talk about the Old Man that way, it perplexed him. Yes, his father was an extraordinary coach, amazing in many ways, inspiring and heroic. But he was also all too human. Couldn't she remember what it was really like?

"Come on, Mother," he would say. "I ... was ... there!"

●

Marie Lombardi died of lung cancer in 1982. She was sixty-seven.

Bart Starr, Forrest Gregg, Ray Nitschke, Herb Adderley, Willie Davis, Jim Ringo, Paul Hornung and Willie Wood joined Lombardi and Taylor in the Hall of Fame.

> *Great stars that knew their days in fame's bright sun.*
> *I hear them tramping to oblivion.*

Not the Green Bay Packers, perhaps, and certainly not the Old Man himself. There are no roadside markers pointing to his childhood home in Sheepshead Bay, nor to his gravesite at Mount Olivet in New Jersey. He is buried next to Marie and Matty and Harry in a modest plot on the back edge of the cemetery, his gray tombstone softened by shrubs on a gentle slope a few steps from a gravel road. Men from the Knights of Columbus attend to the grave, clearing away ice in winter and weeds in summer, and there are often a few weather-worn tokens of worship left behind: seashells with shiny pennies in them, miniature statues of the saints, a green and gold plastic helmet, a felt Packers flag. The remnants of Lombardi's world are fading, yet his legend only grows in memory: the rugged and noble face, commanding voice, flashing teeth, primordial passion, unmatched commitment. In the end it is perhaps Vincent—who had *been there*—who gave him the highest honor. After years of working through the contradictory feelings that he had for his father, the son found his calling. He became a motivational speaker, using for his inspirational material the life and words of Vince Lombardi.

Notes

1: TATTOOS

15   *The ornamentation:* Ints. Madeline Werner, Harold Lombardi, Joe Lombardi, Vincent H. Lombardi, Susan Lombardi, Clara Parvin. Also Clara Parvin and Michelle Walden photograph collections.

16   *Next door to the Lombardis: Fourteenth Census of the United States: 1920—Population. Brooklyn. Enumeration District 114.*

17   *As teenagers from Vietri:* Municipal records, Vietri di Potenza, Italy.

17   *The union of Antonio and Laura:* Ints. Madeline Werner, Clara Parvin, Dorothy Pennell, Harold Lombardi, Joe Lombardi, Anthony Izzo, Eddie Izzo, Jill Couch, Wallace Izzo, Richard Izzo. Also *Twelfth Census of the United States. Schedule No. 1—Population. City of New York. Enumeration District 565.*

18   *Large Italian families: Brooklyn Eagle,* Sept. 26, 1924.

19   *Grandpa Antonio Izzo: Brooklyn Eagle* and ints. Richard Izzo, Eddie Izzo, Anthony Izzo.

20   *His mother's favorite picture:* Ints. Joe Lombardi, Clara Parvin; Parvin photograph collection.

20   *"From the first contact on":* W. C. Heinz notes.

21   *There was in Harry:* Ints. Joe Lombardi, Harold Lombardi, Madeline Werner.

22   *When a painful lesson:* Ints. Joe Lombardi, Harold Lombardi, Vincent H. Lombardi, Madeline Werner, Clara Parvin.

23   *Every weekday morning:* Ints. Joe Lombardi, Madeline Werner, Harold Lombardi, Lucy O'Brien.

25   *Cathedral Prep: Cathedral Annual,* 1929, 1930, 1931, 1932. *The Gargoyle* 1929–30, 1930–31, 1931–32. Also ints. Rev. Joe Gartner and Rev. Larry Ballweg.

28   *None of this meant much:* Ints. Harold Lombardi, Joe Lombardi, Dorothy Pennell. Lombardi's football career at St. Francis drawn largely from detailed notes of W. C. Heinz interviews with Lombardi and Cohane papers; *The SanFran* January, February, March and May 1932.

2: FORDHAM ROAD

31   *The trip by public:* Int. Richard Izzo. Also New York City subway map, 1934.

33   Descriptions of student life at Fordham 1933–37 from interviews with Lombardi classmates Andrew Palau, Frank Mautte, Victor Del Guercio, Ray Walsh, Wellington Mara, Richard Healy, Emmitt Eaton, James Ambury, John Barris, Rev. Francis Culkin, James McCann, John J. Corcoran, Charles Capraro, Peter Purchia, Thomas Rohan, John Sparnicht, Lawrence Sperandei, Daniel Brannigan, James Brearton, Alvin Lucchi, Phillip Castellano, Edwin Hoysradt Jr., Robert L. Kelly, Orville Leddy, David Pflug, Edwin Quinn, Edward Schmidlein, Charles Schweickart, John Madigan. Also *The Fordham Ram* and *Maroon* yearbook, 1934 and 1937.

34   *It took only one day:* Heinz notes and Cohane papers. Also ints. Andrew Palau, Frank Mautte, Richard Healy.

34   *At Lambeau's suggestion:* Cohane papers; Cohane's *Bypaths* (p. 661), Rice's *Tumult:* "The Rock of Notre Dame" (pp. 159–66), "The Coach and the Horsemen" (pp. 57–66); The *Fordham Ram.* Ints. Dom Principe, Andrew Palau, Frank Mautte, Richard Healy, John Druze; *Four Horsemen of the Apocalypse,* directed by Rex Ingram (1921).

38   *The next weekend:* Accounts of VL sophomore season drawn from voluminous Fordham Research Library archives scrapbook with clippings of *The Ram,* New York newspapers, Fordham game programs. Also *Maroon* yearbook, Heinz notes, Cohane papers.

40   *Lombardi's experience with women:* Ints. Dorothy Pennell, Madeline Lombardi, Harold Lombardi, Joe Lombardi, Richard Izzo, Susan Lombardi, Vincent H. Lombardi, Jill Lombardi, Andrew Palau, Richard Healy, Frank Mautte. Also Susan Lombardi papers, Vincent H. Lombardi papers.

42   *The year 1935 in the Bronx:* Fordham Research Library archives scrapbooks.

43   *The professionalization: The New York Times,* Nov. 29, 1935.

44   *His junior year:* Cohane papers, Heinz notes, Fordham scrapbook; ints. Andrew Palau, Frank Mautte, John Druze, Richard Healy.

3: WE DO, OR DIE

48   *Reston appraised this:* Fordham scrapbook.

49   *On the eve:* Account of 1936 season and creation of Seven Blocks of Granite drawn from Heinz notes; Cohane papers (including original copy of Grantland Rice's "Old Gibraltar"); Fordham scrapbook (including originals of Damon Runyon's game coverage in *New York American*); Fordham game programs; 1937 *Maroon* yearbook; ints. Andrew Palau, Frank Mautte, John Druze, Richard Healy, Dom Principe, Fred Russell, Joe Lombardi, Wellington Mara, Ray Walsh, Victor Del Guercio, Rev. Francis Culkin.

59   *That the image was a wall:* Roland Barthes, *Mythologies* (Noonday, 1973), p. 88.

63   *From his playing days:* Cohane papers.

64   *His highest grades:* O'Brien, in *Vince,* p. 37, was first to obtain Lombardi's grades through request of Vincent H. Lombardi and discern that his academic prowess had been exaggerated, as was his later performance in law school.

64   *The values and ideas: The Ram,* Jan. 18, 1929; Cox, *Integral Education and Necessary Inbreeding,* 1934; Cox, "The Catholic Church and Birth Control," *American Medicine,* 1935; Cox, "Radio Chapel Address," *The Living God,* 1950. Cox, *Liberty: Its Use and Abuse,* 1937. Also ints. Wellington Mara, Victor Del Guercio, Frank Mautte, John Barris, Ray Walsh, Charles Capraro, Peter Purchia, Lawrence Sperandei, Ray Schroth, James McCann.

66   *The class of 1937:* The Ninety-Second Annual Commencement Program, June 16, 1937; ints. Frank Mautte, Andrew Palau, Ray Walsh, Wellington Mara, Victor Del Guercio, Joe Lombardi.

4: SAINTS

68   *This life inevitably:* Ints. Richard Izzo, Harold Lombardi, Madeline Werner, Andrew Palau. Also Heinz notes and O'Brien for account of law school grades.

69   *One of Palau's first:* Int. Andrew Palau.

69   *When he took the job:* Heinz notes. Ints. Andrew Palau, Father Tim Moore.

70   *The Saints lost:* Accounts of Saints games from St. Celilia archive; scrapbooks of Joe McPartland and Andrew Palau, with clippings from *Englewood Press* and *The Record,* Heinz notes, Cohane papers. Also ints. Andrew Palau, Joe McPartland, Father Guy McPartland, John DeGasperis, Al Quilici, Don Crane, Joe Lombardi, Dorothy Bachmann.

71   *In his first experience:* Ints. Andrew Palau, Mickey Corcoran, Father Tim Moore.

72   *Late that first season: The Record,* March 1, 1939. A sidebar to the game story featured the headline: "Referee Paid, It's a Swindle." Also ints. Mickey Corcoran, Joe Lombardi, Father Tim Moore.

74   *A date was soon set:* Andrew Palau, Harold Lombardi, Madeline Werner, Father Tim Moore. Vincent H. Lombardi papers; Susan Lombardi papers; letter from Father Nemecek to Marie Lombardi.

74   *Bored and stuck:* Ints. Margaret Palau, Andrew Palau, Harold Lombardi, Madeline Werner.

82   *The Sisters of Charity: Silverian* yearbook, 1947. Ints. Joe McPartland, Father Guy McPartland, Joe Lombardi, Don Crane, Dorothy Bachmann.

84   *Though he was color-blind:* Classification record of Vincent T. Lombardi. U.S. Selective Service System. Local Board No. 7 for Bergen County.

84   *The students at Saints regarded him: The Arcade,* March 20, 1944. Ints. Don Crane, Joe McPartland, John DeGasperis, Al Quilici, Joe Lombardi, Dorothy Bachmann.

87   *Hours after he had informed:* Father Tim Moore, Joe Lombardi, John DeGasperis, Jill Lombardi. Also Vincent H. Lombardi papers.

5: LOST IN THE BRONX

88   *The American life: Brooklyn Eagle,* Sept. 2, 1947. Also ints. Joe Lombardi, Madeline Werner, Clara Parvin, Dorothy Pennell.

89   *Lombardi's official responsibilities:* Fordham Research Library archives; *The Fordham Ram,* 1948 *Maroon* yearbook.

91   *Fordham had never had:* Heinz notes; Cohane papers; Fordham Research Library scrapbooks. Ints. Herb Seidell, Joe Lombardi, John DeGasperis, Dick Tarrant, Andrew Palau, Dominic Principe.

94   *Lombardi neither pushed:* Cohane papers; ints. Wellington Mara, Herb Seidell.

6: FIELDS OF FRIENDLY STRIFE

97   *Lombardi drove north:* Heinz notes; Cohane papers; Blaik, *You Have to Pay the Price,* p. 436.

99   *Lombardi and Warmath had met:* Int. Murray Warmath; 1934 Fordham-Tennessee game program.

100   *When spring practice opened:* Ints. Murray Warmath, Doug Kenna. Also Heinz notes, Cohane papers.

102   *There was one dominating characteristic:* Cohane papers; ints. Doug Kenna, Murray Warmath, O. C. Krueger, Red Reeder.

103   *"Dauntless Doug":* Assembly, Spring 1964: "MacArthur of West Point"; Phillips, "Douglas MacArthur: Father of the New West Point" (senior thesis, United States Military Academy). Ints. Red Reeder, Doug Kenna.

103   *Blaik and MacArthur were regular correspondents:* Blaik-MacArthur letters in West Point Library archives.

104   *Lombardi slept in Cabin No. 2:* Cohane papers; Cohane, *Bypaths,* p. 217; Heinz notes; ints. Murray Warmath, Doug Kenna, Red Reeder, Fred Russell.

106   *West Point then was dominated:* Lombardi speech to *Reader's Digest* executives, May 1970; ints. Red Reeder, Doug Kenna.

106   *They also studied the Michigan offensive players:* Heinz notes; Cohane papers.

108   *In a sense Tim Cohane:* Account of Army-Fordham game from Tim Cohane papers; Cohane, *Bypaths,* p. 7; Heinz notes; ints. Herb Seidell, Doug Kenna, Red Reeder, O. C. Krueger, Joe Lombardi. Also *New York Journal American.*

109   *What about family?* Ints. Red Reeder, Vincent H. Lombardi, Russell Reeder III, Red Reeder, O. C. Krueger, Julia Reeder McCutchen, Susan Lombardi, Doug Kenna, Harold Lombardi.

114   *The overconfident Cadets:* Blaik letter to MacArthur, Dec. 27, 1950; Blaik letter to General D. D. Eisenhower, Dec. 14, 1950; Assembly, January 1951; ints. Doug Kenna, Murray Warmath; Cohane papers.

7: BLAIK'S BOYS

116   *An unraveling had begun:* Ints. Murray Warmath, Doug Kenna, Red Reeder. Also Cohane papers; Blaik letter to Eisenhower, May 1951.

117   *He already seemed besieged:* Blaik cablegrams to MacArthur, Jan. 24, 1951; April 12, 1951; letter to MacArthur, May 28, 1951.

117   *Not long after:* Blaik letter to John O'Donnell, March 24, 1952. West Point Library. Cohane, *Bypaths,* p. 225; Cohane papers.

118   *The spring of 1951:* Account of Lombardi trip to Far East from *Annual Report of the Superintendent, 1951,* USMA. Also ints. Murray Warmath, Doug Kenna, O. C. Krueger, Red Reeder.

120   *The trouble for Blaik's boys:* Proceedings of a Board of Officers, May 28, 1951. This document, known as the Collins report, recorded the USMA's investigation of the cribbing scandal. It was declassified in 1970 and is now on file at West Point. Also, Assembly, Fall 1951, "The Recent Violations of the Honor Code at West Point," Maj. Gen. Frederick A. Irving, U.S.A., Superintendent.

122   *The next afternoon:* Blaik, *Pay the Price,* p. 289; Cohane papers.

124   Cadets 1–5 and A–C: Collins report transcript.

126   *During the third week of July:* Ints. Doug Kenna, Murray Warmath, Red Reeder.

126   *At the end of that week:* Learned Hand reviewed Collins report findings as part of three-board panel with two retired generals, Lt. Gen. Troy H. Middleton and Maj. Gen. Robert M. Danford, July 23–25, 1951.

128   *How did Lombardi behave:* Ints. Murray Warmath, Doug Kenna, Rex Reeder, O. C. Krueger. Also Cohane papers.

129   *Early the next morning:* Blaik, *Pay the Price,* p. 299; Cohane papers.

130   *Blaik returned to Bull Pond:* Account of Blaik press conference at Leone's from Red Smith's "Views of Sport" column, *New York Herald Tribune,* Aug. 10, 1951; *Time,* Aug. 20, 1951; *New York Times,* Aug. 10, 1951. Also ints. Doug Kenna, Red Reeder, O. C. Krueger.

131   *Blaik and his assistants:* Ints. Murray Warmath, Doug Kenna. Also *New York Daily News,* Aug. 14, 1951. Joseph P. Kennedy's anonymous offer was reported by AP from South Bend, Aug. 21, 1951.

132   *With every national scandal:* Dozens of newspaper editorials and sports columns excoriated West Point scandal. Headline over Sokolsky column, Aug. 9, 1951, in *Christian Science Monitor* read: "Nation's Morals the Issue in Scandal at West Point."

133   *In an effort to head off:* Second Board of Officers appointed Aug. 13, 1951 (Bartlett board), issued report Sept. 7, 1951.

8: NO SUBSTITUTE FOR VICTORY

135   *Blaik was so unfamiliar:* Blaik letter to MacArthur, Sept. 4, 1951, West Point Library special collections. Also *New York Times,* Aug. 28, 1951.

136   *For Lombardi:* Ints. Red Reeder, O. C. Krueger, Doug Kenna, Lowell Sisson, Gerald Lodge. Also, Cohane papers, Heinz notes.

137   *"He was a driver":* Time, Dec. 21, 1962.

138   *The technical aspects:* Ints. John Druze, Red Reeder, Herb Seidell.

139   *As the Army coaches:* Ints. Doug Kenna, Vincent H. Lombardi, Red Reeder, Gerald Lodge. Also Cohane papers (Blaik int., May 8, 1967); Blaik, *Pay the Price,* p. 322.

140   *The next July:* Ints. Red Reeder, Russell Reeder III, Vincent H. Lombardi. Also Reeder, *Born at Reveille,* pp. 273–285; Cohane, *Bypaths,* p. 219; O'Brien, *Vince,* pp. 98–99; "Daybreak on D-Day Was Calm," *New York Times,* June 6, 1984; Fred Russell column, *Nashville Banner,* Aug. 3, 1995.

143   *Dear General MacArthur:* Blaik letter to MacArthur, June 24, 1952, West Point Library special collections.

145   *The Cadets were competitive:* Int. Gerald Lodge.

145   *Lombardi's ability to see everything:* Lombardi speech to *Reader's Digest* executives, May 1970; ints. Doug Kenna, Red Reeder, O. C. Krueger.

146   *Lombardi was anxious:* Cohane papers; Cohane, *Bypaths,* p. 225.

146   *In June, Lombardi had turned forty:* Ints. Red Reeder, Russell Reeder III, Vincent H. Lombardi.

147   *Not much was expected:* Account of Army football's 1953 season drawn from Blaik letters to MacArthur, March 26, May 18, Sept. 4, Nov. 4, 20, 30, 1953, West Point Library; Cohane papers; Heinz notes; ints. Gerald Lodge, Lowell Sisson, Doug Kenna, Red Reeder, O. C. Krueger, Tim Cohane Jr., Vincent H. Lombardi; Joe Cahill, "Down the Field," Assembly, September–November 1953; *New York Times,* Oct. 19, 1953; Red Smith column, "Old Soldiers Never Give Up," *New York Herald Tribune,* Oct. 13, 1953.

9: CULT OF THE NEW

150   *Grantland Rice wrote those lines:* Rice, *Tumult;* Cohane papers; *New York Times,* July 13, 1954.

151   *the new age of television:* Greenfield, *Television;* Winship, *Television;* NFL documents; 1954 letters from Commissioner Bell to New York Giants.

151   *"THE LIGHT OF A NEW AGE":* Newsweek, July 5, 12, 19, 26, Aug. 16, 1954.

152   *It was in the spirit of the new:* New York Daily News, Dec. 11, 1953; ints. Wellington Mara, Ray Walsh, Red Reeder, O. C. Krueger, Doug Kenna; Blaik, *Pay the Price;* Whittingham, *Giants,* p. 262; Steinbreder, *70 Years.*

155   *The new job brought the Lombardis:* Heinz notes; Cohane papers; ints. Vincent H. Lombardi, Wellington Mara, Joe Lombardi.

156   *The pros, for their part:* Ints. Bill Austin, Herb Rich, Frank Gifford, Wellington Mara, Ken Kavanaugh. Also Heinz notes.

157   *Young Vincent:* Int. Vincent H. Lombardi.

157   *After his difficult early weeks:* Heinz notes. Ints. Frank Gifford, Wellington Mara, Ray Walsh, Bill Austin; Whittingham, *Giants.*

159   *These were still only faint glimmers:* Int. Herb Rich.

159   *For the league to rise:* Ints. Wellington Mara, Ray Walsh; Heinz notes. Whittingham, *Giants,* p. 90.

160   *Lombardi and Landry:* Ints. Wellington Mara, Ray Walsh, Bill Austin, Frank Gifford; Tom Landry, "Vince Lombardi," *Sport,* 1986; Landry interview in Whittingham, *Giants,* p. 91; *New York World-Telegram,* Nov. 15, 1958.

162   *We do, or die:* "From Rose Hill to Oblivion," *New York Times,* Dec. 17, 1954; Rev. Laurence J. McGinley, S.J., letter to alumni, Dec. 15, 1954, Fordham Research Library Archives; ints. Wellington Mara, Ray Walsh; Vincent H. Lombardi papers; Cohane papers; Cohane, *Bypaths,* p. 3.

10: THIS PRIDE OF GIANTS

166   *No name in sports:* Cohane papers; Heinz notes; Vincent H. Lombardi papers.

167   *Huff, a two-way lineman:* New York Football Giants player file on Robert Lee "Sam" Huff, Giants administrative headquarters, The Meadowlands, N.J.; Whittingham, *Giants,* p. 71; Gifford, *The Whole Ten Yards;* ints. Wellington Mara, Ray Walsh.

168   *The sophistication of his playbook:* Heinz notes; Cohane papers; ints. Ken Kavanaugh, Bill Austin, Frank Gifford.

168   *Special Bulletin No. 12A:* Document from NFL office, July 6, 1956.

169   *It had been seventeen years:* "Crowley Had Role in TV's First Sports Production," *Scrantonian,* May 9, 1982; Stanley Grosshandler, "About 500 Saw the Game," *Fordham Bulletin.*

170   *Another twelve years passed:* Winship, *Television;* int. Ray Scott.

171   *Old pros might not make mistakes:* Heinz notes; Cohane papers.

172   *a sporting intellectual:* Sunday News, Nov. 25, 1956.

172   *Lombardi did not have to wait:* Account of Giants-Bears championship game drawn from ints. Frank Gifford, Bill Austin, Wellington Mara, Ken Kavanaugh, Ray Walsh, Vincent H. Lombardi; Cohane papers; Sports Illustrated, Jan. 7, 1957; Heinz notes; Whittingham, *Giants,* p. 205; *New York Times,* Dec. 30, 31, 1956; Jan. 1, 1957; Red Smith, "Frost on the Punkin' Heads," *New York Herald Tribune,* Dec. 31, 1956; *Chicago Tribune,* Dec. 31, 1956.

175   *Money was just then emerging:* Report of 1st Players Association Meeting (notes taken by Norm Van Brocklin), Dec. 28–29, 1956; *New York Times,* Dec. 30, 1956.

176   *All smiles when the Lombardi family:* Long Branch Daily Record, Dec. 4, 1956. Description of Lombardi family drawn from interviews with Vincent H. Lombardi, Susan Lombardi, Joe Lombardi, Madeline Werner, Dorothy Pennell, Steve Werner, Harold Lombardi, Clara Parvin, DeDe Clark.

176   *Marie had been married to Vince:* Ints. Joe Lombardi, Vincent H. Lombardi, Susan Lombardi, Madeline Werner.

181   *Lombardi's mind was quickly elsewhere:* Heinz notes, Vincent H. Lombardi papers (on Marie's state of mind); Cohane papers; ints. Wellington Mara, Ray Walsh, Vic Del Guercio, Father Tim Moore.

183   *Two minutes left:* Ints. Wellington Mara, Ken Kavanaugh, Ray Walsh, Bill Austin, Frank Gifford. Also Steinbreder, *70 Years,* pp. 43–44; Whittingham, *Giants,* p. 32; *Sports Illustrated,* Dec. 10, 1958; Red Smith column in *Philadelphia Inquirer,* Dec. 30, 1958.

185   *affected by the strike:* Dorothy Schiff Papers at New York Public Library Center for Humanities, Box 132; *New York Times,* Dec. 12–20 (two-page strike edition), 29, 1958; *Editor and Publisher,* Dec. 20, 1958; Columbia School of Journalism Report, Dec. 12–17, 1958.

186   *The weather on December 28:* Account of championship game drawn from ints. Wellington Mara, Ray Walsh, Frank Gifford, Ken Kavanaugh, Vincent H. Lombardi, Joe Lombardi, Susan Lombardi; Heinz notes; Cohane papers; *Sports Illustrated,* Jan. 3, 1959; New York Football Giants archives; Red Smith column in *Inquirer,* Dec. 29, 1958; Whittingham, *Giants,* p. 18; Steinbreder, *70 Years,* pp. 48–49; William Gildea, "The Colts of '58 Have a Fine Time to Remember," *Washington Post,* Nov. 21, 1998.

11: THE FOREIGNER

191   *Christmas Eve 1958:* Ints. Ruth McKloskey, Art Daley, Jerry Van, Tom Van.

191   *Now Scooter was fleeing:* Ints. Bud Lea, Art Daley, Bob Skoronski; *Green Bay Press-Gazette,* Dec. 17, 1958.

192   *Olejniczak had been president:* Ints. Bud Lea, Art Daley, Lee Remmel, Tom Olejniczak; Olejniczak papers; *Press-Gazette,* Jan. 14, 1959.

193   *Scooter chose to hang out with players:* Ints. Gary Knafelc, Tony Canadeo, Paul Mazzoleni, Bert Turek, Art Daley, Ray Scott, Max McGee, Bart Starr, Paul Hornung, Lew Anderson.

195   *Lombardi was in the kitchen:* Heinz notes; Cohane papers.

196   *Even Earl Louis Lambeau:* Ints. Tony Canadeo, Ruth McKloskey, Art Daley. *Press-Gazette* series on Packer history, Feb. 15, 22, March 1, 8, 1998; Lambeau obituary, *Press-Gazette,* June 2, 1965.

198   *Following up on Vainisi:* Ints. Wellington Mara, Tony Canadeo.

199   *Early on the evening of January 22:* Heinz notes; ints. Wellington Mara, Ray Walsh, Tony Canadeo; Wiebusch, *Lombardi,* p. 78; *Press-Gazette,* Jan. 19, 1959; *Philadelphia Inquirer,* Jan. 21–23, 1959.

200   *once he had made a tentative decision:* Cohane papers; Heinz notes; ints. DeDe Clark, Wellington Mara.

201   *The board of directors:* Ints. Art Daley, Lee Remmel, Bud Lea, Tony Canadeo; *Press-Gazette,* Jan. 27, 1959; *New York Times,* Jan. 29, 1959.

202   *There were no round-the-clock:* Ints. Wayne Vander Patten, Mike Blindauer, John Ebert, Art Daley, Bart Starr.

12: PACKER SWEEP

204   *The Lombardis drove to Green Bay:* Ints. Vincent H. Lombardi, Susan Lombardi; Vincent H. Lombardi papers.

205   *Green Bay was more a blur:* Ints. Mary Antil, Mary Jo Johnson, Vincent H. Lombardi, Susan Lombardi, Lois Bourguignon.

206   *The offices of the Green Bay Packers:* Int. Ruth McKloskey.

207   *John Thurman Cochran and John Philip Bengtson:* Ints. Red Cochran, Pat Cochran, Bill Austin, Ruth McKloskey; Bengtson (with Todd Hunt), *Packer Dynasty,* pp. 7–9; Heinz notes.

208   *the antithesis of the happy-go-lucky Scooter:* Ints. Ruth McKloskey, Tony Canadeo; *Press-Gazette,* Feb. 4, 1959.

208   *"We knew Lombardi was going to be disciplined":* Ints. Red Cochran, Bill Austin, Ruth McKloskey; Heinz notes, Cohane papers.

209   *Hornung knew about Gifford:* Int. Paul Hornung.

210   *The dominant figure:* Int. Gary Knafelc; Heinz notes.

211   *Lombardi vacillated:* Ints. Vincent H. Lombardi, Pat Cochran, Ruth McKloskey, Bill Austin, Bart Starr; Heinz notes.

215   *Only a few miles south:* Ints. Gary DeBauche, Father Dennis Burke, Father Thomas Dewane.

215   *On Thursday evening, July 23: Press Gazette,* July 24–27, 1959; Heinz notes; Cohane papers; ints. Bill Butler, Max McGee, Bart Starr, Bob Skoronski, Gary Knafelc.

218   *Young Vincent was there:* Ints. Vincent H. Lombardi, Ray Nitschke, Art Daley, Bud Lea.

219   *The nutcracker was Lombardi's "test of manhood":* Ints. Bob Skoronski, Ray Nitschke, Gary Knafelc, Max McGee.

220   *Images of pain:* Cestaro, *Vietri di Potenza,* pp. 120–121; Levi, *Christ Stopped at Eboli,* p. 42; Whitfield, *Painting in Naples, 1606–1705,* pp. 16–29; ints. Francesco Izzo, Madeline Werner, Harold Lombardi, Joe Lombardi.

221   *Lombardi had used the sweep:* Heinz notes; ints. Red Cochran, Bill Austin, Ken Kavanaugh, Gary Knafelc, Bob Skoronski, Paul Hornung, Bart Starr, Fuzzy Thurston, Ron Kramer, Max McGee.

13: TRINITY

227   *Here stood the Fordham wall: New York World-Telegram,* Aug. 20, 1960; ints. John Druze, Father Tim Moore.

228   *Coach of the Year: Press-Gazette,* Dec. 22, 1959; *Chicago Tribune,* Oct. 13, 1959; *New York World-Telegram,* Oct. 13,

1959; *Sports Illustrated*, Oct. 19, 1959; Heinz notes; Cohane papers; ints. Ron Kramer, Lamar McHan, Bart Starr, Ruth McCloskey, Max McGee; Susan Lombardi tapes (for Frank Gifford radio show, "It's Sports Time," Oct. 1959).

231   *the dawn of a new decade:* Ints. Susan Lombardi, Vincent H. Lombardi, Mary Antil, Lois Bourguignon, Victoria Vidani, Shirley Koeppler, Jack Koeppler, Father Dennis Burke, Tony Canadeo.

237   *Willie Wood seemed an exception:* Ints. Willie Wood, Art Daley, Lee Remmel, Gaylord Nelson, Tony Canadeo, Jack Koeppler; Heinz notes; Cohane papers; "World of Women," *Milwaukee Sentinel*, Nov. 1, 1960.

242   *The trinity of life:* Ints. Susan Lombardi, Vincent H. Lombardi, Joe Lombardi, Harold Lombardi, Father Dennis Burke, Father William Spalding, Father Tim Moore, Eugene Brusky, Jack Koeppler, Gary DeBauche, David Picard, Jim Huxford, Frances Hassell; Lombardi religious books maintained by Vincent H. Lombardi.

246   *The Packers opened the 1960 season:* Ints. Bart Starr, Paul Hornung, Gary Knafelc, Red Cochran, Bill Austin, Willie Wood, Bob Skoronski.

14: Remembering Jack

249   *On the Sunday after Thanksgiving: Press-Gazette*, Nov. 28–29, 1960; Jack Vainisi papers; ints. Jackie Vainisi, Sam Vainisi, Paul Hornung, Art Daley, Lee Remmel, Bud Lea, Bob Skoronski.

254   *The images Riger came away with:* Robert Riger, "Again and Again," *Green Bay Packers Yearbook*, 1961.

255   *He would often tell his cronies:* Ints. Bart Starr, Jack Koeppler, Tony Canadeo, Art Daley, Murray Warmath; Heinz notes; Starr and Olderman, *Starr*, pp. 14–15.

257   *Bart Starr usually slept soundly:* Starr diary, Saturday, Dec. 17, 1960; *Green Bay Packers Yearbook*, 1961. Ints. Bart Starr, Gary Knafelc, Max McGee; *Press-Gazette*, Dec. 19, 1960; *Milwaukee Sentinel*, Dec. 19, 1960.

261   *"From Los Angeles to New York": Philadelphia Inquirer*, Dec. 22, 1960.

261   *Lombardi was in a generous mood:* Account of Packers-Eagles championship game drawn from ints. Bob Skoronski, Bart Starr, Gary Knafelc, Willie Wood, Lew Anderson, Tom Olejniczak, Ray Scott, Steve Sabol, Paul Hornung, Max McGee, Red Cochran; Vincent H. Lombardi, *Coaching for Teamwork*, p. 17; *Green Bay Packers Yearbook*, 1961 (Robert Riger photos and article and reprint of Red Smith column); *Philadelphia Inquirer*, Dec. 24–27, 1960; *Press-Gazette*, Dec. 24–27, 1960.

265   *An important aspect of the mythology:* New York Football Giants document, Jan. 10, 1961; Olejniczak papers; ints. Wellington Mara, Ray Walsh, Father Tim Moore, Tony Canadeo. Dick Young, *New York Daily News*, Dec. 29, 1960; *The Record*, Aug. 8, 1961; *Press-Gazette*, Dec. 28, 1960; Harold Weissman, "The Sports Whirl," *New York Mirror*, Jan. 12, 1961.

268   *Six weeks after Jack Vainisi died:* Int. Jackie Vainisi.

15: Golden

269   *John F. Kennedy, the new president:* Ethel Kennedy letters to Vince Lombardi (1969–70); Lew Anderson notebooks; Vincent H. Lombardi papers.

270   *What was it about Lombardi?* Ints. Susan Lombardi, Lois Bourguignon, Mary Antil, O. C. Krueger, Bud Lea, W. C. Heinz.

270   *Here he is, on the Wednesday evening:* Program, Testimonial Dinner-Dance honoring Vincent Lombardi, April 5, 1961, Clara Parvin papers; photographs of testimonial, Susan Lombardi photographs; ints. Ray Walsh, Victor Del Guercio, Joe Lombardi, Eddie Izzo, Anthony Izzo.

271   *It was a snap to draw:* Ints. Ruth McCloskey, Pat Peppler, Tony Canadeo, Bob Skoronski, Lorraine Keck.

273   *That was true only:* Ints. Bob Skoronski, Gary Knafelc.

274   *Lombardi carried this dread with him:* Heinz notes; Cohane papers; ints. Art Daley, Lee Remmel, Bud Lea, Max McGee, Willie Wood.

275   *The mythmakers were finding their way:* Cohane papers; Cohane, *Bypaths*, p. 11; *Look*, Oct. 24, 1961.

277   *And out came more writers:* Int. Dick Schaap; "The Rough Road Ahead for Paul Hornung," *Sport*, November 1961.

278   *Myth or reality?* Int. Gary Van Ness.

279   *To trade places for a moment:* Ints. W. C. Heinz, Ruth McCloskey, Vincent H. Lombardi, Jack Koeppler.

280   *Paul Hornung never enjoyed much:* Ints. Paul Hornung, George Dickson, John Druze, Max McGee; *Sport*, November 1956; *Family Weekly*, Sept. 24, 1961; Hornung and Silverman, *Football and the Single Man*, p. 61.

282   *His teammates in Green Bay:* Ints. Elijah Pitts, Ron Kramer, Max McGee, Gary Knafelc, Dick Schaap, John Ebert, Tony Canadeo.

284   *Lombardi was openly distraught:* Account of Hornung experience in Army drawn from ints. Paul Hornung, Lew Anderson, O. C. Krueger, Duane Dinius, Gen. John Ruggles, Bud Lea: AP, Oct. 7–10, 1961; UPI, Oct. 27, 1961; *Milwaukee Sentinel*, Nov. 14, 1961; Chief of Staff, U.S. Army memorandum, Oct. 20, 1961; Lew Anderson letter to Dick Voris, Packers director of personnel, Nov. 6, 1961; Lombardi letter to Kenneth O'Donnell, special assistant to the president, March 16, 1962.

291   *The Giants thought they had a chance:* Account of 1961 championship game drawn from ints. Jack Koeppler, Tony Canadeo, Bart Starr, Paul Hornung, Ray Nitschke, Max McGee, Willie Wood, Gary Knafelc, Ron Kramer, Red Cochran, Bill Austin, Wellington Mara, Vic Del Guercio, Father Tim Moore, Vincent H. Lombardi, Lois Bourguignon; Steinbreder, *70 Years*, p. 81; Whittingham, *Giants*, pp. 119–120; *New York Times*, Jan. 1, 1962; *New York Daily News*, Jan. 1, 1962; *Press-Gazette*, Jan. 1, 1962; *Milwaukee Sentinel*, Jan. 1, 1962.

16: A NIGHT AT THE ELKS

295   *On the Monday evening of April 30, 1962:* The Program, Tribute to Vincent Thomas Lombardi.

295   *This was a night for tales:* Account in this chapter drawn from long-playing audiodisks of evening recorded by WJPG in Green Bay, April 30, 1962; Cohane, *Bypaths,* pp. 11–13; *Press-Gazette,* May 1, 1962; *Washington Post,* Nov. 7, 1963; ints. Father Tim Moore, Jack Koeppler, Paul Hornung.

17: DAYLIGHT

304   *The call came one Sunday:* Int. W. C. Heinz.

306   *On the thirtieth of June:* Heinz notes; int. W. C. Heinz.

307   *Nothing came so easily:* Heinz notes, Notebook No. 1.

308   *Lombardi even forgot:* Int. Susan Lombardi.

312   *But did he need the Wisconsin press?:* Ints. Bud Lea, Art Daley, Lee Remmel, Terry Bledsoe, Russ Kriwanek, Wayne Vander Patten, Dave Hrubesky, Jim Irwin, Al Sampson, Al DelGreco, Robert Strom.

316   *It was their defense that made them:* Ints. Ray Nitschke, Art Daley, Willie Wood.

317   *He got the game:* Heinz, *Run to Daylight!,* pp. 208–235; Heinz notes; int. W. C. Heinz.

318   *The astounding team in the heartland:* Herbert Warren Wind, "The Sporting Scene (Packerland)," *The New Yorker,* Dec. 8, 1962.

319   *Detroit had a defense as tenacious:* Account of Thanksgiving Day loss to Lions drawn from ints. Max McGee, Bob Skoronski, Willie Wood, Bart Starr, W. C. Heinz; *Press-Gazette,* Nov. 21–24, 1962.

320   *Heinz had written six chapters:* Int. W. C. Heinz; Heinz, *Run to Daylight!,* pp. 21–193; Flynn, *The Vince Lombardi Scrapbook.*

18: THE END OF SOMETHING

322   *Marie had traveled:* Ints. Susan Lombardi, Vincent H. Lombardi; Vincent H. Lombardi papers.

323   *The entire family:* Time, Dec. 21, 1962.

324   *Of the 54.9 million homes:* NFL Pro Football Review and Analysis prepared by Leo Burnett Company for Philip Morris Inc.

325   *There would be a seamless web:* NFL internal documents and notes of league meetings, 1962.

325   *Vince had made plans to take the family:* Cohane papers; Wiebusch, *Lombardi,* p. 122.

326   *He and Marie had left their daughter:* Int. Susan Lombardi.

327   *By God it was thrilling:* Ints. Bud Lea, Red Cochran; Bengtson, *Packer Dynasty,* p. 60; *Sports Illustrated,* Jan. 7, 1963.

328   *When the bus stopped:* Jerry Kramer interviewed by John Minot on WNFL in Green Bay, December 1996.

328   *But were the Yankees this beat up?:* Ints. Ron Kramer, Paul Hornung; Marie Lombardi tapes; Wiebusch, *Lombardi,* p. 124.

329   *Red, white and blue bunting:* Sports Illustrated, Jan. 7, 1963; Red Smith column reprinted in *Green Bay Packers Yearbook,* 1963; ints. Vincent H. Lombardi, Bart Starr, Paul Hornung, Ray Nitschke, Ron Kramer, Willie Wood.

330   *Up in the auxiliary press box:* Ints. Red Cochran, Ray Scott, Steve Sabol.

330   *Willie Wood kicked off:* Account of 1962 championship game drawn from ints. Willie Wood, Paul Hornung, Ray Nitschke, Bob Skoronski, Gary Knafelc, Ron Kramer, Bart Starr, Max McGee, Tom Brown, Eugene Brusky, Red Cochran, Pat Cochran, Lew Anderson, Bill Austin, Bud Lea, Art Daley, W. C. Heinz, Steve Sabol, Ken Kavanaugh, Susan Lombardi, Vincent H. Lombardi; Jerry Kramer interview with John Minot; *Press-Gazette,* Dec. 31, 1962; Lee Remmel, "Greatest Packers Games," reprinted in the Green Bay Packers Game Program, 1996; *Washington Post,* Dec. 31, 1962; *Sports Illustrated,* Jan. 7, 1963; *Pro Football Illustrated,* January 1963; Whittingham, *Giants,* p. 124; Wiebusch, *Lombardi,* p. 122; Vince Lombardi letter to players, Jan. 4, 1963.

19: FOOT OF THE CROSS

335   *Not long after:* Int. Max McGee.

336   *Hornung's other roommate:* Int. Ron Kramer.

336   *The story of how Paul Hornung:* Int. Paul Hornung; Hornung and Silverman, *Football and the Single Man,* p. 17; *Las Vegas Review-Journal,* Apr. 19, 1963.

338   *Late in the summer:* NFL internal documents and minutes of owners' meetings, 1963.

338   *Lombardi appeared mildly concerned:* Ints. Jack Koeppler, O. C. Krueger; Flynn, *Lombardi Scrapbook,* p. 119.

338   *After the championship game:* Int. Paul Hornung.

339   *At the end of January:* Minutes of special meeting of NFL executive committee, Bal Harbour, Fla., Jan. 28, 1963.

339   *Hornung was home in Louisville:* Int. Paul Hornung.

339   *On the first of April:* NFL documents; Cohane papers; ints. O. C. Krueger, Jack Koeppler.
340   *it came at last on the morning of April 17:* Int. Paul Hornung; NFL Commissioner's Report on Investigation, Apr. 17, 1963; Cohane papers; *New York Times,* Apr. 18, 1963; *Chicago Tribune,* Apr. 18, 1963; (Madison) *Capital Times,* Apr. 18, 1963; *Press-Gazette,* Apr. 19, 1963; *Las Vegas Review-Journal,* Apr. 19, 1963.
341   *The gambling story, Schaap wrote: Sport,* September 1963.
341   *The essential relationship:* Ints. O. C. Krueger, Jack Koeppler, Ray Scott, Paul Hornung.

20: Coming in Second

343   *Only two of Harry Lombardi's three sons:* Ints. Joe Lombardi, Harold Lombardi.
344   *Vince did know that Harold was gay:* Ints. Vincent H. Lombardi, Susan Lombardi, Michelle Walden, Father Guy McPartland, George Dickson.
344   *If there was any awkwardness:* Int. Harold Lombardi.
345   *Bigness is relative:* Int. Dave Robinson; Green Bay Packers publicity memorandum.
346   *How and where:* Ints. Pat Richter, Dave Robinson, O. C. Krueger, Pat Peppler, Ruth McCloskey, Willie Wood.
348   *Lombardi was consumed:* Wiebusch, *Lombardi,* p. 125; O'Brien, *Vince,* p. 164; W. C. Heinz, *Run to Daylight!,* p. 21.
348   *He pushed harder:* Ints. Ruth McCloskey, Lorraine Keck, Jack Koeppler, Eugene Brusky, Red Cochran.
349   *Could the Packers win?:* Ints. Al Sampson, Art Daley, Max McGee, Jack Koeppler, Dave Robinson, Willie Wood, Ray Nitschke, Ruth McCloskey; D'Amato and Christl, *Mudbaths & Bloodbaths.*
351   *President Kennedy was killed: Press-Gazette,* Nov. 24, 1963; *Milwaukee Sentinel,* Nov. 24, 1963; Vincent H. Lombardi memorabilia collection; W. C. Heinz article on Willie Davis in *Once They Heard the Cheers* (Doubleday, 1979), pp. 276–279.
352   *Lombardi later would place:* Lombardi speech to First Friday Club, Los Angeles, Spring 1964.
353   *Paul Hornung, on his knees:* Int. Paul Hornung.
354   *The manner of Ringo's departure:* Ints. Pat Peppler, Bob Skoronski, Bill Austin, Red Cochran; Dowling, *Coach,* p. 28; O'Brien, *Vince,* p. 221; *Milwaukee Journal,* May 6, 1964.
355   *If there was anything in Lombardi's life:* Ints. Jack Koeppler, Eugene Brusky, Bert Turek, Gary DeBauche, Father Dennis Burke, Tony Canadeo, Russell Reeder III, Bob Milward, Tom Hallion, Bob Maahs, Mike Flessner, Walter Davis, Max McGee.
358   *The documentary borrowed the name: Run to Daylight!* documentary, Howard Cosell, producer, Lou Volpicelli, director, W. C. Heinz, writer; ints. W. C. Heinz, Lou Volpicelli.
360   *Much was at stake: Sports Illustrated,* September 1964; Gentile, *The Packer Tapes,* p. 5; ints. Paul Hornung, Max McGee, Pat Peppler.
362   *In private meetings:* Ints. Max McGee, Bob Skoronski, Willie Wood, Tom Brown.
362   *It was an uncertain time for Lombardi:* Olejniczak papers; ints. Tony Canadeo, Susan Lombardi, Vincent H. Lombardi, Jill Lombardi, Jack Koeppler, Shirley Koeppler; *Minot Daily News,* June 23, 1965.

21: Winning Isn't Everything

366   *there was a crucial distinction:* Ints. Red Cochran, Bill Austin, Willie Wood, Tom Brown, Bob Skoronski, Paul Hornung, Bart Starr.
366   *The signature phrase itself:* Int. Melville Shavelson.
367   *The script became the movie: Trouble Along the Way* (1953), Warner Bros., written and produced by Melville Shavelson.
368   *Shavelson had only a passing knowledge:* Int. Melville Shavelson.
369   *If Red Sanders coined the phrase:* Int. Fred Russell; Russell, *Bury Me in an Old Press Box,* pp. 73–75; Cohane papers.

22: It's the Only Thing

371   *"Whadaya think of that?":* Ints. Bud Lea, Art Daley, Tom Brown; O'Brien, *Vince,* p. 173.
373   *"There's an old fable":* Cohane papers; *The New Yorker,* Dec. 8, 1962, Feb. 4, 1967; ints. W. C. Heinz, Steve Sabol, Jack Koeppler, Vincent H. Lombardi.
374   *Was it love or hate?:* Cohane papers; ints. Max McGee, Bob Skoronski, AP, July 12, 1966; *Washington Star,* Aug. 24, 1967; James Maraniss, "Vince Lombardi—Is It Love or Hate That Makes His Team Tick?" (Madison) *Capital Times.*
375   *There was a similar paradox:* Ints. Bob Skoronski, Tom Brown, Dave Robinson, Willie Wood, Pat Peppler, Gary Knafelc, Red Cochran, Bill Austin, Max McGee.
377   *There was a more practical explanation:* Bengtson, *Packer Dynasty,* p. 207; ints. Jack Koeppler, Paul Hornung, Willie Wood, Art Daley, Ray Nitschke, Tom Brown, Max McGee, Dave Robinson.
378   *On the airplane returning from the coast:* George Plimpton, *One More July* (HarperCollins, 1977); ints. Bob Skoronski, Willie Davis.

379 *Hornung seemed rejuvenated: Newsday,* Dec. 13, 1965; *Press-Gazette,* Dec. 13, 1965; Arthur Daley, "The Golden Dome," *New York Times,* Dec. 14, 1965.

380 *The next big game: Press-Gazette,* Dec. 23–27, 1965; *Milwaukee Sentinel,* Dec. 27, 1965; ints. Paul Hornung, Willie Wood, Ray Scott, Red Cochran, Art Daley, Lee Remmel, Bud Lea, Ray Nitschke.

381 *The world championship was played: Press-Gazette,* Jan. 1–3, 1966; Carroll, *Total Football,* p. 136; ints. Paul Hornung, Steve Sabol, Bob Skoronski.

383 *The game on the field:* Ints. Pat Peppler, Jim Grabowski, O. C. Krueger.

385 *On the eleventh of June:* Ints. Vincent H. Lombardi, Jill Lombardi, Susan Lombardi, Ray Scott, Mary Antil, Jack Koeppler, Mary Jo Johnson.

386 *After the game Ken Hartnett:* AP, Oct. 24, 1966; ints. Bud Lea, Art Daley, Chuck Lane, Lee Remmel, Bill Austin.

388 *Lombardi had a need to prevail:* Ints. Art Daley, Russ Kriwanek, Vernon Biever, Lee Remmel, Wayne Vander Patten, Jim Irwin, Al Sampson, Bud Lea, Mike Gourlie.

389 *The pressure of success:* Ints. Chuck Lane, Eugene Brusky, Father Tim Moore, Jack Koeppler, Bill Austin, Red Cochran, Ruth McCloskey.

390 *"LAST GO FOR LOMBARDI?": Dallas Times-Herald,* Dec. 27, 1966; ints. Lee Remmel, Art Daley, Dave Robinson, Elijah Pitts, Jim Grabowski, Tom Brown.

391 *The game was a lower-case phenomenon:* Account of Super Bowl I drawn from ints. Paul Hornung, Max McGee, Bart Starr, Bob Skoronski, Ray Nitschke, Dave Robinson, Tom Brown, Carroll Dale, Willie Wood, Elijah Pitts, Lee Remmel, Art Daley, Bud Lea, Vernon Biever, Tony Canadeo, Vincent H. Lombardi, Ruth McCloskey, Red Cochran, Pat Cochran, Jack Koeppler, Shirley Koeppler, Lois Bourguignon, Steve Sabol. Also Carroll, *Total Football,* p. 101; "Day One," *Sports Illustrated; The New Yorker,* Feb. 4, 1967; *Life,* January 1967.

23: IN SEARCH OF MEANING

397 *The doldrums of 1967:* Ints. Red Cochran, Pat Cochran.

397 *That crossover process had begun:* Int. W. C. Heinz.

398 *When responding to letters:* Ints. Ruth McCloskey, Lorraine Keck; John Minot papers.

398 *The Great Lakes region: Life,* Feb. 10, 1967; *Press-Gazette,* Feb. 2–6, 1967; *New York Times,* Feb. 3–8, 1967.

399 *It was in the midst of this storm:* Int. Christ Seraphim.

399 *At several stops along the route:* Ints. Pat Conway, George Disegni.

400 *They were finishing the salad course:* Ints. George Disegni, Joe Lombardi; *New York Times,* Feb. 9, 1967; AP, Feb. 8, 1967.

401 *Many of Blaik's:* Blaik, *Pay the Price,* p. 413; Cohane papers; archive of Lombardi speeches maintained by Lorraine Keck, standard speech for this chapter based on speech titled "Leadership in Management."

401 *Fifteen years earlier:* Cohane papers; Blaik, *Pay the Price,* p. 524; ints. Doug Kenna, Red Reeder.

403 *When Father Cox:* Cox, *Liberty: Its Use and Abuse.*

403 *Lombardi had mixed feelings about the reforms:* Ints. Jack Koeppler, Father Dennis Burke.

403 *Father Lombardi?* Int. Ruth McCloskey.

403 *Lombardi could adjust:* Murray Olderman, NEA interview, Spring 1970.

405 *This line of thinking went back:* Blaik letters, West Point Research Library.

406 *He was "such a forceful personality":* Int. W. C. Heinz.

406 *Character is an integration:* Cox, *Liberty: Its Use and Abuse.*

406 *Love and loyalty:* Kramer, *Instant Replay,* p. 19.

407 *The loss of Hornung:* Ints. Max McGee, Paul Hornung, Jack Koeppler, Bert Turek.

407 *At seven o'clock:* Fordham Research Library archive; ints. Joe Lombardi, Jack Koeppler.

24: ICE

410 *Ed Sabol could not sleep:* Int. Steve Sabol.

410 *The same words of disbelief:* Ints. Paul Mazzoleni, Willie Wood, Chuck Mercein.

411 *His colleague called at seven:* Ints. Lee Remmel, Chuck Lane.

411 *Dick Schaap led a foursome:* Ints. Dick Schaap, Dave Robinson.

411 *There was a full house:* Ints. Susan Lombardi, Vincent H. Lombardi, Jill Lombardi.

412 *The Sabols were already there:* Int. Steve Sabol.

413 *Chuck Lane was heading out:* Ints. Chuck Lane, Bud Lea, Jim Tunney.

414 *In the locker room:* Ints. Willie Wood, Tom Brown, Dave Robinson, Jim Grabowski.

414 *Of all the major characters:* Ints. Chuck Mercein, Wellington Mara.

415 *When the team returned:* Ints. Willie Wood, Max McGee.

415 *His playing career done:* Int. Gary Knafelc.

416 *To many fans:* Ints. Carol Schmidt, Bob Kaminsky, Jack Koeppler, Jerry Van, Lois Bourguignon, Red Cochran, Gary Van Ness, Mary Turek, Tom Olejniczak, Lorraine Keck, Chuck Mercein.

417 *For the first quarter:* Ints. Tom Brown, Dave Robinson, Ray Nitschke; *Green Bay Packers Yearbook,* 1968.

418 *Willie Wood drops back:* Int. Willie Wood.

418   *Lombardi had little to say:* Ints. Tom Brown, Bob Skoronski, Paul Hornung, Lee Remmel; Kramer, *Instant Replay*, p. 215.

419   *The wives of Dick Schaap and Jerry Kramer:* Int. Dick Schaap.

419   *The third quarter:* Tunney, *Impartial Judgment*, p. 64; ints. Jim Huxford, Ray Nitschke, Chuck Mercein; Gifford, *The Whole Ten Yards*, p. 243.

420   *The press box:* Ints. Chuck Lane, Bud Lea, Lee Remmel, Art Daley, Jim Irwin, Ray Scott.

420   *Willie Wood thought:* Ints. Willie Wood, Ray Scott, Ray Nitschke, Dick Schaap, Vincent H. Lombardi, Clara Parvin, Eugene Brusky, Jim Huxford, O. C. Krueger, Paul Mazzoleni, Steve Sabol.

422   *Before trotting onto the field:* Ints. Bart Starr, Bob Skoronski, Chuck Mercein.

423   *Then came what Starr considered:* Ints. Bart Starr, Chuck Mercein, Art Daley, Jim Huxford.

423   *Starr knows exactly what his coach:* Ints. Bart Starr, Paul Hornung, Chuck Mercein, Max McGee, Bud Lea, Pat Peppler, Willie Wood; *Green Bay Packers Yearbook*, 1968; Green Bay Packers 1967 highlights film; Kramer, *Instant Replay*, p. 216; W. C. Heinz interview of Willie Davis in *Once They Heard the Cheers* (Doubleday, 1979), pp. 276–279.

425   *Vincent has worked his way:* Ints. Vincent H. Lombardi, O. C. Krueger, Dick Schaap, Vernon Biever.

425   *Now the Packers are in the same situation:* Ints. Chuck Mercein, Bob Skoronski, Bart Starr, Vernon Biever, Dick Schaap, Clara Parvin, Ray Scott, Bud Lea, Lee Remmel, Chuck Lane; Kramer, *Instant Replay*, p. 217; Bengtson, *Packer Dynasty*, p. 124; *Green Bay Packers Yearbook*, 1968.

426   *The locker room was a jangle:* Press-Gazette, Jan. 1, 1968; *Milwaukee Sentinel*, Jan. 1, 1968.

426   *Glacial tears:* Ints. Ray Nitschke, Tom Brown, Willie Wood, Jim Grabowski, Dick Schaap, Vincent H. Lombardi, Jill Lombardi, Steve Sabol; Blaik, *Pay the Price*, p. 440.

427   *A few days later:* Int. Chuck Mercein.

428   *A few weeks later:* Int. Dick Schaap.

428   *A few months later:* Ints. Steve Sabol, Vincent H. Lombardi, Jack Koeppler; NFL Films *The Greatest Challenge*.

25: Until Lombardi Loves You

429   *Susan Lombardi had suspected:* Ints. Susan Lombardi, Father William Spalding.

430   *The first report:* Ints. Ray Scott, Hal Scott, Father Dennis Burke, Father William Spalding.

431   *At the final film session:* Ints. Tom Brown, Willie Wood, Jim Grabowski; Kramer, *Instant Replay*, p. 227.

432   *Two and a half weeks after:* Press-Gazette, Feb. 2, 1968; *Wisconsin State Journal*, Feb. 2, 1968; *Milwaukee Sentinel*, Feb. 2, 1968; ints. Chuck Lane, Lee Remmel, Art Daley, Jim Irwin, Tony Canadeo, O. C. Krueger.

432   *Why did Lombardi quit?* Ints. Chuck Lane, Carroll Dale, Father William Spalding, Susan Lombardi, Father Tim Moore, Tony Canadeo.

433   *All of this had come to a climax:* Leonard Shecter, "The Toughest Man," *Esquire*, January 1968. Ints. Dick Schaap, Chuck Lane; Cohane papers; Howard Cosell interview, Summer 1969.

434   *Two other reasons:* Ints. Bert Turek, Gary Knafelc, Vincent H. Lombardi.

435   *On the Friday morning:* Int. Ruth McKloskey; letters from Vincent H. Lombardi papers.

436   *For several years:* Ints. Jack Koeppler, David Carley, Jim Carley, Mitch Fromstein, O. C. Krueger.

437   *As he became more famous:* Ints. Vincent H. Lombardi, Jack Koeppler.

438   *Lombardi now equated money with power:* Ints. David Carley, Jack Koeppler, Mitch Fromstein; Agreement in Principle Between David Carley and Vincent Lombardi, Public Facilities Associates, Inc., David Carley papers.

439   *He had tried to persuade:* Ints. Father Dennis Burke, Jack Koeppler, O. C. Krueger, Tony Canadeo.

439   *Red Blaik was part of the group:* Ints. Doug Kenna, O. C. Krueger, David Carley, Mitch Fromstein, Wellington Mara. O'Brien, *Vince*, p. 328.

439   *"Dear Pete," he wrote:* Personal & Confidential letter from R. B. Levitas to Pete Rozelle, April 22, 1968.

440   *Sides were being taken:* Ints. Bernie Baum, Dave Robinson, Wellington Mara, Pat Richter; Press-Gazette, July 9–14, 1968.

442   *In the old days:* Ints. Chuck Lane, Ruth McKloskey, David Carley, Susan Lombardi, Ray Nitschke, Chuck Mercein, Jim Grabowski, Art Daley, Lee Remmel, Bud Lea, Bob Skoronski, Tony Canadeo.

444   *There was an odd sensation:* Ints. W. C. Heinz, Eddie Izzo, Dorothy Pennell; Calendar of Events for "A Salute to Vince Lombardi," Pro Football Hall of Fame archives; Press-Gazette, Aug. 8, 1968; Recording of "An Evening with Vince Lombardi," WJPG, Aug. 7, 1968.

445   *As Lombardi's audience grew:* Milwaukee Sentinel, May 6, 1968.

446   *This was not merely:* Int. David Carley; *Milwaukee Sentinel*, Aug. 3, 1968; Miles McMillin, "Hello, Wisconsin," (Madison) *Capital Times*, Aug. 27, 1968; Vincent H. Lombardi papers.

447   *Nothing came of this talk:* Int. David Carley.

447   *The first time he and Marie:* Ints. Frank Ripple, Tony Canadeo, W. C. Heinz.

449   *"Look at these people!":* Ints. W. C. Heinz; Chuck Lane, Mitch Fromstein, Tony Canadeo, Ruth McKloskey, Max McGee.

449   *the consequences for Marie were worse:* Ints. Vincent H. Lombardi, Susan Lombardi, Jill Lombardi, DeDe Clark, O. C. Krueger.

450   *As the season entered:* Vincent H. Lombardi papers; int. Pat Peppler.

450   *Lombardi traveled to Washington:* Ints. Lee Remmel, Chuck Lane, O. C. Krueger; Thomas, *The Man to See*, p. 247.

452   *In his search for the old:* Ints. Ruth McKloskey, Chuck Lane; *Press-Gazette*, Dec. 8, 1968.

452   *Super Bowl III:* Ints. Ed Kiely, George Dickson, John Druze, Ben Bradlee; Thomas, *The Man to See*, p. 330.

26: THE EMPTY ROOM

454   *Not since the days:* Ints. Pat Peppler, Chuck Lane; *Press-Gazette,* Jan. 29, 1969.
454   *A short time later:* Int. W. C. Heinz; Dowling, *Coach,* p. 12.
455   *That weekend:* Int. Martie Zad; *Washington Post,* Feb. 1, 1969.
456   *Williams, Bradlee and Art Buchwald:* Bradlee, *A Good Life* (Simon & Schuster, 1995); int. Martie Zad.
456   *Lombardi's mind and spirit:* Int. Lois Bourguignon.
456   *At his stadium office:* Int. Lorraine Keck; copy of letter of resignation, Feb. 4, 1969.
457   *The ability of Lombardi:* Ints. David Carley, Jack Koeppler.
458   *That morning Olejniczak:* Press-Gazette, Feb. 3, 1969; ints. Tony Canadeo, Lee Remmel.
459   *They convened at 6:10:* Press-Gazette, Feb. 6, 1969; *Washington Post,* Feb. 6, 1969; ints. Tony Canadeo, Chuck Lane.
460   *Word of Lombardi's departure: Wisconsin State Journal,* Feb. 6, 1969; ints. Paul Mazzoleni, Lois Bourguignon, Pat Peppler, Chuck Lane.
461   *Lombardi was obsessing again:* Ints. Chuck Lane, Bart Starr.
462   *Perhaps he had been leaving:* Ints. Ruth McKloskey, Lorraine Keck, Bart Starr, Vernon Biever; letter from Starr to Lombardi in Vincent H. Lombardi collection.

27: TAKING CHARGE IN WASHINGTON

464   *Washington, at last: Washington Post,* Feb. 7, 1969; "This Morning with Shirley Povich," *Washington Post,* Feb. 7, 1969; *The Record,* Feb. 8, 1969; Thomas, *The Man to See,* p. 247; ints. Martie Zad, Ben Bradlee, O. C. Krueger, David Slattery.
465   *The fact that the home team:* David Broder, *Washington Post,* Feb. 12, 1969; Art Buchwald, "Hail to the Chief," *Washington Post,* Feb. 11, 1969.
466   *The move to Washington:* Ints. Susan Lombardi, Vincent H. Lombardi, O. C. Krueger; *Washington Post,* Feb. 16, 1969.
466   *The Lombardis stayed:* Medical records of Dr. Landon Bamfield; ints. Jackie Anderson, Connie Boyle, Dr. Phil James, Dr. Landon Bamfield.
467   *Marie's outlook brightened:* Ints. Jackie Anderson, Connie Boyle.
468   *What kind of material?:* Ints. George Dickson, David Slattery, Paul Hornung, Sonny Jurgensen; WTEM radio documentary.
469   *It was typical of Lombardi:* Letter from Joseph Stechshulte concerning Bishop Thomas Lyons.
469   *On the evening of June 9:* Ints. Vincent H. Lombardi, Jill Lombardi. *Minneapolis Tribune,* June 10, 1969.
470   *On June 16:* Ints. Pat Richter, Tom Brown, Sonny Jurgensen, George Dickson, Bill Austin.
471   *When training camp opened:* Ints. Father Tim Moore, Father Guy McPartland, David Slattery, George Dickson, O. C. Krueger, Ben Bradlee, Joe Lombardi, Pat Richter, Tom Brown, Sam Huff, WTEM documentary.
474   *Lombardi was still at training camp:* Ints. Vincent H. Lombardi, Jill Lombardi, Anthony Izzo, Jackie Anderson, O. C. Krueger.
475   *Not long after Vincent:* Letter from Vince Lombardi to Susan Lombardi, Susan Lombardi papers, October 1969.
476   *Ethel Kennedy wrote:* Letter from Ethel Kennedy, Oct. 27, 1969, Susan Lombardi papers; Wiebusch, *Lombardi,* p. 16; O'Brien, *Vince,* p. 361.
477   *Lombardi's reaction:* Int. George Dickson.
478   *This one brought a letter:* President Richard M. Nixon letter, November 1969, Susan Lombardi papers.
478   *she wrote a letter that jolted:* Letter from Marie Lombardi to Vincent H. Lombardi, November 1969, Vincent H. Lombardi papers.
479   *Vincent had a more complicated perspective:* Ints. Vincent H. Lombardi, Jill Lombardi.
480   *Vince called two of his favorite old Packers:* Ints. Paul Hornung, Max McGee, O. C. Krueger, Pat Richter.
481   *He went to Super Bowl IV:* Ints. Ray Scott, O. C. Krueger, Sonny Jurgensen.

28: RUN TO WIN

482   *The work of the NFL league meeting:* Ints. Susan Lombardi, Wellington Mara; Wiebusch, *Lombardi,* p. 188.
483   *In the second week of May:* Ints. Jill Lombardi, Vincent H. Lombardi, Joe Lombardi.
484   *Two days after his New York visit: Milwaukee Sentinel,* May 13, 1970; ints. Jack Koeppler, Chuck Lane, Ruth McKloskey, Lee Remmel, Art Daley, Tony Canadeo, Lois Bourguignon, Tom Olejniczak, Father William Spalding, Father Dennis Burke, Eugene Brusky.
485   *A few weeks later:* Ints. David Carley, Jim Carley, Mitch Fromstein.
485   *Marie had accompanied:* Int. Susan Lombardi.
486   *Patriotism and golf:* Int. Gordon Peterson; Susan Lombardi papers.
486   *During one round Guglielmi:* Int. Ralph Guglielmi.
487   *They arrived in time:* Int. Ralph Guglielmi; *Dayton Journal,* June 23, 1970; *Dayton Daily News,* June 23, 1970; transcript of Lombardi speech to All Pro Mid-America Conference, June 22, 1970.
488   *Georgetown University Hospital:* Georgetown University Hospital medical records and discharge summary for Vincent T. Lombardi, June 27–July 7, 1970.

489   *Marie had suspected it:* Ints. Susan Lombardi, Clara Parvin, Vincent H. Lombardi.

489   *Exploratory abdominal surgery: Washington Post,* June 28, 1970; Georgetown University Hospital medical records.

490   *By July 10:* Georgetown University Hospital medical records; ints. Vincent H. Lombardi, Joe Lombardi, Harold Lombardi, Wellington Mara, Ben Bradlee, Jack Koeppler.

491   *When the players threatened to strike:* Ints. Ed Garvey, Pat Richter, Dave Robinson, David Slattery, Bill Austin, George Dickson, Joe Lombardi, Wellington Mara.

492   *The trip home:* Georgetown University medical records; *Washington Post,* Sept. 2, 1970; Wiebusch, *Lombardi,* p. 207; O'Brien, *Vince,* p. 372; ints. Joe Lombardi, O. C. Krueger, David Slattery.

492   *The next day:* Ints. Pat Richter, Tom Brown, George Dickson, Bill Austin, *Washington Post,* July 26–28, 1970.

493   *On July 27:* Georgetown University medical records; ints. O. C. Krueger, Martie Zad; Susan Lombardi papers.

493   *The card was signed:* Ints. Ed Garvey, Pat Richter, Dave Robinson.

493   *The coach was fading:* Georgetown University Hospital discharge summary records, July 27–Sept. 3, 1970.

494   *Even his eyebrows were growing wild:* Ints. Joe Lombardi, Vincent H. Lombardi, Susan Lombardi, Jackie Anderson, Lew Anderson, O. C. Krueger.

494   *His boys make the pilgrimage:* Ints. Frank Gifford, Willie Wood, Chuck Mercein, Paul Hornung, Max McGee, Bob Skoronski, Bart Starr, Sonny Jurgensen (WTEM documentary), Willie Davis (with W. C. Heinz); Kramer, *Winning Is the Only Thing,* p. 4; Marie Lombardi cassette tape recording of Hall of Fame speech (on Jim Taylor).

496   *Everyone in Washington: Congressional Record,* Aug. 13, 1970; *Washington Post,* Aug. 12, 1970; ints. Clara Parvin, Joe Lombardi, Harold Lombardi, Jackie Anderson, Lew Anderson, O. C. Krueger, Susan Lombardi, Father Tim Moore; Georgetown University Hospital discharge summary report; Marie Lombardi interview with Bob Addie, *Washington Post,* Sept. 1, 1970.

497   *Vincent visited his father's hospital room:* Int. Vincent H. Lombardi.

497   *By August 31:* Georgetown University Hospital medical discharge records; Marie Lombardi interview with Bob Addie; ints. Vincent H. Lombardi, O. C. Krueger, Gordon Peterson, Paul Hornung, Tom Brown, Susan Lombardi, Jackie Anderson, Martie Zad.

498   *Four days after his death: Washington Post,* Sept. 3–8, 1970; *New York Daily News,* Sept. 8, 1970; *Press-Gazette,* Sept. 7–8, 1970; ints. Vincent H. Lombardi, Susan Lombardi, Joe Lombardi, Harold Lombardi, Madeline Werner, Clara Parvin, Anthony Izzo, Tony Canadeo, Lois Bourguignon, Al Quilici, Father Dennis Burke, Father Tim Moore, Paul Hornung, Bart Starr, Willie Wood, Dave Robinson, Bob Skoronski; *Newark Star Ledger,* Sept. 8, 1970; *New York Times,* Sept. 9, 1970; Homily of His Eminence Terence Cardinal Cooke at Funeral Mass of Vincent Lombardi, St. Patrick's Cathedral, Monday, Sept. 7, 1970.

EPILOGUE

500   *"Oh, yecch!":* From cassette tape recording of Marie Lombardi practicing the speech, Vincent H. Lombardi collection.

501   *This was the summer of 1976:* Ints. Susan Lombardi, Vincent H. Lombardi, Jill Lombardi, Pat Cochran, Lois Bourguignon, O. C. Krueger.

502   *Everybody knows about:* Marie Lombardi tape.

502   *Marie still watched pro football:* Ints. Vincent H. Lombardi, Susan Lombardi.

Bibliography

The literature on Vince Lombardi includes two sports classics that framed the glory years of the Green Bay Packers. *Run to Daylight!* is the coach's diary of the week leading up to a game against the Detroit Lions in 1962, written by W. C. Heinz; and *Instant Replay* is Jerry Kramer's diary of the 1967 season, written with Dick Schaap. Any biography is obliged to the works that have gone before it, as I am to those two books. Also of particular note are three other books: Michael O'Brien's *Vince,* the first serious study of his life; Tom Dowling's absorbing *Coach,* an account of his season with the Redskins, and John Wiebusch's *Lombardi,* a trove of interviews compiled shortly after his death. The reference book I turned to more than any other was *Total Football,* edited by Bob Carroll, which I considered my bible on football facts and figures.

Bengtson, Phil, with Todd Hunt. *Packer Dynasty.* Garden City, N.Y.: Doubleday, 1969.
Biever, Vernon J. *The Glory of Titletown.* Dallas: Taylor, 1997.
Blaik, Earl H., with Tim Cohane. *You Have to Pay the Price.* New York: Holt, Rinehart and Winston, 1960.
Burns, James MacGregor. *Leadership.* New York: Harper & Row, 1978.
Bynum, Mike. *A Dynasty Remembered.* Nashville: Athlon, 1994.
Carroll, Bob. *When the Grass Was Real.* New York: Simon & Schuster, 1993.
———. *Total Football.* New York: HarperCollins, 1997.
Cestaro, Antonio. *Vietri di Potenza.* Agrapoli, Italy: Capano, 1996.
Cohane, Tim. *Bypaths of Glory.* New York: Harper & Row, 1963.
Collins, John J. *Saint Cecilia's Parish.* Englewood, N.J.: St. Cecilia, 1967.
Daley, Art, and Jack Yuenger. *Green Bay Packers 1968 Yearbook.* Green Bay, Wis.: Inland Press, 1968.
———. *The Lombardi Era.* Inland, 1968.
D'Amato, Gary, and Cliff Christl. *Mudbaths & Bloodbaths.* Madison, Wis.: Prairie Oak, 1997.
Dowling, Tom. *Coach: A Season with Lombardi.* New York: Norton, 1970.
Flynn, George L. *The Vince Lombardi Scrapbook.* New York: Grosset & Dunlap, 1976.
Fülöp-Miller, René. *The Power and Secret of the Jesuits.* New York: Braziller, 1956.
Gentile, Domenic, with Gary D'Amato. *The Packer Tapes.* Madison, Wis.: Prairie Oak, 1996.
Gifford, Frank. *The Whole Ten Yards.* New York: Ballantine, 1994.
Greenfield, Jeff. *Television: The First Fifty Years.* New York: Abrams, 1977.
Halas, George. *Halas by Halas.* New York: McGraw-Hill, 1979.
Halberstam, David. *The Fifties.* New York: Villard, 1993.
Hallam, Elizabeth. *Saints.* New York: Simon & Schuster, 1994.
Hornung, Paul, with Al Silverman. *Football and the Single Man.* Garden City, N.Y.: Doubleday, 1965.
Huizinga, Johan. *The Autumn of the Middle Ages.* Chicago: University of Chicago Press, 1996. (Translation of 1921 edition.)
Kisseloff, Jeff. *The Box: An Oral History of Television, 1920–1961.* New York: Viking, 1995.
Kramer, Jerry, ed. *Lombardi: Winning Is the Only Thing.* New York: World, 1970.
Kramer, Jerry, with Dick Schaap. *Instant Replay.* New York: New American Library, 1968
———. *Farewell to Football.* New York: World, 1969.
———. *Distant Replay.* New York: Putnam's Sons, 1985.
Leahy, Frank. *Notre Dame Football.* Englewood Cliffs, N.J.: Prentice-Hall, 1949.
Levi, Carlo. *Christ Stopped at Eboli.* New York: Farrar, Straus, 1947.

Lombardi, Vince, and W. C. Heinz. *Run to Daylight!* Englewood Cliffs, N.J.: Prentice-Hall, 1963.
Lombardi, Vincent H. *Coaching for Teamwork.* Bellevue, Wash.: Reinforcement, 1996.
Lombardi, Vince, Jr., and John Q. Baucom. *Baby Steps to Success.* Lancaster, Pa.: Starburst, 1997.
Long, Gavin. *MacArthur as Military Commander.* London: Batsford, 1969.
Manchester, William. *American Caesar.* Boston: Little, Brown, 1978.
Mottola, Anthony, trans. *The Spiritual Exercises of St. Ignatius.* Garden City, N.Y.: Doubleday, 1964.
Newcombe, Jack. *The Fireside Book of Football.* New York: Simon & Schuster, 1964.
O'Brien, Michael O. *Vince: A Personal Biography of Vince Lombardi.* New York: Morrow, 1987.
Oriard, Michael. *Reading Football.* Chapel Hill: University of North Carolina Press, 1993.
Reeder, Red. *Born at Reveille.* Rutland: Vermont Heritage Press, 1966.
Rice, Grantland. *The Tumult and the Shouting.* New York: Barnes, 1954.
Russell, Fred. *Bury Me in an Old Press Box.* New York: Barnes, 1957.
Schiffer, Don. *Pro Football Handbook, 1959.* New York: Pocket, 1959.
———. *Pro Football Handbook, 1961.* Nashville: Nelson, 1961.
Starr, Bart, with Murray Olderman. *Starr.* New York: Morrow, 1987.
Steinbreder, John. *70 Years of Championship Football.* Dallas: Taylor, 1994.
Thomas, Evan. *The Man to See: Edward Bennett Williams.* New York: Simon & Schuster, 1991.
Tunney, Jim. *Impartial Judgment.* New York: Watts, 1988.
Wells, Robert W. *Lombardi: His Life and Times.* Madison: Wisconsin House, 1971.
Whitfield, Clovis, and Jane Martineau. *Painting in Naples, 1606–1705.* New York: Weidenfeld and Nicolson, 1983.
Whittingham, Richard. *Giants, in Their Own Words.* Chicago: Contemporary, 1992.
Wiebusch, John. *Lombardi.* Chicago: Follett, 1971.
Wiebusch, John, and Brian Silverman. *A Game of Passion.* Atlanta: Turner, 1994.
Williams, Edward Bennett. *One Man's Freedom.* New York: Atheneum, 1962.
Wills, Garry. *Certain Trumpets.* New York: Simon & Schuster, 1994.
Winship, Michael. *Television.* New York: Random House, 1988.

Acknowledgments

On July 21, 1995, Nardi Reeder Campion of Hanover, New Hampshire, sent me a letter saying that she had heard on C-Span's *Booknotes* that I might write a book about Vince Lombardi. It was true that when Brian Lamb asked me about my next biographical subject, I mentioned the late coach, but I said it as something of a lark. I was preoccupied with Washington politics at the time, and the day when I might get around to Lombardi seemed distant. A sentence in Mrs. Campion's letter changed all that. "My brother, Colonel Red Reeder, was a close friend of his and his next door neighbor at West Point," she wrote. "Red has a collection of funny Lombardi stories in his remarkable memory. (He is 94 but his memory puts an elephant to shame.)"

A colonel in his nineties with the memory of an elephant was not someone to put off to another year. So I paid a visit to Red Reeder at his retirement home in Fort Belvoir, Virginia, and I found him to be as funny and sharp-minded as his sister promised, and my Lombardi book had begun. Until the day he died three years later, Colonel Reeder was a constant source of encouragement, sending me a stream of delightful postcards signed in his big shaky scrawl, RED.

Among the pleasures of researching this book was the chance to spend time with older and wiser people. Fred Russell, the sportswriting sage of Nashville, showed remarkable recall more than sixty years later of a Vanderbilt road game against Fordham at the Polo Grounds in 1934. I found a new writing hero in the process, W. C. "Bill" Heinz, who wrote the first book about Vince Lombardi, *Run to Daylight!*—the coach's memoir of a week during the 1962 season. From the moment I met Heinz at his hilltop home in Dorset, Vermont, and he showed me his old Remington typewriter and shared notes from interviews he conducted with Lombardi thirty-seven years ago, I realized that I was in the presence of a true pro.

For the winter of 1996–97 my wife and I moved to Green Bay to research the book. We will long remember the clear northern winter, the amazing run of the Packers to the Super Bowl under coach Mike Holmgren and general manager Ron Wolf, and the warm people we met during our stay. Our deepest thanks to Gary and Donna DeBauche, our local guides; to Ron and Helen Desotel, who provided us with a wonderful home in the bayside woods of rural Brussels; to Jack and Rita Earp, our friendly neighbors (Jack, great-grandnephew of Wyatt Earp, rode his tractor snowplow like a horseman); to Judy, the postmistress who delivered our mail through blizzards; to the irrepressible Johnny Maino and Larry McCarren, Michael Bauman, Bud Lea and Art Daley, who welcomed me into the Packer media tribe; to Lee Remmel and his skilled staff at Lambeau; to Vernon Biever, the great photographer; and to Mary Jane Herber at the Brown County Library, whose research assistance was invaluable.

Our two summers of research in New York City were made possible by Robin Becker, the graceful dancer of West 107th Street, and Tom Chulak, my loving cousin. Researchers Gloria Riviera, Ben Maraniss and Libby Estelle were quick and efficient. It was a pleasure to deal with Allen Aimone, the skilled special collections librarian at West Point, Suzanne Christoff, the USMA archivist, and Pat Hanlon, media relations director for the New York Giants. Vic Del Guercio taught me about the Depression-era Fordham. Don Crane and the McPartland brothers brought back the Saints. Tim Cohane Jr. provided me with two blue tubs full of his father's papers. And Joe Lombardi, the Old Man's sweet-natured little brother, showed me around Sheepshead Bay. Michael and Beth Norman, Blaine Harden and Jessica Kowal, Chip Brown and Kate Betts gave us plenty of happy diversions, and Beth, a professor of nursing, also helped as a medical adviser, along with Dr. Dorothy Scott.

Although this was not an authorized biography, the Lombardi family welcomed my project and provided a balanced perspective on St. Vince. His son, Vincent, daughter-in-law, Jill, and daughter, Susan, were open and honest, and I will never forget their generosity. Cousin Clara Parvin and niece Michelle Walden went out of their way to find family photographs. Among the old Packers, special thanks to Bob Skoronski for his incisive comments and to Paul Hornung, who tracked me down in a Louisville hotel room one night and showed that the Golden Boy is a helluva guy.

Vincent H. Lombardi, representing management, and David Meggyesy, representing the union, once almost came to blows on opposite sides of an NFL bargaining table, yet I admire them both greatly. Meggyesy's thoughts on the meaning of football in American culture are always interesting. Thanks to Jim Warren for introducing me to Meggyesy and for providing a clear reading of the manuscript. Preliminary readings by Richard Cohen, Valerie Strauss and Maralee Schwartz gave me an early boost, as did Andrea Dettelbach's energetic research and the art history exuberance of Paul Richard. I am always lucky to have Bob Woodward, Elsa Walsh, Michael Weisskopf, Judith Katz, Frank Roloff, Neil Henry and John Feinstein looking out for me. The memos that Dick Harwood wrote after reading the manuscript were always insightful.

The *Washington Post* was extraordinarily accommodating throughout this project. Don Graham, Leonard Downie Jr., Robert Kaiser, Steve Coll, Karen DeYoung and Bill Hamilton let me keep going on Lombardi even as my former subject, Bill Clinton, found new (or old) ways to make news. George Solomon, the sports editor, generously allowed me to cover the Packers during their 1996 championship run. *Post* researcher Bobbye Pratt once again was a lifesaver. Rafe Sagalyn, my agent, believed in this book from the beginning and was greatly helpful, as were his assistants, Ethan Kline and Dan Kois. This is my fourth book for Alice Mayhew at Simon & Schuster, our first sports book. She can be as tough as Lombardi, and as smart and loving. Thanks also to Carolyn Reidy, David Rosenthal, Victoria Meyer, Kerri Kennedy, Jennifer Thornton, Charlotte Gross, Roger Labrie and Layla Hearth. Near the end of any book, my absentmindness turns to outright carelessness. This time I lost a computer disk with the entire book on it while riding the Metroliner from Washington to New York. Amtrak's Cliff Black to the rescue. He sent a team of employees onto the empty train hours later and miraculously found the disk.

There is nothing that means more to me than having my parents, Mary and Elliott Maraniss, serve as the first readers and editors for my two biographies, and this time they were joined in the process by the Maraniss family's adopted big sister, Whitney Gould, whose comments were all the more valuable because she has no use for football. And thanks finally to Linda, Andrew and Sarah. Linda lived this book as much as I did, moving to Green Bay in the dead of winter and to New York in the brutal summer, and everything I did depended on her incredible support and invariably correct editorial advice. As I wrote once before, paraphrasing the old coach, and say again at the end of my obsession with Lombardi, she and our children are not everything, they are the only thing.

Index

Photo Credits